SALE OF GOODS
AND
CONSUMER CREDIT

PAUL DOBSON, LL.B.

of Lincoln's Inn, Barrister
Visiting Professor of Law at Anglia Polytechnic
University and University of Greenwich

SIXTH EDITION

LONDON
SWEET & MAXWELL
2000

First Edition 1975
Second Edition 1979
Third Edition 1984
Fourth Edition 1989
Fifth Edition 1996
Sixth Edition 2000

Published in 2000 by
Sweet & Maxwell Limited of
100 Avenue Road, Swiss Cottage, London, NW3 3PF
Typeset by Tradespools Ltd, Frome, Somerset
Printed in England by
Clays Ltd, St Ives plc

A CIP Catalogue
record for this book
is available from
the British Library

ISBN 0 421 722 304

SALE OF GOODS
AND
CONSUMER CREDIT

AUSTRALIA
LBC Information Services
Sydney

CANADA and USA
Carswell
Toronto

NEW ZEALAND
Brooker's
Auckland

SINGAPORE and MALAYSIA
Sweet & Maxwell Asia
and Kuala Lumpur

PREFACE

This edition sees the addition of two new chapters: "Distance Selling" and "International Sale of Goods". The latter deals with c.i.f and f.o.b contracts etc. The former is a response to the growth in all forms of distance selling, including e-commerce. It includes coverage of the Electronic Communications Act 2000 as well as the Distance Selling Directive. It also looks briefly at issues of jurisdiction and applicable law in cross-border consumer contracts. The increasing impact of the EU as a source of law in the area of consumer law is evidenced by the fact that the Table of Directives lists 16 Directives of which 10 (or the British legislation resulting from them) are considered in the text. These include the recent Directives on Distance Selling, E-commerce, Injunctions and Consumer Guarantees. Legislative developments reflected in this edition also include the Contracts (Right of Third Parties) Act 1999 whilst detailed changes to consumer credit law reflected in the text include changes to the definitions of certain categories of exempt agreement and to the definition of the total charge for credit.

The Unfair Terms in Consumer Contracts Regulations 1994 have been replaced by a revised 1999 version and have been the subject of a major ruling in the Court of Appeal, *Director General of Fair Trading v. First National Bank* (2000). This decision is explained. Also included is "credit-hire" case of *Dimond v. Lovell* (2000), the first decision of the House of Lords on consumer credit issues. Other decisions taken in include: *Rahman v. Sterling Credit Ltd* (2000) on when a claim to re-open an extortionate credit bargain becomes statute barred; *Stevenson v. Rogers* (1999) on what is meant by "in the course of a business"; *Truk v. Tokmakidis* (2000) on when a buyer is taken to have accepted the goods; *Oceano Grupo Editorial SA v. Rocio Murciano Quintero* (2000) on the court's proper response to an exclusive jurisdiction clause which is unfair within the meaning of the Directive on Unfair Contract Terms.

Where changes to the law are imminent (*e.g.* because an EU Directive so requires) or are presently under consideration, *e.g.* by the Office of Fair Trading, I have tried to summarise the likely or possible changes. In the case of the Consumer Protection (Distance Selling) Regulations 2000, I have been able to go further. Although these regulations (implementing the Distance

Selling Directive) have not yet made their appearance at the time of finalising the text of this book, I have been able (starting at paragraph 16–05) to give an outline of their effect, basing my account on the draft regulations put out for consultation.

I hope that the book will continue to provide a reliable guide for those interested in business and consumer law. I have stated the law as I believe it to be on August 15, 2000.

Woodford Green   Paul Dobson

POSTSCRIPT

The Consumer Protection (Distance Selling) Regulations 2000 were made on August 31, 2000 (coming into force on October 31, 2000). There are some differences from the draft regulations as explained at paragraph 16-05 onwards in this book. The provisions on cancellation remain, apart from the most minor details, accurately set out there. The main differences from what is in the text are:

Para. 16-08. The provisions whereby contracts for construction of buildings and extensions (but not contracts for the supply of goods for incorporation in land) were "excepted" are replaced with a simple provision: a contract for construction of a building is excepted if it also provides for a sale or other disposition of an interest in the land.

Paras 16-10 to 16-13. Contracts are not rendered unenforceable if the information is not given as required (*i.e.* prior to the contract or in a durable medium). The only sanction for failing to give the information as required is that the Director General of Fair Trading (or a Trading Standards Department) may seek an injunction against the trader.

Para. 16-18. The only related credit agreements which are cancelled when a distance contract is cancelled are "fixed-sum" credit agreements. Thus the consumer will not find her credit card agreement cancelled, just because she has used the credit card to make a payment under a distance contract which she later cancels.

Para. 16-21. The regulations contain no provisions dealing with unsolicited emails and other distance communications. The Telecommunications (Data Protection and Privacy) Regulations 1999 control such communications by phone and fax. Mail and email are, however, not controlled by law but only by self regulatory schemes.

Para. 16-22. The only enforcement authorities are the Director General of Fair Trading and local Trading Standards Departments. This may change, however, when the Injunctions Directive is implemented, see para. 18-52.

TABLE OF CONTENTS

	page
Preface	v
Table of Cases	xiii
Table of Statutes	xxix
Table of Statutory Instruments	xxxvii
Table of European Directives	xxxix

PART ONE
SALE OF GOODS

	PARA.
1. INTRODUCTION AND DEFINITION OF CONTRACT OF	
SALE OF GOODS	1–01
Definition	1–04
Sale Distinguished from other Transactions	1–11
The Importance of the Definition	1–18
2. FORMATION AND CANCELLATION OF THE CONTRACT	2–01
Formation of the Contract	2–01
The Price	2–13
Cancellable Agreements	2–18
3. THE PASSING OF PROPERTY AND RISK	3–01
Classification of the Contract	3–03
The Time of the Transfer of Property	3–07
Transfer of Risk	3–30
Unascertained Goods from an Identified Bulk	3–37
Retention of Title Clauses	3–48
4. PERISHING OF GOODS	4–01
Goods Perishing Before the Contract is Made	4–02
Goods Perishing After the Contract is Made	4–08
5. SELLER NOT THE OWNER	5–01
6. MISREPRESENTATION	6–01
What Amounts to an Actionable	
Misrepresentation?	6–02

Remedies   6–03
Exclusion   6–05
Additional or Alternative Defendant   6–06

7. TERMS OF THE CONTRACT   7–01
   Implied Terms—Sections 12–15   7–15
   European Directive on Consumer Guarantees   7–52

8. SUPPLY OF GOODS AND SERVICES ACT 1982   8–01
   The First Set—Contracts for the Transfer of
       Goods   8–02
   The Second Set—Contracts of Hire   8–08
   The Third Set—Contracts for Services   8–09

9. PRODUCT LIABILITY   9–01

10. EXEMPTION CLAUSES AND UNFAIR TERMS   10–01
    Incorporation   10–02
    Misrepresentation   10–10
    Privity of Contract   10–11
    Scope of the Clause   10–13
    Unfair Contract Terms Act 1977   10–18
    The Unfair Terms in Consumer Contracts
        Regulations 1999   10–39
    Criminal Use of Ineffective Exemption Clauses   10–48

11. DELIVERY AND PAYMENT   11–01
    Delivery   11–03
    Payment   11–10

12. SELLER'S REMEDIES   12–01
    Personal Remedies   12–02
    Remedies Against the Goods   12–04

13. BUYER'S REMEDIES   13–01
    Additional or Alternative Defendant   13–14

14. THE MEASURE OF DAMAGES   14–01
    General Contractual Principles   14–01
    Prima Facie Rules   14–02
    Sub-Sales   14–15
    Mitigation   14–19
    Penalties   14–21

15. AUCTION SALES   15–01
     Advertisements Before the Auction Sale   15–02
     Section 57 of the Sale of Goods Act   15–03
     Reserve Price   15–04
     Exemption Clauses   15–05
     Position of the Auctioneer   15–06
     Auctions (Bidding Agreements) Acts 1927–69   15–09
     Mock Auctions Act 1961   15–10

16. E-COMMERCE AND DISTANCE SELLING   16–01
     Distance Selling Regulations   16–05
     Cross Border Contracts   16–23

17. INTERNATIONAL SALES   17–01
     C.I.F. Contracts   17–02
     F.O.B. Contracts   17–09
     Incoterms   17–15
     Other Types of Contract   17–16
     Methods of Payment   17–17

18. TRADES DESCRIPTIONS ADVERTISING, FAIR
     TRADING AND INJUNCTIONS   18–01
     Trade Descriptions Act 1968   18–03
     Misleading Price Indications   18–34
     Misleading Advertisements   18–44
     Fair Trading Act 1973   18–46
     Injunctions Directive   18–52

PART TWO
CONSUMER CREDIT

19. INTRODUCTION AND DEFINITION OF HIRE-PURCHASE   19–01

20. OTHER FORMS OF NEVER-NEVER   20–01
     Some Particular Forms of Security   20–07
     Methods of Providing Credit   20–13
     Parasitic Business   20–27
     Credit Unions   20–34

21. THE CONSUMER CREDIT ACT 1974   21–01
     Definitions   21–05

22. LICENSING   22–01
    Business Needing a License   22–05
    Unlicensed Trading   22–17
    Agreements Rendered Unenforceable   22–18
    Director-General's Licensing Powers   22–22

23. ADVERTISING AND SEEKING BUSINESS   23–01
    Canvassing Off Trade Premises   23–02
    Criminal Offences   23–06
    Advertising   23–08

24. FORMATION OF A CONSUMER CREDIT AGREEMENT   24–01
    Hire-Purchase, Conditional Sale and Credit Sale
        Agreements   24–02
    Other Regulated Agreements   24–16
    Credit-Broker's Fees and Credit Reference
        Agencies   24–29
    Formalities   24–32
    Cancellation   24–48

25. CREDITOR'S LIABILITY IN RESPECT OF THE GOODS
    OR SERVICES SUPPLIED   25–01
    Terms of the Goods or Services Agreement   25–02
    Creditor's Liability for the Supplier's Breach   25–03
    Hire-Purchase   25–09
    Credit Sale and Conditional Sale   25–23

26. ENFORCEMENT BY THE CREDITOR OR OWNER   26–01
    Broad Principles of Enforcement   26–02
    Subsidiary Matters   26–25
    Enforcement of Security   26–40

27. TERMINATION OF HIRE-PURCHASE CONTRACTS   27–01
    Events Causing Termination   27–03
    Operation of an Accelerated Payments Clause   27–13
    Recovery of the Goods by the Creditor from the
        Debtor   27–17
    Protected Goods   27–20
    Money Claim by Creditor from Debtor   27–25
    Powers of the Court in the Case of Regulated
        Agreements   27–36
    Recovery by the Creditor of Goods in the Hands
        of a Third Party   27–38

28. TERMINATION OF CREDIT SALE, CONDITIONAL SALE AND
      CONSUMER HIRE AGREEMENTS   28–01
     Credit Sale Agreements   28–01
     Conditional Sale Agreements   28–02
     Consumer Hire Agreements   28–07

Index   511

TABLE OF CASES

N.B. C.C.L.R. denotes Consumer Credit Law Reports which are to be found in Volumes 3 and 4 of Bennion and Dobson's Consumer Credit Control.

A.E.G. v. Logic Resource Ltd (1995) unreported 10–05
Ailsa Craig Fishing Co. Ltd v. Malvern Fishing Co. Ltd [1983] 1
    W.L.R. 964; [1983] 1 All E.R. 101 .... 10–15, 10–16
Albermarle Supply Co. Ltd v. Hind & Co. [1928] 1 K.B. 307; 97
    L.J.K.B. 25; [1927] All E.R.Rep. 401 27–44
Aldridge v. Johnson [1857] 26 L.J.Q.B. 296; [1857] 7 E. & B.
    885 .... 3–27, 8–04
Allen v. Simmons [1978] 1 W.L.R. 879; 122 S.J. 470; [1978]
    Crim.L.R. 362; [1978] 3 All E.R. 662 15–10
Alliance & Leicester Building Society v. Babbs C.C.L.R. 77; 12
    Tr.L.R. 105 23–06
Aluminium Industrie Vassen BV. v. Romalpa Aluminium Ltd
    [1976] 1 W.L.R. 676; [1976] 2 All E.R. 552 .... 1–17, 3–26, 3–29,
                                    3–48, 3–59
Andrews v. Hopkinson [1957] 1 Q.B. 229; [1956] 3 W.L.R. 732;
    [1956] 3 All E.R. 422 .... 19–10, 24–12
Andrews Bros. Ltd v. Singer & Co. Ltd [1934] 1 K.B. 17; [1934]
    103 L.J.K.B. 90; [1933] All E.R.Rep. 479 .... 10–13, 18–10
Anglo-Auto Finance v. James [1963] 1 W.L.R. 1042; 107 S.J. 534;
    [1963] 3 All E.R. 566 27–33
Ant. Jurgens Margarinefabricken v. Dreyfus (Louis) [1914] 3 K.B.
    40; 111 L.T. 248 12–09
Arcos v. Ronaasen (E. A.) & Son [1933] A.C. 470; [1933] All
    E.R.Rep. 646 7–29
Arenson v. Casson [1975] 3 W.L.R. 815; [1975] 3 All E.R. 901;
    [1976] 1 Lloyd's Rep. 179, HL. 2–16
Armour v. Thyssen Edelstahlwerke AG [1991] A.C. 339; [1990] 3
    W.L.R. 810; [1990] 3 All E.R. 481 3–53
Arthur JS Hall & Co. v. Simons; *The Times*, July 2, 2000, HL . 8–09
Asfar & Co. v. Blundell [1896] 1 Q.B. 123; 73 L.T. 648 4–03
Ashington Piggeries v. Hill (Christopher) [1971] 2 W.L.R. 1051;
    115 S.J. 223; [1971] 1 All E.R. 847 .... 1–13, 3–06, 7–30
Ashley v. Sutton L.B.C. [1995] Crim.L.R. 657 18–17
Associated Distributors Ltd v. Hall [1938] 2 K.B. 83; [1938] 1 All
    E.R. 511 .... 10–46, 27–05, 27–06, 27–33
Aswan Engineering Establishment v. Lupdine [1987] 1 W.L.R. 1;
    [1987] 1 All E.R. 135; [1986] 2 Lloyd's Rep. 191; (1987) 6
    Tr.L. 1 .... 7–37, 7–41
Avery v. Bowden (1856) L.J.Q.B. 3; (1856) 6 E. & B. 953; (1855)
    5 E. & B. 714 4–08

BALDING v. Lew Ways Ltd, *The Times*, 19th March 1995 9–25
Baldry v. Marshall [1925] 1 K.B. 260; [1925] 94 L.J.K.B. 208;
    [1924] All E.R.Rep. 155 7–45

Barber v. NWS Bank [1996] C.C.L.R. 30 . . . 5–08, 7–20, 25–11, 25–12
Barker v. Bell [1971] 1 W.L.R. 983; 115 S.J. 364; [1971] 2 All
    E.R. 867 5–40
Barrow, Lane and Ballard Ltd v. Phillips, Phillips & Co. Ltd
    [1929] 1 K.B. 574; [1929] 98 L.J.K.B. 193; [1928] All
    E.R.Rep. 74 4–03
Bartlett v. Marcus (Sidney) [1965] 1 W.L.R. 1013; 109 S.J. 451;
    [1965] 2 All E.R. 753 . . . . 7–39, 7–47
Beale v. Taylor [1967] 1 W.L.R. 1193; 111 S.J. 668; [1967] 3 All
    E.R. 253 7–26
Beckett v. Cohen [1972] 1 W.L.R. 1593; 116 S.J. 882; [1973] 1
    All E.R. 120 18–19
Behnke v. Bede Shipping Co. Ltd [1927] 1 K.B. 640; [1927] 1
    K.B. 640; [1927] 96 L.J.K.B. 325; [1927] All E.R.Rep. 689 . 13–01
Behrend & Co. v. Produce Brokers' Co. [1920] 3 K.B. 530; [1920]
    90 L.J.K.B. 143; [1920] All E.R. Rep. 125 11–08
Belvoir Finance v. Stapelton (1971) 1 Q.B. 210; [1970] 3 W.L.R.
    530; [1970] 3 All E.R. 664 24–15
Bence Graphics v. Fasson UK Ltd [1997] 3 W.L.R. 205; [1997] 1
    All E.R. 979; [1997] C.L.C. 373; (1996) 93 (40) L.S.G. 24;
    (1996) 146 N.L.J. Rep. 1577; (1996) S.J.L.B. 227, CA. 14–18
Bentinck v. Cromwell Engineering Co. [1971] 1 Q.B. 324; [1971]
    3 W.L.R. 1113; [1971] 1 All E.R. 33 27–23
Benton v. Campbell, Parker & Co. [1925] 2 K.B. 410; [1925] 94
    L.J.K.B. 881; [1925] All E.R.Rep. 187 15–08
Bentworth Finance v. Lubert [1968] 1 Q.B. 680; [1967] 3 W.L.R.
    378; [1967] 2 All E.R. 810 25–17
Bernstein v. Pamson Motors (Golders Green) Ltd [1987] 2 All E.R.
    220; [1987] R.T.R. 384 13–05
Beverley Acceptances v. Oakley [1982] R.T.R. 417 5–13
Birkenhead & District Co-op. Soc. v. Roberts [1970] 1 W.L.R.
    1497; 114 S.J. 703; [1970] 3 All E.R. 391 18–30
Bisset v. Wilkinson [1927] A.C. 177; (1927) 136 L.T. 97; (1927)
    42 T.L.R. 727 6–02
Blackmore v. Bellamy [1983] R.T.R. 303 18–07
Blyth Shipbuilding & Dry Dock Co., Re [1926] Ch. 494; [1926]
    95 L.J.Ch. 350; [1926] All E.R.Rep. 373 3–09
Bond Worth, Re [1980] Ch. 228; [1979] 3 W.L.R. 629; [1979]
    3 All E.R. 919 3–50
Borden UK v. Scottish Timber Products Ltd [1981] Ch. 25; [1979]
    3 W.L.R. 672; [1979] 3 All E.R. 961 3–50
Bowes v. Shand (1877) 2 A.C. 433; 36 L.T. 857. 17–10
Bowmaker v. Wycombe Motors [1946] K.B. 505; [1946] 2 All
    E.R. 113 27–45
Bowmakers v. Barnet Instruments [1945] K.B. 65; [1944] 2 All
    E.R. 579 . . . . 24–15, 27–18
Boyter v. Thomson [1995] 2 A.C. 628; [1995] 3 W.L.R. 36; [1995]
    3 All E.R. 135 7–34
Branwhite v. Worcester Works Finance [1969] 1 A.C. 552; [1968]
    3 W.L.R. 760; [1968] 3 All E.R. 104 . . . . 24–06, 24–08

Breed v. Cluett [1970] 2 Q.B. 459. [1970] 3 W.L.R. 76; [1970] 2
　All E.R. 662 18–19
Bridge v. Campbell Discount Co. [1962] 2 A.C. 600; [1962] 2
　W.L.R. 439; [1962] 1 All E.R. 385 . . . . 27–32, 27–33
Brinkibon Ltd v. Stahag Stahi [1983] 2 A.C. 34; [1982] 1 All E.R.
　293; [1982] Com.L.R. 72 . . . . 2–06, 2–08
British & Benningtons Ltd v. North West Cachar Tea Co. [1923]
　A.C. 48; 92 L.J.K.B. 62; 128 L.T. 422; 20 Com.Cas. 247;
　[1922] All E.R.Rep. 224 (H.L.) 14–09
British Airways Board v. Taylor [1976] 1 W.L.R. 13; 120 S.J. 7;
　[1976] 1 All E.R. 65; [1976] 1 Lloyd's Rep. 167; (1975) 62
　Cr.App.R. 174; 18 Man. Law. 146; affirming [1975] 1
　W.L.R. 1197; 119 S.J. 559; [1975] 3 All E.R. 307; 18
　Man.Law. 46; [1975] 2 Lloyd's Rep. 434; [1975]
　Crim.L.R. 471 18–20
Brookes v. Retail Credit Cards Ltd [1986] C.C.L.R. 5; [1986]
　F.L.R. 86; [1986] Crim.L.R. 22–11
Brown (B.S.) & Son v. Craiks [1970] 1 W.L.R. 752; 114 S.J. 282;
　[1970] 1 All E.R. 823 7–38
Bunge Corp. v. Tradax Export S.A. [1981] 1 W.L.R. 711; [1981] 2
　All E.R. 540; (1981) 125 S.J. 373; [1981] Lloyd's Law Rep.
　1 . . . . 7–14, 17–09
Business Applications Specialists Ltd v. Nationwide Credit Corpn.
　Ltd [1988] C.C.L.R. 135 7–40
Butterworth v. Kingsway Motors [1954] 1 W.L.R. 1286; 2 S.J.
　717; [1954] 2 All E.R. 694 . . . . . 5–39, 7–19, 7–20, 25–13, 27–40

CADBURY v. Halliday [1975] 1 W.L.R. 649; 119 S.J. 219; [1975] 2
　All E.R. 226; 73 L.G.R. 256; [1975] Crim.L.R. 249 . . 18–05, 18–32
Cahn v. Pockett's Bristol Channel Steam Packet Co. [1899] 1 Q.B.
　643; [1899] 68 L.J.Q.B. 515; 80 L.T. 269 . . 5–36, 5–37, 5–36, 5–37
Cammell Laird & Co. Ltd v. Manganese Bronze and Brass Co. Ltd
　[1934] A.C. 402; [1934] 103 L.J.K.B. 289; [1934] All E.R.
　Rep. 1 . . . . 1–13, 7–45
Campbell Discount Co. Ltd v. Gall [1961] 1 Q.B. 431; [1961] 2
　W.L.R. 514; [1961] 2 All E.R. 104 . . . . 24–06, 24–07, 24–35
Car and Universal Finance v. Caldwell [1965] 1 Q.B. 535; [1964]
　2 W.L.R. 606; [1964] 1 All E.R. 290 5–26
Carlill v. Carbolic Smoke Ball Co. [1893] 1 Q.B. 256; [1893] 62
　L.J.Q.B. 257; 67 L.T. 837 9–02
Carlos Federspiel & Co. S.A. v. Twigg (Charles) & Co. [1957] 1
　Lloyd's Rep. 240; [1957] J.B.L. 296 . . . . 3–21, 17–12
Cavendish Woodhouse v. Manley [1984] Crim.L.R. 239 . . 10–29, 10–49
Cehave v. Bremer Handeigeselischaft mbH., Hansa Nord, The
　[1976] Q.B. 44; [1975] 3 W.L.R. 447; 119 S.J. 678; [1975] 3
　All E.R. 739; [1975] 2 Lloyd's Rep. 445 . . . . 7–12, 7–31
Central Newbury Car Auctions v. Unity Finance [1957] 1 Q.B.
　371; [1956] 3 W.L.R. 927; [1956] 3 All E.R. 905 5–06
Chapelton v. Barry U.D.C. [1940] 1 K.B. 532; [1940] 1 All E.R.
　356 10–05
Chapronière v. Mason (1905) 21 T.L.R. 633 9–04

Charge Card Services Ltd *in re.* [1988] 3 W.L.R. 723; [1988] 3
All E.R. 702 . . . . 8–05, 20–21
Charter v. Sullivan [1957] 2 Q.B. 117; [1957] 2 W.L.R. 528;
[1957] 1 All E.R. 809 14–04
Chartered Trust v. Pitcher [1987] C.C.L.R. 71; [1988] R.T.R. 72 . . 27–23
Charterhouse Credit v. Tolly [1963] 2 Q.B. 683; [1963] 2 All E.R.
432 25–21
Chelmsford Auctions v. Poole [1973] 1 Q.B. 542; [1973] 2 W.L.R.
219; [1972] 1 All E.R. 810 . . . . 15–06, 15–07, 15–08
Chubb Cash Ltd v. John Crilley and Son [1983] 1 W.L.R. 599;
[1983] 2 All E.R. 294 27–41
City Fur Manufacturing Co. v. Fureenbond London Ltd [1937] 81
S.J. 218; [1937] 1 All E.R. 799 5–29
Clode v. Barnes [1974] 1 W.L.R. 544; 118 S.J. 257; [1974] 1 All
E.R. 1166 18–09
Close Asset Finance v. Care Graphics Machinery Ltd [2000]
C.C.L.R. 43, QBD. 19–05
Clough Mill Ltd v. Martin [1985] 1 W.L.R. 111; [1984] 3 All E.R.
982 3–51
Cointat v. Myham & Sons (1914) 110 L.T. 749; [1914] 84 L.J.K.B.
2253; [1911–13] All E.R. 724 . . . . 10–08, 10–26
Cottee v. Seaton (Douglas) [1972] 1 W.L.R. 1408; 116 S.J. 821;
[1972] 3 All E.R. 750 18–09
Coupe v. Guyett [1973] 1 W.L.R. 669; [1973] 2 All E.R. 1058 . . . 2–11,
18–32
Coutts & Co. v. Browne Leckey [1947] K.B. 104; [1947] 115
L.J.K.B. 508 2–12
Couturier v. Hastie (1856) 5 H.L.Cas. 673; (1856) 28 L.T.O.S. 240;
(1856) 25 L.J.Ex. 253 . . . . 4–02, 4–06
Cowburn v. Focus Television Rentals Ltd [1983] Crim.L.R. 563 . 18–21,
18–22
Crowther v. Shannon [1975] 1 W.L.R. 30; [1975] 1 All E.R. 139;
[1975] R.T.R. 201; [1975] 1 Lloyd's Rep. 382 . . . . . . 7–39, 7–47
Cuillinane v. British "Rema" Manufacturing Co. [1954] 1 Q.B.
292; [1953] 3 W.L.R. 923; [1953] 2 All E.R. 1257 14–12
Cundy v. Lindsay (1878) 3 App.Cas. 459; (1878) 38 L.T. 573;
[1874–80] All E.R. 1149 . . . . 5–23, 5–24
Curtis v. Chemical Cleaning and Dyeing Co. [1951] 1 K.B. 805;
[1951] 1 T.L.R. 452; [1951] 1 All E.R. 631 10–10

D. & M. TRAILERS (HALIFAX) LTD. v. Stirling [1978] R.T.R. 468;
122 S.J. 625; (1978) 248 E.G. 597 10–06
Daniels v. White [1938] 160 L.T. 128; 82 S.J. 912; [1938] 4 All
E.R. 258 9–04
Davies v. Commissioners of Customs and Excise [1975] 1 W.L.R.
204 . . . . 8–05, 20–18
—v. Sumner [1984] 1 W.L.R. 1301; [1984] 3 All E.R. 831; [1985]
L.G.R. 123; [1985] R.T.R. 95 . . . . 18–07, 18–35
Dawson (G. J.) (Clapham) Ltd v. Dutfield [1936] 2 All E.R. 232 . 1–09,
8–04

Demby Hamilton & Co. v. Barden [1949] W.N. 73; [1949] 1 All
    E.R. 435 3–31
Dennant v. Skinner and Collom [1948] 2 K.B. 164; [1948] L.J.R.
    1576; [1948] 2 All E.R. 29 . . . . 3–08, 3–11, 3–14, 15–05
Derry v. Peek [1889] 14 App.Cas. 337; (1889) 58 L.J.Ch. 864 . . . 6–04
Dimond v. Lovell [2000] 2 W.L.R. 1121; [2000] All E.R. 897;
    [2000] C.C.L.R. 57, HL. 20–26, 21–07, 21–25
Director General of Fair Trading v. First National Bank Plc [2000]
    All E.R. 759, CA. 10–46, 26–08,
                                                                    26–24
Dixons v. Roberts (1984) 82 L.G.R. 689; (1984) 4 Tr.L. 136 18–16
Dodds v. Yorkshire Bank Finance Ltd [1992] C.C.L.R. 92 5–40
Donnelly v. Rowlands [1970] 1 W.L.R. 1600; 114 S.J.863; [1971]
    1 All E.R. 9 18–08
Donoghue v. Stevenson [1932] A.C. 562; [1932] 86 L.Q.R. 454 . . 9–04,
                                                        9–05, 10–16, 19–10
Drummond v. Van Ingen [1887] 12 App.Cas. 284; (1887) 56
    L.J.Q.B. 563; (1887) 57 L.T. 1 7–50
Drury v. Buckland (Victor) Ltd [1941] 85 S.J. 117; [1941] 1 All
    E.R. 269 19–10
Dunlop Pneumatic Tyre Co. Ltd v. New Garage & Motor Co. Ltd
    [1915] A.C. 79, [1915] 83 L.J.K.B. 1574; [1914–15] All
    E.R.Rep. 739 . . . . 14–21, 27–32

EALING L.B.C. v. Taylor [1995] Crim.L.R. 156 18–26
Eastern Distributors v. Golding [1957] 2 Q.B. 600; [1957] 3
    W.L.R. 237; [1957] 2 All E.R. 252 . . . . 5–05, 5–06, 5–07
Edwards v. Ddin [1976] 1 W.L.R. 942; 120 S.J. 587; [1976] 3 All
    E.R. 705; (1976) 63 Cr.App.R. 218; [1976] R.T.R. 508;
    [1976] Crim.L.R. 580 3–27
Edwards (Percy) Ltd v. Vaughan [1910] 26 T.L.R. 545 5–34
Elliott v. Director-General of Fair Trading [1980] 1 W.L.R. 977;
    [1980] I.C.R. 629; [1980] C.C.L.R. 23 . . . . 23 07, 26–39
Ellis Son & Vidler Ltd, Re [1994] 1 W.L.R. 1181; [1995] 1 All
    E.R. 192 3–24
Elson v. Prices Tailors Ltd [1963] 1 W.L.R. 287; 107 S.J. 195 . . . 2–17
Entores v. Miles Far East Co. [1955] 2 O.B. 327; [1955] 3 W.L.R.
    48 2–06
Eshun v. Moorgate Mercantile Co. [1971] 1 W.L.R. 722; 115 S.J.
    301; [1971] 2 All E.R. 402 . . . . 27–08, 27–28
Esso Petroleum Co. v. Commissioners of Customs and Excise
    [1976] 1 W.L.R. 1; 120 S.J. 49; [1976] 1 All E.R. 117 . 1–10, 8–03
Equitable Trust Company of New York v. Dawson Partners Ltd
    (1926) 27 Lloyd's Rep. 49. 17–21

FALCO FINANCE LTD v. Gough [1999] C.C.L.R. 16; 17 Tr. L.R.
    526 26–08
Farnworth Finance Facilities v. Attryde [1970] 1 W.L.R. 1053; 114
    S.J. 354; [1970] 2 All E.R. 774 25–20
Farquharson Bros. & Co. v. King & Co. [1902] A.C. 325; [1902]
    71 L.J.K.B. 667; [1900–03] All E.R.Rep. 120 5–09

Felthouse v. Bindley [1863] 1 New Rep. 401; 7 L.T. 835; (1863) 1
 W.R. 429; Ex.Ch 2–07
Fercometal S.a.r.l. v. Mediterranean Shipping Co. [1988] 3 W.L.R.
 200; [1988] 2 All E.R. 742; [1988] 2 Lloyd's Rep. 199 13–10
Ferrier, Re [1944] Ch. 295; 114 L.J.Ch. 15; 60 T.L.R. 295 .. 3–18
Fibrosa, Spolka Akcyjna v. Fairburn Lawson Coombe Barbour Ltd
 [1943] A.C. 32; [1942] 2 All E.R. 122 4–15
Financings v. Baldock [1963] 2 Q.B. 104; [1963] 2 W.L.R. 359;
 [1963] 1 All E.R. 443 .... 27–28, 27–29, 27–33
—v. Stimson [1962] 1 W.L.R. 1184; [1962] 79 L.Q.R. 33; [1962]
 3 All E.R. 386 .... 24–03, 24–04
Finlay (James) & Co. Ltd v. Kwik Hoo Tong (N.V.) [1929] 1 K.B.
 400; [1929] 98 L.J.K.B. 251; [1928] All E.R.Rep. 110 14–19
Fisher v. Bell [1961] 1 Q.B. 394; [1960] 3 W.L.R. 919; 104 S.J.
 981 2–03
Fletcher v. Budgen, The Times, June 12, 1974 18–06
Foley v. Classique Coaches Ltd [1934] 2 K.B. 1; 103 L.J.K.B. 550;
 [1934] 151 L.T. 242 2–15
Forthright Finance Ltd v. Carlyle Finance Ltd [1997] 4 All E.R.
 90; [1997] C.C.L.R. 84, CA. 19–05
Forthright Finance Ltd v. Ingate [1997] 4 All E.R. 99; [1997]
 C.C.L.R. 95, CA. 24–14
Forward Trust v. Hornsby [1996] C.C.L.R. 18 25–08
Four Point Garage v. Carter, The Times, November 19, 1984 .. 5–36
Frost v. Aylesbury Dairy Co. [1905] 1 K.B. 608; [1905] 74
 L.J.K.B. 386; [1904–07] All E.R.Rep. 132 .... 7–48, 14–13

GALBRAITH AND GRANT LTD v. Block [1922] 2 K.B. 155 [1922]
 91 L.J.K.B. 649; [1922] All E.R.Rep. 443 11–04
Gallie v. Lee [1971] A.C. 1004; [1970] 3 W.L.R. 1078; 3 All E.R.
 961 24–11
Geddling v. Marsh (1920) 1 K.B. 668; (1920) 89 L.J.K.B. 526;
 [1920] All E.R.Rep. 631 7–32
Genn v. Winkel [1912] 107 L.T. 434; [1912] 28 T.L.R. 483;
 [1911–13] All E.R. 910 3–17
George Mitchell Ltd v. Finney Lock Seeds Ltd. See Mitchell
 (George) (Chesterhall) Ltd v. Finney Lock Seeds Ltd. 10–27,
 10–28
Gill & Duffus SA v. Berger & Co. Inc. [1984] 2 W.L.R. 95; (1984)
 1 All E.R. 438 .... 14–09, 17–07
Glencore Grain Rotterclam BV v. Lebanese Organisation for
 International Commerce [1997] 4 All E.R. 514; [1997] 2
 Lloyd's Rep. 386; [1997] C.L.C. 1274, CA. 13–11
Global Marketing Europe v. Berkshire County Council [1995]
 C.C.L.R. 150 .... 18–17, 18–20
Godley v. Perry [1960] 1 W.L.R. 9; [1960] 1 All E.R. 36; 104 S.J.
 16 .... 9–05, 14–17
Goulston Discount Co. Ltd v. Clark [1967] 2 Q.B. 493; (1966) 3
 W.L.R. 1280; [1967] 1 All E.R. 61 .... 19–12, 27–30
Grant v. Australian Knitting Mills Ltd (1936) A.C. 85; (1936) 105
 L.J.P.C. 6; 154 L.T. 18 .... 7–26, 7–45

Green v. Cade (1978) 1 Lloyd's Rep. 602 10–26
Greenwood v. Bennett [1972] 3 W.L.R. 691; 116 S.J. 762; [1972]
    3 All E.R. 586 . . . . 5–02, 5–03
Griffiths v. Conway (Peter) Ltd (1939) 1 All E.R. 685, C.A. 7–44
Groom (C) Ltd v. Barber [1915] 1 K.B. 316. 17–06

HADLEY v. Baxendale (1854) 9 Exch. 341; (1854) 23 L.J.Ex. 179;
    [1843–60] All E.R. 461 . . . . 14–01, 14–10, 14–13, 14–14
Hall and Pim's Arbitration, Re (1928) 139 L.T. 50; [1928] All
    E.R.Rep. 763 14–15
Hamzeh Malas & Sons v. British Imex Industries [1958] 2 Q.B.
    127; [1958] 2 W.L.R. 100; 102 S.J. 68; [1958] 1 All E.R.
    262; [1957] 2 Lloyd's Rep 549, CA. 17–20
Hare v. Schurek [1993] C.C.L.R. 47 . . . . 21–28, 14–15, 22–05
Hargreave v. Spink [1892] 1 Q.B. 25; [1892] 61 L.J.Q.B. 318; 65
    L.T. 650 5–21
Haringey London Borough v. Piro Shoes Ltd [1976] Crim.L.R.
    462 18–29
Harling v. Eddy [1951] 2 K.B. 739; [1951] 2 T.L.R. 245; [1951] 2
    All E.R. 212 10–09
Harlingdon and Leinster Enterprises v. Christopher Hull Fine Art
    [1991] 1 Q.B. 564; [1990] 3 W.L.R. 13; [1990] 1 All E.R.
    737 7–27
Harris v. Nickerson (1873) L.R.8 Q.B. 286; (1873) 42 L.J.Q.B.
    171; 28 L.T. 414 15–02
Harrop v. Thompson [1975] 1 W.L.R. 545; 118 S.J. 753; [1975] 2
    All E.R. 94 15–09
Hartley v. Hymans [1920] 3 K.B. 479; [1920] 90 L.J.K.B. 14;
    [1920] All E.R.Rep. 328 7–13
Hartog v. Colin and Shields [1939] 3 All E.R. 566. 2–08
Havering, London Borough of v. Stevenson [1970] 3 All E.R. 609;
    (1970) 114 S.J. 664 . . . . 7–17, 18–07
Healey v. Howlett & Sons [1917] 86 L.J.K.B. 337; [1917] 86
    L.J.K.B. 252; 116 L.T. 591 . . . . 3–25, 3–33
Heil v. Hedges [1951] 1 T.L.R. 512; 95 S.J. 140 9–01
Helby v. Matthews [1895] A.C. 471; [1895] 72 L.T. 841; [1895–
    99] All E.R. 821 . . . . 1–15, 5–34, 5–40, 19–02, 19–03, 19–04,
                               19–05, 19–07, 20–13, 27–39, 27–40
Hendy Lennox Ltd v. Grahame Puttick Ltd [1984] 1 W.L.R. 485;
    [1984] 2 All E.R. 152 3–50
Herne Bay Steamboat Co. v. Hutton [1903] 2 K.B. 683; [1903] 72
    L.J.K.B. 879; 89 L.T. 422 4–12
Hill v. Crowe (James) [1978] I.C.R. 298; [1978] 1 All E.R. 812;
    [1977] 2 Lloyd's Rep. 450 9–04
Hoffberger v. Ascot International Bloodstock Bureau (1976) 120
    S.J. 130 14–20
Hollier v. Rambler Motors [1972] 2 Q.B. 71; [1972] 2 W.L.R. 401;
    [1972] 1 All E.R. 399 10–07
Horn v. Minister of Food [1948] 65 T.L.R. 106; [1948] 2 All E.R.
    1036 . . . . 4–03, 4–10

Horsfall v. Thomas (1862) 1 H. & C. 90; (1862) 10 W.R. 650;
    (1862) 6 L.T. 462 6–02
Household, Fire & Carriage Accident Insurance Co. v. Grant
    (1879) 48 L.J.Q.B. 577; [1879] 41 L.T. 298; [1894] 4 Ex.D.
    216 2–06
Howard Marine & Dredging Co. Ltd v. Ogden [1978] Q.B. 574;
    [1978] 2 W.L.R. 515; [1978] 2 All E.R. 1134; [1978] 1
    Lloyd's Rep. 334; (1977) 122 S.J. 48 6–04
Howell v. Coupland (1876) 1 Q.B.D. 258; (1876) 46 L.J.Q.B. 147;
    [1874–80] All E.R. Rep. 878 .... 4–10, 4–11, 4–14, 4–16
Hurley v. Martinez [1991] C.C.L.R. 1; (1990) 9 Tr.L.R. 189 9–25, 18–27

INGHAM v. Emes [1955] 2 Q.B. 366; [1955] 2 All E.R. 740 8–06
Interfoto Picture Library v. Stiletto Visual Programmes [1988] 2
    W.L.R. 615; [1988] 1 All E.R. 348 .... 7–06, 7–07, 10–05
Inter-Office Telephones Ltd v. Freeman (Robert) Co. Ltd [1958] 1
    Q.B. 190; 101 S.J. 958, C.A.; [1957] 3 W.L.R. 971; [1957] 3
    All E.R. 479 25–18

JACKSON v. Rotax Motor and Cycle Co. [1910] 2 K.B. 937; [1910]
    80 L.J.K.B. 38; 103 L.T. 411 11–08
Jarrett v. Bardays Bank Plc [1997] 2 All E.R. 484; (1997) 6 Bank
    L.R. 66; (1997) C.L.C. 391; [1997] C.C.L.R. 32; (1996)
    N.P.C. 159; (1996) 140 S.J.L.B. 252, CA. ... 16–28, 16–29
Jenkins v. Lombard North Central [1983] C.C.L.R. 15; [1984] 1
    W.L.R. 307; [1984] 1 All E.R. 828 .... 23–08, 23–12
John v. Matthews [1970] 2 Q.B. 443; [1970] 2 W.L.R. 1246;
    [1970] 2 All E.R. 643 .... 10–21, 18–04
Johnson v. Agnew [1970] A.C. 367; [1979] 2 W.L.R. 487; 123 S.J.
    217; [1979] 1 All E.R. 983 14–08
Johnson v. Taylor Bros [1920] A.C. 144; (1920) 122 L.T. 130. 17–06
Julian Hodge Bank Ltd v. Hall [1998] C.C.L.R. 14, CA. . . 26–29, 27–22

KARLSHAMNS Oiefabriker v. Eastport Navigation Corp., The Elafi
    [1982] 1 All E.R. 208; [1981] 2 Lloyd's Rep. 679; [1981]
    Com.L.R. 149 3–29
Karsales (Harrow) Ltd v. Wallis [1956] 1 W.L.R. 936; 100 S.J.
    548; [1956] 2 All E.R. 866 25–14
Kendall v. Lillico [1969] 2 A.C. 31; [1968] 3 W.L.R. 110; [1968]
    2 All E.R. 444 .... 10–07, 10–26
Kinchin v. Ashton Park Scooters Ltd (1984) 148 J.P. 540; (1984)
    134 J.P.N. 459 18–16
Kirkham v. Attenborough [1897] 1 Q.B. 201; [1895–99] All E.R.
    Rep. 450; 75 L.T. 543 3–17
Kolfar Plant Ltd v. Tilbury Plant Ltd (1977) 121 S.J. 390 13–02
Kursell v. Timber Operators & Contractors [1927] 1 K.B. 298; 95
    L.J.K.B. 569; 135 L.T. 223 .... 3–04, 3–05
Kwei Tek Chao v. British Traders [1954] 2 Q.B. 459; [1954] 1 All
    E.R. 779; [1954] 2 W.L.R. 365 .... 3–29, 17–07

LAMBERT v. Lewis [1982] A.C. 225; [1981] 2 W.L.R. 713; [1981]
   1 All E.R. 1185; [1981] Lloyd's Rep. 17; [1981] R.T.R. 346;
   125 S.J. 310 . . . . 7–49, 9–05
Lazenby Garages v. Wright (1976) 14–04
Leaf v. International Galleries [1950] 2 K.B. 86; [1950] 66 T.L.R.
   (Pt. 1) 1031; [1950] 1 All E.R. 696 . . . . 6–02, 6–03
Lee v. Butler [1893] 2 Q.B. 318; [1893] 62 L.J.Q.B. 591; [1891–
   94] All E.R. Rep. 1200 . . . . . 5–34, 16–02, 19–03, 19–04, 19–05,
                                              19–07, 28–03
—v. York Coach and Marine [1977] R.T.R. 35 . . . . 7–39, 13–05
Lesters Leather and Skin Co. v. Home and Overseas Brokers
   [1948] W.N. 437; (1848) 64 T.L.R. 569; 92 S.J. 646, C.A. . . 14–19
L'Estrange v. Graucob Ltd [1934] 2 K.B. 394; [1934] 103 L.J.K.B.
   730; (1934) 152 L.T. 164 . . . . 10–03, 10–14
Lewin v. Fuell [1991] 10 Tr.L.R. 126; [1990] Crim.L.R. 658 . . . 18–11,
                                                  18–14
Lewis v. Averay [1972] 1 Q.B. 198; [1971] 3 W.L.R. 603; [1971]
   3 All E.R. 907 5–25
Lloyds Bank v. Bank of America National Trust & Savings
   Assocn. [1938] 2 K.B. 147; [1938] 107 L.J.K.B. 538; [1938]
   2 All E.R. 63 5–17
Lloyds Bowmaker Leasing Ltd v MacDonald [1993] C.C.L.R. 65   24–49
Lockett v. A. & M. Charles Ltd [1938] 159 L.T. 547; [1938] 4 All
   E.R. 170 1–13
Lombard North Central p.l.c. v. Butterworth [1987] Q.B. 527;
   [1987] 2 W.L.R. 7; [1987] 1 All E.R. 267; [1987] C.C.L.R.
   41 . . . . 27–28, 27–29
Lombard North Central v. Stobart [1990] C.C.L.R. 53; 9 Tr.L.R.
   105 26–27
London Wine Co. (Shippers) [1986] P.C.C. 121 . . . . . 3–04, 3–23, 3–24
Long v. Lloyd [1958] 1 W.L.R. 753; 102 S.J. 488; [1958] 2 All
   E.R. 402 6–03
Lowther v. Harris [1927] 1 K.B. 393; [1927] 96 L.J.K.B. 170;
   [1926] All E.R. 352 5–13
Lyons v. May & Baker [1923] 1 K.B. 695; [1923] 92 L.J.K.B. 675 . . 13–02

M.F.I. FURNITURE CENTRES v. Hibbert *The Times*, July 21, 1995   18–35
M.F.I. Warehouses v. Nattrass [1973] Crim.L.R. 196; [1973] 1 All
   E.R. 762 18–22
McDougall v. Aeromarine of Emsworth Ltd [1958] 1 W.L.R. 1126;
   102 S.J. 860; [1958] 3 All E.R. 431 . . . . 3–06, 3–09, 3–20
McManus v. Fortescue [1907] 2 K.B. 1; [1907] 76 L.J.K.B. 393;
   [1904–07] All E.R. Rep. 707 15–04
McRae v. Commonwealth Disposals Commission (1951) 84 C.L.R.
   377 4–06
Manbre Saccharine Co. Ltd v. Corn Products Co. Ltd [1919] 1
   K.B. 189. 17–06
Maple Flock v. Universal Furniture Products Ltd [1934] 1 K.B.
   148; [1934] 103 L.J.K.B. 513; [1933] All E.R. Rep. 15 11–08
Mash & Murrell Ltd v. Joseph J. Emanuel [1961] 1 W.L.R. 862;
   105 S.J. 468; [1961] 1 All E.R. 485 7–42

Mathew v. T.M. Sutton [1994] 1 W.L.R. 1455; [1944] 4 All E.R.
    793; [1994] C.C.L.R. 140 26–47
May & Butcher Ltd v. R. [1934] 2 K.B. 17; [1934] 103 L.J.K.B.
    556; (1934) 151 L.T. 246 . . . . 2–14, 2–15
Melachrino v. Nickoll and Knight [1920] 1 K.B. 693; 89 L.J.K.B.
    906; 122 L.T. 545; 36 T.L.R. 143; 25 Com.Cas. 103; [1918–
    19] All E.R. Rep. 856 14–08
Mercantile Credit Co. v. Cross [1965] 2 Q.B. 205; [1965] 2 W.L.R.
    687; [1965] 1 All E.R. 577 27–23
—v. Hamblin [1965] 2 Q.B. 242; [1964] 3 W.L.R. 798; [1964] 3
    All E.R. 592 . . . . 5–07, 5–10
Mercantile Union Guarantee Corpn. Ltd v. Wheatley [1938] 1 K.B.
    490; [1938] 107 L.J.K.B. 158; [1937] 4 All E.R. 713 25–10
Microbeads v. Vinhurst Road Markings [1975] 1 W.L.R. 218; 119
    S.J. 81; [1975] 1 All E.R. 529 . . . . 7–25, 25–11
Mitchell (George) (Chesterhall) Ltd v. Finney Lock Seeds Ltd
    [1983] 3 W.L.R. 163; [1983] 2 All E.R. 737 . 10–15, 10–17, 10–28
Mitsui v. Flota Mercante Grancolombiana, The Ciudad de Pasto
    [1988] 1 W.L.R. 1145; (1988) 132 S.J. 1182; [1988] 2
    Lloyd's Rep. 208, CA. 17–12
Moore and Landauer, Re [1921] 2 K.B. 519; 90 L.J.K.B. 731;
    125 L.T. 372; [1921] All E.R. Rep. 466 . . . . 7–03, 13–03
Moorgate Mercantile v. Twitchings [1976] 3 W.L.R. 66; 120 S.J.
    470; [1976] 2 All E.R. 641; [1976] R.T.R. 437 5–08
Moorgate Mercantile Leasing Ltd v. Gell and Ugolini [1988]
    C.C.L.R. 1 24–28
Moorgate Services Ltd v. Kabir [1995] C.C.L.R. 74 24–50
Mordaunt Bros. v. British Oil & Cake Mills Ltd [1910] 2 K.B.
    502; [1910] 79 L.J.K.B. 967; 103 L.T. 217 12–08
Morgan v. Russell & Sons [1909] 1 K.B. 357; [1909] 78 L.J.K.B.
    187; (1909) 100 L.T. 118 1–07
Moss v. Hancock [1899] 2 Q.B. 111 1–08
Mount v. Jay & Jay Ltd [1960] 1 Q.B. 159; [1959] 3 W.L.R. 537;
    [1959] 3 All E.R. 307 . . . . 5–37, 12–10
Muskham Finance v. Howard [1963] 1 Q.B. 904; [1963] 2 W.L.R.
    87; [1963] 1 All E.R. 81 24–11

NANKA-BRUCE v. Commonwealth Trust Ltd [1926] A.C. 77;
    [1926] 94 L.J.P.C. 169; (1926) 134 L.T. 35 3–16
Nash v. Inman [1908] 2 K.B. 1; [1908–10] 77 L.J.K.B. 626;
    (1908) 98 L.T. 658 2–11
National Cash Register Co. v. Stanley [1921] 3 K.B. 292; [1921]
    90 L.J.K.B. 1220; (1921) 125 L.T. 765 25–15
National Employers Mutual General Insurance Assoc. Ltd v. Jones
    [1988] 2 W.L.R. 952; [1988] 2 All E.R. 425; [1988] R.T.R.
    289 3–39
Newell and Taylor v. Hicks (1984) 128 S.J. 63; (1984) 148 J.P.
    308; (1984) 81 L.S. Gaz 354; [1984] Crim. L.R. 241; (1984)
    R.T.R. 135, D.C. 18–16, 18–17
Newtons of Wembley v. Williams [1965] 1 Q.B. 560; [1964] 3
    W.L.R. 888; [1964] 3 All E.R. 532 . . . . 5–35, 5–38

Niblett Ltd v. Confectioners Materials Co. [1921] 3 K.B. 387;
  [1921] 90 L.J.K.B. 984; [1921] All E.R. 459 .... 7–24, 7–25
Nichol v. Godts (1854) 10 Exch. 191; (1854) 23 L.J.Ex. 314;
  (1854) 23 L.T.O.S. 162 7–28
Nicholson v. Harper [1895] 2 Ch. 415; [1895–99] 64 L.J.Ch. 672;
  [1895–99] All E.R. Rep. 882 5–30
Norman v. Bennett, *The Times*, July 12, 1974 18–11

OCEANO GRUPO EDITORIAL SA v. Rocio Murciano Quintero,
  June 27, 2000 C-240/98, ECJ 10–44
Ogiersson v. Kitching [1986] 1 W.L.R. 304; [1986] 1 All E.R. 746;
  [1988] R.T.R. 129 .... 18–32, 18–43
Olley v. Marlborough Court [1949] 1 K.B. 532; [1949] L.J.R. 360;
  (1949) 65 T.L.R. 95 10–02
Oppenheimer v. Attenborough & Son [1908] 1 K.B. 221; [1908]
  77 L.J.K.B. 209; [1904–07] All E.R. Rep. 1016 ..... 5–18, 5–19
Overstone v. Shipway [1962] 1 W.L.R. 117; 106 S.J.14; [1962] 1
  All E.R. 52 27–27

PACIFIC MOTOR AUCTIONS v. Motor Credits [1965] A.C. 867;
  [1965] 2 W.L.R. 881; [1965] 2 All E.R. 105 3–29
Pagnan v. Feed Products [1987] 2 Lloyd's Rep. 601 2–15
Pagnan & Fratelli v. Corbiss Industrial Agropacuaria [1970] 1
  W.L.R. 1306; 114 S.J. 568; [1971] 1 All E.R. 165 .. 14–03, 14–05,
                                                          14–06
Panchaud Freres S.A. v. Etablissements General Grain Co. [1970]
  1 Lloyd's Rep. 53, CA. 17–08
Parker, *Re* (1885), 14 Q.B.D. 636; (1885) 29 Ch.D. 199;
  (1885) 54 L.J.Ch. 959 27–47
Parsons (H.) (Livestock) v. Uttley Ingham [1978] Q.B. 791; [1977]
  3 W.L.R. 990; 121 S.J. 811; [1978] 1 All E.R. 525; [1977] 2
  Lloyd's Rep. 522 14–14
Pavia and Co Spa v. Thurmann Nielsen [1952] 2 Q.B. 84; [1952] 1
  All E.R. 492; [1952] 1 Lloyd's Rep. 153, CA. 17–19
Payza Ltd v. Saunders [1919] 2 K.B. 581; [1919] 89 L.J.K.B. 17;
  [1918–19] All E.R. Rep. 961 14–19
Peachdart, *Re* [1983] 3 All E.R. 204 3–50
Pearson v. Rose and Young [1951] 1 K.B. 275; [1951] 66 T.L.R.
  (Pt. 2) 886; [1950] 2 All E.R. 1027 5–15
Perdana Properties v. United Orient Leasing Co. [1981] 1 W.L.R.
  1496; [1982] 1 All E.R. 193; 125 S.J. 791 27–47
Pfeiffer G.m.b.h. v. Arbuthnot Factors [1988] 1 W.L.R. 150 3–54
Pharmaceutical Society of Great Britain v. Boots Cash Chemists
  [1952] 2 Q.B. 795; [1952] 2 T.L.R. 340; 96 S.J. 513 ... 2–02
Phillips v. Brooks Ltd [1919] 2 K.B. 243; [1918–19] 88 L.J.K.B.
  953; [1918–19] All E.R. Rep. 246 .... 5–24, 5–25
Photo Production v. Securicor Transport [1980] A.C. 827; [1980] 2
  W.L.R. 283; 124 S.J. 147; [1980] 1 Lloyd's Rep. 545; [1980]
  1 All E.R. 556 10–15
Pignataro v. Gilroy [1919] 1 K.B. 459; [1919] 88 L.J.K.B. 726;
  [1919] 120 L.T. 480 .... 3–27, 3–30

Pinnock Bros. v. Lewis and Peat Ltd [1923] 1 K.B. 690; [1923] 92
  L.J.K.B. 695; 129 L.T. 320   7–30
Plasticmoda Spa v. Davidsons (Manerester) Ltd. [1952] 1 Lloyd's
  Rep. 527, CA. 17–19
Porter v. General Guarantee Corporation [1982] R.T.R. 384; [1982]
  C.C.L.R. 1 25–07
Pound (A.V.) & Co. v. Hardy (M.W.) & Co. [1956] A.C. 588;
  [1956] 2 W.L.R. 683; 100 S.J. 208; [1956] 1 All E.R. 639,
  CA. 17–14
Priest v. Last [1903] 2 K.B. 148; [1903] 72 L.J.K.B. 657   7–43
Purnell Secretarial Services v. Lease Management Services [1994]
  C.C.L.R. 127 . . . . 24–09, 24–28

R. v. Anderson, *The Times*, December 31, 1987   18–10
—v. Baldwin's Garage [1988] Crim.L.R. 438 21–38
—v. Bevelectric Ltd, *The Times*, 7th Sept 1992   18–20
—v. Breeze [1973] 1 W.L.R. 994; [1973] 2 All E.R. 1141; [1973]
  Crim.L.R. 458 18–17
—v. Coventry City Justices, *exp.* Farrand [1988] R.T.R. 273 . .   18–05
—v. Marshall [1989] C.C.L.R. 47 22–05
—v. Ford Motor Co., *The Times*, July 17, 1974   18–10
—v. McHugh [1977] R.T.R. 1; (1976) 64 Cr.App.R. 92; [1977]
  Crim.L.R.   3–27
—v. Piper [1995] Crim.L.R. 827 16–14
—v. Shrewsbury Magistrates Court, ex. p. Simon Dudley Ltd,
  [1996] C.C.L.R. 22 18–33
—v. Southwood [1987] 3 All E.R. 556; (1987) 85 Cr.App.Rep.
  272 18–13
—v. Sunair Holidays [1973] 1 W.L.R. 1105; 117 S.J. 429; [1973]
  2 All E.R. 1233; 57 Cr.App.R. 782; [1973] Crim.L.R. 587 . . 18–20
—v. Thompson Holidays [1974] Q.B. 592; 2 W.L.R. 371; [1974] 1
  All E.R. 823 18–02
R & B Customs Brokers Co. Ltd v. United Dominions Trust Ltd
  [1988] 1 W.L.R. 321; [1988] 1 All E.R. 847; [1988] R.T.R.
  134: [1988] 65 . . . . 7–34, 7–36, 10–23, 18–07
Rahman v. Sterling Credit Ltd, July 20, 2000, (CA, unreported) . . 26–07
Rank Xerox v. Hepple and Fenneymore [1994] C.C.L.R. 1 24–44
Rasbora Ltd v. J.C.L. Marino Ltd [1977] 1 Lloyd's Rep. 645 10–22
Reardon Smith Line v. Yngvar Hamsen-Tangen [1976] W.L.R.
  989; 120 S.J. 719; [1976] 3 All E.R. 570 . . . .   7–12, 7–31
Regent v. Francesco [1981] Com.L.R. 78; [1981] 3 All E.R.
  327 11–07
Rickards (Charles) v. Oppenheim [1950] 1 K.B. 616; [1950] 66
  T.L.R. (Pt. 1) 435; [1950] 1 All E.R. 420 . . . .   7–14, 13–09
Riley v. Webb [1987] C.C.L.R. 65; [1987] Crim.L.R. 447   9–17
Robinson v. Graves [1935] 1 K.B. 597; [1935] 104 L.J.K.B.
  441   1–12
Rogers v. Parish (Scarborough) Ltd [1987] Q.B. 933; [1987] 2
  W.L.R. 353; [1987] 2 All E.R. 232; [1987] R.T.R. 312   7–40
Rolls Razor Co. v. Cox [1967] 1 Q.B. 552; [1967] 2 W.L.R. 241;
  [1967] 1 All E.R. 397   5–13

Rondel v. Worsley [1696] 1 A.C. 191; [1967] 3 W.L.R. 1666; 111
S.J. 927; [1967] 3 All E.R. 993 8–09
Rosenthal & Sons v. Esmail [1965] 1 W.L.R. 1117; 109 S.J. 553;
[1965] 2 All E.R. 860 11–08
Rotherham Met. Borough Council v. Raysun [1989] C.C.L.R. 1 .. 9–25
Rover Group Limited and Rover Group Finance Ltd v. Sumner
[1995] C.C.L.R. 1 23–09
Rowland v. Divall [1923] 2 K.B. 500; [1923] 92 L.J.K.B. 1041;
[1923] All E.R.Rep. 270 .... 4–12, 7–18, 13–13, 20–07,
25–12
Ruben (E.S.) v. Faire Bros. & Co. [1949] 1 K.B. 254; [1949]
L.J.R. 800; [1949] 1 All E.R. 215 7–50
Rutter v. Palmer [1922] 2 K.B. 87; 91 L.J.K.B. 657; [1922] All
E.R. Rep. 367 10–12

ST ALBANS AND DISTRICT COUNCIL v. International Computers Ltd
[1994] T.L.R. 579, CA 1–14, 7–32, 10–28
St. Albans District Council v. I.C.L. [1996] 4 All E.R. 481; [1997]
Info T.L.R. 58; (1996) 15 Tr. L.R. 444; (1997) 20(2) I.P.D.
20020; [1996] Masons C.L.R. 13, CA. 1–14, 7–32, 10–29
Sainsbury (H.R. and S.) v. Street [1972] 1 W.L.R. 834; 116 S.J.
483; [1972] 3 All E.R. 1127 .... 3–06, 4–14
Samuels v. Davis [1943] K.B. 526; [1943] 112 L.J.K.B. 561 1–13,
1–16, 1–17, 23–04
Saunders v. Anglia Building Society [1971] A.C. 1004; [1970] 3
W.L.R. 1078; 114 S.J. 885; [1970] 3 All E.R. 961 5–10
Scammell v. Ouston [1941] A.C. 251; [1941] 110 L.J.K.B. 197;
[1941] 1 All E.R. 14 .... 10–11, 24–05
Scruttons v. Midland Silicones [1962] A.C. 446; [1962] 2 W.L.R.
186; [1962] 1 All E.R. 1 10–11
Selectmove, Re [1995] 1 W.L.R. 474; [1995] 2 All E.R. 531 . 2–07
Shaw v. Commissioner of Police for the Metropolis [1987] 1
W.L.R. 1332; [1987] 3 All E.R. 405 5–09
Shine v. General Finance Co. Ltd [1988] C.C.L.R. 14; [1988] 1
All E.R. 911 7–40
Shipton, Anderson & Co. v. Well Bros. & Co. [1912] 1 K.B. 574;
[1912] 81 L.J.K.B. 910; 106 L.T. 272 11–07
Simmons v. Potter [1975] R.T.R. 347; [1975] Crim.L.R. 354 18–26
Slater v. Finning Ltd. [1997] A.C. 473; [1996] 3 W.L.R. 190;
[1996] 3 All E.R. 398; (1996) 2 Lloyd's Rep. 353; 1997
S.C.(HL) 8; (1996) C.L.C. 1236; (1996) 15 Tr. L.R. 458,
HL. 7–44
—v. Ravenhill [1984] Tr.L. 29 18–31
Smith v. Land and House Property Corporation (1884) 28 Ch.D. 7;
(1884) 51 L.T. 718; (1884) 49 J.P. 182, C.A. 6–02
Smyth (Ross) & Co. Ltd v. Bailey Son & Co. [1940] 3 All E.R.
60; (1940) 164 L.T. 102 11–08
Snell v. Unity Finance Co. [1964] 2 Q.B. 203; [1963] 3 W.L.R.
559; 107 S.J. 533 24–15
Soper v. Arnold [1889] 14 App.Cas. 429; [1889] 59 L.J.Ch. 214;
(1889) 61 L.T. 702 2–17

Southern and District Finance plc v. Barnes [1995] C.C.L.R. 62 . 26–21, 26–23

Southwark London Borough (1983) 147 J.P. 470; (1983) 2 Tr.L. 13 . . . . 9–19, 18–07

Stadium Finance Co. v. Robbins [1962] 2 Q.B. 664; [1962] 3 W.L.R. 453; [1962] All E.R. 633 . . . . 5–16, 5–18

Sterns Ltd v. Vickers Ltd [1923] 1 K.B. 78; [1923] 92 L.J.K.B. 331; [1922] All E.R. Rep. 126 . . . . 3–33, 3–34, 3–45

Stevenson v. Beverley Bentinck [1976] 1 W.L.R. 483; 120 S.J. 197; [1976] 2 All E.R. 606; [1976] R.T.R. 543; 19 Man.Law 2 5–40

Stevenson v. Rogers [1999] 1 All E.R. 613; *The Times*, December 31, 1998, CA. 7–34, 10–23, 18–07

Sunair Holidays v. Dodd [1970] 1 W.L.R. 1593; 114 S.J. 372; [1970] 2 All E.R. 410 18–18

TAI HING COTTON MILL LTD v. Kamsing Knitting Factor [1978] 2 W.L.R. 62; (1977) 121 S.J. 662; [1978] 1 All E.R. 515 14–07

Teheran-Europe v. Belton (S.T.) [1968] 2 Q.B. 545; [1968] 3 W.L.R. 205; [1968] 2 All E.R. 886 7–45

Tesco Supermarkets v. Nattrass [1972] A.C. 153; [1971] 2 W.L.R. 116; [1971] 2 All E.R. 127 . . . . 18–23, 18–28

Thompson v. Robinson [1955] Ch. 177; [1955] 2 W.L.R. 185; [1955] 1 All E.R. 154 14–04

Thornett and Fehr v. Beers & Son [1919] 1 K.B. 486; [1919] 88 L.J.K.B. 684; (1919) 120 L.T. 570 7–35

Thornton v. Shoe Lane Parking Co. [1971] 2 Q.B. 163; [1971] 2 W.L.R. 585; (1970) 115 S.J. 75 2–05

Times Furnishing Co. Ltd v. Hutchings [1938] 1 K.B. 775; [1938] 107 L.J.K.B. 432; [1935] 1 All E.R. 422 27–47

Toys 'R' Us v. Gloucestershire CC [1994] Tr.L.R. 276; [1994] Crim.L.R. 521 18–38

Truk (UK) Ltd v. Tokmakidis GmbH [2000] 1 Lloyd's Rep 543 . . 13–06

U.C.B. LEASING v. Holtom [1987] C.C.L.R. 101 25–21

Underwood Ltd v. Burgh Castle Brick & Cement Syndicate [1922] 1 K.B. 343; [1922] 91 L.J.K.B. 355; [1921] All E.R. Rep. 515 . . . . 3–13, 3–14, 3–22

Union Transport Finance v. British Car Auctions [1978] 2 All E.R. 385 27–42

United City Merchants Investments Ltd. v. Royal Bank of Canada [1983] 1 A.C. 168; [1982] 2 W.L.R. 1039; [1982] 2 All E.R. 720; [1982] Lloyd's Rep. 1; [1982] Com L.R. 142, HL. 17–22

United Dominions Trust (Commercial) Ltd v. Ennis [1968] Q.B. 54; [1967] 3 W.L.R. 1; [1967] 2 E.R. 345 . . 22–08, 27–07, 27–22

— v. Taylor, 1980 S.L.T. 28; [1980] C.C.L.R. 29 25–08

United Dominions Trust Ltd v. Western [1976] Q.B. 513; [1976] 2 W.L.R. 64; 119 S.J. 792; [1975] 3 All E.R. 1017 . . . 5–10, 24–08, 24–11, 27–33

VACWELL ENGINEERING CO. v. B.D.H. Chemicals [1971] 1 Q.B.
88; [1969] 3 W.L.R. 927; [1969] 3 All E.R. 1681 14–13
Varley v. Whipp [1900] 1 Q.B. 513; [1900] 69 L.J.Q.B. 333;
[1900] 48 W.R. 363 . . . . 3–06, 3–12
Victoria Laundry v. Newman Industries Coulson & Co. [1949] 2
K.B. 529; [1949] 65 T.L.R. 274; [1949] 1 All E.R. 997 . . . 14–01,
14–05
Vitol S.A. v. Norelf Ltd [1995] 3 W.L.R. 549; [1995] 3 All E.R.
971 13–06

WADHAM STRINGER LTD v. Meaney [1981] 1 W.L.R. 39; [1980] 3
All E.R. 789; [1981] R.T.R. 152; [1980] Com.L.R. 7; 124 S.J.
807; [1987] C.C.L.R. 18 . . . . 27–15, 27–16
Wait, Re [1927] 1 Ch. 606; 71 S.J. 56; [1926] All E.R. Rep.
433 . . . . 3–04, 3–05, 13–01
Walker v. Simon Dudley Ltd; Sub nom. Shopshire C.C.V. Simon
Dudley Ltd. (1997) 16 Tr. L.R. 69; (1997) 161 J.P. 224;
(1997) 161 J.P. N285, QBD. 18–06
Wallis, Son and Wells v. Pratt and Haynes [1911] A.C. 394; [1911]
80 L.J.K.B. 1058; [1911–13] All E.R. Rep. 989 . . . . 7–10, 10–13
Ward v. Bignall [1967] I Q.B. 534; [1967] 2 W.L.R. 1050; [1967]
2 All E.R. 449 . . . . 3–08, 12–12
Wardars (Import & Export) v. Norwood [1968] 2 Q.B. 663; [1968]
2 W.L.R. 1440; [1968] 2 All E.R. 602 3–26
Warlow v. Harrison (1859) 1 E. & E. 309; (1859) 29 L.J.Q.B. 14;
[1843–60] All E.R. Rep. 620 15–02
Warman v. Southern Counties Car Finance Corporation [1949] 2
K.B. 576; [1949] L.J.R. 1182; [1949] 1 All E.R. 711 . 18–43, 25–12
Warwickshire County Council v. Johnson [1993] A.C. 583; [1993]
2 W.L.R. 1; [1993] 1 All E.R. 299 . . . . 18–35, 18–37
Weiner v. Gill [1906] 2 K.B. 574; [1906] 75 L.J.K.B. 916; [1904–
07] All E.R. Rep. 773 . . . . 1–17, 3–18, 5–32
—v. Harris [1910] 1 K.B. 285; [1910] 79 L.J.K.B. 342; (1910) 101
L.T. 647 1–17
Wertheim v. Chicoutimi Pulp Co. [1911] A.C. 301; [1911] 80
L.J.P.C. 91; [1909–10] All E.R. Rep. 707 14–17
Westminster City Council v. Ray Allen (Manshops) Ltd [1982] 1
W.L.R. 383; 126 S.J. 115; [1982] 1 All E.R. 771 18–16
Wickens Motors (Gloucester) v. Hall [1972] 1 W.L.R. 1418; 116
S.J. 744; [1972] 3 All E.R. 759 18–05
Wickham Holdings v. Brooke House Motors [1967] 1 W.L.R. 295;
[1967] 1 All E.R. 117 . . . . 27–18, 27–40, 27–41
Williams Bros. v. Ed. T. Agius Ltd [1914] A.C. 510; [1914] 83
L.J.K.B. 715; [1914–15] All E.R. Rep. 97 14–15
Wills v. Wood [1984] C.C.L.R. 7 22–06
Wimble & Sons v. Rosenberg [1913] 3 K.B. 743. 17–11
Wings v. Ellis [1985] A.C. 272; [1984] 3 W.L.R. 965; [1984] 3 All
E.R. 577; [1985] L.G.R. 193 18–24
Woodchester Equipment (Leasing) Limited v. BACFID [1995]
C.C.L.R. 51 24–28

Woodchester Lease Management Services Ltd. v. Swain & Co. [1999] C.C.L.R 8. . . . . 26–10, 27–08

Worcester Works Finance v. Cooden Engineering [1972] 1 Q.B. 210; [1971] 3 W.L.R. 661; 115 S.J. 605; [1971] 3 All E.R. 708 5–31

Workman Clark & Co. Ltd v. Lloyd Brazileno [1908] 1 K.B. 968; [1908] 77 L.J.K.B. 953; 99 L.T. 477 12–02

Wormell v. R.H.M. Agriculture [1987] 1 W.L.R. 1091; [1987] 3 All E.R. 75 7–32

Wycombe Marsh Garages v. Fowler [1972] 1 W.L.R. 1156; 116 S.J. 467; [1972] 3 All E.R. 248 18–05

YEOMAN CREDIT v. Latter [1961] 1 W.L.R. 828; 105 S.J. 300 . . . 2–12

—v. Waragowski [1961] 1 W.L.R. 1124; 105 S.J. 588; [1961] 3 All E.R. 145 . . . . . . 27–27, 27–28, 27–29, 27–32, 27–33, 27–35

Young & Marten v. McManus Childs [1969] 1 A.C. 454; [1968] 3 W.L.R. 630 [1968] 2 All E.R. 1169 1–11

Young (Thomas) & Sons v. Hobson & Partner (1949) 65 T.L.R. 365, C.A. 11–09

ZAWADSKI v. Sleigh (1975) 119 S.J. 318 [1975] R.T.R. 113; [1975] Crim.L.R. 180 18–12

Zoan v. Rouamba [2000] 2 All E.R. 620; [2000] C.C.L.R 18. 21–25

TABLE OF STATUTES

1677 Statute of Frauds (29
      Cha. 2, c. 3) . . 19–12,
                         24–47
1867 Policies of Assurance
      Act (30 & 31
      Vict., c. 144). . 24–47
1872 Pawnbrokers Act (35
      & 36 Vict., c.
      93) 21–01, 26–40
1878 Bills of Sale Act (41
      & 42 Vict., c.
      31) 20–09, 24–47
1882 Bills of Sale Act
      (1878)
      Amendment Act
      (45 & 46 Vict.,
      c. 43). 24–47
1889 Factors Act (52 &
      53 Vict., c. 45)   5–11
      s. 1(1)   5–12
      s. 2 . . . 5–13, 5–14, 5–17
        (1).   5–11
        (3).   5–15
        (4).   5–15
      s. 8 . . 5–26, 5–28, 12–12
      s. 9 . . 5–32, 5–33, 5–34,
      5–37, 5–38, 12–09, 19–04,
            27–39, 28–03, 28–05
1893 Sale of Goods Act
      (56 & 57 Vict.,
      c. 71).   1–03,
                    7–02, 7–16
      s. 25(1) 5–28, 5–30
1900 Moneylenders   Act
      (63 & 64 Vict.,
      c. 51).   20–01
1908 Law   of   Distress
      Amendment Act
      (8 Edw. 7, c.
      53)   27–46
1925 Law of Property Act
      (15 & 16 Geo.
      5, c. 20).   9–01
      s. 136 . . . . 9–01, 24–47

1927 Auctions   (Bidding
      Agreements)
      Act (17 & 18
      Geo. 5, c. 12) .   15–09
      Moneylenders   Act
      (17 & 18 Geo.
      5, c. 21).   19–01
1943 Law   Reform
      (Frustrated
      Contracts) Act
      (6 & 7 Geo. 6,
      c. 40).   4–16
1948 Companies Act (11
      & 12 Geo. 6, c.
      38)   3–50
      s. 94   3–50
1960 Pawnbrokers Act (8
      & 9 Eliz. 2, c.
      24) 21–01, 26–40
1961 Consumer Protection
      Act (9 & 10
      Eliz. 2, c. 40)9–15, 9–19
      Mock Auctions Act
      (9 & 10 Eliz. 2,
      c. 47).   15–10
1964 Hire Purchase Act
      (c. 53)Part III .   5–39,
      7–20, 19–06, 21–01, 27–39,
            27–42, 28–05, 28–13
      s. 27   7–20
        (6).   7–20
      Trading Stamps Act
      (c. 71)   8–07
      s. 4   8–07
1965 Industrial   and
      Provident
      Societies Act (c.
      12)   20–34
      Hire Purchase Act
      (c. 16)   20–01,
            20–02, 27–23
1967 Misrepresentation
      Act (c. 7). . . .   1–03
      s. 2(1)   6–04
        (2).   6–04
      s. 3 . . . . . . 6–05, 10–34

1967 Advertisements (Hire
    Purchase) Act
    (c. 42) 20–01
1968 Trade Descriptions
    Act (c. 29) . . . 6–01,
    7–34, 18–01, 18–03,
    18–14, 18–49, 23–09
    s. 1 . . . . . 18–05, 18–09,
    18–16, 18–28, 18–32
      (1). 18–05
        (a). 18–13
        (b). . 18–13, 18–31
    s. 2 18–05
    s. 4(3) . . . 18–06, 18–10
    s. 6 . . . . . 18–14, 18–29
    s. 11 . . . . 18–23, 18–34
    s. 14 . . . . 18–02, 18–05,
    18–14, 18–15, 18–16,
    18–17, 18–18, 18–19,
    18–20, 18–21, 18–23,
    18–25, 18–32
    s. 19 18–33
    s. 23 . . . . 18–32, 18–43
    s. 24 . . . . 18–11, 18–26,
    18–27, 18–32, 18–42,
    18–49, 21–07, 23–10
      (1). . . . 18–26, 18–31
      (3). 18–31
    s. 25 . . . . 18–11, 18–26,
    18–31, 18–32, 18–49
    s. 35 18–03
1969 Family Law Reform
    Act (c. 46) . . . 2–11
1971 Unsolicited Goods
    and Services
    Act (c. 30) . . . 2–09
    s. 1 2–09
    s. 2 2–09
    s. 4 2–09
1972 Defective Premises
    Act (c. 35) . . . 9–09
1973 Supply of Goods
    (Implied Terms)
    Act (c. 13) . . . 1–03,
    1–18, 7–16, 7–33, 10–18,
    10–27, 25–09
    ss. 8–11 . . . 8–07, 25–09,
    25–22
    s. 8 25–10
      (1)(a). . 25–10, 25–12
      (b). 25–11

1973 Supply of Goods (Im-
    plied Terms) Act
    (c. 13)—cont.
      (2). 25–10
    s. 9 25–14
      (1). 25–14
      (1A) 25–14
      (2). 25–14
    s. 10 25–15
    s. 11 25–16
    s. 14 25–23
    Fair Trading Act (c.
    41) 10–47, 18–01,
    18–46
    Pt. I. 18–46
    Pt. III 18–46
    s. 2 18–48
    s. 13 18–48
    s. 14 18–48
    FTA s. 17. 18–48
    s. 22 18–48
    s. 25 18–49
    ss. 27–33 18–49
    ss. 34–43 18–50
    s. 34 18–50
    ss. 118–123 18–47
    s. 119 18–47
    s. 120(3) 18–47
    Powers of Criminal
    Courts Act (c.
    62) 18–02
    s. 35 18–02
1974 Prices Act (c. 24). . 18–41
    Consumer Credit
    Act (c. 39). . 1–03,
    2–22, 5–10, 5–33, 16–03,
    16–07, 16–18, 16–20, 18–01,
    18–30, 18–52, 19–01, 19–04,
    19–05, 19–07, 21–01, 21–05,
    26–27
    ss. 8–20 21–04
    s. 8(1) 21–06
      (2). 21–06
    s. 9(1) . . . 19–07, 21–06
      (3). 21–06
    s. 11 21–19
    s. 12 21–20
    s. 13 21–20
    s. 14 26–39
    s. 15 21–15
    s. 16 21–25

1974 Prices Act (c. 24)
—*cont.*

s. 17 . . . . 21–27, 24–32
s. 19 21–27
  (3). . . . 21–29, 21–31
s. 20 . . . . 21–36, 21–39
s. 21 22–07
s. 23(1) 22–17
  (3). 23–04
s. 39(1) 22–17
  (2). 22–17
s. 40 . . . . 22–19, 22–20,
            22–21
s. 43 23–08
s. 45 23–09
s. 46 . . . . 18–33, 23–09
s. 48 . . . . 22–03, 23–03
s. 49 23–04
  (3). 23–04
s. 50 23–06
s. 51 . . . . 23–07, 26–35,
            26–39
s. 56 . . . . . 6–06, 24–10,
    24–13, 24–18, 24–19,
    24–20, 24–23, 24–24,
    24–26, 24–27, 25–05
  (1)(b). 24–13
  (2). . . 24–10, 24–19
s. 57 . . . . 24–04, 24–17,
       24–22, 24–23
s. 58 . . . . 24–40, 24–41
ss. 60–65 24–32
s. 60 24–34
s. 61 . . . . 24–34, 24–35
  (1)(b). 24–34
  (2). 24–40
ss. 62–64 26–46
s. 62 . . . . 24–36, 24–38,
       24–41, 24–42
s. 63 . . . . 24–36, 24–38,
    24–41, 24–42, 24–33
s. 64 . . . . 24–39, 24–42,
           24–53
s. 65 24–44
s. 66 26–36
ss. 67–73 24–48
s. 67 . . . . 24–49, 24–50
s. 68 . . . . 24–51, 24–52,
           24–53
s. 69 . . . . 21–29, 24–17,
       24–22, 24–52

1974 Prices Act (c. 24)
—*cont.*

  (1). 21–31
  (2). 24–57
  (7). 24–53
s. 71 24–58
s. 72 24–26
s. 74 . . . . 24–32, 24–35,
           24–51
s. 75 . . . . . 6–06, 13–14,
   24–24, 24–25, 24–26,
   25–03, 25–04, 25–05,
      25–06, 25–07
s. 76 . . . . 26–17, 26–18,
   27–10, 27–11, 28–04,
           28–09
ss. 77–79 . 24–38, 26–26
s. 78(4) 26–27
  (5). 26–27
s. 81 . . . . 26–28, 27–22,
           27–35
s. 82 . . . . 26 30, 27–01
  (1). 26–30
  (2). 26–30
  (3). 26–31
  (4). 26–31
s. 83 . . . . 26–32, 26–34
s. 84 . . . . 26–32, 26–34,
           26–37
s. 85 26–35
s. 86 . . . . 26–12, 26–13,
   26–14, 28–04, 28–09
  (1). 26–12
s. 87 . . . . 26–09, 26–10,
   26–18, 26–19, 27–08,
   27–11, 27–15, 27–42,
   28–04, 28–08, 28–09
  (1). . . . 26–09, 26–10,
   26–12, 26–14, 26–17,
           26–18
s. 88 . . . . 26–09, 26–19
s. 89 27–11
s. 90 . . . . 27–21, 27–23,
           28–04
  (2). 27–21
s. 91 . . . . 27–23, 28–04
s. 92 . . . . 27–19, 28–11
s. 93 26–05
s. 94 . . . . 26–04, 28–01
s. 95 . . . . 26–11, 27–16
s. 96(1) 21–31

1974 Prices Act (c. 24)
—*cont.*
s. 97 .... 26–26, 26–27
s. 98 .... 26–17, 26–18,
 27–10, 28–04, 28–09
s. 99 .... 27–05, 27–06,
 27–15, 27–16, 27–22,
 27–34, 28–04
s. 100 ... 27–05, 27–34,
 28–01
 (2). ... 27–35, 28–04
 (5). ... 27–19, 27–21
s. 101 ... 28–09, 28–10
s. 102 ... 24–13, 24–17,
 21–26
s. 103 26–26
s. 105 24–47
ss. 107–109 26–42
ss. 107–110 26–26,
 26–27
s. 111 26–41
ss. 112–114 26–46
s. 113 ... 21–03, 24–44,
 24–47, 26–43, 26–44,
 27–30
ss. 114–121 26–46
s. 126 26–45
s. 127 ... 24–42, 24–44,
 24–47
s. 129 ... 26–19, 27–15,
 27–36, 28–01, 28–04
s. 130 27–45
 (2). 26–20
s. 132 28–12
s. 133 ... 27–37, 28–04
 (4). 27–37
s. 135 ... 24–44, 24–47,
 26–22
 (3). ... 24–44, 28–07
s. 136 ... 24–47, 26–08,
 26–23
ss. 137–140 21–13,
 26–06, 26–07
s. 138 26–06
s. 139(2) 26–07
s. 141 26–03
s. 145 22–15
 (1). 22–10
s. 146 ... 22–10, 22–15
 (5). 22–16
s. 147 22–21

1974 Prices Act (c. 24)
—*cont.*
s. 148 22–20
s. 149 22–21
s. 151 23–08
s. 153 23–05
s. 154 23–05
s. 155 24–30
ss. 157–159 24–30
s. 157 24–31
s. 158 24–31
s. 159 24–31
s. 168 23–10
s. 171 26–37
 (7). 26–06
s. 172 ... 26–26, 26–27
s. 173 ... 21–03, 27–05,
 28–10
 (3). 25–10
s. 175 22–14
s. 187(3) 21–23
s. 189 ...24, 46, 26–14,
 26–16
 (1). ...21–28, 22–08,
 22–09, 25–05, 26–14,
 26–16, 26–40
 (2). 22–05
 Sched. 4. 28–05
1977 Torts (Interference
 with Goods) Act
 (c. 32) ... 5–03, 5–40,
 27–18, 27–40
 Unfair Contract
 Terms Act
 (c. 50) ... 1–03, 6–05,
 7–02, 7–07, 10–01, 10–11,
 10–12, 10–19, 10–22,
 10–27, 10–30, 10–36,
 10–37, 10–45, 10–47,
 11–07, 13–03, 13–07,
 15–05, 16–31, 18–07,
 19–07, 25–05, 25–22
s. 1 10–38
s. 2 ..... 10–32, 10–33,
 10–35, 10–36, 10–38
s. 3 ..... 10–30, 10–32,
 10–33, 10–34, 10–35,
 10–36, 10–38
 (2). 10–31
s. 5 ..... 9–03, 10–33,
 10–35, 10–48

1977 Unfair Contract
    Terms Act (c.
    50)—*cont.*
    s. 6 . . . . . 10–20, 10–24,
      10–32, 10–33, 10–35,
      10–47, 10–48
    s. 8 . . . . . 10–32, 10–34,
      10–35, 10–36
    s. 11 6–05
    s. 12 10–21
    s. 13 10–18
    s. 14 10–35
    Sched. 2. . 10–25, 10–32
1978 House Purchase
    Assistance and
    Housing
    Corporation
    Guarantee Act
    (c. 27) 21–25
    Consumer Safety Act
    (c. 38) 9–15
1979 Credit Unions Act
    (c. 34) 20–34
    s. 11 20–35
    Sale of Goods Act
    (c. 54) . . . 1–01, 1–03,
      1–18, 3–01, 3–05, 4–03,
      7–01, 8–01, 8–02, 9–06,
      9–10, 10–05, 24–51
    s. 2(1) .1–04, 1–05, 1–12
    s. 3(1) 2–11
    (2). 2–11
    (3). 2–11
    s. 5(1) 3–06
    s. 6 . . 4–02, 4–03, 4–04,
      4–05, 4–06, 4–08, 4–09,
      4–10, 4–11
    s. 7 . . 4–08, 4–09, 4–10,
      4–11, 4–12, 4–13,
      4–15, 4–16
    s. 8 2–15
    (1). 2–13
    (2). 2–13, 2–14, 2–16
    (3). 2–13
    (9). 2–16
    ss. 10–15 25–23
    s. 10 7–13
    s. 11 . . . . 10–24, 11–08
    (2). 13–09
    s. 11(4) . . .7–13, 11–08,
      25–20, 25–23

1979 Sale of Goods Act (c.
    54)—*cont.*
    ss. 12–15 . . .7–09, 7–13,
      7–33, 8–02, 8–07, 8–08,
      9–01, 10–18, 10–20,
      10–21, 10–30, 10–32,
      10–36, 25–02, 25–09,
      25–22
    s. 12 . . . . . .7–17, 7–18,
      7–19, 7–21, 7–22, 7–25,
      10–24, 15–08, 25–10,
      25–12, 27–41
    (1). 7–17
    (2). 7–17
    (3). 7–17, 7–22, 7–23
    (5A) 7–17
    ss. 13–15 . 10–24, 10–35,
      10–47, 13–02, 15–05
    s. 13 . . . . . .7–11, 7–26,
      7–31, 8–04, 10–26,
      11–07, 13–03, 25–14
    (1). 7–26
    (1A) 7–26
    (2). 7–26, 7–28
    (2c)(a)–(c) . . 7–33
    s. 13(3) 7–26, 7–28
    s. 14 . 7–11, 7–13, 7–31,
      7–32, 7–34, 8–03,
      8–04, 10–22,10–35,
      10–36 13–03, 19–10,
      25–15, 25–23
    (1). 7–32
    (2). 7–32, 7–33,
      7–35, 7–43, 7–36
    (2A) 7–33, 7–37
    (2B)7–33, 7–37, 7–40
    (a). . . .7–33, 7–37
    (b). . . .7–33, 7–40
    (c). . . .7–33, 7–40
    (e). . . .7–33, 7–42
    (2C) 7–33
    (b). 7–35
    (3). 7–32, 7–36,
      7–37, 7–43, 7–45
    (b). 25–15
    (5). 7–33
    s. 15 . 7–11, 7–32, 7–50,
      10–35, 13–03, 25–16
    (1). 7–50
    (2). 7–50
    (a). 7–50

1979 Sale of Goods Act (c.
      54)—*cont.*
           (c).   7–50
      s. 15A   13–03
      ss. 16–18   3–48
      ss. 16–19   3–07
      s. 16 . . . . . .3–09, 3–25,
                       3–37, 3–38
      s. 17 . . . . . .3–08, 3–09,
                      3–10, 19–03
      s. 18 . . . . . .3–08, 3–09,
                3–10, 3–18, 3–21,
                      3–27, 19–03
      s. 18, rule 1 3–11,
           3–12, 3–13, 3–14,
                3–16, 19–05
           2. . . . .3–15, 3–16
           3.   3–16
           4. . . . .3–17, 3–18
           5. . . . 3–09, 3–10,
                     3–19, 3–27
           (1). .3–19, 3–21,
                 3–27, 3–43
           (2). . 3–19, 3–25
           (3). . 3–28, 3–39
           (a)–(b) . . . 3–28
           (4). 3–28
      s. 19 . . . . . . 3–25, 3–29
      s. 20 . . . . . .3–02, 3–30,
           3–32, 3–35, 3–45
           (1). 3–27
           (2). . 3–21, 3–31
           (3). 3–32
      s. 20A 3–09, 3–24,
           3–38, 3–39, 3–46,
                3–47, 4–17
      s. 20B   3–43
      s. 21(1) 5–02, 5–04
           (2)(a).   5–40
           (b).   5–41
      s. 22(1)   5–20
      s. 23 . . . . . . 5–21, 5–25
      s. 24 . .3–42, 3–44, 5–26
      s. 25 . . . . . .5–32, 5–33,
           5–34, 5–35, 5–37, 5–38,
                5–39, 12–09, 12–10,
                19–04, 27–39, 28–03,
                            28–05
           (2). 5–33, 28–05
      s. 28 11–02,11–10,
                      12–02, 12–05

1979 Sale of Goods Act (c.
      54)—*cont.*
      s. 29(1)   11–04
           (2). . . . 10–30, 11–04
           (3). 11–04
           (5). 11–05
           (6). 11–06
      s. 30 . . . . .11–07, 11–08
           (1). 11–07
           (2). 11–07
           (2A)(a).   11–07
              (b).   11–07
           (2B)   11–07
           (2C)   11–07
           (2D)   11–07
              (a).   11–07
              (b).   11–07
           (2E).   11–07
           (3). 11–07
           (5). 11–07
      s. 31(2)   11–08
      s. 32(1)   11–09
           (2). . . . 11–09, 13–03
           (3). 11–09
      s. 33   3–35
      s. 35 . . . . .7–19, 13–04,
                     13–06, 13–07
           (7). 13–07
      s. 35A   13–07
           (1). 13–07
           (2). 13–07
           (3). 13–07
           (4). 13–07
      s. 36 13–02
      s. 37 . . . . 12–02, 14–04
           (1). 12–02
           (2). 12–02
      s. 38 . . . . . 8–05, 12–04
      s. 41(1) . . 12–05, 12–09
      s. 42 12–05
      s. 43(1)   12–07
      s. 44 12–11
      s. 45 12–11
      s. 46 12–11
      s. 47 12–09
           (1). 12–09
           (2). . . .12–09, 12–10,
                            12–11
      s. 48 12–12
           (1). 12–12
           (2). 12–12

1979 Sale of Goods Act (c.
       54)—*cont.*
         (3).   12–12
         (4).   12–12
       s. 49 . . . . . 3–02, 11–02,
                    12–02, 12–03
       s. 50 . . . . 12–03, 14–06,
                          14–07
         (1).   14–03
         (2).   14–03
         (3).   14–03
       s. 51 . . . . 14–05, 14–07
         (1).   14–04
         (2).   14–04
         (3).   14–04
       s. 52   13–01
       s. 53   14–11
         (1).   14–14
         (2).   14–12
         (3).   14–18
         (4).   14–15
       s. 54   11–10
       s. 55(1) . . . 7–02, 10–01,
                          10–19
       s. 57   15–03
         (1).   15–03
         (2). 2–04, 15–03
         (3). . . . 15–03, 15–04
         (4).   15–03
         (5).   15–03
         (6).   15–03
       s. 61 . 1–06, 1–08, 3–04,
                    11–03, 19–02
         (1).   7–10
         (4).   12–05
         (5).   3–13
       s. 62(2)   4–04
       Sched. 4.   5–33
1981 Supreme Court Act
       (c. 54)   5–42
       s. 138   5–42
1982 Civil Jurisdiction and
       Judgments Act
       (c. 27) . . . 9–11, 16–23
       Supply of Goods and
       Services Act (c.
       29)   1–18,
              8–01, 10–38, 25–02
       ss. 1–5 25–02
       s. 1 8–02
         (1).   8–07

1982 Supply of Goods and
       Services Act (c.
       29)—*cont.*
         (2).   8–07
       ss. 2–5 . . . . .8–02, 8–05,
                          10–37
       s. 2   8–02
       s. 3   8–02
       s. 4 . . . . 8–02, 8–03
       s. 5   8–02
       ss. 6–10 . . . 8–08, 10–37
       s. 7   8–08
       s. 8   8–08
       s. 9   8–08
       s. 10   8–08
       ss. 12–16   8–01
       ss. 13–15   8–09
       s. 13 . . . . . 8–09, 10–38,
                          25–02
       s. 14 . . . . 10–38, 25–02
         (1).   8–09
         (2).   8–09
       s. 15   10–38
         (1).   8–09
         (2).   8–09
       Insurance Companies
         Act (c. 50) . . .   2–19
       ss. 75–77   21–33
1985 Companies Act (c. 6)   3–50,
                                3–54
       s. 365   3–50
1986 Financial   Services
         Act (c. 60) . . .   2–19
1987 Minors'   Contracts
         Act (c. 13) . . .   2–10
       s. 2 2–12
       s. 3 2–11
       Banking Act (c. 22)   2–19
       s. 89 21–23
       Consumer Protection
         Act (c. 43) 1–18, 7–54,
              9–28, 10–12, 10–18,
                   10–33, 10–36
       CPA Pt. I   9–06,
                     9–18, 10–11
       Pt. II 9–15, 9–18,
                     9–19, 18–01
       Pt. III . . . 18–01, 18–28,
                          18–34
       s. 1(2)   9–09
       s. 2 . . . . 9–07, 9–11

1987 Consumer Protection
Act (c. 43)
—*cont.*
s. 3 9–08
(2). 9–08
s. 4 9–12
s. 5 9–10
s. 6(1) 9–13
s. 7 . . . . . . 9–14, 10–18
s. 10 . . . . . .9–17, 9–18,
9–20, 16–34
s. 13 9–16
s. 14 9–16
(7). 9–16
s. 20 . . . . 18–34, 18–37,
18–38, 18–39
(1). 18–35
(2). 18–35
s. 21 18–34
s. 23 18–43
s. 24 18–41
s. 25 . . . . 18–34, 18–38
s. 26 . . . . 18–40, 18–41
s. 31 9–16
s. 39 . . . . . .9–16, 9–17,
18–37, 18–43
CPA s. 40. 18–43
s. 41(4) 10–18
s. 45 9–09
1988 Control of Mis-
leading Adver-
tisements Set. . 18–01
Criminal Justice Act
(c. 33) 18–02
s. 104 18–02
1989 Law of Property
(Miscellaneous
Provisions) Act
(c. 34) 2–10
s. 2 2–10

1990 Education (Student
Loans) Act (c.
6) . . . .
21–26, 23–06
Contracts (Applicable
Law) Act (c.
36) 16–23
1994 Sale of Goods
(Amendment)
Act (c. 32) . . . 5–20
Sale and Supply of
Goods Act (c.
35) 1–03, 7–11,
7–16, 7–37, 13–03
1995 Sale of Goods
(Amendment)
Act (c. 29) . . . 1–03,
3–28, 3–37, 3–45,
4–17
1998 Data Protection Act
s. 7 (c. 29) . . . 24–31
1999 Contracts (Rights of
Third Parties)
Act (c. 31) . . . 7–03,
7–04, 7–45, 9–01,
10–11
s. 1 7–03
(1). 7–03
(2). 7–03
(3). 7–03
(4). 7–03
s. 2 7–05
2000 Electronic Com-
munications Act
(c. 7). . . 16–02, 16–04
Financial Services
and Markets Act
(c. 8) 20–36

TABLE OF STATUTORY INSTRUMENTS

Mail Order Transactions (Information) Order (S.I. 1976 No. 1812) 18–44, 18–49

Consumer Transactions (Restrictions on Statements) Order (S.I. 1976 No. 1813) 10–47, 10–48, 18–49

Consumer Credit (Notice of Variation of Agreements) Regulations (S.I. 1977 No. 328) 26–30

Business Advertisements (Disclosure) Order (S.I. 1977 No. 1918) 18–44, 18–49

Price Marking (Bargain Offers) Order (S.I. 1979 No. 364) 18–34

Consumer Credit (Total Charge for Credit) Regulations (S.I. 1980 No. 51) . . . . 21–36 to 21–39, 23–12

Consumer Credit (Agreements) Regulations (S.I. 1983 No. 1553) . 24–34, 24–35, 24–42, 24–43, 24–46, 26–31
Sched. 6 22–41

Consumer Credit (Guarantees and Indemnities) Regulations (S.I. 1983 No. 1556) 24–47

Consumer Credit (Cancellation Notices and Copies of Documents) Regulations (S.I. 1983 No. 1557) 24–38, 24–41

Consumer Credit (Repayment of Credit on Cancellation) Regulations (S.I. 1983 No. 1559) 24–58

Consumer Credit (Linked Transactions) (Exemptions) Regulations (S.I. 1983 No. 1560) 21–32, 24–54

Consumer Credit (Enforcement, Default and Termination Notices) Regulations (S.I. 1983 No. 1561) 26–09, 26–17

Consumer Credit (Rebate on Early Settlement) Regulations (S.I. 1983 No. 1562) 26–04, 27–16

Consumer Credit (Pawn Receipt) Regulations (S.I. 1983 No. 1566) 26–46

Consumer Credit (Realisation of Pawn) Regulations (S.I. 1983 No. 1568) 26–47

Consumer Credit (Exempt Advertisements) Order (S.I. 1985 No. 621) 23–08

Consumer Protection (Cancellation of Contracts concluded away from Business Premises) Regulations (S.I. 1987 No. 2117) . . 2–18, 16–05, 16–07, 24–32, 24–48, 24–51

Control of Misleading Advertisements Regulations (S.I. 1988 No. 915) 10–48, 18–45

Consumer Credit (Exempt Agreements) Order (S.I. 1989 No. 869) 21–26

Consumer Credit (Advertisements) Regulations (S.I. 1989 No. 1125) 23–11

Toys (Safety) Regulations (S.I. 1989 No. 1680) 9–25

County Courts (Interest on Judgment Debts) Order (S.I. 1991 No. 1184) 26–24

Price Marking Order (S.I. 1991 No. 1382) 18–40

Price Indications (Bureaux de Change) (No. 2) Regulations (S.I. 1992 No. 737) 18–40

General Product Safety Regulations (S.I. 1994 No. 2328) . 18–01, 9–17, 9–19 to 9–28

Unfair Terms in Consumer Contracts Regulations (S.I. 1994 No. 3159) 10–01, 10–38

Education (Student Loans) Regulations (S.I. 1998 No. 211) 21–26
Unfair Terms in Consumer Contracts Regulations (S.I. 1999 No. 2083) 7–02, 10–01, 10–38, 10–45, 15–05, 26–24, 27–31, 27–33
Consumer Credit (Content of Quotations) and Consumer Credit (Advertisements) (Amendment) Regulations (S.I. 1999 No. 2725) 23–14
Consumer Protection (Distance Selling) Regulations 2000 . . . . . . 2–23, 16–05 to 16–22, 18–52, 24–48
Consumer Protection (Product Liability) (Modification) Order 2000 9–09

TABLE OF EUROPEAN DIRECTIVES

Misleading Advertisements (84/450/EEC) 18–45, 18–52
Product Liability (85/374/EEC) 9–06
Doorstep Selling (85/557/EEC) 2–18, 18–52
Consumer Credit (87/102/EEC) 18–52
TV Broadcasting (89/552/EEC) 18–52
Package Travel, Package Holidays and Package Tours (90/
      314/EEC) 18–52
Advertising of Medicinal Products for Human Use (92/28/
      EEC) 18–52
General Product Safety (92/59/EEC) 9–20
Unfair Terms in Consumer Contracts (93/13/EEC) . . 10–40, 18–52
Timeshare (94/47/EC) 18–52
Distance Selling (97/7/EC) 2–09, 16–05, 18–52
Injunctions (98/27/EC) 18–01, 18–52, 18–53
Product Liability Amendment (1999/34/EC) 9–09
Consumer Guarantees (1999/44/EC) . . . 7–05, 7–52 to 7–54, 9–03,
                                               13–06
Electronic Signatures (1999/93/EC) 16–02
Electronic Commerce Directive (2000/31/EC) 16–04, 18–52

PART ONE
SALE OF GOODS

CHAPTER 1

INTRODUCTION AND DEFINITION OF CONTRACT OF SALE OF GOODS

THE sale of goods is the most common type of commercial transaction. The term "sale of goods" embraces agreements which are apparently very different. For example, the sale of a newspaper for 30p from a stand in the street, the sale of industrial machinery for millions of pounds to a large company and the sale of aircraft to the government are all equally contracts (*i.e.* agreements) of sale of goods. The bulk of the first part of this book is devoted to the contractual relationship between the buyer and seller, *i.e.* the rights and duties between them. A clue to these will often be found in the Sale of Goods Act 1979. Reference will constantly be made to sections of this Act. **1–01**

It must be remarked at the outset that it is principally between the buyer and seller that rights and obligations exist. These arise out of their bargain (*i.e.* their contract of sale). It is commonly thought, but wrongly so, that the buyer's best legal rights exist against the manufacturer. This common misconception is fostered and perhaps shared by a great many retailers. Of course, a manufacturer does enjoy the rights and incur the obligations of a seller but these exist as between himself and the person(s) to whom he sells his goods. Similarly, he has the rights and obligations of a buyer as against the person from whom he purchases his raw materials. A manufacturer does have some obligations which arise independently of his position as buyer or seller. Reference will be made to manufacturers as well as to auctioneers who also have liabilities (and rights) distinct from those of the seller or buyer. **1–02**

One matter in particular will not figure much in Part One. This is where goods are taken on hire purchase, credit sale or conditional sale terms. These types of agreement will be considered in Part Two.

Before the definition of a contract of sale of goods is considered, something must be said of the history and sources of **1–03** the law relating to sale of goods. The Sale of Goods Act 1979, only the second such Act to have been passed in this country, replaced the original Sale of Goods Act 1893. The original Act had been amended in the years before 1979 by such Acts as the Misrepresentation Act 1967, the Supply of Goods (Implied Terms) Act 1973, the Consumer Credit Act 1974 and the Unfair Contract Terms Act 1977. These amendments, though significant, were principally changes of detail and were not substantial in extent. Thus the 1893 Act remained largely in the form in which it was originally enacted. The current Act, the Sale of Goods Act 1979, did not seek to make further changes in the law, but was a consolidation measure which reproduced (with a few technical amendments) the provisions of the 1893 Act as amended. Thus the provisions of the 1979 Act are in large part the very same ones as those originally passed in 1893. Indeed, the majority of the section numbers are the same as they were in the 1893 Act. The 1979 Act has itself been amended, principally by the Sale and Supply of Goods Act 1994 and the Sale of Goods (Amendment) Act 1995. Nevertheless, it is still true to say that much of the law of sale of goods today is basically the common law, *i.e.* the law as stated over the years by judges in the process of deciding cases before them. The 1893 Act was intended, not to effect radical changes in the law, but to codify it, *i.e.* to put the common law into one statute to which it was easy to refer. The 1979 Act once again put the law into one statute by incorporating all the amendments which had been made in the original Act. However, decided cases still have to be referred to in two situations. The first is where the Act is silent or ambiguous on any given point and the second is where the court in a decided case has given a particular interpretation to a section of the Act (or to the same section in the original Act of 1893). In the case of a conflict between the pre-existing common law and any statute, the latter prevails. In this book references to sections of the Sale of Goods Act are references to sections of the current Act, the Sale of Goods Act 1979.

DEFINITION

1–04 Section 2(1) of the Sale of Goods Act defines a contract of sale of goods as: "a contract whereby the seller transfers or agrees to transfer the property in goods to the buyer for a money consideration, called the price." Three elements in this definition require explanation, "property", "goods" and "money consideration".

"Property" means ownership. Selling is the most common **1–05** method by which ownership is transferred from person to person. Sometimes the contract provides that ownership will be transferred at some later date. Such a contract is termed "an agreement to sell" but it is still a contract of sale within the definition because of the words in section 2(1), "agrees to transfer". Of course, a contract which lacks any agreement to transfer property (ownership) at all, will fall outside the definition, *e.g.* a contract where one person agrees simply to borrow or hire another person's goods. This type of contract, *i.e.* where possession, but not ownership, is agreed to be transferred, is altogether different and is called a contract of bailment.

"Goods" is defined by section 61 to include "emblements, **1–06** industrial growing crops and things attached to or forming part of the land which are agreed to be severed before sale or under the contract of sale". Thus, a contract to sell crops which are growing or to be grown—whether they mature within a year (*e.g.* wheat) or not (*e.g.* timber)—is a contract of sale of goods. The only exception to this is when the crops are sold along with the land on which they are growing or to be grown. In this case the crops are not "agreed to be severed before sale or under the contract of sale".

Things—other than crops—which are "attached to or form part **1–07** of the land" are "goods" only if they are identifiable as being distinct from the land. *Morgan v. Russell & Sons* (1909 DC) concerned the sale of some slag and cinders which were lying on a particular piece of ground. They were not in identifiable heaps but had melted into the soil. It was held that the slag and cinders were not distinct from the land itself and therefore were not "goods".

Other things which are not "goods" are "things in action and **1–08** money" (section 61). Things in action include cheques and stocks and shares. Although money is not normally "goods", a coin which is sold as a curio piece and not as currency, is regarded as goods: *Moss v. Hancock* (1899 DC). Apart from the exceptions mentioned, "goods" include "all chattels personal", *i.e.* all tangible moveable things.

The third element of the definition is "money consideration". **1–09** A contract of barter, *i.e.* where goods are exchanged for other goods—lacks this element and is not a contract of sale. However, where goods are exchanged for a combination of money and other goods, the contract is one of sale of goods. In this case there is a money consideration even though goods are also given. In *Dawson v. Dutfield* (1936 KB), two lorries worth £475 were to be paid for by a combination of two "trade-in" lorries worth £250 and the balance in cash. The buyer paid the cash sum but failed to deliver the two "trade-in" lorries. It was held that there was a contract of sale of goods and that the sellers could sue for the outstanding balance of the price.

1–10   Whether there was a "money consideration" was in issue in *Esso v. Commissioners of Customs and Excise* (1976 HL). Esso devised a petrol sales promotion scheme whereby a World Cup coin was given away at Esso petrol stations with every four gallons of petrol purchased. Posters displayed at petrol stations read "Free World Cup Coins". "One coin given away with every four gallons of petrol". There could be no doubt that when a garage proprietor sold petrol to a customer he made a contract of sale (*i.e.* of the petrol) with the customer, since the customer agreed to pay a "money consideration", the price. Did the garage proprietor also make a contract of sale in relation to the World Cup coins? If he did, then Esso were liable to pay purchase tax (since abolished) in respect of all the World Cup coins they had produced. Esso advanced two arguments. First, they claimed that the garage proprietor made no contract at all with the customer in relation to the World Cup coins. The coins had a small intrinsic value and therefore the offer in the posters could not have been intended to create a legally binding relationship (*i.e.* a contract) between the garage proprietor and the customer. The majority of their lordships rejected this argument and held that it had been intended that a customer who accepted the offer by buying four gallons would thereby become entitled in law to have a World Cup coin. Esso's second argument succeeded. It was held that the contract in relation to the World Cup coins was not a contract of sale. There was not just one contract made between the garage proprietor and the customer. There were two. Beside the contract of sale of the petrol there was a separate collateral contract relating to the World Cup coins. The posters amounted to an offer by the garage proprietor to supply a World Cup coin if the customer would buy four gallons of petrol. That offer was accepted by the customer making a contract to buy four gallons. The consideration which the customer gave for the garage proprietor's promise to supply a World Cup coin was the making of a contract to buy four gallons of petrol. The making of a contract to buy four gallons of petrol was not a "money consideration". (For a further discussion of this case and of contracts of barter, see paragraphs 8–03 and 8–04 below.)

SALE DISTINGUISHED FROM OTHER TRANSACTIONS

We have already examined the difference between sale and **1–11** barter. More can be learned about the nature of sale from a comparison of it with other contracts.

Contracts for labour and materials supplied

These contracts are not uncommon. Take an example: a builder sub-contracts the job of putting the roof on a house which he is building. The sub-contract requires the sub-contractor to supply the tiles. This is not a contract of sale of goods because its principal object is the provision of services: *Young & Marten v. McManus Childs* (1968 HL).

The words in section 2(1), "transfers or agrees to transfer the **1–12** property in goods to the buyer", have been interpreted by the courts to require that the transfer of ownership to the buyer should be the main object of the agreement. If the main purpose is something else (*e.g.* the provision of labour) then the agreement is not a contract of sale. This is so even though an incidental or ancillary object of the contract is the transfer of ownership in some goods. In *Robinson v. Graves* (1935) the Court of Appeal held that a contract whereby an artist agreed to paint a client's portrait for him was not a contract of sale of goods. Even though, when finished, the canvas would be transferred to the buyer's ownership, the substance of the agreement was the provision by the artist of his skill and labour. If, on the other hand, the client selected from the artist's studio a finished painting and agreed to pay for it, that agreement would be a contract of sale of goods. In that case the artist would be agreeing, not to provide his skill and labour, but simply to part with the ownership of a finished canvas, the fruit of his past efforts. The substance of such an agreement is the transfer of ownership.

It is not always easy to decide what is the substance of the **1–13** contract, the provision of services or the transfer of ownership. It may be helpful to know that the courts have treated the following as contracts of sale—contracts: to make and supply ships' propellers according to a specification, *Cammell Laird v. Manganese Bronze & Brass* (1934 HL); to prepare and supply food in a restaurant, *Lockett v. A. & M. Charles Ltd* (1938 KB); to compound and supply animal foodstuff according to a formula setting out the ingredients and their proportions, *Ashington Piggeries v. Hill* (1971 HL). A borderline case, *Samuels v. Davis*, came before the Court of Appeal in 1943. It concerned a contract to provide a made-to-measure set of teeth and it arose because they did not fit. The Court sidestepped the question of whether it was a contract of sale or for services, by holding that, whichever it was, there was an implied term of the contract that the goods should be reasonably fit for the purpose for which they were intended. The seller was therefore liable.

Contracts to supply computer software

1–14   Here the contract may or may not involve the transfer of goods. Thus if the software is transferred by simply being downloaded on to the purchaser's machine from the internet or from a disk temporarily supplied by the software supplier, the contract is not one of sale of goods, since the program or software, not being tangible, does not amount to "goods", *St Albans District Council v. ICL* (1996 CA). Nevertheless, if the program is intended by the parties to enable a computer to achieve specified functions, there will be an implied term at common law that the program is reasonably fit for this purpose. If, however, the software is supplied on a permanent medium such as a disk, the contract will be one of sale of goods. It is then no different from a book (or video or audio cassette). In that case there will be the statutory implied terms that the goods will be of satisfactory quality and reasonably fit for their purpose. According to the *St Albans* judgment, the statutory implied obligations extend not only to the physical disk, book or video but also to its contents. Thus supplying an instruction manual containing wrong instructions would amount to a breach of these terms, as would supplying a disk with defective software.

Contracts of hire-purchase

1–15   It is the hall mark of a contract of sale that seller and buyer each enter a commitment that there will be a transfer of ownership from the seller to the buyer. A hire-purchase agreement lacks this. Under a hire-purchase agreement the hirer undertakes to hire the goods for a specified period at a specified rent and he is given an option to buy the goods when he has paid all the specified rent. Since he has only an option and does not legally commit himself to buy the goods, the contract is not one of sale: *Helby v. Matthews* (1895 HL). For a fuller explanation see paragraph 19–02, below.

Contracts of agency

Sometimes X sells goods to Y who in turn sells them to Z. **1–16**
Sometimes, however, Y acts as X's agent in selling to Z. In the
former case Z buys his goods from Y and if they are not
delivered or are defective Z can look to his seller, Y, and if
necessary can sue him for breach of his contract of sale. In the
latter case Z buys from X through X's agent Y; it is with X that
he made his contract and if things go wrong, he can look to his
seller, X, for a remedy. The answer to the question "who sold to
Z?" depends upon whether Y was a buyer and reseller or whether
he was merely an agent for X. The answer is not helped by the
fact that people who are in fact buyers and resellers are often
termed in the trade "agents". Car dealers, for example, may be
called "Vauxhall agents" but they are not merely agents for the
manufacturer. They themselves buy new cars and resell them to
members of the public. The true nature of the transaction can be
ascertained only by examining the terms of the contract between
X and Y. If it is clear that Y is buying the goods for himself,
albeit with a commitment or an intention to resell, then Y is a
buyer and reseller.

The problem can arise acutely in a situation where Y takes **1–17**
goods from X on "sale or return" terms. Is Y a buyer and reseller
or is he X's agent? In either case he does not run the risk of
being left with the goods; if he cannot find a purchaser he can
return them to X. The answer is that he is X's agent if under the
terms of his contract with X he has no right himself to buy the
goods but can only sell to a third party: *Weiner v. Harris* (1910
CA). Contrariwise, if he has the right himself to buy the goods he
is a buyer and the contract between X and Y will be one of sale
of goods and not one of agency: *Weiner v. Gill* (1906 CA).

The problem can also arise where Y takes goods from X under
a sale of goods contract which contains a retention of title clause,
i.e. a clause stating that Y is not to become the owner unless and
until he has paid for them and that if Y resells them before
paying for them, X's ownership is to transfer from the goods to
the proceeds of the resale received by Y. Suppose Y sells the
goods to Z before he has paid X for them. Clearly, although he is
not yet the owner of the goods, he has the authority of the owner,
X, to resell them. In this situation is Y a buyer and reseller or is
he merely X's agent for selling the goods to Z? This question
will be important if Z wishes to sue his seller for breach of
contract (*e.g.* if the goods are defective) or if Z fails to pay the
price. Whom can Z sue and who can sue Z? To put it another

way, who is the other party to the contract by which Z purchased the goods? Who is the seller who sold the goods to Z? The answer is twofold. First, as between X and Y, Y is acting as X's agent in selling to Z; secondly, as between Y and Z, Y is selling as principal: *Aluminium Industrie Vaasen BV v. Romalpa Aluminium* Ltd (1976 CA). For a fuller account see paragraph 3–49 below). Thus, although Y owes X the duties which an agent owes to his principal, it is Y who as seller can sue Z for the price and be sued by Z for breach of the contract of sale.

THE IMPORTANCE OF THE DEFINITION

1–18   Contracts other than contracts of sale of goods are not governed by the provisions of the Sale of Goods Act 1979. Although they will often be governed by some other Act of Parliament, none of them is governed by an Act which is as comprehensive as the Sale of Goods Act. Later in this book, some of these other Acts of Parliament are considered, including the Supply of Goods (Implied Terms) Act 1973 (Chapter 25) and the Supply of Goods and Services Act 1982 (Chapter 8). Another important statute, the Consumer Protection Act 1987, which deals with manufacturers' liability, is also considered later (Chapter 9).

CHAPTER 2

FORMATION AND CANCELLATION OF THE CONTRACT

FORMATION OF THE CONTRACT

A CONTRACT of sale is an agreement by which the seller and 2–01 buyer undertake mutual obligations. At the very least the seller agrees that the buyer shall become the owner and the buyer agrees to pay the price. Often there are more obligations than just these. The number and extent of the obligations can be ascertained only by reference to the terms expressly agreed in the contract and to those extra terms which the law automatically implies into it. These will be discussed later. At present we are concerned with what amounts to an enforceable agreement (*i.e.* a contract). If there is no contract or it is unenforceable, then neither the buyer nor the seller can complain that the other has broken it.

Time of making the contract

It is important to know exactly when a contract is made 2–02 because until that time either party is free to back out. An agreement is made when one person makes an offer to another and that other accepts it. Until there is an offer which is accepted, there is no contract. An offer is something which is clearly intended if accepted to form a binding agreement. Thus it has been held that the display of goods on the shelves of a self-service shop is not an offer: *Pharmaceutical Society of Great Britain v. Boots Cash Chemists* (1952 DC). The customer who takes them from the shelf therefore does not accept an offer. Rather, the offer is made by the customer when he takes the goods to the cash desk and it is accepted by the assistant at the cash desk. At any time before that, either party can back out. In

11

particular the customer can restore the goods to the shelf and will be under no obligation to pay for them.

2–03   Similarly, the display of goods in a shop window does not amount to an offer: *Fisher v. Bell* (1961 DC). The person who enters the shop and asks to buy goods displayed in the window does not therefore accept an offer. He in fact makes an offer which the shopkeeper is free to accept or to reject. The display of goods in the shop window or on the shelves of a supermarket is an invitation to treat, *i.e.* an invitation to members of the public to make an offer to buy. The acceptance of an invitation to treat does not make a contract.

2–04   The difference between an offer and an invitation to treat can most clearly be seen in auction sales. The auctioneer asks for bids. He many receive quite a lot of bids and will usually accept the highest. When the auctioneer asks for bids he is making, not an offer, but an invitation to treat. Each bid is a separate offer and a contract is not made until the auctioneer accepts one of them. Thus section 57(2) of the Sale of Goods Act reads:

> "A sale by auction is complete when the auctioneer announces its completion by the fall of the hammer, or in other customary manner; and until the announcement is made any bidder may retract his bid."

2–05   Another problem which has sometimes exercised the minds of academics is, "At exactly what stage is the contract concluded in the case of a purchase from an automatic vending machine?" Is it when the purchaser puts his money in or is that merely an offer which the machine accepts? Some words of Lord Denning M.R. in *Thornton v. Shoe Lane Parking* (1971 CA) are helpful in this context. The case actually involved a contract made between a motorist wishing to park his car and the proprietor of a car park with an automatic entrance barrier. His Lordship, however, also spoke about a machine which issues railway tickets and his comments would appear to apply equally to a machine selling goods. Referring to the customer, he said:

> "He was committed at the very moment that he put his money into the machine. The contract was concluded at that time. It can be translated into offer and acceptance in this way. The offer is made when the proprietor of the machine

holds it out as being ready to receive the money. The acceptance takes place when the customer puts his money into the slot."

It seems then that the display of goods in an automatic vending machine—unlike that in a shop window or on the shelves of a supermarket—is not merely an invitation to treat but is an offer.

Once an offer can be identified there is not usually any **2–06** difficulty in ascertaining whether it has been accepted. The general rule is that an acceptance takes effect when it is actually communicated to the offeror: *Entores v. Miles Far East Company* (1955 CA); and *Brinkibon Ltd v. Stahag Stahl* (1982 HL). There are, however, two or three exceptions to this. First, in circumstances where the post is expected to be used as the means of communication between the seller and the buyer, an acceptance takes effect when it is posted. Thus there is still a contract even if the letter of acceptance is lost in the post: *Household, Fire & Carriage Insurance Company v. Grant* (1879 CA). Secondly, where the offeror expressly or implicitly waives the need for the acceptance to be communicated to him, the acceptance will take effect when the acceptor does whatever act is necessary to indicate his acceptance. The vending machine situation provides a good example of this. The contract is complete when the customer puts his money in the slot. He is certainly not expected to telephone or to write a letter to the proprietor of the machine.

Even if the offeror waives the need for communication to him, **2–07** there must always be some act to indicate acceptance. The offeror cannot say "if you do nothing you will thereby accept my offer!" In *Felthouse v. Bindley* (1863 QB) the offeror wrote to his nephew offering to buy the latter's horse. In the letter he said, "If I hear no more about him, I consider the horse mine". The nephew sent no reply and the court held that no contract was made. A contract is an agreement. It follows that one person cannot impose a contract upon another. If, on the other hand, the person to whom an offer is made says, for example, "If you do not hear from me within a week, you can assume I have accepted your offer", then that will amount to an acceptance unless he communicates otherwise within the week. In *Re Selectmove Ltd* (1995 CA), Gibson L.J. said:

"Where the offeree himself indicates that an offer is to be taken as accepted if he does not indicate to the contrary by an ascertainable time, he is undertaking to speak if he does

13

not want an agreement to be concluded. I see no reason in principle why that should not be an exceptional circumstance such that the offer can be accepted by silence".

There may be a third exception to the general rule that an acceptance takes effect when it is actually communicated to the offeror. In *Brinkibon Ltd v. Stahag Stahl* (1982 HL) the House of Lords confirmed the decision in *Entores v. Miles Far East Company*, that normally in the case of a telephone conversation or a telex communication the postal exception does not apply and therefore the acceptance takes effect when (and where) it is actually communicated to the offeror. Their lordships did, however, state that a different result might apply to a telex message which was not a direct communication in office hours between the acceptor and the offeror, *e.g.* if it was sent at night or was sent or received through telex machines operated by third persons. In such a case the acceptance could take effect upon despatch or upon communication to the machine at the receiving end of the telex link or upon actual communication to the offeror. A court would have to decide that issue by reference to the intention of the parties, to sound business practice and to its own judgment as to where the risk should lie.

Sales via the internet

2–08   Doubtless, the advertising of goods (or indeed services) will normally amount to no more than an invitation to treat. Someone responding to such an advertisement and submitting an order via an email may then be making what is in law an offer. If so, the advertiser is then free to accept or not. Assuming that the advertiser accepts by email, there will presumably be the same uncertainty as to when the contract is made, as was expressed in the *Brinkibon* case about the position where the parties were not in direct telex communication in office hours. It would seem absurd, however, for the result to be that the contract is not made until the offeror decides to log on and check his emails (perhaps a week or more later?). In one widely publicised instance in 1999 Argos, a catalogue shopping company, advertised on its website a television set for £3 instead of £300. Apparently many orders for these televisions were placed via the internet before the company realised its mistake. For those people who had not received any confirmation of their order, it seems reasonably clear there was no contract. Apparently, however, some had received confirmation by email. This was, arguably, an acceptance. This unfortunate incident gave rise to no reported decision. It seems probable, however, the contract was unenforceable by any of the buyers since they surely must have known that the bargain (a television for £3) was not intended by the seller and the law does not allow one party to snatch a bargain which he knows is not intended by the other, *Hartog v. Colin and Shields* (1939 KBD).

For coverage of recent legislation relevant to internet sales, e-commerce and distance selling, see Chapter 16 below.

Unsolicited goods and services

Goods are sometimes sent without prior request. The recipient might become worried if successive letters then come threatening that action will be taken to obtain the price. Clearly, the recipient who does nothing does not enter into a contract to buy the goods and therefore is not bound to pay. In spite of the lack of any right to payment, some unscrupulous firms have in the past found it profitable to market their wares by sending them out unsolicited. This had two undesirable results. One was that some members of the public were unaware that they need not pay and gave in to the pressure of successive threatening letters. The other was that the goods, if they were not purchased by the recipient, still belonged to the sender. Therefore the recipient did not dare to throw them away and was in effect forced to give them house room. The Unsolicited Goods and Services Act 1971 tackles these two social problems. Section 2 makes it a criminal offence to make a demand for payment for unsolicited goods without reasonable cause to believe there is a right to it. Section 1 provides that after six months, unsolicited goods are deemed to be an unconditional gift to the recipient. Further, if the recipient does not wish to wait six months he can serve a notice on the sender in which case, if the sender does not come within one month to collect them, they then become an unconditional gift.

The 1971 Act will no doubt shortly be amended in order to bring it into line with Article 9 of the Distance Selling Directive (97/7/EC) which was supposed to be implemented by June 14 2000. First, section 1 is likely to amended with the effect that unsolicited goods will be deemed to be an unconditional gift immediately (or after one month), *i.e.* not after six months. Secondly the criminal offence in section 2 will be extended to cover demanding payment for unsolicited services as well as for unsolicited goods.

Form of the contract

2–10   The law on this is very easy and is contained in section 4:

> "...a contract of sale may be made in writing (either with or without seal), or by word of mouth, or partly in writing and partly by word of mouth, or may be implied from the conduct of the parties."

In this respect contracts of sale of goods are different from contracts for the sale of land. Whereas there are no particular formalities for the former, a contract for the sale of land can only be made in writing incorporating all the terms which the parties have expressly agreed and signed by or on behalf of each party: Law of Property (Miscellaneous Provisions) Act 1989, s.2. The distinction between goods and land (see paragraph 1–07) is therefore important.

Capacity

2–11   Certain persons lack the legal capacity to make a contract. Thus contracts are not generally binding on the following people: persons who at the time of making the contract were either minors, or so insane or drunk as not to know what they were doing. Such a person can enforce the contract against the other party but can not generally himself be sued. An exception to this, however, is found in section 3:

> "(1) Capacity to buy and sell is regulated by the general law concerning capacity to contract and to transfer and acquire property.
>
> (2) Where necessaries are sold and delivered to a minor or to a person who by reason of mental incapacity or drunkenness is incompetent to contract, he must pay a reasonable price for them.
>
> (3) In subsection (2) above 'necessaries' means goods suitable to the condition in life of the minor or other person concerned and to his actual requirements at the time of the sale and delivery."

In one case a minor undergraduate bought 11 fancy waistcoats: *Nash v. Inman* (1908 CA). It was held that the tailor could not sue for any money because the goods were not necessaries; the minor was already well supplied with waistcoats. The result of this decision was that not only was the minor under no obligation to pay for the waistcoats but also, apparently, he could keep them! Now, however, the law is different. Section 3 of the Minors' Contracts Act 1987 empowers the court, where it would be "just and equitable" (*i.e.* fair) to do so, to require the minor to return property which he has acquired under a contract which is unenforceable against him.

The Family Law Reform Act 1969 reduced the age of majority to 18 so that only people under that age enjoy the privileged status of minor.

Not surprisingly some traders are reluctant to deal with minors on any basis other than that the minor pays cash before taking the goods away. On the other hand, to refuse to give credit can be to turn away valuable business. Thus sometimes a trader will agree to give credit to a minor providing an adult (usually a parent) signs a document guaranteeing the minor's debt. Until 1987, however, a guarantee was no safeguard because the legal nature of guarantee is that it is subsidiary to, and dependent upon, the contract which is guaranteed. If the latter was void, then the trader had no recourse against the guarantor: *Coutts & Co. v. Browne-Lecky* (1946 KB). If, on the other hand, the adult had signed a contract, not of guarantee, but of indemnity, that contract could be enforced against the adult even if the minor's contract was void: *Yeoman Credit Ltd v. Latter* (1961). Thus the difference between a contract of guarantee and one of indemnity was vital. Now, however, where a contract is unenforceable against someone merely because he is a minor, a contract of guarantee is enforceable against the guarantor (Minors' Contracts Act 1987, s.2).   **2–12**

THE PRICE

The amount

Section 8 provides: **2–13**

   "(1) The price in a contract of sale may be fixed by the contract, or may be left to be fixed in a manner agreed by the contract, or may be determined by the course of dealing between the parties.

   (2) Where the price is not determined as mentioned in subsection (1) above the buyer must pay a reasonable price.

(3) What is a reasonable price is a question of fact dependent on the circumstances of each particular case."

2–14   The price is normally a basic part of the agreement and normally it will be expressly agreed. It might appear from section 8(2) that, if no price is agreed and there is no method of ascertaining it, a reasonable price is automatically payable. This is not necessarily so. The price is so basic that, if the parties have expressly left it over for later agreement, the court may well conclude that the parties did not intend to make, and have not made, a contract. This was the conclusion of the House of Lords in *May & Butcher v. R.* (1934) where an agreement for the purchase of government tentage provided that the price, the manner of delivery and dates of payment were to be agreed upon from time to time. If the contract had simply failed to mention these items, they could have been resolved by applying the provisions of the Sale of Goods Act. Equally, if the contract had provided for the price to be fixed by the seller (or the buyer), that would have been binding. However, the contract expressly left the price and other items over for later agreement. That being so, and the items being so basic, their Lordships held that the parties had not intended to make a contract but had simply agreed to agree. There was therefore no contract.

2–15   If, however, a relatively minor matter is left over for later agreement it does not necessarily follow that there is no contract. It is perfectly possible in law for parties to make an interim agreement for the sale of goods which requires further negotiation to iron out the less important details of the transaction: *Pagnan S.p.A. v. Feed Products* (1987 CA). All the circumstances must be examined to see if the parties intended to leave over the entire agreement or whether they intended to make a binding contract, albeit one with some details still outstanding. In *Foley v. Classique Coaches Ltd* (1934 CA) the defendants bought some land from the claimant and it was a condition of the purchase that the defendants agreed to buy petrol (for their coach business) only from the claimant. The agreement provided for the price of the petrol "to be agreed by the parties from time to time" and, failing agreement, to be settled by arbitration. It was held there that the parties had made a binding contract, albeit with the price still outstanding.

Clearly if there is no contract, as in *May & Butcher v. R*, no price is payable and section 8 is irrelevant. If there is a contract the price is ascertained by the relevant method in section 8—in *Foley's* case by arbitration, the manner agreed in the contract.

Valuation

Valuation by a third party is one method the parties can **2–16** stipulate for ascertainment of the price. Section 9 provides that where he cannot or does not make the valuation, the contract is avoided. In that case there is no obligation on the seller to deliver the goods and none on the buyer to pay. Section 9 has one exception to this:

> "...if the goods or any part of them have been delivered to and appropriated by the buyer he must pay a reasonable price for them."

Section 9(2) provides that where the valuation is prevented by the fault of one of the parties, the other may maintain an action for damages against the party at fault. Where the valuer makes the valuation, then, unless the valuer was acting fraudulently in connivance with one of the parties, the valuation will be binding as between the parties. If, however, the valuation was arrived at negligently, the victim (*i.e.* the buyer or seller, depending upon whether the valuation was too high or too low) will have a claim in negligence against the valuer: *Arenson v. Casson* (1977 HL).

Deposits

It is not uncommon for the buyer to pay part of the price at the **2–17** time of making the contract to buy. This payment could be either a deposit or mere part payment. The effect of a deposit or mere part payment is a matter of agreement between the parties. In the absence of any agreement to the contrary, a deposit is generally forfeited by the buyer if the sale falls through because of his fault. A mere part payment, however, is returnable. A deposit is, in the words of Lord Macnaghten in *Soper v. Arnold* (1889 HL), "a guarantee that the purchaser means business". It is a security for the completion of the purchase.

As so often, the law endeavours to discover the intention of the parties. It examines all the circumstances to see whether they intended the money to be a deposit or merely a payment on account. If the parties actually used the word "deposit", then unless there is evidence to the contrary it will be assumed that that is what they meant: *Elson v. Prices Tailors Ltd* (1963 ChD).

Of course, if the seller has a claim against the buyer either for the price or for damages (see Chapter 12) he will in making his claim have to bring into account any money already received—whether as a deposit or merely as a part payment. The seller cannot expect on the one hand to be fully compensated for the sale falling through and on the other to be allowed in addition to retain a deposit already received.

CANCELLABLE AGREEMENTS

2–18   The general rule is that, once a contract is made, neither party is free to back out. To that rule there is an exception created by the Consumer Protection (Cancellation of Contracts Concluded away from Business Premises) Regulations 1987. These Regulations give effect to the Doorstep Selling Directive (85/557/EEC) and, broadly speaking, give a cooling-off period of seven days to a customer who enters a contract (to buy goods or services) as a result of doorstep canvassing. The customer is given the right to cancel the contract during the cooling-off period. This gives him an antidote to the high pressure selling techniques sometimes employed by door-to-door salesmen. The Regulations are intended to protect ordinary consumers and therefore do not apply where the customer is a company or corporate body or where the customer is making the contract for his business purposes.

The Regulations apply when the customer makes the contract during an unsolicited visit by the trader (or his representative) to the customer's home, to someone else's home or to the customer's place of work. The visit is not "unsolicited", and therefore the Regulations do not apply, if the customer has expressly requested the visit, *e.g.* by completing and returning a reply paid card asking for the visit or by telephoning asking for it. If, on the other hand, the trader (without the customer having requested him to do so) has telephoned the customer indicating that he is willing to make a visit, the trader's subsequent visit *will* be unsolicited and the Regulations will apply. Similarly, if the trader makes an unsolicited visit during which he indicates that he is willing to make a further visit to the customer, the trader's subsequent visit will also be unsolicited and the Regulations will apply.

Suppose that the customer has expressly requested a visit for one purpose (say, a possible purchase of kitchen fitments) and that during the visit the trader talks the customer into buying something else, say a television. In that case the contract to buy the television will be cancellable provided the customer did not know, and could not reasonably have known, that the trader sold televisions. Obviously, if the customer had been prompted to request the visit by an advertisement indicating that the trader sold televisions as well as kitchen fitments, the contract to buy the television will not be cancellable.

We have seen that a contract *made* during an unsolicited visit is cancellable. This will be the case where an offer is made by one side which during the visit is accepted by the other. It could occur, however, that the visiting salesman gets the customer to complete an application or proposal form (*i.e.* an offer to buy) and that the salesman takes the form away saying that the customer will receive a reply later. If a few days later the salesman's firm sends the customer a letter accepting the customer's offer, the contract is made, not during the visit, but a few days later. Nevertheless the Regulations still apply to such a contract.

In addition to the contracts mentioned so far, the Regulations also apply to contracts made during an excursion organised by the trader away from his trade premises. This is a trading practice (more common on the Continent than in the United Kingdom) whereby a trader organises a coach or boat trip and then during the trip gets the travellers to buy or offer to buy goods or services. The resulting contracts are cancellable under the Regulations. This does not, however, apply to a contract made by someone visiting, say, the Ideal Home Exhibition and making a contract at a trader's exhibition stand. Even if such a customer is on an excursion, it is not one organised by the trader.

Excepted contracts

There are some important exceptions to what has been said so   **2–19**
far. Certain contracts are excepted and are therefore not cancellable under the Regulations (even if made during or following an unsolicited visit or an excursion), namely any contract:

(1) where the price (including VAT) is £35 or less;

(2) to buy, sell, dispose of, lease or mortgage land;

(3) to finance, or provide bridging finance for, the purchase of land;

(4) for the construction or extension of a building or other erection on land (nevertheless contracts for repairs and improvements are *not* excepted unless they are secured by a land mortgage);

(5) for the supply of food, drink or other goods intended for current consumption by use in the household and supplied by regular roundsmen.

Also excepted are certain contracts which are governed by some other piece of legislation: contracts of insurance to which the Insurance Companies Act 1982 applies; investment agreements within the meaning of the Financial Services Act 1986; and certain agreements for the making of deposits within the meaning of the Banking Act 1987.

There is a further exception for certain mail order (and other) "catalogue" agreements which give the customer equal rights. Such a contract is excepted if three conditions are all satisfied:

(i) its terms are set out in a catalogue which is readily available to be read by the customer in the absence of the salesman before the contract is made;

(ii) there is to be a continuing contact between the trader (or his representative) and the customer;

(iii) the contract expressly gives the customer the right to return any goods within seven days of receiving them and to cancel the agreement.

Finally, a contract is excepted if it provides credit of £35 or less (unless it is a hire-purchase or conditional sale agreement). This last exception leads to an absurdity whereby a contract (say, to install new kitchen units for a cash price of £2,000 payable immediately on completion of the work) which would otherwise be cancellable, will be excepted if it contains a term that £35 of the price is not payable until, say, six months after completion.

Cooling-off period

2–20   Where the Regulations apply, they give a cooling-off period entitling the customer to cancel the agreement at any time "within the period of 7 days following the making of the contract". Thus where during the trader's unsolicited visit an offer is made which is accepted only later, the customer effectively has a longer cooling-off period. The cooling-off period does not expire until the end of seven days following the acceptance.

The Regulations require the trader to give the customer a notice of his cancellation rights and a detachable form must also be provided for the customer's use. These must be in the form required by the Regulations and must be given to the customer during the trader's visit (or during the excursion). If the trader fails to comply with these requirements, he is not allowed to enforce the agreement against the customer. [He also commits a criminal offence].

The customer is entitled to cancel the agreement by giving the trader within the cooling-off period written notice of his intention to cancel the contract. He does not have to use the detachable form provided by the trader. If the customer posts his notice of cancellation, it will be effective to cancel the agreement provided it is *posted* within the cooling-off period, *i.e.* even if it does not reach the trader until later or even if it never reaches him.

Effect of cancellation

Broadly speaking, the customer is entitled to be repaid any money he has already paid before cancellation and must return any goods he has received. He need not, however, transport the goods but can wait for the trader to come and collect them. The customer's duty to take care of the goods ceases 21 days after he cancelled the agreement, unless before then he has received from the trader a written signed request to hand them over. By way of exception, goods in the following four categories are not returnable and the customer will remain liable to pay for them (and for the provision of any services in connection with their supply):

    (i) perishable goods;

    (ii) consumable goods which have been consumed before cancellation;

    (iii) goods supplied to meet any emergency;

    (iv) goods (*e.g.* bricks or plants) which before cancellation have been incorporated in land.

Subject to having to pay for goods in the last four categories, the customer is entitled to be repaid any money he has already

2–21

paid. He is also given a lien on any goods which he is himself supposed to return. This entitles him to refuse to hand them over until he has been repaid the money repayable to him.

If as part of the cancelled contract the customer has traded in goods in part-exchange, the trader must return those goods (in substantially the same condition) to the customer within 10 days beginning with the date of cancellation. If he does not, the customer is entitled to their part-exchange allowance instead. The customer can use his lien to enforce this: he can refuse to hand over any goods which are returnable by him, until he receives the part-exchange goods or the part-exchange allowance.

Relationship with cancellation provisions of Consumer Credit Act.

2–22   A number of contracts cancellable under the Regulations will also be cancellable under the Consumer Credit Act 1974. The latter provisions are fully explained in Part Two of this book at paragraph 24–48 onwards. The rules are very similar, the main difference being that in most cases the cooling-off period under the Consumer Credit Act will be longer. From the trader's point of view the position is straightforward. If the contract is cancellable under the Consumer Credit Act as well as under the Regulations, it is only the provisions of the former with which he must comply—*i.e.* provisions as to giving the customer notice of his cancellation rights.

It should also be noted that in the case of some excepted contracts (*i.e.* where the Regulations therefore do not apply), there will be provisions of the Consumer Credit Act giving protection to the customer. Thus a contract for house repairs or improvements which is secured by a mortgage of the house will normally be subject to a compulsory pre-contract consideration period (see paragraph 24–40 below).

Relationship with distance-selling provisions

2–23   Where a contract is made exclusively by distance communication, the consumer is given a right of cancellation by the Consumer Protection (Distance Selling) Regulations 2000. These provisions are fully explained at paragraph 16–05 below. Since the 1987 Regulations cannot in practice apply unless there has been some face to face contact with the consumer, there is no chance of a contract being cancellable under both the 1987 and the 2000 regulations.

CHAPTER 3

THE PASSING OF PROPERTY AND RISK

A CONTRACT of sale is made in order to transfer ownership from **3–01** the seller to the buyer. This transfer of ownership is called by the Sale of Goods Act "the Transfer of Property". It often takes place on the very instant that the contract is made. However, it can occur at almost any time from the making of the contract onwards—perhaps months or years later. Until it does so, the goods remain the property of the seller. The word "property" as used in the Sale of Goods Act means ownership. When considering the passing of property from the seller to the buyer, we are therefore dealing with something different from the physical handing over (*i.e.* delivery) of the goods. The transfer of ownership and the transfer of physical possession, often do not occur simultaneously. Thus, sometimes a seller will find himself still in possession of goods after the ownership in them has passed to the buyer. Equally, it is possible for goods to be delivered to the buyer some time before they become his property.

Contrary to common belief, the buyer's right to obtain **3–02** possession of the goods does not depend upon him being the owner. Unless the parties agree otherwise, he has the right to take delivery upon payment of the price and to do so irrespective of whether property has passed to him. Why then does it matter at what point in time the property passes? The answer is that four important things depend upon the passing of property.

    (i) Unless the parties agree a different time for payment, the seller can sue for the price only after property has passed—section 49 (see paragraph 12–02).

    (ii) Unless and until the buyer has the ownership in the goods he cannot transfer that ownership on to any further person. This rule is subject to a number of exceptions (see Chapter 5).

(iii) Risk, prima facie, passes with property—section 20. The risk of accidental damage is borne (unless otherwise agreed) by the owner. This rule is of questionable merit. It would seem sensible to link risk with possession rather than with ownership, because the person in possession of the goods is in the best position to see that they come to no harm. Still, section 20 represents the law and we shall return to it later.

(iv) In the event of either the seller or buyer becoming bankrupt (or, in the case of a company, going into liquidation), the rights of the other party over the goods may well depend upon whether property has passed to the buyer.

CLASSIFICATION OF THE CONTRACT

3–03   We cannot pinpoint the exact time that property passes without first classifying the contract. It will be one of two types, being either (i) for the sale of specific goods, or (ii) for the sale of unascertained goods.

Specific goods
3–04   These are defined in section 61 as "goods identified and agreed upon at the time a contract of sale is made and includes an undivided share, specified as a fraction or percentage, of goods identified and agreed as aforesaid". If, at the time the contract is made, it is possible to point out the particular goods upon which the parties have agreed, then those goods are specific. For example second-hand car deals are usually contracts for the sale of specific goods. At the time of the contract the parties know which particular car is being sold and bought. They have "identified and agreed upon" that car. Similarly, most contracts made in supermarkets are purchases of specific goods. At the time of the contract (*i.e.* at the cash desk) the parties have identified and agreed upon the goods (*i.e.* those brought by the customer to the cash desk).

Kursell v. Timber Operators (1927 CA) concerned the sale of timber which at the time the contract was made was still growing in a Latvian forest. The buyer was to fell and take away the trees for himself. The trees which he was entitled to fell and remove (*i.e.* which he was buying) were described in the contract as "all trunks and branches of trees, but not seedlings and young trees of less than six inches in diameter at a height of four feet from the ground". They were to be measured at the time of felling and the buyer was given 15 years in which to do the felling. Until the time for felling, it therefore could not be said which trees were within the contract. They were not "identified" at the time the contract was made. It was held that they were not, therefore, specific goods.

An agreement to sell some unspecified goods out of a larger specified quantity, as in *Kursell v. Timber Operators*, is not a contract for the sale of specific goods. The goods actually being sold must be identified. Contracts to sell the following are therefore not contracts for the sale of specific goods: "a bottle of port from the seller's stock"; or, "one of the seller's current stock of 12 bottles of port"; or, "12 of the seller's stock of 13 bottles of port". This description does not tell us which 12 out of the specified 13 are being sold. *Re Wait* (1927 CA) involved a contract to sell 500 tons of wheat out of the cargo of 1,000 tons in the ship *Challenger*. The 500 tons were not specific goods because, in the words of Lord Hanworth M.R., "There was no ascertainment or identification of the 500 tons out of the cargo in bulk". Even if the 500 tons were subsequently separated from the bulk of the cargo and thereby identified, this would not make them "specific goods". The relevant time is when the contract is made. Only if they are at that time identified and agreed upon will they be specific goods. This is clear from the definition in section 61.

Suppose a seller with just 12 bottles of port in stock agrees to sell 12 bottles of port to a particular buyer. Even this may not be contract for the sale of specific goods. Even if the seller has every intention of supplying the buyer with the 12 bottles currently in stock, it still may not be a contract for the sale of specific goods. In order to determine whether it is, the terms of the contract must be examined and, if necessary, construed (*i.e.* interpreted). If the terms are such as to leave the seller free, if he should wish to do so, to obtain more wine of the same description for delivery to the buyer, then the contract goods have not been identified and agreed upon at the date of the contract and the contract is not one for the sale of specific goods: *Re London Wine Co. (Shippers)* (1986 QBD). There is a difference between a contract to sell "12 bottles of port" and one to sell "the 12 bottles of port which I have now in stock". The former is not a contract for the sale of specific goods; whereas, if the seller has just 12 bottles of port in stock, the latter *is* a contract for the sale of specific goods.

The words in the definition of specific goods referring to "an undivided share, specified as a fraction or percentage, of goods identified and agreed as aforesaid" deal with the position where what is sold is a share in goods which are identified. A typical example would be the sale of "a 10 per cent share in the race horse White Rum". The horse, White Rum, is identified and agreed upon at the time of the contract. Provided (a) that it is an *undivided* share that is being sold (*e.g.* not the right back leg!) and (b) that the share is expressed as a fraction or percentage, the contract will still be one for the sale of specific goods.

Unascertained goods

3–05   If the contract is not for the sale of specific goods then it must be for the sale of unascertained goods. This was the position in both *Kursell v. Timber Operators* and *Re Wait*. However, within the category of unascertained goods the Sale of Goods Act distinguishes between two types:

   (i) A specified quantity of unascertained goods out of an identified bulk—*e.g.* "500 tons of wheat from the cargo of 1,000 tons on the Challenger."

   (ii) Purely generic unascertained goods—*e.g.* "500 tons of wheat".

In the former the seller can fulfil his contract only by delivery of 500 tons from the specified cargo, whereas in the latter he can fulfil his contract by supplying 500 tons from any source. This difference, however, does not alter the fact that both are contracts for the sale of unascertained goods.

Having been told that there can be a contract either for the sale of specific goods or for the sale of unascertained goods, one might ask, "Is there not a third category? Can there not be a contract for the sale of ascertained goods?" The answer is that there is no third category. If at the time the contract is made, the goods are ascertained (*i.e.* identified and agreed upon), then the contract is one for the sale of specific goods. If they become ascertained only after the contract was made, the contract at the time of its creation was for sale of unascertained goods. The time for classification is when the contract is made. Therefore there are only two possible categories of contract, for the sale of specific goods and for the sale of unascertained goods. The word "ascertained" is used in the Sale of Goods Act to mean goods which become identified and agreed upon only after the contract is made.

Future goods

Section 5(1) reads: 3–06

> "The goods which form the subject of a contract of sale may be either existing goods, owned or possessed by the seller, or goods to be manufactured or acquired by him after the making of the contract of sale, in this Act called 'future goods'."

The problem here is to decide into which category future goods fall. Are they specific or are they unascertained? Examples of future goods are:

> 275 tons of barley to be grown by the seller (see *Sainsbury v. Street* (1972 Assizes));
>
> Animal feedstuff to be made according to a specification supplied by the buyer (see *Ashington Piggeries v. Hill* (1971 HL));
>
> A ship to be built by the seller to a specification (*McDougall v. Aeromarine of Emsworth* (1958 QB)).

Although these particular examples each concern a contract for the sale of unascertained goods, it is not true that all future goods automatically fall into that category. For example X may agree to sell to Y "the Morris car, registration number ABC 123, at present in the ownership of Q and to be acquired from him by X". This is a contract for the sale of specific goods. In *Varley v. Whipp* (1900 QB) the contract was for the sale of a specified second-hand reaping machine which at the time of the contract the seller did not own but had still to acquire. The court nevertheless regarded the reaping machine as specific goods.

THE TIME OF THE TRANSFER OF PROPERTY

The rules as to the time that property passes are contained in   3–07
sections 16–19 and they differ according to whether the contract is for the sale of specific or unascertained goods.

Specific goods

3–08   Section 17 says that property in specific goods passes to the buyer at such time as the parties intend it to be transferred. It also says that the intention of the parties can be determined by reference to the terms of the contract, the conduct of the parties and the circumstances of the case. If the contract expressly states when property is to pass then that is fine. Often, however, it does not do so. The seller is concerned about being paid and the buyer about getting hold of the goods. It is not unusual therefore for the contract expressly to deal with the time for payment and the time for delivery but to be silent about the time of the transfer of property. In such a case, one must still examine all the circumstances of the case in order to discern what was the parties' intention as to the passing of property. For example, a clue may be obtained from the time that the parties have stipulated for delivery and/or payment. In *Ward v. Bignall* (1967 CA), Diplock L.J. said "...in modern times very little is needed to give rise to the inference that property in specific goods is to pass only on delivery or payment".

One is attempting to discover what was the intention of the parties at the time they made the contract. If their intention subsequently changes, that is irrelevant and the property will pass in accordance with their intention at the time of making the contract. In *Dennant v. Skinner* (1948 KB) the buyer had a van knocked down to him at an auction. Shortly after this he paid for it by cheque and on request signed a statement that property in the van was not to pass to him until the cheque was cleared. The court in attempting to discover the intention of the parties ignored the signed statement because it had been made after the making of the contract.

Often even the diligent searcher will fail to discover when the parties intended property to pass. In this case property passes according to whichever of the rules in section 18 is relevant (see below). This is what occurred in *Dennant v. Skinner*.

Unascertained goods

3–09   Section 16 says:

> "Subject to section 20A below where there is a contract for the sale of unascertained goods no property is transferred to the buyer unless and until the goods are ascertained."

This is no more than common sense. Until the parties have identified the goods which the buyer is to have, no property can pass from the seller to the buyer for the simple reason that it is impossible to tell in which goods the property is passing. So, in a case where the seller was to build a yacht for the buyer and they agreed that on payment of the first instalment the vessel and all materials used in its construction should become the absolute property of the buyer, the court held that nevertheless no property passed on payment of the first instalment because at that time the boat's construction had not commenced and the materials to be used had not yet been identified: *McDougall v. Aeromarine of Emsworth Ltd* (1958 QB). A similar contract was involved in *Re Blyth Shipbuilding and Dry Dock Co.* (1926 CA), but in that case the vessel was already in course of construction when the first instalment was paid. It was held that property in the incomplete ship passed on payment of the first instalment but that no property passed at that time in some materials which were lying in the ship yard and might be used in the ship's construction. The reason was that it was not at that time ascertained that those materials were definitely to be used.

Suppose a seller, S, has contracted with A in Aylesbury to sell him 60kg of potatoes and with B in Bristol to sell him 25kg and with C in Cardiff to sell him 15kg. Suppose also that the seller despatches a lorry carrying 100kg of potatoes to make delivery to A, B and C in that order. Until the lorry has unloaded both A's and B's deliveries, the potatoes are all mixed up and C's 15kg are unascertained. As soon as A's and B's deliveries have both been made, C's 15kg become ascertained by exhaustion, since it is then possible to say that all the potatoes left on the lorry are destined for C. Now suppose that before the lorry is despatched, C sells his 15kg to B and arranges with S that the lorry shall drop 40kg to B in Bristol. In that case B's 40cwt become ascertained by exhaustion as soon as A's 60kg have been unloaded. That is so even though B's 40kg may not have been subdivided or allocated as between the separate contracts by which he bought them: *Karlshamns Oliefabriker v. Eastport Navigation Corporation, The Elafi* (1982 QB).

No property can pass in goods until they are ascertained. There is one exception to this. It is that there are special rules, introduced in 1995 and stated in section 20A, which apply to a contract to sell a specified quantity of unascertained goods out of a specified bulk and these rules provide for a special kind of proprietary interest to pass even before the goods have become ascertained. These special rules are dealt with later at paragraphs 3–37 to 3–47. So now we leave that exception aside for the moment and consider the ordinary rules which govern the passing of property in both contracts for the sale of specific goods and contracts for the sale of unascertained goods.

Although, apart from the exception just mentioned, no property can pass until the goods have become ascertained, it does not follow that the property will necessarily pass as soon as the goods are ascertained. Property passes when the parties intend it to— section 17. Section 17 applies to ascertained goods in exactly the same way as it does to specific goods. Again, as in the case of specific goods, if the intention of the parties is not apparent, then property passes according to the relevant rule in section 18, *i.e.* in the case of a contract for the sale of unascertained goods, usually rule 5.

Rules in section 18

3–10   Section 17 is the governing section and the rules in section 18 are to be consulted only if the parties have not evinced their intention as to when property is to pass. This is clear from the opening words of section 18:

> "Unless a different intention appears, the following are rules for ascertaining the intention of the parties as to the time at which the property in the goods is to pass to the buyer."

3–11   "*Rule 1:* Where there is an unconditional contract for the sale of specific goods, in a deliverable state, the property in the goods passes to the buyer when the contract is made, and it is immaterial whether the time of payment or the time of delivery or both be postponed."

The essence of this is that if the goods are identified and agreed upon and ready to be handed over, the parties are taken to have intended the buyer to become the owner immediately, *i.e.* at the very instant that the contract is made. In *Dennant v. Skinner* (1948 KB) a van was auctioned and knocked down to a Mr King. Hallet J. quoted rule 1 and continued:

> "Accordingly, on the fall of the hammer the property of this car passed to King unless that prima facie rule is excluded

from applying because of a different intention appearing or because there was some condition in the contract preventing the rule from applying."

He held that therefore the van became King's immediately.

It is not completely settled what is the meaning in rule 1 of "an unconditional contract". This could refer to a contract without any conditions whatsoever. Such an interpretation, however, would be absurd, since any contract of sale must have a condition somewhere at its core. It is difficult to imagine one without at least two conditions, namely, that the buyer will pay the price and that the seller will deliver the goods. The words "unconditional contract" therefore do not mean a contract without conditions in the sense just referred to, *i.e.* important terms of the contract (see Chapter 7). It seems sensible therefore to assume that they mean a contract which contains no condition preventing rule 1 from applying. An example of such a condition would be if, to the buyer's knowledge at the time the contract was made, the seller was not the owner of the goods. In that case ownership will not pass to the buyer before the seller has himself succeeded in acquiring that ownership. This was precisely the position in the case, referred to earlier, of *Varley v. Whipp*, where at the time of the contract the seller still had to acquire the second-hand reaping machine which he was agreeing to sell. It was held that the contract was not "unconditional" and that therefore rule 1 did not apply.

3–12

The words "deliverable state" are defined in section 61(5) as, goods "in such a state that the buyer would under the contract be bound to take the delivery of them". Thus if the goods require anything to be done to them in order for them to be ready for delivery or in order to make them comply with the contract, they will not be in a deliverable state. In *Underwood v. Burgh Castle Brick & Cement Syndicate* (1922 CA) the contract was to sell a 30-ton condensing machine which at the time of the contract was standing bolted to a concrete emplacement in which it had become embedded because of its weight. It was an expensive and time-consuming task to remove it. In the contract the sellers had agreed to do this and to deliver the machine f.o.r. (free on rail) which meant that they undertook to see that the machine was conveyed to and loaded upon the train. The Court of Appeal had two reasons for deciding that rule 1 did not apply. First, the parties had, by making an f.o.r. agreement, indicated their intention that property should pass when the goods were loaded

3–13

on to the rail. Secondly, the machine was not at the time of the contract in a deliverable state, since it still had to be removed from the concrete emplacement.

3–14   We now come to the closing words of rule 1, "it is immaterial whether the time of payment or the time of delivery, or both, be postponed". From these, it is clear that a buyer can be owner of the goods even though he has not paid for them and even though they remain in the seller's possession. As we shall see in Chapter 12, the seller usually has the right to retain possession of the goods until the buyer pays. This does not alter the fact that if rule 1 applies the buyer becomes owner at the instant the contract is made. As Hallett J. explained in *Dennant v. Skinner*, "the passing of property and the right to possession are two different things. Here, in my judgment, the property had passed on the fall of the hammer, but still the (seller) had a right to retain possession of the goods until payment was made."

In other words, what occurs after the contract is made, in relation either to the possession of the goods or to the payment of the price, can have no bearing upon the operation of rule 1. However, what might affect it is if at the time of the making of the contract the parties make an *agreement* about delivery and/or payment, *e.g.* that they be postponed. Such an agreement could easily give rise to the inference that they intended the passing of property to be similarly postponed (see *Underwood v. Burgh Castle Brick & Cement Syndicate*, above). In that situation none of the rules in section 18 would apply since those rules are only relevant "unless a different intention appears".

3–15   "*Rule 2:* Where there is a contract for the sale of specific goods and the seller is bound to do something to the goods, for the purpose of putting them into a deliverable state, the property does not pass until the thing is done, and the buyer has notice that it has been done."

One unanswered question here is what "notice" means. Suppose the seller puts a letter in the post informing the buyer that the goods are in a deliverable state. Does property pass when the letter is posted or when it arrives? "Notice" probably means actual knowledge in which case the property passes when the letter arrives. So, if the letter is lost in the post, property does not pass until the buyer actually discovers that the goods are in a deliverable state.

"Rule 3: Where there is a contract for the sale of specific   **3–16**
goods in a deliverable state, but the seller is bound to
weigh, measure, test or do some other act or thing with
reference to the goods for the purpose of ascertaining the
price, the property does not pass until the act or thing is
done and the buyer has notice that it has been done."

It is important here to note that rule 3 applies only if it is the
seller who is to do the weighing, measuring, testing, etc.

In *Nanka Bruce v. Commonwealth Trust Ltd.* (1926 PC) it was
agreed that the buyer would pay 59s. per 60lb. The buyer was
going to resell the goods and it was recognised that the buyer's
sub-purchaser would test the weight and thus ascertain the precise
sum to be paid to the seller. The Privy Council held that property
passed from the seller before the sub-purchaser had tested the
goods for weight. Thus, where specific goods are to be weighed
or tested, etc., by some person other than the seller, property will
pass under rule 1 or rule 2 unless the parties have agreed
otherwise.

"Rule 4: When goods are delivered to the buyer on   **3–17**
approval or on sale or return or other similar terms the
property in the goods passes to the buyer:

(a) when he signifies his approval or acceptance to the
    seller or does any other act adopting the transaction;

(b) if he does not signify his approval or acceptance to the
    seller but retains the goods without giving notice of
    rejection, then if a time has been fixed for the return
    of the goods, on expiration of that time and, if no time
    has been fixed, on the expiration of a reasonable
    time."

It is sometimes difficult to know whether the purchaser has
done an act adopting the transaction. He will have done such an
act if he does something which substantially impedes his ability
to return the goods by the end of the period (whether that be a
stipulated period or a reasonable length of time). Thus he
"adopts" the transaction when he resells the goods or when he
pledges them with a pawnbroker (*Kirkham v. Attenborough* (1897
CA)). What is the position, though, where the buyer resells the
goods on sale or return terms? Passages from the judgments from

Genn v. Winkel (1911 CA) are particularly helpful here. Fletcher Moulton L.J. said:

> "A person who receives goods on sale or return and at once passes them on to someone else under a like contract is entitled to demand them from that third person just as soon as the original owner of the goods has the right to demand them from him, but I am clear that, if he allows a period to elapse before he hands them on to a third person on sale or return, he has done an act which limits and impedes his power of returning the goods. If 14 days be a reasonable length of time in such a contract in this particular trade, and if he waits seven days before entrusting the goods to a third person on sale or return, that third person has the right to keep them as against him for 14 days, whereas the original owner has a right to the return of them within seven days from that date and I think that is clearly an act inconsistent with anything but his having adopted the transaction."

Buckley L.J. said:

> "If A delivers goods to B on sale or return and B having received them immediately delivers them to C on sale or return, the reasonable time in the one case must, I think, be co-extensive with that in the other case and if that reasonable time elapses and C brings back the goods to B and B takes them back to A, everybody is acting within his rights, and it appears to me that property never passes...if under like circumstances A delivers goods to B and B delivers them to C in each case on sale or return and the reasonable time be, let us say, 14 days, and C after four days sells the goods or elects to buy the goods, I think property will have passed, because C will have done an act which renders it impossible for B to return the goods to A."

3–18   Two further points need to be made about rule 4. First, if the cause of the purchaser being unable to return the goods within the approval period is something which occurs entirely without his fault and beyond his control (*e.g.* if the goods are stolen or accidentally destroyed) he can offer that as an excuse and property will not pass: *Re Ferrier* (1944 Ch).

Secondly, as with all the rules in section 18, rule 4 is irrelevant if the parties when making the contract express their intentions as to when property shall pass. Thus in *Weiner v. Gill* (1906 CA) although jewellery sold on approval was subsequently resold by the buyer, the Court held that property had not passed because of an express statement in the original contract that property was not to pass until the seller was paid.

> "*Rule 5:* (1) Where there is a contract for the sale of unascertained or future goods by description, and goods of that description and in a deliverable state are unconditionally appropriated to the contract, either by the seller with the assent of the buyer, or by the buyer with the assent of the seller, the property in the goods then passes to the buyer; and the assent may be express or implied, and may be given either before or after the appropriation is made. **3–19**
>
> (2) Where, in pursuance of the contract, the seller delivers the goods to the buyer or to a carrier or other bailee or custodier (whether named by the buyer or not) for the purpose of transmission to the buyer, and does not reserve the right to disposal, he is taken to have unconditionally appropriated the goods to the contract."

There are many contracts for the sale of unascertained goods where the parties do not express their intention as to when property shall pass. Rule 5(1) applies to these contracts. It contains two basic requirements for property to pass. First, goods complying with the contract must be unconditionally appropriated to the contract by one of the parties. Secondly, the other party must give his assent.

Take an example: Mrs Jones telephones her coal merchant asking him to deliver six bags of coal. He agrees. Next day the merchant, his lorry loaded with 200 bags of coal, sets out to make deliveries. He arrives at Mrs Jones's door with 150 bags left on the lorry. He knocks at her door. She unlocks the coal house door for him. He goes to his lorry where he drags six bags to the edge of the lorry's platform. He takes one of them, brings it to the coal house and empties it there. He repeats this with each of the other five bags. At what time does the property in the coal pass to Mrs Jones? It is not when the merchant set out on his round because at that time Mrs Jones' coal was as yet unascertained—*McDougall v. Aeromarine of Emsworth* (above). **3–20**

For the same reason, it did not pass when the merchant drew up outside her house.

3–21   Rule 5(1) tells us that property passes when it is unconditionally appropriated by one party with the other's assent. In *Carlos Federspiel & Co. v. Charles Twigg & Co.* (1957 QB) Pearson J. had to consider what amounted to an "unconditional appropriation". He said:

> "A mere setting apart or selection by the seller of the goods which he expects to use in performance of the contract is not enough. If that is all, he can change his mind and use those goods in performance of some other contract and use some other goods in performance of this contract."

Thus, in our example, property did not pass when the merchant moved the six bags towards the edge of the lorry's platform. Pearson J. went on:

> "To constitute an appropriation of goods to the contract, the parties must have had, or be reasonably supposed to have had, an intention to attach the contract irrevocably to those goods."

3–22   It would seem then that in our example there was an unconditional appropriation of the contents of each bag as when it was emptied into Mrs Jones' coal house. Pearson J. was considering a contract where the seller had agreed to despatch goods f.o.b. (free on board) a ship, *i.e.* the seller undertook to convey the goods to the ship and to load them.

He had got as far as packaging and labelling them at his premises prior to taking them to the ship. Pearson J. held that property had not passed under rule 5(1) for two reasons. First, section 18 was irrelevant since the parties by making an f.o.b. contract had indicated their intention that property was to pass as and when the goods were loaded on to the ship (see *Underwood v. Burgh Castle Brick & Cement Syndicate*, above). Secondly, the goods had been merely set aside and not unconditionally appropriated.

3–23   *Re London Wine Co. (Shippers)* (1986 QBD) also illustrates the principle that for an appropriation there has to be an apparent intention to attach the goods irrevocably to the contract. The selling company dealt in wine and maintained considerable stocks. It contracted to sell wine on terms that after the contract the wine would be stored for the purchaser by the vendor. The company issued each purchaser with a document confirming that the purchaser was the sole owner of the wine he had purchased. In one instance a contract was made to sell to one purchaser a quantity of a given type of wine which exactly equalled the seller's stock of it. In another instance several contracts with different purchasers exhausted the seller's stock of another type of wine. Each purchaser was given a document stating him to be the owner of the quantity he had purchased of the wine in question. It was held, nevertheless, that in neither instance was there an appropriation. Where there were several purchasers of the same type of wine, it was impossible to say who owned which of the bottles of wine in the seller's stock. Even where there was only one purchaser, there was nothing to identify the particular cases of wine in stock as the subject-matter of the purchaser's contract. It was quite open to the selling company, if it wished, to obtain more wine of the same description for delivery to the purchaser. Thus no property passed in any of the wine remaining in the seller's stock.

The decision in *Re London Wine Company (Shippers)* was **3–24** distinguished in *Re Ellis Son & Vidler* (1995 QBD), where again wine was sold on terms that after the sale it would be stored for the purchasers by the vendor. In this case, however, there was to be, and was, a segregation of wine within the seller's warehouse, so that upon a contract being made, wine of the appropriate year and description was segregated from the general trading stock of the seller and kept together with other wine bought by customers and stored for them by the seller. Within the segregated part of the warehouse, wine of any particular year and description was kept together but was not further allocated to the different customers who had bought wine of that year and description. When later (perhaps years later) a customer asked for delivery of; say, a case of his Chateau Plonk 1976, that request would be fulfilled by the seller taking and delivering any case from the quantity of Chateau Plonk 1976 stored in the segregated part of the warehouse. The judge dealt with this situation in a combination of two novel ways. First, he held that since the contract contemplated no immediate delivery of the goods but merely a segregation in the hands of the seller for retention purposes, the wine became sufficiently ascertained when that segregation occurred. That was so, even though the cases of wine were not at that stage allocated to each individual customer. Secondly, he held that property passed when the parties intended it to, namely when the wine was set aside for storage. Since at that time the cases of wine in storage were not allocated as between the different purchasers, the nature of the property right which passed to the buyer was unusual. Thus each set of cases of identical wine which was held by the seller, not mingled with the trading stock, but segregated and in store for a group of customers, was the property of that group of customers, each customer holding the wine as tenant in common. This means that each such customer had an undivided share in the set of cases, a share proportionate to the number of cases he had bought. The key distinctions between this case and *Re London Wine* were, first, that in this case there was to be a segregation of the wine by the seller for storage purposes and, secondly, that the London Wine Company, unlike the seller in the present case, was free to sell its stock and satisfy its customers from any other available source. The ruling in the present case anticipated the rules relating to a specified quantity of unascertained goods out of a identified bulk which were shortly afterwards introduced by section 20A (see paragraphs 3–37 to 3–47 below).

3–25 When goods have to be despatched by a carrier (*e.g.* the Post Office) rule 5(2) is often helpful. Thus the goods will normally be unconditionally appropriated when handed over to the carrier. However, there are two limitations to this. First, there is no unconditional appropriation when the seller reserves the right of disposal—see section 19 (below). The other limitation is that property cannot pass in unascertained goods—see section 16 (above). To put it another way, goods are not appropriated unless it is clear which goods are appropriated. This is neatly illustrated by *Healy v. Howlett* (1917 KB). The seller contracted to sell 20 boxes of mackerel f.o.r. (free on rail). He despatched by rail all at the same time 190 boxes to go to various customers. He did not label the boxes to go to particular destinations but left it to the rail company to allot the appropriate number of boxes to the various destinations. Ridley J. held that putting the 190 boxes on the rail was not in this case an unconditional appropriation because it was impossible to say which of them was appropriated to any given buyer. They therefore were still unascertained goods. Property therefore could not pass until the railway company made the allotments.

3–26 The problem of when does an unconditional appropriation occur can arise in a very different situation; when the buyer has to collect the goods, not from the seller, but from a third person. There is an unconditional appropriation when the goods are identified and the third person acknowledges that he now holds them for the buyer: *Wardars (Import & Exports) v. W. Norwood* (1968 CA). This case concerned the sale of 600 cartons of frozen kidneys out of a bulk of 1,500 cartons stored for the seller at a cold store. The buyer's carrier went to the cold store with a delivery order. He found that 600 cartons had been set aside ready for him. He handed over his delivery order to an official who thereupon gave instructions for loading to commence. The Court of Appeal held that there was an unconditional appropriation when the delivery order was accepted and loading allowed to commence.

Under rule 5(1) an unconditional appropriation will not pass property unless the other party assents. This assent could sometimes be difficult to establish but fortunately rule 5 allows it to be implied and to be given in advance. Thus, in our earlier example, Mrs Jones's assent can be inferred from the fact that she unlocked the coal house door. Similarly, in *Aldridge v. Johnson* (1857 QB) where the buyer supplied bags for the seller to put the goods (barley) into, it was held that property passed when the seller filled the bags. An easy and neat example of assent can also be found in the case of a purchase of petrol at a garage. If a petrol pump attendant puts the petrol into the customer's car, that is an unconditional appropriation to which the buyer's assent is clearly implied: *Edwards v. Ddin* (1976 DC). At a self-service garage it is the motorist who unconditionally appropriates the petrol by pouring it into his tank, the assent of the seller being equally clearly implied. Thus at a self-service station, as in the case of a non-self-service one, property in the petrol passes to the buyer when it is poured into his tank: *R. v. McHugh* (1977 DC).

3–27

On the other hand, assent is sometimes given only after the unconditional appropriation is made. In that case the property passes not upon appropriation but when the other party's assent is subsequently given. This was the position in *Pignataro v. Gilroy* (1919 KB) where the sale concerned some unascertained bags of rice which the buyer was to collect. The sellers got the rice completely ready for collection and were requested by the buyer for a delivery order enabling him to collect the rice. They sent him a delivery order but he failed to come and collect the rice. He did nothing. The buyer's assent to the appropriation made by the sellers was inferred from his failure to object after receiving the delivery order. Therefore property passed to him when, after a reasonable length of time, he had failed to object.

3–28   "*Rule 5:* (3) "Where there is a contract for the sale of a specified quantity of unascertained goods in a deliverable state forming part of a bulk which is identified either in the contract or by subsequent agreement between the parties and bulk is reduced to (or less than) that quantity, then, if the buyer is the only buyer to whom goods are then due out of the bulk,

   (a) the remaining goods are to be taken as appropriated to that contract at the time when the bulk is so reduced; and

   (b) the property in those goods then passes to the buyer.

(4) Paragraph (3) above applies also (with the necessary modifications) where a bulk is reduced to (or to less than) the aggregate of the quantities due to a single buyer under separate contracts relating to that bulk and he is the only buyer to whom goods are then due out of that bulk."

Rules 5(3) and (4) were added to the section by the Sale of Goods (Amendment) Act 1995. They give statutory authority to the decision in *Karlshamns Oliefabriker v. Eastport Navigation Corporation, The Elafi* (1982), explained at paragraph 3–09 above. The principle involved is one of ascertainment and appropriation by exhaustion. Where the buyer agrees to buy goods out of a specified bulk, *e.g.* "50 tonnes out of the 110 tonnes of potatoes currently in the seller's Bedford warehouse", the complete property in the remaining potatoes at the warehouse passes to the buyer at the moment that the 110 tonnes is reduced to 50 tonnes (or less). At least that is so provided that (a) the goods are in a deliverable state, (b) the buyer is the only buyer remaining entitled to potatoes from that warehouse, (c) the buyer has assented to the appropriation and (d) the parties have not made an agreement for property to pass at some later stage. In the absence of some particular evidence to the contrary, the buyer's assent is likely to be implied from the mere fact that he agreed to buy from the specific bulk, since he must have meant to leave the seller free to deal with the remaining 60 tonnes and that automatically must involve the buyer assenting to the remaining ones being thereby appropriated to him. It makes no difference if it is under more than one contract that the buyer is entitled to the whole of the remaining quantity of the outstanding bulk: rule

5(4). Of course, if the 110 tonnes have become reduced to less than 50 tonnes, then, whilst property in whatever tonnage is left will at that stage pass to the buyer, the buyer may well have a claim against the seller for breach of contract for delivery of less than the contract quantity. Nor can the seller within the terms of the contract make up the shortfall from another source.

On the question of what proprietary interest the buyer gets in the bulk *before* property passes under rule 5(3) and (4), see paragraphs 3–37 to 3–47 below.

Section 19

Section 19 provides that, if the seller reserves a right of disposal of the goods until certain conditions are fulfilled, property does not pass until those conditions are fulfilled. Thus if a seller entrusts identified and appropriated goods to a carrier with instructions that they be conveyed to the buyer but not handed over until the buyer has paid, the goods will remain the seller's property until the buyer pays for them. 3–29

It is quite common in an import or export sale for the seller to agree to arrange the carriage of the goods by ship to the buyer and also to arrange for their insurance en route. Such contracts are termed c.i.f. because the cost (*i.e.* the price paid by the buyer to the seller) includes the insurance and freight. In this case the bill of lading (*i.e.* the document given by the shipowner acknowledging that he has received the goods) will usually indicate that the goods are held according to the seller's instructions. The seller will normally send by air to the buyer some documents: one will be the bill of lading transferred to the buyer to enable him to collect the goods at their port of destination; another will be a bill of exchange which the buyer will normally sign and return thereby undertaking to pay for the goods on the date specified on the bill of exchange. If the buyer finds that the bill of lading is not in order, *i.e.* it indicates that the contract has not been complied with, he can refuse to accept it and will therefore refuse to sign the bill of exchange. In such a case no property passes to the buyer—section 19. Also, section 19 requires the buyer to return the bill of lading to the seller. If on the other hand the buyer finds the bill of lading in order he will retain it and will sign and return the bill of exchange. When he does this, property will pass. This, of course, does not preclude the buyer from refusing to accept the goods if when they arrive they do not comply with the contract. If he does that, then property will pass back to the seller: *Kwei Tek Chao v. British*

Traders (1954 QB). C.I.F. and other international sale agreements are further explained in Chapter 17.

TRANSFER OF RISK

Section 20

3–30   Unless the parties agree otherwise, risk passes with property—section 20(1). Thus if the goods are damaged or stolen this loss falls on the seller if it occurs before property has passed; otherwise it falls on the buyer. This is so irrespective of whose possession the goods were in at the time. This is illustrated by *Pignataro v. Gilroy* (1919 KB) where we have seen that property passed to the buyer under section 18, rule 5. The buyer failed to collect them and they were stolen from the seller's warehouse. It was held that the buyer must bear this loss because property had passed to him before the goods were stolen.

The basic rule that risk passes with property is subject to three limitations; they are section 20(2) and (3) and the fact that section 20(1) only applies unless otherwise agreed.

Section 20(2)

3–31   "But where the delivery has been delayed through the fault of either buyer or seller the goods are at the risk of the party at fault as regards any loss which might not have occurred but for such fault."

This was applied in *Demby Hamilton v. Barden* (1949 KB) where the buyer was supposed to take delivery of some apple juice in weekly loads. The buyer held up delivery and the juice went bad as a result. It was held that the buyer must bear the loss.

Section 20(3)

3–32   "Nothing in this section shall affect the duties or liabilities of either seller or buyer as a bailee or custodier of the goods of the other party."

This means that the person in possession must take reasonable care of the goods even if the ownership is with the other party. Thus if the goods are damaged or stolen because of his negligence he will have to bear the loss even though at the time he was not the owner. To put it another way, the risk which under section 20 passes with property (*i.e.* which falls upon the owner) does not include the risk of loss or damage due to the other party's negligence.

"Unless otherwise agreed"

The parties can agree when risk shall pass. They can select a   **3–33** time before or after the passing of property. In order for their agreement to have any effect it must be part of the contract. It may be remembered that in *Healy v. Howlett* no property passed in the mackerel put by the sellers on to the rail because the consignment was not allotted as to the various destinations. After putting them on the rail the sellers sent the buyers an invoice stating "At sole risk of purchaser after putting fish on rail here". Ridley J. said, "I do not see how those words form part of the contract". He therefore ignored them. The mackerel went bad before the railway had allocated particular boxes to particular destinations. Therefore, since property had not passed, the loss fell on the seller.

An agreement that the passing of risk shall not be simultaneous with the passing of property can be inferred from the circumstances. An example is the difficult case of *Sterns v. Vickers* (1923 CA). The sellers owned 200,000 gallons of white spirit stored for them by an independent person, X, in his tanks. They sold to the buyers 120,000 out of the 200,000 gallons and gave the buyers the benefit of free storage at X's for a given period, *i.e.* down to January 31. It was agreed that the buyers would make their own arrangement for storage thereafter. The sellers gave the buyers a delivery note to enable them to collect the spirit from X. However, the buyers chose to keep it at X's and did not come to remove it for some months by which time it had deteriorated. Clearly, property had not passed because, until collected, the 120,000 gallons out of the 200,000 remained unascertained. In spite of this, the Court of Appeal held that the parties intended risk to pass when the buyers accepted the delivery note. The buyers therefore had to bear the costs of the deterioration. There are three things to note about this case.

First, the agreement that risk should pass independently from property was not express but inferred by the court from the circumstances of the case. Secondly, that agreement resulted in risk passing before property. Thirdly, it resulted in the risk passing in unascertained goods.

3–34   This last point is not without difficulty. Which goods were at the buyer's risk? Clearly no more than 120,000 gallons—but which 120,000 gallons? If, say, only 100,000 out of the 200,000 gallons had deteriorated, it would have been difficult to allocate the loss as between seller and buyer. Presumably it would be done pro rata, *i.e.* the buyer would bear

$$\frac{120,000}{200,000} (= 3/5) \text{ of the loss.}$$

This is possible where, as in *Sterns v. Vickers*, the contract is for the sale of unascertained goods out of a specified bulk. One can identify the bulk, calculate the total loss and make the buyer bear a proportion according to his share of the bulk. This could not be done where the contract was for the sale of purely generic goods. In that case until the goods are ascertained it is impossible for risk to pass. Not only would it be impossible to identify the goods which were at the buyer's risk but also it would be impossible to identify any goods which were pro rata at his risk.

There is now a fourth point which can be made about the case. It is that if the facts had arisen after 1995, there would have to be a qualification to the statement that property had not passed to the buyer. The qualification is that, under the law as it now is, the buyer (assuming he had paid for the goods) would have acquired an undivided share of 60 per cent of the 200,000 gallons and thus when all the gallons deteriorated, he would have had to bear the loss in so far as it affected his 60 per cent. In other words the net result would still be the same if the facts of *Sterns v. Vickers* occurred again today (as to the buyer getting an undivided share in an identified bulk, see paragraphs 3–37 to 3–47 below).

3–35   Let us now turn to a less difficult situation where the rule in section 20 may be affected, *i.e.* where the seller undertakes to deliver the goods. The seller does not have to agree to this and if he does, that will not normally affect the operation of section 20. Thus the risk of loss or damage (other than that caused by late delivery or the seller's negligence) will pass at the same time as the passing of property. If on the other hand the seller agrees to deliver "at his own risk" this will alter the operation of section

20. Its effect will be that even if property passes earlier to the buyer, the goods will remain at the seller's risk until their arrival. However, even in this case, unless the parties agree otherwise, the buyer must bear the "risk of deterioration necessarily incident to the course of transit"—section 33. Thus where the seller agrees to deliver the goods "at his own risk" the buyer will bear the risk of any unavoidable deterioration in the goods in transit but the seller will have to bear the risk of them being stolen from his lorry *en route*.

Effect of loss falling on one party

If because risk had passed to him the buyer has to bear some **3–36** loss, it follows that he is not excused from carrying out the contract. Thus, if he refuses to accept the goods or to pay because they have deteriorated, he is in breach of contract. The seller will have all the usual seller's remedies. If, because risk had not passed to the buyer, the seller has to bear the loss, this does not necessarily excuse him from performing the contract. It will do so only if it frustrates the contract (*i.e.* renders it impossible to carry it out—see Chapter 4). Unless the contract is frustrated, the seller will still have to carry out the contract and if he delivers goods which do not comply with it, he will be in breach of contract.

UNASCERTAINED GOODS FROM AN IDENTIFIED BULK

Until 1995 there was no statutory provision dealing expressly **3–37** with the situation where the subject matter of the contract was a specified quantity of goods from an identified source, *e.g.* "nine bottles of the seller's current stock of 1992 Chateau Plonk", or "400 of the 1,000 tonnes of wheat currently in the Wally's Warehouse at Woodford". Since such a contract is for the sale of unascertained goods, it followed (by virtue of the rule in section 16) that no property could pass to the buyer until his nine bottles or his 400 tonnes had become ascertained. This was less than ideal in the situation where the buyer had paid the price and the seller had become insolvent before the particular goods to be supplied to the buyer had become identified. This was because in that situation the goods remained the property of the seller and hence became the property of the seller's trustee in bankruptcy and the buyer became simply an unsecured creditor. It was to remedy this defect in the law that the Sale of Goods (Amendment) Act 1995 was passed.

3-38   This Act created a qualification to the rule in section 16 of the Sale of Goods Act. It did this by inserting into the Sale of Goods Act a new section, section 20A. This section applies to any contract for the sale of a specified quantity of goods which is part of an identified bulk. Its effect is that as soon as the buyer pays the price (or part of it), the buyer acquires property in an undivided share in the bulk, becoming thereby an owner in common of the bulk. The buyer's share is "such share as the quantity of goods paid for and due to the buyer out of the bulk bears to the quantity of goods in the bulk". So, if the buyer has agreed to buy "400 tonnes out of the 1,000 tonnes of wheat in Wally's Woodford Warehouse", and he has paid for his 400 tonnes, then provided there are 1,000 tonnes of wheat in the warehouse, the buyer will own an undivided share of 40 per cent of the 1,000 tonnes. If the seller should subsequently remove 200 tonnes from the bulk (*e.g.* to supply a second buyer), then the bulk is reduced by that amount. In that case the first buyer's undivided share will automatically become a larger proportion of the reduced bulk, *i.e.* it will then amount to 50 per cent of the now remaining 800 tonnes. Thus, although no property in the buyer's particular 400 tonnes can be transferred to the buyer until his particular 400 tonnes have been identified, he does acquire a proprietary right in the form of this undivided share in the bulk.

3-39   This cannot occur before payment and in any case the effect of section 20A is subject to contrary agreement by the parties. The parties can by agreement decide that section 20A will not apply at all (*i.e.* that the buyer will not get an undivided share in the bulk) or that the property in an undivided share will pass at some point of time *after* payment. They cannot agree to it passing at any earlier stage.

Of course, in the example given above the seller could remove all of the rest of the bulk, *i.e.* so that only 400 tonnes were left. In that case the buyer would cease to have an undivided share, but would then have complete property in the bulk by virtue of section 18, rule 5(3): see paragraph 3-28 above.

Insufficient quantity in the bulk

3-40   What then is the position if the bulk becomes reduced to less than the quantity to which the buyer is entitled? This could happen in several different ways.

(1) The seller makes contracts under which the total quantity contracted to be sold out of the bulk is greater than the total quantity in the specified bulk

Suppose the seller has 1,000 tonnes of wheat in the warehouse. Suppose that he agrees to sell 500 tonnes of the bulk to A, 400 tonnes of it to B and 300 tonnes of it C. Suppose also that each of A, B and C have paid the seller in full. Suppose also that the contracts are made and the payments are made in that order, *i.e.* A first, B second and C third. In that situation, while the bulk is still undivided, it is obvious as a matter of common sense that A, B and C cannot each have an undivided share in a bulk of 1,200 tonnes, since the bulk contains only 1,000 tonnes. The result therefore has to be one of the two following: **3–41**

(i)   the seller can and does give to C only that which the seller has still got, namely an undivided share in one-tenth of the bulk of 1,000 tonnes;

(ii) C is introduced as an extra purchaser having an undivided share of three-twelfths of the bulk, thereby diluting A's and B's undivided shares to five-twelfths and four-twelfths respectively.

The second of these two solutions cannot apply because of the rule that the seller cannot give that which does not have; he can give only that which he has got. This rule is known by its Latin: *nemo dat quod non habet* (no one can give that which he does not have) and is fully explained in Chapter 5. Since, immediately prior to the sale to C, the seller has only an undivided share in one-tenth of the bulk of 1,000 tonnes, that is all that C can get. Thus A's and B's shares remain undiluted and C gets an undivided share in one-tenth of the bulk of 1,000 tonnes. Suppose now, however, that the seller delivers to C, pursuant to the seller's contract with C, 300 tonnes out of the bulk. If at the time of that delivery C takes in good faith, unaware of A's and B's contracts, C will obtain complete property in the 300 tonnes delivered. This is because of section 24 of the Sale of Goods Act, which creates an exception to the rule that the seller cannot pass property (*i.e.* ownership) which he does not have. Section 24 applies where a person, having sold goods, continues in possession and then delivers the goods under any sale or other disposition to another person who takes them in good faith and without notice of the **3–42** previous sale. (Section 24 is dealt more fully at paragraph 5–27 below.) When in these circumstances C obtains property in the 300 tonnes that are delivered to him, A's and B's rights are reduced to undivided shares in the reduced bulk of 700 tonnes, shares of five-ninths and four-ninths respectively. That is the effect of section 20A(4) which provides that where the aggregate of the undivided shares of buyers in a bulk would exceed the whole of the bulk, the undivided share of each buyer is reduced proportionately so that the aggregate of the undivided shares is equal to the whole bulk. If the next thing that happens is that the seller becomes bankrupt, A and B will be entitled to take the remaining 700 tonnes and divide it between themselves in the proportions five to four. This will of course leave each of them with a shortfall and to that extent they will become unsecured creditors of the seller.

3–43 Of course it could have happened that, shortly before becoming insolvent, the seller delivered out of the remaining bulk of 700 tonnes to one or other of A or B. Suppose then that, before becoming insolvent and bankrupt, the seller delivered to B 400 tonnes from the bulk pursuant to B's contract. In that case complete property in the 400 tonnes will have at that point passed to B, by virtue of section 18, rule 5(1) (see paragraph 3–19 above). At the moment of the delivery to B, A will have become the only buyer entitled to the remaining bulk which at a mere 300 tonnes was less than he contracted to buy. Thus at that moment complete property in the remaining 300 tonnes will have passed to A. So far as his shortfall of 200 tonnes is concerned, his only claim is as an unsecured creditor against the seller. Thus the effect of the delivery to B is to transfer to A the full effect of the shortfall. At least, that is so unless there was an express contractual arrangement to the contrary between A and B. This is because section 20B provides that each owner in common of the bulk (here A, B and C) is deemed to have consented to delivery out of the bulk to any other owner in common of the bulk.

(2) The seller delivers goods out of the bulk to another buyer in pursuance of a contract other than one to supply goods from that particular bulk

3–44 Suppose that the bulk is 1,000 tonnes and that A is the only buyer to whom the seller has contracted to sell goods (500 tonnes) from that particular bulk and suppose that A has paid for them. In that case a delivery to another buyer (X) of 100 tonnes will simply reduce the bulk to 900 tonnes and A will then have an undivided share of five-ninths of the 900 tonnes remaining. Now, however, suppose that the quantity sold and delivered to X is 600 tonnes out of the bulk. The effect of this delivery is to reduce the remainder of the bulk to 400 tonnes. Obviously, complete property in the remaining 400 tonnes will pass to A. The sale and supply of 600 tonnes to X appears to have reduced A's rights by 100 tonnes. How can A's proprietary rights in 100 tonnes be given to X? The answer lies again in section 24 that, despite the fact that the seller does not have a right to any more than 500 of the 1,000 tonnes, he can nevertheless pass to X good title to goods already sold to A. This occurs, by virtue of section 24, provided X takes in good faith and unaware of A's contract.

(3) The bulk is destroyed, reduced or damaged by accident or act of God

Suppose that there are 1,000 tonnes in the bulk and that A has contracted to buy, but has not yet paid for, 500 tonnes of them. In that case A will have acquired no property, not even an undivided share in the goods. That being so, no risk will have passed to A, unless the parties have agreed otherwise or else the seller can establish that delivery has been delayed through A's own fault (see section 20 at paragraph 3–30 above). A's contract will be frustrated at common law if the contract has become impossible, *e.g.* if the bulk is totally lost in an act of God, such as an accidental fire. (For more explanation of frustration see paragraph 4–11 below.)

3–45

Now, however, suppose that A has paid for his 500 tonnes before the fire occurs and suppose that there is no other buyer with an interest in the 1,000 bulk. A and B each had an undivided share of 50 per cent in the 1,000 tonnes. Normally, risk passes with property. So, assuming the whole of the 1,000 tonnes are lost, each of A and B loses his entire interest in the bulk. The position is different, however, if the fire destroys only part of the bulk. According to the Law Commission Report whose recommendations the Sale of Goods (Amendment) Act 1995 was passed to implement, "...the risk of partial destruction of the goods rests with the seller (in the absence of agreement to the contrary) so long as the quantity destroyed is within the quantity retained by the seller". To put it another way, in any case of destruction of any of the bulk, it is assumed that the share in the goods retained by the seller is destroyed first. Only when that has all been destroyed, do the various buyers with undivided shares begin each to suffer a loss proportionate according to the size of their respective undivided shares. Of course it is possible that none of the goods are destroyed but that some or all of them are damaged. In that case the same principle applies. The damage is taken to have occurred first to the share of the goods retained by the seller. Of course if the damage is to all of the bulk equally, then the seller and the buyer(s) will bear the loss in proportion to their respective shares. So if the buyer has agreed to buy (and has paid for) 120,000 gallons out of a bulk of 200,000 gallons and the whole bulk is damaged equally, the buyer will have to bear 60 per cent and the seller 40 per cent of that loss (see *Sterns v. Vickers*, paragraph 3–33 above for a case where similar facts arose before the advent of the new law on undivided shares).

Limits to the new rules

3–46   For the rules in section 20A to apply, the agreement must be for a specified quantity of goods forming part of an identified bulk. This section, whereby the buyer may acquire an undivided share in the bulk, applies only where the parties agree that the goods are to come from that bulk. It is not enough that each of the parties had in his mind this particular source for the goods, if they have not actually agreed it. If they have agreed simply that the seller will supply "500 tonnes of wheat", then the contract can be fulfilled by the seller supplying wheat from any source, even though they may both have assumed that this particular source would be used. Section 20A applies only where the particular bulk is identified either by the contract or else by subsequent agreement between the parties. Even then, the section will not apply unless that identified source amounts to a "bulk" which means:

"a mass or collection of goods of the same kind which

(a) is contained within a confined space or area, and

(b) is such that any goods in the bulk are interchangeable with any other goods therein of the same number or quantity."

3–47   Even then section 20A will still not apply unless the agreement is for a "specified quantity" (*e.g.* 500 tonnes, 40 cases, nine bottles) of goods from the bulk. Thus a contract for the sale of "500 tonnes of the 1,000 tonnes of wheat in the seller's warehouse at Woodford" is one for unascertained goods and section 20A will apply to it. On the other hand, a contract to purchase a percentage or a fraction (*e.g.* 10 per cent or one-half) of the bulk is an example of a contract for the purchase of specific goods and section 20A will not apply to it. Thus a contract for the sale of "half of the 1,000 tonnes of wheat currently in the seller's warehouse at Woodford" is a contract for the sale of specific goods. Although the Act still has no provision for such a contract (beyond stating that it is a contract for specific goods), it is nevertheless still presumably intended by the parties that the buyer will acquire an undivided share in the bulk. The property in that undivided share will pass when the parties intend it to. If it turns out that the bulk is greater or less than the 1,000 tonnes, then the buyer will either gain or lose in comparison with his expectations. If it turns out to be less, presumably he may have a claim for misrepresentation or for breach of contract, since the seller had informed and/or promised him that the bulk comprised 1,000 tonnes. It may be that the example of "half of a bulk of 1,000 tonnes of wheat" is unrealistic because the parties would be much more likely to state "500 tonnes out of the bulk of 1,000 tonnes". The percentage or fraction approach is more likely to be adopted by parties who are selling and buying part of an item which is essentially indivisible, *e.g.* a racehorse.

RETENTION OF TITLE CLAUSES

In business it is not uncommon for a seller (X) to sell large   **3–48** quantities of a commodity to a buyer (Y Ltd) in the knowledge that Y Ltd will be able to pay for them only out of the proceeds of reselling them. It may be that Y Ltd is only a buyer and reseller, *i.e.* only a link in the chain of distribution. Alternatively it could be that Y Ltd is a manufacturer and that the commodity he buys from X is part of his raw materials. In either case the problem for X is the same, namely what is X's position if Y Ltd having taken delivery then becomes insolvent and goes into liquidation before paying for the goods? Has X got property rights over the goods entitling him to recover the goods (or their value) in priority to any other creditors of Y Ltd, or, on the other hand, is he merely an unsecured creditor having only a right to sue for the price? The latter will be the case if property has passed to Y Ltd. In that situation X, being an unsecured creditor, is likely to obtain no more than a small percentage of the price he is owed. In the absence of a contrary statement in the contract between X and Y Ltd, property will normally have passed by virtue of sections 16–18 of the Sale of Goods Act (paragraphs 3–07 to 3–24). However, a provision in the contract to the effect the property does not pass until Y Ltd has paid the price, will not entirely meet X's needs. Y Ltd has got to be allowed to sell the goods; otherwise Y Ltd may never be able to pay X. How can X protect himself against the possibility that Y Ltd, having sold the goods, might then go into liquidation before paying X? The way to do so was demonstrated by the Dutch sellers in *Aluminium Industrie Vaasen BV v. Romalpa Aluminium Ltd* (1976 CA).

The *Romalpa* case

3–49   The contract was for the sale by a Dutch company of aluminium foil some of which the buyers (an English company) were to use in their manufacturing process. At the time of manufacture the foil would obviously become mixed with other materials. The buyers took delivery of the foil but never made full payment. Later they became insolvent and a receiver was appointed. At that time the buyers still had some of the foil which had not yet been taken into the manufacturing process (*i.e.* unmixed foil). They had also sold some of the foil, some unmixed and some mixed (manufactured). The Dutch sellers now relied upon a clause (clause 13) in their contract of sale with the buyers and claimed therefore to have proprietary rights entitling them to have priority over the buyers' other creditors. This claim, however, was limited to unmixed foil and the proceeds of the sale of unmixed foil. Clause 13 was in two parts. The first part dealt with unmixed foil and stated that ownership in the foil would transfer to the buyers only when they had paid all that was owing to the sellers. The second part dealt with mixed foil and stated that the ownership of the sellers would transfer from the foil used in the manufacture to the finished products and that these would remain the property of the sellers until full payment had been made to them. Furthermore the buyers were to keep the finished goods as "fiduciary" for the sellers. The second part of clause 13 also authorised the buyers to sell these finished goods, on condition that they would if requested transfer to the sellers the benefit of those sales.

Foil (mixed or unmixed) which had been sold by the buyers clearly now belonged to whoever had bought it, since the Dutch sellers had expressly authorised the buyers to sell it. Any unmixed foil unsold by the buyers clearly still belonged to the Dutch sellers by virtue of the first part of clause 13. Ownership passes when (and not before) the parties intend it to. In relation to the unmixed foil which the buyers had sold, the Court of Appeal held that the Dutch sellers were entitled to receive from the buyers the proceeds of the sales by the buyers. The Dutch sellers were entitled to those proceeds of sale in priority to the buyers' other creditors (secured and unsecured). This was because of the right of an owner (here, the Dutch sellers) to "trace". This is a right to follow, and take, the proceeds of a sale where the owner's goods are disposed of by someone in a fiduciary relationship with the owner. It was held that clause 13 clearly imposed that fiduciary relationship upon the buyers.

In relation to the unmixed goods the clause worked by a combination of two things. First, it reserved title to the sellers and secondly it imposed a fiduciary duty upon the buyers which enabled the sellers to trace into the proceeds of sale.

Mixed goods

What would be the position with mixed goods? The answer is   **3–50** that the clause would, because it said so, give the sellers property rights over the mixed (manufactured) goods. This, however, is not because title in the mixed goods is reserved to the sellers. It is possible to *reserve* title only in goods in which one has got title to start with, *i.e.* the unmixed goods. In *Re Peachdart* (1983 ChD) the sellers of leather which the buyers then made into handbags could reserve title in the leather which they supplied but could not *reserve* title in the handbags which were newly created goods. When made into handbags, the leather ceased to exist as separate goods and became absorbed into the handbags. The contract of sale of the leather stated that the ownership in any mixed goods (*i.e.* handbags) should also be and remain with the sellers. The ownership which the sellers were thus given in the handbags was not, however, *reserved* to the sellers but was granted to them by those who would otherwise have been the owners, namely the buyers of the leather. This property right was therefore a charge created by the buyers of the leather. It was void because any charge created by a company is void unless registered: Companies Act 1948, (now the Companies Act 1985, s.365). It seems then that a *Romalpa* clause will, if properly worded, work in the case of unmixed goods and the proceeds of sale of unmixed goods, but that in the case of mixed goods (and their proceeds of sale) will work only it if is registered as a charge created by the buying company.

Where goods subject to a retention of title clause are used by the buyer in a manufacturing process, it is a question of fact whether or not, like the leather in *Re Peachdart*, they have lost their identity and therefore ceased to be the property of the seller. Grapes made into wine, olives into oil, wheat into bread, all clearly do thereby lose their identity. The following have been held similarly to have lost their identity: resin used to make chipboard (*Re Bond Worth* (1979)); and Acrilan made into yarn and then into carpet (*Borden U.K. v. Scottish Timber Products Ltd* (1979 CA)). In *Hendy Lennox Ltd v. Grahame Puttick Ltd* (1984 QED) a diesel engine in which the seller had reserved title was used by the buyer as major component of a diesel generating set which the buyer made. The engine remained unchanged and readily identifiable by a serial number and could be disconnected relatively easily from the generator in a matter of hours by undoing bolts and other connections. Distinguishing *Re Peachdart* and the other cases above, the judge held that the engine's incorporation did not preclude the seller from being entitled to retake the engine upon the buyer's liquidation. The engine had remained an engine, albeit connected to other things.

Unmixed goods

3–51   In *Clough Mill Ltd v. Martin* (1985) the Court of Appeal confirmed that the seller can, by the terms of the contract, effectively retain title in unmixed goods which the buyer has not resold. Such a clause does not require registration under the Companies Act because the buyer is not creating a charge over his (the buyer's) assets. Rather the goods do not become the buyer's assets until the buyer has paid. Thus if the buyer goes into liquidation before fully paying for the goods, any of the goods which have not been resold by the buyer and which remain unmixed will belong to the seller. The seller, not the buyer's other creditors, will be entitled to take those goods. Assuming that the seller can then resell them elsewhere for the same price as the buyer had agreed to pay, the seller will suffer no loss. If the seller is able to sell the goods elsewhere for more than the buyer had agreed to pay, the seller will in fact make a profit (*i.e.* will be better off than if the buyer had fully paid the seller before going into liquidation).

3–52   It is possible that before going into liquidation the buyer had paid *part* of the price to the seller. Clearly, if the seller has been able to sell the goods elsewhere for the same price as the buyer had agreed to pay (or a greater price) the seller must refund the buyer's part payment. That part payment will then be available for the buyer's other creditors. If, however, the seller has been able to resell the goods elsewhere only at a loss (*i.e.* for less than the buyer had agreed to pay) the seller is entitled to deduct that loss from the refund. The loss (*i.e.* the amount to be deducted) is the difference between the price the buyer had agreed to pay and the lower price which the seller is able to get on a resale elsewhere. Suppose the buyer had agreed to pay £2,000 and at the time of liquidation had paid only £1,000. Assuming that the seller had retained title to the goods, the seller must refund the £1,000 unless the seller is unable to resell the goods elsewhere for at least £2,000. If the seller was only able to sell the goods elsewhere for £1,800, then the seller must refund £800.

Now, suppose that the buyer had agreed to pay £2,000 (for the goods, a load of timber) and had actually paid the £2,000 but that the contract reserved title to the seller until the buyer had satisfied *all* his liabilities towards the seller (*i.e.* under not only this contract but also any *other* contracts there might be between them). Suppose also that at the time the timber was delivered and through to the time of the buyer's liquidation the buyer owed £500 to the seller under another contract. In *Armour v. Thyssen* (1990) the House of Lords upheld the validity of "all liabilities" retention of title clauses. Thus the retention of title clause would entitle the seller to take and resell such of the timber he had supplied under this contract as remained unsold and unmixed in the buyer's possession. The seller would then be entitled to deduct from the £2,000 refund, not only any loss on reselling the timber but also the £500 just mentioned. If, on the other hand, the seller were able to sell the goods for more than £2,000, say £2,200, the extra value would belong to the seller (see *obiter dicta* in *Armour v. Thyssen*). In this respect "all liabilities" clauses are no different from other retention of title clauses. Thus, in the example just given, if the seller resells the goods for £2,000 or for a higher sum, the seller will still be refunding the same net figure of £1,500. **3–53**

Proceeds of sale of unmixed goods

In the *Romalpa* case, not only was the seller entitled, as owner, to the unmixed goods which the buyer had not sold, but the seller was also entitled to the proceeds of the sale which the buyer had received from sub-sales of unmixed goods. This was because the terms of the contract between seller and buyer made it clear that the buyer in reselling the goods was doing so, not for his own **3–54** account, but as agent for, and on account of, the seller. This is not, however, the normal effect of a clause authorising the buyer to sub-sell the goods. The normal effect of such an authorisation is that the buyer is sub-selling for his own account. In *Pfeiffer GmbH v. Arbuthnot Factors* (1988 QBD), there was a clause retaining title for the seller and nevertheless authorising the buyer to make sub-sales. The contract required the buyer to pass on to the seller all the buyer's rights under the sub-sales contracts. However, it required this to be done only up to the amount of the buyer's outstanding indebtedness to the seller. It was held that this did not entitle the seller to take from the buyer the proceeds of the sub-sales of his (the seller's) property; instead it merely created a charge in favour of the seller which was void because it was not registered under the Companies Act. In order, without being registered, to entitle the seller to take the proceeds of sale in priority to the buyer's other creditors, the contract should, it seems:

(1) reserve the seller's title to the goods themselves (*i.e.* until either the buyer has paid or else the goods are sold by the buyer or lose their identity in the buyer's manufacturing or other process), and

(2) expressly state one or more of the following things:

    (a) that the buyer is (until title passes) in possession of the goods as bailee of the seller;

    (b) that the buyer, in having possession of the goods and in selling them, is in a "fiduciary" relationship with the seller;

    (c) that the buyer in selling them, does so on account of, and as agent for, the seller and

(3) not provide that the buyer's duty to account to the seller for the proceeds of sub-sales is limited to the buyer's outstanding indebtedness to the seller.

These provisions would give the seller a kind of property right over, and thereby give the seller entitlement to, *all* the proceeds of the sub-sales of unmixed goods (except those sub-sales made after title has already passed to the buyer). To make commercial sense of this arrangement, the contract would also need to contain a provision placing a duty on the seller to account to the buyer for any amount by which the proceeds of sub-sales of unmixed goods exceed the amount of the buyer's indebtedness to the seller.

CHAPTER 4

PERISHING OF GOODS

IN the last chapter we considered the problem of who is to bear **4–01**
the loss when goods perish. We now face a different problem—
namely, what effect does the perishing of the goods have upon
the contract? In other words, must both parties still fully carry out
the contract and, if not, to what extent is either party excused?

GOODS PERISHING BEFORE THE CONTRACT IS MADE

Section 6 provides: **4–02**

> "Where there is a contract for the sale of specific goods,
> and the goods without the knowledge of the seller have
> perished at the time when the contract is made, the contract
> is void."

If the parties have made an agreement about goods which do
not exist, it is an agreement about nothing. Thus in *Couturier v.
Hastie* (1856 HL) a contract to sell a cargo of corn was held to
be void because, unknown to the seller, the ship's master had
already sold it in Tunisia, as it had begun to ferment *en route*. At
the time of the contract the cargo no longer existed.

The words "void contract" are a contradiction in terms; a void
contract is no contract at all. Thus neither party is under any
obligation to carry it out. In *Couturier v. Hastie*, where the seller
was suing the buyer for the price, the action therefore failed. It
follows that if the buyer had paid he could have recovered that
money.

One must not be misled by the apparent simplicity of section 6
and *Couturier v. Hastie*. There are in fact some considerable
difficulties.

(i) "Perish"

4–03   The meaning of this word as used in the Sale of Goods Act is in doubt. In *Horn v. Minister of Food* (1948 KB), Morris J. considered that potatoes which had become seriously rotten had not "perished" because they were still potatoes, albeit worthless ones. From this it appears that they would have to become unrecognisable as potatoes before they could have been said to have perished. This view seems a little extreme and in *Asfar v. Blundell* (1896 CA) it was held that dates, which were under water for two days and became impregnated with sewage, had perished—*i.e.* in a commercial sense. They could no longer be bought and sold as dates. Whichever of these two cases correctly reflects the meaning of "perish", one thing seems clear—goods which have deteriorated to some slight extent but not sufficiently to change their commercial character, have not "perished".

It was held in *Barrow, Lane & Ballard v. Phillips* (1929 KB) where goods had disappeared—presumably stolen—that they had perished within the meaning of section 6. The case involved the sale of a specific lot of 700 bags of nuts lying in the seller's warehouse. Unknown to the parties, 109 of the bags had already disappeared. Wright J. applied section 6 and held that the contract was void. Because the contract was indivisible it was entirely void. Had it been severable, *i.e.* if it had been the sale of separate lots to be separately paid for, then presumably the contract would have been void only as to those lots which were not complete at the time of the contract. In that case the seller would have had to deliver and the buyer to pay for the lots remaining complete. The decision in *Barrow, Lane & Ballard v. Phillips* clearly indicates that if only some of the goods have perished that is sufficient to make the contract void.

4–04   There remains one further point about the word "perish". Goods that never existed cannot perish. It follows that if A agrees to sell specific goods to B which both A and B believe to exist but which never have existed, section 6 cannot apply. However, the contract would still be void, because at common law a contract is void if it is made on a false assumption that its subject-matter is in existence. Section 6, like many other sections of the Act, is no more than an attempt to put into an Act of Parliament a rule of common law. It was not intended to oust or restrict any of the common law rules (section 62(2)). Thus in our example where no goods perished because none ever existed, the contract is void at common law. The reason is that right from the start the contract is impossible to carry out. It is an agreement built upon a non-existent foundation.

All of this in no way affects the ability to make a contract for the sale of future goods. Such goods are expected to materialise. It cannot be said at the outset that it is impossible for the contract to be carried out. A contract for the sale of future goods is not made on any false assumption that the goods are in existence at the time of the contract. Indeed, we saw in the last chapter that a contract for the sale of future goods is quite possible.

(ii) Unascertained goods

Section 6 applies only to specific goods. However, again the common law may declare void a contract which does not fall within section 6. A contract for the sale of unascertained goods may or may not be void because of the fact that certain goods have perished or do not exist at the time of the contract. It will be void if that fact makes it impossible right from the outset to carry out the contract. It is important to remember the distinction explained in the last chapter between purely generic unascertained goods (*e.g.* "500 tonnes of wheat") and unascertained goods from an identified bulk (*e.g.* "500 tonnes of wheat out of the 1,000 tonnes in the vessel *Neptune*"). In the case of purely generic goods, if the particular goods which the seller had in mind to supply had in fact perished at the time of the contract this would not make it impossible for him to perform the contract. He could fulfil the contract by supplying wheat from any source; the contract is therefore not void. On the other hand, if he has to supply goods from a particular source and at the time of the making of the contract that source has ceased to exist (*e.g.* the *Neptune* has sunk) the contract is void at common law.

(iii) Contrary agreement

Both section 6 and the common law rule making contracts void apply only in the absence of any agreement of the parties to the contrary. It is a matter of examining the contract to see whether the parties intended it to remain valid even if the goods were not in existence or had perished. For example, the buyer may have agreed to buy *a spes* (*i.e.* a chance). He may have agreed that if the goods were in existence he would acquire the ownership of them and if they were not in existence he would get nothing, but that in either event he would pay the price. If that were the agreement made by the parties the contract would be valid, even if the goods were not in existence, and the buyer would be liable

4–05

4–06

to pay the price. In *Couturier v. Hastie*, the House of Lords said it was a matter of construing the contract and it was only after doing so that their Lordships held that the buyer had not agreed to buy *a spes* and that the contract was therefore void. It will be relatively seldom that a buyer will agree to buy *a spes*. He will certainly be most unlikely to agree a very high price if he is to run the risk of getting absolutely nothing for his money.

A different possible interpretation of a contract is that not the buyer but the seller has undertaken to accept the risk that the goods might not exist, *i.e.* he has undertaken as part of the contract that the goods do in fact exist. In this case, if it turns out that the goods do not exist at the time of the contract, the seller will be liable in damages to the buyer for breach of his contractual undertaking. This is exactly what happened in the Australian case of *McRae v. Commonwealth Disposals Commission* (1951). The Disposals Commission agreed to sell a wreck on the Jourmand Reef off the coast of Papua. The buyer subsequently discovered that the wreck had never existed and that, indeed, neither had the reef! The Australian court construed the agreement and concluded that the contract was not void, because the sellers had impliedly warranted that the wreck existed at the spot specified. The sellers were therefore liable in damages to the buyer.

4–07   To sum up: a contract is void if, at the time the contract is made and unknown to the parties, goods have perished or do not exist, thereby rendering it impossible for the contract to be performed; this, however, is subject to the qualification that the contract will not be void if the parties expressly or impliedly agreed otherwise.

GOODS PERISHING AFTER THE CONTRACT IS MADE

4–08   Section 7 provides:

> "Where there is an agreement to sell specific goods, and subsequently the goods, without any fault on the part of the seller or buyer, perish before the risk passes to the buyer, the agreement is avoided."

Like section 6, this section is only part of a wider principle of common law. The principle this time relates to frustration of contract. It applies when, through no fault of either party, events take an unexpected turn making it impossible to carry out the contract as originally conceived. In such circumstances the contract is frustrated or (in the terminology of section 7) avoided. This can occur not only if the goods subsequently perish but also, for example, if after the contract is made, it becomes illegal to carry it out. It happened in *Avery v. Bowden* (1855 QB) where there was a contract to bring goods from Russia. Before the ship was due to be loaded, the Crimean War broke out, making it illegal to trade with Russia (the enemy). It was held that no claim could be brought against the defendant for failing to load because the contract had been frustrated by illegality before the time for loading.

It can be seen that in the event of specific goods perishing, the contract may be avoided by section 7 but if in any other case the contract becomes impossible or illegal to perform, it will be frustrated at common law.

Again, there are some difficulties:

(i) The time of perishing

Both section 7 and the common law doctrine of frustration are concerned with events occurring after the contract was made. If the goods had already perished at the time the contract was made, then section 6 is the appropriate section. If section 6 applies, the contract is void. Where the events occur after the contract was made and the contract is avoided or frustrated the effect is not the same (see below).

4–09

(ii) "Perish"

The word "perish" presumably means the same as in section 6. Indeed, one of the cases quoted above, *Horn v. Minister of Health*, was a case on section 7.

4–10

The point was made in relation to section 6 that goods cannot perish if they never have been in existence. Thus a contract for the sale of future goods (*e.g.* a crop to be grown on a specific farm) will not be avoided by section 7 if the goods do not materialise. Nevertheless such a contract may be frustrated at common law. In *Howell v. Coupland* (1876 C.A.), the seller agreed to sell 200 tons of the potato crop on a specific piece of land, which would normally have produced easily that amount. However, the crop failed due to blight. The Court held that the seller was not liable for non-delivery of the goods because the contract had been made on the assumption that the crop would materialise. The crop failure was an unexpected turn of events rendering it impossible to perform the contract which was therefore frustrated.

(iii) Unascertained goods

4-11   Again like section 6, section 7 applies only to specific goods. However, a contract for the sale of unascertained goods can be frustrated at common law if it subsequently becomes impossible to perform because of an unexpected turn of events, as in *Howell v. Coupland*. As with section 6, it is important to remember the difference between unascertained goods out of a specific bulk (*e.g. Howell v. Coupland*) and purely generic goods. In his judgment in *Howell v. Coupland*, Blackburn J. said:

> "Had the contract been simply for so many tons of potatoes of a particular quality then, although each party might have had in his mind when he made the contract this particular crop of potatoes, if they had all perished, the defendant would still have been bound to deliver the quantity contracted for."

Thus a great deal turns on the exact terms of the contract— whether it stipulates "200 tonnes of potatoes to be grown on Blackacre" or simply "200 tonnes of potatoes". The failure of the crop of Blackacre will render it impossible to perform the contract in the first example, whereas in the latter case the contract can be fulfilled by supplying potatoes from any source.

(iv) The passing of risk and property

4-12   Once risk has passed to the buyer the contract cannot be avoided by section 7. Equally, a contract for the sale of unascertained goods out of a specific bulk will not be frustrated by the perishing of the bulk if this occurs after risk has passed to the buyer. All of this should be easily understood when it is realised that the effect of the contract being avoided or frustrated is generally that the parties are no longer required to carry out the contract; they are excused. So, for example, the buyer is under no obligation to pay. If this were to be the position when goods perish after the risk has passed to the buyer, it would be a contradiction in terms. In such a case the only way to make sense of the rule that the buyer must bear the loss is still to make him pay whilst allowing him to take whatever remains of the goods. That is exactly the legal position. The contract in such a case is most certainly not frustrated or avoided.

Neither will the contract be avoided or frustrated if at the time the goods perish, property has already passed to the buyer. Section 7, on its wording, applies only to agreements to sell. An agreement to sell becomes a sale when property passes to the buyer. The common law doctrine of frustration applies only where the main purpose of the contract has become impossible to achieve: *Herne Bay Steam Boat Co. v. Hutton* (1903 CA). The main purpose of a contract of sale of goods is that the buyer should become owner of the goods: *Rowland v. Divall* ((1923 CA), see paragraph 7–18 below). That purpose is achieved the instant that property passes to the buyer. The contract cannot be frustrated by the goods perishing after that moment.

(v) Effect of the contract being frustrated or avoided

The main effect is that the parties are excused from further **4–13** performance of the contract. The seller need not deliver the goods and the buyer need not pay for them. The law is putting into effect what it reasonably presumes would have been the intention of the parties. It presumes, although the parties did not anticipate the contract becoming impossible or illegal to perform, that nevertheless, if they had thought about it, they would have stated that further performance was to be excused.

Thus, if the parties did actually turn their minds to the possibility that such things might happen (*e.g.* that the goods might perish) and provided in the contract for that eventuality, then the effect of the event occurring will be whatever is stated in their contract. In this case it is not in fact accurate to say that the contract is avoided or frustrated; the contract remains and its provisions apply. Indeed, section 7 applies only in the absence of contrary agreement.

Usually it is reasonable to presume that (if the parties had **4–14** considered the eventuality that the contract would become impossible or illegal to perform), they would have intended all further performance to be excused. However, the law will not excuse all further performance of the contract if that, on the facts of the particular case, is an unreasonable presumption of what the parties would have intended. *Sainsbury v. Street* (1972 Assizes) is a more recent case with facts similar to those in *Howell v. Coupland*. The contract was an agreement to sell 275 tons of barley to be grown by the seller on his farm. In the event the crop was an unexpectedly poor one and amounted to only 140 tons. Clearly, following the decision in *Howell v. Coupland*, the seller was excused his obligation to deliver 275 tons. The question was whether he was entirely excused from performance for he had not offered to supply the reduced amount of 140 tons but had instead sold it to someone else. MacKenna J. held that there was an implied term that in such a case the seller was not completely excused from all performance but that the buyer had the option of accepting delivery of the reduced quantity, at a pro rata price. Therefore the seller was liable in damages for non-delivery of 140 tons. So it can be seen that the parties will usually be excused further performance of the contract, either partly or entirely, according to what is a reasonable presumption of what the parties would have intended.

4-15   A problem can arise for the buyer if, before the contract was frustrated or avoided, he has paid all or part of the price. Can he recover his money? The answer differs according to whether the contract was avoided by section 7 or frustrated at common law. In the former case there is an "all or nothing" rule. The buyer is entitled to the return of his money in full provided he has suffered a total failure of consideration, *i.e.* has received no benefit under the contract: *Fibrosa Spolka Akcyjna v. Fairburn Lawson Combe Barbour Ltd* (1943 HL). This will be the position provided the goods perished before any had been delivered to the buyer. If, however, he had any benefit under the contract, *i.e.* some use of the goods, before the goods perished, then he will be unable to recover any of the money he has paid. It will, of course, seldom happen that after the buyer has had some benefit, the contract is avoided by section 7 because usually by the time the goods are delivered to the buyer risk will have passed to him; section 7 applies only where the goods perish before the risk passes to the buyer.

4-16   On the other hand, if the contract is frustrated at common law (as occurred in *Howell v. Coupland*) the position as to the return of the price to the buyer is now regulated by the Law Reform (Frustrated Contracts) Act 1943 (which does not apply to contracts avoided by section 7). The position under this Act is that the buyer can recover his money but the court can deduct from that a sum towards expenses incurred by the seller in performing the contract. Further, the 1943 Act empowers the court to order the buyer to pay a reasonable sum for any benefit he has received under the contract. This will occur if for example the buyer has had some use of the goods and subsequently they perished, thereby frustrating the contract. It should be emphasised again that this last situation will occur only very seldom, because usually by the time the buyer gets possession of the goods risk will have passed to him and, if the goods perish after risk has passed to the buyer, that will not frustrate the contract. If the contract is not frustrated, the buyer will not be entitled to the return of any money and will have to pay any money still outstanding.

(vi) Effect of section 20A

Section 20A was introduced into the Sale of Goods Act in 1995. As was explained in the last chapter, it gives a proprietary interest to someone who buys and pays for goods which are agreed to be part of an identified bulk. Such a buyer has an undivided share in the bulk. We saw that, as between the seller and buyer, this has the effect that any destruction of the goods is taken to destroy the seller's share of the bulk first. What, however, is the position where more than the seller's share is destroyed? In that case some of the buyer's share of the goods is then taken to be destroyed and thus, if the whole bulk is destroyed, the whole of the buyer's as well as the whole of the seller's shares are destroyed. Section 20A thereby imposes on the buyer the risk of any loss which would prevent the seller being able to carry out the contract. Let us return to the example where the contract is for the sale of "400 tonnes out of the 1,000 tonnes of wheat stored in Wally's Woodford Warehouse". Let us also assume that the buyer has paid for his 400 tonnes and that the seller has not contracted to sell any of the 1,000 tonnes to anyone else. In those circumstances, if, say, 700 tonnes of the bulk are destroyed by lightning, then it is assumed that 600 of those tonnes were the seller's and that the buyer has thus lost only 100 tonnes. That does of course render it impossible for the seller to fulfill his contract to supply the buyer with 400 tonnes from the stock in the warehouse. Nevertheless, the contract is not frustrated because, if it were, that would make nonsense of providing that the buyer must bear the loss of the 100 tonnes. Thus the buyer is not entitled to the return of any of the price though he is of course entitled to take delivery of the remaining 300 tonnes.

4–17

SELLER NOT THE OWNER

SOMEONE not having the authority to do so sells or otherwise **5–01** disposes of goods which do not belong to him. This may involve an element of roguery but the knotty question which often comes before the courts is "Who is the owner?" Is it the original owner or is it the innocent purchaser? Whichever of these two is the loser usually suffers a considerable loss. If it is the buyer he will have to give up goods (or their value) for which he has paid good money. It is true that whichever is the loser will have a remedy against the unauthorised seller. However, if the latter is a rogue he is likely to have disappeared and if he can be found will probably be penniless.

There is, then, a problem of ownership and remember, the law uses three words all meaning the same thing, "ownership", "property" and "title". In choosing between the original owner and the innocent purchaser, the law is having to choose between upholding the sanctity of property and giving effect to a commercial transaction. There is no obvious answer. The law's solution is to have a general principle in favour of the original owner with a number of exceptions in favour of the innocent purchaser. The goods will therefore be regarded as belonging to the original owner unless one of the exceptions applies.

The general principle—*"Nemo dat quod non habet"*

The general principle is in section 21(1): **5–02**

> "Subject to this Act, where goods are sold by a person who is not their owner, and who does not sell them under the authority or with the consent of the owner, the buyer acquires no better title to the goods than the seller had, unless the owner of the goods is by his conduct precluded from denying the seller's authority to sell."

This rule that someone without title cannot without authority transfer title is illustrated by the decision in *Greenwood v. Bennett* (1972 CA). Bennett, the original owner of a Jaguar car, entrusted it to one Searle for some repairs to be carried out. Searle was a rogue and used it for his own purposes. He had a crash and damaged it extensively. Entirely without authority he sold it for £75 to Harper, a garage proprietor who was unaware that Searle was not the owner. Harper spent £226 on repairing it and sold it to a finance company. The Court held that the car still belonged to Bennett. Searle did not have title and therefore could not transfer it to Harper. For the same reason Harper did not transfer title to the finance company. (There was one further point: Harper carried out work in good faith believing the car to be his; because of this Bennett recovered a car worth more than it would otherwise have been. It was held that Bennett must compensate Harper for that work by paying him £226.)

A claim for conversion

5–03   An owner who wishes to bring a claim to recover possession of his goods from someone who has refused to return them can bring a claim for conversion (Torts (Interference with Goods) Act 1977). If the owner wishes to bring a claim against someone who has wrongfully sold the owner's goods, his claim will again be for conversion. Suppose the goods are sold by X to Y who in turn sells them to Z. Suppose the goods belong to O and that X sold them wrongfully and without authority. We have just seen that the general rule is that since X is not the owner he cannot confer ownership on Y, who similarly cannot confer ownership on Z. If Z refuses to return the goods to O, O has a claim against Z for conversion of the goods. Alternatively, O may choose to bring a claim for conversion against X or Y. Where O brings his claim against Z, Z will naturally wish to claim against Y who sold to him. He can do this. He can claim the return of the price he paid to Y. This claim is based upon a breach of contract by Y in that Y did not have the right to sell the goods and failed to confer any ownership upon his buyer, Z (see paragraph 7–17 below). The fact that Y may have been quite innocent and have genuinely believed at the time that the goods were his to sell gives him no defence either to a claim by Z for breach of contract or to a claim by O for conversion. Y can also reclaim from X the price Y paid to X.

Now suppose that Y had improved the goods (just as Harper did in *Greenwood v. Bennett*). The Torts (Interference With

Goods) Act 1977, passed after the decision in *Greenwood v. Bennett*, provides a mechanism by which the innocent improver is to be reimbursed. If O sues Y for conversion (*i.e.* for selling O's goods to Z), then O will obtain judgment against Y for damages equal to the value of the goods on the date of the sale to Z, less the deduction of an improvement allowance. That allowance is the proportion of the value of the goods which is attributable to the improvement by Y. If O does not sue Y but instead sues Z for conversion, then Z gets the benefit of the improvement allowance. The judgment obtained by O against Z will not normally be an order to Z to return the goods. Such an order will be granted only where damages would not be an adequate remedy (*e.g.* if the goods were unique, or virtually so). O may, however, obtain judgment against Z in the alternative, *i.e.* judgment ordering Z either to return the goods or to pay damages equal to their value. Z is thereby given the option. In either case Z gets the benefit of the improvement allowance. In the latter case it is deducted from the damages he has to pay O. Where he returns the goods to O, O must pay Z the improvement allowance. In our example, this allowance relates to improvements performed by Y. Thus in a claim by Z against Y, Y is entitled to deduct the improvement allowance when returning Z the price paid by Z.

In all of this it has been assumed that the general rule applies and that X, not being the owner could not confer ownership on Y who in turn could not confer ownership on Z. It now remains to examine those exceptional situations where the original owner may lose his ownership, *i.e.* where title may be conferred by someone who himself has no title.

Estoppel

When an estoppel is raised, the original owner is estopped **5–04** (precluded) from asserting that the sale was unauthorised. Thus if an estoppel is raised the unauthorised sale takes effect as if it was authorised—*i.e.* it transfers ownership to the buyer in the ordinary way (see section 21(1), above).

An estoppel is raised when the original owner by his statements or conduct leads the innocent purchaser to believe that the unauthorised seller in fact has the right to sell the goods. More accurately, for the innocent purchaser to obtain a good title by estoppel, all the following requirements must be fulfilled:

(i) The original owner must have made a representation (by statement or conduct) that the seller was entitled to sell the goods.

(ii) The representation must have been made intentionally or negligently.

(iii) The representation must have misled the innocent purchaser.

(iv) The innocent purchaser must have bought (and not merely agreed to buy) the goods.

5–05   One problem with the first requirement is what conduct by the original owner will amount to a representation that the seller has the right to sell the goods. A case where a plea of estoppel succeeded and the innocent purchaser therefore obtained a good title was *Eastern Distributors v. Goldring* (1957 CA). The facts, however, can be appreciated only with a knowledge of the role of the finance company in a modern hire-purchase transaction (for a full explanation see paragraph 19–07, below). Briefly, the customer sees at a trader's premises the item he wishes to acquire. He asks for credit terms and, at the trader's suggestion, he fills in a finance company's hire-purchase proposal form, which is in fact an offer made by the customer and addressed to the finance company to acquire the item from the finance company on hire-purchase terms. The customer will leave the completed form with the trader. The trader himself will fill in another form offering to sell the same item to the finance company. He will then send both forms to the finance company which will either accept or reject both offers. If it accepts, it thereby agrees to purchase the item for cash from the trader and at the same time agrees to transfer it on hire-purchase terms to the customer.

In *Eastern Distributors v. Goldring*, the customer wished to raise a loan on his van. He and a motor trader got together to deceive the finance company. They each filled in their respective forms as if the van belonged to the trader and as if the customer wished to acquire the van on hire-purchase terms. Everything appeared in order to the finance company, which accepted the forms believing the trader to be the owner of the van. Thus it bought the van from the trader and transferred it on hire-purchase to the customer. The customer did not pay his instalments under the hire-purchase agreement and sold the van to X, an innocent purchaser. The finance company discovered the fraud and the question arose as to who was the owner. The customer was the original owner and, provided he had not in the interim lost his ownership, he transferred that ownership to X. However, the Court upheld the finance company's claim that the customer had by the doctrine of estoppel lost his ownership to the finance company. He had submitted through the trader a form offering to acquire the van on hire-purchase terms. Thereby he had represented to the finance company that the van was not his but that it belonged to the trader. This was an intentional deception. Since the customer was therefore stopped from asserting his ownership, the finance company obtained good title when it bought the van from the dealer. It still had that ownership because under a hire-purchase agreement property does not pass until the customer has paid all his instalments (see paragraph 1–15 and Chapter 19). Thus the car did not belong to the customer who therefore could not transfer ownership to X.

In *Goldring's* case, the customer had done something clearly   **5–06**
conveying to the finance company that he did not own the van and that so far as he was concerned the seller (the trader) had every right to sell it. An act which does not clearly convey that fact is not sufficient to raise an estoppel. So, if the owner of goods merely allows another person to have possession of them, (e.g. at a left luggage office) that act will not raise an estoppel for it does not convey to others that he considers the person in possession to have the right to dispose of them. If O lends his car to Q who then unauthorisedly sells it to P, O is still the owner and he can assert that ownership. In *Central Newbury Car Auctions v. Unity Finance* (1957 CA) a customer wished to acquire a car on hire-purchase. He and the motor trader filled in the usual forms. Before the finance company's reply was received, the trader allowed the customer to take delivery of the car (together with its registration document). The customer sold the car to X. The finance company rejected the offers. It was held that the car still belonged to the trader. His allowing the customer to have possession of the car did not amount to a representation that the customer had the right to sell it. His giving him possession also of the registration document made no difference since a registration document is not in the eyes of the law a document of title.

An estoppel will not be raised unless the representation was   **5–07**
intentional or negligent. In *Eastern Distributors v. Golding* the original owner (the customer) clearly intended to make the

deception. In *Mercantile Credit Co. v. Hamblin* (1964 CA) the customer had no such intention. Like the customer in the former case, Mrs Hamblin wished to raise a loan on her vehicle. She went to a motor trader who told her this could be done. He agreed that he would enquire as to what terms could be obtained from a finance company and would then telephone Mrs Hamblin to see if they were acceptable. He got her to sign a proposal form of a particular finance company. She believed this to be an application to the finance company for a loan on the security of her car. In fact it was the usual proposal form to acquire the car on hire-purchase terms. Placing her confidence and trust in him she was guided by the trader and signed the form in blank and agreed with the trader that, if he succeeded in obtaining terms acceptable to her, he would then be able to fill in the details on the form and send it to the finance company. However, the trader subsequently filled in the form without having reported back to her and therefore without her authority. He also filled in the usual trader's form offering to sell the car to the finance company and sent both forms off to the finance company. The finance company accepted the proposals. Who now owned the car? Mrs Hamblin had not intended to make it appear that the car belonged to the trader. The Court held that neither was she negligent. She knew nothing of financial matters and had acted quite reasonably in placing her trust and confidence in a motor trader who had a good reputation in the area. In the absence of intention or negligence, no estoppel could be raised against her. The car was therefore still hers.

5–08   The question of negligence was discussed in *Moorgate Mercantile v. Twitchings* (1976 HL). Moorgate Mercantile were a finance company which owned a car. They let it on hire-purchase terms to a customer. Before completing his instalments, the customer without authority sold the car to Twitchings, a car dealer. Moorgate Mercantile and Twitchings were both members of H.P. Information Ltd (H.P.I). H.P.I. was an organisation which operated a register where finance companies could register their hire purchase agreements so that any other member (*e.g.* a car dealer) could, before buying a second-hand car, check with H.P.I. to see if the car was the subject of a registered hire-purchase agreement. On this occasion Moorgate Mercantile had carelessly failed to register their hire-purchase agreement with the result that Twitchings was told by H.P.I. that there was no hire-purchase agreement registered in connection with this particular car. Twitchings claimed that Moorgate Mercantile were estopped from denying that their hire-purchase customer was the owner of the car. This claim failed. Moorgate Mercantile had not made any representation to Twitchings. The only statement to Twitchings had been made by H.P.I., namely that there was no registered hire-purchase agreement relating to the car in question. That statement had been true and had in any case not been made by Moorgate Mercantile, since H.P.I. was not an agent of Moorgate Mercantile for the purpose of making such a statement. As to negligence it was true that Moorgate Mercantile had been careless in failing to register their hire purchase agreement. However, carelessness did not amount to negligence unless the carelessness was a breach of a legal duty to take care. Moorgate Mercantile were under no legal duty to join H.P.I. and, having joined, were under no legal duty to take care to register their hire-purchase agreements. Thus in the absense of either a deliberate misleading by Moorgate Mercantile or negligence on their part, no estoppel could be raised against them. Moorgate Mercantile therefore succeeded in their claim against Twitchings for conversion of the car. (Since 1995 H.P.I., now run by Equifax, has offered a service to traders and to ordinary members of the public enabling them, on payment of a small fee, to have a search of the H.P.I. register carried out and also to be given a guarantee of compensation if the information given is incorrect or incomplete. The H.P.I. report will cover not just existing finance agreements relating to the vehicle but also whether it has ever been: stolen, an insurance "write-off", or the subject of a number plate change. For an account of the interrelated provisions of the law in this area, see "Risks in Buying a Used Car" (1996) 140 S.J. 1180. See also paragraph 5–40 and *Barber v. N.W.S. Bank* at paragraph 7–20 below).

An estoppel can be raised only if the representation misled the innocent purchaser. In *Farquharson Bros. v. King* (1902 HL) a timber firm owned some timber which was in the possession of a dock company. The firm told the dock company to deal with the timber according to the instructions of a clerk of the firm. The clerk, a rogue, instructed the dock company to hold the timber to the order of "Brown" (which was the clerk under an assumed name). In his assumed name of Brown he sold the timber to an innocent purchaser. To whom did the timber belong? The House of Lords held that it still belonged to the timber firm. The statement made by the timber firm to the dock company had not come to the attention of the innocent purchaser; it therefore could not have misled him. The only thing which misled the purchaser

5–09

was Brown's roguery. No estoppel could be raised against the timber firm.

Where an innocent purchaser is able to rely upon an estoppel, property in the goods passes to him in the normal way, *i.e.* as if his seller himself has good title to give. Thus he will obtain good title if, and when, according to the terms of his contract of purchase, property in the goods is to pass to him. To put it another way, someone who has "bought" goods (*i.e.* to whom property has passed under his contract of purchase) can rely upon an estoppel. Someone who has only agreed to buy (*i.e.* to whom property has not yet passed) cannot do so: *Shaw v. Commissioner of Police for the Metropolis* (1987 CA). In this case the innocent purchaser had agreed to buy a car from, as he later discovered, someone who did not own it, on terms that property in the car would pass to him upon payment of the price. It was held that since he had not paid the price, no property in the goods could have passed to him. Therefore he could not claim a good title by raising an estoppel against the true owner.

Owner's signature on document intended to have legal effect

5–10   Quite apart from the doctrine of estoppel, there may be another alternative basis on which the owner may be precluded from denying the seller's authority to sell—namely where the owner has signed a document clearly conveying the implication that the seller is entitled or authorised to sell the goods. There is a rule that normally a person is bound by his signature: *Saunders v. Anglia Building Society* (1970 HL). This rule is not confined to someone signing a fully completed document. It applies also to someone signing a document with the blanks for the particular transaction not filled in but agreeing to, or authorising, another to fill in those blanks later: *United Dominions Trust v. Western* (1975 CA). Thus in *Mercantile Credit v. Hamblin* (paragraph 5–07 above), if Mrs Hamblin had authorised or agreed to the trader filling in the proposal form, the result of the case would have been different. Mrs Hamblin would have been precluded from denying the trader's authority to sell the car. This would have been not because of the doctrine of estoppel (which would have required either a deliberate misleading or negligence by her), but because of her signature on a document which, as was apparent on the face, was intended to have legal effect and which she had authorised the trader to complete.

There are two particular exceptions to this rule, *i.e.* where the signer will not be bound by his signature. The first is where he can plead *non est factum*. This plea will succeed where he can show two things: (i) that he was *radically* mistaken about the nature or effect of the document; and (ii) that he was not careless in signing it (*Saunders v. Anglian Building Society*). The mistake in *Mercantile Credit v. Hamblin* would not have been sufficiently radical to justify a plea of *non est factum*. The hire-purchase proposal (*i.e.* involving the sale of the car by the trader to the finance company and the reacquisition of the car by Mrs Hamblin on hire-purchase terms) was not radically different in substance from a loan on the security of the car.

The second exception could arise in a *Mercantile Credit v. Hamblin* type of situation. It would arise if the motor trader were the agent of the finance company in dealing with the customer. At common law the dealer is not normally the agent either of the finance company or of the customer. However, section 56 of the Consumer Credit Act 1974 now makes him in most cases the statutory agent of the finance company (see paragraph 24–10 below). The customer cannot be bound to the finance company by his signature on a document which the finance company's agent knows does not reflect the customer's intention.

Mercantile agents

The Factors Act 1889, s. 2(1) provides: **5–11**

> "Where a mercantile agent is, with the consent of the owner, in possession of goods or of the documents of title to goods, any sale, pledge or other disposition of the goods, made by him when acting in the ordinary course of business of a mercantile agent, shall, subject to the provisions of this Act be as valid as if he were expressly authorised by the owner of the goods to make the same; provided that the person taking under the disposition takes in good faith, and has not at the time of the disposition notice that the person making the disposition has not authority to make the same."

There are here six requirements to be fulfilled in order for an unauthorised sale by a mercantile agent to confer good title upon an innocent purchaser.

(i) The seller must be a mercantile agent, *i.e.* a factor.   **5–12**

Broadly, a mercantile agent is an independent agent acting in a way of business to whom someone else entrusts his goods and upon whom is conferred authority of a type referred to in the Factors Act 1889, s.1(1). That section provides:

> "The expression 'mercantile agent' shall mean a mercantile agent having in the customary course of his business as such agent authority either to sell goods or to consign goods for the purchase of sale, or to buy goods, or to raise money on the security of goods."

This statutory definition is not complete. In order to be a mercantile agent, an agent must have not merely the customary authority referred to in the statue but also three further characteristics.

5–13   First, he must be independent from the person (his principal) for whom he is agent. A "mere servant or shopman" or "caretaker" is therefore not a mercantile agent. Secondly, he must be acting as agent in a way of business. This "business" characteristic does not require that he should regularly carry on business as an agent but simply that on the occasion in question he was acting as a business proposition. In *Lowther v. Harris* (1926 KB) an agent was entrusted with a tapestry with a view to selling it. He was instructed not actually to conclude a sale without first referring back to his principal; he was to receive commission if a sale was concluded. In fact, he sold the tapestry to an innocent purchaser without first having referred back to his principal. Wright J. held that the agent who had no general occupation as an agent, who normally bought and sold goods on his own account and who was the agent for only the one principal, was nevertheless a mercantile agent. Therefore since all the requirements in section 2 of the Factors Act were fulfilled, the innocent purchaser had good title to the tapestry.

The third characteristic referred to above is that the agent must be authorised to deal with goods in his own name without disclosing his agency. In *Rolls Razor Co. v. Cox* (1967 CA) the court had to consider the status of some travelling salesmen. Lord Denning M.R. said:

> "The usual characteristics of a factor are these. He is an agent entrusted with the possession of goods of several principals, or sometimes only one principal, for the purpose of sale in his own name without disclosing the name of his principal and he is remunerated by a commission. These salesmen lacked one of those characteristics. They did not

sell in their own names but in the name and on behalf of their principals, the Company. They are agents pure and simple and not factors."

Before leaving the question of who is a mercantile agent, it should be said that someone who is not an agent cannot be a mercantile agent. It can be difficult sometimes when someone takes goods on "sale or return" terms to decide whether he was acting as an agent or as principal (see Chapter 1).

> (ii) The mercantile agent must be in possession of the goods or documents of title; and he must have that possession at the time he sells, pledges or otherwise disposes of the goods.

An example of a document of title is a bill of lading (*i.e.* the document given by a shipowner acknowledging that he has received goods which have been shipped). A motor vehicle's registration document is not, however, a document of title. Thus, a mercantile agent in possession of the registration book but not of the vehicle itself can not confer good title under section 2 of the Factors Act: *Beverley Acceptances v. Oakely* (1982 CA).

A mercantile agent in possession of the vehicle itself might well be able to confer good title on an innocent purchaser, but the sale to the latter must occur whilst the mercantile agent is still in possession. Imagine a mercantile agent who obtains possession of the goods (perhaps by borrowing them from the owner) and who shows them to X, an innocent prospective purchaser. The mercantile agent then will not confer good title on X under section 2 of the Factors Act if he does not make the contract of sale with X until after he has returned the goods to their true owner: *Beverley Acceptances v. Oakley.*

> (iii) The mercantile agent must be in possession of the **5–14** goods or documents of title in his capacity as a mercantile agent.

The car owner who leaves his car with a garage for repairs to be carried out does not consent to the garage having possession in its capacity as a mercantile agent (*i.e.* as a dealer). Therefore the garage cannot confer good title under section 2 of the Factors Act.

5-15   (iv) The mercantile agent must be in possession of the goods or document of title with the consent of the owner.

This consent is presumed in the absence of evidence to the contrary and withdrawal of consent is of no effect until that withdrawal is brought to the notice of the person taking the goods—Factors Act, s.2(3) and (4). The fact that consent was obtained by a trick or by fraud is irrelevant so long as the consent was given the agent in his capacity as a mercantile agent. For the consent to be operative it must be such as to clothe the agent with apparent authority to sell the goods. This would occur in the case of a second-hand car only if the owner consented to the dealer having possession not only of the car but also of the registration book and the ignition key. Two cases illustrate the point. In *Pearson v. Rose and Young* (1950 CA) the owner left his car with a dealer with instructions for the latter not to sell it but to see what offers could be obtained for it. The owner did not intend to leave the registration document but showed it to the dealer who arranged a trick whereby the owner was called away on an imaginary emergency thereby forgetting the registration document. The dealer sold the car. The dealer was in possession of the car with consent and in his capacity as a mercantile agent, since the possession was with a view to an eventual sale, but he was not in possession of the registration document with the consent of the owner.

5-16   As regards the registration document, it was not a case of obtaining consent by a trick; he had obtained the possession by a trick but he had obtained no consent at all to that possession. This case was followed in *Stadium Finance v. Robbins* (1962 CA) where the owner left his car with a dealer with instructions to see what offers could be obtained for it. He retained the ignition key though he accidentally left the registration document locked in the glove compartment. The dealer supplied his own key, found the registration document and sold the car. It was held that the owner had not clothed the dealer with apparent authority since he had retained the ignition key and not consented to the dealer having possession of the registration document. In each of these cases, therefore, the innocent purchaser acquired no title to the car which still belonged to the original owner. This was extremely harsh on the innocent purchaser who bought goods in good faith from a mercantile agent and who could not reasonably have suspected that anything was wrong.

Sometimes the ownership of goods is split. This occurs for **5–17** example when goods are pledged as security for a loan. The pledgor gives the pledgee (the lender) some rights but does not part with all rights of ownership. The pledgor and pledgee together combine to constitute "the owner". Someone in possession with the consent of them both can be said to be in possession "with consent of the owner". *Lloyds Bank v. Bank of America* (1938 CA) involved dealings not with goods but with documents of title. The owner, a mercantile agent, pledged bills of lading with Lloyds Bank. Lloyds Bank released the bills back to him so that he could sell them and thereby obtain the money to pay off the loan from the bank. However, instead of selling them, he pledged them, without authority from Lloyds, with the Bank of America. It was held that all the requirements of section 2 of the Factors Act were complied with including the requirement that the mercantile agent be in possession of goods or of the documents of title with the consent of "the owner". Therefore the Bank of America took its title entirely free from the interest of Lloyds Bank. Thus Lloyds Bank lost its security.

> (v) The mercantile agent in disposing of the goods must **5–18** have been acting in the ordinary course of business of a mercantile agent.

Clearly, selling a second-hand car without an ignition key or registration document would not be acting in the ordinary course of business. This was taken one step further in *Stadium Finance v. Robbins* where it was held that this requirement was not complied with. Willmer L.J. said:

> "A sale involving delivery to the hirer of the car without its registration book would not in my judgment be in the ordinary course of business. Following Pearson's case, I think the same applies to a sale involving delivery...of a registration book obtained by larceny or fraud or other unlawful means."

On the other hand, the agent does not have to have been acting within the ordinary course of his own particular business or even within the normal course of business of his particular type of trade. It is sufficient that he was acting within the ordinary course of business of mercantile agents generally. The mercantile agent in *Oppenheimer v. Attenborough* (1908 CA) was a diamond broker. Without authority he pledged the diamonds entrusted to him. Although diamond brokers do not ordinarily have authority to pledge diamonds in their possession it was held that the broker had acted in the ordinary course of business of a mercantile agent. The pledgee therefore obtained good title to the diamonds.

5–19   (vi) The person taking the goods must have taken them in good faith without notice of the agent's lack of authority.

The burden of proof lies on him to prove that he was in good faith, etc. *(Heap v. Motorists Advisory Agency* (1923)). He will find it difficult to do this in circumstances where he is "put upon notice". An example can be found in the judgment of Lord Alverstone C.J. in *Oppenheimer v. Attenborough:*

> "there may be particular agents, such for instance as auctioneers, by whom a pledge would be such a departure from the ordinary course of their business as to put the pledgee upon notice."

Market overt
5–20   Until 1995 there was a statutory rule in section 22(1) of the Sale of Goods Act that a sale by a trader in market overt (*i.e.* a shop in the City of London or an open market) passed good title to an innocent purchaser even if the trader did not have title to the goods. The rule was abolished, by the Sale of Goods (Amendment) Act 1994 which repealed section 22(1) of the Sale of Goods Act.

Sale under a voidable title
5–21   Section 23 of the Sale of Goods Act provides:

> "Where the seller of goods has a voidable title to them, but his title has not been avoided at the time of the sale, the buyer acquires a good title to the goods, provided he buys them in good faith and without notice of the seller's defect of title."

A voidable title is less than perfect and yet section 23 allows a seller with a voidable title to confer a perfect title upon an innocent purchaser. A void title on the other hand is no title at all

84

and an innocent purchaser who buys from someone with a void title can derive no benefit from section 23 (although, of course, he might acquire good title by virtue of some other exception to the *nemo dat* principle).

What is a voidable title and how it differs from a void title can best be shown by an example: A owns some goods which he sells to B who in turn sells them to C. If the first contract (*i.e.* between A and B) is valid then title passes from A to B. If it is void for any reason then it is no contract at all and no ownership passes to B. If it is voidable then it is initially valid but can be avoided (set aside) later. Under a voidable contract ownership passes to B in the normal way but will pass back to A if and when the contract is later avoided. The commonest example of a voidable contract is one where a party has by making a misrepresentation induced the other party to enter the contract. This gives the latter (the innocent party) the right subsequently to avoid the contract (see Chapter 6). In our example, if B has induced A to sell him the goods by making a misrepresentation, then B will acquire only a voidable title. A will have the right to set the contract aside and to demand the return of the goods. If, however, B sells the goods to C before A finds out that he has been duped, then C (provided he was innocent) will get a perfect title by virtue of section 23 and A will therefore be unable to recover the goods. **5–22**

Although a misrepresentation by B can render the contract between A and B voidable, there can be present some factor which renders that contract completely void. The difficulties have arisen mainly in cases where B has misrepresented to A his (B's) identity. In these circumstances, the contract between A and B is void if the two following characteristics are both present: **5–23**

(i) The buyer's identity was a vital factor for the seller (A) in deciding to make the contract.

(ii) The seller when making the contract was intending to deal with someone other than B.

In *Cundy v. Lindsay* (1878 HL) the seller, Lindsay, received a letter from a rogue called Blenkarn from an address at 37, Wood Street, Cheapside. The letter ordered some goods and was signed by Blenkarn in such a way that the signature looked like "Blenkiron & Co.". Lindsay knew of a reputable firm Blenkiron & Co. who traded from 123, Wood Street. Without checking Blenkiron's address, Lindsay despatched the goods to "Messrs.

Blenkiron & Co., 37, Wood Street". Blenkarn received the goods but never paid for them and sold them to Cundy who knew nothing of his fraud. The House of Lords held that the contract between Lindsay and Blenkarn was void and that therefore the goods still belonged to Lindsay.

5–24   *Cundy v. Lindsay* involved a transaction (between Lindsay and Blenkarn) conducted through the post. In a contract made between parties face to face the seller will find it difficult to show that to him the identity of the buyer was a vital factor in deciding to make the contract. In the absence of strong evidence to the contrary, the law presumes that in face to face agreements the seller is prepared to deal with the person in front of him— whoever that may be. This is particularly so in the case of a shopkeeper. In *Phillips v. Brooks* (1919 KB) a rogue called North entered a jeweller's shop, selected some items including a ring and asked to pay by cheque and to take the ring with him. The shopkeeper agreed to this after the rogue told him that he (the rogue) was Sir George Bullough. The rogue took the ring to Brooks, a firm of pawnbrokers, and pledged it with them for £350. The cheque given to the jeweller proved worthless and he sued the pawnbroker to recover the ring. It was held that the contract between the jeweller and rogue was not void but merely voidable. Since it had not been set aside before the pawnbroker took the ring, the pawnbroker acquired good title to the ring. Of course, he did not get complete ownership for he did not buy the ring but the limited title he got was perfectly valid and he could enforce that against the jeweller.

5–25   *Phillips v. Brooks* was followed by the Court of Appeal in *Lewis v. Averay* (1971). Lewis advertised his car for sale. A rogue responded to the advertisement. He told Lewis that he was Richard Green, a well-known film actor (which was untrue). They agreed on a price of £450 and after seeing "proof" of the buyer's identity as Richard Green (a pass for Pinewood Studios), Lewis agreed to accept a cheque. The rogue took the car and registration documents. The cheque was worthless. The rogue posed as Mr Lewis in selling the car to Averay, an innocent purchaser. The Court held that there was a contract between Lewis and the rogue and that therefore Averay now had perfect title to the car. Lord Denning M.R. said:

> "When a dealing is had between a seller like Mr Lewis and a person who is actually there present before him, then the presumption in law is that there is a contract, even though

there is a fraudulent impersonation by the buyer representing himself as a different man than he is. There is a contract made with the very person there who is present in person. It is liable no doubt to be avoided for fraud but it is still a good contract..."

In both the last cases, the innocent purchaser (the pawnbroker in *Phillips v. Brooks*, and Mr Averay in *Lewis v. Averay*) acquired the goods before the contract between the original owner and the rogue had been avoided. If, before the innocent purchaser bought the goods, the original owner had avoided his contract with the rogue, ownership in the goods would have reverted to the original owner. If this had happened the rogue could not have conferred title upon the innocent purchaser (unless under some other exception to the *nemo dat* principle) for the rogue would no longer have had a voidable title.

The normal method of the original owner to "avoid" the **5–26** contract is for him to inform the rogue that he does so. However, it is often impossible to locate the rogue. In this case the contract is avoided as soon as the original owner has done all that he reasonably can. *Car and Universal Finance v. Caldwell* (1965 CA) was another case where a rogue bought a car and by fraud induced the seller to accept a cheque which proved to be worthless. On discovering this the seller immediately informed the police and the Automobile Association. It was held that this operated to avoid the contract. After this, but before the car or rogue had been traced, the rogue sold the car to an innocent purchaser. Since, at the time the rogue sold the car, his title had been avoided, it was held that the purchaser acquired no title under section 23.

Seller in possession

Two provisions in two different statutes are almost identical, **5–27** section 24 of the Sale of Goods Act and section 8 of the Factors Act 1889. Section 8 provides:

"Where a person, having sold goods, continues, or is, in possession of the goods or of the documents of title to the goods, the delivery or transfer by that person, or by a mercantile agent acting for him, of the goods or documents of title under any sale, pledge, or other disposition thereof, or under any agreement for sale, pledge or other disposition thereof, to any person receiving the same in good faith and without notice of the previous sale, shall have the same effect as if the person making the delivery or transfer were expressly authorised by the owner of the goods to make the same."

This relates to the situation where A sells or agrees to sell goods to B and then later sells or agrees to sell them to C. To whom do the goods belong? If under the contract between A and B property had not yet passed to B (see Chapter 3), then A was still the owner when he sold to C. Still being the owner, A could pass that ownership to C. One has to examine the two contracts, B's and C's, and find out under which of them property was to pass first. If it is C's then C will be the owner.

5–28   Usually (*i.e.* in the case of a sale of specific goods in a deliverable state, see Chapter 3), property will have passed first to B (*i.e.* at the time he made his contract). In this case, following the *nemo dat* principle, B is now the owner; they were B's goods at the time A sold them to C and therefore A could not, without B's authority, confer title upon C. This result would be, different, however, if C could show that C's contract with A fell within one of the exceptions to the *nemo dat* principle.

5–29   The statutory provisions in section 8 of the Factors Act and section 24 of the Sale of Goods Act constitute one of those exceptions and were designed specifically to help someone in C's position. In order for C to acquire good title under these provisions, a number of requirements must be fulfilled:

(i) The seller must have been in possession of the goods or documents of title.

The point here is that the first purchaser can safeguard himself by taking immediate delivery and not leaving the goods or documents of title with the seller. The seller's possession does not have to be a "personal possession". If they were in the possession of a warehouseman (or other agent) holding them on behalf of the seller, that is sufficient. In *City Fur Manufacturing Co. v. Fureenbond* (1937 KB) A owned some skins which were stored for him at an independent warehouse. A sold them to B who did not collect them. Later, A pledged them to C. On A's instructions the warehouseman handed them over to C who therefore acquired good title to the goods under section 25(1) of the Sale of Goods Act 1893 (now section 24 of the Sale of Goods Act 1979).

The nature of the seller's possession is immaterial. So if A sells goods to B who then decides to leave them for A to repair, A is a person who "having sold goods continues or is in possession of the goods": *Pacific Motor Auctions v. Motor Credits* (1965 PC). If A then sells and delivers them to an innocent purchaser, the latter will acquire good title. It does not matter that A was at the time in possession in his capacity, not as seller, but as repairer.

(ii) There must be a delivery to the subsequent purchaser of the goods or documents of title.   **5–30**

In *Nicholson v. Harper* (1895) A owned some goods stored for him at a warehouse. He sold them to B who did not take delivery. The warehouse proprietor was unaware of B's purchase and himself bought them from A. It was held that the warehouse proprietor did not acquire good title, since being already in possession of the goods he did not take delivery under the contract of sale.

(iii) The subsequent purchaser must be "in good faith and without notice of the previous sale".

In *Worcester Works Finance v. Cooden Engineering* (1971 CA) all the requirements of the section were fulfilled. X sold a car to Y (a car dealer) who in turn sold it to Z (a finance company). The reason for the sale by Y to Z was that Z at the same time accepted a hire-purchase proposal relating to the same car from M, a customer of Y's. Y (the car dealer) was fraudulent and two things occurred which ought not to have done. First, the cheque which Y had given X when Y took delivery of the car from X was dishonoured. Secondly, Y never gave possession of the car to his customer (M) as he should have done after the finance company (Z) had accepted the hire-purchase proposal. After Y's cheque to X was dishonoured, X (with Y's acquiescence) repossessed the car from Y's premises. At the time of this repossession by X the car clearly belonged to Z. This was because X had sold it to Y who had sold it to Z. It was held, however, that Y, in allowing X to repossess the car, was within the section. Having sold the car to Z, Y was a seller in possession of it. Since he had not delivered it to his customer (M) he had "continued" in possession (albeit wrongfully). His allowing X to repossess the car amounted to a "delivery or transfer" of it under a   **5–31** "disposition". This was because it amounted to a transfer back to X of *property* in the car (because Y's cheque had not been met) in return for X waiving any right to enforce payment from Y. At the time of the repossession, X was unaware of Y's sale to Z and thus, by repossessing the car with Y's acquiescence, X obtained ownership of it by virtue of section 25(1) of the 1893 Act (*i.e.* section 24 of the Sale of Goods Act 1979).

Buyer in possession

5–32   There is normally no problem because a buyer in possession of goods will usually in fact be the owner of them, *i.e.* property will have passed to him (see Chapter 3). Being the owner, if he sells the goods he will be able to pass on that ownership to his purchaser. If he himself has not paid for them then the person who sold him the goods will be able to sue him for the price but will have lost any chance of recovering the goods.

However, it is possible in some circumstances for the buyer to take delivery of the goods before property has passed to him. This is most likely to occur where he agrees with his seller that property shall not pass to him until he has paid for them. This occurred in *Weiner v. Gill* (see paragraph 3–18). In this situation he cannot confer good title on the sub-purchaser unless that sale falls under an exception to the *nemo dat* principle.

5–33   The most likely exception is that contained in two almost identical statutory provisions, section 25 of the Sale of Goods Act and section 9 of the Factors Act 1889. This latter reads:

> "Where a person, having bought or agreed to buy goods, obtains with the consent of the seller possession of the goods or documents of title to the goods, the delivery or transfer, by that person or by a mercantile agent acting for him, of the goods or documents of title, under any sale, pledge, or other disposition thereof, or under any agreement for sale, pledge or other disposition thereof, to any person receiving the same in good faith and without notice of any lien or other right of the original seller in respect of the goods, shall have the same effect as if the person making the delivery or transfer were a mercantile agent in possession of the goods or documents of title with the consent of the owner."

5–34   The requirements for the operation of this exception to the *nemo dat* principle are as follows:

(i) The person selling (pledging, etc.) must be someone who has "bought or agreed to buy".

Someone who has taken only an option to buy has not "bought or agreed to buy". This excludes someone who has taken goods on "sale or return" terms: *Edwards v. Vaughan* (1910 CA). For the same reason, someone hiring goods under a hire-purchase agreement is also excluded. Therefore if the hirer sells the goods, section 25 of the Sale of Goods Act and section 9 of the Factors Act will not operate to give his purchaser a good title. This is apparent from *Helby v. Matthews*, where someone who was hiring a piano on hire-purchase terms, sold it to an innocent purchaser. The House of Lords held that the hirer had not "bought or agreed to buy" the piano which therefore still belonged to the person from whom it had been hired. In the light of this decision it is easy to understand why hire-purchase has become popular with traders and finance companies as a means of supplying goods on credit. (For full discussion of the distinction between hire-purchase and sale, see paragraph 19–02 below).

It has been held that a buyer under a conditional sale agreement is someone who "bought or agreed to buy": *Lee v. Butler* (see Chapter 19). However, that position has been radically altered by the Consumer Credit Act 1974. A buyer under a conditional sale agreement which is a consumer credit agreement within the meaning of that Act (see Chapter 19), is for the purposes of section 25 of the Sale of Goods Act and section 9 of the Factors Act, not someone who has "bought or agreed to buy" (Consumer Credit Act 1974, Sched. 4 and section 25(2) of the Sale of Goods Act).

We have already seen that someone with a voidable title can **5–35** nevertheless transfer to an innocent purchaser a perfect title, provided he does so before his title is avoided. However, if the transaction falls within section 25 (or section 9 of the Factors Act), he can pass on a good title even after his voidable title has been avoided: *Newtons of Wembley v. Williams* (1965 CA). The reason is that, even though his title has been avoided, he is still someone who has "bought or agreed to buy" the goods. In *Newtons of Wembley v. Williams* a rogue bought a car and persuaded the seller to accept a cheque. When the cheque was dishonoured the seller did all he could to trace the rogue and car and he informed the police. After this but before the rogue was traced, the rogue took the car along to a market in Warren Street (where dealers commonly sold cars) and he sold it to an innocent purchaser. The Court of Appeal held that the innocent purchaser acquired good title under section 9 of the Factors Act.

> (ii) The person selling the goods must have been a buyer "in possession", *i.e.* he must have obtained "with the consent of the seller, possession of the goods or documents of title to the goods".

5–36   Two principles derive from *Cahn v. Pockett's Bristol Channel Steam Packet Co.* (1899 CA). First, it is sufficient that he *obtains* possession with the seller's consent and it is immaterial whether that consent is later withdrawn. Secondly, it is immaterial whether or not he had obtained possession before he made the contract with the innocent purchaser; it is sufficient that the possession was obtained before he transferred or delivered the goods or documents of title to the innocent purchaser. The facts were that B agreed to buy goods from S. S sent to B a bill of lading together with a bill of exchange (see Chapter 3, paragraph 3–29 above). B did not, as he should have done, sign and return the bill of exchange. This meant that property did not pass to B (see section 19, paragraph 3–29 above). However, B had already agreed to sell the goods to Cahn and, on receiving the documents from S, he transferred the bill of lading (the document of title to the goods) to Cahn. It was held that Cahn acquired good title to the goods by the operation of section 25 of the Sale of Goods Act.

The question whether the person selling had been a buyer "in possession" arose in *Four Point Garage Ltd v. Carter* (1985 CA). An innocent purchaser, Mr Carter, agreed to buy a new Ford Escort XR3i from X, a car dealer. X, who did not have one in stock, contracted to buy one from Four Point Garage. Under the terms of this contract, property in the car was not to transfer to X until he had paid Four Point Garage. Mr Carter paid X for the car. At X's request Four Point Garage delivered the car direct to Mr Carter, who believed himself to be taking delivery from X. X became insolvent without ever paying Four Point Garage. The latter claimed that the car was still theirs since X had never paid and property had therefore never passed to X. It was held, however, that Mr Carter had obtained good title under section 25. When Four Point Garage, at X's request, delivered direct to Mr Carter, it was exactly the same as if X had taken delivery from Four Point Garage and himself delivered the car to Mr Carter. In other words, X was deemed to have been a buyer "in possession" and deemed to have delivered the car to the innocent purchaser.

(iii) There must be a delivery or transfer of the goods or documents of title to the innocent sub-purchaser.

Where documents of title are involved it will usually turn out **5–37** that the buyer transfers to his sub-purchaser the same document of title which he received from his seller. This occurred in *Cahn v. Pockett's*. The requirement is equally complied with if he receives a document of title from his seller and then transfers to the innocent sub-purchaser a different document of title relating to the same goods: *Mount v. Jay* (1960 QB).

(iv) The buyer in possession must have acted in the normal course of business of a mercantile agent.

This may seem a little absurd since the buyer in possession **5–38** may well not be a mercantile agent. It is, however, implicit in the closing words of both section 9 of the Factors Act and section 25 of the Sale of Goods Act. This was held to be so by the Court of Appeal in *Newtons of Wembley v. Williams*. The sale in that case (see above) was in fact in the ordinary course of business of a mercantile agent, since car dealers did commonly sell cars in Warren Street.

(v) The sub-purchaser must be bona fide and unaware that the original seller has any rights in respect of the goods.

The seller's lien and other rights will be explained in Chapter 12.

If any one of the above requirements is not fulfilled, the sub- **5–39** purchaser will not acquire good title by virtue of the two sections under consideration. However, it is always possible that the person who sold him the goods later acquires the title to them. This can happen if, for example, the sub-purchaser bought the goods from someone who was hiring them on hire-purchase terms. Normally under a hire-purchase agreement as soon as the hirer pays off all moneys due under the agreement, the goods become the hirer's property. Thus if the hirer subsequently pays off all the remaining instalments, ownership will pass to the hirer and straight on to the purchaser from the hirer. This process is known as "feeding the title". It means that the purchaser from the hirer does eventually acquire good title, albeit somewhat delayed: *Butterworth v. Kingsway Motors* (see paragraph 7–19 below).

We have seen that section 25 of the Sale of Goods Act and section 9 of the Factors Act typically apply where a seller lets his buyer take possession but retains property (title to the goods) until the buyer pays the price. There is then a risk that the buyer, before he has paid and therefore before he has acquired title, sells and delivers the goods to a sub-purchaser who is unaware that he is buying from someone who has no title. The theory behind the sections is that, if an owner of goods agrees to sell them to someone and retains title but nevertheless lets the buyer have possession, that owner must bear the consequences (*i.e.* loss of title) if the buyer then sells and delivers the goods to an innocent sub-purchaser. Thus the sections give good title to the innocent sub-purchaser. Typically then they operate to defeat the title of the unpaid seller (let us call him C) who has entrusted his goods to a buyer who, without paying C, has in turn sold them to an innocent purchaser. In *National Mutual General Insurance Association Ltd v. Jones* (1988 HL) the issue was whether the sections could operate to defeat the title of someone much earlier in the chain of events than C. Thieves had stolen a car and sold it to A who sold it to C (a car dealer) who sold it to D (another car dealer) who sold it to Jones. Jones claimed to have good title by virtue of the two sections, thereby defeating the title of the owner from whom the thieves had stolen the car. The House of Lords rejected this argument and held that the two sections could defeat the title only of an owner who had entrusted possession of his goods to a buyer. Therefore the two sections could not take title away from the owner from whom the goods had been stolen.

Disposition of motor vehicles under the Hire Purchase Act 1964, Part III

5–40   Part III is all that remains of the 1964 Act. The rest has been repealed.

We have just seen that a hirer under a hire-purchase agreement is not someone who has "bought or agreed to buy" for the purpose of section 25 of the Sale of Goods Act. This meant that an innocent purchaser could buy a car from such a hirer only to discover at some later date that the car did not after all belong to him. The owner could reclaim the car and was entitled to come along and seize it. Part III of the 1964 Act was designed to protect the innocent purchaser in this situation. The purchaser acquires good title provided the following requirements are fulfilled:

    (i) The seller must be someone who is hiring the vehicle under a hire-purchase agreement or buying it under a conditional sale agreement.

The nature of these two types of agreement will be explained in Chapter 19.

    (ii) The purchaser must be a "private purchaser".

That is, someone who is not a dealer (or finance house) carrying on business in the motor trade. Dealers do not need the same protection since they know the importance of checking to see whether the seller is the owner of the car. Thus a car dealer does not obtain the protection and that is so even if he is buying the vehicle for his own private purposes and not for his business purposes: *Stevenson v. Beverley Bentinck* (1976 CA).

It is possible for Part III of the 1964 Act to operate even though the hirer sells the car to a dealer. Although the Act gives no protection to a dealer, it will give protection to the first private purchaser providing he was bona fide, etc. So if the dealer sells the car to an innocent private purchaser, the latter will acquire good title.

    (iii) The goods involved must be a motor vehicle.

Thus the decision would be the same today, if the facts of *Helby v. Matthews* (a piano) were again to come before the courts.

    (iv) The private purchaser must be bona fide and unaware of any relevant hire-purchase or conditional sale agreement.

In *Barker v. Bell* (1971 CA) the private purchaser of a motor car believed what he was told by the vendor—namely that the latter had bought the car under a hire-purchase agreement from B finance company. The vendor showed him a receipt from B finance company across which was written "final payment". In fact, unknown to the purchaser, the vendor was hiring the car under a hire-purchase agreement with A finance company. It was held that the purchaser was unaware of any relevant hire purchase agreement. Lord Denning M.R. said:

"...a purchaser is only affected by notice if he has actual notice that the car is on hire purchase. He is not affected merely by being told that it was previously on hire purchase. which has now been paid off."

The purchaser therefore obtained good title to the car.

The test of the private purchaser's bona fides and unawareness of the hire purchase agreement is a subjective one. It is not one of whether the private purchaser ought to have been suspicious or less gullible. It is a purely subjective question of honesty. Good faith is equated with honesty and bad faith with dishonesty. Also, the relevant time to apply the test is when the private purchaser makes his purchase. Thus a private purchaser who had suspicions that the motor vehicle was the subject of a hire purchase agreement, but whose suspicions had at the time of the purchase been laid to rest, was a purchaser in good faith without notice of the hire purchase agreement, who therefore obtained good title: *Dodds v. Yorkshire Bank Finance Ltd* (1992 CA).

    (v) The transaction under which the private purchaser buys the goods must be an ordinary sale, or a hire-purchase or conditional sale agreement.

Thus the 1964 Act gives no protection in the event of a pledge.

Having looked at the requirements, it remains to point out that there are no financial limits on the operation of the 1964 Act. It is immaterial for how much the car was being hired or bought, or how much credit was involved, and equally it is immaterial whether the hirer or buyer was a body corporate.

The 1964 Act, then, gives protection to a bona fide private purchaser who buys a motor vehicle unaware that the seller is hiring or buying it under a hire-purchase or conditional sale agreement. For example, O supplies a car to P on hire-purchase terms and P, before he has finished paying off his instalments, sells the car to a bona fide private purchaser, Q, who is unaware of the hire purchase agreement. The Act gives good title to Q, *but only as against* O. Thus, if O were not the owner but had, for example stolen the car (or bought it from someone who had stolen it) then the true owner (*i.e.* from whom the car was stolen)

96

will still have good title (*i.e.* unless one of the other exceptions to the *nemo dat* principle applies).

Finally, it is now possible for a buyer (whether a trade purchaser or a private purchaser) to have check carried out to discover whether a motor vehicle is subject to an existing finance agreement, has ever been an insurance "write-off" or has been stolen—see paragraph 5–08 above.

Sale under a common law or statutory power

Certain persons are given the right by common law or statute   **5–41**
in certain circumstances to sell the goods of another. Examples are a pawnbroker selling the pledgor's goods when the loan is not repaid and an innkeeper selling the guest's property when the bill is not paid. When a sale is made under a common law or statutory power the purchaser acquires good title to the goods— Sale of Goods Act, s.21(2)(a).

It is also to be noted that under the Torts (Interference with Goods) Act 1977 a person such as a repairer, improver, valuer or storer has the right to sell uncollected goods. He must first serve upon the bailor (*i.e.* the person who left the goods for repair, treatment or valuation, etc.) a notice containing certain details of the intended sale. If after expiry of the notice the goods remain uncollected and the right of the sale is duly exercised, the purchaser will obtain good title as against the bailor. However, if the bailor was not the owner but had, for example, stolen them before leaving them for repair or treatment, etc., then the true owner will still have good title (*i.e.* unless one of the other exceptions to the *nemo dat* principle applies).

Sale under a court order

The High Court has power in certain circumstances to order the   **5–42**
sale of goods. If it exercises this power, the purchaser acquires good title, notwithstanding any claim by the original owner—Sale of Goods Act, s.21(2)(b).

Effect of writ of execution

When judgment is given in court for a sum of damages, the   **5–43**
defendant usually pays up. If he does not, the successful claimant can enforce the judgment by causing a writ of execution to be issued. It is then the sheriff's duty to carry it out. He has the legal right to seize enough of the defendant's goods to satisfy the judgment. He has this right in relation to goods which the defendant owns at the time the sheriff receives the writ. Anyone

who after that time purchases goods from the defendant therefore runs the risk of having them seized by the sheriff. However, section 138 of the Supreme Court Act 1981 protects the purchaser from this provided that when he bought the goods he was bona fide and unaware of any writ of execution relating to the defendant.

CHAPTER 6

MISREPRESENTATION

THE seller who makes a false statement in connection with the   6–01
supply of goods can find himself liable in one or more of a
number of ways. There are three principal ways. First, he may be
liable to conviction of an offence under the Trade Descriptions
Act 1968. This will be considered in Chapter 18. Secondly, he
may be liable to his purchaser for breach of a term of his
contract—a matter to be considered in the next chapter. Thirdly,
the purchaser may have a remedy for misrepresentation.

WHAT AMOUNTS TO AN ACTIONABLE MISREPRESENTATION?

A misrepresentation is a false statement of fact made by one   6–02
party (or his agent) which is intended to and does induce the
other party to enter the contract. A statement may be made in
writing, orally or even by conduct, for example, by making the
goods tell a lie about themselves as in the case where the seller
patched up a crack in the barrel of a cannon so as to make it
appear unfractured: *Horsfall v. Thomas* (1862).

A mere statement of opinion, provided the opinion is genuinely
held, is not a statement of fact: *Bisset v. Wilkinson* (1927 PC).
However, a statement of opinion by someone in a position to
know the facts will be regarded as a statement of fact. In *Smith v.
Land & House Property Corporation* (1884 CA) the seller of
some premises described them as "let to Mr Frederick Fleck (a
most desirable tenant)". In fact it had been only with difficulty
that the seller had managed to get rent from Mr Fleck, who was
still in arrears. It was held that the seller made a
misrepresentation.

A mere trader's puff is not a statement of fact. Thus the car
dealer who describes a second-hand car as "a beautiful looking
car" makes no misrepresentation. However, the distinction
between a trader's puff and a statement having legal significance
is a fine one. The car dealer who tells his purchaser "It's a good

little bus. I would stake my life on it", will not be able to claim either that it was a mere trader's puff or that it was a mere statement of opinion. After all, the dealer is in a position to know whether the car has any serious defects.

The statement need not be made fraudulently. Although the remedies available may be less extensive, a statement made quite innocently can nevertheless amount to a misrepresentation, as in *Leaf v. International Galleries* (1950 CA) where the sellers incorrectly stated that a painting was by Constable, a statement which they genuinely believed.

A statement is not an actionable misrepresentation unless it induces the other party to enter the contract. It does not have to be the only thing which persuaded him to do so but it does have to have been a factor in influencing him. If he placed no reliance at all upon it, he cannot complain of a misrepresentation. Thus in *Horsfall v. Thomas*, above, the purchaser lost his case because he had not bothered to examine the cannon before purchasing it and therefore was unaware of the misrepresentation. Equally, if the purchaser, though aware of the statement, chooses to place no reliance upon it, he cannot subsequently complain of it. This would be the position if a potential purchaser, on being told that a car was mechanically sound, nevertheless insisted, before buying, on having his own mechanic examine it.

REMEDIES

6–03   There are two possible remedies:

Rescission

A misrepresentation by one party makes the contract voidable at the option of the other. This means that the latter can rescind the contract. This involves the parties being returned to their positions as they were before the contract, *i.e.* the return of the price to the buyer and the goods to the seller. If the innocent party is the buyer and he has not paid then he may simply refuse to do so and return the goods if he has already received them.

Rescission is an equitable remedy which means that it is not available if that would be unfair. Thus it is not available in the following situations:

(i)   Where it is impossible to restore the parties to their pre-contract positions, *e.g.* if the purchaser has consumed the goods.

(ii) Where it would involve upsetting the rights of an innocent third party, *e.g.* if the purchaser has sold the goods to an innocent sub-purchaser.

(iii) Where there has been a lapse of more than a reasonable length of time from the time the contract was made. Thus in *Leaf v. International Galleries*, above, the purchaser was unable to rescind the contract some five years after it was made. (In the case of a fraudulent misrepresentation, the purchaser is allowed a reasonable length of time from when he discovers it to be untrue.)

(iv) Where the innocent party has affirmed the contract, *i.e.* indicated his intention of continuing with it in spite of the misrepresentation. In *Long v. Lloyd* (1958 CA) the seller had claimed that the lorry was in excellent condition and was capable of 40 m.p.h. and 11 m.p.g. On the first run the purchaser discovered a number of faults; the dynamo did not work and the lorry consumed petrol at the rate of 5 m.p.g. He telephoned the seller and complained. The seller offered to meet half the cost of repairing the dynamo. The buyer accepted that offer. When the lorry broke down again, the purchaser indicated that he was rescinding the contract. It was held that he could not, since by accepting the seller's offer on the telephone he had accepted the goods and thereby affirmed the contract.

Affirmation, which defeats the buyer's right to rescission for misrepresentation, is similar to "acceptance", which defeats the buyer's right to reject the goods and regard the contract as repudiated for breach of condition (see paragraph 13–04 below).

Damages

Damages may be claimed on their own or in addition to rescission. Unlike rescission, damages are not available for all misrepresentations and the state of mind of the person who made the misrepresentations is important.   **6–04**

(i) A fraudulent misrepresentation is one made (a) without belief in its truth, or (b) with such a degree of recklessness as amounts to dishonesty (careless whether it be true or false). For a fraudulent misrepresentation, damages are available in deceit: *Derry v. Peek* (1889 HL).

(ii) A negligent misrepresentation is one made by someone who believes it to be true but has no reasonable grounds for so believing, *e.g.* a car dealer who claims as having been made in 1989, a car of a type not manufactured before 1990. Damages are available for a negligent misrepresentation—Misrepresentation Act 1967, s.2(1).

(iii) A completely innocent misrepresentation is one made by someone who genuinely and on reasonable grounds believes it to be true. Damages are not normally available for this sort of misrepresentation, although the court does have a discretion to award damages instead of (but not in addition to) rescission—Misrepresentation Act 1967, s.2(2).

The burden of proof is upon the defendant to prove that he had reasonable grounds for believing his statement. Otherwise it will be presumed to have been a negligent one—Misrepresentation Act 1967, s.2(1).

In *Howard Marine & Dredging Co. Ltd v. Ogden* (1978 CA) the owner of a vessel which a customer was considering hiring told the customer that its payload was 1,600 tons, whereas its payload was in fact only 1,055 tons (so stated in the ship's documents). After the contract was made, the hirer brought a claim for damages for misrepresentation. The owner claimed to have had reasonable grounds to believe the truth of his misrepresentation because the Lloyd's Register had (in a rare mistake) wrongly stated the payload as 1,800 tons. It was held that in showing that he relied upon the figures in Lloyd's Register and had disregarded the figure in the ship's documents, he had failed to prove that he had had reasonable grounds to believe the truth of his misrepresentation. The hirer therefore won his claim for damages.

EXCLUSION

6–05   Any provision in a contract which would have the effect of excluding or restricting liability for a misrepresentation is ineffective, except to the extent that the clause is shown to satisfy the requirement of reasonableness—Misrepresentation Act 1967, s.3 as amended by the Unfair Contract Terms Act 1977. The requirement of reasonableness is set out in section 11 of the Unfair Contract Terms Act (see paragraphs 10–24 to 10–29 below).

ADDITIONAL OR ALTERNATIVE DEFENDANT

We are in this chapter considering misrepresentations made to the buyer by the seller (or the seller's agent). It follows that the remedies we have discussed are those which the buyer has against the seller. Normally the seller will be the only person against whom the buyer will be entitled to make a claim. However, there is an exception, created by section 75 of the Consumer Credit Act 1974. So, where the buyer bought the goods under a credit agreement of a certain type he will be able to bring against the creditor a claim similar to that which he can bring against the seller. The most common type of situation where this will occur is where the buyer uses his credit card to buy an item costing over £100. The credit card company is the person who provides the credit (*i.e.* is the creditor) and therefore the buyer may be able to bring a claim against the credit card company for a misrepresentation by the seller. The circumstances in which section 75 of the Consumer Credit Act applies will be more fully considered in Chapter 25.

Section 56 of the Consumer Credit Act also can operate to entitle a buyer in some cases to sue the creditor (*e.g.* a credit card company) in respect of a misrepresentation by the seller. Section 56 is more fully considered in Chapter 24 (paragraph 24–18 below).

6–06

CHAPTER 7

TERMS OF THE CONTRACT

CONTRACTS of sale vary enormously. At one extreme one may **7–01** find a written contract containing many detailed clauses setting out the terms of the contract. At the other extreme, the parties may have expressly agreed only as to which goods were being sold and how much the price was. In the latter case the parties have left much unsaid, *e.g.* as to delivery, payment, the transfer of ownership, the quality of the goods, etc. Many provisions of the Sale of Goods Act were designed to remedy such deficiencies in the contract.

Freedom of contract

The original Sale of Goods Act of 1893 was intended not to **7–02** dictate to the parties what the terms of their bargain should be, but only to provide solutions to problems and questions unforeseen and unconsidered by the parties. Thus most of the sections of the Act originally applied only in the absence of contrary agreement by the parties. The Act was based upon the notion of freedom of contract, *i.e.* that the parties were free to make their contract upon whatever terms they pleased. In relation to exemption clauses, however, the Unfair Contract Terms Act 1977 has made a large inroad into this notion and section 55(1) of the Sale of Goods Act 1979 now reads as follows:

> "Where a right, duty or liability would arise under a contract of sale of goods by implication of law, it may (subject to the Unfair Contract Terms Act 1977) be negatived or varied by express agreement, or by the course of dealing between the parties, or by such usage as binds both parties to the contract."

The provisions of the Unfair Contract Terms Act 1977 will be considered in Chapter 10. In the present chapter we shall consider terms other than exemption clauses. The Unfair Terms in

Consumer Contracts Regulations 1999 represent a further inroad into the doctrine of freedom of contract. These Regulations, which are capable of applying to other terms as well as to exemption clauses, will also be considered in Chapter 10.

Rights of Third Parties

7–03   As a general rule only the buyer and seller can sue or be sued on a contract of sale. This results from the two aspects of the privity of contract doctrine. First, the contract can be enforced only against someone who is a party to it. Secondly, only someone who is a party to the contract can enforce it. The Contracts (Rights of Third Parties) Act 1999, however, created an exception to the latter. Section 1 provides:

> "(1) Subject to the provisions of this Act, a person who is not a party to a contract (a "third party") may in his own right enforce a term of the contract if—
>   (a) the contract expressly provides that he may, or
>   (b) subject to subsection (2), the term purports to confer a benefit on him.
>
> (2) Subsection (1)(b) does not apply if on a proper construction of the contract it appears that the parties did not intend the term to be enforceable by the third party.
>
> (3) The third party must be expressly identified in the contract by name, as a member of a class or as answering a particular description but need not be in existence when the contract is entered into.
>
> (4) ..."

7–04   Suppose X buys an item, informing the retailer that it is a gift for Y (whom he names) and arranging that the retailer will send it to Y at her address. If the item proves to be defective can Y rely on this provision to enable her to claim against the retailer under the terms in the contract governing the quality of the goods? The answer is not easy. The effect of the 1999 Act is to enable Y to enforce a *term* which purports to confer a benefit upon her. Arguably the only term which purports to confer a benefit on Y is the term as to delivery, thereby giving her a right to sue the retailer if the item is not delivered. Much depends upon judicial interpretation of the 1999 statute and of the circumstances presented. Will the courts read the situation as one where there was a term of the contract that Y was to have the benefit of *all* the terms in the contract which give rights to the buyer? A similar situation arises where M buys a wedding present for P & Q from the shop where P & Q have informed M that they have arranged their wedding present list.

Where the 1999 Act gives a third party a right to enforce a **7-05** contract term, that right is subject to any other relevant terms of the contract such as a clause expressly limiting such a claim—although no term will be effective to exclude or limit a right to sue for death or personal injury caused by negligence. Where the third party's right exists, the judicial remedies available to the third party for breach of the contract term are the same as if the third party had been a party to the contract, *e.g.* damages and/or rejection of the goods and return of the price (see Chapter 13). Also the Act limits the ability of the parties to the contract subsequently to remove or alter the third party's right, *e.g.* by varying the contract. Unless the contract otherwise provides, they cannot (s. 2) do so without the third party's consent, if:

"(a) the third party communicated his assent to the term to the promisor [*i.e.* to the party who was contracted to perform the term in question], or

(b) the promisor is aware that the third party has relied on the term, or

(c) the promisor can reasonably be expected to have foreseen that the third party would rely on the term and the third party has in fact relied upon it."

When the third party seeks to enforce his right under the Act, the defendant is entitled to rely upon any defence (or set-off) which would have been available to the defendant if either (a) the other party to the contract had brought the claim, or (b) the third party had been a party to the contract.

For discussion of the effect of the 1999 Act, see an article *Removing a Blot on the Landscape* by Meryll Dean, [2000] J.B.L. 143. For the third party's right to rely on an exemption clause, see paragraph 10–11 below and for a much larger potential inroad into the doctrine of privity, see the Directive on Consumer Guarantees, paragraph 7–54 below.

Express terms

Although the parties are free to agree what terms they choose, **7-06** they will not be bound by any term which is not properly incorporated in the contract. In the case of terms in a written contract signed by both parties, there will be no doubt that the terms have been properly incorporated. Often, however, the terms will not be in a signed contract. It is perfectly possible for the parties to incorporate terms by agreeing to them orally or in writing whether or not signed. Chapter 10 deals with the position where one of the terms is an exclusion clause. In that case, the party whom the clause favours (usually the seller) will not be found to have incorporated it in the contract unless either it was in a contractual document signed by the other party or else reasonable steps had been taken to bring it to the attention of the other party. This rule applies not only to exclusion clauses but to any clause which is particularly onerous or unusual and unlikely to be known to the other party: *Interfoto Picture Library v. Stiletto Visual Programmes* (1988 CA). In that case an advertising agency telephoned a transparency library with whom the agency had never previously dealt. The agency asked to hire some transparencies of the 1950s. Accordingly the library sent 47 transparencies with a delivery note clearly requiring that they be returned by March 19. The delivery note included nine conditions, printed in four columns, which the agency never read. Condition 2 stated that a charge of £5 plus VAT per transparency was payable for each day they were late being returned. After the agency returned the transparencies 14 days late, the library claimed over £3,500 under this condition. The Court refused to allow the claim, holding that the clause (imposing an exorbitant charge) was particularly onerous and unusual and the library had not taken all reasonable steps to bring it to the attention of the agency. Presumably the library should at least have highlighted it in some way such as printing it in red, on the *front* of the delivery note, perhaps with a large red hand pointing to it. As Bingham L.J. put it, "...the more outlandish the clause, the greater the notice which the other party, if he is to be bound, must in all fairness be given".

7–07 As a general rule, if sufficient notice is given and the clause is therefore incorporated, the court will enforce it. That is unless it is: (i) an exclusion clause made unenforceable by the Unfair Contract Terms 1977 (see Chapter 10); (ii) a clause made unenforceable by the Unfair Terms in Consumer Contracts Regulations 1999 (also see Chapter 10); or (iii) a penalty clause. Curiously, the clause in *Interfoto Picture Library v. Stiletto Visual Programmes* was almost certainly a penalty and unenforceable even if it had been properly incorporated (see paragraph 14–21 below).

Terms which are not expressly agreed between the parties but **7–08** are inserted by law into the contract are called implied terms. Any term, express or implied, may be a condition or a warranty.

Warranties and conditions

The law classifies breaches of contract into two categories, first, **7–09** breaches of a less serious nature which entitle the innocent party only to damages and secondly, more serious breaches which give him also the option to regard the contract as repudiated. The difference is that with the first type, the innocent party, though entitled to damages, must still perform his part of the bargain, whereas with a repudiatory breach he may, in addition to claiming damages, regard himself as discharged from his obligations under the contract. The former and less serious type is a breach of warranty and the latter is a breach of condition.

It is therefore important to know which terms are conditions **7–10** and which merely warranties. With the terms implied by sections 12–15 of the Sale of Goods Act it is easy because the Act makes it clear. With terms expressly agreed by the parties it is not always so easy. It is a matter of construing (interpreting) the contract—conditions being those terms which "go to the root" of the contract or are "of the essence" of it. In *Wallis & Wells v. Pratt and Haynes* (1911), Fletcher Moulton L.J. said that conditions "go so directly to the substance of the contract or, in other words, are so essential to its very nature that their non-performance may fairly be considered by the other party as a substantial failure to perform the contract at all". Warranties "are other obligations which, though they must be performed, are not so vital that a failure to perform them goes to the substance of the contract". Section 61(1) of the Sale of Goods Act defines a warranty as:

> "...an agreement with reference to goods which are the subject of a contract of sale, but collateral to the main purpose of such contract, the breach of which gives rise to a claim for damages, but not to a right to reject the goods and treat the contract as repudiated."

The neat classification, just explained, of contract terms into **7–11** two categories, conditions and warranties, has begun to crumble in recent years. So far as the effect of a breach of condition is concerned, the position, with one exception, remains unaltered. If the seller commits any breach (even a minor one) of a term which is clearly a condition, the buyer will be entitled not only to damages but also to reject the goods and treat himself as discharged from his obligations. The exception was created by the Sale and Supply of Goods Act 1994 and applies where the following three circumstances are all present:

(i) the buyer is not dealing as a consumer;

(ii) the condition broken is one relating to description, quality or sample implied by sections 13, 14 or 15 of the Sale of Goods Act;

(iii) the breach is so slight that it would be unreasonable for the buyer to reject the goods.

This limitation on the right to reject is further explained in Chapter 13.

7–12   Where there is a breach of any term which is not a condition, that breach could be either repudiatory (*i.e.* equivalent in effect to a breach of condition) or a mere breach of warranty (*i.e.* giving rise only to a claim to damages). It is a matter of looking at the extent of the actual breach which has occurred. If that breach "goes to the root of the contract" or deprives the other party of "substantially the whole benefit of the contract", then it entitles the latter to treat the contract as repudiated and himself as discharged from it. This approach was clearly adopted by the Court of Appeal in *Cehave v. Bremer (The Hansa Nord)* (1975) and approved by the House of Lords in *Reardon Smith Line v. Hansen-Tangen* (1976). In *Cehave*, a written contract for the sale of fruit pellets contained the express term "Shipment to be in good condition". On shipment some (about a third) of the pellets were not in "good" condition. However, although they were worth less on the open market than if they had been in "good" condition, they were still fit for the purpose for which the buyer wanted them (making into cattle food) and were still so upon arrival. It was held that there was no breach of the condition implied by the Sale of Goods Act as to merchantable quality, because the pellets were still saleable, albeit at a reduced price. Also the express term was not a "condition" in the contract. Therefore, since the sellers' breach had not been serious enough to go to the root of the contract, the buyers were entitled only to damages. It seems that an express stipulation will not easily be construed by the court as a "condition". It will be a condition only if either there is an earlier case establishing that such a clause is a condition (*i.e.* "of the essence") or else it was clearly intended by the parties when they made the contract that *any* breach of that term would entitle the other party to repudiate the contract and reject the goods.

Stipulations as to time

There is a presumption that the time of payment is not "of the essence" (section 10), although the parties could expressly agree otherwise. However, a stipulated time for delivery is likely to be more important and therefore in an ordinary commercial transaction a delivery date is normally "of the essence": *Hartley v. Hymans* (1920 KB). Similarly, if a date is specified for shipment by the seller, that will be "of the essence". So, if a delivery or shipment date is not met, the buyer, as well as claiming damages, can if he wishes regard the contract as repudiated, *i.e.* reject the goods and reclaim any money paid. Of course, if delivery is late the buyer may accept late delivery, thereby waiving his right to treat the contract as repudiated. If he does, he loses his right to reject the goods but still has a right to damages—section 11(4). **7–13**

In *Rickards v. Oppenheim* (1950 CA) the seller contracted to build a car for the buyer, the car to be built by March 20. It was not ready by that date. The buyer did not repudiate the contract but pressed for early delivery. When at the end of June it still was not finished, the buyer informed the seller that if it was not ready in another four weeks he would then regard the contract as repudiated. It was held that the buyer had acted within his rights. By his waiver he had lost his right to regard the contract as repudiated on March 20, but in the circumstances it was a condition of his waiver that delivery should take place as soon as possible. He could therefore revive his right by giving reasonable notice. At the end of the four weeks, the car was still not ready. Therefore the buyer was under no obligation to buy it. **7–14**

Suppose that under a contract, the seller is to deliver the goods to a ship and that the buyer is to nominate the ship so that delivery can be made. Then, if there is a stipulation as to the time by which the buyer must make his nomination, that stipulation as to time relates to delivery and will be "of the essence": *Bunge Corporation v. Tradax* (1981 HL). Thus, if the buyer is late in making his nomination, the seller is entitled, if he wishes, to regard the contract as repudiated (*i.e.* entitled to refuse to supply the goods).

IMPLIED TERMS—SECTIONS 12–15

7–15   The expression "buyer beware" is not entirely reflected in the law. It is true that in the law relating to misrepresentation, the seller cannot be liable for failing to disclose defects in the goods but only for any actual statements made by him or his agents. However, the terms implied by sections 12–15 are designed to see that the buyer receives certain basic benefits from the transaction. They relate to title, description, quality and sample. In spite of this, the words "buyer beware" still carry a very real warning in one type of purchase and that is what is colloquially called a private sale. The reason, as will be seen, is that the implied terms as to quality (in section 14) apply only where goods are sold in the course of a business.

7–16   Before turning to the detail of sections 12–15 it must be noted that under the original Sale of Goods Act of 1893 the wording of some of these sections was different. The Supply of Goods (Implied Terms) Act made some slight changes and, in relation to the implied condition as to merchantable (now satisfactory) quality, the Sale and Supply of Goods Act 1994 made more significant changes. Thus some of the cases which will be discussed in the next few pages were decided on sections which were not absolutely identical with the current provisions. However, because the changes were not substantial, this does not significantly diminish the authority of those cases, except (and it will be indicated) in relation to some cases on merchantable quality. The current wording of the sections will be used in this book.

Title—section 12

7–17   Section 12(1) and (2) reads:

> "(1) In a contract of sale, other than one to which subsection (3) below applies, there is an implied term on the part of the seller that in the case of a sale he has a right to sell the goods, and in the case of an agreement to sell he will have such a right at the time when the property is to pass.

(2) In a contract of sale, other than one to which subsection (3) below applies, there is also an implied term that—

  (a) the goods are free, and will remain free until the time when the property is to pass, from any charge or encumbrance not disclosed or known to the buyer before the contract is made, and

  (b) the buyer will enjoy quiet possession of the goods except so far as it may be disturbed by the owner or other person entitled to the benefit of any charge or encumbrance so disclosed or known."

Section 12(5A) makes it clear that the term in section 12(1) is a condition and the term in section 12(2) is a warranty. Most important is the implied condition that the seller has a right to sell the goods. This condition is commonly broken by someone selling goods which are not his. Chapter 5 was devoted to the question of who then owns the goods, the purchaser or the original owner. If the purchaser does so, then he has no quarrel with his seller. If, however, the original owner still owns them, the purchaser has an action against his seller for breach of condition; he can claim damages and/or a return of the price.

Rowland v. Divall (1923 CA) has attracted considerable criticism. Three months after buying and taking delivery of a car, the purchaser discovered that it had not belonged to the seller and still belonged to its original owner. It was returned to the latter and the purchaser brought an action against the seller under section 12. It was held that he was entitled to the return of the price, on the ground that he had suffered a "total failure of consideration". The whole object for a buyer in making a purchase is to obtain legal ownership of the goods. If he does not obtain that, then he suffers a total failure of consideration and is entitled to the return of the price. Thus, in effect, the buyer had over three months' free use of the car.   **7–18**

If the buyer does obtain ownership, then he does not suffer a total failure of consideration. It can happen that at the time of the sale the seller is not the owner (and thus is in breach of the condition in section 12) but that he subsequently obtains that ownership, *e.g.* by buying the goods from their owner. This "feeds" the purchaser's title (see paragraph 5–39). Thus good title is conferred upon the purchaser but at a date later than it should have been. If this occurs, the buyer can no longer claim to have suffered a total failure of consideration. The goods will be   **7–19** his, he will not be able to reject them (because he will have "accepted" them, section 35, paragraph 13–04 below) and his only claim will be for damages. However, at any time before the purchaser's title is fed (*i.e.* before the seller obtains ownership), the buyer is entitled by virtue of the seller's breach of condition to regard the contract as repudiated, to reject the goods and thus to reclaim the price on a total failure of consideration. These principles were applied in *Butterworth v. Kingsway Motors* (1954 QB). Miss A acquired a car on hire-purchase terms. Before completing her payments and therefore before the car was hers, she sold it to B. B sold it to C, who sold it to Kingsway Motors, who in turn sold it to Butterworth. In all this time Miss A still had not completed her payments. It followed that each seller was liable to his buyer for breach of the condition in section 12. After using the car for 11 months, Butterworth discovered that he was not the owner. He thereupon immediately wrote to Kingsway Motors informing them of the situation and claiming the return of his purchase price. A week later Miss A completed her payments under her hire-purchase agreement and in doing so fed title down the line of purchasers. The process of feeding stopped at Kingsway Motors who thus became owners of the car. Ownership did not pass to Butterworth who by his letter had already indicated that he regarded his contract as repudiated. It was held that Butterworth had suffered a total failure of consideration and was entitled therefore to the return from Kingsway Motors of his purchase price. However, neither Kingsway Motors nor C nor B had suffered a total failure of consideration because their title had been fed. Once they had "accepted" the goods (see paragraph 13–04 below) and their title had been fed, they lost the right to reject the goods for breach of condition. Kingsway Motors, C and B obtained only damages from their respective sellers. Kingsway Motors' damages were assessed as the difference between the value of the car when ownership should have passed to them (*i.e.* when they bought it) and its lower value when ownership actually passed to them (*i.e.* when title was fed). C obtained the same sum from B and B from Miss A.

7–20 *Butterworth v. Kingsway Motors* involved a motor vehicle and was decided before the enactment of the Hire Purchase Act 1964, Pt. III. We have seen (paragraph 5–40 above) that by virtue of section 27 of the 1964 Act where someone, who has possession of a motor vehicle under a hire purchase or conditional sale agreement, sells the vehicle before making all the payments under the agreement (*i.e.* before acquiring property in the vehicle), the first private purchaser (provided he was innocent and bona fide) will become the owner. Thus, if the facts of *Butterworth v. Kingsway Motors* were to arise again today, Butterworth would acquire title to the car provided that the first private purchaser (either B, C or Butterworth himself) was innocent and bona fide. Would that prevent Butterworth being entitled to reject the car? The answer depends upon whether on the one hand B or C was the innocent bona fide first private purchaser or whether on the other hand B and C were trade purchasers and Mr Butterworth was himself the first private purchaser. If it were the former, then Kingsway Motors would have good title (acquired from C) and therefore Kingsway Motors would not be in breach of the term that they had the right to sell the car. If it were Mr Butterworth who was the first private purchaser, then Kingsway Motors would still be in breach of the term as to title and Mr Butterworth's right to reject the car for that breach of condition would be unaffected by the 1964 Act. This was held in *Barber v. NWS Bank* (1996 CA), relying upon section 27(6) of the 1964 Act which provides that "...nothing in this section shall exonerate [the] trade or finance purchaser who becomes a purchaser of the vehicle and is not a person claiming under the first private purchaser, from any liability (whether civil or criminal) to which he would be subject apart from this section".

It can happen that the ownership of one person is subject to certain rights which someone else has over the goods. This could occur where someone has a lien over the goods, *i.e.* a right to retain possession of them until a debt is paid. For example, when goods are entrusted to a repairer for repair, he has a lien over them to compel payment of his repair bill. The owner can still sell the goods even though they are in possession of the repairer who is exercising his lien. In this case the seller will not be in breach of the terms implied by section 12, provided that before the contract was made he disclosed to the buyer the existence of the lien. **7–21**

It can happen that there is some doubt about someone's title to goods, *e.g.* a finder's title. A finder does have title to the goods (a "possessory" title) but it is subject to the title of the original owner. The latter, if he ever turns up, can therefore reclaim the goods. A finder who sells goods without first disclosing that he has only a finder's title is in breach of the condition in section 12. However, if he has disclosed that fact so as to indicate that he is transferring to the purchaser only his own possessory title, then he will not be in breach of the condition—section 12(3). **7–22**

7–23   Section 12(3) applies to a contract where it appears from the contract or is to be inferred from the circumstances that the parties intended that the seller should transfer only a limited title (whether it be the limited title of the seller himself or of some third person from whom the seller would obtain it). In such a contract there is no implied condition that the seller has or will have a right to sell the goods. There are, however, implied warranties of quiet possession, etc. The seller will be in breach of these if all charges and encumbrances (*e.g.* liens) known to him were not made known to the buyer before the contract was made.

7–24   So far it may have appeared that the condition in section 12 will be broken only if the seller turns out not to be the owner, anything less serious being merely a breach of one of the warranties. There is, however, some overlap between the warranties and the condition in section 12. The condition is broken if for any reason (undisclosed to the buyer) the seller does not have the right to sell the goods. The sellers in *Niblett Ltd v. Confectioners' Materials Co.* (1921 CA) agreed to sell tins of condensed milk. They supplied tins labelled "Nissly Brand". This infringed the Nestlé trade mark. Nestlé Co. could have obtained an injunction restraining the sale of those tins and they required the buyers not to resell them without first removing the labels. The buyers claimed damages from the sellers. It was held that the sellers were in breach both of the condition that they had the right to sell the goods and also of the warranty of quiet possession.

7–25   *Niblett's* case was considered in *Microbeads v. Vinhurst Road Markings* (1975 CA). Shortly after the sale of some road marking machines, a company unconnected with the contract of sale obtained a patent relating to road marking machines. This entitled them to bring a patent action against the buyers to enforce the patent. The buyers sued the sellers under section 12 claiming a breach of the condition as to title and a breach of the warranty of quiet possession. It was held that there had been no breach of the condition as to title because that condition related to the time of the sale. At that time no patent had been obtained; the buyers could use the machines undisturbed; and the sellers thus had the right to pass the ownership in the machines and to confer undisturbed possession upon the buyers. The warranty as to quiet possession, however, relates to the future. It states that the buyer "*will* enjoy quiet possession". The sellers were liable to the buyer in damages for breach of warranty.

Description—section 13

Section 13 reads:

"(1) Where there is a contract for the sale of goods by description, there is an implied term that the goods will correspond with the description.

(1A) As regards England and Wales and Northern Ireland, the term implied by subsection (1) above is a condition.

(2) If the sale is by sample as well as by description it is not sufficient that the bulk of the goods corresponds with the sample if the goods do not also correspond with the description.

(3) A sale of goods is not prevented from being a sale by description by reason only that, being exposed for sale or hire, they are selected by the buyer."

The condition is implied only where there is a sale by description. Clearly, goods are sold by description where the purchaser has not seen the goods but is relying on the description alone. Equally, in the words of Lord Wright in *Grant v. Australian Knitting Mills* (1936 PC):

"there is a sale by description even though the buyer is buying something displayed before him on the counter; a thing is sold by description, though it is specific, so long as it is sold not merely as the specific thing but as a thing corresponding to a description."

In that case the sale of woollen underwear across the counter was held to be a sale by description. The essence of a sale by description is that in deciding to buy the buyer placed some (but not necessarily exclusive) reliance upon the description. In *Beale v. Taylor* (1967 CA) the buyer saw an advertisement for a "Herald, convertible, white, 1961". He answered the advertisement, inspected the car and bought it. Although the buyer had inspected the car, he had relied not purely on his own assessment of its value, but to some extent on the description. The seller was held liable under section 13, since the car consisted of the rear half of a 1961 car and the front half of an earlier model.

7–27   In most cases the mere fact that a description was given (*e.g.* "good condition" or "1996 model") will be sufficient and convincing evidence that the sale was by description. It will be obvious that the buyer has relied, at least to some extent, upon the description. If in fact, however, it is clear that there was no reliance at all upon the description, the sale will not be a sale by description. In *Harlingdon & Leinster Enterprises Ltd v. Christopher Hull Fine Art Ltd* (1990 CA), an art dealer contacted another art dealer informing him that he had two paintings by Gabriele Munter (an artist of the German expressionist school). The latter visited the former (the seller) and inspected the paintings. The seller, as the buyer knew, had no expertise in, or knowledge of, the German expressionist school. Hence, the buyer placed no reliance upon the seller's attribution but relied solely upon his own judgment and assessment. It was held that, since it was not within the reasonable contemplation of the parties that the buyer was relying upon the seller's attribution, there was no sale by description.

7–28   A sale in a supermarket is usually a sale by description. The reason that the buyer selects a packet labelled, say, "cocoa" from the shelf is that she wants cocoa and she is relying on the description "cocoa" accurately to identify the packet and its contents. It is a sale by description even though it is the customer who decides which particular goods to select from the display— section 13(3). Occasionally, goods, *e.g.* vegetables, are displayed without any label or notice describing them. It would seem that such goods are not sold by description.

A sale by sample will often be a sale also by description. Section 13(2) embodies a principle illustrated by *Nichol v. Godts* (1854). The buyer bought by sample "foreign refined rape oil". It was held that the goods must correspond not only with the sample but must also be "foreign refined rape oil".

7–29   In order to determine whether the goods correspond with the contractual description it may be necessary to determine the exact scope and meaning of the description. Obviously, the more detailed it is, the more stringent is the seller's obligation to supply goods corresponding with it. A contract to supply "staves" is one thing, but a contract to supply "staves, half an inch thick" is altogether more onerous. If in the latter case the seller supplies staves between half an inch and nine-sixteenths of an inch thick, he is in breach of the condition as to description: *Arcos v. Ronaasen* (1933 HL). If the seller wants a margin, he must stipulate for it in the contractual description.

The fact that the goods are of defective quality is usually 7–30
irrelevant in deciding whether they correspond with their
description. *Pinnock Bros. v. Lewis & Peat* (1923 KB) involved a
contract for the sale of "copra cake" which was to be used to
feed cattle. The goods actually supplied consisted of copra cake
combined with a quantity of castor oil, the latter being poisonous
to cattle. The sellers were in breach of the condition as to
description. However, this was not because the goods were unfit
for use but rather because they included goods of a different
description. *Ashington Piggeries v. Hill* (1971 HL) involved a
contract for the sale of "Norwegian herring meal fair average
quality for the season, expected to analyse..." which was to be
used to feed mink. The sellers supplied Norwegian herring meal,
i.e. Norwegian herrings plus preservative. The herrings and
preservative had reacted together and produced a chemical which
was poisonous to mink. Here, the sellers were not in breach of
the condition as to description since, unlike *Pinnock's* case, there
was no addition of goods outside the contractual description. The
key to section 13 was said to be "identification" not "quality".
Hence the expression "fair average quality for the season" was
held not to be part of the contract description, since it did not
"identify" the goods sold. Goods which are useless or unsuitable
for any normal purpose will still correspond with their description
(here "Norwegian herring meal") if it accurately identified them.
A balloon, though punctured, is nevertheless accurately identified
and described as a "balloon".

Re Moore and Landauer (1921 CA) is now a controversial 7–31
decision. The sellers had agreed to sell a quantity of tinned pears
which were to be packed in cases containing 30 tins each. They
had delivered the correct total quantity of tins but half of them
were packed in cases of 24 tins each. It was held that the contract
requirement that they be packed in cases of 30 was part of the
contract description. Therefore the buyers were entitled to refuse
to accept delivery because the sellers had committed a breach of
condition (*i.e.* of section 13) and the buyers were entitled to do so
even if they would have suffered no loss by having the tins
packed in cases of 24 instead of cases of 30. The correctness of
the decision in *Re Moore and Landauer* has, however, been
doubted by Lord Wilberforce in *Reardon Smith Line v. Hansen
Tangen* (1976 HL). Because section 13 is an implied *condition*,
anything which is regarded by the court as part of the contract
description automatically becomes "of the essence" and, if not
complied with, has until recently automatically given the buyer

the right to reject the goods for breach of condition, no matter how slight the breach was. The modern trend has therefore been to regard as part of the contract description only those contract words which help in "identifying" the goods. Other expressions in the contract (such as "fair average quality for the season" or "packed in cases of 30") can then be regarded not as part of the contract description, but as express terms of the contract in their own right. Unless the contract clearly indicates otherwise, these express terms (not being stipulations as to the time of delivery) will then normally be warranties and not conditions. Thus if the seller is in breach of one of them, the buyer will not be entitled to reject the goods unless the seller's breach is such as to deprive the buyer of substantially the whole benefit of the contract: *Cehave v. Bremer*, paragraph 7–12 above. Of course, if there is a defect of quality, a buyer who wishes to reject the goods may still be able to do so, *i.e.* if he can show that there has been a breach of one of the conditions implied by section 14. Even then, however, a buyer who is a non-consumer will not be entitled to reject the goods if the breach was so slight as to make rejection unreasonable (see paragraph 13–03 below).

Quality—section 14

7–32   There are two conditions which may be implied by section 14—as to satisfactory quality (section 14(2)) and as to fitness for purpose (section 14(3)). Before considering in what circumstances these conditions will be implied, note should be made of section 14(1) which reads:

> "(1) Except as provided by this section, and section 15 below and subject to any other enactment, there is no implied term about the quality or fitness for any particular purpose of goods supplied under a contract of sale."

The two conditions implied by section 14 extend, not only to the goods actually bought, but also to goods "supplied under" the contract, *e.g.* a returnable bottle: *Geddling v. Marsh* (1920 KB). They also extend to the instructions. It would, for example, be no defence for the seller to say that his farm fertiliser was perfectly safe and effective when applied in the right concentration (at the right time of the year) if the instructions supplied with the fertiliser stated in error the wrong concentration, whether too weak to be effective or so strong as to kill the crops. The law does not consider just the goods. It asks whether the goods with their instructions were of satisfactory quality and reasonably fit for their purpose: *Wormell v. R.H.M. Agriculture (East)* (1987 CA). In the case of a book, video cassette, or computer disk containing a software program, the two conditions extend, apparently, not just to the physical book, disk or video, but also to the contents (see *St Albans District Council v. ICL*, paragraph 1–14 above).

Satisfactory quality—section 14(2)

Section 14(2), (2A), (2B) and (2C) read: **7–33**

"(2) Where the seller sells goods in the course of a business, there is an implied term that the goods supplied under the contract are of satisfactory quality.

(2A) For the purposes of this Act, goods are of satisfactory quality if they meet the standard that a reasonable person would regard as satisfactory, taking account of any description of the goods, the price (if relevant) and all the other relevant circumstances.

(2B) For the purposes of this Act, the quality of the goods includes their state and condition and the following (among others) are in appropriate cases aspects of the quality of goods:
  (a) fitness for all the purposes for which goods of the kind in question are commonly supplied;
  (b) appearance and finish;
  (c) freedom from minor blemishes;
  (d) safety; and
  (e) durability.

(2C) The term implied by subsection (2) above does not extend to any matter making the goods unsatisfactory:
  (a) which is specifically drawn to the buyer's attention before the contract is made;
  (b) where the buyer examines the goods before the contract is made, which that examination ought to reveal; or
  (c) in the case of a contract for sale by sample, which would have been apparent on a reasonable examination of the sample."

The implied term as to satisfactory quality is a condition. It is **7–34** implied only if the goods are sold "in the course of a business".

These words were new in section 14 by virtue of the Supply of Goods (Implied Terms) Act 1973. Someone can sell "in the course of a business" without being a dealer in, or a regular seller of, goods of the description sold. The phrase is simply there to distinguish between a sale made in the course of a seller's business and a purely private sale outside the confines of any business. Of course a butcher selling meat or a baker selling bread are each selling in the course of their business. Equally, the baker sells his bread van in the course of a business when he part-exchanges it for a new one. The solicitor who sells off old office furniture or a computer no longer wanted for the practice, similarly is selling in the course of a business. This meaning of the phrase was established in *Stevenson v. Rogers* (1999 CA), in which a sale of his fishing boat by a fisherman was held to be a sale in the course of a business. This case casts doubt upon an earlier decision, *R & B Customs Brokers v. U.D.T.*, giving the phrase a much narrower meaning in the Unfair Contract Terms Act 1977 (see paragraph 10–23 below). It seems clear, however, that a similar phrase in the Trade Descriptions Act 1968 does indeed have a narrower meaning (see paragraph 18–07 below). Section 61(1) of the Sale of Goods Act states that:

> "'business' includes a profession and the activities of any government department (including a Northern Ireland department), or local or public authority."

Thus someone buying goods from the local council does have the benefit of the implied condition that they shall be of satisfactory quality. Suppose that the seller is a private seller not selling in the course of a business, but that he gets an agent to make the sale for him. Suppose also that the agent is acting in the course of a business. In that case the seller is treated as if he were selling in the course of a business, unless either the buyer knew that he was not doing so or else reasonable steps had been taken to bring that fact to the buyer's attention before the contract was made: section 14(5) and *Boyter v. Thomson* (1995 HL).

7–35   There are three exceptions in section 14(2). First, the buyer cannot complain of defects which had been specifically drawn to his attention, although naturally the condition will still apply in relation to other defects rendering the goods of unsatisfactory quality. The second exception applies "where the buyer examines the goods before the contract is made". So, if the buyer does, he cannot complain of defects which he ought thereby to have discerned. In *Thornett & Fehr v. Beers* (1919 KB) the buyers of some barrels of glue had examined only the outside. It was held that a normal examination would have involved looking inside and that they could not complain of defects in the glue which an inspection inside would have revealed. This decision might not be the same today, because the wording of section 14(2C)(b) now refers to defects which "*that* examination ought to reveal" and the word "that" must refer to the examination actually made and not to any examination which ought to have been made. One could not say (it is arguable) that the examination actually made in *Thornett* (*i.e.* of the outside of the barrel) ought to have revealed defects apparent only on an examination which was not made (*i.e.* of the inside). Nevertheless, the buyer's legal position may be better if he made no examination than if he made merely a superficial examination. This is not the case, however, where there is a sale by sample. The third exception prevents any liability under section 14(2) in respect of any defect which would have been apparent on a reasonable examination of the sample, *i.e.* even if no such examination was carried out.

Returning to the second exception, suppose the buyer examines   **7–36**
the goods, discovers a defect but decides nevertheless to buy, taking the view that the defect is one that can be easily remedied. If it is easily remedied, then clearly the buyer cannot complain of the defect in question. If it turns out to be incapable of being remedied, the result may well be different. If at the time of making the contract, the buyer was unaware, and could not reasonably have been aware, of the gravity of the defect, then the court would probably hold that the condition as to satisfactory quality was implied. In *R & B Customs Brokers Co. Ltd v. United Dominions Trust Ltd* (1988 CA) the buyer had discovered that the car had a leak but did not discover until after the contract the gravity of the leak or that it was incurable. Neill L.J. said:

"I am not at present persuaded, however, that the condition in section 14(2) is excluded if at the time the contract is made the buyer is reasonably of the opinion that the defect can be, and will be, rectified at no cost to himself."

The Court of Appeal side-stepped having to decide that issue, by holding that the buyer was entitled anyway to rely on section 14(3) (paragraph 7–43 below); the car was not reasonably fit for the particular purposes (driving upon the roads in England—in

English weather) for which the buyer had informed the seller that he wanted it.

7–37 Prior to 1994 the implied term in section 14(2) was an implied condition that the goods would be of *merchantable* quality. The Sale and Supply of Goods Act 1994 amended section 14(2). It replaced the word merchantable with the word *satisfactory* and introduced a new definition set out in section 14(2A) and (2B). According to that definition it is important to assess the quality of the goods against the description applied to them. Clearly, goods sold as "mink food" will not be of satisfactory quality if it is poisonous to mink. That is so even if it is perfectly wholesome for other animals. What, however, is the position if it is sold as "animal food"? Under the previous law, there was clear authority that the goods did not have be fit for all the purposes for which goods of that kind were commonly bought; it was sufficient if they were fit for one or more of those purposes: *Aswan Engineering Establishment v. Lupdine* (1987 CA). Now, however, section 14(2B)(a) seems to require the goods to be fit for all the purposes for which goods of that kind are commonly bought. Thus if the goods are sold as "animal food" and animal food is commonly bought to feed to mink, then if the food is poisonous to mink, it would appear that it is not of satisfactory quality.

7–38 The definition also states that the price can be relevant. This appears to be no change from the previous law relating to merchantable quality. The relevance of the price was discussed in *Brown v. Craiks* (1970 HL) which involved the sale of industrial fabric. The buyer found it unsuitable for making into dresses. It was, however, perfectly suitable for other industrial purposes and could be sold for such—albeit at a slightly lower price. The House of Lords held that it was of merchantable quality because it was saleable without any substantial reduction of the price. Their Lordships said that if it had been saleable only at a "throw away" price, that would indicate that it was not of merchantable quality.

7–39 The word "satisfactory" in the definition indicates that the goods are not necessarily required to be of the very best quality but that the level of quality demanded depends upon the circumstances of the case, including the price. In this respect the law has not changed. For example, second-hand goods can hardly be expected to be in perfect condition. In *Bartlett v. Sydney Marcus* (1965 CA) the seller, a car dealer, told the buyer that the car had a defective clutch and that if he bought it as it was he could have it for £550 but that if the seller were to repair it first, the price would be £575. The buyer opted to take the car as it was. About a month later the buyer had the clutch repaired at a cost of £45 and claimed this sum from the seller, alleging that the car was not of merchantable quality and not reasonably fit for the purpose of being driven on the road. The claim failed. "A buyer should realise that, when he buys a second-hand car, defects may appear sooner or later." The car came up to the standard required. On the other hand major defects in a second-hand car might well mean that it is not of satisfactory quality (see *Crowther v. Shannon*. paragraph 7–47 below). A second-hand car which is not safe to be driven on the road (for example because the brakes are in such a state that they would fail if the driver had to carry out an emergency stop) is clearly not of satisfactory quality: *Lee v. York Coach and Marine* (1977 CA)—unless of course the car was only sold for scrap.

In *Rogers v. Parish (Scarborough) Ltd* (1986) the Court of **7–40** Appeal gave an authoritative ruling on how the old definition of merchantable quality applied in the case of a motor vehicle. It seems very likely that this ruling will be held to be equally applicable to the new definition of satisfactory quality. The old definition referred, as the new one does in section 14(2B), to the purposes for which goods of that kind are commonly bought. In *Rogers v. Parish* it was held that in the case of motor vehicles those purposes include not merely the purpose of driving it from place to place but of doing so with the appropriate degree of comfort, ease of handling and pride in the vehicle's outward and interior appearance. The appropriate degree varies with the price, the description and other relevant factors. The relative weight to be attached to the different characteristics of the vehicle depends upon which market it is aimed at. On a vehicle sold as new, the performance and finish to be expected are those of a model of average standard with no mileage. No less is to be expected of a vehicle sold with a manufacturer's warranty. This authoritative ruling made it clear that defects in appearance, if of sufficient degree, could render a vehicle unmerchantable. That is true also of the new definition of satisfactory quality (see section 14(2B)(b)). The merest blemish on a Rolls Royce might render it unsatisfactory whereas it might not on a humbler car (see section 14(2B)(c)). The concept of satisfactory quality is one of degree. Deficiencies which are unacceptable on a car sold as new might be acceptable on a second-hand car. Nevertheless the general approach laid down in *Rogers v. Parish (Scarborough) Ltd* applies equally to second-hand vehicles (*Business Applications Specialists*

Ltd v. Nationwide Credit Corpn. Ltd (1988 CA)) and, as noted earlier, sufficiently serious defects can render even a second-hand car of unsatisfactory quality. Thus in *Shine v. General Guarantee Finance Co. Ltd* (1988 CA) a 20-month-old Fiat was held to be unmerchantable because, unknown to the buyer, it had eight months earlier been totally submerged in water for over 24 hours and had consequently been treated as a "write off" by its insurer. The car would equally be of unsatisfactory quality under the new definition.

7–41   It is of interest to speculate whether the decision in *Aswan Engineering Establishment v. Lupdine* (1987 CA) would be the same under the new definition of satisfactory quality. In that case some heavy-duty buckets (which were suitable for most purposes for which such buckets were normally bought or used) collapsed when left by the buyer for several days stacked in extreme heat such that the contents reached $70°C$ ($156°$ Fahrenheit). It was held that they were of merchantable quality because the definition of merchantable quality did not require the goods to be suitable for all the purposes for which such goods were commonly bought. It seems highly likely that the same result would be achieved under the new definition but by a slightly different line of reasoning, namely that the definition of satisfactory quality does not require that the goods be fit for extreme or outlandish purposes but just for such uses as such goods are commonly, *i.e.* normally, used. Leaving the buckets stacked in such extreme temperatures could well be held to be an extreme, abnormal use.

7–42   Where perishable goods are to be despatched to the buyer by carrier, it is reasonable to expect the goods to be of such a quality as to be able to withstand a normal journey—*Mash & Murrell v. Joseph Emmanuel* (1961 QB). More generally, it is now clear that durability is part of the definition of satisfactory quality—section 14(2B)(e). It may be accurate to say that the goods must be of satisfactory quality for a reasonable period after delivery so long as they remain in the same apparent state as that in which they were delivered, apart from normal wear and tear. That would bring section 14(2) into line with the implied condition as to fitness for purpose (see paragraph 7–43 below).

Fitness for purpose—section 14(3)

7–43   Section 14(3) reads:

>   "(3) Where the seller sells goods in the course of a business
>   and the buyer, expressly or by implication, makes

126

known (a) to the seller or (b)..., any particular purpose for which the goods are being bought, there is an implied term that the goods supplied under the contract are reasonably fit for that purpose, whether or not that is a purpose for which such goods are commonly supplied, except where the circumstances show that the buyer does not rely, or that it is unreasonable for him to rely, on the skill or judgment of the seller..."

(For an explanation of the omitted words see paragraph 25–23 below.)

This is a condition and, like the one in section 14(2), is implied only where the goods are sold in the course of a business. Further, the buyer must have made known to the seller the particular purpose for which he was buying the goods. With goods having only one normal use the mere fact of the purchase will, by implication, make it known that this is what the buyer wants them for, *e.g.* a hot-water bottle, as in *Priest v. Last* (1903 CA).

Someone who buys goods having more than one common use **7–44** or who wants goods for an abnormal purpose will not benefit from section 14(3) unless the seller was expressly informed of the particular purpose for which they were required. In *Griffiths v. Peter Conway* (1939 CA) the purchaser of a tweed coat contracted dermatitis from wearing it. Someone with normally sensitive skin would not have been affected but the purchaser had abnormally sensitive skin. Not having made that fact known to the seller, she lost the case. This decision was approved in *Slater v. Finning* (1996 HL), where a boat owner had bought and had installed in his boat engine a new part, a camshaft. It failed while at sea as did two further replacement camshafts. The expert evidence was that the cause of the failures was excessive torsional resonance excited by some cause external to the engine and the camshaft. It was held that the camshaft was fit for the purpose for which the seller had been informed that it was required, namely use as a component part of the engine in the buyer's boat, *i.e.* an ordinary boat, the sellers not having been informed of any special characteristic of the boat. There is no breach of the implied condition where the failure of the goods arises from some idiosyncrasy, not made known to the seller, in the buyer or in the circumstances of the planned use of the goods. That is so even if the buyer is himself unaware of that abnormal feature or idiosyncrasy.

7–45   If the buyer does not rely, or it is unreasonable for him to rely, on the seller's skill or judgment he will have no claim under section 14(3). However, the courts seem quite ready to infer the necessary reliance. Lord Wright, in *Grant v. Australian Knitting Mills* (1935 PC) said:

> "…thus to take a case like that in question of a purchase from a retailer the reliance will be in general inferred from the fact that a buyer goes to the shop in confidence that the tradesman has selected his stock with skill and judgment."

On the other hand, if the buyer asks for an article by its trade or brand name and does so in such a way as to exclude any discussion of its suitability, then he is not relying on the seller's skill or judgment: *Baldry v. Marshall* (1924 CA).

Sometimes there will be partial reliance, the buyer relying in some respects upon the seller's skill and judgment and in others upon his own. Should the goods prove unfit for their purpose, the buyer will have a claim only if their unfitness relates to the sphere of reliance placed upon the seller. In *Cammell Laird v. Manganese Bronze & Brass* (1934 HL) the sellers were to supply a particular ship's propellers which they were to make according to a specification supplied by the buyer. The seller's skill and judgment were relied upon as to matters not within the buyer's specification. This included ensuring that adequate materials were used and that the specification was embodied in the propellers. It also included other matters not provided for in the specification. In fact the propellers were unfit for their purpose because they were not thick enough, a matter not included in the buyer's specification. The sellers were liable.

7–46   In *Teheran—Europe v. S. T. Belton* (1968 CA) tractors were purchased for the purpose of exporting and reselling in Persia. They in fact infringed Persian regulations and the buyer was fined by a Persian criminal court. He sued the seller. It was held that since the buyer knew much more about Persia than the seller, he must have been relying on his own judgment as to whether the tractors were suitable for the Persian market. The buyer lost.

7–47   The words "reasonably fit" do not require the goods to be of the very best quality. The quality to be expected will depend upon all the circumstances of the sale. Second-hand goods cannot be expected to be perfect. Minor defects must, for example, be expected to materialise in a second-hand car (see *Bartlett v. Sydney Marcus* above). However, major defects existing at the time of the sale are another matter. In *Crowther v. Shannon* (1975 CA) a car dealer sold for £390 an eight-year-old Jaguar car with 82,000 miles on the milometer. Three weeks and 2,300 miles later, the engine seized up. It needed replacing. It was held that the fact the engine seized up after only three weeks was evidence that at the time of the sale the car was not reasonably fit for the purpose of being driven on the road. The seller was liable for breach of the condition of fitness for purpose.

Although the words "reasonably fit" do not require the goods to be of the very best quality, they do impose upon the seller an absolute obligation. It is no defence that he acted reasonably if in fact the goods are not reasonably fit for their purpose. In *Frost v. Aylesbury Dairy* (1905 CA) milk was sold containing typhoid germs. It was no defence that the sellers had taken all reasonable precautions as to hygiene.   **7–48**

It is at the time of delivery that the goods must be reasonably fit for the purpose for which the buyer indicated he wanted them. They must also continue to be so for a reasonable time after delivery. In *Lambert v. Lewis* (1981 HL) Lord Diplock said that the condition of fitness for purpose was a continuing obligation "that the goods will continue to be fit for that purpose for a reasonable time after delivery, so long as they remain in the same apparent state and condition as that in which they were delivered, apart from normal wear and tear." In that case a farmer had bought from a dealer a towing coupling for his Land Rover. He continued to use the coupling after it had become apparent to him that the locking mechanism of the coupling was broken. Subsequently, due to defective design (*i.e.* not the broken locking mechanism), the coupling failed while in use and a road accident occurred as a result of the trailer becoming detached from the Land Rover. Clearly, the farmer had been supplied with a coupling which was not reasonably fit for the purpose for which he had indicated he wanted it. Nevertheless, he was unable, on the basis of that breach of condition, to claim from the seller any of the damage and losses which the farmer suffered in the accident. Once it had become apparent to the farmer that the locking mechanism was broken, that brought to an end the seller's obligation that the coupling continue to be reasonably fit for its purpose.   **7–49**

Sample—section 15

Section 15 provides: **7–50**

"(1) A contract of sale is a contract for sale by sample where there is an express or implied term to that effect in the contract.

(2) In the case of a contract for sale by sample there is an implied term—

   (a) that the bulk will correspond with the sample in quality;

   (b) . . .

   (c) that the goods will be free from any defect, making their quality unsatisfactory, which would not be apparent on reasonable examination of the sample."

Section 15 applies only if there is a term of the contract that it is a contract of sale by sample. In the case of a written contract the sale will be by sample only if that is included in the writing. Merely exhibiting a sample during the negotiations will not make it a sale by sample unless the parties agree that it is a sale by sample. In *Drummond v. Van Ingen* (1887 HL) Lord MacNaghten explained the function of a sample:

"The office of a sample is to present to the eye the real meaning and intention of the parties with regard to the subject-matter of the contract which, owing to the imperfection of language, it may be difficult or impossible to express in words. The sample speaks for itself."

The term is section 15(2) is a condition. Under section 15(2)(a) it is no defence that the bulk can easily be made to correspond with the sample. In *E. & S. Ruben v. Faire Bros.* (1949 KB) Linatex was sold which was crinkly, whereas the sample was soft. The seller was liable even though by a simple process of warming, the bulk could have been made soft.

The buyer cannot complain under section 15(2)(c) of defects which he could reasonably have discovered on an examination of the sample. This is similar to the position under section 14(2) above.

Remedies

7–51   For breach by the seller of any term of the contract, the buyer can sue for damages. In the case of a breach of condition the buyer normally has the additional right to reject the goods and recover the price. The buyer however may lose the right to reject the goods either by waiver of that right or by "acceptance" of the goods. "Acceptance" has a technical meaning. This will be explained in Chapter 13 which deals with the buyer's remedies.

EUROPEAN DIRECTIVE ON CONSUMER GUARANTEES

This Directive (1999/44/EC) is to be implemented in member states by January 1, 2002. Despite its title, it is concerned more with the consumer's rights against the seller than with those against the manufacturer or distributor. It deals with aspects of the sale of consumer goods and associated guarantees. Consumer goods include any tangible moveable item, except for water and gas not put up for sale in a limited quantity or volume. A consumer is an individual purchasing for purposes unrelated to his trade, business or profession. Member states are allowed to have more stringent provisions for the protection of the consumer than those required by the Directive. They are also allowed to exempt second-hand goods sold at public auction where consumers have the opportunity of attending in person. Thus an auction of second-hand goods conducted solely over the internet will not be exempt.

7–52

The Directive requires goods to conform with the contract of sale, involving in particular:

- complying with the description given by the seller,

- being fit for the purposes for which goods of the same type are normally used,

- being fit for any particular purpose for which the consumer required them and which was made known to the seller and accepted by him,

- being of satisfactory quality and performance.

The seller is to be made liable for failure to conform. English law will have to be amended—probably by amendments to the Sale of Goods Act—in order to comply with some of the details of the Directive. Some of these follow—

1. Any lack of conformity becoming apparent within six months of delivery is to be presumed to have existed at the time of delivery, unless the contrary is proved or the

presumption is incompatible with the type of goods or the nature of the lack of conformity (*e.g.* perishable ones).

2. The buyer is to be given a range of remedies in the event of lack of conformity, including, if the seller has not remedied the defect within a reasonable period, an appropriate reduction in the price or rescission of the contract. The latter is achieved in English Law by the buyer's right to reject the goods. That right, however, can be lost by "acceptance". The doctrine of acceptance does not fit very easily with the Directive which allows member states to create a pre-condition for the consumer to benefit from his rights, namely that the consumer informs the seller of the lack of conformity within two months of detecting the lack of conformity. English Law will have to be changed to ensure that the consumer is not taken to have "accepted" the goods before the end of that two month period. (On "acceptance" see Chapter 13).

3. The seller is to be made liable to the consumer for any lack of conformity of the goods with the public statements (*e.g.* by advertisements) made by the producer or manufacturer. Exceptions are allowed where, (a) the seller did not know, and could not have known, of the statement in question, (b) the seller corrected the statement at the time of the sale, or (c) the consumer's decision to buy could not have been influenced by the statement.

7–53   The Directive also deals with "commercial guarantees". A commercial guarantee is one given by a seller or producer. Thus this aspect of the Directive does affect manufacturer's liability. A commercial guarantee will be enforceable and must be such as to place the consumer in a better position than he would be without it, *i.e.* it must enhance his rights over and above what the law would otherwise give him. This, when enacted in English law, will remove the uncertainty as to the legal enforceability of a manufacturer's guarantee given by means of a registration card included within the packaging of goods. [For manufacturers' guarantees see also paragraphs 9–02 to 9–03 below.]

7–54   Finally, the Directive commits the European Commission to producing by July 2006 a report which considers whether to introduce direct liability of the producer/manufacturer. The manufacturer is already directly liable for personal injury and damage caused by defective products (under the Consumer Protection Act 1987, see paragraph 9–06 below). Making the manufacturer directly liable to the consumer for non-conformity with the contract of sale would, if it ever happened, create a much larger inroad into the doctrine of privity of contract than does the Contracts (Rights of Third Parties) Act 1999 (see paragraph 7–03 above).

[For further discussion of the Directive, see an article by Shears, Zollers and Hurd at [2000] J.B.L 262.]

CHAPTER 8

SUPPLY OF GOODS AND SERVICES ACT
1982

THIS Act is mainly concerned with certain types of contract **8–01** which are not contracts of sale of goods. Nevertheless, some of these contracts are closely related to sale of goods ones and much of the law in the Act is modelled on parts of the Sale of Goods Act. Furthermore, some of the Act's provisions (sections 12–16) will apply to certain contracts of sale of goods, *i.e.* where these contracts involve also the provision of some service or services. For these reasons a full account of the 1982 Act is given here. In this chapter references to sections are to sections of the 1982 Act unless otherwise stated. The Act consists of three sets of implied terms. Each set is implied in a defined category of contracts. The extent to which the parties can contract out of these terms will be explained in Chapter 10 (paragraph 10–37).

THE FIRST SET—CONTRACTS FOR THE TRANSFER OF GOODS

The first set of implied terms (sections 2 to 5) applies, with **8–02** certain exceptions, to contracts which are not contracts of sale of goods or hire-purchase but where nevertheless one person transfers, or agrees to transfer, property (ownership) in goods to another, section 1. The main kinds of contracts affected are contracts of exchange or barter (which are not contracts of sale of goods because of lack of a *money* consideration) and contracts (*e.g.* of repair) where, although some goods are supplied, the substance of the contract is the provision of services. Customers under such contracts are given rights in relation to title, description, quality and sample which are identical to those conferred by the Sale of Goods Act upon a buyer under a sale of goods contract. The first set of implied terms consists of terms as to: title, freedom from encumbrances and quiet possession (section 2); description (section 3); satisfactory quality and fitness for purpose (section 4); and sample (section 5). These terms relate to the goods supplied and are implied in identical circumstances and are to an identical effect as the terms implied by sections 12–15 of the Sale of Goods Act.

Even though the implied terms in sections 2 to 5 of the 1982 Act are identical to those in sections 12–15 of the Sale of Goods Act, it still may be necessary to distinguish between on the one hand a contract governed by sections 2–5 of the 1982 Act and on the other a contract of sale of goods. Two particular reasons spring to mind. First, the doctrine of "acceptance" (paragraph 13–04 below) applies only to sale of goods contracts. The result is that a customer under, say, a contract of barter may have longer in which to reject the goods for breach of condition than does a buyer under a sale of goods contract. In this respect all non-sale of goods contracts are the same, *i.e.* the question whether the customer has lost his right to reject the goods for breach of condition is determined not by whether he has "accepted" the goods but by whether he has affirmed the contract. For a discussion of the doctrine of affirmation in relation to hire-purchase agreements, see paragraph 25–20 below. The second reason for distinguishing between sale of goods contracts and others is that the Sale of Goods Act applies only to contracts of sale of goods and the Supply of Goods and Services Act 1982 does not contain provisions corresponding to any other than sections 12–15 of the Sale of Goods Act. So, for example, there are no statutory rules relating to the passing of property and risk under a contract of barter. It is therefore a matter of common law and there is not much English case law on the matter. Consider now some different types of contract.

1. Collateral contracts which are not contracts of sale of goods

8–03   It will be remembered that if there is no money consideration, a contract will not be a sale of goods contract. Hence, in *Esso v. Commissioners of Customs and Excise* (paragraph 1–10 above), although there was a contract of sale of goods in relation to the petrol, the collateral contract relating to the World Cup coin was not a contract of sale of goods. It is difficult, perhaps, to imagine a dispute about title, description, quality or sample arising in relation to a World Cup coin. Consider, however, the situation where an electrical retailer advertises that with every refrigerator sold in November a free electric toaster will be supplied. According to the reasoning in the Esso case, the advertisement is an offer (*i.e.* to supply a toaster). A member of the public can accept that offer during November by entering a contract to buy a refrigerator from the retailer. The consideration given by the customer for the toaster is not money but is the entering of the contract to buy the refrigerator. The result is that if the *toaster* is not of satisfactory quality the customer's claim is under section 4 of the Supply of Goods and Services Act, but if the *refrigerator* is not of satisfactory quality his claim is under section 14 of the Sale of Goods Act. In the latter case the buyer could exercise his right to reject the refrigerator for breach of condition and then recover the price on a total failure of consideration. He would still presumably be entitled to retain the toaster which he obtained under a separate collateral contract. If, however, the toaster and not the fridge had been of less than satisfactory quality, then there would be no point in rejecting the toaster for breach of condition, since under the contract (*i.e.* the one relating to the toaster) no price was payable by the customer and therefore none would be recoverable. Nevertheless, the customer could of course sue for damages.

2. Contracts of barter or exchange

Where goods are swapped for other goods, then there is no   **8–04** contract of sale of goods since there is no *money* consideration. What, however, about the situation where goods are swapped for a combination of money and other goods? This problem typically occurs where goods are part-exchanged or "traded in". For example, a customer buying a new car with a cash price of £5,000 might get the garage to allow him £500 part-exchange allowance on his old car. In this case there is still a contract of sale of the new car because there is for it a money consideration (of £4,500): *Dawson v. Dutfield* (paragraph 1–09 above). The position is still the same even if the part-exchange allowance is for most or nearly all of the price—say, in our example, £4,800— because there is still a money consideration, albeit a small one: *Aldridge v. Johnson* (below). Thus, if the new car proves not to match the description by which it was sold or not to be of satisfactory quality the customer's claim is founded on sections 13 or 14 of the Sale of Goods Act.

Consider now the traded-in car. At first sight it appears that there is no money consideration given by the garage for the traded-in car. However, it is usual in the car trade for a value to be agreed for the traded-in car as well as for the new car, *i.e.* the trade-in allowance is a precise stated figure (*e.g.* £500). In this case it may be correct to regard the traded-in car, not as exchanged or bartered towards the new car, but as sold for £500 which sum the customer uses towards payment for his new car. Looked at in this way, the whole transaction between the garage and customer is not a sale of a new car and a part-exchange (or barter) of the old, but represents a sale of each. In *Aldridge v. Johnson* (1875 QB) barley valued at £215 was sold in return for £23 and bullocks valued at £192. The court considered that, each set of goods having been allocated a price, there were mutual sales. It seems to follow that if X agrees to swap his coat for Y's jacket, there is a contract of barter, but if in making the contract they allocated a value or price of say, £20 to each item, there would be mutual sales.

3. Contracts where payment for goods is made by cheque, trading check, credit card, or other voucher

8–05   Are these contracts of sale of goods or are they contracts under which the customer gives no money consideration? Clearly, where the payment is by cheque, the contract is one of sale of goods. Indeed, section 38 of the Sale of Goods Act expressly contemplates this possibility. If the cheque bounces (*i.e.* is dishonoured), the seller will be able to sue for the price because acceptance of payment by cheque will have been conditional (*i.e.* upon the cheque being honoured).

Where a trading check is used to pay for goods, the contract is one of sale of goods: *Davies v. Commissioners of Customs and Excise* (1975 DC). With a trading check, although the buyer does not actually hand over any cash, he does hand over something having an agreed cash value (*i.e.* agreed between himself and the seller). Just as it is sale of goods when a customer trades in a car in part exchange for another (see paragraph 8–04 above), so it is a sale of goods when a retailer supplies goods in return for a trading check. In each case the seller (*i.e.* the customer trading in his car and the retailer providing goods in return for the trading check) receives no actual cash, but he receives something having an agreed cash value. The same can be said where payment is made by means of a credit (or charge) card. The seller, in accepting payment by the card, is taking something having an agreed cash value. Therefore, provided that the commodity being bought is goods (as opposed to services) the contract between seller and buyer is one of sale of goods. This is so despite the fact that the contract is in one respect different from that where payment is made by cheque. Where payment is made by means of a credit (or charge) card, that is an absolute, not a conditional, payment: *Re Charge Card Services Ltd* (1988 CA). Thus if the card company fails to pay the seller, *e.g.* because the card company is insolvent, the seller is not entitled to recover payment from the card holder. Accounts of how trading checks and credit cards work are given at paragraphs 20–18 and 24–23 below.

Where a voucher, other than a trading check or credit card, is used (*e.g.* a book-token) there is no case law telling us into which category the contract falls. Where the voucher is used together with cash to buy goods, clearly there is a sale of goods contract. Where the voucher alone is used, presumably the same reasoning used in the last paragraph will apply. Thus, where, as in the case of a book-token, the voucher is used as having an agreed cash value (*i.e.* as a cash equivalent), the contract is one of sale of goods. Record-tokens and shop gift vouchers would come into this category also. Imagine, however, an offer on the top of a soap powder packet, "Send three coupons for a free teddy bear", there being a coupon printed on the side of each soap powder packet. The customer who sends his coupons and obtains the teddy bear, obtains it, not under a sale of goods contract, but under a contract of barter or exchange, because the coupons are not used as representing any particular cash value. If the teddy bear infringes one of the implied conditions, *e.g.* is not of satisfactory quality, then the customer's claim lies under sections 2–5 of the 1982 Act.

4. Contracts for work with materials supplied

Where the main purpose or "substance" of the contract is the **8–06** provision of services then it is not a sale of goods contract even though there is to be a transfer of ownership in some goods (see paragraph 1–12 above). Two examples are construction contracts (where the customer will become owner of the bricks and tiles, etc., used) and repair contracts (where the customer will become owner of any spare parts used). In these cases the first set of implied terms in the 1982 Act will apply in relation to the *goods* supplied under the contract. Suppose an electrician is called in to repair the television and suppose that shortly afterwards the television breaks down again. This could be due to (i) faulty replacement parts fitted by the electrician or (ii) failure to exercise due care and skill by the electrician or (iii) some other reason, such as failure of some other part in the television. Only if it is the first of these will the customer have a claim under the first set of implied terms in the 1982 Act. If his claim relates not to the goods but to the quality of service provided, then the relevant law is that contained in the third set of implied terms in the 1982 Act (paragraph 8–09 below).

Sometimes goods are used (*i.e.* consumed) by someone in the course of providing a service. An example is the use of shampoo or hair-dye by a hairdresser. In cases such as this, there is no transfer to the customer of property (ownership) in the goods. Thus the contract is not governed either by the Sale of Goods Act or by the first set of implied terms in the 1982 Act. In these cases although there are no *statutory* implied terms relating to the goods, it seems that similar terms are implied at common law: *Ingham v. Emes* (1955 CA). So, if for example the hair-dye is not of merchantable (*i.e.* satisfactory) quality and makes the customer's hair fall out, she will have a common law claim.

5. Excepted contracts

8–07   The first set of terms in the 1982 Act are implied in any contract where one person transfers or agrees to transfer property (ownership) in goods to another—section 1(1). There are, however, five categories of contract which are excepted from that—section 1(2). The first three are contracts of sale of goods, hire-purchase contracts and contracts by which property in goods is obtained in exchange for trading stamps. The reason for these exceptions is that each of these three is governed by its own set of statutory implied terms. The relevant statutory provisions are as follows: in the case of sale of goods contracts, sections 12–15 of the Sale Of Goods Act 1979; in the case of hire-purchase agreements, sections 8–11 of the Supply of Goods (Implied Terms) Act 1973 (see paragraph 25–09 below); in the case of trading stamp agreements, section 4 of the Trading Stamps Act 1964. The two other excepted contracts are, first, where the property is transferred under a deed (covenant) gratuitously made and, secondly, any contract intended to operate by way of mortgage, pledge, charge or any other security.

THE SECOND SET—CONTRACTS OF HIRE

8–08   A contract of hire is a contract of bailment. Under it, the hirer (the bailee) obtains possession but not property (*i.e.* not ownership). Since there is no transfer, or agreement to transfer, property (ownership) to the hirer, the first set of implied terms in the 1982 Act is not implied in a hire contract. Sections 6–10 of the Supply of Goods and Services Act 1982 apply to contracts of hire, other than hire-purchase agreements. The intention behind them is to imply in hire contracts, terms similar to those implied in sale of goods contracts by sections 12–15 of the Sale of Goods Act. In fact the implied terms as to description (section 8), satisfactory quality and fitness for purpose (section 9) and sample (section 10) are identical in effect to the corresponding Sale of Goods Act provisions. Section 7 of the 1982 Act contains (i) a condition as to title, namely that the bailor has (or, in the case of an agreement to bail in the future, will have) a right to transfer possession to the bailee (hirer) for the period of the hire, and (ii) a warranty of quiet possession during the period of the hire except in so far as the bailee's (hirer's) possession may be disturbed by someone entitled to the benefit of any charge or encumbrance disclosed or known to the bailee (hirer) before the contract.

THE THIRD SET—CONTRACTS FOR SERVICES

The third set of terms is implied into any contract where one party (the supplier) has agreed to carry out any service (whether or not he has also agreed to supply goods). By way of exception, however, these terms are not implied in any contract of employment or apprenticeship. It is clear that these terms are implied not only in contracts where the supply of service is the substance of the contract but also in contracts of hire and of sale of goods where, although the substance of the contract is the hire or transfer of owner-ship of goods, there is nevertheless an undertaking by the seller that he will provide a service (*e.g.* of installing the goods). These terms are implied by the Supply of Goods and Services Act 1982, sections 13–15:   **8–09**

> "13. In a contract for the supply of a service where the supplier is acting in the course of a business, there is an implied term that the supplier will carry out the service with reasonable care and skill.
>
> 14.—(1) Where, under a contract for the supply of a service by a supplier acting in the course of a business, the time for the service to be carried out is not fixed by the contract, left to be fixed in manner agreed by the contract or determined by the course of dealing between the parties, there is an implied term that the supplier will carry out the service within a reasonable time.
>
> (2) What is a reasonable time is a question of fact.

15.—(1) Where, under a contract for the supply of a service, the consideration for the service is not determined by the contract, left to be determined in a manner agreed by the contract or determined by the course of dealing between the parties, there is an implied term that the party contracting with the supplier will pay a reasonable charge.

(2) What is a reasonable charge is a question of fact."

The Secretary of State has power by statutory instrument to exclude one or more of the terms in the third set from applying to specified services. One such exclusion order has so far been made, excluding section 13 from applying to :

(i) the services of an advocate in court or before any tribunal, inquiry or arbitrator and in carrying out preliminary work directly affecting the conduct of the hearing; and

(ii) the services rendered to a company by a director of a company in his capacity as such.

The first of these was to prevent section 13 sweeping away the immunity from an action in negligence conferred upon advocates (notably solicitors) by the decision in *Rondel v. Worsley* (1969 HL). The exclusion order was not necessary in order to preserve the immunity of barristers because a barrister does not have a contractual relationship with his client and therefore section 13 would not apply to him anyway. The Advocates' immunity has since been removed by the decision in *Arthur JS Hall & Co. v. Simons* (2000 HL).

The third set of terms does not apply to contracts of employment. The exclusion of section 13 from applying to the services of a director is thus necessary in order to prevent it discriminating unfairly against non-employed directors. If section 13 had applied to directors it would have imposed on them an objective standard of care. That would have been a rather higher standard of care than the law in fact imposes upon directors. This matter is dealt with in books on company law.

CHAPTER 9

PRODUCT LIABILITY

A MANUFACTURER of a defective product may find himself liable   9–01
on any one of a number of grounds. There are five principal
grounds.

1. The contract of sale

Like any other seller of goods, a manufacturer can be liable for
a breach of a term of his contract of sale. This liability benefits
only the immediate purchaser from the manufacturer, because
liability for breach of contract exists only between parties to the
same contract. In the case of direct marketing the immediate
purchaser may be the actual consumer. Where goods are marketed
via wholesaler and retailer the person who buys goods from the
retailer cannot complain that the manufacturer was in breach of
his contract of sale with the wholesaler. He can of course sue
upon his own contract of sale, *i.e.* sue the retailer. The implied
terms in sections 12–15 of the Sale of Goods Act are often seen,
and correctly so, as important safeguards for the consumer.
Nevertheless one must remember that, although they enhance the
purchaser's contractual rights against his seller, they do not confer
upon him any rights against other persons. Indeed, if X buys
goods and passes them as a gift to Y, those implied terms are of
no benefit at all to Y—unless the contract purports to confer that
benefit upon him thereby enabling him to rely on the Contracts
(Rights of Third Parties) Act 1999 (see paragraph 7–03 above).

There is another way, assignment, by which Y can be given the
benefit of the purchaser's (X's) rights against the seller. The most
effective way of doing this is for X to comply with the provisions
of section 136 of the Law of Property Act 1925, *i.e.* to give Y a
written notice, signed by X, unconditionally assigning to Y all
X's rights as buyer under the contract of sale. X can do this at
the time of giving the goods to Y or at any later stage. Of course
in transferring his rights to Y, X is losing them himself. The
consent of the seller is not needed for such an assignment.

However, X cannot without the seller's consent assign his burdens under the contract (*i.e.* the obligation to pay).

2. Collateral contract or guarantee

9–02   Where goods are marketed indirectly and the manufacturer therefore does not sell directly to the consumer, it can nevertheless happen that the manufacturer makes a collateral contract with the consumer. The classic case of this was *Carlill v. Carbolic Smoke Ball Co.* (1893 CA) where the defendants published an advertisement claiming that their product was a cure and preventative of any number of illnesses. In particular, the company promised in the advertisement to pay £100 to anyone who contracted influenza after using a carbolic smoke ball as instructed for a specified period. Mrs Carlill saw the advertisement, purchased a smoke ball, used it as instructed for the specified period and nevertheless caught 'flu. Although she had not bought the smoke ball from the company, it was held that there was a contract between her and the company, albeit not a contract of sale. A contract is a bargain and the bargain was that the company made her the promise in the advertisement and she in return bought one of their smoke balls from a retailer. The company made her an offer in the advertisement which she accepted by buying a smoke ball from a retailer.

It can be seen then that manufacturers' "guarantees" (or "warranties") often form the basis of a contract between manufacturer and customer similar to that in *Carlill v. Carbolic Smoke Ball Co.* It is true that often they do not specify a sum of money and sometimes contain many qualifications. Nevertheless if a guarantee promise (*e.g.* "The goods are warranted to be in perfect condition on leaving the factory") is broken, then the manufacturer is liable, subject to the qualifications in the guarantee. An example of such a qualification might occur where the manufacturer promises to refund the purchase price "provided the goods are first returned carriage paid to manufacturer".

9–03   Sometimes a guarantee does more than qualify the benefits which it gives. It may take away or qualify other rights of the consumer which are quite independent of the guarantee. In particular it may claim to restrict or remove the consumer's ability to bring an action for negligence (see below). This may be achieved by some clause in the guarantee such as "Apart from his obligations under the terms of this guarantee, the manufacturer shall not be liable for any loss howsoever arising". This type of guarantee was in the past commonly created by the manufacturer supplying with the goods a reply paid postcard which the purchaser was asked to fill in and post, thereby accepting its terms. Now, by virtue of section 5 of the Unfair Contract Terms Act 1977, a clause in a manufacturer's or distributor's guarantee cannot operate to exclude or restrict the manufacturer's or distributor's liability to the consumer. This is so provided three conditions are all satisfied:

(i) the goods are of a type ordinarily supplied for private use or consumption;

(ii) they prove defective whilst "in consumer use" (*i.e.* not used exclusively for the purposes of a business);

(iii) the manufacturer or distributor in question is not also the person who sold the goods to the consumer.

This last point seems to suggest that where the consumer buys the goods direct from the manufacturer, the manufacturer is free to exclude his liability. However, this is not necessarily so. In that case, although section 5 of the Unfair Contract Terms Act will not apply, other sections of the same Act are most likely to apply and to prevent the seller from excluding his liability. These other sections will be considered in Chapter 10.

The European Directive on Consumer Guarantees, when implemented, will confirm the validity of manufacturers' guarantees, though not of any exclusion clause which they may contain (see paragraph 7–53 above).

3. Negligence

Donoghue v. Stevenson (1932) was a landmark in legal   **9–04** development. The House of Lords established the principle that a consumer who suffers damage because of a manufacturer's negligence can sue the latter for damages and can do so irrespective of whether the consumer bought the goods. Mrs Donoghue and a friend went into a café. The friend bought for Mrs Donoghue a bottle of ginger beer, manufactured by Stevenson. Mrs Donoghue drank some. When the remainder was poured out, she noticed that the bottle contained two half-decomposed snails. She suffered some shock as well as some gastro-enteritis.

From the consumer's point of view, there is a considerable drawback to an action in negligence; he has to prove that the manufacturer (or one or more of his employees) was negligent.

145

This involves showing that reasonable care was not taken in the manufacture. This can be difficult because the consumer has no means of knowing what goes on (or went on) in the factory. Sometimes it may seem obvious that there must have been negligence, as in the case of the purchaser of a bath bun who found a stone in the middle of it (*Chaproniere v. Mason* (1905 CA)). In such a case, the facts may be said to speak for themselves—*res ipsa loquitur*. Then it is up to the manufacturer to prove that there was no negligence, *i.e.* that all reasonable care was taken. In *Chaproniere v. Mason* the manufacturer brought evidence to show that he had a safe system of operations such as to prevent alien matter entering the food. The Court held that this did not show an absence of negligence since someone must have been careless in not following the proper system. The manufacturer was therefore liable.

A similar situation arose in *Daniels v. White* (1938) where some carbolic acid got into a bottle of lemonade. The consumer pleaded *res ipsa loquitur*. The manufacturer brought evidence that he had a safe system of operating and adequate supervision to ensure that the system was followed. Here it was held that this showed that all reasonable care had been taken. The manufacturer was therefore not liable. However, the reasoning behind the decision in *Daniels v. White* seems questionable. If there was in operation a good system to prevent alien matter entering the lemonade then someone who worked there must have been very negligent if alien matter got in despite the system. An employer is answerable for the negligence of his employees. Therefore in *Daniels v. White* it would seem that the employer (the defendant) ought to have been held liable. The decision has been criticised and in *Hill v. James Crowe* (1978 QBD) MacKenna J. refused to follow it.

It should be pointed out that an action in negligence is not restricted to shock and personal injuries but may also include damage to property or even sometimes purely financial loss.

It should also be pointed out that *Donoghue v. Stevenson* established a principle of wider application than it may so far have appeared. Anyone (whether he is a manufacturer or not) who ought to appreciate that his acts or omissions may well cause harm to another may be liable to that other for any damage caused by his negligence in carrying on those activities.

9–05   Suppose a manufacturer of catapults sells some to a wholesaler, who sells some to a retailer who in turn sells one to a young boy. Suppose also that, because it has a latent defect, the catapult is not of satisfactory quality and that it breaks in use and injures the boy's eye as a result. The boy will no doubt succeed in his claim for breach of contract against the retailer, as will the retailer succeed against the wholesaler and the wholesaler against the manufacturer: *Godley v. Perry* (1960 QB). The retailer's claim against the wholesaler is a claim for indemnity. This simply means that the retailer is entitled to claim from the wholesaler (as damages for breach of contract) the whole amount which the retailer is himself liable to pay his buyer. That is the amount of the retailer's loss arising from the wholesaler's breach of contract. On the same reasoning the wholesaler is entitled to indemnity from the manufacturer. In this way, liability is passed back up the chain of distribution to the manufacturer. What if there is a blockage in the process? This could happen if, for example, the wholesaler has gone out of business or if in the contract between the wholesaler and the retailer there is a valid exemption clause which prevents the wholesaler being liable to the retailer. In this case, the retailer is liable to his buyer, the boy, but now has no contract under which he can recover indemnity. We have already seen that if the defect was due to the negligence of the manufacturer, the boy could himself have sued the manufacturer direct for negligence. That, however, is not much use to the retailer if the boy has chosen instead to sue the retailer for breach of contract. In *Lambert v. Lewis* (1981 HL) Lord Diplock suggested that in that case someone down the chain of distribution who suffers economic loss (*i.e.* because he has to pay out damages for breach of contract), might well be able to claim indemnity direct from the negligent manufacturer under the principle in *Donoghue v. Stevenson.*

4. Product liability

From the consumer's point of view, the drawback to the implied terms in the Sale of Goods Act is that only the buyer can sue the seller. If someone other than the buyer was injured by the goods, the Sale of Goods Act gives him no rights—other than in the exceptional case where the Contracts (Rights of Third Parties) Act 1999 applies (see paragraph 7–03 above). A claim in negligence, on the other hand, can be brought by any consumer. The drawback to this claim is that the defendant (usually the manufacturer) must be shown to have been negligent. Part I of the Consumer Protection Act 1987 implemented the Product Liability Directive (85/374/EEC) and gives the consumer an additional right to make a claim which is free of both these

9–06

drawbacks. Under this Act, anyone who is injured by a defective product can sue the manufacturer, irrespective of whether the manufacturer was negligent. Damage caused to non-business property can be claimed if it exceeds £275 in value. In giving this right, the Act does not remove or alter any other rights of the consumer, *e.g.* under the Sale of Goods Act or the law of negligence.

Basis of the claim—section 2

9–07 To succeed under Part I of the Consumer Protection Act, the plaintiff must establish four things, namely that:

(a) *a product* contained a *defect*;

(b) the plaintiff suffered *damage*;

(c) the damage was caused by the defect;

(d) the defendant was, *producer*, *own-brander* or *importer* into the European Community (or, sometimes, supplier) of the product.

Defect—section 3

9–08 A product is defective "if the safety of the product is not such as persons generally are entitled to expect". Safety includes safety in the context of risks of damage to property as well as in the context of risks of death or personal injury. Thus new furniture would be defective if it contained live woodworm, even though the presence of the woodworm posed no threat of personal injury. Safety is a relative, not an absolute, concept. A sharp kitchen knife cannot be made absolutely safe if it is to be any use as a kitchen knife. If, however, it were marketed as a child's toy or the blade were such that when used to peel potatoes it disintegrated into splinters, then it would not be as safe as people generally were entitled to expect. Thus section 3(2) provides that in determining whether a product is defective all the circumstances are to be taken into account, including:

"(a) the manner in which, and purposes for which, the product has been marketed, its get-up, the use of any mark in relation to the product and any instructions for, or warnings with respect to, doing or refraining from doing anything with or in relation to the product;

(b) what might reasonably be expected to be done with or in relation to the product; and

(c) the time when the product was supplied by its producer to another;

and nothing in this section shall require a defect to be inferred from the fact alone that the safety of a product which is supplied after that time is greater than the safety of the product in question."

As in the knife example earlier, the marketing and/or labelling will affect the use to which the product is likely to be put. Something advertised as a toy is likely to be used by children. If something is advertised and sold as a hover-mower, is it reasonable to expect it to be used as a hedge-trimmer? If not, then it is not defective just because it is dangerous when used in that way.

Public expectations as to safety are to be judged as at the time the *producer* supplied the product in question. A producer is not required to meet expectations of safety which arise after *he* has supplied the product. Suppose manufacturer A has for some years produced a razor which will not normally cut the user unless it is slid sideways across the skin. Suppose that in May 2001 manufacturer B markets a razor which is equally efficient but which will not normally cut the user, even when slid sideways. Imagine that a razor supplied by manufacturer A in February 2000 is bought from a retailer in June 2001 and when used in July 2001 cuts the user's face when slid sideways across it. The fact that manufacturer B produced a safer razor after the razor in question had been supplied by manufacturer A is not enough to enable us to say that manufacturer A's razor was defective. If, however, another user is cut by a razor which manufacturer A supplied after May 2001, this user can point to the safer design of manufacturer B's razor as evidence that the razor which cut him was not as safe as persons were (at the time manufacturer A supplied it) entitled to expect.

Product—section 1(2)

The definition of product is very wide. Thus there is liability **9–09** for defects in virtually anything which might conceivably be considered a product, including goods, electricity, gas and vapours. There is an exception in the case of land.

Liability is imposed for defective goods, not for defective land. "Goods" include "things comprised in land by virtue of being attached to it"—section 45. A building is land. A builder will therefore not be liable under the Act for damage caused by a defect in the building because it was badly built, *e.g.* because the foundations were inadequate, though he might be liable under some other legal provision (*e.g.* negligence or the Defective Premises Act 1972). A brick or tile used in the construction of a building is a thing comprised in land by virtue of being attached to it. Therefore, if a tile, because it is defective, breaks and falls on to a passer-by, the manufacturer of the tile will be liable under the Act.

Under the Act as originally enacted, agricultural produce and game were excluded from liability under the Act unless it had undergone an "industrial process" giving it "essential characteristics". These expressions were not defined in the Act. Presumably the freezing or canning of peas or the turning of meat into sausages would amount to such an industrial process. In that case, the industrial processor was regarded as the producer and could be liable to anyone injured by a defect in the peas or sausages. That is so even if the defect (*e.g.* salmonella) was present in the produce before it reached the industrial processor. These provisions making the industrial processor liable as producer remain. However, in accordance with an amendment to the Product Liability Directive (1999/34/EC) and with effect from December 4, 2000, the immunity (*i.e.* of farmers) from liability in respect of primary agricultural produce and game has been removed. This was done by the Consumer Protection Act 1987 (Product Liability) (Modification) Order 2000.

Damage—section 5

9–10   Under Part I of the 1987 Act damages can be claimed for death or personal injuries and also for loss of, or damage to, property (including land) which is:

    (a) of a description of property ordinarily intended for private use, occupation or consumption; and

    (b) intended by the person suffering the loss or damage mainly for his own private use, occupation or consumption.

Damage to business property cannot be claimed under the Act. Furthermore the claimant cannot claim even for his private (non-business) property loss or damage unless it exceeds £275. This is to prevent trivial claims for property damage. If, however, the amount of damage done to the claimant's private property exceeds £275, then the whole amount is recoverable, including the first £275. (Someone suffering property damage not exceeding £275 may, of course, be able to claim for it in negligence or under the implied terms in the Sale of Goods Act.)

A claim under Part I of the Consumer Protection Act cannot be made for any damage to the defective product itself. Thus if a defective toaster catches fire damaging the house and contents, one adds up the value of the damage done (but not including either the toaster itself or any property used mainly for business purposes, *e.g.* a word-processor). If the value exceeds £275, then it can be claimed under the Act. If the defect had been in a component of the toaster, say the heating element, the result would still be the same unless the heating element had not been supplied as part of the toaster (*e.g.* had been bought as a replacement later). If the defective element had not been supplied with the toaster, then the value of the damage done to the toaster (but not to the element) could be included in the claim. (In this case, of course, the claim would not be against the toaster manufacturer but against the manufacturer of the heating element.) The rule is that one cannot claim for damage to the defective product itself or to any product which was supplied with the defective product comprised within it.

Where a defective product is used as a component by another manufacturer, there will be *two* defective products and *two* producers. Under the Act the claimant can sue either. Whichever he sues, he cannot include a claim for damage done to the component or to the larger item which was supplied with the component comprised in it.

The defendant—section 2

Under the 1987 Act a claim can be brought against the producer, the own-brander or the importer. The producer is the manufacturer. In the case of products (like salt, oil or coal) which are won or abstracted, the person who wins or abstracts them is the producer. In the case of other products (*e.g.* agricultural produce) which are not manufactured, the producer is the farmer

9–11

or the person who carries out an industrial process (*e.g.* freezing) which gives them essential characteristics.

An own-brander is liable if he has own-branded the goods in such a way as to hold himself out as being the producer. If Superstores own-brands the coffee it sells, it can avoid liability by labelling it with a statement such as "Made for Superstores by Coffee Fellers Inc.".

The only importer liable under the Act is the person who imported the product into the European Community. If a product was made in France and brought to England, there is no importer to sue, but only a French producer. If the product was made in the United States and brought to France before being brought to England, then the person who imported it into France is liable. If judgment is obtained in this country against someone in France (or most other Community states), that judgment can be enforced in the country in question by virtue of the Brussels Convention (on Jurisdiction and Enforcement of Judgments) 1968 (see Chapter 16). The same is also true vice versa under the Civil Jurisdiction and Judgments Act 1982.

Where there is a long chain of distribution, the claimant may find it difficult to identify who was the producer or importer into the European Community. He may ask anyone who has supplied the product in question, *e.g.* retailer, wholesaler or distributor, to identify the producer, own-brander or importer into the European Community. If the supplier fails to make the identification and also fails to identify the person who supplied the product to him, the supplier is liable as if he had himself been the producer.

Defences—section 4

9–12   Section 4 provides the following defences:

1. The defect is due to compliance with any statutory requirement or rule of the European Community.

2. The defendant did not supply the product, *e.g.* it was stolen from his premises.

3. The defendant supplied the product otherwise than in the course of a business *and* the defendant did not produce it (or own-brand it or import it into the European Community) with a view to profit. This lets off grandad who makes grandson John a toy and gives

152

it to him for Christmas. Similarly a tourist returning from Japan with a gift for a friend in Britain will not be liable either as supplier or as importer.

4. The defect did not exist in the product at the time it was supplied by the defendant (*i.e.* the producer, own-brander or importer). Thus the defendant would not be liable if chocolates he had made and supplied were poisoned by saboteurs at the retailer's premises.

5. A component manufacturer is not liable where the defect is attributable to the design of the larger product in which the product is included or where the defect is attributable to instructions given by the manufacturer of the larger product. In such circumstances, the defence will not, of course, be available to the producer of the larger product.

6. The "development risks" defence is available where the defendant shows "that the state of scientific and technical knowledge at the relevant time was not such that a producer of products of the same description as the product in question might be expected to have discovered the defect if it had existed in his products while they were under his control". In short, a producer relying on this defence needs to show that the defect was not discoverable at the time he supplied the product. Suppose that in 2001 a pair of gloves supplied by the manufacturer in 1993 is proved to have caused arthritis to the wearer because the gloves were made with polyester. To succeed under the Consumer Protection Act, the claimant would have to establish that in 1993 people generally were entitled to expect the gloves not to carry the risk of causing arthritis (see paragraph 9–08 above). If the claimant can establish that, then the manufacturer will have a defence if he can show that in 1993, given the then state of scientific and technical knowledge, the risk of the polyester causing arthritis was not discoverable. Establishing the defence might be very important to the manufacturer if over the years he has supplied a lot of such gloves and a lot of wearers have suffered arthritis because of them.

9–13   Whichever of these six defences in section 4 is raised, the burden of establishing it rests upon the defendant.

The same is true of the defence of contributory negligence—section 6(1). With this defence the defendant is saying that the claimant has failed to take reasonable care and has thereby been partly responsible for his own injuries, loss or damage. This could apply where the claimant has made an unreasonable use of the product. In fact an unreasonable use of the product might allow the defendant three different arguments in his own defence. So suppose an adult sniffs glue, making himself very ill and subsequently sues the glue manufacturer. The latter could argue:

(i) That there was no defect in the glue, *i.e.* it was as safe as persons generally were entitled to expect. This argument would be especially strong if there were no commercially viable way of producing glue without the risk of toxic fumes and if the container had carried a clear warning of the risks.

(ii) That the claimant's illness was caused not by the alleged defects in the product but entirely by his own decision to sniff the glue.

(iii) That the claimant by his own failure to take reasonable care for his own safety contributed to his own illness.

In this example it is difficult to know which of these arguments would find favour with a court. If either of the first two did so, the defendant would not be liable. If only the third found favour, the damages awarded would be a reduced proportion of what would be awarded for such an illness in the absence of contributory negligence.

Exclusion of liability and limitation

9–14   No exclusion or limitation of liability clause can exclude or limit the liability imposed by Part I of the Consumer Protection Act (section 7).

The rules on limitation are an entirely different matter. These are rules laid down by law which allow a claim to be brought only if legal proceedings are commenced before the expiry of a deadline. There are two such rules which apply to claims for product liability under the Consumer Protection Act:

1. Proceedings must be commenced within three years of when the injury or damage occured or, if the injury, etc., was not discovered until later, within three years of when the claimant became aware of the injury or damage.

2. No proceedings may be commenced more than 10 years after the producer supplied the product. If the own-brander or importer is being sued, then the 10 years run from when *he* supplied the product.

The 10 years begin to run the moment that the particular product in question was supplied by its producer (own-brander or importer). If those 10 years have expired, it is immaterial that the defendant continued—even is still continuing—to manufacture and supply identical products.

5. Part II of the Consumer Protection Act 1987

Part II does four things. First, it empowers the Secretary of **9–15** State to make safety regulations governing the making and supplying of goods, *i.e.* regulations designed to secure that goods are safe, that appropriate information is supplied with them and inappropriate information is not supplied. Thus, for example, regulations may govern the composition or design of goods, may require goods to conform to a certain standard (*e.g.* a British Institute Standard) and may require a warning or instructions to be given with the goods. Some regulations made under earlier Acts continue to be effective under the 1987 Act. They relate to such things as children's nightdresses, carrycot stands, electric blankets, prams and pushchairs, cosmetics, colour coding of electrical appliances and upholstered furniture. The regulations will sometimes affect only a manufacturer (*e.g.* where they govern design or composition). Other regulations may affect any supplier, whether manufacturer, wholesaler or retailer (*e.g.* regulations requiring information to be supplied with goods). It is a criminal offence to infringe the regulations.

The second thing Part II does is to enable quick action to be **9–16** taken against the marketing of unsafe goods. Section 13 gives the Secretary of State powers to issue two types of instruction:

(i) a "prohibition notice" can be issued to prevent the trader upon whom it is served from supplying any specified type of goods which the Secretary of State considers unsafe;

(ii) a "notice to warn" can require the trader upon whom it is served to take specified steps to warn consumers about unsafe goods which that trader supplies or has already supplied.

A "notice to warn" might well be served, for example, upon a car manufacturer if it appears that a certain model had a dangerous design fault. The notice will specify what steps the manufacturer must take. It may require him to publish a warning in the newspaper or it could, for example, require him to write individually to all purchasers of that model. Failure by a trader to comply with a prohibition notice or notice to warn is a criminal offence.

A prohibition notice can in practice be made only when the fact that there are dangerous goods on the market has come to the attention of the Secretary of State. It has sometimes been the case, however, that unsafe imported goods have been in the shops and bought in considerable quantities before the Secretary of State has learnt of their presence in the country. Hence each enforcement authority (*i.e.* local trading standards department) now has power to serve a "suspension notice" upon a trader where it has reasonable grounds to think legal safety requirements have been infringed—section 14. The notice will prohibit the trader from supplying specified goods for up to six months. If it turns out that there had been no infringement of the law in relation to the goods in question, the trader may be entitled to compensation from the enforcement authority—section 14(7). In order to catch suspect goods at the ports, customs officers have power to seize and detain goods for up to two working days in order to enable local trading standards officers to examine them to determine whether they infringe legal safety requirements—section 31.

9–17 The third aspect of Part II is that section 10 makes it an offence for a trader to supply consumer goods which fail to comply with a general safety requirement. This offence has, however, been rendered virtually redundant by the General Product Safety Regulations 1994. These regulations create an offence similar to that in section 10 and are explained at paragraph 9–20 below.

The fourth aspect of Part II of the Consumer Protection Act **9–18** relates to civil liability. The Act entitles a consumer to bring an action for damages against any trader in respect of damage or loss suffered by the consumer because of an infringement by the trader of safety regulations. Thus a child whose nightdress catches fire because when supplied it did not comply with the safety regulations will be able to claim compensation for her burns from the manufacturer. This is so even if she did not buy it direct from the manufacturer (or, indeed, even if she did not buy it). She does not have to prove any negligence on the part of the manufacturer and does not even have to rely upon the product liability provisions of Part I of the Act. Civil liability under the Act cannot be excluded or restricted by any exemption clause.

Criminal and civil liability under Part II of the Consumer **9–19** Protection Act attaches only to persons who are acting "in the course of carrying on a business". The defendant in *Southwark London Borough v. Charlesworth* (1983 DC) was a shoe repairer who also carried on a secondary business as seller of second-hand goods. At his shop he sold an electric fire which infringed safety regulations (under the Consumer Protection Act 1961). The fire had come from his home and the money from the sale of the fire did not go through the books of the business. Nevertheless, there was no differentiation in the shop between the fire and other goods he was selling in his secondary line of business. That being so, the court held that the sale was a sale in the course of a business. The result might have been different if there had been a notice attached to the goods making it clear that these goods had nothing to do with the defendant's business as a dealer in second-hand goods but had come from his home and that the sale of the goods was to be a private transaction.

6. The General Product Safety Regulations 1994

These Regulations implement the Directive on General Product **9–20** Safety (92/59/EC). They create criminal offences which are concerned with the marketing of unsafe products. Regulation 5 prevents any overlap with the criminal offence created by section 10 of the Consumer Protection Act 1987. It makes the offences in the Regulations the primary offences. The Regulations potentially apply (and section 10 does not apply) if a product:

(i) is placed on the market by a producer; or

(ii) is supplied by a distributor.

For this purpose, placing on the market includes offering or agreeing to place on the market or exposing or possessing a product to place on the market. Supplying includes offering or agreeing to supply or exposing or possessing a product to be supplied.

Scope of the Regulations

9–21   The Regulations apply to the situation where a producer, in the course of a commercial activity, places on the market any product intended for consumers or likely to be used by consumers. They also impose requirements of care on a distributor of such a product.

- By regulation 7, the producer commits an offence if he "places a product on the market" which is not a "safe" product.

- By regulation 9(a) a distributor commits an offence if he does not act with due care in order to help ensure compliance with regulation 7.

This latter requires, for example, that a distributor does not supply any products "which he knows, or should have presumed, on the basis of the information in his possession and as a professional, are dangerous". The Regulations do not apply to any product which is used exclusively in the context of a commercial activity, *e.g.* a machine tool supplied to be used in a factory, or a typewriter to be used by a firm's secretary. Of course, if that same typewriter were instead sold direct to the secretary for her private use at home, then the Regulations would apply. " 'Commercial activity' includes a business and a trade." This expression does not expressly include a profession. Apparently, for example, if that same typewriter were supplied for use in the parish office of a church that would still be within the Regulations, since presumably the church could not be said to be a business or a trade.

9–22   There is only a very short list of products excluded from the Regulations. Second-hand goods, demonstration models and reconditioned goods are all included. The only products excluded are:

- second-hand *antiques:*

- products supplied *for* repair or reconditioning before use, provided the supplier clearly informs the customer to that effect;

- any product where there are specific provisions in the rules of Community law governing *all* aspects of the safety of the product.

Meaning of "safe"

Safety is defined in terms of risk to persons, not property. A **9–23** safe product "means any product which, under normal or reasonably foreseeable conditions of use, including duration, does not present any risk or only the minimum risk compatible with the product's use, considered as acceptable and consistent with a high level of protection for the safety and health of persons". Few products will be considered totally safe. It is enough, however, if three requirements are satisfied: (i) the risks presented are the minimum risk compatible with the product's use; (ii) those risks are "acceptable"; (iii) those risks are consistent with a high level of protection for the safety and health of persons. The following factors, in particular, are to be taken into account:

- the characteristics and composition of the product, its packaging and instructions for assembly and maintenance;

- its effect on other products, where it is reasonably foreseeable that it will be used with other products;

- its presentation, labelling, any instructions for use and disposal and any other information provided by the producer;

- the categories of consumers at serious risk when using the product, especially children.

Obviously articles such as toys that are likely to be used by children will have to be safe for that group of consumers. The reference to instructions for disposal leaves open the possibility of a product being found to be unsafe because of the risks it poses when it is to be disposed of, *i.e.* after its useful life is over. This could well catch products which contain toxic chemicals. The reference to a product being used with other products might well apply, for example, to a shelf support bracket. Clearly such a bracket is likely to be used together with other products, *i.e.* the shelf and the items to be placed on the shelf. The strength of the bracket will in that situation clearly be a feature of its safety.

9–24   The giving of information is a key feature. Thus regulation 8 requires a producer to provide information to enable consumers to assess the risks inherent in it throughout the normal or reasonably foreseeable period of its use, where those risks are not immediately apparent without adequate warnings. It also requires producers to take measures, commensurate with the characteristics of the product, to enable consumers to be informed of risks and to enable the producer, if necessary, to withdraw the product. In the case of many products, this in effect requires the producer to use a batch number system, so that different batches of the product can be identified from a mark or number on the product itself. It may also require sample testing of marketed products, the investigation of complaints and keeping distributors informed of risks which materialise after marketing.

In relation to many products there are published standards. Sometimes these are embodied in safety regulations, or they may be Community technical specifications, or they may be national voluntary standards, or contained in codes of good practice, etc. There is no absolute defence in respect of a product which complies with safety regulations. There is in that case, however, a presumption, until the contrary is proved, that the product is safe. So far as concerns other types of standards, these are things to be taken into account in determining the safety which consumers may reasonably expect and hence whether the risks presented by the product are acceptable.

Who is liable?

9–25   Primarily, it is the "producer". There are, however, various people who may be regarded as the producer and thus liable. They are: the manufacturer provided that the manufacturer is established in the European Community; any own-brander in the Community (*i.e.* someone who presents himself as the manufacturer by affixing to the product his name, trade mark or other distinctive mark); anyone reconditioning the product; the importer of the product into the Community (*i.e.* if the manufacturer is not himself established, and has no representative established, in the Community); the manufacturer's established representative in the Community. As seen above, a distributor also can be liable, *i.e.* for failing to act with due care to help to ensure compliance.

Defences

The defence of due diligence is available to anyone charged **9–26** with an offence under the Regulations. The defence is commonly found in consumer protection legislation and is for example, also a defence to someone charged with an offence under section 10 of the Consumer Protection Act or under safety regulations. It is that the defendant took all reasonable steps and exercised all due diligence to avoid committing the offence. An importer or wholesaler will not be able to rely on this defence if he has taken no steps to require his supplier to supply goods which correspond with the relevant legal requirements. This may mean not only placing specific contractual obligations upon his supplier but also making tests on more than infrequent random samples of the goods supplied: *Riley v. Webb* (1987 DC); and *Rotherham M.B.C. v. Raysun* (1988 DC).

The amount of care required before the defendant can be said to have taken all reasonable steps and exercised all due diligence will be a question of fact in each case. In a situation where the defendant had imported goods from a source (*e.g.* the German wine industry) where there is a known thorough system of verification and testing to see the correct standard has been reached, he may not be expected to sample at all: *Hurley v. Martinez* (1991 DC). When considering whether he should sample, the degree of risk to be guarded against is an important factor. Thus, it is noticeable that in cases (such as *Rotherham M.B.C. v. Raysun*) where the defendant is relying on the defence of due diligence to a consumer safety charge, the court is much more likely to demand a thorough sampling system than it is in cases (such as *Hurley v. Martinez*) where the defendant is relying on the same defence to a misleading statement charge. In *Hurley v. Martinez*, the defendant was charged over a misstatement of the alcoholic strength (as 8 per cent instead of 7.2 per cent) on German wine.

Of course, taking steps to ensure that goods comply with a British Standards specification is not capable of being sufficient to satisfy the defence of due diligence, unless compliance with the

British Standards specification will automatically involve compliance with the provisions (*e.g.* of the Toys (Safety) Regulations 1989) under which the proceedings are brought: *Balding v. Lew Ways Ltd* (1995 DC).

9–27   By way of exception, a distributor who is charged with an offence, under the Regulations, of failing to act with due care to help ensure compliance with the requirement that the product is safe, will not be able to rely upon the defence of due diligence unless, within the limits of his activities, he has participated in monitoring the safety of the products placed on the market, in particular by passing on information on product risks and co-operating in any action taken to avoid those risks. Thus, for example, a car dealer who failed to co-operate in attempts to recall a model identified as being within a defective batch would not be able to rely upon the defence.

Prohibition notices, notices to warn suspension notices

9–28   Prohibition notices, notices to warn and suspension notices are all notices which can be issued under the terms of the Consumer Protection Act 1987. The Regulations make it clear that the powers to issue those notices extend also to products within the meaning of the Regulations, *i.e.* to products intended for consumers to use or likely to be used by consumers. For an explanation of those three kinds of notice, see paragraph 9–16 above.

CHAPTER 10

EXEMPTION CLAUSES AND UNFAIR TERMS

AN exemption clause is a term of the contract intended to exclude **10–01** or restrict the liability of one of the parties, usually the seller. Sometimes a seller is so financially powerful that he can blatantly insist on such a clause being included in the contract; he can adopt a "take it or leave it" attitude. More common is the seller who, having inserted an exclusion clause into his conditions of sale, relies on his buyer not bothering to read (or not understanding) the small print; for example, the exclusion clause may be contained in the small print of a guarantee which he gives to the buyer.

An exemption clause may, contrary to appearances, have little or no effect. Such clauses are not looked upon with favour either by the courts or by Parliament. They are subject to several common law rules evolved by the courts as well as to certain pieces of legislation. In this respect the Unfair Contract Terms Act 1977 is particularly important. This Act will be considered later in the chapter. At the moment it is worth recording that section 55 (1) of the Sale of Goods Act reads:

> "Where a right, duty or liability would arise under a contract of sale of goods by implication of law, it may (subject to the Unfair Contract Terms Act 1977) be negatived or varied by express agreement, or by the course of dealing between the parties, or by such usage as binds both parties to the contract."

As well as the 1977 Act there are the Unfair Terms in Consumer Contracts Regulations 1999. These Regulations render invalid certain exemption clauses and also other terms of the contract which are unfair. These Regulations will be considered at the end of this chapter. Before turning to the 1977 Act and the 1999 Regulations we shall first examine the common law rules relating to incorporation, misrepresentation, privity of contract and scope of the clause.

INCORPORATION

10–02   A clause is of no effect unless it is incorporated (included) as a term in the contract. It must be incorporated when the contract is made. Any attempt to incorporate it after the contract is made will be unsuccessful. Thus a document which is first brought to the purchaser's notice after the contract is made will not incorporate into the contract terms printed on the document. It is for this reason that a seller will usually be unable to rely on an exclusion clause printed on a receipt. Receipts are not usually handed over until after the purchaser has paid (*i.e.* after the contract has been made). This rule, that a clause cannot subsequently be incorporated, was applied in *Olley v. Marlborough Court* (1949 CA). There the claimant had booked in at the reception desk of a hotel and only subsequently, on entering her room, did she discover behind the door a notice which claimed to exclude the hotel's liability for guests' property. The Court of Appeal held that the notice was not incorporated in the contract, since it was not displayed at a spot visible to claimant before she made the contract. The defendant would have been better advised to display his notice in a prominent position near the reception desk.

We can now consider individually the different methods of incorporation.

Oral agreement between buyer and seller

10–03   This method is not commonly used for two main reasons. First, it involves bringing the exclusion directly to the attention of the buyer. Secondly, there may be difficulty in proving that the buyer orally agreed to the exclusion.

Signed contractual document

10–04   The buyer will find it difficult to argue that the clause was not agreed upon if it is contained in a document signed by him. It will not help him to plead that he had not read the clause or was unaware of its existence. In *L'Estrange v. Graucob* (1934 CA) a café proprietress bought a vending machine on the terms of a sales agreement which she signed without having read. Although she had been unaware that the small print contained a wide exclusion clause, the Court of Appeal held that the clause protected the seller from liability in respect of defects in the machine.

A clause will not be incorporated by a document which is not a contractual document. A document will be "contractual" if a reasonable person in the position of the prospective buyer would expect it to contain terms affecting his rights and liabilities. A buyer who has taken the formal step of signing a document will therefore find it difficult to show that it was not a contractual document.

Unsigned contractual document

There are two significant differences between signed and unsigned documents. First, an exclusion clause in an unsigned document is not incorporated unless at the time of making the contract either the buyer was aware of its existence or else reasonable steps had been taken to bring it to his attention. The harsher the clause, the greater the effort needed to bring it to the attention of the buyer (see *Interfoto Picture Library v. Stiletto Visual Programmes*, paragraph 7–06 above). In *A.E.G. Ltd v. Logic Resource Ltd* (1995 CA), the seller's confirmation of order form stated "Orders are subject to our conditions of sale—for extract see reverse". The term which excluded liability for breach of the implied terms in the Sale of Goods Act and left the buyer with no choice but to return defective goods was not included in the extract on the reverse. The Court of Appeal held that insufficient steps had been taken to bring the exclusion clause to the buyer's attention and therefore the clause was not incorporated into the contract. Secondly, in the case of an unsigned document the buyer may find it easier to establish that it was not a contractual document. In *Chapelton v. Barry U.D.C.* (1940 CA) Mr Chapelton wanted to hire a deck chair on the beach. He saw a pile of them and a notice nearby, "Hire of chairs 2d. per session of three hours". The notice continued by "respectfully requesting" the hirer to obtain a ticket from the attendant. This he did. He later brought an action claiming damages for injuries he received when his chair collapsed. As a defence, the Council pleaded an exemption clause printed on the back of the ticket. As Mr Chapelton had obtained his ticket from the attendant at the time of making the contract (*i.e.* when he collected his chair from the pile), the ticket had changed hands in sufficient time. The Court of Appeal rejected the Council's defence on the ground, not that the ticket changed hands too late, but that it was not a contractual document; for no reasonable person would expect to

10–05

find contractual terms in a document which was no more than a receipt for him to prove that he had paid and which in many instances (*i.e.* in the absence of the attendant) would not change hands until long after the contract was made.

Displayed notices

10–06   As with an unsigned contractual document, this method of incorporation will work only if at the time of making the contract the buyer actually knew of the existence of the terms or else reasonable steps had been taken to bring them to his attention. Thus the notice must be reasonably large and prominently displayed at a spot visible to the buyer when the contract is made. Exactly what amounts to "reasonable steps" is a question of fact in each case. The wider and more drastic the clause, the more care must be taken to bring it to the buyer's attention.

Even if reasonable steps have been taken to bring the exemption clause to the notice of the buyer, it will not be incorporated if it does not clearly cover the particular transaction in question. In *D & M Trailers (Halifax) Ltd v. Stirling* (1978 CA) an extensive exemption clause was included in the conditions of sale posted up around an auction room. One of these conditions stated, " 'Sale' used in these conditions shall include sale by private treaty as well as sale by auction". Mr Stirling attended the auction and bought some vehicles. On returning a day or two later to pay for them, he saw in the yard a Scania tractor which had been included but not sold at the auction which he had attended. He spoke privately with the auctioneers and agreed to buy the Scania (*i.e.* he agreed by private treaty and not in an auction). The Scania soon proved to be seriously defective and not of satisfactory quality. The buyer's claim for breach of condition succeeded. The Court held that the exemption clause, though it had been incorporated in the auction sales, had not been incorporated in the later sale by private treaty. This was a separate transaction from the auction and the auctioneers had not made it clear that the exemption clause was being incorporated into it.

Previous course of dealing

10–07   If, in the past, parties have regularly made contracts with each other upon the same terms (including exempting terms), then that course of dealing can incorporate those same terms into a later contract between them. This later contract must be merely the latest in the established course of dealing. Thus three requirements must be satisfied before a course of dealing can incorporate an exemption clause into a later contract:

(i) The transactions between the parties must have been sufficiently numerous to constitute a "course of dealing".

(ii) The established course of dealing must have been consistent.

(iii) The established course of dealing must not have been deviated from on the occasion in question.

In *Hollier v. Rambler Motors* (1972 CA) the first of these requirements was not satisfied. The Court of Appeal held that three or four transactions in the course of five years were not sufficient to establish a course of dealing.

In *Kendall v. Lillico* (1969 HL) all the requirements were fulfilled. Just as he had done on over 100 occasions during the previous three years, the seller sold some animal food to the buyer. As had always previously happened, they made an oral agreement followed by the seller giving to the buyers a "sold note" which had on the back an exclusion clause. Plainly the clause was not on this occasion incorporated by virtue of the sold note, which had been handed over only after the bargain was struck. However, there had been a long and consistent course of dealing which was adhered to on this occasion. It was by virtue of this that the clause was incorporated. The House of Lords held this to be so, even though the buyers were unaware of the precise terms on the sold notes. Lord Pearce said:

"The only reasonable inference from the regular course of dealing over so long a period is that the buyers were evincing an acceptance of, and a readiness to be bound by, the printed conditions of whose existence they were well aware although they had not troubled to read them."

Trade usage

Whereas a course of dealing can incorporate a term that has in effect become customary between the two parties in question, trade usage can incorporate a term that has become a custom amongst all the buyers and sellers dealing in the environment in question. In the latter case there is no need for the particular   **10–08** seller and buyer to have dealt previously with each other, or, indeed, previously in the particular environment. It is sufficient that the custom was established in the market in which on this occasion the buyer bought from the seller. By dealing in this market, they are taken, unless they expressly agreed otherwise, to have been dealing in accordance with all the customs of the market. Thus in *Cointat v. Myham* (1913 CA) where the claimant bought bad meat in the Central London Meat Market, it was held that any warranty as to the fitness or quality of the meat was excluded, because there was an established custom of the market to that effect.

Overriding oral warranty

10–09   An exclusion clause which would otherwise be incorporated by one of the methods referred to above may nevertheless be overriden by later statements made by the seller to the buyer. The plaintiff in *Harling v. Eddy* (1951 CA) bought a heifer at a cattle auction. One of the printed conditions of sale in the auction catalogue was that no warranty was given in respect of any animal sold. However, when there had been some difficulty in getting the bidding started, the seller announced that there was nothing wrong with the heifer and he would absolutely guarantee her. After this the heifer was knocked down to the claimant. The Court of Appeal held that the oral statement overrode the exclusion clause which therefore did not form part of the contract.

MISREPRESENTATION

10–10   The seller cannot rely on any exclusion clause, no matter what liability it claims to exclude, to the extent that he or his agent has misrepresented the effect of the clause. In *Curtis v. Chemical Dyeing Co.* (1951 CA) the claimant took a wedding dress to the defendants for cleaning. The shop assistant asked her to sign a receipt, telling her that this was because the cleaners took no responsibility for damage to beads and sequins on the dress. In fact this was literally true but the clause on the receipt went further. It claimed to exempt the defendants from liability for "any damage howsoever caused". The claimant signed the receipt without reading it. The assistant had not deliberately or knowingly misled the claimant. Nevertheless she had, by revealing part of the clauses's effect, concealed its full effect. This amounted to a misrepresentation. The Court of Appeal held the defendants liable in negligence for damage caused to the dress. The misrepresentation, albeit an innocent one, "was a sufficient misrepresentation to disentitle the cleaner from relying on the exemption, except in regard to beads and sequins".

PRIVITY OF CONTRACT

The privity of contract principle is that someone who is not privy to (*i.e.* not a party to) a contract can neither rely upon the contract nor be bound by it. Generally, a contract can affect the rights and liabilities only as between the parties to it. Thus an exclusion clause in a contract is a defence available, generally, only to a contracted party and only against the other contracted party: *Scruttons v. Midland Silicones* (1962 HL). The Contracts (Rights of Third Parties) Act 1999, however, creates a limited exception whereby a third party, who is described or identified in the contract, can rely on an exclusion clause if either (a) the parties expressly provide that he may or (b) the exclusion clause purports to enable the third party to rely on it (see paragraph 7–03 above). Consider a common situation: a manufacturer sells a number of his products to a wholesaler, the wholesaler sells some of them to a retailer and the retailer sells one of them to a consumer. Here there are three separate contracts of sale. If the product proves to be defective, then this could give rise to three separate claims for damages for breach of contract—one by the consumer against the retailer, one by the retailer against the wholesaler and one by the wholesaler against the manufacturer. There is a chain of contracts and a breach of one may well cause a chain reaction, *i.e.* a breach of each of the others—see paragraph 9–05 above. The law does not allow the consumer to ignore the intermediate links in the chain. He cannot sue the manufacturer for breach of the latter's contract of sale. However, in certain circumstances, the law of tort gives a consumer a right to sue a manufacturer with whom he has no contract (see Chapter 9). In our example, if the manufacturer was careless in the manufacture of his product and this had injured the consumer, the latter will have a claim (in the law of tort) in negligence against the manufacturer even though he did not buy the goods from him. Whilst an exclusion clause in the manufacturer's contract of sale could provide the manufacturer with a good defence to a claim by the wholesaler, it would provide him with no defence to a claim in negligence by the consumer. Similarly, an exclusion clause in

10–11

the contract between the retailer and the consumer could not be relied upon by the manufacturer—unless the clause or contract purported to confer that right on the manufacturer. In the latter case the clause might nevertheless be rendered ineffective by the Unfair Contract Terms Act 1977.

10–12   Sometimes a manufacturer sells directly to a member of the public, *e.g.* by mail order or by door-to-door salesman. In such a case an exclusion clause could, if appropriately worded (and, again, subject to the provisions of the Unfair Contract Terms Act), provide the manufacturer with a good defence against a claim by the purchaser in negligence. However, someone other than the purchaser could be injured on account of the article's negligent manufacture and an exclusion clause would provide no defence in an action brought by him against the manufacturer. Furthermore, a manufacturer can now be liable to his immediate purchaser or to anyone else who is caused injury (or private property damage) by a defective product. This liability, under Part I of the Consumer Protection Act 1987, cannot be limited or excluded at all—see paragraphs 9–06 to 9–14 above.

SCOPE OF THE CLAUSE

10–13   An exclusion clause is construed *contra proferentem, i.e.* narrowly against the interest of the person relying upon it. An exclusion clause is usually inserted for the sole benefit of one of the parties: in a contract of sale, the seller. The court, in interpreting the clause, leans against the seller. If the clause is ambiguous, the court will adopt the meaning less favourable to the seller and any ground of liability not clearly excluded will remain. In *Andrews v. Singer* (1934 CA) the claimant made a written contract to buy a "new Singer car". The car delivered to him had in fact done a considerable mileage. It was held that a clause excluding all "implied conditions and warranties" did not exclude the seller's liability for breach of the *express* condition that he would supply a "new" car. A further illustration is to be found in *Wallis & Wells v. Pratt and Haynes* (1911 HL) where the House of Lords held that the clause "Sellers give no warranty, express or implied" did not exclude conditions. A clause which does not expressly mention conditions will not normally exclude liability for breach of condition.

Old approach to interpretation

Until the 1970s there was no statutory control upon exemption **10–14** clauses. So, if an exemption clause was part of the contract and if on its wording it excused one party from a given liability, then the court had to give effect to the clause, *i.e.* that party (usually the seller) had a valid defence. That is what happened in *L'Estrange v. Graucob* (paragraph 10–04 above). The courts, however, did not very much like this sort of result and, when interpreting an exemption clause, used to adopt a hostile approach. There were two particular aspects to this. First the court would sometimes place a strained or tortured meaning on the words of the exemption clause in order to deprive it of effect. Secondly, the courts developed the doctrine of fundamental breach of contract. According to this doctrine, a party who had committed a fundamental breach of contract could not (at least, sometimes could not) rely for his defence upon an exemption clause. This doctrine was never, however, approved by the House of Lords.

New approach to interpretation

As will be explained later in this chapter, Parliament in the **10–15** 1970s passed legislation which renders certain exemption clauses absolutely ineffective and imposes a test of reasonableness on many others. This means that, even though an exemption clause on its wording apparently provides a defence, it may nevertheless be ineffective. This enabled the court to adopt a less hostile approach to the interpretation of the wording of exemption clauses.

In *Photo Production Ltd v. Securicor Transport Ltd* (1980) the House of Lords swept away the doctrine that a fundamental breach of contract could prevent an exemption clause from providing a defence. Their Lordships overruled earlier decisions saying otherwise. After the *Photo Production* case there were two more decisions of the House of Lords, *Ailsa Craig Fishing Co. Ltd v. Malvern Fishing Co. Ltd* (1983) and *George Mitchell Ltd v. Finney Lock Seeds Ltd* (1983). From this trilogy of cases the modern approach to the interpretation of exemption clauses emerged.

Exemption clauses are still construed *contra proferentem*, *i.e.* if **10–16** a clause is ambiguous the court will adopt the meaning which is less favourable to the party (usually the seller) wishing to rely upon the clause. The court will not, however, read an ambiguity into clear words by giving them a strained or tortured meaning.

Clear and plain words will be given their clear meaning. One aspect of the *contra proferentem* rule is that, if there is more than one possible head of liability one of which is liability for negligence, then an exemption clause will not be interpreted as excluding liability for negligence unless it does so in clear terms. For example a manufacturer who sells his goods to a wholesaler may in the contract exclude his liability in respect of defects in the goods. This clause might well be interpreted as excluding the manufacturer's liability to the wholesaler under the implied terms as to satisfactory quality and fitness for purpose. In the absence of clear words, however, it will not be interpreted as excluding the manufacturer's liability to the wholesaler for negligence (*i.e.* under the principle in *Donoghue v. Stevenson*, see paragraph 9–04 above). On the other hand the *Ailsa Craig* case established that the *contra proferentem* rule is not applied quite as rigorously in interpreting clauses which merely *limit* the defendant's (usually the seller's) liability, as it is to clauses which claim to *exclude* his liability.

10–17   In *George Mitchell Ltd v. Finney Lock Seeds Ltd* some farmers contracted to buy from some seed merchants 30lb of Finney's "Late Dutch Special" cabbage seed. Unknown to the buyers, the sellers negligently delivered the wrong seed. The buyers planted the seed but only leaves came up and the crop proved worthless, causing the buyers a loss of £61,000. In defence to a claim for that loss, the sellers sought to rely upon a contractual clause limiting the sellers' liability to the cost of replacement of the seeds, *i.e.* the clause excluded the sellers' liability for any consequential loss arising from "use or failure in performance of or any defect in any seeds or plants supplied or for any other loss or damage whatsoever", except for the cost of replacement of the seed. In interpreting the clause, their Lordships observed that this was a limitation of liability clause and not a complete exclusion clause. They unanimously held that on its wording it *limited* the sellers' liability to the cost of replacing the seed. That was so even though the breach of contract had been a negligent one. That, however, did not mean that the clause necessarily gave the sellers a valid defence because the clause still had to satisfy the legislation on exemption clauses (see further paragraph 10–28 below).

UNFAIR CONTRACT TERMS ACT 1977

10–18   The Unfair Contract Terms Act 1977 is a major landmark in the development of the law of contract. It deals with exemption clauses and it replaced and greatly extended certain provisions previously in the Supply of Goods (Implied Terms) Act 1973. The 1973 Act was confined to exemption clauses which claimed to exclude or restrict the statutory implied terms relating to title, description, quality and sample (implied by sections 12–15 of the Sale of Goods Act). The 1977 Act places severe curbs upon the effectiveness of exemption clauses of many sorts. The 1977 Act does not, however, deal with liability under the Consumer Protection Act 1987 (explained at paragraphs 9–06 to 9–14 and 9–18 above). The Consumer Protection Act itself provides, in sections 7 and 41(4), that such liability cannot be excluded or limited.

Two preliminary matters must be explained. First, the 1977 Act applies to exemption clauses and these include not only clauses which claim to exclude liability for breach of contract but also (by section 13 of the 1977 Act) those which claim:

(i) to prevent liability from arising in the first place (*e.g.* "Seller gives no warranty as to fitness for purpose or satisfactory quality");

(ii) to restrict liability (*e.g.* to a maximum amount);

(iii) to restrict the buyer's remedies (*e.g.* to prevent him from rejecting the goods and to confine him to damages for breach of condition);

(iv) to restrict the time within which a remedy may be claimed (*e.g.* "No claims to be made more than six weeks after purchase"). The general rule is that a claim for damages for breach of contract can be brought at any time up to six years after the breach occurred. If the claim is for personal injuries the period is reduced to three years. A clause claiming to shorten these periods is an exemption clause;

(v) to make the enforcement of any remedy subject to a restrictive condition (*e.g.* "Seller accepts no liability unless the goods are first returned to him carriage paid").

The other preliminary matter is that the Unfair Contract Terms **10–19** Act 1977 does not tell you whether the seller is liable. To put it another way, it does not alter the basis of liability. It simply curbs the effectiveness of exemption clauses. Suppose a contract of sale contains an exemption clause; suppose also that exemption clause is rendered ineffective by the Unfair Contract Terms Act. There still remains the question "What, if any, is the liability of the seller?" That question can be answered only by examining the express and implied terms of the contract, including those implied by the Sale of Goods Act. Now let us turn to exemption clauses and the effect upon them of the provisions of the Unfair Contract Terms Act.

Section 55(1) of the Sale of Goods Act was quoted at paragraph 10–01 above. It allows an exemption clause to take effect subject to the common law rules already outlined and subject also to the provisions of the Unfair Contract Terms Act 1977. We shall examine first the effect of the 1977 Act upon exemption clauses which claim to exempt from liability under the statutory implied terms as to title, description, quality and sample and then its effect upon other exemption clauses.

Exemption from sections 12–15 of the Sale of Goods Act—section 6

10–20   Section 6 of the Unfair Contract Terms Act applies to any clause claiming to exempt the seller from any of the terms implied by sections 12–15 of the Sale of Goods Act, *i.e.* the terms as to title description, satisfactory quality, fitness for purpose and sample. The effect of section 6 depends upon whether the buyer was "dealing as a consumer".

Consumer deals

10–21   In any case where the buyer "deals as consumer" it is impossible for the seller to exempt himself from any of his liability under sections 12–15 of the Sale of Goods Act. Section 12 of the Unfair Contract Terms Act tells us when a buyer "deals as consumer";

> "(1) A party to a contract "deals as consumer" in relation to another party if—
>   (a) he neither makes the contract in the course of a business nor holds himself out as doing so; and
>   (b) the other party does make the contract in the course of a business; and
>   (c) ...the goods passing under or in pursuance of the contract are of a type ordinarily supplied for private use or consumption.

(2) But on a sale by auction or by competitive tender the buyer is not in any circumstances to be regarded as dealing as consumer.

(3) Subject to this, it is for those claiming that a party does not deal as consumer to show that he does not.''

Thus the following are not consumer deals:

(i) The sale of goods for the purpose of resale by the purchaser to a wholesaler, retailer or distributor.

(ii) The sale of goods for use by the purchaser in an industrial process, *e.g.* manufacturing.

(iii) The sale of goods for use by the purchaser in the running of his business, *e.g.* a typewriter for use in a firm's office.

(iv) The sale of goods by a private individual.

(v) The sale of goods by auction or competitive tender.

Clearly the sale of cigarettes to a publican for the purpose of resale across the counter is not a consumer sale. It may be that the sale of cigarettes for the same purpose to a working men's club is a consumer sale. Cigarettes are a type of goods ordinarily bought for private use or consumption and it has been held (for the purpose of the Trade Descriptions Act 1968) that a private members' club is not a business: *John v. Matthews* (1970 DC), see paragraph 18–04 below.

The question as to whether the contract was a consumer deal **10–22** arose in *Rasbora Ltd v. J.C.L. Marine Ltd* (1977 QBD). A contract was made between a Mr Atkinson and J.C.L. Marine Ltd, a Norfolk boat builder, for J.C.L. Marine to build a boat for Mr Atkinson. This contract included a clause claiming to exclude the sellers' (J.C.L. Marine's) liability for breach of the statutory implied terms as to quality and fitness for purpose. Subsequently Rasbora Ltd, a company incorporated in Jersey, was substituted as buyer in place of Mr Atkinson. This was done by novation, *i.e.* by agreement between Mr Atkinson, J.C.L. Marine Ltd and Rasbora Ltd. A novation is an extinguishing of rights under the earlier contract and the creation of a new contract. Rasbora Ltd was wholly owned by Mr Atkinson and, being a Jersey company, did not have to pay VAT (valued added tax) on the boat. Shortly after it was purchased, the boat caught fire and sank off

Dungeness. The buyers, Rasbora Ltd, sued the sellers for breach of the implied term as to merchantable (now satisfactory) quality. The sellers tried to rely upon the exemption clause. The judge held that the contract originally made between Mr Atkinson and J.C.L. Marine was a consumer deal and that the new one made between Rasbora Ltd and J.C.L. Marine was also a consumer deal, *i.e.* that the novation did not alter the consumer nature of the contract. How was it that a limited company made a contract otherwise than in the course of its business? His Lordship pointed out that Rasbora Ltd had been formed by Mr Atkinson for the purpose of buying the boat and with the intention that the boat was to be used only by Mr Atkinson and his friends; there was no intention to hire it out. It being a consumer deal, the condition as to merchantable quality could not be excluded and the sellers were therefore liable.

10–23   In *R & B Customs Brokers v. United Dominions Trust* (1988) the Court of Appeal held that a company making a purchase (or sale) was not doing so "in the course of a business" unless it made that type of purchase (or sale) regularly. A company (whose business was shipping brokerage) had bought a car for the use of its directors. This was only the second or third time in its five years existence that the company had bought a car. It was held that the company had dealt as a consumer in buying the car, because it had not bought it "in the course of a business". The decision was almost certainly wrong. It was distinguished in *Stevenson v. Rogers* (1999) where the Court of Appeal held that a sale was a sale "in the course of a business" (for the purposes of the Sale of Goods Act, s.14) unless it was a purely private sale outside the confines of any business (see paragraph 7–34 above). In *R & B Customs Brokers*, the Court should have held the sale to be a non-consumer sale.

Non-consumer deals

10–24   Where the buyer is not "dealing as consumer" the effect of section 6 of the Unfair Contract Terms Act is as follows. It is impossible for the seller to exempt himself from liability under section 12 of the Sale of Goods Act. It is, however, possible for the seller to be exempted from liability under sections 13 to 15 of the Sale of Goods Act, but only in so far as the seller can show that the exemption clause satisfies the requirement of reasonableness, *i.e.* that it was a "fair and reasonable one to be included having regard to circumstances which were, or ought reasonably to have been, known to or in the contemplation of the parties when the contract was made" (section 11).

Schedule 2 provides "guidelines" for the application of the reasonableness test:

10–25

"The matters to which regard is to be had in particular...are any of the following which appear to be relevant—

    (a) the strength of the bargaining positions of the parties relative to each other, taking into account (among other things) alternative means by which the customer's requirements could have been met;

    (b) whether the customer received an inducement to agree to the term, or in accepting it had an opportunity of entering into a similar contract with other persons, but without having to accept a similar term;

    (c) whether the customer knew or ought reasonably to have known of the existence of the term (having regard, among other things, to any custom of the trade and any previous course of dealing between the parties);

    (d) where the term excludes or restricts any relevant liability if some condition is not complied with, whether it was reasonable at the time of the contract to expect that compliance with that condition would be practicable;

    (e) whether the goods were manufactured, processed or adapted to the special order of the customer."

It would appear from paragraph (a) that a seller who has a monopoly over the supply of the kind of goods in question is unlikely to convince the court of the reasonableness of a wide exemption clause, especially if it was a large demand for the product which enabled him to insist on the clause being in the contract. In the light of paragraph (b) the seller having a monopoly will be more likely to succeed if the buyer had been offered the chance of buying the goods, perhaps at a slightly higher price, on terms not including the exemption clause. Obviously, if the alternative offer had involved a considerably or prohibitively higher price, that would tell against the seller.

Paragraph (c) would appear not to affect decisions in cases such as *Kendall v. Lillico* (see paragraph 10–07) and *Cointat v.*

10–26

Myham (see paragraph 10–08), cases where the purchaser chooses to buy goods for his business from a seller whose terms he has in a consistent course of dealing been apparently quite happy to accept or where the purchaser buys goods in a market in which a trade custom shows that merchants have found exclusion terms to be acceptable.

In the light of paragraph (d), a clause excluding, for example, all liability "other than that in respect of defects and defaults notified to the seller within three days of purchase" would clearly not be reasonable: *Green v. Cade* ((1978 Q.B.), paragraph 10–28 below). Paragraph (e) would be particularly relevant where the purchaser required the goods to be made or adapted from some use for which the seller did not normally supply goods. It would seem reasonable for the seller to stipulate that he will not guarantee the goods' suitability for that purpose.

Paragraphs (a) to (e) are only guidelines and all the circumstances of the case should be taken into account. So, for example, the scope and harshness (or otherwise) of the clause will also be relevant.

10–27   The leading case on the requirement of reasonableness arose, not under the Unfair Contract Terms Act 1977, but under the earlier provisions of the Supply of Goods (Implied Terms) Act 1973 which were replaced by the 1977 Act. The requirement of reasonableness under the earlier Act was different in two respects. First, the onus of proof was upon the buyer to show that the exemption clause did not pass the test, whereas under the 1977 Act the onus is on the seller to show that the clause passes the test. Secondly, under the 1973 Act the test was whether it was fair and reasonable to allow reliance upon the exemption clause, whereas under the 1977 Act the test is whether the clause was a fair and reasonable one to have been included in the contract. Nevertheless the former test and the current test are very similar and indeed the "guidelines" laid down by the two Acts are the same. The leading case is *George Mitchell v. Finney Lock Seeds* (for the facts see paragraph 10–17 above). There the exemption clause, according to its wording limited the liability of some seed merchants (for supplying defective seed) to the cost of replacing the seed; it excluded liability for consequential loss of the buyers' crop. These limitation terms were incorporated in all contracts between seedsmen and farmers and had been for many years. They had not been negotiated by any representative body of farmers, such as the National Farmers' Union. They had been introduced by seed merchants putting them into their catalogues and invoices—and never objected to by farmers. It was held that the exemption clause did not in the circumstances pass the test of reasonableness and that therefore the sellers could not rely upon it to limit their liability. The relevant circumstances were that: (i) the limitation terms had not been negotiated by any representative body; (ii) the buyers could not have discovered the error (*i.e.* that the wrong seed had been delivered) until after the crop was sown, whereas the sellers were in a position to have known; (iii) the buyers could not reasonably have been expected to cover such a risk (*i.e.* of crop failure) by insurance, whereas it was possible for seedsmen to cover their liability by insurance at a modest premium which would not have put up the cost of seeds by very much; (iv) the error could not have occured without some negligence on the part of the sellers.

George Mitchell v. Finney Lock Seeds was different from **10–28** *Green v. Cade* (1978 QB), which had involved the sale of seed potatoes on the standard terms of the National Association of Seed Potato Merchants. In that case one clause which on its wording excluded liability if the buyers had not given notice of any defects within three days of purchase was held to fail the reasonableness test. Another clause, restricting the sellers' liability for a consequential loss and limiting that liability to the amount of the contract price, was held to pass the reasonableness test. The latter clause, however, had had the approval of negotiating bodies representing both potato merchants and farmers; no blame for the infection of the seed potatoes was attributable to either side, and, further, the buyers, if they had so wished, could have bought at a small extra cost, seed potatoes certified by inspectors of the Ministry of Agriculture.

In *St Albans City and District Council v. International* **10–29** *Computers Ltd* (1996 CA) the court had to apply the requirement of reasonableness to a limitation of liability clause in an international computer firm's standard conditions in a contract made with a local council to supply the council with a database for a community charge register. At that time the community charge was a local tax. The clause limited the computer firm's liability to a maximum of £100,000. The database supplied was defective in that it overstated the local population by 2,966. This in turn had the effect that the rate of tax levied was lower than it would have been if the population had been accurately stated. This in turn caused a loss of tax revenue to the council of over £1.3 million. The relevant factors taken into account by the court were: (a) the parties were of unequal bargaining power; (b) the figure of £100,000 was small in relation to the potential and the actual risk; (c) the computer firm was insured for an aggregate sum of £50 million worldwide; (d) it was in practical terms easier for the computer firm to secure insurance and to pass the cost of that on to its customers and it was not unreasonable that the firm which made the profit by supplying the program should carry the risk. Thus the clause failed to satisfy the requirement of reasonableness and was unenforceable. (On the question of whether the contract in this case was a sale of goods contract see paragraph 1–14 above.)

Exemption from other terms of the contract—section 3

10–30   We have just considered the extent to which the Unfair Contract Terms Act allows the seller to exclude his liability under section 12–15 of the Sale of Goods Act. However, the contract will doubtless contain other terms, some of them expressly agreed between the parties (*e.g.* the date of delivery) and some of them implied (often by other sections of the Sale of Goods Act—*e.g.* as to the place of delivery, section 29(2)). The Unfair Contract Terms Act does not totally prohibit the seller from exempting himself from liability for breach of these other terms. Section 3 of that Act, however, does, in certain circumstances, render such an exemption clause subject to the requirement of reasonableness. This section applies if two conditions are both satisfied:

    (i) the seller's liability is "business liability"; and

    (ii) in buying the goods, the buyer "deals as consumer" or on the seller's written standard terms of business.

The first of these requirements will clearly be satisfied where the seller sells the goods in the course of his business. The meaning of "deals as consumer" has already been considered (at paragraph 10–21). The Act does not define "written standard terms of business". This expression clearly covers the situation where a seller insists that all (or a considerable proportion of) his buyers buy on the terms of his written contract, there being no variation in the terms from one buyer to another. This would still seem to be so if most, though not all, the terms are standard—if, say, there are minor variations from one buyer to another (*e.g.* as to the commodity or the quantity bought or the price to be paid). Even where the only "standard" terms of the seller are those in the exemption clause itself, still a buyer whose contract includes that exemption clause could well be regarded as buying on the seller's "written standard terms of business".

Where the two conditions mentioned above are satisfied, section **10–31** 3 applies and its effect is that the seller can not (section 3(2)):

"(a) when himself in breach of contract, exclude or restrict any liability of his in respect of the breach; or

(b) claim to be entitled—

(i) to render a contractual performance substantially different from that which was reasonably expected of him or

(ii) in respect of the whole or any part of his contractual obligation, to render no performance at all, except in so far as the contract term [*i.e.* exemption clause] satisfies the requirement of reasonableness."

There is a great deal of room for the courts to interpret these words. Confining ourselves to the obvious, it is clear that for paragraph (a) to apply the seller must be in breach of contract. Clearly, therefore, a maximum damages clause would be caught by it.

Three important points must be made. First, section 3, where it **10–32** applies, does not render a clause ineffective if the clause is shown to satisfy the requirement of reasonableness. This requirement has already been explained in relation to section 6 of the Unfair Contract Terms Act (paragraphs 10–24 to 10–25 above). It is exactly the same here except that the Act does not say that the "guidelines" in Schedule 2 should be referred to. Nevertheless it seems likely that similar factors will in fact be taken into account by the courts. Secondly, an exemption clause may be partially effective if it is shown to be to some extent reasonable. A clause might for example claim (i) to exclude liability for certain fundamental breaches of contract and (ii) to limit any damages to a maximum of £5,000. A court might well be persuaded that the clause is reasonable as to (ii) but not as to (i).

The third point is that where an exemption clause is not invalidated (or not completely so) by section 3 of the Unfair Contract Terms Act, the buyer may still be able to defeat the exemption clause by relying on section 6, section 8 or section 2 of that Act. Section 6 has already been considered and applies where the buyer's claim is based upon a breach by the seller of the terms implied by sections 12 to 15 of the Sale of Goods Act.

Section 8 applies where the claim is based upon misrepresentation and will be returned to later. Section 2 applies where the claim is based upon negligence.

Exemption from liability for negligence—section 2

10–33   In Chapter 9 we saw that a manufacturer can be liable to a consumer for any loss or damage caused by the negligence of the manufacturer or any of his employees. This is so irrespective of whether the consumer bought the goods from the manufacturer. A distributor or seller who was not the manufacturer (*e.g.* a retailer) could also be liable under the same principle if he was negligent, *e.g.* if he negligently failed to pass on to the customer a warning label ("Not to be taken internally") which he had received with a bottle of medicine. We have also seen that a manufacturer or distributor who does not supply the goods directly to the consumer cannot (*e.g.* in a guarantee document) exclude any liability for negligence that he may have towards the consumer— see section 5 of the Unfair Contract Terms Act (paragraph 9–03 above). What about the trader who does sell directly to the consumer? This could be a manufacturer or, say, a retailer. Can he exclude his liability for negligence? Section 2 of the Unfair Contract Terms Act applies here. Its effect is twofold. First, it is impossible to exclude liability for death or personal injuries caused by negligence. Secondly, it is possible to exclude or restrict liability for other loss or damage (*e.g.* to property) caused by negligence, but only to the extent that the exemption clause is shown to satisfy the requirement of reasonableness. The requirement of reasonableness is exactly the same here as it is in relation to section 3 (paragraph 10–32 above).

There are three final points about section 2. First, like sections 3 and 5, it applies only to "business liability". Secondly, where an exemption clause is not invalidated by section 2, the buyer may be able to sue the seller for breach of contract and to defeat the exemption clause by virtue of sections 6 or 3 of the Unfair Contract Terms Act. Thirdly, he may be able to establish a claim for product liability under the Consumer Protection Act 1987— such liability cannot be excluded (paragraph 9–06 above). Alternatively, he may be able to sue for misrepresentation.

Exemption of liability for misrepresentation—section 8

10–34   Section 8 of the Unfair Contract Terms Act has amended section 3 of the Misrepresentation Act 1967 (see paragraph 6–05 above). The latter section, as amended, renders any exemption clause ineffective except to the extent that the clause is shown to satisfy the requirement of reasonableness. This requirement is exactly the same here as it is in relation to section 3 of the Unfair Contract Terms Act (paragraph 10–32 above).

Business liability

Some sections (2, 3 and 5) of the Unfair Contract Terms Act   **10–35**
apply to exemption clauses only where those clauses claim to exempt from "business liability". " 'Business' includes a profession and the activities of any government department or local or public authority"—section 14. Thus a private house-holder selling his old lawn mower or even his second-hand car is free to insist on an exemption clause excluding his liability for, say, negligence. Such a clause will be effective, subject only to the common law rules outlined earlier in this chapter. Two sections of the Unfair Contract Terms Act apply both to business and to non-business liability—sections 6 and 8. Thus, by section 8, the private seller cannot exempt himself from liability for misrepresentation unless he can show that the exemption clause satisfies the requirement of reasonableness. By section 6, the position is the same if he tries to exempt himself from sections 13–15 of the Sale of Goods Act. This is because it is not a consumer deal if the seller does not sell in the course of a business. All of this does not, however, mean that if the goods prove defective the private seller can easily be made liable for breach of the terms of sections 13–15 of the Sale of Goods Act. He is unlikely to have sold by sample; that rules out section 15. By definition the private seller did not sell in the course of a business; that rules out the conditions in section 14 (*i.e.* as to satisfactory quality and fitness for purpose). Finally, provided the goods correspond with the description, there will be no liability under section 13.

Mixed exemption clauses

Suppose one exemption clause falls within more than one   **10–36**
section of the Unfair Contract Terms Act. Suppose, for example, it claims to exclude all the following liabilities of the seller; for misrepresentation, for negligence and also for breach of the terms implied by sections 12 to 15 of the Sale of Goods Act. Which section of the Unfair Contract Terms Act is relevant? The answer depends upon what claim the buyer makes. Section 8 of the Unfair Contract Terms Act is relevant to a claim for misrepresentation; section 2 to a claim for negligence; section 6

to a claim under sections 12–15 of the Sale of Goods Act; and section 3 to a claim for any other breach of contract. Following a consumer deal in which the consumer bought a hot bottle direct from the manufacturer, the consumer may claim for damage to his bed after the bottle burst. It is possible here that his claims (if any) against the manufacturer for misrepresentation or negligence will fail because of an exemption clause which satisfies the requirement of reasonableness (imposed by sections 8 and 2 of the Unfair Contract Terms Act). A claim for product liability under the Consumer Protection Act 1987 will also fail unless the damage to the bed exceeds £275 in value (see paragraph 9–10 above). A claim under section 14 of the Sale Goods Act will, however, succeed because section 6 of the Unfair Contract Terms Act totally prevents the exclusion from a consumer deal of the terms implied by sections 12–15 of the Sale of Goods Act.

Contracts other than for the sale of goods

10–37   The Unfair Contract Terms Act applies to hire-purchase contracts in exactly the same way as it does to contracts of sale of goods. This will be explained in Chapter 25. There are certain other contracts which are not contracts of sale of goods but which are analogous contracts because the ownership of goods passes under them, *e.g.* contracts of exchange and barter and contracts for labour and materials supplied (see Chapter 8 above). The Unfair Contract Terms Act 1977 applies to these analogous contracts in the same way as it applies to contract of sale of goods. The statutory terms (as to title, description, quality and sample) implied by sections 2–5 of the Supply of Goods and Services Act 1982 are dealt with in the same way as the corresponding terms implied in contracts of sale of goods. There is the same distinction between "consumer deals" and others— the distinction having exactly the same effect.

Turning to hire contracts, it will be remembered that there are statutory implied terms as title, description, quality and sample implied by sections 6–10 of the Supply of Goods and Services Act 1982 (see paragraph 8–08 above). The Unfair Contract Terms Act applies, with one small difference, to hire contracts as it does to contracts of sale of goods, hire-purchase, barter and exchange, etc. Thus, its effect is the same in relation to a clause claiming to exempt the supplier from liability under the terms relating to description, quality or sample. It is impossible to exclude such liability in a consumer deal and in any non-consumer deal the clause is subject to the requirement of reasonableness. The one difference is that in a hire contract the terms as to title and quiet possession can be excluded or restricted by an exemption clause provided that exemption clause satisfies the requirement of reasonableness.

Finally, let us turn to the third set of terms implied by the **10–38** Supply of Goods and Services Act 1982. These are the terms implied in a contract where the supplier has agreed to carry out a service (paragraph 8–09 above). These are terms that: the supplier acting in the course of a business will carry out the service with reasonable care and skill (section 13); within a reasonable time (section 14); and that the customer will pay a reasonable charge (section 15). An exclusion clause, which purports to exclude or limit liability under these terms, is subject to the rules already outlined in this chapter, including the rules laid down in the Unfair Contract Terms Act 1977. In particular, section 3 of that Act will apply (paragraph 10–30 above). Thus a clause purporting to exclude or limit the supplier's liability will be subject to the requirement of reasonableness, provided the supplier's customer was either dealing as a consumer or else had contracted on the supplier's written standard terms of business. A further explanation is required in relation to the term as to reasonable care and skill implied by section 13 of the Supply of Goods and Services Act 1982. This is because a claim for a breach of that term is treated by the Unfair Contract Terms Act, s.1, as a claim for negligence. Thus, liability for death or personal injury arising from such a breach of contract can not be excluded or restricted at all; liability for other loss or injury arising from such a breach can be excluded only in so far as the exclusion clause satisfies the requirement of reasonableness—Unfair Contract Terms Act 1977, s.2 (see paragraph 10–33 above).

THE UNFAIR TERMS IN CONSUMER CONTRACTS REGULATIONS 1999

These Regulations are virtually identical in their effect on **10–39** contracts as were the Unfair Terms in Consumer Contracts Regulations 1994 which they replaced. They apply to a wide range of contracts. Where they apply they make any unfair term not binding on the consumer.

Contracts to which the Regulations apply

The basic rule is that these Regulations apply to any contract **10–40** where a trader is contracting to supply goods or services to a private consumer. Put more precisely, they apply to a contract between on the one hand a seller or supplier (of goods or services) who is acting for purposes relating to his business and, on the other hand, an individual consumer who is acting for purposes which are outside his business. The Regulations apply where goods or services are being sold or supplied. Certainly, therefore, they apply to a situation where goods are being hired because, though not a sale, such a contract does involve a supply of goods.

It is possible, however, that for these purposes "goods" also includes land. These Regulations implement the Directive on Unfair Terms in Consumer Contracts (93/13/EEC). The word "goods" is not defined in the directive or in the Regulations. In some countries' text of the Directive the word used is not a word confined in its meaning to what we would call chattels. Thus the French language version of the directive includes the word *"biens"*, which includes both goods and land. If this is what is meant by "goods", then a contract between a house-builder/estate developer and the first-time private house purchaser is subject to these Regulations. On any view, a contract where a private house owner is engaging an estate agent to sell the house for him is subject to the Regulations, since clearly the estate agent is providing a "service" to the consumer. Equally, a residential mortgage contract is simply a contract for a loan on the security of a mortgage, and where the borrower (mortgagor) is a private house buyer the lender is providing the service of lending money to the borrower; thus such a contract is subject to the Regulations.

Turning to financial services, there is no doubt, for example, that a contract between a stockbroker and a private client is subject to the Regulations, since the former in the course of his business is providing a service to the consumer.

Clarity and interpretation

10–41   Any written term must be expressed in plain, intelligible language. If there is doubt about the meaning of a written term, the interpretation most favourable to the consumer prevails.

What is an unfair term?

10–42   This is any term "if, contrary to the requirement of good faith, it causes a significant imbalance in the parties' rights and obligations under the contract to the detriment of the consumer". The requirement of good faith is not defined. Nor do the Regulations state upon whom rests the burden of proof, *i.e.* to establish fairness or unfairness. In determining whether the term is unfair the court must take into account the nature of the goods or services and must refer to: all the circumstances attending the making of the contract; all the other terms of the contract and of any contract upon which it is dependent.

In Schedule 2 to the Regulations there is an indicative list of **10–43** the sorts of terms which *may* be regarded as unfair. The list, which is not exhaustive, includes exemption clauses, limitation of liability clauses, penalty clauses, and clauses:

- which the consumer had no real opportunity to become acquainted with before the contract;

- giving the seller/supplier the discretion to terminate the contract without conferring the same right upon the consumer;

- giving the seller/supplier the power to terminate a contract of indefinite duration without giving reasonable notice (except where there are serious grounds to do so);

- automatically extending a contract of fixed duration unless the consumer indicates to the contrary within an unreasonably early deadline;

- enabling the seller/supplier to retain a deposit or part payment when the consumer cancels the contract, without also giving the consumer a similar right to compensation where it is the seller/supplier who cancels it;

- enabling the seller/supplier to retain a deposit or part payment for services not yet supplied when it is the supplier who cancels the contract;

- enabling the seller/supplier to vary the agreement unilaterally for an invalid reason or for a reason not specified in the contract;

- providing for the seller/supplier to raise the price without at the same time giving the consumer the right in such a case to cancel the contract if the price is then high as compared with the original contract price;

- providing for the price to be determined at the time of delivery but not allowing for the consumer to cancel the agreement if the price is then high as compared with the original contract price;

- giving the seller/supplier the exclusive right to interpret any term of the contract;

- giving the seller/supplier the right to determine whether goods or services are in conformity with the contract;

- giving the seller/supplier the possibility of transferring his obligations under the contract, where this may reduce the guarantees for the consumer, without the consumer's agreement;

- excluding or hindering the consumer's right to take legal action or take any other legal remedy, particularly by requiring the consumer to take disputes exclusively to arbitration not covered by legal provisions.

10–44   Two kinds of term are not subject to the requirement to be fair: (i) a term which is individually negotiated; (ii) core terms of the contract (in so far as they are in plain an intelligible language). The burden to establish that a term was individually negotiated rests on the seller/supplier. A term will not be regarded as individually negotiated if it was drafted in advance and the consumer was therefore unable to influence its substance.

Core terms are those that:

- define the main subject-matter of the contract;

- concern the adequacy of the price or remuneration for the goods or services supplied.

Thus the terms that are subject to the Regulations are those that are ancillary, *e.g.* those relating to: quality; time (of delivery/completion and of payment); arbitration; making complaints; giving (and forfeiting) deposits or down payments; cancellation; powers to vary the agreement, etc. *Oceano Grupo Editorial SA v. Rocio Muriciano Quintero*, 2000, ECJ involved a number of contracts by a company which had its principal place of business in Barcelona, each such contract being a contract to sell, on instalment credit terms, an encyclopedia to a consumer domiciled in another part of Spain. Each contract contained a clause, not individually negotiated, giving exclusive jurisdiction to the Barcelona courts, which is where the seller commenced proceedings against consumers who had defaulted on their repayments. The European Court clearly considered the clause to be unfair (within the meaning of the Directive). It was held that the Barcelona court should of its own motion (a) determine whether the jurisdiction clause was unfair and, (b), it being unfair, should decline the jurisdiction it conferred.

Effect of a term being unfair
The contract is treated as if the unfair term were not in it. **10–45** Thus, provided the contract is capable of subsisting without the unfair term, the rest of the contract survives.

Relationship with other legislation
In making these Regulations the Government implemented a **10–46** European directive. The Regulations are clearly capable of applying to exclusion clauses. Any such clause held to fail the fairness requirement cannot be relied upon against the consumer. These Regulations have not repealed or amended any other legislation. In particular, the Unfair Contract Terms Act 1997 remains fully in force. Thus there are now two separate pieces of legislation which can potentially be used to render an exclusion clause ineffective; the consumer who is trying to prevent the trader relying on such a clause can rely on either the Regulations or the 1977 Act or both. The Regulations are wider in one respect than the Act, since the Regulations can apply to any term, whether or not it is an exclusion clause. As we have seen above, they could for example apply to a liquidated damages clause (see paragraph 14–21 below); to a penalties clause (see paragraph 27–32 below); or indeed to something which, though not a penalty, is nevertheless very close to being one (see for example *Associated Distributors v. Hall* at paragraph 27–33 below). On the other hand, in a different respect the 1977 Act is wider than the Regulations, since the Act, though confined to exclusion clauses, is capable of applying to such a clause if it is standard term used in a contract between two businesses.

So far, reported cases under the Regulations have involved, not exclusion clauses but clauses in credit agreements which, though not extortionate, could be regarded as somewhat oppressive. These cases, including *Director General of Fair Trading v. First National Bank* (2000 CA), are explained at paragraphs 26–08 and 26–24 below.

Power of the Director-General of Fair Trading
One imagines the Regulations being of significance in **10–47** contractual disputes between consumer and trader. However, the Regulations also give a power of enforcement to the Director-

General. He can, on receiving a complaint that a contract term is unfair, bring proceedings for an injunction to stop a trader using an unfair term. He is given the power to accept undertakings from traders and will take these into account in determining whether to start proceedings for an injunction. The 1999 Regulations now give similar enforcement powers to other regulatory bodies (*e.g.* water and gas regulators) and to local Trading Standards Departments. In addition, the power to seek an injunction has now been extended to a non-statutory body, the Consumers' Association.

CRIMINAL USE OF INEFFECTIVE EXEMPTION CLAUSES

10–48   At one time it was not uncommon for a retailer to display an exemption clause in his premises or include it in a written contract even though that clause was rendered totally ineffective by Act of Parliament. The clause, though having no legal validity, would very likely mislead the consumer as to his rights. The Unfair Contract Terms Act does not in any way prevent that practice. However, the Consumer Transactions (Restrictions on Statements) Order 1976 was made under the Fair Trading Act 1973 (the procedure for making these orders is explained at paragraph 18–48 below). The 1976 Order (as amended by a further order in 1978) applies to any exemption clause claiming in a consumer deal to exclude liability under sections 13–15 of the Sale of Goods Act. There are four aspects to the Order, First, it makes it a criminal offence for anyone in the course of a business to display at a place where consumer deals are likely to be made (*e.g.* at a shop or garage) a notice of an exemption clause which is void by virtue of section 6 of the Unfair Contract Terms Act. Secondly, it is similarly an offence for someone in the course of a business to publish such a notice in any advertisement (or catalogue or circular) or to supply goods bearing any such notice. Thirdly, it is an offence for someone in the course of a business to furnish the consumer with a written contract (or other written document) containing such a notice. Fourthly, it is an offence for someone in the course of a business to supply goods bearing any statement about the seller's liability in respect of description, quality or fitness for purpose unless the statement also makes it clear that the statement does not affect the statutory rights of the consumer.

10–49   The Order applies only to clauses rendered void by section 6 of the Unfair Contract Terms Act. Section 6, however, does not render a clause void unless the clause, *properly interpreted*, purports to exclude or limit liability under sections 13–15 of the Sale of Goods Act. Thus, whereas an ambiguous clause, such as "bought as seen", might be understood by a buyer to exclude such liability, it might equally well, as a matter of correct legal interpretation, be held not to have that effect. If so, the clause is not caught by the 1976 Order: *Cavendish Woodhouse Ltd v. Manley* (1984 DC). Though of no legal effect, it can be used, apparently with impunity, to mislead a buyer about his rights.

The Order applies only to exemption clauses relating to "consumer deals" and only to exemption clauses affected by section 6 of the Unfair Contract Terms Act. Thus a manufacturer commits no offence by including on the goods he supplies to his wholesaler a notice which reads "The manufacturer accepts no liability in respect of death or personal injuries arising from negligence". Nor will the wholesaler commit any offence in supplying the goods thus labelled to the retailer, nor the retailer in similarly supplying them to the consumer. No offence is committed even though this notice will have no effect (see section 5 of the Unfair Contract Terms Act, paragraph 9–03 above). It should be noted that if any of these ineffective exclusion clauses are included in an advertisement, the trader responsible will expose himself to the risk of proceedings against him under the Control of Misleading Advertisements Regulations 1988 (see paragraph 18–45, below).

CHAPTER 11

DELIVERY AND PAYMENT

THE parties can make what agreement they wish about the time, **11–01** place and manner of delivery and payment. What follows is an explanation of the rights and duties between the seller and buyer when they have not agreed anything different in their contract.

Concurrent conditions

Section 28 provides: **11–02**

> "Unless otherwise agreed, delivery of the goods and payment of the price are concurrent conditions. . ."

Thus, although section 49 states that the seller can sue for the price in certain circumstances (see Chapter 12), he will nevertheless not be able to do so unless he is also ready and willing to deliver the goods. Equally, the buyer will not be able to sue for non-delivery unless he was ready and willing to pay or else it had been agreed that he could have credit. The rule that delivery and payment are concurrent conditions ties in with the unpaid seller's lien (see Chapter 12) which entitles him in the absence of contrary agreement to retain the goods until payment.

DELIVERY

Delivery is the voluntary transfer of possession from one person **11–03** to another—section 61. Delivery may be achieved in one of several ways. The seller may physically hand over the goods. He may hand over the means of control of the goods, *e.g.* the key to the premises where they are housed. He may, where the goods are at the time of the sale in the possession of a third party (*e.g.* at a warehouse), instruct the third party to hold the goods to the order of the buyer. In that case, delivery occurs when the third party attorns, *i.e.* acknowledges to the buyer that he holds the goods on his behalf—section 29(4). Delivery can be made in an appropriate case by the transfer of a document, or documents, of title, as in c.i.f. contracts (see paragraph 3–29). Sometimes there could be confusion between the last two methods of delivery. For example, X could own a cargo in course of transit which is therefore in the hands of a third party, the carrier. If X sells it by dealing with the documents of title, then delivery occurs when he transfers the bill of lading to the buyer, irrespective of whether the carrier attorns—section 29(4).

Place of delivery

11–04   Section 29 provides:

> "(1) Whether it is for the buyer to take possession of the goods or for the seller to send them to the buyer is a question depending in each case on the contract, express or implied, between the parties.
>
> (2) Apart from any such contract, express or implied, the place of delivery is the seller's place of business, if he has one, and if not, his residence: except that, if the contract is for the sale of specific goods, which to the knowledge of the parties when the contract is made are in some other place, then that place is the place of delivery."

Thus, unless otherwise agreed, it is not for the seller to convey the goods to the buyer but for the latter to collect them. If the seller does agree to convey them, he must do so within a reasonable length of time—section 29(3). If on arrival he hands them over to someone whom he reasonably assumes to be authorised to receive them, then he has carried out his duty of delivery: *Galbraith and Grant v. Block* (1922 KB).

Time of delivery

11–05   We have already seen (paragraph 7–13) that, in a commercial contract, the time of delivery is normally "of the essence", *i.e.* if a delivery date is stipulated and the seller cannot make delivery by that date, that is a breach of condition and the buyer is entitled to repudiate the contract and sue for non-delivery.

When no time is stipulated and it is for the buyer to collect, the seller must be ready to hand over the goods (against payment) to the buyer on demand (provided made at a reasonable hour—section 29(5)) at any time after the making of the contract. If he fails to do so, he is in breach of condition; the buyer can treat the contract as repudiated and sue for non-delivery.

Expenses

Unless otherwise agreed, the seller must bear the expenses, if any, connected with putting the goods into a deliverable state— section 29(6).

11–06

Delivery of wrong quantity

Section 30 provides:

"(1) Where the seller delivers to the buyer a quantity of goods less than he contracted to sell, the buyer may reject them, but if the buyer accepts the goods so delivered he must pay for them at the contract rate.

11–07

(2) Where the seller delivers to the buyer a quantity of goods larger than he contracted to sell, the buyer may accept the goods included in the contract and reject the rest, or he may reject the whole.

(2A) A buyer who does not deal as consumer may not—
    (a) where the seller delivers a quantity of goods less than he contracted to sell, reject the goods under subsection (1) above, or
    (b) where the seller delivers a quantity of goods larger than he contracted to sell, reject the whole under subsection (2) above,
if the shortfall or, as the case may be, excess is so slight that it would be unreasonable for him to do so.

(2B) It is for the seller to show that a shortfall or excess fell within subsection (2A) above.

(2C) Subsections (2A) and (2B) above do not apply to Scotland.

(2D) Where the seller delivers a quantity of goods—
    (a) less than he contracted to sell, the buyer shall not be entitled to reject the goods under subsection (1) above,
    (b) larger than he contracted to sell, the buyer shall not be entitled to reject the whole under subsection (2) above,

unless the shortfall or excess is material.

195

(2E) Subsection (2D) above applies to Scotland only.

(3) Where the seller delivers to the buyer a quantity of goods larger than he contracted to sell and the buyer accepts the whole of the goods so delivered he must pay for them at the contract rate.

(4) (*Subsection (4) was repealed in 1995.*)

(5) This section is subject to any usage of trade, special agreement, or course of dealing between the parties."

The law ignores trifling breaches of contract. In *Shipton, Anderson v. Weil Bros.* (1912 KB) the sellers were entitled to deliver 4,950 tons. They in fact delivered 4,950 tons 55lb. It was held that this did not entitle the buyers to reject the whole consignment.

A breach of the obligations to deliver the contract quantity will be a breach of the condition implied by section 13 (see paragraph 7–26). This leads to the observation that section 30(5) must presumably be read subject to the provisions of the Unfair Contract Terms Act 1977 which has drastically reduced the ability of the parties to exclude or restrict the seller's liability (see paragraphs 10–18 onwards).

Section 30(1) and 30(2) allows the buyer to reject the goods (all of them) if too many or too few are delivered. In the case of a buyer who is not dealing as a consumer, this is now subject to the rule in subsection (2A) that the buyer does not have this right of rejection if the shortfall or excess is so slight as to make rejection unreasonable. For an explanation of who "deals as a consumer", see paragraphs 10–21 to 10–23 above.

Section 30(1) entitles the buyer to reject all the goods if less than the contract quantity is delivered. Section 30(1) does not, however, apply where a contract is severable, *i.e.* where the parties have agreed that delivery can be made in instalments and, on a true construction of the contract, the parties did not intend that a breach of one consignment was to justify rejection of them all: *Regent v. Francesco* (1981 QB). In that case a shortfall in one instalment will normally only justify a rejection of that one instalment. It would not entitle the buyer to reject all other instalments unless the seller's breach was so serious as to amount to a repudiation of the contract (see paragraph 11–08 below).

Delivery by instalments

There are three possible situations: **11–08**

(i) The parties did not agree that delivery could be by instalments. In this case the buyer is not bound to accept delivery by instalments. In *Behrend v. Produce Brokers* (1920 KB) part of the goods were delivered which the buyers accepted. It was held, applying section 30, that the buyers were entitled to refuse to accept later delivery of the rest of the goods and that they should pay pro rata for those they had accepted.

(ii) The parties agreed that delivery could be by instalments but the contract is not severable. A breach of condition (*e.g.* as to quality) in relation to the first instalment will entitle the buyer to repudiate the whole contract. If, however, he has accepted one or more instalments (or any part thereof), he will not be able to reject later instalments if there is a breach of condition in relation to them—section 11(4) (unless he can bring himself within section 30 (above)). This appears to remain the position even after the introduction in 1995 of the right of partial rejection (see paragraph 13–07 below).

(iii) The parties agreed that delivery could be made by instalments (either on specified dates or "as required") and the contract is severable (divisible). The contract is severable if, on its true construction, the parties did not intend that a breach as to one consignment would justify rejection of all the consignments. If the parties had agreed that each consignment was to be separately paid for, the court will normally construe the contract as severable. That, however, is not an essential requirement of a severable contract. In the case of a severable contract, acceptance of one or more instalments does not preclude rejection of later instalments for breach of condition—section 11(4). In *Jackson v. Rotax Motor and Cycle Co.* (1910 CA) the buyer accepted as satisfactory the first delivery of motor horns but claimed to reject the later deliveries because they were not of merchantable quality. It was held that he was entitled to do this.

A more difficult question in relation to severable contracts is whether a breach of condition in relation to one or more instalments entitles the innocent party to regard the whole contract as repudiated or whether it is a severable breach confined to the instalments in question. It is a question of fact in each case depending upon the circumstances—section 31(2). *Maple Flock Co. v. Universal Furniture Products (Wembley)* (1933 CA) concerned a severable contract for the sale of 100 tons of flock by instalments. The first 15 instalments were satisfactory, the sixteenth was defective, and there were four more satisfactory deliveries. The buyers claimed to regard the whole contract as repudiated. It was held that they could not. The court said that whether the breach was a repudiatory one depended on two factors: (i) the ratio the breach bore quantitatively to the whole contract; and (ii) the likelihood of the breach being repeated in later instalments. On neither factor did the breach appear serious in this case. Sometimes the contract includes a clause such as "each instalment to be considered as a separate contract". This has little effect and the courts will still regard the contract as one contract (albeit a severable one) and therefore it is possible for a sufficiently serious breach to be a repudiation of the whole contract: *Smyth (Ross) v. Bailey* (1940 HL).

The problem of classifying the contract as either non-severable (*i.e.* (ii) above) or severable (*i.e.* (iii) above) arose in *Rosenthal v. Esmail* (1965 HL). Under a c.i.f. contract which provided "each shipment to be regarded as a separate contract", the sellers had an option whether to send separate shipments or to send all the goods by one shipment. They close the latter course but they sent to the buyer separate shipping documents in respect of two different lots in the one ship. The buyer claimed that the contract was severable, accepted one lot and rejected the other for breach of condition. The House of Lords held that since the sellers had opted for the one shipment, albeit with separate documents, the contract was not severable. Therefore the buyers having accepted part of the goods could not reject the rest—section 11. This decision must now, however, be read in the light of the right of partial rejection introduced in 1994 (see paragraph 13–07 below).

Delivery to a carrier

11–09   Where the seller is authorised or required to send the goods to the buyer, delivery to a carrier for that purpose will normally constitute complete performance of the seller's duty of delivery—section 32(1).

The seller must, unless otherwise authorised, make the best reasonably possible contract with the carrier on behalf of the buyer—section 32(2). In *Thomas Young v. Hobson* (1949 CA) the seller made a contract for the goods to be carried at the "owner's risk". The carrier would have agreed to carry them for the same price at the carrier's risk. The goods were damaged in transit and it was held that the seller was in breach of his duty under section 32(2) and the buyer was entitled to reject the goods. (As to risk generally during transit, see paragraphs 3–35 and 7–42)

Where customary, the seller must give sufficient information to the buyer to enable him to insure the goods whilst in transit by sea—section 32(3).

Payment

Normally, in the absence of contrary agreement, the buyer need **11–10** not make payment until delivery is made—section 28. However, where the goods have been destroyed or stolen at a time when they were at the buyer's risk (see paragraph 3–36), then of course he is under a duty to pay, even though delivery is impossible.

Apart from that situation, if the buyer has paid and the goods are not delivered, he is entitled to recover the price because he has received no consideration for it—section 54.

Two matters are dealt with elsewhere, the amount of the price (see paragraphs 2–13 to 2–17) and when the seller can sue for the price (see paragraph 12–02).

CHAPTER 12

SELLER'S REMEDIES

A seller has two sets of remedies available, personal remedies **12–01** enforceable by taking action in the courts against the buyer and remedies exercisable against the goods.

PERSONAL REMEDIES

The seller has two possible actions; for the price or for **12–02** damages for non-acceptance.

The price

Section 49 allows the seller to maintain an action for the price where both the following conditions are fulfilled:

(i) The buyer has wrongfully refused or neglected to pay according to the terms of the contract.

(ii) Either property has passed to the buyer or "the price is payable on a day certain irrespective of delivery".

The buyer's refusal or failure to pay must have been wrongful. It is not wrongful if he has rightfully rejected the goods for breach of condition. Similarly, he is entitled (subject to contrary agreement) to refuse to pay except in exchange for taking delivery of the goods—section 28. Therefore the seller will be unable to sue for the price unless, at the time of the neglect or refusal to pay, he was ready and willing to deliver. Again, if the seller has granted the buyer credit, he cannot sue for the price before the end of the agreed credit period; until then the buyer's failure to pay is not wrongful.

In relation to the second requirement, if a particular date has been stipulated for payment then an action can be maintained after that date irrespective of whether property has passed to the buyer. When no "day certain" has been agreed, the seller will succeed only if property has passed to the buyer. A "day certain" may be a fixed date or could be fixed by reference to the seller's performance of his part of the contract. Different days certain may be agreed for the payment of different instalments of the price. In *Workman Clark v. Lloyd Brazileno* (1908 CA) the seller was building a vessel for the buyer and the price was to be paid by instalments on dates to be determined by reference to the stage of construction. It was held that at the relevant stages the seller could sue for the instalments then due.

In addition to an action for the price, the seller may have a claim under section 37 which provides:

"(1) When the seller is ready and willing to deliver the goods, and requests the buyer to take delivery, and the buyer does not within a reasonable time after such request take delivery of the goods, he is liable to the seller for any loss occasioned by his neglect or refusal to take delivery, and also for a reasonable charge for the care and custody of the goods.

(2) Nothing in this section affects the rights of the seller where the neglect or refusal of the buyer to take delivery amounts to a repudiation of the contract."

This might apply, if, for example, the goods had perished or contaminated others.

Where a buyer has paid with a cheque which has been dishonoured, he is still liable to pay and can be sued for the price. Where, however, he has paid with credit or charge card and then the card issuing company fails to pay, the seller is not able to sue the buyer for the price. (See generally paragraph 8–05 above and also 12–04 below).

Damages for non-acceptance

12–03 If the seller cannot maintain an action under section 49, he may still have a claim for damages which he can bring under section 50 "where the buyer wrongfully neglects or refuses to accept and pay for the goods". The measure of damages is considered in Chapter 14. Usually damages will be much less than the price and the seller also has the inconvenience of having to find another buyer.

REMEDIES AGAINST THE GOODS

There are three possible remedies against the goods—lien, **12–04** stoppage in transit and resale. They are available to an "unpaid seller". By section 38 a seller is an "unpaid seller",

"(a) when the whole of the price has not been paid or tendered;

(b) when a bill of exchange or other negotiable instrument has been received as conditional payment, and the condition on which it was received has not been fulfilled by reason of the dishonour of the instrument or otherwise."

A cheque is a bill of exchange. Thus a seller who in the normal way has accepted a cheque which is later dishonoured, is an unpaid seller.

Lien

The unpaid seller has a right in the circumstances provided by **12–05** section 41(1) to retain possession of the goods until he is paid or payment is tendered to him. As a matter of strict terminology, this right is called a "lien" if property has passed to the buyer and a "right of retention" if property is still with the seller—section 39(2). This right complements the rule in section 28 that, in the absence of contrary agreement, payment and delivery are concurrent conditions. By section 41(1) the right exists in each of the following circumstances:

"(a) where the goods have been sold without any stipulation as to credit;

(b) where the goods have been sold on credit, but the term of credit has expired;

(c) where the buyer becomes insolvent."

Obviously, agreement by the seller to allow credit is agreement contrary to the rule in section 28. In such circumstances the seller is not entitled to refuse delivery unless the agreed period has already expired. Usually by that time, delivery will already have been made, thus depriving the seller of his lien. Section 41(1)(c) represents an exception to the rule that the seller has no lien during an agreed period of credit. In spite of having agreed to grant credit, the seller does have a lien if, before the seller relinquishes possession, the buyer becomes insolvent. A person is insolvent (whether or not he is bankrupt) "if he has either ceased to pay his debts in the ordinary course of business or he cannot pay his debts as they become due"—section 61(4).

The seller's lien relates only to the price. He is not entitled to withhold the goods until other debts owed to him by the buyer are paid. Thus there is no lien for damages due by the buyer under section 37 (see paragraph 12–02 above).

12–06 Where delivery is made in instalments, the extent of the unpaid seller's lien depends upon whether the contract is severable. If it is not severable, the seller can retain any part of the goods to compel payment of any part or all of the price. Section 42 provides:

> "Where an unpaid seller has made part delivery of the goods, he may exercise his lien or right of retention on the remainder, unless such part delivery has been made under such circumstances as to show an agreement to waive the lien or right of retention."

A severable contract is generally one where goods are to be delivered in instalments which are to be separately paid for (see paragraph 11–08 above). In this case the seller has no lien over one instalment of goods to compel payment for a different (earlier) instalment. However, if the buyer's failure to pay amounts to a repudiatory breach of contract (see paragraph 11–08 above), the seller can refuse to make further deliveries, not by virtue of any lien, but because the buyer's repudiatory breach excuses the seller from further performance of his contractual obligations. If the reason for the buyer's failure to pay is his insolvency then the breach is a repudiatory one, although in this case the seller must deliver those instalments which have actually been paid for.

12–07 The seller's lien is lost if any of the following situations arises:

(i) The seller ceases to be unpaid, *i.e.* if the whole of the price is paid or tendered to him.

(ii) One of the terminating events in section 43 occurs.

(iii) An innocent third party acquires title free from the lien, under one of the exceptions to the *nemo dat* principle.

The last two of these require explanation. Section 43 states:

"(1) The unpaid seller of goods loses his lien or right of retention in respect of them

(a) when he delivers the goods to a carrier or other bailee or custodier for the purpose of transmission to the buyer without reserving the right of disposal of the goods;

(b) when the buyer or his agent lawfully obtains possession of the goods;

(c) by waiver of the lien or right of retention."

Although delivery to a carrier without the reservation of a right of disposal terminates the unpaid seller's lien, he may still be able to recover the goods by exercising his right of stoppage in transit. Lawful acquisition of possession by the buyer will deprive the seller of his rights of lien and stoppage and those rights will not revive even if the buyer later returns the goods to the possession of the seller. Allowing the buyer to have access to the goods, *e.g.* to paint or repair, will not amount to giving him possession provided the seller retains control over the goods. If the buyer without authority from the seller seizes possession of the goods that is unlawful and does not destroy the seller's lien.

Waiver of his lien by the seller may take the form of first an **12–08** express agreement to forego the lien, or secondly an act clearly indicating an intention to forego it, or thirdly a wrongful act inconsistent with delivery to the buyer. Examples of the last of these are consumption of the goods by the seller or a resale of them by the seller when he has no right to resell. In these cases the buyer can lawfully bring an action for damages against the seller but the damages will be awarded only after deducting the price still owed by the buyer. An example of the second form of waiver is assent by the seller to a sub-sale by the buyer. To amount to a waiver it must be such an assent as to show that the seller intends to renounce his rights against the goods. In *Mordaunt v. British Oil & Cake Mills Ltd* (1910 KB) the seller was told of the sub-sale by the buyer only after it had been made. It was held that the seller's acknowledgment of the existence of the sub-sale was not assent such as to defeat his lien. In spite of the sub-sale the seller was entitled to retain possession of the goods until they were paid for.

If the buyer disposes of the goods within one of the exceptions **12–09** to the *nemo dat* principle (see Chapter 5), the innocent sub-purchaser obtains title free from the seller's lien. In this case the seller must surrender the goods to the sub-purchaser and will be reduced to pursuing his personal remedies against the buyer. Most of the exceptions to the *nemo dat* principle apply only if the goods are disposed of by someone in possession of them and if the buyer is lawfully in possession of the goods the seller's lien is lost anyway (section 43(1)(b)). The exceptions may, however, be relevant where the buyer has unlawfully obtained possession. Further, certain exceptions can apply where the buyer has possession only of documents of title. The seller can lose his lien by virtue of one of these. The provisions of section 25 of the Sale of Goods Act and section 9 of the Factors Act have already been considered (see paragraph 5–32 above). However, there is a further provision by virtue of which an innocent sub-purchaser may acquire title free from the seller's lien, section 47. It reads:

"(1) Subject to this Act, the unpaid seller's right of lien or retention or stoppage in transit is not affected by any sale, or other disposition of the goods which the buyer may have made, unless the seller has assented to it.

(2) Where a document of title to goods has been lawfully transferred to any person as buyer or owner of the goods, and that person transfers the document to a person who takes it in good faith and for valuable consideration, then—

(a) if the last-mentioned transfer was by way of sale the unpaid seller's right of lien or retention or stoppage in transit is defeated; and

(b) if the last-mentioned transfer was made by way of pledge or other disposition for value, the unpaid seller's right of lien or retention or stoppage in transit can only be exercised subject to the rights of the transferee."

Subsection (2) was applied in *Ant. Jurgens Margarinefabrieken v. Louis Dreyfus & Co.* (1914 KB). Some mowra seed was sold. The buyers paid by cheque and the sellers gave the buyers a delivery order which the buyers endorsed and transferred to a sub-purchaser. The cheque was dishonoured and the sellers claimed to have a lien over the mowra seed which was still in their possession. It was held that since all the requirements of subsection (2) were fulfilled, the seller's lien was defeated. Subsection (2) is clearly an exception to the *nemo dat* principle, since the buyers were able to confer upon the sub-purchaser a title better than that which the buyers had themselves, namely, a title free from the sellers' lien and which therefore gave to the sub-purchaser the right to immediate possession.

In the last mentioned case the delivery order transferred by the **12–10** buyers to the sub-purchaser was the same document as that which has been transferred to the buyers by the sellers. If, instead of transferring the same document, the buyers had transferred a different one, then section 47(2) would not have applied. This was held by Salmon J. in *Mount v. Jay & Jay Ltd* (1959 QB) where the buyers wrote their own delivery order which they sent off to the sub-purchaser. His Lordship thought, however, that section 25 applied to defeat the sellers' lien (see paragraph 5–37 above). Nevertheless, he did not base his decision upon section 25, but held that the sellers' lien was defeated because the sellers, who knew in advance of the sub-sale, had assented to it in a way that indicated their intention to forego the lien.

Stoppage in transit

Section 44 provides that the seller can resume possession of the **12–11** goods and retain them until payment or tender of the price to him, if two conditions are both fulfilled:

(i) The buyer has become insolvent.

(ii) The goods are "in course of transit".

The meaning of "insolvent" has already been considered when dealing with the seller's lien.

Section 45 is a long section dealing with the "course of transit". Broadly, goods are in course of transit from the time that they are delivered to an independent middleman for the purpose of transmission to the buyer, until the time that the buyer actually obtains or is entitled to obtain possession. The carrier will of course be paid for his service by the buyer or seller. Apart from that, however, he must be independent. If, for example, the buyer sends his own lorry driven by one of his own employees to collect the goods, then the goods, once loaded on to the lorry, are not in the course of transit but are in the buyer's possession.

The course of transit ends:

(i) when the buyer obtains delivery, or

(ii) when the carrier acknowledges that he holds for and on behalf of the buyer, *e.g.* by accepting and acting upon the buyer's instructions not to convey the goods as far as their original destination or to convey them to a further destination, or

(iii) when the carrier wrongfully refuses to deliver the goods to the buyer.

Part delivery to the buyer does not prevent the remainder being stopped in transit unless the part delivery is made under such circumstances as to show an agreement to give up possession of the whole of the goods.

Section 46 deals with how stoppage in transit may be effected, by the seller either taking actual possession of the goods or giving notice of his claim to the carrier. The carrier is under a duty to comply with the seller's instructions as to redelivery, although the seller must bear the expenses involved. The seller can give his instructions to the person in actual possession of the goods, but it may be difficult for him to discover who that is, if, for example, the goods are on the railways. If, as is more likely, the seller gives his instruction to that person's employer or principal, he must allow reasonable time for the instructions to be communicated to the person in actual possession before delivery is made to the buyer.

With one exception, the right of stoppage in transit is lost in the same circumstances as is the seller's lien. It can therefore be lost by waiver or the operation of section 47(2), etc. The exception is of course that delivery to a carrier without the reservation of a right of disposal will terminate the seller's lien whereas it marks the commencement of the "course of transit".

Resale

12–12   Section 48 governs the right of the unpaid seller to resell the goods. Section 48(1) reads:

> "(1) Subject to this section, a contract of sale is not rescinded by the mere exercise by an unpaid seller of his right of lien or retention or stoppage in transit."

Since the contract is not rescinded by the seller exercising his rights of lien or stoppage, the seller's obligations under the contract remain, including his obligation to deliver the goods against payment of the price. Thus he has no right to resell the goods other than that allowed him by later subsections of section

48. In fact sections 48(3) and (4) allow him quite generous rights of resale:

> "(3) Where the goods are of a perishable nature, or where the unpaid seller gives notice to the buyer of his intention to resell, and the buyer does not within a reasonable time pay or tender the price, the unpaid seller may resell the goods and recover from the original buyer damages for any loss occasioned by his breach of contract.
>
> (4) Where the seller expressly reserves the right of resale in case the buyer should make default, and on the buyer making default, resells the goods, the original contract of sale is rescinded, but without prejudice to any claim the seller may have for damages."

When the seller exercises his right of resale—whether under subsection (3) or under subsection (4)—the contract with the first buyer is thereby rescinded. The effect of rescission is that property (title), if it had passed to the buyer, reverts to the seller. Thus, on exercising his right of resale, the seller resells as owner. Since he resells as owner it follows that he can keep any profit he makes by reselling at a higher price than the original buyer had agreed to pay. That is in addition to keeping any deposit he obtained from the original buyer (see paragraph 2–17 above). In the more likely event that the seller makes a loss on the resale, he can claim that loss from the original buyer as damages together with any other damage caused to him by the buyer's failure to pay.

Ward v. Bignall (1967 CA) concerned a contract for the sale of two cars for £850. After paying a deposit of £25 the buyer refused to pay the rest. The seller informed the buyer in writing that, if he did not pay the balance by a given date, the seller would try to resell the cars. The buyer still did not pay. The seller sold one car for £350 but failed to find a purchaser for the other. He brought a claim against the original buyer for the balance of the purchase price (£475) and advertising expenses (£22 10s.). It was held that the seller could not recover any of the price since the buyer was no longer the owner of either of the cars, the ownership having reverted to the seller on the resale. The seller was entitled to damages. The remaining car being worth £450, the seller's loss on the resale was £850 minus (£450 plus £350) equals £50. From that figure was deducted the amount (£25) of the deposit paid by the original buyer. The seller was also entitled to his reasonable advertising expenses for the resale, *i.e.* £22 10s. Therefore the damages awarded to him totalled £47 10s.

It is, of course, possible for the unpaid seller to resell the goods in circumstances where he has no right to do so. If he does, he will confer good title on the new purchaser provided the resale falls within one of the exceptions to the *nemo dat* principle. One particular exception which may well apply is that contained in sections 8 of the Factors Act and 24 of the Sale of Goods Act. This exception applies where the seller continues or is in possession of the goods or documents of title and subsequently delivers them to a new innocent purchaser. It was considered in paragraph 5–27 above. A further exception is to be found in section 48(2) of the Sale of Goods Act:

> "(2) Where an unpaid seller who has exercised his right of lien or retention or stoppage in transit resells the goods, the buyer acquires a good title to them as against the original buyer."

This provision can apply in much the same circumstances as section 24, namely where someone who has sold goods to one person then later resells them to another. However, for the subsequent purchaser to acquire good title under this provision there are different requirements to be fulfilled:

(i) The seller must have been "unpaid" by the first buyer.

(ii) He must also have exercised his right of lien or retention or stoppage in transit.

(iii) He must "sell" the goods. Thus someone taking only a pledge cannot acquire good title by virtue of this provision.

Unlike section 24, section 48(2) has no requirement that there be a delivery to the second purchaser and no requirement that the latter should be bona fide.

Finally it should be noted that if the seller does resell the goods and confer good title upon the new purchaser, the original buyer will be able to bring an action against the seller for non-delivery, provided the seller did not have the right to resell.

CHAPTER 13

BUYER'S REMEDIES

Specific performance

SECTION 52 allows the court to make an order of specific **13–01** performance against the seller in the case of a contract to deliver specific or ascertained goods. Thus the order cannot be made in the case of a contract for the sale of unascertained goods which have not been appropriated to the contract—*Re Wait* (see paragraph 3–04 above).

An order for specific performance is one which requires the seller actually to deliver the goods and does not give him the option of paying damages instead. Even in the case of specific or ascertained goods the court will not make such an order unless damages for non-delivery would not be an adequate remedy. This is likely to be the case only where similar goods are unobtainable elsewhere, *e.g.* if the goods are unique or virtually so, as in *Behnke v. Bede Shipping Co.* (1927 KB). A German shipowner had agreed to buy for immediate use a specific ship, the *City*, which had engines and boilers which were practically new and satisfied German regulations. There was only one other such ship afloat. An order for specific performance was granted since damages would not have been an adequate remedy.

Rejection of the goods

A breach of condition by the seller gives the buyer, as well as **13–02** a claim to damages, the right to reject the goods (and therefore not to have to pay for them). The buyer can exercise this right by refusing to take delivery or informing the seller that he rejects the goods. He need not return them to the seller, who if he wants them must come and collect them—section 36. If the seller fails to collect goods which the buyer has rightly rejected and as a result the buyer reasonably incurs storage expenses, the buyer is entitled to claim those expenses from the seller as damages for breach of contract: *Kolfor Plant Ltd v. Tilbury Plant Ltd* (1977 QB). The buyer has no lien over rejected goods and therefore must hand them over on request even though he has not received the return of his purchase money: *Lyons v. May & Baker* (1923 KB). He can bring an action to recover his price on the ground of a total failure of consideration.

The right of rejection is not given for an ordinary breach of warranty. Unless the seller commits a breach of condition or commits a breach of warranty which is so serious as to deprive the buyer of substantially the whole benefit of the contract, the buyer has no right to reject the goods or recover the price (see paragraph 7–12 above). If he unjustifiably rejects them, the seller may sue him for damages for non-acceptance or, possibly, will have an action for the price (see paragraph 14–03 and Chapter 12).

Trivial breaches of implied condition

13–03   The normal rule is that any breach of condition by the seller, however small or trivial, entitles the buyer to reject the goods. Section 15A creates an exception where there is a minor breach of one of the implied conditions as to description, quality and sample contained in sections 13, 14 and 15. Section 15A provides that if the breach "is so slight that it would be unreasonable for him to reject them...the breach is not to be treated as a breach of condition but may be treated as a breach of warranty". This is the position "unless a contrary intention appears in, or is to be implied from, the contract". It would seem extremely likely that if this provision had been in force at the time, the decision in *Re Moore and Landauer* ((1921), see paragraph 7–31 above) would have been different. In that case the only breach by the seller was that, although he had delivered the correct quantity of tins of pears, he had delivered them packed in cases of 24 tins instead of in cases of 30 tins. In a situation where this breach would cause the buyer no loss or inconvenience, this breach would seem to be so slight that it would be unreasonable for the buyer to reject the goods. Section 15A, which denies the buyer the right to reject for a slight breach of condition, applies only to breaches of the conditions in sections 13–15. Even in relation to those conditions, it does not apply to a buyer who "deals as a consumer", the definition of this latter expression being the same as that used in the Unfair Contract Terms Act 1977 (see paragraphs 10-21 to 10-23 above).

Acceptance

Faced with a breach of condition, the buyer's choice is either **13–04** to reject or to accept the goods. Acceptance of any part of the goods will preclude the buyer from later rejecting the goods accepted and may cause him to lose the right to reject other goods under the contract.

Simply taking delivery does not amount to acceptance. Acceptance may take one of three forms—section 35:

(i) If the buyer informs the seller that he has accepted the goods.

(ii) If the buyer takes delivery and he does some act inconsistent with the seller being the owner of them (*e.g.* by selling them).

(iii) If the buyer retains the goods for more than a reasonable length of time without informing the seller that he rejects them.

Neither of the first two of these, however, will amount to acceptance unless either the buyer examined the goods before the contract was made or, alternatively, has had a reasonable opportunity after delivery of the goods to examine the goods for the purpose of ascertaining whether they are in conformity with the contract—section 35(2). Thus, reselling the goods does not constitute acceptance unless the buyer has had a reasonable opportunity of examining them. For example, where a manufacturer sells goods in sealed containers to a distributor who resells them, that distributor does not thereby lose his right of rejection. If the distributor's buyer opens them up and finds them not to comply with a condition in his contract he may reject them. If they also do not comply with a condition in the contract between the manufacturer and distributor, the latter may also reject them.

In *Lee v. York Coach and Marine* (1977 QB), the buyer had **13–05** been supplied in March with a second-hand car which was not of merchantable quality because its brakes were defective. Because the buyer did not claim to reject the car until September, it was held that she had accepted it and that therefore she was entitled only to damages. This is an example of the third form of acceptance, which occurs if the buyer retains the goods for more than a reasonable length of time without intimating to the seller that he is rejecting them. It used to be thought that this meant a reasonable length of time to try the goods out (*i.e.* a relatively short period) and not a reasonable length of time in which to discover any defects there might be in the goods: *Bernstein v. Pamsons Motors (Golders Green) Ltd* (1986 QB). In that case the buyer of a new Nissan car had had it for less than three weeks and had made two or three short journeys in it for the purpose of trying it out, before the engine seized up because of a latent manufacturing fault. Rougier J. held that, before the seizure the buyer had already had the car a reasonable length of time for trying it out generally. Therefore the buyer had accepted the car and was entitled only to damages. Since then, however, section 35 has been amended by the Sale and Supply of Goods Act 1994. Thus we now know that in measuring whether a reasonable length of time has elapsed, the court has to take into account whether the buyer has had a reasonable opportunity of examining the goods for the purpose of ascertaining whether they are in conformity with the contract.

13–06   The 1994 amendments to section 35 brought two further new provisions which clarify what is not acceptance. First, the buyer will not be deemed to have accepted the goods merely because he asks for, or agrees to, their repair by or under an arrangement with the seller. Secondly, he will not be deemed to have accepted the goods merely because they are delivered to another under a sub-sale or other disposition. Suppose, however, that the sub-purchaser retains the goods for more than a reasonable length of time so that, *vis-à-vis* the buyer, the sub-purchaser has accepted them. In that case the buyer will *then* be deemed to have accepted the goods *vis-à-vis* his seller. These provisions were considered in *Truk (UK) Ltd. v. Tokmakidis GmbH*, 2000, QBD. It involved a contract between two businesses for the sale and fitting of some lifting equipment to be paid for six months after delivery. The equipment was to be fitted to, and form part of, a towing vehicle which the buyer was then going to re-sell. Approximately six months after delivery the buyer was informed by a potential purchaser of the towing vehicle that the equipment was defective. The buyer immediately informed the seller and refused to pay the price pending investigation (by an appropriate company). About three months later, promptly upon receipt of the result of the investigation which confirmed the allegation, the buyer unequivocally rejected the goods. The judge held as follows. Where goods as sold for resale, a reasonable time in which to give notice of rejection should normally be the time actually taken to resell the goods, together with an additional period in which they can be inspected and tried out (by the sub-purchaser). Where the price is payable at a date after delivery, that reasonable period of time should normally last at least until the date for payment. The reasonable time had not expired when about six months after delivery, the buyer first questioned compliance. The buyer was entitled to a further period in which to investigate that issue. Accordingly the buyer had not accepted the goods when he (validly) rejected them nine months after delivery.

The law on acceptance as just set out is the law as it currently is. By January 1, 2002, however, it will need to have been changed in order to comply with the European Directive on Consumer Guarantees—probably by a provision stating that the buyer, if a consumer, will not be taken to have accepted the goods before the lapse of two months from when the buyer discovers a defect in the goods. For more details, see paragraph 7–52 above.

Partial rejection

Until section 35 was amended by the 1994 Act, there was a **13–07** rule that acceptance by the buyer of all or any part of the goods precluded the buyer from being able to reject any of the goods. There were exceptions to that rule: (a) in the case of a severable contract, where acceptance of goods under one severable part of the contract did not preclude the possibility of rejecting the goods under another part; (b) where goods more than the contract quantity were delivered, in which case the buyer had the option of accepting the contract quantity and rejecting the rest. These two exceptions remain. However, there is also now a general exception to that rule. Section 35A was inserted into the Sale of Goods Act and it states:

"(1) If the buyer—

    (a) has the right to reject the goods by reason of a breach on the part of the seller that affects some or all of them, but

    (b) accepts some of the goods, including, where there are any goods unaffected by the breach, all such goods, he does not by accepting them lose his right to reject the rest.

(2) In the case of a buyer having the right to reject an instalment of goods, subsection (1) above applies as if references to the goods were references to the goods comprised in the instalment.

(3) For the purposes of subsection (1) above, goods are affected by a breach if by reason of the breach they are not in conformity with the contract.

(4) This section applies unless a contrary intention appears in, or is to be implied from, the contract."

Thus, in order to exercise a right of partial rejection under this provision, the buyer must first have a right to reject the goods, *e.g.* because of a breach of condition, and must secondly accept all the goods which comply with the contract. Providing he accepts all the goods which comply with the contract, he is not precluded from rejecting some, or all, of those which do not. It should be observed that although section 35A(4) states that this section applies only if a contrary intention does not appear, nevertheless, a clause in a contract which purported to deprive the buyer of his right of partial rejection would be an exclusion clause and therefore could well be rendered ineffective by the Unfair Contract Terms Act 1977.

13–08   There is one qualification to the right of partial rejection just mentioned. This lies in the concept of a "commercial unit". A commercial unit is a unit of goods, "division of which would materially impair the value of the goods or the character of the unit". An example might be a two-volume dictionary, the first volume dealing with, say, A to K and the second with L to Z. Suppose that one of the volumes is, and the other is not, of satisfactory quality. By virtue of section 35(7), a buyer accepting any goods in the commercial unit is deemed to have accepted all the goods in that unit. Thus the buyer could not accept one of the volumes and reject the other.

Waiver

13–09   The buyer may lose his right to reject by waiver of that right— section 11(2). This may be particularly relevant where the seller is, to the buyer's knowledge, in breach of condition before the goods are delivered. If the buyer indicates that he will nevertheless accept delivery in spite of the breach of condition, that may well amount to waiver (see *Rickards v. Oppenheim*, paragraph 7–14 above).

Treatment of contract as repudiated

13–10   The buyer's right to treat the contract as repudiated arises in the same circumstances as his right to reject the goods, *i.e.* if the seller commits a breach of condition or a breach of warranty which deprives the buyer of substantially the whole benefit of the contract (see paragraphs 7–09 to 7–12, above). Often the buyer will exercise both remedies at once, *i.e.* will reject the goods and will also indicate that he is not going on with the contract, *e.g.* by demanding his money back. He can, however, reject the goods without treating the contract as repudiated. If he does, then the seller is at liberty, if he can do so, to re-tender goods which comply with the contract. If the seller does so, he will be entitled to the price. It can of course also occur that the buyer treats the contract as repudiated by the seller and yet does not reject any goods. This could occur if the breach by the seller is a failure to deliver the goods by the contractual delivery date, or if the seller commits an anticipatory repudiation, *e.g.* informs the buyer that he will not be delivering or will not be delivering by the contractual delivery date. In the circumstances where the buyer accepts the seller's breach as a repudiation of the contract, the buyer will be entitled to damages assessed as for non-delivery of the goods (see Chapter 14). To exercise his right to treat the contract as repudiated by the seller's repudiatory breach, the buyer must inform the seller that he regards the contract as at an end.

Suppose the seller commits a wrongful anticipatory repudiation **13–11** which the buyer does not accept as a repudiation. This latter point would be clear if, for example, the buyer responded to the anticipatory breach by indicating that due delivery was still expected. If then the seller duly makes delivery in accordance with the contract, the buyer must accept it. This is because an anticipatory repudiation terminates a contract only if it is accepted by the innocent party: *Fercometal S.a.r.l. v. Mediterranean Shipping Co.* (1988 HL). If after having failed to accept the seller's breach as a repudiation, the buyer himself subsequently repudiates the contract, *e.g.* by rejecting goods which conform to the contract, he will himself be liable to the seller for damages assessed as for non-acceptance (see Chapter 14). These principles work exactly the same vice versa. Thus where the buyer commits an anticipatory repudiation which the seller fails to accept as terminating the contract, the seller will be liable if he himself subsequently fails to perform the contract.

Where one of the parties, say the buyer, treats the contract as repudiated giving a bad reason (*e.g.* simply that he has changed his mind about buying) or even giving no reason at all, that repudiation will not be wrongful if at the time of the repudiation he in fact had a valid reason for it. A party who gives a bad reason for his refusal to perform the contract, does not thereby deprive himself of a justification which in fact existed, whether or not he was aware of it, *Glencore Grain Rotterdam BV v. Lebanese Organisation for International Commerce* (1997 CA). The only exceptions to this are: (i) where that party is estopped from relying on the valid reason by virtue of an earlier representation of his, (ii) where the valid reason later relied upon is one which if given at the time, could have been put right by the other party. In this regard, however, note that in the case of a c.i.f. contract, the fact that goods were not shipped in conformity with the contract, does not justify the buyer in rejecting documents which conform to the contract (see paragraph 17–07).

Action for damages

13–12   The buyer can claim damages for non-delivery or for breach of any other condition or warranty. This right is an addition to any right to reject the goods or to recover the purchase price. The measure of damages will be considered in Chapter 14.

Recovery of the purchase price

13–13   Where the consideration has totally failed, the buyer can recover any payments he has already paid. This rule clearly applies in the case of a non-delivery. It also applies where the buyer exercises his right to reject the goods and treat the contract as repudiated because of a breach of condition. We have also seen a surprising application of it in the case of *Rowland v. Divall* (see paragraph 7–18 above).

Of course, in the situation where the buyer can and does accept part and reject part of the goods, (see paragraph 13–07 above), he is entitled to recover any part of the price that he has paid in respect of the rejected part of the goods and remains liable to pay, if he has not done so already, pro rata for the goods he has accepted.

ADDITIONAL OR ALTERNATIVE DEFENDANT

13–14   Of course, the seller will be liable for his own breach of contract. However, as an exception to the general rule, section 75 of the Consumer Credit Act 1974 allows the buyer in certain circumstances to bring against someone else (the creditor) a claim for the seller's breach of contract or misrepresentation. Section 75 has already been noted in connection with misrepresentation (see paragraph 6–06). It applies in exactly the same way in the case of a breach of contract by the seller. The claim that the buyer can bring against the creditor (*e.g.* the credit card company when the buyer has used his credit card to buy an item for more than £100) is the same as that which he can bring against the seller. The section only enhances the buyer's rights and therefore does not in any way reduce his right to sue the seller. The circumstances in which section 75 applies are set out in Chapter 25.

CHAPTER 14

THE MEASURE OF DAMAGES

GENERAL CONTRACTUAL PRINCIPLES

ACCORDING to the rules in *Hadley v. Baxendale* (1854) damages **14–01** for breach of contract can be obtained for two kinds of loss:

(i) any loss naturally arising from the breach;

(ii) any loss which at the time of making the contract the defendant could have predicted as likely (or not unlikely) to result from the breach of it.

These principles were applied in *Victoria Laundry v. Newman Industries* (1949 CA) where the laundry had agreed to buy a new (larger) boiler. In breach of contract the boiler was delivered five months late. For that period the buyers were therefore without its larger capacity and therefore unable to cater for a larger volume of business. They were awarded damages for this loss of ordinary business which arose naturally from the late delivery. They received no damages for the loss of some exceptionally lucrative government dyeing contracts which they would have secured if the boiler had been delivered on time. This loss did not arise naturally—in the usual course of business. Neither was it within the second type of loss above, because the sellers were unaware of the buyers' chance of obtaining those lucrative contracts.

PRIMA FACIE RULES

The general principles just outlined apply in sale of goods, for **14–02** although there are sections of the Sale of Goods Act governing the assessment of damages, those sections do little more than embody the general principles.

Non-acceptance

14–03   Section 50 provides:

> "(1) Where the buyer wrongfully neglects or refuses to accept and pay for the goods, the seller may maintain an action against him for damages for non-acceptance.
>
> (2) The measure of damages is the estimated loss directly and naturally resulting, in the ordinary course of events, from the buyer's breach of contract.
>
> (3) Where there is an available market for the goods in question the measure of damages is prima facie to be ascertained by the difference between the contract price and market or current price at the time or times when the goods ought to have been accepted, or (if no time was fixed for acceptance) at the time of the refusal to accept."

Subsection 3 lays down the prima facie measure of damages. The idea is that if the seller can sell the goods elsewhere at the same or a higher price than the buyer had agreed to pay, the seller has lost nothing, in which case he will receive only nominal damages. However, if the market price is less than the contract price, the difference between the two represents the seller's loss. The market price for these purposes is the price which in normal business dealings those goods would have fetched on the date when the buyer should have accepted the goods. If the market price subsequently rose or fell, that is irrelevant, even if the seller actually sold at that subsequent greater or lower price. This is clear from some words of Salmon L.J. in *Pagnan v. Corbisa* (1970 CA) which are quoted below.

14–04   The measure of damages in subsection 3, being prima facie, does not apply where it does not represent the seller's loss. In *Thompson v. Robinson* (1955 QB) the purchaser ordered from a motor trader a Vanguard car and later refused to accept it. The price of Vanguard cars did not fluctuate and the contract price and market price at the date of the buyer's breach were the same. However, the trader's loss was not merely nominal because he had lost a sale. It was held that the prima facie rule was displaced and the seller received as damages his loss of profit on one transaction. This was his loss "directly and naturally resulting".

That case was distinguished in *Charter v. Sullivan* (1957 CA) where the buyer refused to accept a Hillman Minx which he had ordered from a trader. The difference was that in *Charter v.*

Sullivan there was a shortage of Hillman Minx cars. The number of sales the trader could make was limited to the number of cars he could get. Demand exceeded supply. Thus when one purchaser backed out, the trader did not lose a sale. He received only nominal damages.

Thompson v. Robinson was distinguished also in *Lazenby Garages v. Wright* (1976 CA) where Mr Wright refused to accept a second-hand car which he had previously agreed to buy for £1,670 from a car dealer. The dealer sold it a little later to another buyer for £1,770. The dealer claimed from Mr Wright the loss of profit on one sale. However, it could not be said with any certainty that because Mr Wright had backed out, the dealer had sold one car less. This was because second-hand cars are all unique. It was held that since the dealer had sold the car for more than the price Mr Wright had agreed to pay, he had suffered no damages at all.

Even when it is not displaced, the prima facie rule does not exclude any further loss which was reasonably foreseeable as a result of the buyer's breach. So, for example, the seller will also be able to recover any reasonable extra storage expenses he has had to incur— section 37.

Non-delivery
Section 51 provides: **14–05**

"(1) Where the seller wrongfully neglects or refuses to deliver the goods to the buyer, the buyer may maintain an action against the seller for damages for non-delivery.

(2) The measure of damages is the estimated loss directly and naturally resulting, in the ordinary course of events, from the seller's breach of contract.

(3) Where there is an available market for the goods in question the measure of damages is prima facie to be ascertained by the difference between the contract price and market or current price of the goods at the time or times when they ought to have been delivered, or (if no time was fixed) at the time of the refusal to deliver."

This section is converse of section 50. If on the date the seller fails or refuses to deliver, the buyer can buy similar goods from elsewhere at the same or a cheaper price, then prima facie the buyer's damages are only nominal. If the market price is higher, then the prima facie measure of damages is the extra, *i.e.* the difference between the contract price and the market price on the date of the seller's breach. Again, it is the market price on the date of the breach which is important. In *Pagnan v. Corbisa* (1970 CA) Salmon L.J. explained the prima facie rule:

> "...the innocent party is not bound to go on the market and buy or sell at the date of the breach. Nor is he bound to gamble on the market changing in his favour. He may wait if he chooses; and if the market turns against him this cannot increase the liability of the party in default; similarly, if the market turns in his favour, the liability of the party in default is not diminished."

Thus, if the buyer does not immediately buy replacement goods but does so subsequently and at a different price from the market price at the date of the breach, that is normally irrelevant. His subsequent purchase is an "independent and disconnected" transaction.

14–06 The prima facie rule would be displaced by a subsequent transaction which was not "independent and disconnected", as illustrated by the facts in *Pagnan v. Corbisa*. The sellers delivered goods which did not comply with the conditions of the contract. The buyers rejected them but, before doing so, obtained from an Italian court a sequestration order which gave them the right to detain the goods against payment of damages. They then negotiated a new contract with the sellers whereby they bought the goods at a price considerably less than the market price—the price being depressed because of the sequestration order. The buyers nevertheless claimed under the first contract damages based on the difference between the contract price and market price on the date of the breach. The claim failed. The second contract could not be ignored since it was not an "independent and disconnected" transaction; the same buyer bought the same goods from the same seller. On the facts, the benefit of the second contract price being depressed was greater than the loss caused by the breach of the first contract. Therefore the buyers obtained no damages.

Anticipatory breach

14–07 Often a contract is to be performed in the future, *i.e.* delivery of the goods is to be in the future, either at a fixed date or within a reasonable length of time. In such a case it is possible for either the seller or the buyer to commit an anticipatory breach of contract, *i.e.* to repudiate the contract before the time for performance. This can be done by the seller informing the buyer that he will not deliver the goods or the buyer informing the seller that he will not accept them. When one side commits an anticipatory breach, the other party (the innocent party) is given an option. Either he can at once accept the anticipatory breach as a repudiation and immediately claim damages or else he can refuse to accept it as a repudiation and wait until there has been actual failure to perform the contract (as opposed to an anticipatory one).

If the innocent party adopts the latter alternative then he can claim damages if and when the actual breach (non-delivery or non-acceptance) occurs. In that case his damages are assessed on the principles already given (sections 50 and 51 above, paragraphs 14-03 to 14-06). Thus the measure of damages is the difference between the contract price and the market price on the date for *actual* performance. *Tai Hing Cotton Mill Ltd v. Kamsing Knitting Factory* (1978 PC) established that the same principle applies where the innocent party immediately accepts the anticipatory breach as a repudiation of the contract. The measure of damages is still the difference between the contract and the market price. The relevant market price is still that prevailing on the date for *actual* performance and not that prevailing on the earlier date of the anticipatory breach. This is so irrespective of whether the contract had a fixed future date for delivery or whether delivery was to be within a reasonable length of time.

Consider an example. On May 1, B agrees to buy from S 50 tonnes of cob nuts at £100 per tonne, delivery to be on December 1. On June 1, when the market price of cob nuts is £101 per tonne S informs B that S will not supply the nuts. B may refuse to accept that as a repudiation by S. In that case B will be able to sue for damages for non-delivery if on December 1 S does not deliver. The market price of cob nuts on December 1 is £110 per tonne. Thus B is entitled to the market price (£110 × 50) less the contract price (£100 × 50) = £500. Suppose that B had in June accepted S's repudiation of the contract. Then the assessment of B's damages would be on the same basis and B would similarly be entitled to £500.

There are just two qualifications to this last point, *i.e.* which apply where the innocent party immediately accepts the repudiation. First, if B's claim for damages comes to trial before **14-08**

225

December 1 (*i.e.* before the actual date of delivery), the court must determine the market price on that future date as best it can: *Melachrino v. Nickoll and Knight* (1920 KB). This will often be little more than guesswork. The second qualification is that an innocent party who accepts an anticipatory breach becomes under a duty to mitigate (minimise) his loss. Thus if B accepts S's repudiation in June and he sees the market price begin to rise, he has a reasonable opportunity to minimise his loss by buying replacement nuts immediately at less than £110 per tonne. In that case the court may well reduce his damages from the £500. It will do so irrespective of whether the buyer actually used the opportunity to buy replacement nuts.

Suppose now, however, that B, having accepted S's repudiation in June, sees the market beginning to rise rapidly in July and, in an attempt to minimise his loss before the market rises further, buys replacement goods on July 15 at £115 per tonne—only to discover that by the delivery date under the original contract (December 1) the market price has fallen back to £110 per tonne. In that case the court has a discretion (in order to avoid injustice) to award damages at the higher level of £750 (*i.e.* by reference to the market price at July 15 instead of the later contract delivery date of December 1): *Johnson v. Agnew* (1979 HL).

The duty to mitigate does not apply where the innocent party refuses to accept the anticipatory breach as a repudiation. Because he is waiting to see if the anticipatory breach turns into non-performance in fact, he is not expected to buy any replacement goods until the date of actual non-performance.

14–09 Now suppose that the buyer commits a wrongful anticipatory repudiation of the contract and the seller immediately accepts that repudiation as terminating the contract and sues for damages. Clearly the seller does not have to remain ready and willing to deliver. The buyer is the only party to have broken the contract and the seller will be entitled to damages from him according to the principles just outlined. What, however, is the position if, at the time of the buyer's wrongful anticipatory repudiation, the seller had already been disabled from completing the essential terms of the contract (*e.g.* the seller's factory making the goods was already so far behind in production that the seller could not possibly have delivered the goods by the contractual delivery date)? In that case the seller's damages would be reduced from the prima facie level in section 50: *British & Benningtons v. North West Cachar Tea Co.* (1923 HL). To achieve a reduction, however, the burden of proof rests upon the buyer to show that the seller would have been unable to comply with the essential terms of the contract if it had not been terminated: *Gill & Duffus v. Berger & Co.* (1984 HL). Even if the buyer were able to do that, the greatest reduction the buyer could achieve would still leave the seller entitled to nominal damages.

Late delivery

Late delivery by the seller will normally be a breach of condition (see paragraph 7–13 above). If the buyer rejects the goods for breach of condition, his damages are assessed as in the case of non-delivery. If it is only a breach of warranty or if the buyer accepts the goods, the damages are prima facie assessed according to the difference between the value of the goods on the date they should have been delivered and their value (if lower) when actually delivered. **14–10**

As always, the prima facie method of assessment may be displaced and damages awarded for any loss which falls within the rules in *Hadley v. Baxendale*. *Victoria Laundry v. Newman Industries* (above) is an example of this.

Breach of condition

If the buyer rejects the goods, damages are assessed as in the case of non-delivery. If he accepts the goods, the damages are assessed as if it were a breach of warranty—section 53. **14–11**

Breach of warranty

Section 53(2) and (3) provide: **14–12**

"(2) The measure of damages for breach of warranty is the estimated loss directly and naturally resulting, in the ordinary course of events, from the breach of warranty.

(3) In the case of breach of warranty of quality such loss is prima facie the difference between the value of the goods at the time of delivery to the buyer and the value they would have had if they had fulfilled the warranty."

The prima facie rule in subsection (3) can be termed a "capital value" assessment. In fact the buyer has a choice. He can claim either his capital loss or his loss of profit. He cannot claim both: *Cullinane v. British Rema* (1953 CA). In that case the sellers had warranted that a clay pulverising machine would process clay at six tons per hour. In fact it could not do so. The purchaser claimed under two heads, first for the capital loss and secondly for his loss of profits—the latter head being based on the difference over three years between the profits made at the machine's actual rate of output and the higher profits which would have been made at the warranted rate of output. The Court of Appeal held that both claims could not succeed and disallowed the first (that being the smaller claim). It was also pointed out that the buyers could have claimed loss of profits for the whole of the estimated useful life of the machine (10 years in this particular case).

14–13   In addition to a claim for capital loss or loss of profits, a claim can be made for any consequential loss which falls within the rules in *Hadley v. Baxendale, i.e.* loss of a type which at the time of the contract could reasonably have been predicted by both parties as liable (*i.e.* not unlikely) to occur in the event of the breach. Indeed this is sometimes the only claim made, as in *Frost v. Aylesbury Dairy Co.* (see paragraph 7–48 above). It does not matter that the extent of the damage could not have been foreseen. Damage is recoverable provided the type of damage and the way it occurred were predictable. In *Vacwell Engineering v. B.D.H. Chemicals* (1969 QB) the sellers supplied (in glass ampoules) a chemical for use in the buyer's factory. The chemical was liable to explode on contact with water. No warning was given of this. Indeed, the sellers were unaware of it. The sellers were in breach of the implied condition that the goods should be reasonably fit for their purpose. Had the sellers known, they could have predicted that perhaps water would come into contact with the contents of an ampoule and cause an explosion. This is what occurred in the buyer's factory but, because a number of ampoules were being washed together, the explosion was much greater than might have been predicted and the damage much more extensive. Rees J. held that nevertheless the sellers were liable for all the damage.

14–14   It should be apparent from this case that in assessing what damages are recoverable (*i.e.* within the rules in *Hadley v. Baxendale*) for breach of a term as to quality, one does not ask simply "What type of damage could the seller at the time of the contract have predicted?" Rather one asks, "Had he known of the defect, what type of damage could the seller at the time of the contract reasonably have predicted?" A similar point arose in *Parsons v. Uttley Ingham* (1978 CA). The buyers, who were pig farmers, bought a 28ft-high hopper which, as the sellers knew, the buyers intended to use for the storage of pig nuts. On delivery the ventilator on top of the hopper was shut and nobody noticed. As a result nuts stored in the hopper became mouldy. A large number of the buyers' pigs died from an infection, *E. Coli*, triggered off by eating the mouldy pig nuts. The sellers were in breach of the implied condition that the hopper would be reasonably fit for the purpose for which the buyers required it. Was the resulting loss of the pigs recoverable under the rules in *Hadley v. Baxendale*? *E. Coli* was a hitherto unknown disease and also, apparently, it could not reasonably have been expected that pigs would become ill from eating mouldy pig nuts. However, the breach of contract by the sellers consisted not of feeding mouldy pig nuts to the buyers' pigs, but of supplying an unventilated hopper. If the sellers had known they were supplying an unventilated hopper, could they reasonably have regarded illness in pigs as a not unlikely consequence of that breach? It was held that they could and were therefore liable for the loss of the pigs. It was immaterial that the seller could not have predicted either the particular illness that resulted or the severity of it.

Section 53(1) allows the buyer to set off damages due to him for breach of warranty against the price he owes the seller. He can of course sue for any excess—section 53(4).

SUB-SALES

Non-delivery

Suppose that on December 1, X agreed to buy from Y for £100 **14–15** one tonne of corn to be delivered on January 1. Y does not deliver the corn and market price on January 1 is £105. Prima facie X is entitled to £5 damages. Suppose further that on December 15, X had agreed to sell a tonne of corn to Q, delivery to be on January 1. That sub-sale can affect X's loss. His loss could be less than £5 if, for example, in his contract with Q the price was £104. Alternatively, it might be greater if for example the price in Q's contract was £106 or if he himself is liable to Q for breach of contract. Does the law take sub-sales into account?

Generally, the effect of a sub-sale is ignored and the prima facie rule prevails. In *Williams v. Agius* (1914 HL) Williams agreed to buy from Agius a cargo of coal at 16s. 3d. per ton. Later he agreed with a sub-purchaser to sell him a similar cargo at 19s. per ton. Agius failed to deliver. Williams' damages were assessed at the difference between the contract price (16s. 3d.) and the market price on the date when delivery should have been made (23s. 6d.).

14–16   In *Re Hall & Pim's Arbitration* (1928) the House of Lords established an exception. The prima facie rule will be displaced and a sub-sale taken into account when the following circumstances all exist:

(i) The first contract contemplated the creation of sub-sales—so that the seller could predict from the outset that in the event of non-delivery the buyer might suffer loss in connection with sub-sales.

(ii) The sub-contract was for the sale, not merely of similar goods, but of the very same goods as were to be supplied under the first contract.

(iii) The sub-contract was not an extravagant or unusual bargain.

(iv) The sub-contract was created before the delivery date under the first contract.

If these circumstances all exist then the loss connected with the sub-sale(s) falls within the second rule in *Hadley v. Baxendale*. This was the position in *Re Hall & Pim's Arbitration*. On November 3 the buyers agreed to buy a cargo of wheat at 51s. 9d. per quarter. The contract clearly referred to the possibility of sub-sales. On November 21 the buyers made a sub-sale of the same cargo at 56s. 9d. per quarter. On March 22, when the seller refused to deliver, the market price was 53s. 9d. per quarter. The buyers were awarded damages assessed at 5s. per quarter and also damages which the buyers had to pay to their sub-buyer.

Late delivery

14–17   From *Wertheim v. Chicoutimi Pulp Co.* (1911 PC) it appears that sub-sales are taken into account more readily in the case of a late delivery. The contract price was 25s. per ton. Before the delivery date, the buyer made a sub-contract to sell similar goods at 65s. per ton. On the date when delivery should have been made under the first contract, the market price was 70s. When delivery was actually made, the market price had dropped to 42s. 6d. The buyer used the goods to fulfil his sub-contract. The Privy Council took the buyer's sub-sale into account and awarded damages assessed at only 5s. per ton.

Breach of term as to quality

Here also sub-sales are taken into account more readily than in **14–18** the case of non-delivery. The buyer can include in his claim for damages the amount of the damages he has had to pay out to his sub-purchaser for breach of contract, see *Godley v. Perry* (paragraph 9–05 above). For this, it is sufficient that the seller knew or ought to have known that the buyer bought the goods for resale.

Sub-sales which are within the reasonable contemplation of the parties, can result in the seller's damages being either more or less than the prima facie measure laid down in section 53(3). *Bence Graphics v. Fasson UK* (1996 CA) involved the sale of vinyl film. The sellers knew that the buyer was going to make it into decals (identification labels for bulk containers) and sell them to companies involved in the international container business. Over a period of years the sellers supplied the buyer with vinyl film which, in breach of an express contract term, was not such that it would survive in good legible condition for at least five years. This was discovered only much later. The value of the film supplied with this latent defect was in fact zero and thus the prima facie measure of damages laid down in section 53(3) (*i.e.* difference between the value the goods should have had on delivery and the lower value of the goods actually supplied) was the whole of the contract price. The breach meant, however, that the buyer was exposed to the risk of claims by their sub-buyers, which could have greatly exceeded that prima facie amount. Nevertheless no such claims were made. The Court of Appeal held that the prima facie measure of damages was displaced. Just as the buyer could have claimed a greater figure if he had had to meet claims in excess of the prima facie amount, equally the sellers did not have to pay the prima facie amount where it exceeded the buyer's actual loss.

MITIGATION

The innocent party is under a duty to take reasonable steps to **14–19** mitigate (minimise) his loss. Any loss which he could reasonably have avoided will be deducted from his damages.

His duty is to act reasonably. So, in the case of non-delivery, the buyer is not expected to hunt the globe to find similar goods: *Lesters Leather & Skin Co. v. Home & Oversees Brokers* (1948 CA). Similarly, a purchaser need not force defective goods upon his sub-purchaser (even if contractually entitled to do so) if that would involve damaging his own commercial reputation: *Finlay v. Kwik Hoo Tong* (1928 CA).

Sometimes the party in default makes an offer to put things right, *e.g.* the seller offers to buy back defective goods. If the offer is a reasonable one then it is likely to be reasonable to accept it. An unreasonable refusal will be a breach of the duty to mitigate: *Payzu v. Saunders* (1919 CA).

14–20   Occasionally, albeit rarely, steps taken by the claimant in an attempt to minimise his loss result in fact in increasing it. In that case the extra loss is recoverable in a claim for damages. The defendants in *Hoffberger v. Ascot International Bloodstock Bureau* (1976 CA) had contracted to buy a mare from Mr Hoffberger for £6,000 in October 1973 provided that on that date the mare was in foal. When the time came the mare was in foal but they failed to buy her and finally refused to do so in December 1973. Mr Hoffberger was unable to sell the mare at the December 1973 sales because she was ill. In an attempt to obtain a good price, he paid a stud fee of over £1,400 to have her covered again so that he would be able to sell her in foal at the December 1974 sales. In fact the market fell and the mare in foal fetched only £1,085 at those sales. Mr Hoffberger was awarded damages of over £7,000. This sum included all the loss and expenses he had incurred in attempting to mitigate his damages. This was because those steps had been reasonable ones to take even though they had in the event aggravated the losses.

PENALTIES

14–21   Sometimes the contract stipulates how much is to be paid by the party in breach, *e.g.* "£100 per day for each day delivery is delayed". Such a clause is a liquidated damages clause and is binding upon the parties provided it is not a penalty. If it binds the parties, the stipulated amount is the amount payable and that is the case, whether the loss actually caused is greater or smaller.

It is a penalty if it was not a genuine attempt by the parties to pre-estimate the likely damages but was intended to hang in terror over one party to ensure that he carried out the contract. Some sentences of Lord Dunedin's in *Dunlop Pneumatic Tyre Co. v. New Garage Motor Co.* (1915 HL) are particularly instructive:

> "Though the parties to a contract who use the words 'penalty' or 'liquidated damages' may prima facie be supposed to mean what they say, yet the expression used is

not conclusive. The court must find out whether the payment stipulated is in truth a penalty or liquidated damages...

It will be held to be a penalty if the sum stipulated for is extravagant and unconscionable in amount in comparison with the greatest loss that could conceivably be proved to have followed from the breach...

There is a presumption (but no more) that it is a penalty when 'a single lump is made payable by way of compensation, on the occurrence of one or more or all of several events, some of which may occasion serious and others but trifling damage...'

On the other hand: it is no obstacle to the sum stipulated being a genuine pre-estimate of damage, that the consequences of the breach are such as to make precise pre-estimation almost an impossibility. On the contrary, that is just the situation when it is probable that pre-estimated damage was the true bargain between the parties."

If it is a penalty, the clause is void and the innocent party can sue in the usual way for whatever is his actual loss. That loss will be calculated according to the principles outlined in the earlier parts of this chapter. Finally, a penalty within a consumer contract might well be rendered ineffective by the Unfair Terms in Consumer Contracts Regulations even if it were not struck down by the doctrine of penalties (see paragraphs 10–39 to 10–45 above).

CHAPTER 15

AUCTION SALES

IN most respects a purchase made at an auction constitutes an **15–01** ordinary contract for the sale of goods. Except in so far as the parties agree otherwise, the provisions of the Sale of Goods Act apply.

ADVERTISEMENTS BEFORE THE AUCTION SALE

An advertisement that an auction is to be held is not an offer **15–02** or a promise that the auction will be held. There is no liability if the auction is not in fact held. In *Harris v. Nickerson* (1873) the claimant travelled to the advertised place for the auction sale which he then found to be cancelled. It was held that he was not entitled to claim his travelling expenses from the advertiser.

It seems, however, that if the auction is in fact held, then anything advertised to be "without reserve" must be sold to the highest bidder. If it is withdrawn, then the advertiser is in breach of contract with any bidder who had come in response to the advertisement: *Warlow v. Harrison* (1859).

SECTION 57 OF THE SALE OF GOODS ACT

Section 57 states: **15–03**

"In the case of a sale by auction—

(1) Where goods are put up for sale by auction in lots, each lot is prima facie deemed to be the subject of a separate contract of sale.

(2) A sale by auction is complete when the auctioneer announces its completion by the fall of the hammer, or in other customary manner; and until such announcement is made any bidder may retract his bid.

(3) A sale by auction may be notified to be subject to a reserve or upset price, and a right to bid may also be reserved expressly by or on behalf of the seller.

(4) Where a sale by auction is not notified to be subject to a right to bid on behalf of the seller, it is not lawful for the seller to bid himself or to employ any person to bid at such a sale, or for the auctioneer knowingly to take any bid from the seller or any such person.

(5) A sale contravening subsection (4) above may be treated as fraudulent by the buyer.

(6) Where, in respect of a sale by auction, a right to bid is expressly reserved (but not otherwise) the seller or any one person on his behalf may bid at the auction."

With reference to subsections 5(4) and (5) the consequence of the buyer being allowed to treat the sale as fraudulent is that he can bring an action for damages and that he can rescind the contract, *i.e.* refuse to pay or take delivery or, if he has paid, demand the return of the price.

RESERVE PRICE

15–04   A problem arises if the seller (*i.e.* the person who puts the goods into the sale) imposes a reserve price and the auctioneer nevertheless accepts a bid for less than the reserve price. If the reserve price had been notified as allowed by section 57(3), then the bidder has no claim against the seller or auctioneer who will not be liable for refusing to deliver the goods: *McManus v. Fortescue* (1907 CA). If the reserve price had not been notified and the bidder had no reason to know of it, then the bidder will have an action against the auctioneer for breach of the auctioneer's warranty of authority. That is the implied warranty given by any agent (whether auctioneer or not) that he is acting within his principal's (in this case the seller's) authority.

EXEMPTION CLAUSES

15–05   The principles that apply are those applicable to sale of goods contracts generally. An illustration is provided by *Dennant v. Skinner* (see paragraph 3–08 above) where, after the goods had been knocked down to him, the buyer was persuaded to sign a statement that property was not to pass until his cheque was paid. The signed statement was held to be ineffective since it was given after the contract was made and therefore could not incorporate terms into the contract.

The usual method of incorporation is for the exemption terms to be set out in printed conditions which are commonly attached to or referred to in the auction catalogue and copies of which are usually displayed on the premises.

A sale by auction will not be a consumer deal for the purposes of the Unfair Contract Terms Act 1977. Therefore any contractual clause exempting from the provisions of sections 13–15 of the Sale of Goods Act will normally be effective provided it is shown to satisfy the requirement of reasonableness in the Unfair Contract Terms Act (see paragraph 10–24 onwards).

The Unfair Terms in Consumer Contracts Regulations 1999 apply to any auction sale where the seller is a trader and the buyer is buying for a purpose outside any business. They render ineffective any term which is unfair (see paragraphs 10–39 to 10–45 above).

POSITION OF THE AUCTIONEER

In selling goods, an auctioneer is an agent of the owner. In **15–06** *Chelmsford Auctions v. Poole* (1973 CA) Lord Denning M.R. explained that on a sale by auction there are three contracts. They are:

(i) Between the owner (vendor) and the highest bidder (purchaser).

(ii) Between the owner (vendor) and the auctioneer.

(iii) Between the auctioneer and the highest bidder (purchaser).

The first of these is a simple contract of sale to which the auctioneer is no party. The auctioneer's rights and obligations arise under the other two contracts.

Contract between auctioneer and owner (vendor)
Of this contract Lord Denning said,   **15–07**

> "The understanding is that the auctioneer should not part with possession of them (the goods) to the purchaser except

against payment of the price; or if the auctioneer should part with them without receiving payment, he is responsible to the vendor for the price...The auctioneer is given as against the vendor, a lien on the proceeds for his commission and charges."

This last means that the auctioneer when he receives payment from the purchaser can deduct his commission charges before passing on the money to the vendor. *Chelmsford Auctions v. Poole* involved the sale of a car which the auctioneers knocked down to the purchaser for £57. The purchaser paid an immediate deposit of £7. The auctioneers retained possession of the car. The auctioneers, without waiting for further payment from the purchaser, paid to the vendor the full amount of the price less their commission charges (£3.50). This deduction was quite proper. Subsequently the auctioneers, as they were entitled to, sued the purchaser for the outstanding balance of the price.

The terms of the contract between the auctioneer and the vendor can of course be varied by contrary agreement (*i.e.* usually by the printed auction conditions).

Contract between auctioneer and highest bidder (purchaser)

15–08   In the absence of contrary agreement, the common law implies the following terms into the contract:

   (i) a warranty by the auctioneer that he has authority to sell;

  (ii) a warranty by the auctioneer that he will give the purchaser possession of the goods against the price paid into his hands;

 (iii) a warranty by the auctioneer that the possession given to the purchaser will be undisturbed by the vendor or by himself;

  (iv) a warranty that he knows of no defect in the vendor's title.

The auctioneer, however, does not warrant the vendor's title in the case of a sale of specific goods (or unascertained goods out of a specific bulk) which the purchaser knows do not belong to the auctioneer. In *Benton v. Campbell, Parker Co.* (1925 KB) the auctioneer knocked down the car to the highest bidder. It turned out that the person who put the car into the auction (the vendor) was not the owner. It was held that the auctioneer was not liable to the purchaser. (The purchaser could, of course, have brought an action against the vendor under section 12 of the Sale of Goods Act.)

As well as giving the implied warranties listed above, the auctioneer has certain rights at common law. He has a special property in the goods, which gives him a lien over the goods until the whole of the price is paid or tendered. In *Chelmsford Auctions v. Poole* it was held that he also had the right personally to sue the purchaser for the price. Lord Denning further pointed out.

> "...the purchaser cannot avoid his liability to the auctioneer by paying the vendor direct without telling the auctioneer. If he does so, the auctioneer can make the purchaser pay the full price again, even though it means that the purchaser pays twice over."

These rights and obligations can be varied by the auction conditions.

AUCTIONS (BIDDING AGREEMENTS) ACTS 1927–69

These Acts are aimed at preventing auction rings. A ring is an **15–09** arrangement whereby several dealers all of whom are interested in a given item agree not to compete in outbidding each other at the public auction but instead to allow one of their number to buy it as cheaply as possible. The idea is that they subsequently hold their own private auction amongst themselves. Under the Acts it is a criminal offence for a dealer to offer or agree to give an inducement or reward to another for abstaining or having abstained from bidding. If goods are sold at an auction to someone who has been a party to such an agreement to abstain from bidding, then the seller can rescind the contract.

It should be noted that these rules relate only to agreements where at least one dealer is involved and also that they do not apply in the case of an agreement to purchase the goods bona fide on a joint account, *e.g.* where two dealers in partnership together wish to purchase goods for their business and agree that only one of them will bid. For the purpose of the Acts a dealer is "a person who in the normal course of his business attends sales by auction for the purpose of purchasing goods with a view to reselling them".

Apart from cases where the Auctions (Bidding Agreements) Acts apply, there is nothing illegal in two potential bidders agreeing that one of them will not bid with the result that the one who does bid obtains the property more cheaply than he otherwise would. The auction sale to the one who does bid remains perfectly valid: *Harrop v. Thompson* (1975 ChD).

MOCK AUCTIONS ACT 1961

15–10 This Act applies to auction sales where the goods include "any plate, plated articles, linen, china, glass, books, pictures, prints, furniture, jewellery, articles of household or personal use or ornament or any musical or scientific instrument or apparatus". It makes it an offence to promote or conduct or assist in the conduct of a mock auction. The Act defines a mock auction as an auction where persons are invited to buy goods by way of competitive bidding and:

(i) any goods listed above are sold to a bidder for less than his highest bid or part of the price is repaid or credited to him (or stated to be so);

or (ii) the right to bid for any goods listed above is (or is stated to be) restricted to persons who have bought or agreed to buy one or more articles;

or (iii) any articles are given away or offered as gifts.

"'Competitive bidding' includes any mode of sale whereby prospective purchasers may be enabled to compete for the purchase of articles, whether by way of increasing bids or by the offer of articles to be bid for at successively decreasing prices or otherwise." The defendant in *Allen v. Simmons* (1978 QBD) offered just one set of glasses and asked his audience who would pay him 30 pence for the set. A number of hands went up. The defendant then selected one of them and then sold the set to that person for one penny. It was held that the defendant was guilty, since in raising their hands the members of the audience were engaging in competitive bidding—namely in competing against one another for the chance of getting in first by raising a hand before anyone else or for the chance of attracting the defendant's favour in selecting the lucky buyer.

CHAPTER 16

E-COMMERCE AND DISTANCE SELLING

THIS chapter concentrates on legislation relevant to the increasing **16–01** trend towards the buying and selling of goods and services at a distance—including cross-border transactions—whether by mail, telephone, the internet or any other means. This chapter deals with a number of recent and proposed European Directives before concluding with an outline of the law's approach to questions, relevant to cross border contracts, of which countries have jurisdiction, and which country's law applies. For the principles of offer and acceptance applied to sales via the internet, see paragraph 2–08 above.

Electronic Communications Act 2000

The Electronic Signatures Directive (1999/93/EC) is **16–02** implemented in the United Kingdom by the Electronic Communications Act 2000. This Act does two main things. First, it creates a statutory approvals scheme for businesses and other organisations providing cryptography services. Cryptography services are essential for ensuring that electronic signatures fulfill their purposes. The statutory approvals scheme is no more than a scheme for giving a mark of quality, *i.e.* approval. It is not a licensing system and there is no legal requirement for anyone to have the statutory approval. Indeed the government has said that it will not bring the statutory approval scheme into force if the industry creates its own approval scheme. Secondly, the Act provides for the legal recognition of electronic signatures. An electronic signature is something in electronic form which:

"(a) is incorporated into or otherwise logically associated with any electronic communication or electronic data; and

(b) purports to be so incorporated or associated for the purpose of being used in establishing the authenticity of the communication or data, the integrity of the communication, or both"

16–03   The purposes served by an electronic signature are thus twofold: to confirm both authenticity (that the communication comes from the person it purports to come from, and is accurately timed and dated and intended to have legal effect) and also integrity (that it and the communication have not been tampered with).

The effect of the Act on electronic signatures is twofold. First it makes them admissible as evidence of authenticity and integrity. Secondly it gives relevant government ministers the power to amend any legislation for the purpose of authorising or facilitating the use of electronic communications and storage. This power is yet to be exercised. It presents a formidable task, given the multitudinous examples of legislation requiring something to be done "in writing". At present, for example, the provisions of the Consumer Credit Act 1974 and regulations made under it lay down very detailed requirements as to the form, contents and signatures of regulated agreements and for the giving of copies of it to the consumer.

Electronic Commerce Directive
16–04   In 1999 the European Commission issued this draft (proposed) directive. Some of its proposals have already been enacted in the United Kingdom. These include ensuring unsolicited e-mails are not sent to those who do not want them (see Distance Selling, paragraph 16–05 below). They also include ensuring that the making of contracts by electronic means is facilitated and not hampered by legal obstacles—a process begun in the United Kingdom by the Electronic Communications Act 2000 (above). Other proposals are requirements that: service providers acknowledge receipt of customer's orders; contract terms are made available; commercial communications are identified as such; prices are clearly indicated; promotional offers are clearly identified as such. The drawing up of codes of conduct for electronic commerce is encouraged.

DISTANCE SELLING REGULATIONS

16–05   The Distance Selling Directive (97/7/EC) aimed to ensure a common degree of consumer protection throughout the European Union where a consumer makes a contract without any face to face communication with the supplier. The consumer protection includes both ensuring that the consumer gets good information prior to the contact being made and also giving the consumer a right to cancel the contract during a subsequent cooling off period. Further protection extends to prevention of inertia selling, exempting the consumer from having to pay for unsolicited supplies and protection in the event of fraudulent use of a payment card.

In Britain the Directive will be implemented by the Consumer Protection (Distance Selling) Regulations 2000. *At the time of writing (August 15, 2000) these Regulations have not been made. The following text (paragraphs 16–06 to 16–22) is therefore based on the draft regulations which are likely in large measure to be reflected in the final version.*

Contracting-out

It is not possible to contract out of the regulations. Any contract term is void to the extent that it is inconsistent with any provision of the regulations for the protection of the consumer. **16–06**

Distance contracts

The regulations apply only to distance contracts. A contract is a distance contract if: **16–07**

1. it concerns goods or services,

2. it is between a supplier (acting for commercial or professional purposes) and a consumer (a natural person acting for purposes outside his business),

3. it is concluded under an organised distance sales or service provision scheme run by the supplier, and

4. the supplier makes exclusive use of distance communication up to, and at the moment, when the contract is made.

Distance communication is any means of communication not involving the simultaneous presence of the consumer and the supplier (or the supplier's representative)—*e.g.* telephone, mail order, letter, fax, e-mail, television. A transaction where initial contact is made by distance communication but where the contract is made face to face is not subject to the regulations. There is thus no chance of a contract being cancellable both under these regulations and also under either the Consumer Protection (Cancellation of Contracts Concluded away from Business Premises) Regulations 1987 or the Consumer Credit Act 1974, since the latter two sets of provisions in practice cannot apply where there has been no face to face contact between the parties. (For these two sets of provisions, see paragraphs 2–18 and 24–48).

The expression "an organised distance sales or service provision scheme" is obscure. What about a telephone enquiry by a consumer as a result of consulting Yellow Pages which leads to a contract being made during that telephone conversation? The fact that the supplier, *e.g.* a department store, has placed an advertisement in such a telephone directory does not in itself show that the supplier has a "distance sales scheme". On the other hand if it advertises its telephone number and runs a "home delivery service" then it does run such a scheme. The requirement for an "organised distance sales...scheme" will certainly exclude the regulations from applying to a supplier who does not normally indulge in distance sales but who does, for example, on a one-off occasion agree to take an order from a customer by telephone.

Excepted contracts

16–08   Even if a contract apparently falls within the definition of "distance contract", the regulations do not apply to it if it is an excepted contract. There are two groups of excepted contracts. The first group includes contracts: for the sale or disposition of an interest in land (except for rental); for a land mortgage; to finance (or to provide a bridging loan for) the purchase of an interest in land; for the construction or extension of a building or other erection on land. A contract is not excepted, however, if it is for the supply of goods and their incorporation in land, or for the repair or improvement of a building where the contract is not secured by a land mortgage. Thus, whereas a contract to have a garden shed made on site (from timber etc) seems to be excepted, a contract to have a ready-made garden shed supplied and erected would apparently not be. Clearly, a contract to have a tree supplied and planted would not be excepted; nor would a contract to have one's house decorated. The second group of excepted contracts comprises: contracts made at auction; contracts for the supply of financial services; contracts concluded via automated machines or premises *(e.g.* vending machines and automated car parks); contracts (for telephone calls) made by the consumer using a public pay phone. The regulations do not apply at all to excepted contracts.

16–09   There are two further groups of contracts to which the main provisions of the regulations (*i.e.* the requirements on prior information and the cancellation provisions) do not apply. The first of these are contracts for the supply of food, beverages or other goods intended for everyday consumption supplied to the consumer's residence or workplace by regular roundsmen. This group includes, for example, doorstep deliveries by the milkman. The second such group comprises contracts for the provision of accommodation, transport, catering or leisure services, where the supplier undertakes, at the time the contract is made, to provide those services on a specific date or within a specific period. This group includes, for example, the following when ordered or booked over the telephone or internet: hotel rooms; mini-cabs; theatre tickets; home delivery of a pizza; railway tickets (unless they are open dated). Whether this group also includes a hair "wash and cut" booked over the telephone, depends upon whether that is a "leisure" service. A contract to hire a marquee and have it erected in the consumer's garden for a party on a specific date might well be made over the telephone. Presumably this is not "accommodation". Very likely, however, it is a "leisure" service. If it is not, then the contract would seem to be fully subject to the regulations.

Information to consumer

Pre-contract information

The information required is: 1. The supplier's identity and, where **16–10** payment in advance is required, the supplier's address. 2. A description of the main characteristics of the goods or services. 3. The price, including all taxes. 4. Any delivery costs. 5. The arrangements for payment, delivery or performance. 6. The existence of a right of cancellation (except where there is no such right). 7. The cost of using the means of distance communication. 8. The period for which the offer, or the price, remains valid. 9. The minimum duration (where appropriate) in the case of contracts for the supply of products or services to be performed permanently or recurrently. This information must be provided:

(1) "in good time" prior to the making of the contract, and

(2) "in a clear and comprehensible manner appropriate to the means of distance communication used, with due regard, in particular, to the principles of good faith in commercial transactions and the principles governing the protection of those who are unable to give their consent."

The burden of proof rests on the supplier to show that he provided the required information in accordance with these requirements. Failure to do so renders the contract unenforceable against the consumer. It may be appropriate to provide the information other than in writing (*e.g.* in the case of a contract made by telephone). If it is provided in writing, the required information must be easily legible and be at least as prominent as any other information in the document (except the heading, the names of the parties to the contract and any information in handwriting). However it is provided, the supplier must when providing it make clear his commercial purpose. In the case of a contract made during a telephone conversation, the supplier must, at the beginning of the conversation, have made clear his identity and the commercial purpose of the telephone call. If he did not, the contract is unenforceable against the consumer.

Information in durable form

16–11   The requirement to give pre-contract information can be satisfied by provision of the required information in a non-permanent form (provided it is a form appropriate to the means of communication used). However, there is a requirement to give that same information to the consumer either in writing or in another durable medium which is available and accessible to the consumer. This must be provided either

    (a) prior to the making of the contract, or

    (b) in good time before or during performance of the contract.

Where the contract concerns goods (not for delivery to third parties) this information in durable form must be provided at the latest at the time of delivery of the goods. It seems likely that where the contract is made over the internet, provision of the information in writing in an e-mail would satisfy the requirement that it be in a "durable medium available and accessible to the consumer". If the information is not provided as required, the contract is unenforceable against the consumer.

Notice of cancellation rights and where to complain etc

16–12   Further information also has to be provided to the consumer. Again, if it is not, the contract is unenforceable against the consumer. This information is: (i) the supplier's geographical business address to which complaints may be addressed; (ii) information on any after-sales service and guarantees; (iii) the conditions for cancelling the agreement, where its duration exceeds a year or is unspecified; (iv) the supplier's name; (v) the supplier's reference number or code or other details (*i.e.* to enable the contract to be identified); (vi) a notice of the consumer's cancellation right and where and how it may be exercised. The consumer may be given a cancellation form which the consumer can use to cancel the contract.

There is an exemption from the requirement to give the further information in the case of a distance contract where services are supplied on one occasion only and are invoiced by the operator of the means of distance communication. This would apply, for example, in the case of information provided over the telephone via a premium rate call. Even in this exceptional case, however, the supplier must, when requested, provide the consumer with a geographical address of the supplier's place of business to which complaints can be addressed. Failure to do so renders the contract unenforceable against the consumer. **16–13**

Cancellation

Cancellable agreements

The regulations give the consumer a right to cancel a "distance contract" the agreement during a short period after the contract has been made. As has been seen, however, some distance contracts are excepted from the application of the regulations or the main part of the regulations (see paragraphs 16–08 to 16–09 above). The regulations deny the right of cancellation in certain other cases as well: (a) in the case of a contract for the provision of services, if performance of the contract has begun with the consumer's consent before the end of the cancellation period; (b) a contract where the price of the goods or services is dependent on fluctuations in the financial market which cannot be controlled by the supplier; (c) a contract for the supply of goods made to the consumer's specifications or clearly personalised or which by their nature cannot be returned or are liable to deteriorate or expire rapidly (*e.g.* flowers); (d) a contract for the supply of audio or video recordings or computer **16–14** software which have been unsealed by the consumer; (e) a contract for the supply of newspapers, periodicals or magazines; (f) a contract for gaming or lottery services. In any case where the regulations do not confer a right of cancellation, it is, of course, possible for the contract expressly to do so.

Cancellation notice

16–15   The consumer can exercise her right of cancellation by serving, within the cancellation period, a written notice of cancellation (whether or not by using a cancellation form provided by the supplier) indicating her intention to cancel the agreement. The notice of cancellation must be served on the supplier or on the person specified in the information given to the consumer as being a person to whom such a notice may be sent.

Cancellation period

16–16   Normally, the cancellation period expires:

- in the case of goods, at the end of a period of seven working days after the goods are delivered", and

- in the case of services, at the end of a period of seven working days after the contract is made.

The cancellation period is extended where, at the time of delivery (in the case of goods) or the making of the contract (in the case of services), the supplier has failed to comply with the requirement to supply certain information in writing or in another durable medium. In that case the cancellation period will expire at the *earlier* of the following two times:

(i) the end of a period of seven working days after the supplier complies with the requirement to provide the required information in a durable medium;

(ii) the end of a period of three months and seven working days after delivery (in the case of goods) or after the making of the contract (in the case of services).

Effect of cancellation

Broadly the position after cancellation is that the consumer is **16–17** entitled to recover any payments she had already made and any goods given in part-exchange (or their part-exchange allowance) and is under a duty to allow the supplier to recover possession of any goods supplied. In fact the legal position is virtually identical to the position following cancellation under the Consumer Protection (Cancellation of Contracts Concluded away from Business Premises) Regulations 1987—for details see paragraph 2–21. The main difference between the two sets of regulations is that whereas under the 1987 regulations the consumer does not have to return perishable goods or goods which have been consumed before cancellation but remains under a duty to pay for them, under the 2000 regulations contracts for those two types of goods are, as we have seen at paragraph 16–14, not cancellable at all. The net result, however, is the same.

Cancellation (under the 2000 regulations) of a distance contract, **16–18** also results in the automatic cancellation of any related credit agreement, *i.e.* any agreement whereby the supplier or a third party (acting under arrangements with the supplier) provided (or was to provide) credit to the consumer. Presumably this means that the related credit agreement is cancelled to the extent that it was to provide credit to finance the consumer's duty to pay the price under the distance contract. In such a case, if the credit provider is a different person from the supplier, the latter is under a duty to inform the credit provider as soon as the supplier receives the consumer's notice of cancellation. The consequences of cancellation of the related credit agreement (or that aspect of it involving credit to finance the distance contract) are virtually identical to those applicable when a cancellable debtor-creditor agreement is cancelled under the cancellation provisions of the Consumer Credit Act 1974. Those consequences are explained at paragraph 24–55 below.

Performance

The regulations require that: Unless the parties agree **16–19** otherwise, the supplier shall perform the contract within a maximum of thirty days beginning with the day following that on which the consumer forwarded his order to the supplier.

Where the supplier is unable to perform the contract, he must inform the consumer and repay any sum paid by the consumer as soon as possible and in any event within thirty days of his informing the consumer of his inability to perform. In the case of outdoor leisure events which by their nature cannot be rescheduled, however, the requirement to make a refund does not apply if the parties have so agreed. The requirement to give notice of inability to perform (and to make a refund) is subject to the possibility of the supplier being allowed to provide substituted performance in the form or goods or services of equivalent quality and price. This is allowed, however, only if three conditions are all satisfied:

    (i) The possibility (of the substituted performance) was provided for, either in the contract or prior to its making.

    (ii) The consumer was informed of this possibility in a clear and comprehensible manner.

    (iii) The cost of returning the goods in the event of the consumer exercising her right of cancellation is to be borne by the seller and the consumer is informed of this.

Presumably failure to comply with the requirement to perform within the 30 day period renders the seller/supplier liable to pay damages.

Fraudulent use of payment cards

16–20   The regulations entitle the consumer to "cancel a payment" where "fraudulent use" has been made of her payment card in connection with a contract to which the regulations apply. This provision applies not just to regulated credit cards but also, for example, to current account debit cards (*e.g.* Delta or Swift) and to charge cards (*e.g.* American Express and Diners Club), which are exempt from being regulated by the Consumer Credit Act 1974. The regulations do not explain what is meant by "fraudulent" use of the card. Presumably it covers, not only use by someone who has stolen the card from the cardholder (*e.g.* by taking the cardholder's handbag), but also by someone who has simply noted the card number and then, without any authority from the cardholder, used that number to make a payment over the telephone. The regulations do not, however, apply where a rogue uses the card to withdraw some money from the cardholder's bank account via an automated teller machine

(ATM), since the rogue is not in that instance using the card to make a "payment". Nor do the regulations apply where the rogue uses someone else's card to make a payment when buying goods or services over the counter, since they apply only to distance contracts. In these cases the cardholder would have to rely on the cardholder's rights under the Banking Code of Practice or, in the case of a card regulated by the Consumer Credit Act, that Act (see paragraphs 26–35 to 26–38).

Restrictions on use of distance selling communications

The Regulations impose restrictions upon the use of distance   **16–21** communications for distance selling purposes. The use of e-mail, faxes and automatic calling systems (*i.e.* ones which when activated, operate without human intervention) is prohibited unless the consumer has opted in, *i.e.* has previously notified the supplier that he consents to such communications being sent by or on behalf of the supplier. The use of other means of distance communication (*e.g.* telephone or the post), is prohibited if the consumer has opted out, *i.e.* has previously notified the seller that she does not consent to receive them or is listed in the record held of persons who have indicated that they do not wish to receive such communications. These prohibitions are enforceable by the Data Protection Commissioner. Also the recipient of a prohibited communication may be able to claim compensation from the sender. The latter may be able to establish the defence of due diligence (that he took reasonable care to comply with the regulations).

Enforcement

Certain bodies may consider complaints about alleged   **16–22** contraventions of the regulations, including: the Data Protection Commissioner, the Director General of Telecommunications, Weights and Measures Authorities (*i.e.* local Trading Standards Departments) and the Consumers' Association. There are provisions for such a body to notify the Director General of Fair Trading that it is considering a complaint. In the absence of such a notification, the Director General of Fair Trading is under a duty to consider any such complaint he receives. All these bodies have power to ask the court for an injunction against an offending trader.

CROSS BORDER CONTRACTS

16–23   We are dealing with the situation where someone in England buys goods (or services) from, or sells them to, someone in another country, principally where the other country is an EU country. There are three important issues: (i) jurisdiction, (ii) applicable law, (iii) enforcement of judgments. The rules on the first two vary according to whether the buyer is a consumer, *i.e.* someone buying for a purpose outside her trade or profession. In the EU, the law on the first and third of these issues is in the Brussels Convention 1968 (as amended), which was incorporated in United Kingdom law by the Civil Jurisdiction and Judgments Act 1982. [By virtue of the Lugano Convention 1988, the law on these issues is virtually identical in the case of a contract between someone in an EU state and someone in an EFTA state which is not part of the EU (Iceland, Norway and Switzerland).] The rules as to the applicable law were established by the Rome Convention 1980 which was incorporated into United Kingdom law by the Contracts (Applicable Law) Act 1990. The Rome Convention is not confined, however, to EU countries.

As a result of the Treaty of Amsterdam, the matters covered by these conventions have moved into the mainstream of EU business. Thus it is intended that the Brussels Convention will be replaced, in an amended form, by an EU Regulation, probably before the end of 2001. Eventually, the Rome Convention also will be replaced by an EU Regulation.

Jurisdiction

16–24   The general rule is that jurisdiction for contract claims lies with the country where the defendant is domiciled (Brussels Convention, Article 2). Thus normally the defendant must be sued in his own country. An individual is domiciled in a country if he resides there and has a substantial connection with it. A company or other corporate body is domiciled in the country where it has its seat, *i.e.* if either (i) it was incorporated there and has its registered office or some other office address there or (ii) its central management or control is exercised there. There are exceptions or variations to the general rule. The main ones applicable in the context of contracts to supply goods or services are as follows.

Branch or agency

Where a defendant company is domiciled in an EU country and **16–25**
the proceedings arise out of the operations in another EU country
of a branch, agency or other establishment of the defendant
company, the defendant company can be sued in the country
where the branch, agency or other establishment is situated. Even
where the defendant company is not domiciled in the EU, a
consumer can bring a contract action in an EU country if the
proceedings arise out of the operation in that EU country of a
branch, agency or other establishment of the defendant company.

Country of performance

A contract claim can be brought either in the country where the **16–26**
defendant is domiciled or in the country where the obligation in
question was to be performed (Article 5(1)). This would seem to
seem to allow, for example, proceedings to be brought in England
against a German seller who has contracted to deliver the goods
in England. The position is more doubtful, however, where all
that the German seller has agreed to do is to package them up
and send them to England.

Claim by consumer

Article 13 gives a consumer the option of suing in the country **16–27**
where the consumer is domiciled. Thus a consumer who buys
goods or services from a seller/supplier in another EU country,
can bring proceedings in the consumer's own country. This
applies to contracts for the sale of goods on instalment credit
terms and to contracts for loans repayable by instalments or for
any other form of credit made to finance the sale of goods. It also
applies to other contracts made by a consumer to buy goods or
services, but only if:

> "(a) in the State of the consumer's domicile the conclusion
> of the contract was preceded by a specific invitation
> addressed to him or by advertising, and
>
> (b) the consumer took in that State the steps necessary for
> the conclusion of the contract".

Thus Article 13 applies where an English consumer makes a
contract in response to an international mail order catalogue or a
newspaper advertisement in England by a French seller/supplier.
On the other hand, an English consumer who buys goods whilst

visiting France, will not be able to take advantage of Article 13 in the event that she wishes to sue the French seller. This is because the consumer did not in her own state, take the steps necessary for the conclusion (the making) of the contract. Imagine an English consumer who responds to a Belgian car seller's newspaper advertisement in England and who while at home (in England) makes a contract to buy a car from the Belgian seller, agreeing to collect the car herself and drive it home from Belgium. This consumer would be able to rely on Article 13. It is not absolutely clear, however, that Article 13 applies in the situation where a consumer buys goods (or services) over the internet from someone in another EU state. This is because it is not clear that "advertising" within Article 13 covers the advertising by a seller in one EU state on a website which can be accessed by consumers in other EU states. In the EU Regulation which will replace the Brussels Convention, it is expected that this uncertainty will be removed and that Article 13 will clearly apply to goods and services bought over the Internet unless the advertiser has expressly made clear on his website that his goods or services are not available in the consumer's home state.

16–28   In any situation where Article 13 does not apply, it may nevertheless still be possible for the consumer to bring a claim in England (for the seller/supplier's breach of contract) against the bank or finance company whose credit the consumer used to make the overseas purchase in question. An example is where the consumer has used her English credit card to pay for an item (costing over £100) in another country. (See *Jarrett v. Barclays Bank* in the next paragraph.)

Claim relating to land

16–29   In the case of a claim relating to immovable property, the general rule (giving jurisdiction to the country of the defendant's domicile) is displaced. Instead the country where the property is situated has exclusive jurisdiction (Article 16). This applies to tenancies and also even to short term lets or licences to occupy premises—the only exception being where the object of the claim is a let for temporary private use for a maximum period of six months and where the parties are both natural persons who are domiciled in the same country. Timeshare agreements are almost always made by *companies* supplying the timeshares to consumers and thus in such cases the country where the timeshare property is situated has exclusive jurisdiction. The English purchaser of a timeshare in Portugal will therefore not be able to sue the timeshare supplier other than by bringing proceedings in Portugal. That is so even if the timeshare supplier was domiciled in England. If, however, the timeshare purchase was financed by a regulated consumer credit agreement made in England between the purchaser and, say, a bank, the purchaser may well be able to bring a "like" claim against the bank (instead of against the Portuguese timeshare supplier) under section 75 of the Consumer Credit Act 1974. In that case the proceedings against the bank could be brought in England, *Jarrett v. Barclays Bank and Royal Bank of Scotland* (1999 CA). For the ability (under section 75) to be able to sue a "connected lender" for breaches of contract by the supplier, see 25–03 below.

Non-European connection

The Brussels Convention does not apply where the overseas **16–30** country of the buyer or seller is a non-European one. In this case the English courts will take jurisdiction in the following cases:

   (i) The defendant is present in person when served with the claim form. A company is present if it has a place of business in England or if it has filed with the registrar of companies the name of a person authorised to accept service on behalf of the company.

  (ii) The defendant submits to the jurisdiction by accepting service of the claim form.

 (iii) The court gives permission for service of the claim form outside the jurisdiction.

The court will not grant such permission unless England is a convenient forum for the dispute to be litigated (taking into account such matters as whether the witnesses are present in England, the place of residence of the parties, whether the law applicable to the agreement is English law). In any case, permission can be granted only if it falls within one of the following four categories:

  (a) The contract was made in England.

(b) The contract was made through an agent trading or residing in England on behalf of the defendant who was trading or residing elsewhere.

(c) The law applicable to the contract is English law.

(d) The contract states that the High Court shall have jurisdiction.

Applicable Law

16–31   The law which will be applied to the contract is not necessarily the law of the country which has jurisdiction and where the proceedings take place. Thus if proceedings are brought in England for breach of a contract to which French law applies, the English court will apply French law. Under the Rome Convention, the applicable law is the law chosen by the parties and, failing any choice having been made by the parties, it is the law of the country with which the contract is most closely connected. There is a presumption that this is the law of the party who has to effect "the performance which is characteristic of the contract". In effect therefore, unless the parties have expressly chosen a different law, the applicable law will usually be that of the seller rather than that of the buyer.

Where the parties have themselves chosen a law, that law may or may not be the law of an EU country. It is not possible, however, by choosing a different law to avoid the "mandatory provisions" of the law of the country where the litigation takes place. Where the litigation takes place in England, those mandatory provisions include the Unfair Contract Terms Act 1977, the Unfair Terms in Consumer Contracts Regulations 1999 and the Consumer Protection (Contracts Concluded by Means of Distance Communication) Regulations 2000. These mandatory provisions will apply to the contract, even if the law of another country is chosen by the parties as the applicable law.

Where an English buyer or seller deals with a seller or buyer in an overseas country to which the Rome Convention does not apply (*i.e.* country which has not become a signatory to the Convention, usually a country outside Europe), the rules as to which law applies to the contract are common law rules but are roughly similar in effect to the rules applicable under the Rome Convention.

Enforcement of a foreign judgment

The Brussels Convention applies in the case of a judgment in   **16–32**
an EU country which relates to a civil or commercial matter (*e.g.*
a breach of contract). Such judgments are enforceable in England
by a simple process of registration in the High Court. An
application to enforce in England a judgment from another EU
state is made "without notice" to the defendant, *i.e.* so as not to
give him notice and thus enable him to avoid enforcement. There
is a variety of procedures for enforcing judgments obtained in
non-European countries.

CHAPTER 17

INTERNATIONAL SALES

WHEN goods are sold by a seller in one country to a buyer in **17–01** another, there will be a delay between the contract being made and the goods reaching the buyer. Someone has to be responsible for arranging transport. It has also to be determined when and how the buyer is to pay, and in which country. The parties can make what arrangements they wish. C.I.F. and F.O.B. contracts are two classic types of contract used when goods are to be conveyed internationally by sea from seller to buyer. In each case, however, the parties are free to vary what would otherwise be the legal effect of making a C.I.F. or F.O.B. contract. There are a lot of other labels (*e.g.* "ex-works" "F.A.S."), some of which are merely variations on one of these main two. In order to encourage a consistent understanding of expressions such as C.I.F. and F.O.B. , the International Chamber of Commerce (the ICC) long ago produced a set of terms, INCOTERMS, which the parties can choose to adopt. The latest set are INCOTERMS 2000. In some respects INCOTERMS, if adopted, amend what would otherwise be the effect of the contract in English Law. They also add provisions to enable, for example, the use of modern communications systems to be used instead of paper. Throughout this chapter is it assumed that the contract is governed by English Law. First the effect of C.I.F. and F.O.B. contracts, in English Law, will be set out. Then the effect of the parties incorporating INCOTERMS will be outlined.

C.I.F. CONTRACTS

This type of sale contract enables the parties to base their **17–02** dealings as much as possible on documents. Apart from paying for the goods, the buyer does not expect to have to do anything in relation to the goods until they reach their destination port. Thus where goods are sold "c.i.f. Liverpool", the seller's duties include: (i) getting the goods to Liverpool, *i.e.* arranging their sea transport, and (ii) insuring them during the voyage under a marine insurance policy. In a C.I.F. contract, the Cost (*i.e.* the price) includes both the Insurance and the Freight. Payment is usually made during the voyage. The classic method of payment was by the buyer "accepting" a bill of exchange. In a simple case, the chronologically works as follows.

1. The seller arranges the insurance and sea transport.

2. The seller obtains an insurance certificate.

3. Upon the goods being received on board the vessel, the master of the ship gives the consignor (*i.e.* the seller) a receipt, termed a bill of lading. This is evidence of the contract of carriage and is also a transferable document enabling the holder to claim the goods on arrival at the destination port.

4. Within a reasonable time after shipment, the seller sends to buyer by post the following documents, (i) the insurance policy or certificate, (ii) the bill of lading, (iii) a commercial invoice for the goods, (iv) a bill of exchange drawn on the buyer for the price, payable by the buyer on the date stated in the contract (*e.g.* "30 days after shipment").

5. The buyer receives the documents and then "accepts" the bill of exchange which he returns to the seller. "Accepting" it, means signing it thereby indicating his liability to pay on presentation of it to him on its due date. If the buyer does not "accept" the bill of exchange, he is obliged to return the documents, including the bill of lading, to the seller, s. 19 (see paragraph 3–29 above.)

The end result of this is:

- the buyer has (via the bill of lading) the ability to collect the goods at the port of destination, and/or, if necessary to sue the carrier for breach of the contract of carriage.

- the buyer has (via the insurance certificate) the ability to claim on the insurance policy for any loss of the goods or damage to them during the voyage,

- the buyer has (via the commercial invoice) the ability to get the goods through customs,

- the seller has the ability (via the bill of exchange) to secure payment.

The bill of exchange is a negotiable instrument payable by the **17–03** buyer on the date stated. Once the buyer has accepted it, the seller can immediately sell it to a bank (at a discount), thus transferring to the bank the right to recover the money from the buyer on the date stated on the bill of exchange. The value of the bill of exchange will be the contract price. That price will have been fixed by the parties in the knowledge (a) that the price includes the cost of the insurance and the freight, and (b) that the seller will have to sell the bill at a discount to obtain immediate payment. (For the bank's role in collecting payment, see paragraph 17–18 below.)

Sub-sales

The above account assumes that the seller is in country X and **17–04** the buyer in country Y. It is quite possible that having made the contract, the buyer then sells the very same cargo under a C.I.F. contract which he makes with his sub-buyer. The buyer has then sold, and the sub-buyer bought, goods which were already afloat. This is perfectly permissible in the case of C.I.F. contracts subject to English Law. (For the position where INCOTERMS have been incorporated see paragraph 17–15 below). It is not uncommon for a cargo to be the subject of a string of sub-sales before it arrives at its destination. There is no difficulty about this because in each case the buyer can pass on to his sub-buyer documents (bill of lading, certificate of insurance etc) which he received from his seller. The buyer at the end of the string, the ultimate buyer, will be able to use the bill of lading entitling him to secure possession of the goods and the certificate of insurance to enable him if necessary to claim for loss or damage which occurred at any stage during the voyage, including any such loss or damage which occurred before he bought the goods. The ultimate buyer will have to pay the cost of unloading and any import duties at the destination port.

Property

In a C.I.F. contract, property passes when it is intended to pass, **17–05** namely when the buyer takes up the documents (at 5 in the chronology at paragraph 17–02 above). At least, this is so provided that the goods were at that time ascertained (see section 16 at paragraph 3–09 above). If the goods were merely a specified quantity out a larger bulk, *e.g.* a part of larger consignment, then the buyer could, once he had paid, acquire an undivided share in the bulk under section 20A (see paragraph 3–38 above). That, however, would be irrelevant in relation to the passing of risk because in making a C.I.F. contract, the parties have also agreed that risk passes before property.

Risk

17–06   Risk passes to the buyer when the goods pass over the ship's rail into the vessel at the port of loading: *Johnson v. Taylor Bros* (1920 HL). Normally the buyer will be able to claim on the marine insurance policy for loss or damage suffered during the voyage. Even if the loss is not one normally covered by such policies and not covered by the particular policy in this case, the buyer still bears any loss or damage to the goods occurring during the voyage and is thus required to pay the price in the usual way, *i.e.* the buyer must take up the documents: *C. Groom Ltd. v. Barber* (1915 KB). Even if the loss or damage (during the voyage) occurred before the documents were tendered to the buyer (*i.e.* before property passed to the buyer), that loss still falls on the buyer. Thus the seller can make a valid tender of documents, even though the goods have already been lost or damaged on the voyage: *Manbre Saccharine Co. Ltd. v. Corn Products Co. Ltd.*(1919 KB). Of course, it is possible that the goods were, unknown to the seller, already destroyed (*e.g.* the ship had sunk) before the contract was even made, *e.g.* if the contract was the last in a string of C.I.F. contracts. In that case, on ordinary contract principles, the contract would be void and no risk would pass to the buyer: see section 6 (paragraph 4–02 above).

Rejection

17–06   The buyer has two rights of rejection, (i) he can reject the documents if they do not conform to the contract and, (ii) he can reject the goods if upon their arrival if there is a breach of condition which was not apparent on the face of the documents. These rights reflect corresponding, and separate, duties of the seller (i) to ship goods which conform to the contract (or to buy afloat goods which were already shipped in accordance with the contract), (ii) to tender documents conforming to the contract. If the buyer rejects documents which conform to the contract, that is a repudiation of the contract, which the seller is then entitled to accept as putting an end to the contract and therefore as relieving the seller of any duty to deliver the goods. The buyer's rejection of conforming documents is still a wrongful repudiation, even if the buyer subsequently discovers that the goods were themselves not in accordance with the contract: *Gill & Duffus v. Berger & Co.* (1984 HL). This can be seen as an exception to the general rule that a party who gives a bad reason for a repudiation can later rely on a valid justification, even if he had been unaware of it at the time of his repudiation (see paragraph 13–11 above). The fact is, however, that he would not be entitled to reject conforming documents even if he knew at that time that the goods did not comply with the contract. Of course if the buyer does not reject the documents, or alternatively the seller does not accept the buyer's rejection of them as ending the contract, the buyer will be able later to reject the goods, if they were shipped in breach of a condition of the contract, *e.g.* did not match the contract description. At least, he will have that right unless the breach was a breach of one of the implied conditions in sections 13–15 and the breach was so slight that to reject the goods would be unreasonable (see paragraph 13–03 above).

It is normally a stipulation of the contract that the goods be **17–08** shipped on, or before, a stated date or within a stated range of dates (*e.g.* during July 2000). This will be a condition. If the documents (*i.e.* usually, the bill of lading or the commercial invoice) show that this condition or any other condition of the contract was broken, then the buyer has the right to reject the documents. If the buyer nevertheless accepts the documents, he thereby waives his right to rely on the breach in question. This causes the doctrine of estoppel to apply; the buyer will be unable subsequently to rely on a breach as entitling him to reject the goods, if that breach was disclosed on the face of the documents: *Panchaud Freres S.A. v. Etablissement General Grain Co.* (1970 CA).

When the buyer accepts the documents, property in the goods passes to the buyer. If he subsequently exercises his right to reject the goods, that property reverts to the seller: *Kwei Tek Chao v British Traders* (1954 QB, see paragraph 3–29 above).

F.O.B. Contracts

17–09   A contract "F.O.B. Southampton" is one where the goods are to be loaded onto the ship at Southampton. It is for the buyer to arrange and pay for the sea transport of the goods. It is for the buyer (unless he has made different arrangements with the seller) to procure space in a vessel and to nominate that vessel to the seller in time for the seller to be able to have the goods loaded within the contract period for shipment. The seller's duty is to have the goods loaded. The contract price does not include the cost of the sea freight. If the contract is an "extended F.O.B." contract and specifically provides for the seller to arrange (and pay for) the sea freight on behalf of the buyer, he is entitled to invoice the buyer for that cost in addition to the contract price.

Time

17–09   In a commercial contract time is, of course, of the essence. Failure to have the goods loaded within the dates allowed by the contract is a breach by the seller entitling the buyer to regard the contract as repudiated: *Bowes v. Shand* (1877 HL). Equally a contract requirement for the buyer to nominate the ship by a certain date is also a condition, breach of which entitles the seller to regard the contract as repudiated: *Bunge Corporation v. Tradax* (1981 HL) (see paragraph 7–14 above). Even if there is no such express term, there must be an implied term that the buyer will nominate the vessel to the seller in sufficient time to allow the seller to have the goods loaded on the first day of the contractual period for loading.

Passing of risk

17–10   Under an F.O.B. contract the parties intend the risk to pass when the goods are loaded, *i.e.* when they pass over the ship's rail. That is when risk passes, even if property does not pass until later. It is thus in the buyer's interest to make sure that he has insurance cover from that moment. Unless the parties have expressly agreed it, it is not the seller's duty to arrange insurance cover for the benefit of the buyer. It is the seller's duty to give such notice to the buyer as enables the buyer to take out the insurance cover during the voyage, s. 32(3). In the case of a strict F.O.B. contract, the buyer will already have such notice, by virtue of his own arranging of vessel and the loading date, and therefore will have no claim if the seller gives him no further notice,

Wimble & Sons v. Rosenberg (1913 CA). The position would be different, however, in the case of an "extended F.O.B." contract, *i.e.* where the parties had agreed that the seller, instead of the buyer, was to book the space on the vessel and deliver the goods on board that vessel. The seller would then have to give the necessary notice.

Passing of property

> "The expression f.o.b. determines how the goods shall be   **17–12**
> delivered, how much of the expense shall be borne by the
> sellers and when the risk of loss or damage shall pass to
> the buyers. It does not necessarily decide when the
> property is to pass." per Staughton L.J. *Mitsui v. Flota
> Mercante Grancolombiana, The Ciudad de Pasto* (1989
> CA).

Property passes when the parties intend it to: s.17. Normally in an F.O.B. contract the parties will be assumed to have intended property to pass upon loading, *i.e.* when the good pass over the ship's rail: *Carlos Federspiel v. Twigg* (1957 QB). Thus assuming that the goods have by then been ascertained (*i.e.* are not merely part of a larger bulk), property will pass upon loading, unless there is something to indicate that the parties had a different intention. There is, however, a rather large exception to this normal position. Where the seller has, upon having the goods loaded, obtained a bill of lading by which the goods are deliverable to the order of the seller, this normally raises the presumption that he has reserved a right of disposal until certain conditions are satisfied—the usual condition being that property is not to pass until the seller has been paid in full. In that situation, property does not pass upon loading but only when the buyer has paid the full price: *The Ciudad de Pasto* (above). The effect of this is that the buyer does not have property in the goods and thus lacks the capacity to sue a third party for damage done to the goods by that third party before the buyer has paid for the goods. The third party could for example be the master of another ship who by his negligence collides with and sinks the ship containing the contract goods. This makes it the more important for the buyer have insurance cover for the goods from the moment of loading. For the presumption of a reservation of a right of disposal, see section 19 (paragraph 3–29 above).

Rejection and payment

17–13   The buyer has two rights of rejection, (i) of the documents, (ii) of the goods. The position is just as it is in the case of a C.I.F. contract (see paragraph 17–07 above). As in the case of C.I.F. contracts, except where the seller has agreed to give credit, it is quite common for the contract to require payment against documents, which in the case of an F.O.B. contract will include a commercial invoice but will not necessarily include a bill of lading (but may simply be a master's receipt which enables the buyer to acquire a bill of lading) and will not include an insurance policy or certificate. For the role of bankers in presenting documents on behalf of the seller in exchange for payment by the buyer, see paragraphs 17–17 to 17–22 below.

Export duties

17–13   Whose duty it is to secure, or to use his best endeavours to secure, an export licence, depends on the provisions of the contract. The expression "subject to licence" usually means that the seller will use his best endeavours to obtain a licence. If the contract contains no express statement at all about the matter, then in an F.O.B. contract (or a F.A.S. contract) between parties in different countries, the seller is likely to be held under a duty to use his best endeavours to obtain any necessary licence: *AV Pound and Co. v. MW Hardy and Co.* (1956 HL). In that case if, despite the seller's best endeavours, a necessary export licence is not obtained, the contract will be frustrated. For the effect of INCOTERMS on this, see below.

INCOTERMS

17–14   Where the parties have incorporated INCOTERMS in their C.I.F. or F.O.B. contract, their rights and obligations will be much the same as those which would be applicable in English Law anyway. The main difference is that INCOTERMS allow the parties, where they have agreed to communicate electronically, to use the electronic version of documents such as a bill of lading or commercial invoice.

Another difference is that in the case of a C.I.F. contract under INCOTERMS the seller is, unless the parties agreed otherwise, bound to ship the goods himself and is not entitled to supply goods bought afloat.

In the case of an F.O.B. contract INCOTERMS make clear the position as regards the duty to secure export and import licences.

The seller has the duty to obtain any necessary export licence and the buyer any necessary import licence.

OTHER TYPES OF CONTRACT

There are 13 INCOTERMS in all. There now follows very **17–16** briefly an explanation of the 11 other types of contract of sale, some of which are merely variations on the classic C.I.F. and F.O.B. contracts. Just as for C.I.F. and F.O.B. contracts, so for each of these types of contract there is set of INCOTERMS which the parties can expressly incorporate. In each case, the rights and duties (summarised very briefly below) are subject to any contrary agreement by the parties. INCOTERMS specifically cater for multi-modal forms (*e.g.* by sea and land) of carriage, *e.g.* with CPT, CIP, DDU and DDP contracts.

Ex works

Here the seller's only responsibility is to make the goods available at his own premises. He has no responsibility for loading.

FCA Free carrier (at a named place)

The seller's responsibility is to transfer the goods into the hands of the carrier at the named place. Risk passes to the buyer at that stage. It is for the buyer to arrange the carrier.

FAS—Free Alongside Ship

Very similar to an F.O.B. contract, except that the seller has no duty to load the goods. He simply has to put them (*e.g.* in barge or tug) alongside the ship notified to him by the buyer. Risk passes when they are put alongside.

CFR—Cost & Freight (to a named destination)

Similar to a C.I.F. contract except that the seller has no duty to insure the goods during the voyage.

CPT—Carriage Paid To (a named place)

This requires the seller to put the goods into the custody of a carrier, carriage paid to the named place in the country of destination. Risk passes to the buyer when the goods are delivered to the carrier.

CIP—Carriage and Insurance Paid (to a named place)

This is the same as CPT except that here the seller also arranges insurance, at his expense, up to the named place in the country of destination.

DAF—Delivered at frontier (at named place)

The seller bears the expense of getting goods to the named place and risk passes on delivery at that place.

DES—Delivered ex ship (at named port)

This is an "arrival" contract. The seller bears all the costs of getting the goods to the named destination port. The goods are at the seller's risk until they reach are ready for collection at a usual unloading point at the destination port. The buyer incurs unloading costs.

DEQ—Delivered ex quay

This is the same as DES except that here the seller bears the unloading costs and the risk does not pass until the goods have been unloaded onto the quay or wharf.

DDU—Delivered Duty Unpaid

The seller pays all costs of getting goods to the named place of destination, except for import taxes and charges. Risk passes on delivery at place of destination.

DDP—Delivered Duty Paid

The same as DDU, except that the seller pays all charges, including import duties and charges.

METHODS OF PAYMENT

It may be that the buyer agrees to pay in advance. Contrariwise, **17–17** the seller may agree to provide goods on credit, especially to a valued customer about whom the seller has no financial worries— and in such a case the use of a retention of title clause will provide some security for the seller (see paragraph 3–48 above). Apart from these situations, the seller is keen not to part with the goods without being sure of payment and the buyer is not keen to pay for the goods until sure that he is getting hold of them. The following arrangements and bankers documentary credits go some way to meeting these concerns.

Collection arrangements

The basic means of payment by a bill of exchange has been **17–17** explained above. For the seller, however, it is risky to send the bill of lading and other documents directly to the buyer together with a bill of exchange for the buyer to accept. The risk is that the buyer does not return the bill of exchange and keeps (though he should not) the bill of lading. Thus the parties may agree that the seller will make the documents available at a bank (usually in the buyer's country). The bank, instructed by the seller perhaps via a bank in the seller's country, will not release the shipping documents to the buyer except in return for the buyer paying the price, or accepting the bill of exchange. If the bank releases the shipping documents without securing (as the case may be) either payment or the buyers' acceptance on the bill of exchange, the bank will be liable for any loss incurred by the seller as a result. The buyer will not be bound to pay (or accept the bill of exchange) if the documents presented by the bank do not conform to the contract.

Documentary credits

Where the contract provides for payment via a banker's **17–18** documentary credit, the buyer will arrange for a bank in his country (the issuing bank) to open a credit with a bank in the seller's country (the advising bank). The credit must conform to the requirements agreed in the contract between the buyer and the seller. The advising bank will advise the seller that the credit has been opened and of its terms. The contract between the buyer and seller will have specified the terms in which the credit must be opened. If the contract does not specify a date but does specify a shipment period, the credit must opened before the shipment

period: *Pavia and Co SPA v. Thurmann-Neilsen* (1952 CA). If
there is a fixed date for shipment it must be opened a reasonable
time before that date: *Plasticmoda SPA v. Davidson (Manchester)
Ltd.* (1952 CA). Once the seller has been advised that the credit is
open, he will feel comfortable in then performing his side of the
contract. He will then tender the documents (bill of lading etc) to
the advising bank. The advising bank will satisfy itself that the
documents are conforming documents before then paying the
seller (or, on behalf of the buyer, accepting the seller's bill of
exchange drawn on the buyer).

Irrevocable and confirmed credits

17–20   The seller will feel more secure if the credit which has been
opened is one which the bank has guaranteed that it will honour.
An *irrevocable* credit is one which the issuing bank guarantees to
the seller that he will be paid (against conforming documents).
An irrevocable and *confirmed* credit is one where the advising
bank adds its own guarantee that the credit will be honoured.
This gives the seller a commitment from a bank in the seller's
own country, that if he tenders the correct documents within the
stipulated period, the credit will be honoured. If it is not, the
bank is liable directly by the seller. The contract of sale may
require the buyer to open an irrevocable and confirmed letter of
credit. If it does and he fails to do so, that is a breach of contract
entitling the seller to regard the contract as repudiated. Once a
confirmed letter of credit has been opened, it cannot be cancelled
on the buyer's instructions. The bank has an absolute obligation
to the seller to pay, notwithstanding any dispute between the
seller and buyer: *Hamzeh Malas & Sons v British Imex Industries*
(1958 CA). This is because the contract between the bank and the
seller, though it was occasioned by the existence of the contract
of sale between buyer and seller, is independent of that contract.

The contract may require the credit to be a transferable one.
This is a credit which, once opened, the seller can use to finance
his purchase of goods (perhaps the very goods he is to supply to
the buyer)—though in that case the amount payable will usually
be less thereby enabling the seller to retain his profit.

Strict compliance

17–20   The buyer must, of course, open a credit which complies with
the requirements agreed in the contract of sale. The credit is in
effect an instruction to the advising bank to pay the seller if the

seller tenders documents conforming to the requirements laid down by the buyer. These requirements (*e.g.* as to the period within which the shipment stated should have occurred) should be consistent with the terms of the contract of sale. The bank is under a duty to comply strictly with those instructions. If it fails to pay according to the terms of the credit, it will be liable to the seller (if the credit was confirmed). If it pays out when the conditions for payment set out in it were not satisfied, then it may be unable to recover that amount from the buyer: *Equitable Trust Company of New York v. Dawson Partners Ltd* (1926 HL).

So important is it that sellers can place total reliance upon letters of credit, that, even when there are allegations of fraud, the bank is not lightly excused from its duty to honour a credit. Thus the bank is not excused from honouring a letter of credit unless the bank is satisfied not only that the documents tendered are fraudulent (*e.g.* forged or falsified) but also that the seller was a party to the fraud. If it is so satisfied, it should refuse to honour the credit: *United City Merchants Investments Ltd v. Royal Bank of Canada* (1982 HL).

17–22

CHAPTER 18

TRADE DESCRIPTIONS, ADVERTISING, FAIR TRADING AND INJUNCTIONS

THIS chapter deals with important bits of legislation which protect   **18–01**
the consumer in ways other than conferring right upon individual
consumers: the Trade Descriptions Act 1968; the Fair Trading Act
1973; Part III of the Consumer Protection Act 1987; the Control
of Misleading Advertisements Regulations 1988; the Injunctions
Directive. Some of these pieces of legislation confer powers on
enforcement authorities to secure court orders against traders
guilty of malpractices. Many of them create criminal offences. In
relation to these offences, powers of enforcement are given to
weights and measure authorities (which is the statutory name for
local Trading Standard Departments). Other measures which
create criminal offences designed to secure consumer protection
include the General Product Safety Regulations 1994 and the
Consumer Credit Act 1974. The former have already been
considered (paragraph 9–20) and the latter will figure prominently
in following chapters.

Now, the fact that a criminal offence is committed by a trader   **18–02**
or creditor does not confer upon the consumer any right to bring
an action or obtain redress in the civil courts. Someone who
commits an offence can be prosecuted in a criminal court and
fined (or, sometimes, imprisoned). However, the Powers of
Criminal Courts Act 1973, s.35, enables the criminal court to give
redress to the victim of the offence. After the offender has been
convicted, it can order the offender to pay compensation to the
victim. This can be done irrespective of whether it was the victim
who brought the prosecution and, if the court fails to make a
compensation order in a case where it is empowered to do so, it
must give reasons. In the case of magistrates' courts the amount
is subject to a maximum of £5,000 per conviction. A particularly
important decision was that in *R. v. Thomson Holidays* (1973 CA)
where the defendants had already been convicted of an offence
under section 14 of the Trade Descriptions Act 1968 by making

false statements in a holiday brochure. It was held that they could
be convicted a second time and made to pay compensation to a
second victim who had read a copy of the same brochure. This
was possible because someone can be tried once and convicted
once for each separate offence he commits and an offence under
section 14 is committed every time someone reads the brochure—
since a false statement is made every time it is communicated to
someone. Thus there was as many offences as there were readers.
This case turned upon the wording of section 14 which is set out
a little further on. However, the case is significant in showing that
the court did not regard as an abuse of the court's process a
second prosecution whose principal objective was to obtain
redress for a second victim.

TRADE DESCRIPTIONS ACT 1968

18–03   This Act creates criminal offences to protect the consumer.
However, it in no way enhances his contractual rights (Trade
Descriptions Act 1968, s.35). It aims to secure both that the
consumer is not misled and also that he is not left in ignorance of
matters of which he should be informed.

The Act has three main sets of provisions. First, the
Department of Trade and Industry is empowered to make certain
orders. These can specify and require information to be included
in advertisements or descriptions of goods; they can specify and
require instructions to be supplied with the goods.

Secondly, there are offences intended to prevent anyone
wrongly claiming to have supplied goods to the Queen (or to
anyone else) or wrongly claiming royal approval, *e.g.* by
displaying an emblem resembling that of the Queen's Award to
Industry.

18–04   Thirdly, and most significantly, the Act creates two offences
relating to misdescriptions of goods, and misleading statements
about services. Before considering these offences we must note
that the Act is aimed at trade and business. Its scope does not
include the private transaction. So, for example, the private man
who sells his car—whether privately or to a dealer—cannot be
caught by this Act. In *John v. Matthews* (1970 DC) a packet of
cigarettes, displayed in the bar of a working men's club bore the
statement "3d. off". It was later sold for the full usual retail
price. This was not an offence under the Act because it does not
extend to the domestic situation and a club having a private
membership enjoys a private or domestic status.

Sale or supply of goods with a misleading trade description—section 1

The principal offence relating to the supply of goods is in **18–05** section 1(1):

"Any person who, in the course of a trade or business
(a) applies a false trade description to any goods; or

(b) supplies or offers to supply any goods to which a false trade description is applied

shall, subject to the provisions of this Act, be guilty of an offence."

No offence is committed under section 1 unless a false "trade description" is applied. No statement is a trade description unless that statement relates to one of the items listed in section 2. The long list in section 2 includes such things as the quantity, composition, method of manufacture, fitness for purpose and date of manufacture of the goods. In *Cadbury v. Halliday* (1975 DC) it was decided that the words "Extra value" written on the wrapper of chocolate bar did not relate to any of the items listed in section 2 and neither could they reasonably be taken to do so. Thus they were not a "trade description" and no offence was committed. All the items listed in section 2 were matters in which truth or falsity could be established as a matter of fact. That could not be said of "value", which was a matter of opinion and not fact.

The courts have added a gloss to the words of section 1—namely that the offence is committed only if the application of the false trade description was associated with the sale or supply of goods. If it is associated with the supply only of services, then section 14 (see below) deals with that. In *Wycombe Marsh Garages Ltd v. Fowler* (1972 DC) the garage conducted a MOT test on a car and stated on the notification of refusal of a certificate that the car's tyres were suffering from "tread lift". Subsequent expert examination revealed that they had only the harmless condition known as "mould drip". It was held that the garage had not committed an offence under section 1 because the false description was not associated with the supply or sale of any goods. If, however, an MOT certificate, which falsely stated the car's approximate age, were shown by a car dealer to a potential buyer of the car, that false statement would be associated with the sale or supply of the car and the car dealer could be guilty: *R. v. Coventry City Justices, ex. p. Farrand* (1988

DC). The principle in *Wycombe Marsh Garages v. Fowler* was applied in *Wickens Motors (Gloucester) Ltd v. Hall* (1972 DC) where the defendants in fact had sold a car. Subsequently the purchaser had complained about its performance and in particular about its steering. He was told, "There is nothing wrong with the car". This occurred some 40 days after he bought the car. The car was in fact unroadworthy and had been so when sold. The court held that the false description 40 days later was not associated with the sale and therefore no offence was committed under section 1.

18–06 This case can be compared with *Walker v. Simon Dudley* (1997), where the sellers had contracted to supply the buyer with a fire engine corresponding to the buyer's specification and later supplied one which conspicuously did not. It was held that the seller was properly convicted of supplying goods to which a false trade description, the contract specification, was applied. The court applied section 4(3) which provides: "Where goods are supplied in pursuance of a request in which a trade description is used and the circumstances are such as to make it reasonable to infer that the goods are supplied as corresponding to that trade description, the person supplying the goods shall be deemed to have applied that trade description to the goods". In these circumstances a breach of contract (delivering goods differing from the contract description) amounts to a criminal offence.

The offence is not one which can be committed only by the supplier. In *Fletcher v. Budgen* (1974 CA) a car dealer who was negotiating to buy a car told the seller that there was no possibility of repairing it and that it was fit only to be scrapped. The seller then sold it to the dealer for £2. The dealer subsequently repaired it and advertised it for sale at £136. The Court held that the section applied to people who in the course of a trade or business applied false trade descriptions and that that could include the buyer.

18–07 Apart from adding a gloss to the section, the courts have had to interpret the actual wording. In *Havering London Borough v. Stevenson* (1970 DC) the question was whether the defendant had applied the false trade description "in the course of a trade or business". He ran a car hire business. As was his normal practice, he sold one of the hire cars when it was no more use to the business. A false indication was given as to the mileage it had covered. The court held that this false description was applied "in the course of a trade or business". This was so even though the business was not that of a car dealer. Therefore the defendant was guilty. The opposite conclusion was reached in *Davies v. Sumner* (1984 HL) where the defendant was a self-employed courier who used his car almost exclusively in connection with his business as a courier. He sold the car in part exchange for another vehicle (which was also for his business use). It was held that his sale of his old car was not in the course of his business. Where a transaction (here selling a car) is merely incidental to the business, that transaction is not made in the course of the business unless the business regularly makes transactions of that type. The distinction between this case and *Havering v. Stevenson* is that in the latter the defendant had a regular practice of selling his ex-rental cars and also in selling those cars he was selling something akin to stock-in-trade. *Davies v. Sumner* thus gives a meaning to the expression "in the course of a business", which is narrower than the expression "in the course of a business" where it appears in the Sale of Goods Act 1979 and the Unfair Contract Terms Act 1977. Where, in *R & B Customs Brokers v. UDT* (1988), the Court of Appeal adopted the *Davies v. Sumner* approach in relation to the Unfair Contract Terms Act 1977, it was almost certainly wrong to do so (see *Stevenson v. Rogers*, at paragraphs 7–34 and 10–23 above).

If a defendant merely carries on a hobby, *e.g.* of buying, refurbishing and reselling cars, a court might find that a transaction made in pursuance of the hobby, *e.g.* when he sells one of the refurbished cars, is not "in the course of a trade or business": *Blackmore v. Bellamy* (1983 DC). However, if he happens also to run a business and sells one of the cars in circumstances suggesting that he is selling it in the course of that business, then he is likely to be regarded as doing just that: *Southwark London Borough v. Charlesworth* (paragraph 9–19 above).

In *Donnelly v. Rowlands* (1971 DC) the question was whether **18–08** there was a "false" trade description. The defendant, a milk retailer, had supplied his milk in bottles each of which was capped with a foil top bearing his name and address. The bottles themselves were embossed variously with "C.W.S.", "Express", "Goodwins", etc. In determining whether there is a false trade description the court looks at the situation as an ordinary purchaser would. Lord Parker C.J. said:

> "The words on the foil cap were an accurate trade description of the milk, and in their context the words on the bottle did not refer to the milk which had already been accurately described, but merely conveyed, as the fact was, that it was a bottle belonging to the person whose name

was embossed. Looked at in that way, which is the way that
a member of the public would look at it, there was no
falsity at all in the trade description."

18–09 Section 1 is a powerful deterrent. Traders do well to be careful
in describing their merchandise, for the section may catch not just
the deliberate liar but also the honest trader who carelessly
misdescribes his goods. In *Cottee v. Douglas Seaton (Used Cars)
Ltd* (1972 DC) the court had to decide to what extent an honest
man could be guilty under the section. The case concerned a
rusty old car which had belonged to one M. The structure of the
car had rusted at the sides of the engine compartment and M had
attempted to repair this with plastic body filler. He made no
attempt to disguise it and sold the car to a firm of car dealers.
They, however, did disguise it by smoothing it down and then
repainting. They then sold the car to W, another dealer, who,
although he inspected it, remained unaware that there was
anything wrong with it. He resold it. Did W commit an offence
under section 1? The court accepted that an alteration of the
goods which causes them to tell a lie about themselves may be a
false description. It accepted that someone could be guilty even
though unaware of the falsity of the description and even though
the description was applied to the goods by another person.
However, W was unaware that the description had been applied
to the goods at all. The court, in deciding that W was not guilty,
said that a supplier of goods does not commit an offence under
section 1 if he does not know at the time of supply or offer to
supply that the trade description was applied to the goods.
Nevertheless, it seems that there is an exception even to this
principle—in the case of partners. In *Clode v. Barnes* (1974 DC)
one partner in selling a car applied a false trade description to it.
It was held that the other partner, who was unaware of the
transaction in question, nevertheless also committed the offence in
section 1 because, as he was a partner, he joined in selling the
car. Perhaps he would have fared better if he pleaded one of the
defences in section 24 (see paragraphs 18–26 to 18–31 below).

18–10 *R. v. Ford Motor Company* (1974) caused the Court of Appeal
to consider two questions—(i) Had the defendants "applied" the
trade description "new" when a car was supplied by them to a
dealer for him to sell to a customer? (ii) Was the trade description
"new" a false one in this case? The dealer had ordered a car
from the Ford Motor Company. The word "new" did not actually
appear on the order form but nevertheless it was clear from the

form that the car would come either from the manufacturer's stock at the factory or off the production line. It was held that the Ford Motor Company had applied the trade description "new" since the car was supplied in response to a request containing an indirect indication of that description and, in the words of section 4(3), it was "reasonable to infer that the goods [were] supplied as goods corresponding to that trade description".

The problem in relation to whether the car was new arose because, before the car was delivered to the dealer, it had suffered some damage in a collision in a compound. The damage had been repaired before delivery to the dealer—at a cost of £50. Ford won their appeal, the Court holding that a new car which is damaged but then repaired so as to be "as good as new" can still be regarded as new. It is clear from that case that much depends upon (a) the type of damage and (b) the quality of the repairs. Thus a car which is so seriously damaged that its chassis is distorted could no longer be accurately described as new, even after being repaired, whereas if only the engine were damaged the car could be restored to newness by a new engine being installed. It also seems clear from the case that a car could no longer answer the description "new" once the mileage it had travelled under its own power significantly exceeded the distance from the point of manufacture to the dealer. That view is in line with the decision in *Andrews v. Singer*, a civil case referred to earlier (paragraph 10–13). The expression "new" in relation to a vehicle is capable of meaning not just in new condition but also that the car has not been registered. In *R. v. Anderson* (1987 CA) the defendant had sold as new a Nissan which, though in mint unused condition, had been registered in the retailer's name. The practice of registering new cars in the retailer's name was not unusual when retail sales were slack. This was because car manufacturers gave retailers bonus payments if there were sufficient new registrations during a given period. The Court of Appeal upheld the defendant's conviction because there was ample evidence that a purchaser would understand the description "new" to indicate that the vehicle had had no previous owner and no previous registered keeper.

A number of successful prosecutions have been brought against **18–11** car dealers who have had cars for sale on which the odometers (milometers) showed mileages different from those which the car had actually travelled. Odometer readings are of course notoriously unreliable as a guide to the distance travelled by the car. But what is to be done by the honest car dealer, who wishes

to avoid committing an offence? Although there are in sections
24 and 25 some general defences (*i.e.* available in relation to any
offence under the Act), they have not in the odometer type of
case always proved a reliable line of defence. However, the car
dealer will not need to rely upon those defences if he ensures that
a false trade description is not applied. He can do that by either
of two methods—by covering up the mileage reading, or by
displaying a notice disclaiming the accuracy of the mileage
reading. A disclaimer would not be effective if it were merely
contained in the small print of a contract or if it were simply the
subject of a casual remark by the salesman during negotiations.
To be effective the disclaimer has to be as bold, precise and
compelling as the trade description itself (*i.e.* the mileage reading)
and it has to be as effectively brought to the notice of any person
to whom the goods might be supplied: *Norman v. Bennett* (1974
CA). A disclaimer can be used in relation to any trade description
of any goods and is not confined to odometers on motor cars.
Norman v. Bennett was in fact concerned with an inaccurate
odometer reading where there was a written disclaimer which
was, however, not as bold, precise and compelling as the
odometer reading. Nevertheless the defendant was acquitted, for
he was on the occasion in question selling the car to another
experienced car dealer who well knew from past dealings that the
defendant did not guarantee the accuracy of odometer readings on
his cars. It was not the written disclaimer but the understanding
between the buyer and seller which meant that the false trade
description was not applied in this case.

18–12 A disclaimer is an obvious and simple device for a trader to
use to avoid committing an offence. An oral disclaimer can
suffice provided that it is bold and compelling enough to
neutralise the effect of the odometer reading. Thus at a car
auction a categoric and clear oral disclaimer announced by the
auctioneer immediately before he accepts bids on a particular car
could be an effective disclaimer in relation to the odometer
reading on that car and in that case the disclaimer would protect
both the auctioneer and the vendor. It is irrelevant on whose
behalf the disclaimer was made: *Zawadski v. Sleigh* (1975 DC).
In this case, however, the defence failed because although the
auctioneer had regularly made reference to the fact that he did
not guarantee the mileage of any car, he had not made an oral
disclaimer before accepting bids on the particular car in question
and the disclaimer in the written conditions of the auction sale
had not been sufficiently brought to the attention of the buyer.

Thus the effect of the odometer reading had not been sufficiently neutralised. To be effective, a disclaimer, whether oral or written, must not only be bold, precise and compelling, but must be made at or before the time when the offence would otherwise be committed. If the seller offers for sale goods to which a false trade description is applied and then subsequently issues a disclaimer, that disclaimer can be no defence: *Lewin v. Fuell* (see paragraph 18–14 below).

Before leaving the matter of odometers and disclaimers, an **18–13** important distinction must be made. On the one hand is the car dealer who buys and displays for sale a car which someone else has previously "clocked", *i.e.* turned back the odometer. This car dealer commits an offence, not under section 1(1)(a), but only under section 1(1)(b) because he has not himself applied a false trade description. The defence of disclaimer is available to someone charged under section 1(1)(b). On the other hand is the car dealer who "clocks" the odometer himself and then displays the car for sale. This dealer commits an offence under section 1(1)(a) and the defence of disclaimer is no defence whatsoever to someone charged under section 1(1)(a): *R. v. Southwood* (1987 CA). In this case the Court also said the trader who "clocks" the odometer to zero (or some other figure so absurdly low that a customer who reads it would not believe it) would still be guilty. Zeroing it amounts to the application—within section 1(1)(a)—of a false trade description. If the trader knows that the car he wishes to sell has already been "clocked", the way for him to avoid committing an offence is, not to "clock" it further himself, but to give the customer a candid intimation of its falsity, *i.e.* a disclaimer. However, it will be no good him doing this *after* offering the "clocked" car for sale.

Before leaving section 1, mention should be made of one **18–14** defence which is not available. It is not a defence for the defendant to claim he was not "offering" his goods but was making only an invitation to treat.

Section 6 reads:

> "A person exposing goods for supply or having goods in his possession for supply shall be deemed to offer to supply them."

Thus, the shopkeeper who displays his goods with a false description commits an offence under section 1. In *Lewin v. Fuell* (1990 DC), the trader displayed for sale watches which were replicas of Cartier and Rolex watches and which bore those brand names. To anyone who enquired about the watches he gave a clear oral disclaimer. It was held that the disclaimer could not provide a defence because by then the offence had already been committed by virtue of the watches having already been displayed.

False statements as to services—section 14

18–15   Section 14 makes it an offence:

> "For any person in the course of any trade or business, (a) to make a statement which he knows to be false; or (b) recklessly to make a statement which is false; as to any of the following matters..."

There then follows a list of matters all connected with "services, accommodation or facilities provided in the course of any trade or business".

18–16   Thus, whereas section 1 deals with false statements associated with the supply of goods, section 14 deals with false statements associated with the provision of services. This dichotomy was highlighted by the decision in *Westminster City Council v. Ray Allen (Manshops) Ltd* (1982 DC). The defendants displayed outside their Oxford Street shop a sign reading "Closing Down Sale" and were still trading from that shop 18 months later. Dismissing a charge under section 14, the court held that since section 14 did not deal with a sale of goods, a reference to a shop sale was not a reference to a "facility" within the meaning of section 14. Similarly in *Newell v. Taylor* (1983 DC) a false statement offering to supply a free gift with a purchase of goods (when in fact it was not free) was held not to fall within section 14 because it was a statement relating to the supply of goods and therefore did not relate to the provision of services or facilities. In this case the court gave a further reason why the false statement was not caught by section 14, namely that it related to the price at which the goods were offered for supply and section 14 did not cover false statements about prices. This was applied in *Dixons Ltd v. Roberts* (1984 DC) where it was held that section 14 did not catch a trader who gave a false indication that a refund would be given on any goods purchased, if within seven days the customer was able to buy the same products locally more cheaply. It seems absurd, but it also seems to the law that a recklessly-made false statement that free insurance will be given with every motor cycle purchased is caught by section 14 (since it relates to the provision of a "service"), whereas the section does not catch a false statement that a free helmet will be given: *Kinchin v. Ashton Park Scooters Ltd* (1984 DC).

In *Newell v. Taylor* the court defined the word "services" as **18–17** "doing something for somebody". That definition was applied in *Global Marketing Europe v. Berkshire County Council* (1995 DC) where the defendant in attempting to sell timeshares invited customers by telephone to timeshare presentations, describing these presentations variously as "leisure exhibition" or a "holiday presentation", promising a free holiday at a resort of their choice provided that the customers attended at the defendant's premises. In each case the statement was false about what was to be done for the customers. In each case the customers had something quite different foisted upon them, namely a timeshare sales pitch. The timeshare presentation was a service and the statements as to the nature of that service were false. Thus in this case the service about which the false statements were made was not the eventual item (the timeshare) which the defendant was attempting to sell, but rather a preliminary item (the timeshare presentation). *Newell v. Taylor* was again distinguished in *Ashley v. Sutton London Borough Council* (1995 DC) where the defendant advertised a strategy and guide (a book) to winning on fixed odds football pools. He offered a guarantee of a refund of the price if the purchaser was not satisfied, but refunds were in fact refused. It was held that the defendant had supplied a service, since the inflated price (between £55 and £179) reflected the cost of the information rather than of the book which was merely the means by which the strategy was set out. It was also held that the representation about the refund was not a representation as to price and therefore *Newell v. Taylor* did not apply. It is in fact difficult to see how this decision fits with *Newell v. Taylor* or, more especially, *Dixons v. Roberts*. It would be better to regard the guarantee of a refund as a service and as containing the implied statement (apparently false in this case) that the defendant intends to honour the guarantee. The fact that the service (the guarantee) is supplied together with goods (the book) should not stop it being a service. On that basis *Dixons v. Roberts* was wrongly decided. This area of the law which defines the scope of section 14 by distinguishing between on the one hand statements as to services and, on the other, statements as to goods or as to price, now needs overhauling by the Court of Appeal or the House of Lords.

Although a service is said to be "doing something for
somebody", it has been held that falsely claiming to have a
qualification (as a qualified architect in *R. v. Breeze* (1973 CA) or
to be a member of guild (of master craftsmen in *R. v. Piper*
(1995 CA) can be a false statement if it is a statement made in
connection with the supply of services, *e.g.* of drawing up plans
for a house or carrying out building works.

18–18   It is more difficult to obtain a conviction under section 14 than
under other sections of the Act because the prosecution must
show that the defendant either knew the statement to be false or
made it recklessly, *i.e.* regardless of whether it was true or false.
It must show that the defendant had this knowledge or
recklessness at the time he made the statement. Subsequent
recklessness will not render criminal an earlier statement. In
Sunair Holidays v. Dodd (1970 DC) advertising literature
described a package holiday in Majorca. It described the double
rooms as having "private bath, shower, W.C. and terrace". The
holiday firm had a contract with the hotel under which the hotel
was required to supply rooms fitting that description. Nevertheless
on the occasion in question, a double room was provided which
had no terrace. The holiday firm had not checked that its
customers were provided with the correct rooms. The court held
that this negligence subsequent to the statement being made could
not render the statement a reckless one. The statement was not
made recklessly.

18–19   Another decision along similar lines was that in *Beckett v.
Cohen* (1972 DC). The accused agreed to build a garage "within
10 days" and to build it "as the existing garage". He defaulted
on both these commitments. However, he was not guilty of an
offence because section 14 has no application to statements as to
the future, which can be neither true nor false. The builder, by
breaking his commitments, no doubt exposed himself to an action
by his customer for breach of contract. That did not make him a
criminal under section 14. Whereas a statement about services to
follow will not be rendered "false" by the services not matching
up to the earlier statement, a subsequent statement which is false
when made can attract liability. This is so even though it had
absolutely no contractual effect and operated to no one's
detriment. The defendant in *Breed v. Cluett* (1970 DC) entered a
contract whereby he agreed to sell a bungalow. Twenty days later,
while he was doing some finishing off work on the bungalow, he
recklessly made a false statement, *i.e.* he told the purchaser that
the bungalow was covered by the National House Builders

Registration Council's 10-year guarantee. It was held that he committed an offence under section 14.

Sometimes it can be difficult to decide whether a statement **18–20** relates only to the future and therefore cannot infringe section 14 or whether on the other hand it relates partly or entirely to some past or present fact. Consider, as an example, a package holiday firm which in December sends out a brochure advertising holidays for the next summer. Suppose that the brochure mentions a particular hotel and states that it is not yet completed. Clearly in that case any statements about the services at the hotel can relate only to the future. Suppose the brochure mentions another hotel, stating that it has been open for several seasons and that it closes every year from November to March. Clearly statements about the service (*e.g.* that English meals are provided or that special dishes for children can be obtained) cannot relate to present facts, for the simple reason that the hotel is closed in December when the brochure is sent out. The statements could relate to past facts (*i.e.* they could mean that those services were provided last season) or they could relate only to the future (*i.e.* that they will be provided next season). In the latter case there can be no liability under section 14. If a prosecution were brought it would be for the court to decide what the statements meant. It is the meaning they were likely to convey to the person to whom they were addressed that matters and not the meaning they might, on analysis, bear to a trained legal mind. This was the approach laid down by the Court of Appeal in *R. v. Sunair Holidays* (1973) and confirmed by the House of Lords in *British Airways Board v. Taylor* (1976). In the latter case a traveller applied for aircraft tickets and received a letter saying "I have pleasure in confirming the following reservations for you..." and giving dates, times and numbers of the flights. The airline which sent the letter had an overbooking policy. This meant that after accepting the traveller's booking, the airline accepted more bookings for the flight than there were seats on the aircraft. When he turned up, the traveller was thus not allowed to travel on his booked flight and had instead to travel the next day. Was the reservation letter received by him merely a promise as to the future or was it a statement of present fact? It was held (a) that it was a statement of present fact, namely that at the time the letter was sent the traveller had a definite and certain booking, (b) that that statement was false because the airline's overbooking policy meant that the traveller's booking was exposed to a risk that it might not give a seat on the aircraft, and (c) that the airline made the false statement knowingly (and not merely recklessly) since the airline was well aware of its own overbooking policy. It should be noted that the airline's offence lay not in having an overbooking policy but in making a false statement in its letter to the traveller. The offence could have been avoided by a clear statement in the letter explaining the overbooking policy and the consequent risk to the "reservations".

It is clear then that a statement cannot attract liability unless it relates to some past or present fact. Provided, however, that it does relate to some past or present fact, it can still attract liability even if it relates to some services already provided. The false statement must of course be connected with, or associated with, the supply of the services in question. In *R v. Bevelectric Ltd* (1992 CA) the defendant company carried on a business of repairing washing machines. The company had represented to a customer that the motor needed replacing. This representation implied that a genuine assessment had been made of the extent of any repair necessary. This was a false statement about a past fact and also related to a service which, if it had been provided at all, had already been provided, namely the service of making the assessment of the need for a replacement motor. This was a service that the customer might well not be expected to pay for, being a preliminary service by which the defendant hoped to secure custom. A false statement about such a service can attract liability under section 14 and the defendant company's conviction was upheld. The approach in this case was similar to that in *Global Marketing Europe v. Berkshire C.C.* (paragraph 18–17 above) where it was held that a false statement about a preliminary service (a timeshare presentation) could attract liability.

18–21   It has been seen that for an offence to be committed under section 14 two things need to be present at the same time. First, the statement must be false and, secondly, there must on the part of the defendant be either knowledge of the falsity or recklessness as to it. The time at which these two factors must be present is when the statement is made. Subsequent facts will not make the statement false; subsequent recklessness will not make it reckless. Similarly, subsequent facts will not make a false statement true. In *Cowburn v. Focus Television Rentals Ltd* (1983 DC) the defendants advertised "Hire 20 feature films absolutely free when you rent a video recorder". As a customer subsequently discovered from the document he was sent upon renting a video recorder, there were two things wrong with the advertisement.

First, he was entitled to only six films and secondly the hire of them was not "absolutely free" because he had to pay postage and packing. He complained and when the defendants were made aware of his complaint they made sure he received 20 free films and reimbursed him his postage and packing. It was held that nevertheless the defendants were guilty because the statements in the advertisement were false when made and had been made recklessly. The defendants' conduct in subsequently honouring the advertisement was irrelevant as it occurred after the offence had been committed.

The question of what amounts to recklessness was considered **18–22** in *M.F.I. Warehouses v. Nattrass.* The defendants, a mail order firm, issued an advertisement offering their louvre doors on 14 days' free approval and indicating the price and the carriage charge. In the same advertisement they offered a set of "Folding Door Gear (Carriage Free)". They intended, when supplying both a louvre door and a set of folding door gear, not to charge carriage on the latter. However, on the occasion in question, a purchaser wrote ordering only the folding door gear. He was required to pay not only the price but also a carriage charge. The court found as a fact that a reasonable person would interpret the advertisement as offering the folding door gear as a separate item for 14 days' free approval carriage free. This had not been appreciated by the defendants' chairman who had considered the advertisement for some five to ten minutes before approving it, but who had not sufficiently thought through the implications of it. It was held that this amounted to recklessness. Recklessness does not necessarily involve dishonesty. The duty not to be reckless places upon the advertiser the positive obligation to have regard to whether his advertisement is true or false—a point reiterated in *Cowburn v. Focus Television Rentals,* above.

We have seen that a defendant, to be convicted under section **18–23** 14, must be proved to have known that the statement was false or to have been reckless as to its falsity. The *defendant* must be proved to have had this mental state, *i.e.* knowledge or recklessness. It is not enough for the prosecution to show that some employee of the defendant had that mental state. What then if the defendant is a company? Since we are dealing with a criminal offence, the general principles of the criminal law apply. These require that where a company is charged, the mental state (*i.e.* of knowledge or recklessness) must be proved to have existed in the mind of a person who was or formed part of the directing mind of the company. This means that one of the following

people must be proved to have had the necessary knowledge or to
have been reckless: the "directors, the managing director" or
perhaps "other superior officers of the company": *Tesco
Supermarkets v. Nattrass* (1972 HL). The result is that if it was
some lesser employee of the company (*e.g.* a mere store manager
or area manager) who put out the offending brochure or
advertisement, it may be difficult to get a conviction.

18–24   In *Wings v. Ellis* (1984 HL) the directors of a travel company
discovered that one of their holiday brochures contained a false
indication that the rooms in one of their holiday hotels were air-
conditioned. They recalled copies of the brochure. Seven or eight
months later a customer booked a holiday, relying on an old
unamended copy of the brochure. The House of Lords held that
the company had correctly been convicted of making a statement
which it knew to be false. A false statement in a brochure is
made when the brochure is published and is made again (or
alternatively, continued) when read at a later stage in an
uncorrected form by a member of the public. Thus a defendant
who has no knowledge of the falsity (and was not reckless as to
it) when the brochure was published, could still be guilty if he
had acquired that knowledge before the brochure was
subsequently read. It is irrelevant that the defendant did not
know that the brochure had been read (*i.e.* that the false
statement had been made). Thus, once the defendant has
discovered the falsity of his brochure, he is liable to commit an
offence each time someone subsequently reads the uncorrected
brochure. For his defence, he would have to rely on one of the
defences in section 24 (paragraph 18–26 below), which would
involve showing that he had taken all reasonable steps (to
withdraw the brochure, etc.) to avoid committing the offence. In
Wings v. Ellis the defendant mysteriously did not rely upon any
such defence.

18–25   In 2000 the DTI issued a consultation paper on Trade
Descriptions. The principal proposal was to revise the offence in
section 14 by: (i) removing the requirement for the prosecution to
prove that the defendant knew the statement was false or was
reckless as to its falsity; (ii) making it clear that it catches
misleading statements as well as false ones; (iii) making it clear
that it catches misleading and false statements as to the future.
These proposals, it is said, will bring section 14 which deals with
statements about services into alignment with section 1 which
deals with statements about goods. It is fair guess that the
government will have the most difficulty with the last element

above, since it appears to come perilously close to turning breaches of contract into crimes.

Defences—sections 24 and 25

If the defendant can establish any of the defences mentioned in section 24(1) he has a good defence to any charge under the Trade Descriptions Acts.

18–26

He must prove:

"(a) that the commission of the offence was due to a mistake or to reliance on information supplied to him or to the act or default of another person, an accident or some other cause beyond his control; and

(b) that he took all reasonable precautions and exercised all due diligence to avoid the commission of such offence by himself or any person under his control."

There are several defences here. Whichever defence is relied upon, the onus of proof is firmly upon the defendant to prove both ingredients. In *Simmons v. Potter* (1975 DC) the defendants, second-hand car dealers, succeeded in proving that the commission of the offence was due to "reliance upon information supplied to him" but failed to prove that they themselves had taken "all reasonable precautions", etc. They had sold a car with the wrong mileage recorded on the odometer. Before doing this they had first made enquiries about the car's history from its previous owner and learnt nothing suggesting that the odometer reading was false. It was held that the defendants had no defence under section 24 because they had, in failing to display a disclaimer, failed to take *all* reasonable precautions. They had failed to adopt an obvious and easy method of avoiding commission of the offence. If they had displayed a disclaimer (sufficiently bold, precise and compelling) they would have avoided commission of the offence even without having to rely upon section 24 (see paragraph 18–11). There is, however, no absolute rule that a failure to display an effective disclaimer will rule out the defences in section 24. There can be exceptional cases where, despite a failure to display an effective disclaimer, the defendant might be held to have taken all reasonable precautions. Thus in *Ealing L.B.C. v. Taylor* (1995) the Divisional Court declined to overturn the magistrates' finding that the defendant car dealer had taken all reasonable precautions (in relation to the mileage reading) in checking the consistency of the

condition of the car with the recorded mileage and in obtaining
from the person who sold him the car a signed warranty
guaranteeing the accuracy of the mileage reading.

18–27   In *Hurley v. Martinez* the defendant had supplied bottles of
German wine on which the labels indicated the alcoholic strength
as 8 per cent instead of 7.2 per cent, the bottles having come to
him from Germany thus labelled. It was held that the defendant
could rely upon the defence in section 24, it not being necessary
for him to have indulged in sample testing the accuracy of the
statement on the labels. For a comparison with the defence of due
diligence when used by someone charged with a consumer safety
offence, see paragraph 9–26 above.

18–28   When the defence relied upon is "act or default of another
person", the defendant will have a good defence only if he has
also made available to the prosecution such information as he has
identifying that other person. This is to enable the prosecution to
find and charge the other person. The other person will often be
the employee of the defendant, as he was in *Tesco Supermarkets
Ltd v. Nattress* (1971 HL). There, the defendant company, which
operated a large number of supermarkets, had instituted in their
stores an effective system to prevent the commission of an
offence. One of their employees, a store manager, failed properly
to carry out the system with the result that Radiant washing
powder was advertised in the window at 2s. 11d. when in fact the
only packets available in the shop were 3s. 11d. (Section 11 of
the Trade Descriptions Act which made this an offence has since
been repealed and replaced by Part III of the Consumer Protection
Act 1987, see paragraph 18–34 below.) The House of Lords held
that the defendant company was not guilty; the commission of the
offence was due to the default of "another person" (the store
manager) and the defendant company had, by instituting an
effective system, taken all reasonable precautions, etc., in the
circumstances.

18–29   Thus where, for example, the defendant owns a chain of stores
he can rely upon the acts of a store manager provided that the
defendant can show that he (the defendant) took all reasonable
precautions to avoid the commission of the offence. These
precautions will usually consist of instructions sent out to
managers. The defendant must show that he sent out *adequate*
instructions. He will have no defence if the instructions were such
that even if they were followed the offence was still likely to be
committed. *In Haringey London Borough v. Piro Shoes Ltd* (1976
DC) the defendants owned shoe shops in one of which some

shoes were sold which were not made entirely of leather but were labelled "all leather". The defendants had previously sent the shop manager a letter instructing him that these shoes were not to leave the shop without the label first being removed. It was held that this instruction was inadequate to prevent the commission of the offence (under section 1). The offence in section 1 was committed by goods with a false trade description being "offered" for sale. By section 6 they were offered for sale if they were "exposed for supply" (see paragraph 18–14 above). Thus the letter to the shop manager should have instructed him that the goods should not be exposed or displayed or offered for sale without the label first being removed. Since the defendants had therefore not taken all reasonable precautions, they had no defence.

When the proper defence is that of "act or default of another **18–30** person", the defendant cannot rely upon the defence of mistake. Thus, the defence of mistake is available only when the mistake was that of the defendant himself: *Birkenhead & District Co-op Society v. Roberts* (1970 DC). In that case the defendant pleaded the defence of mistake, the mistake being that of a shop assistant who in a lapse of concentration put the wrong label on a piece of meat. It was held that this was no defence for the defendants who should have relied upon the defence of "act or default of another person".

Section 24(3) provides a defence which is available only on a **18–31** charge under section 1(1)(b) of the Act. It provides:

> "...it shall be defence for the person charged to prove that he did not know, and could not with reasonable diligence have ascertained, that the goods did not conform to the description or that the description had been applied to the goods."

This defence is capable of applying to the car dealer who has sold a car with a "clocked" odometer. We have already seen that if the car dealer did the "clocking" himself, he will have no defence at all, not even if he used a disclaimer (paragraph 18–11 above). If he bought the car already "clocked" he could use a disclaimer. If he has not used a disclaimer or has not used an adequate one, then he will have difficulty in establishing any of the defences in section 24(1) (paragraph 18–26 above). The defence in section 24(3) may therefore be a last resort. If the car dealer had made extensive enquiries of previous owners as to the

accuracy of the odometer reading, then the defence is likely to
succeed, especially if the general condition of the car was
consistent with the mileage recorded on the odometer. Where,
however, the recorded mileage was exceptionally low for the age
of the vehicle and the defendant had failed to make any enquiries
even of the car's immediate previous owner, the defence is likely
to fail: *Simmons v. Ravenhill* (1983 DC).

It falls finally to mention the defence in section 25 (available
on any charge under the Trade Descriptions Acts). This is a
defence of innocent publication of an advertisement. So, for
example, a newspaper which innocently publishes a misleading
advertisement will have a good defence provided the
advertisement was received in the ordinary course of business.

Additional or alternative defendant—section 23

18–32   The object of section 23 is to ensure that the person who really
is to blame can be convicted. It provides:

> "Where the commission by any person of an offence under
> this Act is due to the act or default of some other person
> that other person shall be guilty of the offence..."

In order for the "other person" to be convicted, two
requirements must be fulfilled:

  (i) The first person must have been guilty of conduct which
  either was an offence under the Act or would have been
  but for a defence in sections 24 or 25: *Coupe v. Guyett*
  (1973 DC).

  (ii) The situation in (i) must have been due to the act or
  default of the "other person".

Under sections 1 and 14 someone can be guilty only if he
makes a false statement "in the course of a trade or business".
Under section 23, however, it is possible for someone who is not
a trader to be convicted. A private motorist who "clocks" his car
before selling it to a car dealer may well find that he is guilty
under section 23, since it may well be his act which causes the
car dealer to commit an offence under section 1: *Olgiersson v.
Kitching* (1986 DC).

Cadbury v. Halliday (1975 DC) also involved a prosecution
under section 23. It was alleged that the retailer committed an

offence under section 1 by selling bars of chocolate bearing the misleading label "Extra value" and that this was due to the act or default of the defendants, the manufacturers. If the retailer had committed an offence it would have consisted of giving an indication that the bars labelled "Extra value" gave better value than other bars of Cadbury's chocolate in his shop. This indication was false since the bars labelled "Extra value" contained slightly less chocolate for the sale price as the bars not so labelled. As we have seen (at paragraph 18–05), it was held that the retailer did not commit any offence under section 1 because indications as to value are not "trade descriptions". If the retailer had committed an offence under section 1, could Cadbury have properly been convicted under section 23? Cadbury had labelled and then supplied the chocolate packed in sealed cases which were not opened until they reached the retailer. Cadbury had changed their labelling policy and had issued no warning to retailers. Nevertheless it was held that any false indication given by the retailer could not be said to be due to the act or default of Cadbury since the retailer could quite easily have compared the weights and prices of his existing stock and the new bars to see if the label "Extra value" was justified.

Enforcement and time limit

The task of seeing that the Act is complied with is given to **18–33** local weights and measures authorities, *i.e.* local trading standards or consumer protection departments. In order that they may collect evidence, the Act empowers them to make test purchases, to enter premises and to inspect and seize goods. It is an offence wilfully to obstruct them.

No prosecution for an offence under the Act can be commenced after either (i) the expiration of three years from the commission of the offence, or (ii) the expiration of one year from the prosecutor's discovery of the offence, whichever is earlier— section 19. The prosecutor is the person laying the information and an offence is discovered for this purpose once the prosecutor has knowledge of all the facts material to found the charge: *R v. Shrewsbury Magistrates' Court, ex p. Simon Dudley Limited* (1996 D.C.) If time has expired, then it may be that, depending on the circumstances, the defendant could instead be prosecuted under another provision which is not subject to a time limit, *e.g.* section 46 of the Consumer Credit Act (see paragraph 23–09 below).

MISLEADING PRICE INDICATIONS

18–34   Part III of the Consumer Protection Act 1987 replaced earlier provisions dealing with misleading price indications. These were the Trade Descriptions Act 1968, s.11 and the Price Marking (Bargain Offers) Order 1979. These provisions had loopholes and proved technical and obscure with the result that enforcement was difficult. Part III of the 1987 Act takes a different approach to the problem of defining the mischief which it seeks to stamp out, *i.e.* the giving of misleading price information. It contains a statement of the offence (section 20) and a generally worded definition of "misleading" (section 21) and provides for a code of practice to be approved by the Secretary of State which gives practical guidance (section 25).

Section 20—the offence

18–35   Section 20(1) provides that a person commits an offence:

> "...if, in the course of any business of his, he gives (by any means whatever) to any consumers an indication which is misleading as to the price at which any goods, services, accommodation or facilities are available (whether generally or from particular persons)."

Section 20(2) goes on to deal with the position where price information is correct when given but becomes false afterwards. If in that situation some consumers might reasonably be expected to rely on the misleading information, the trader commits an offence unless he has taken all reasonable steps to prevent them from doing so. This could apply where a trader's brochure is accurate when put out and accurate when read by the consumer but becomes inaccurate after that.

It is only if the misleading price indication is given in the course of a business that an offence is committed. For the meaning of a similar expression in the Trade Descriptions Act, see *Davies v. Sumner* at paragraph 18–07 above. Also, since the defendant has to have been acting "in the course of a business of his", a mere employee cannot be guilty: *Warwickshire C.C. v. Johnson* (see paragraph 18–36 below).

The purpose of the offence is to prevent consumers being misled, though it is not necessary for the prosecution to produce an individual consumer to whom the misleading price was indicated. On the other hand, a price indication given only to potential customers who might be interested only in the course of their trade or profession would not be caught by the offence. It would not be an offence for a wholesaler to give a misleading indication to a retailer buying for retail sale. Nor would it be an offence to give a misleading indication as to the price of goods which by their nature could not be intended for private use or consumption, for example dental equipment which would be used only by a professional dentist: *M.F.I. Furniture Centres v. Hibbert* (1995 DC).

Section 21—"misleading"

Whether a price indication is misleading depends, not upon what the trader intended to convey, but upon what a consumer might reasonably understand from what he reads or is told. Thus it is for the trader to resolve ambiguities in his price indications. The following are misleading:

18–36

(a) an understatement of the price;

(b) the stating of the price without making it clear, if it is the case, that it applies only to cash customers or that it does not apply to part-exchange deals or applies only in certain circumstances or does not apply in certain other circumstances;

(c) failing to make it clear, if it is the case, that service is charged extra or that some other additional charge is made;

(d) a false indication that a price is expected to be increased or reduced or maintained (whether or not for a particular period);

(e) making a false price comparison, *e.g.* falsely stating that the price is reduced or comparing the price of a car with that of another model without stating that the price for the other model has since been reduced.

The advertisement in *Warwickshire County Council v. Johnson* (1993 HL) was found to be misleading. The advertisement, outside a branch of Dixons, an electrical shop, read "We will beat any TV HiFi and Video price by £20 on the spot". A customer saw the notice, saw a TV on sale elsewhere at £159.99 and sought to buy the same model from the Dixons shop at £139.99. The manager had one in stock but refused to sell at that

18–37

price. The manager was charged under section 20. It was held
that the notice was misleading as to the price at which the goods
were offered, since the statement was a continuing indication and
whether it was misleading or not could only be tested by
somebody taking it up. It had been so tested and found to be
misleading. Nevertheless the manager's conviction was quashed
because section 20 is designed to catch the employer, not a mere
employee. This is clear from the wording of section 20 which
makes someone guilty if "in the course of any business of his"
he gives a misleading price indication. It was not in the course of
a business of *his* that the manager gave the misleading indication.
This suggests that the prosecution should have been brought
against the manager's employer, the company. In such a case the
company may well have sought to rely upon the defence of due
diligence in section 39 (see paragraph 18–42 below). To succeed
with such a defence the company would have had to show that
they had taken all reasonable steps and exercised all due diligence
to avoid the commission of the offence. That would require them
to show such things as adequate training of managers in such
matters and a careful monitoring system to prevent the
commission of such offences.

18–38   In *Toys 'R' Us. v. Gloucestershire C.C.* (1994 DC) the court
had to consider the situation where goods are labelled with one
price and the bar code indicates a different price. In that situation,
is the price label a misleading price indication? The retailer in
fact had a policy which required a cashier to check the price on
any item after the cashier had scanned the bar code and revealed
a price for the item at the cash till. If the cashier found a price on
the ticket lower than the price displayed on the till, the cashier
was under instructions to charge the lower price. It was held that
the relevant time for the purposes of section 20 was when the
price indication was given. That was when an item was on the
shelf with a price attached to it. The offence could be established
only if it could be shown that, despite the retailer's policy, the
goods were not in fact available at the price indicated on the
label. This would require the prosecution to show that cashiers
and customers did not notice discrepancies and correct them. This
the prosecution had failed to do.

Section 25—code of practice

18–39   The Code of Practice which the Secretary of State has approved
is intended to give traders practical guidance. However,
compliance with the code is not necessarily a complete defence.

Compliance or non-compliance is simply something to be taken into account by the court in determining whether an offence under section 20 has been committed. It is therefore possible, in theory at least, for a court to find that a trader has complied with the code but that such compliance nevertheless involved giving a misleading indication. In such a case the compliance would doubtless be a strong factor in mitigation of sentence.

Section 26—regulations

This section empowers the Secretary of State to make **18–40** regulations regulating the giving of price information. Such regulations could make specific practices a criminal offence and the giving of specific information mandatory. The Price Indications (Method of Payment) Regulations 1991 have been made under this section. These deal with the situation where a trader's price is not the same for all methods of payment and they require the customer to be informed of those methods of payment to which the indicated price does not apply. Also there are the Price Indications (Bureaux de Change) (No. 2) Regulations, dealing with prices shown by bureaux de change. In addition to these Regulations made under section 26, note should also be made of the Price Marking Order 1991, made under the Prices Act 1974. This Order applies to goods sold by retail and to advertisements for such goods and with certain exceptions requires the selling price to be indicated in writing. It has specific provisions on the price marking of goods sold from bulk or prepackaged, and has special provisions dealing with the price marking of motor fuel, precious metals, and general price reductions (as in sales). It generally requires prices on consumer goods to be VAT-inclusive.

Defences

Under section 24 the defendant has a defence if he can prove **18–41** any one of the following:

(a) his acts or omissions were authorised by regulations made under section 26;

(b) the offending price indication was given, other than in an advertisement, in the media (*i.e.* radio, television, cable programme service, newspaper, magazine, film or book);

(c) he was an innocent publisher or advertising agency who was unaware, and had no grounds for suspecting, that the advertisement contained a false price indication;

(d) the misleading price indication related to a recommended price, which did not apply to the price at which the item was available from the defendant, and which the defendant could reasonably believe was generally being charged, and which was false only because a supplier was not following the recommendation.

This last defence might well be available to a book publisher. The publisher might well include the recommended retail price on the cover of the book (or in an advertisement), only to be surprised subsequently to learn that a retailer has been selling at a different price.

18–42   In addition to the defences above, it is a defence for anyone charged under the Consumer Protection Act to show that he took all reasonable steps and exercised all due diligence to avoid committing the offence—section 39. This defence is now a standard defence often to be found in consumer protection measures, including for example—and in a slightly different form—section 24 of the Trade Descriptions Act 1968 (paragraph 18–26 above). The defence in section 39 itself has already been discussed (at paragraph 9–26 above) in relation to safety regulations and the product safety provisions in section 10 of the Consumer Protection Act.

Additional or alternative defendant

18–43   Section 40, like section 23 of the Trade Descriptions Act 1968 (paragraph 18–32 above), deals with the situation where A commits an offence because of the fault of B. It enables B to be convicted where A has been guilty of conduct which either was an offence under the Consumer Protection Act or would have been one but for one of the statutory defences. Clearly relevant here is the case law on section 23 (see paragraph 18–32)—except for *Olgiersson v. Kitching*. The latter is not relevant because under section 40 B is not guilty unless his act or default which led to A's conduct in question was committed by B "in the course of any business of his". (See *Warwickshire C.C. v. Johnson* at paragraph 18–37 above.)

MISLEADING ADVERTISEMENTS

It has been seen that there are a number of criminal offences **18–44** relating to advertising. Another is to be found in the Business Advertisements (Disclosure) Order 1977, which is designed to prevent a business advertising goods, *e.g.* in the small ads of a newspaper, without the advertisement making clear that the seller is indeed carrying on a business. It makes it a criminal offence for the advertiser to fail to make it clear that he is selling in the course of a business. A further offence is to be found in the Mail Order Transactions (Information) Order 1976, whereby written advertisements in which someone in the course of a business invites from consumers mail orders for goods, with payment in advance, must include a legible description of the name and address of the person inviting the orders.

With any system of control by criminal offences there is always **18–45** the risk that someone may find a loophole, a way which misleads the public without amounting to an offence. The Control of Misleading Advertisements Regulations 1988 deal with this possibility. They implement the Misleading Advertisements Directive (84/450/EEC). They require the Director-General of Fair Trading to consider complaints (other than vexatious or frivolous ones) about misleading advertisements. He can bring proceedings for a High Court injunction to stop the publication of a misleading advertisement. The Director-General, before considering a complaint, may require the complainant to satisfy him that alternative methods of dealing with the matter have been tried and found inadequate. Thus where the advertisement constitutes a criminal offence, it would seem pointless to complain to the Director-General. It would be more sensible to complain to the local trading standards department. Even where the advertisement does not amount to an offence, the Director-General may consider that an approach to the Advertising Standards Authority (a non-statutory body with no legal powers) would be an adequate way of dealing with the complaint. The Regulations clearly could be useful as a last resort, where the advertisement is not caught by any other legal provision and there is no other effective way of dealing with it, *e.g.* an advertisement falsely stating "closing down sale" (see paragraph 18–16 above). Before the Director-General can take action under the Regulations, the advertisement must be such that it *both* deceives or is likely to deceive *and* is likely to affect the economic behaviour of those whom it reaches or to injure a competitor of the trader (usually the advertiser) whose interests the advertisement is promoting.

By way of exception, the Regulations do not give the Director-General powers in relation to commercial radio and television advertisements or to cable advertisements. Instead, the IBA and the Cable Authority, respectively, are given powers to consider whether such advertisements are misleading.

FAIR TRADING ACT 1973

18–46   This Act created the office of Director General of Fair Trading, giving that official certain functions in relation to consumer affairs. It does not enhance consumers' individual rights. Part II of the Act established a mechanism for creating new criminal offences to combat, as they arise, trading malpractices adverse to consumers. Part III gives the Director General powers of enforcement against traders guilty of malpractices. In addition the opportunity was taken to deal with pyramid selling, a particular malpractice which had become a nuisance at the time the Act was being passed. This will be now be considered first, before we turn to Parts II and III.

Pyramid selling
18–47   In their heyday, before 1973, pyramid selling schemes worked something like this. The typical scheme was ostensibly concerned with marketing goods or services through a chain of private distributors. An individual was persuaded to join the scheme as a "distributor" (or "agent" or "representative" or whatever). He may have been persuaded to pay a large sum of money (perhaps hundreds or thousands of pounds) for the privilege of joining. Whether he could recover this sum would depend upon whether he could introduce further people into the scheme, for he would receive a payment for each new participant whom he introduced. Sometimes the fee he paid for joining was expressed to be payment for a consignment of the goods which the scheme was supposed to be marketing. However, he could still find it difficult to recoup his joining fee if he could not find new members for the scheme, because he would find it difficult to sell the goods. It was not always easy for a private householder to find buyers for a large number of packets of soap!

Sections 118–123 deal with pyramid selling. Section 120(3) makes it an offence for a promoter or participant to receive any payment (or the benefit of any payments) which some other participant is induced to make by reason that the prospect is held out to him of receiving payments or other benefits for introducing other persons into the scheme. Further, section 119 empowers the Secretary of State to make regulations for the purpose of preventing participants being unfairly treated. These powers have been used thereby effectively banning pyramid selling as it was previously practised.

Creation of criminal offences

The aim is to discover, and by ministerial order prevent, **18–48** consumer trade practices which adversely affect the economic interests of consumers. A "Consumer trade practice" (see section 13) is one which relates to:

(a) The terms upon which goods or services are supplied.

or (b) The manner in which those terms are communicated to the consumer.

or (c) The promotion (*e.g.* by advertising or labelling) of the supply of goods or services.

or (d) Methods of salesmanship employed in dealing with consumers.

or (e) The way in which goods are packed or otherwise got up for the purpose of being supplied.

or (f) The method of demanding or securing payment for goods or services.

The Director or any other government department can refer a consumer trade practice to the Consumer Advisory Protection Committee on the question of whether the practice adversely affects the economic interests of consumers—section 14. The Advisory Committee's only function is to report on such references. A reference by the Director may include a proposal for a ministerial order dealing with the consumer trade practice—section 17. Section 22 then empowers the Secretary of State to make an order regulating the trade practice but he cannot do so unless the Advisory Committee has agreed with the Director's proposed Order (either as it stood or subject to modifications).

18–49   One important order made under this procedure is the Consumer Transactions (Restrictions on Statements) Order 1976, which bans the use of certain void exemption clauses (see paragraph 10–48 above).

Contravention of one of these orders is a criminal offence of the same type as those in the Trade Descriptions Act. Thus section 25 provides defences which are the same as those in sections 24 and 25 of the 1968 Act (above). Also, enforcement is carried out in the same way by the weights and measures authorities—sections 27–33.

The procedure, just outlined, for the creation of new criminal offences has fallen into disuse. Intended to be a quick method of banning undesirable trade practices having an adverse impact on consumers, it proved to be slow, largely because of the time needed for the Advisory Committee to report. Only three orders were ever made under it, the other two being the Mail Order Transactions (Information) Order 1976 and the Business Advertisements (Disclosure) Order 1977 (both explained at paragraph 18–44 above). However, in a consultation paper in 2000 the DTI announced proposals to revise and revive the procedure, the main proposed revision being the abolition of the Advisory Committee, which will enable the Secretary of State to make an Order following a proposal from the Director.

Power to enforce the general law on protection of consumers

18–50   Part III of the Act (sections 34–43) gives the Director power to act against someone who in the course of business persistently breaks the law (civil or criminal) in a way detrimental to the interests of consumers. These provisions, unlike those just outlined, are concerned not only with the economic interests of consumers but also their "interests in respect of health, safety or other matters"—section 34. The Director can ask the offender for an assurance that he will abandon the conduct in question. If that fails, or if the offender breaks his assurance, the Director can take proceedings to obtain a court order that the course of conduct be abandoned. These powers can be exercised irrespective of whether other proceedings (civil or criminal) have been brought.

Proposals for change

18–51   In a consulation paper in 2000, the DTI announced proposals to revise the Part III provisions. The main changes proposed to the existing "course of conduct" procedure are:

- removal of the "persistence" requirement, since the courts require proof of a very large number of instances before finding that the trader has *persistently* broken the law;

- removal of the requirement (but not the power) that before applying for a court order the Director must have used his best endeavours to obtain from the trader an assurance of good behaviour;

- giving powers of enforcement to local trading standards departments as well as the Director General of Fair Trading;

- addition of "anti-avoidance" provisions designed to prevent traders against whom an order has been made from starting up similar practices again, either under the guise of a "one man band" company, or by having his spouse of other relative carry on the practice in their own name but under his influence.

Additionally, the consultation paper proposes the creation of a further type of order, a banning order. The court, on an application by the Director (or a trading standards department) or the Secretary of State, could issue an order banning the trader, not just from the trading malpractice(s) identified, but from carrying on business (or a specified kind of business) with consumers at all. Such an order could be made if the trader was found to have:

- broken an order under the Act to abandon a specified trading malpractice;

- committed an offence of fraud, dishonesty or violence; or

- engaged in conduct unfair and prejudicial to consumers of such frequency, or length of time or geographical area as to demonstrate his unfitness to engage in business with consumers.

It is not yet clear how the above proposals will dovetail with the requirements of the Injunctions Directive.

INJUNCTIONS DIRECTIVE

18–52   The Injunctions Directive (98/27/EC) has to be implemented by
1 January 2001. Its purpose is to permit consumer protection
bodies to apply to the courts, both in their own and in other
Member States, for orders to stop traders infringing legislation
implementing Directives where those infringements "harm the
collective interests of consumers". It is not intended as a means
of securing redress for individual consumers. It applies to
legislation implementing the following Directives:

- Misleading Advertisements (84/450/EEC)—implemented
  in the UK by the Control of Misleading Advertisements
  Regulations 1988 (paragraph 18–45 above).

- Doorstep Selling (85/557/EEC)—implemented in the UK
  by the Consumer Protection (Contracts Concluded away
  from Business Premises Regulations 1987 (paragraph
  2–18 above).

- Consumer Credit (87/102/EEC)—already implemented in
  the UK by virtue of the Consumer Credit Act 1974.

- Distance Selling (97/77/EC)—implemented in UK by the
  Consumer Protection (Distance Selling) Regulations 2000
  (paragraph 16–05 above).

- Unfair Terms in Consumer Contracts (93/13/EEC)—
  implemented in UK by the Unfair Terms in Consumer
  Contracts Regulations 1999 (paragraph 10–39 above).

- Electronic   Commerce   Directive   (2000/31/EC)—
  (paragraph 16–04 above).

- Package Travel, Package Holidays and Package Tours
  (90/314/EEC).

- Timeshare (94/47/EC).

- TV Broadcasting (89/552/EEC).

- Advertising of Medicinal Products for Human Use
  (92/28/EEC).

The first six of these Directives are relevant to the subject
matter of this book, indicated by the paragraph references given
above.

18–53   The DTI's consulatation document (February 2000) indicates
how it proposes to implement the Directive. In relation to the

legislation implementing each Directive, it proposes to have a lead body, with other bodies designated as also having powers to seek a court injunction against an infringing trader. The lead body would have a duty to consider any complaint alleging trader infringements, unless another designated body had agreed to do so. The body dealing with any particular complaint would be able to accept an undertaking from the trader instead of immediately commencing proceedings for a court order. There will be liaison provisions, including a requirement on non-lead bodies to notify the lead body of assurances accepted, investigations undertaken etc. The Director General of Fair Trading is expected to be the lead body in relation to the first eight Directives listed above (except for certain investment advertisements and medicines advertising).

A system such as is required, already exists in this country in relation to the Unfair Terms in Consumer Contracts Directive and the Distance Selling Directive. The Director General is the lead body and other regulatory bodies, trading standards departments and also the Consumers' Association, subject to their duty to liaise, all have powers to apply for an injunctions against an offending trader (see paragraphs 10–47 and 16–22 above).

PART TWO
CONSUMER CREDIT

INTRODUCTION AND DEFINITION OF HIRE-PURCHASE

A CONTRACT of hire-purchase, as its name suggests, contains two **19–01** elements. It is a contract of hire which also gives the hirer an option to purchase the goods. Hire s a form of bailment which is a word used to describe the situation where one person is put in possession of goods belonging to another. The hirer is a bailee. Thus a hire-purchase agreement is an agreement for the bailment of goods whereby the bailee has an option to purchase them.

Two particular contracts relating to goods have long been recognised by the law, one of bailment and one of sale. Of which type, then, is a hire-purchase agreement? Is it bailment or is it sale? To put it another way, is it hire or is it purchase? The emphatic answer is that it is not a contract of sale. Thus the parties to a hire-purchase agreement are termed, not "seller" and "buyer", but "owner" and "hirer". Under the Consumer Credit Act 1974 they are termed "creditor" and "debtor".

Distinction between hire-purchase and sale

It is the hall mark of a contract of sale of goods that the parties **19–02** enter into a mutual commitment that the buyer thereby acquires or shall acquire ownership of the goods. A "buyer" is described in section 61 of the Sale of Goods Act as a "a person who buys or agrees to buy goods". If the buyer does not commit himself to acquire ownership of the goods there is no contract of sale and indeed it is inaccurate to describe him as "buyer". This was made clear by the House of Lords in the leading case of *Helby v. Matthews* (1895). The agreement in that case was between the owner of a piano (a dealer) and his customer. The latter agreed to hire the piano for 36 months at a rent of 10s. 6d. per month. The agreement provided that the piano would become the property of the customer on payment of all the instalments of rent but that he could at any time before then terminate the hiring by returning the piano to the dealer. In the event of the hiring being terminated, the hirer would be liable only for arrears of rent in respect of the period prior to the termination. The House of Lords held that this agreement was not a contract of sale and that the customer was not a "buyer". The fact that he could terminate the hiring meant that he was under no commitment to acquire ownership of the goods. He had in effect an option to purchase, which he could exercise by not terminating the agreement and by paying all 36 monthly instalments. An option is not a commitment. Their Lordships said that the option was an irrevocable offer by the owner to sell. That offer could be accepted only when the option was exercised. Until then there was no purchase and no contract of sale. Therefore the hire-purchase agreement was not a contract of sale within the meaning of the Sale of Goods Act. Thus a hire-purchase contract is a contract a bailment, albeit one with a difference—namely an option to purchase.

19–03 In deciding *Helby v. Matthews* their Lordships distinguished the case of *Lee v. Butler* (1893). In that case the agreement provided that the customer should have immediate possession of the goods (furniture) and should pay £1 on May 6 and £96 on August 1. These sums were termed "rent". The agreement further provided that the furniture would become the customer's property when the instalments had both been paid and not before. There was no clause in the agreement giving the customer the right to terminate it, although there were provisions entitling the dealer to do so (and to repossess the goods) if the customer defaulted. The Court of Appeal held that this agreement was a contract of sale. The difference between this and *Helby v. Matthews* is that here the customer was committed to making all the payments and therefore to acquiring ownership of the goods.

It will be observed that in *Lee v. Butler* the goods were not to become the buyer's property until he had paid all the money. This, however, did not prevent the agreement from being a contract of sale. Indeed, as we saw in Chapter 3, sections 17 and 18 of the Sale of Goods Act expressly recognise that property passes to the buyer at the time the parties intend it to.

19–04 In each of the cases mentioned above, the customer disposed of the goods (in return for money) to an innocent third person and he did so before completing his payments. The importance of the distinction between hire-purchase and sale becomes apparent when it is realised that different legal results followed. In neither case was the customer owner of the goods at the time he disposed of them. In *Helby v. Matthews* he was merely hiring them and in

Lee v. Butler it had been expressly agreed that the furniture was not to become his property until the payments had been completed. However, in *Lee v. Butler* he was a "buyer" in possession of the goods and thus, although he was not the owner, he could pass good title to an innocent purchaser (Factors Act s.9, see Chapter 5 above). So in *Lee v. Butler* the dealer could not recover the goods from the innocent purchaser to whom his customer has sold them. In *Helby v. Matthews*, on the other hand, the dealer was held entitled to recover the goods. Someone hiring goods under a hire-purchase agreement is not a "buyer" and therefore cannot pass good title under either the Factors Act, s.9 or the Sale of Goods Act, s.25. Therefore, from the dealer's point of view, the hire-purchase transaction has the advantage that he will not be prevented by either of those sections from recovering the goods after they have been passed on by the hirer to an innocent third party. It should be remembered that there are other provisions which could in certain circumstances prevent him from doing so (see Chapter 5 above). In particular the Hire Purchase Act 1964, Pt. III can have this effect in the case of a motor vehicle. Also note that, since *Lee v. Butler*, sections 9 of the Factors Act and 25 of the Sale of Goods Act have been amended. The result is that the rule in *Lee v. Butler* (that under those sections a buyer under a conditional sale agreement can pass good title to an innocent purchaser) applies only if the conditional sale agreement is not regulated by the Consumer Credit Act 1974 (see paragraph 5–34 above).

Since the House of Lords decision in *Helby v. Matthews*, the **19–05** hire-purchase agreement has become very common indeed. The usual form it has come to take is an agreement whereby the customer (a) agrees to hire the goods for an agreed fixed period (*e.g.* 48 months) in return for a monthly payment, and (b) is given an option to purchase the goods for a nominal amount (*e.g.* £1) which option is exercisable only after the customer has first completed payment of all the monthly instalments. In economic terms the customer has paid for the goods by means of the monthly instalments. Having paid all the monthly instalments, he would be mad not to exercise his option to buy for the nominal amount. Nevertheless he is not legally bound to do so and thus the agreement is still only a hire-purchase agreement and is not a contract of sale unless and until the customer exercises his option to buy: *Close Asset Finance v. Care Graphics Machinery Ltd* (2000 QBD). Suppose, on the other hand, that the customer is contractually bound to pay all the monthly instalments, is not required to pay anything at all for exercising his "option to buy" and is deemed to have exercised that option simply by completing his instalment payments without informing the owner that he wishes not to exercise it. In that unusual case, the agreement is a sale of goods contract (a conditional sale agreement) and not a hire-purchase agreement: *Forthright Finance Ltd. v. Carlyle Finance Ltd* (1997 CA).

Conditional sale and credit sale agreements

19–06   Each of these is a type of contract of sale of goods and each has the characteristic that the buyer is committed to acquiring ownership of the goods. "Conditional" and "Credit" are commonly used to describe contracts of sale of goods where the price is payable in instalments. In that respect they therefore have some similarity with hire-purchase agreements.

At common law there is only one difference between a credit and a conditional sale agreement. It is that in a conditional sale agreement the passing of property to the buyer is expressly postponed until some condition (usually all the instalments being paid) is fulfilled. So, the agreement in *Lee v. Butler* can be described as a conditional sale agreement. In a credit sale agreement there is no such condition to the passing of property and the goods therefore normally become the buyer's immediately the contract is made (Sale of Goods Act, s.18, r.1). Thus under a credit sale agreement, the buyer will, as soon as he takes delivery, be in possession of goods of which he is the owner. Under a conditional sale agreement the buyer will be in possession of goods which will continue to belong to the seller until all the instalments have been paid. Apart from this, there is at common law no difference between credit sale and conditional sale agreements.

Although this is the position at common law, we shall see that the Consumer Credit Act 1974 radically alters the position with respect to conditional sale agreements regulated by its provisions, thus making them significantly different in effect from credit sale agreements.

The finance company

19–07   In both *Helby v. Matthews* and *Lee v. Butler*, the customer took the goods under an agreement between himself and the dealer. There was no intermediate party. No doubt some dealers still do business in that way. Today, however, it is common for the dealer to sell goods for cash to a finance company which then parts with them on instalment terms to the customer. Thus today's customer often finds that he is hiring or buying the goods, not from the dealer, but from a remote and powerful finance company. This is a classic example of a weak party (the customer) contracting with a strong one (the finance company). Finance companies, by adopting a "take it or leave it" attitude, used to insist on inserting terms that were very onerous for the customer—terms to the effect that all implied conditions and warranties were excluded; that in the event of the customer's payments falling into arrears the finance company could repossess the goods; that in order to repossess the goods the company's agents could trespass upon the customer's premises; that in the event of the customer terminating the agreement he should pay a large sum of money to the finance company, etc. The Consumer Credit Act 1974 and the Unfair Contract Terms Act 1977 largely prevent these abuses, but it is true that, in so far as those Acts allow them to, finance companies still insist on the terms being as beneficial to themselves as possible. Finance companies have now also to take account of the Unfair Terms in Consumer Contracts Regulations 1999.

The usual process by which the contract is made is as follows. **19–08** The customer selects the goods from the dealer's stock. He asks for instalment terms. At the dealer's request (and sometimes with his assistance) he fills in a form. This form will have been supplied to the dealer by a finance company with whom the dealer maintains regular contact. When completed and signed by the customer, it will constitute an offer to the finance company by the customer to take the goods either on hire-purchase or on credit sale or conditional sale terms. The customer will leave that form with the dealer. The dealer will himself complete another form which will constitute an offer by him to the finance company to sell it the goods. The dealer will send both forms to the finance company which will either accept or reject both offers. It will accept offers only if made on its own forms and thus incorporating the terms that it wishes to include. If it accepts the offers, the finance company will have agreed with the dealer to buy the goods from him and with the customer to supply the goods to him on hire-purchase (or credit sale or conditional sale) terms.

The dealer

Much of the following chapters is devoted to the contractual **19–09** relationship between the customer and the person (often a finance company) from whom he hires or buys the goods. However, a little time should be spent considering the position of the dealer who sells his goods to the finance company.

(i) Dealer and customer

19–10   The relationship between these two is not that of seller and buyer, because the dealer has sold the goods, not to the customer, but to the finance company. It follows that, if the goods prove defective, the customer has no action against the dealer under section 14 of the Sale of Goods Act: *Drury v. Victor Buckland* (1941 CA). Nevertheless he may well still have a remedy against the dealer. In *Andrews v. Hopkinson* (1956 QB) the dealer told the customer "It's a good little bus. I would stake my life on it". After this the customer made a hire-purchase contract, in the usual way, with a finance company. Soon after taking delivery of the car, he had a crash in it, due to its defective steering mechanism. McNair J. held that the dealer was liable in damages to the customer for two reasons. (i) There was a contract, albeit not one of sale, between the dealer and the customer. The contract consisted of the dealer promising that the car was a "good little bus" in return of the customer applying to the finance company to acquire it on hire-purchase terms. The dealer was therefore liable for breach of his warranty (*i.e.* his promise). (ii) The defect in the steering mechanism was due to negligent lack of inspection and servicing by the dealer who was therefore liable—irrespective of whether there was a contract—to anyone foreseeably injured by his negligence. This was an application of the general principle in *Donoghue v. Stevenson* (see paragraph 9–04 above).

(ii) Dealer and finance company

19–11   The relationship of dealer and finance company is primarily that of seller and buyer. Their contract will therefore, in the absence of contrary agreement, be subject to the provisions of the Sale of Goods Act. However, the finance company will often require the dealer to take on further obligations and to enter into a recourse agreement. The extent of the dealer's liability under one of these will depend upon the terms of his particular agreement. Often it will be worded so as to constitute a contract of indemnity under which the dealer must make good any loss suffered by the finance company in the event of the customer defaulting on his payments or terminating his agreement.

The question of to what extent the dealer in dealing with the customer is the agent of the finance company will be discussed in Chapter 24.

Guarantors and indemnifiers

There are risks involved in credit trading. Apart from the chance that the customer may default on his payments (perhaps even go bankrupt), there is the risk that he may also sell, damage or even destroy the goods. In the typical transaction, it is the finance company which runs these risks. The finance company can to some extent safeguard itself by including certain terms in the contract it makes with the customer. For example, in the case of a motor vehicle the contract may require the hirer/buyer to have comprehensive insurance. However, this does not provide any safeguard against the irresponsible customer who does not comply with such terms of the agreement or against the out and out rogue who, having paid his initial deposit, disappears with the goods without trace.

19–12

Thus it is quite possible for a finance company to insist that some third person acts as a safeguard against the finance company making a loss on the transaction. The contract made between the third person and the finance company will, depending upon its terms, be a contract either of guarantee or of indemnity. The difference between these two types of contract has already been considered (in Chapter 2, paragraph 2–12 above). From the finance company's point of view a contract of guarantee is the less satisfactory, for two reasons. First, it is enforceable only if there is sufficient written evidence of its existence (Statute of Frauds 1677), though this is perhaps not very important since the agreement will usually be in writing anyway. Secondly, a contract of guarantee is enforceable only if the principal contract is valid (*i.e.* the one between the finance company and the customer). To put this another way, if the customer has a defence to a claim against him under the hire-purchase agreement, then any guarantor will also be able to use the same defence. An indemnifier, however, can be liable when the customer has a valid defence and can sometimes be liable to a greater extent than the customer (see *Goulston Discount Co. Ltd v. Clark*, paragraph 27–30 below).

It is useful at this stage to indicate that guarantors and indemnifiers are of two types, those who act as such at the request of the customer and those who were not requested by the customer to do so. An example of the latter is the dealer who has a recourse agreement with the finance company.

CHAPTER 20

OTHER FORMS OF NEVER-NEVER

WITH the coming of the affluent society the consumer credit **20–01** business has boomed. In earlier days, having goods on hire-purchase or similar terms came to be known colloquially as having them on the "never-never"—because the repayment periods were so long it sometimes seemed as though they would never be paid for. Hire-purchase is today only one of the ways in which the consumer can obtain credit. This chapter is a "whistle-stop tour" of the rest of the never-never land, a quick passing look at a number of different ways in which credit is provided and security taken. It is concerned not so much with the law as with the way business is carried on.

Hire-purchase, conditional sale and credit sale have in common **20–02** that the goods and the credit are provided in the same agreement. The same agreement regulates both the supply of the goods and also the indebtedness of the hirer or buyer. However there is no legal or practical reason why this should be the case with every credit agreement. Take the typical situation where a finance company lets goods on hire-purchase terms to a customer. From a practical view (though not a legal one) the finance company is not really the supplier of the goods. The dealer is the real supplier of the goods. Indeed, when the agreement has been made, it is from the dealer that the customer will collect the goods which he is hiring on hire-purchase terms from the finance company. Practically speaking, the finance company is in business, not really to sell or hire out goods, but to give loans. It supplies goods (*i.e.* purchases them from the dealer and lets them to the borrower on hire-purchase terms) in order to make the loan and at the same time to retain some collateral for the loan. The collateral is the finance company's right to recover possession of the goods in the event of the hirer defaulting on his payments or disposing of the goods.

Why does the finance company not achieve the same result (*i.e.* the giving of a loan on the collateral of the goods) by granting a loan to the purchaser and taking a mortgage of the goods? This is how house purchases are financed and it would have the advantage that the borrower buys the goods directly from the person who is actually the supplier of them, *i.e.* the dealer. The finance company would not then be cast in the role of a seller or owner (*i.e.* supplier) of the goods. The reason that finance companies do not commonly take mortgages of goods lies in the Bills of Sale Acts (see "Mortgages of Goods", below).

20–03   However, there are various methods in use today by which credit is quite commonly granted under an agreement which is separate from that which regulates the selling or hiring of the goods, *e.g.* the customer borrows the money from X and uses it to buy the goods from Y. We are about to examine some of these methods but two preliminary points need to be made. First, the credit (*i.e.* the loan) does not necessarily have to be for the supply of goods. It could be for the purchase of services (*e.g.* a holiday or the erection of a garage) or for the purchase of a plot of land or for any other use to which the borrower wants to put it. Secondly, the two agreements (*i.e.* loan and purchase) could be with the same person, *e.g.* the borrower borrows money from X and uses it to buy goods also from X. Now let us examine first some general categories and then some more particular examples.

Unsecured loan

20–04   The notion of an unsecured loan is very simple. It consists of the lender giving money to the borrower in return for a promise by the borrower to repay it. The only means for the creditor to enforce the agreement is for him to sue the borrower in the courts. If the borrower becomes insolvent or bankrupt, the creditor has no other remedy open to him and therefore runs a considerable risk of losing part or all of his money. Since the lender runs high risks, the cost of the loan (*i.e.* the interest) will usually be high. Unsecured loans can be obtained from various sources, mainly banks and finance companies.

It is worthwhile comparing an unsecured loan with a credit sale agreement. The effect of both is that the creditor provides unsecured credit. Under a credit sale agreement the credit is, by the nature of the transaction, directly related to the purchase of the goods in the credit sale agreement, *i.e.* the credit is for the purchase of particular goods. (Incidentally, this last statement is true also of hire-purchase and conditional sale agreements.) A direct loan, on the other hand, need not be associated with the purchase of a specific item or items. The vast majority of hire-purchase, conditional sale and credit sale agreements involve the giving of credit by a finance company which has business connections with the dealer. These agreements often arise out of a regular relationship between a dealer and a finance company to whom the dealer regularly introduces potential purchasers who require credit terms. A direct loan may also be given by such a connected lender but, equally, may be given by a lender completely unconnected with the dealer (*i.e.* a lender contacted by the borrower for himself, whether it be a bank, a finance company or even a friend).

Unsecured credit

An unsecured loan is only one type of unsecured credit and is in reality no different from any other form. The word "loan" conjures up a picture of money passing physically from the lender to the borrower who then uses it as desired and makes repayments later. A loan is but one way of creating a debt and a credit. (It must of course create both, since one person's debt is another person's credit.) However, a debt can be created in other ways. Whenever there is an agreement that a debt may be paid later there is something which can be called a credit agreement. A credit sale agreement provides an excellent example. Others (*e.g.* credit card and trading check agreements) will be given shortly.

20–05

Secured credit

The purpose of security for the creditor is to reduce the risk for him that he will not recoup the debt that is owing to him—the main risks being either that the debtor does not have the means to pay (*i.e.* becomes insolvent) or that he disappears without trace. The main advantage to the debtor of giving security is that the creditor, because the risks are reduced, may offer better terms (*i.e.* charge less interest).

20–06

Generally, the fact that a credit agreement is secured does not in any other way alter its nature. Generally, even if for some reason the security fails, the creditor will still be able to sue the debtor on his promise to repay.

SOME PARTICULAR FORMS OF SECURITY

What follows is no more than a very general outline of some of the more common forms of security.

20–07

Guarantee or indemnity

20–08   The notion of someone acting as guarantor or indemnifier has already been considered in relation to hire-purchase agreements (see paragraph 19–12). His position and function are exactly the same in relation to any other credit agreement. He does in a very real sense provide security. He is someone to whom the creditor can look if the debtor defaults. He may be the only security that the creditor has or, equally, may be additional to security in one of the following forms.

Mortgage of goods (chattel mortgage)

20–09   A mortgage of goods is created when the owner of goods (the borrower) transfers ownership to the lender (*e.g.* a finance company) on condition that the lender will retransfer the ownership when the loan is duly repaid. The borrower retains possession throughout. The borrower could create a mortgage over goods he has owned for some time or could do it at the time he purchases them. Mortgages of goods are seldom used, because any document creating one must comply with the very technical and obscure requirements of the Bills of Sale Acts 1878–1882 and must be registered. Failure to comply with these requirements is likely to render the security void.

Pledge

20–10   A pledge is created when the owner of goods transfers possession of them (or of the documents of title) to a lender as security for a loan. A pledge differs from a mortgage in that with a pledge the borrower retains his ownership throughout and parts with possession, whereas with a mortgage of goods the borrower parts with ownership and retains possession throughout.

Mortgage of land

20–11   This is a particularly sound form of security—more so than any security over goods, which can be lost, stolen or destroyed or can simply depreciate in value. Land on the other hand tends to increase in value and cannot be moved. It is this last fact which has made land mortgages increasingly widely used in the consumer credit field. It is well known that someone who buys a house is able to mortgage the house as security for the loan of the money to buy it. After he has occupied it for a while it may have increased in value and would be good security for a further loan. Thus there exists what might be termed second mortgage companies which will give the house owner a loan and take a second mortgage as security for the loan. The agreement will usually allow the borrower to use the loan for whatever he likes.

Assignment of life assurance endowment policy

A policy of this type presents for the assured person a means 20–12 of saving combined with seeing that in the event of his premature death his dependents are not left without money. The policy is an agreement whereby he agrees to pay for, say, 20 years a regular premium to the insurance company. In return, the company agrees to pay him a fixed sum (perhaps plus bonuses) at the end of the period; it further agrees that if he dies earlier it will immediately pay the fixed sum (perhaps plus any bonuses already accumulated). That is a typical agreement. Now, suppose the agreement has been running for 10 years. It has by then got some value and could, for example, be sold (*i.e.* surrendered) back to the insurance company for an immediate cash payment.

Instead of doing that, the insured could obtain a loan and assign (*i.e.* transfer the benefit of) the policy to the lender until the loan is repaid. A bank will sometimes accept an assignment of such an insurance policy as security for a loan and may then charge a lower rate of interest.

METHODS OF PROVIDING CREDIT

Arrangements vary. There are three different roles which may 20–13 or may not be combined in one person:

(i) That of creditor, *i.e.* the lender, the person who provides the credit for the debtor.

(ii) That of seller/supplier, *i.e.* the person who makes a contract with the debtor to supply him with goods or services.

(iii) That of dealer, *i.e.* the retailer of the goods (or services).

There are three common combinations:

(a) All three roles are combined in the same person, *e.g.* when a dealer makes a credit sale or hire-purchase agreement directly with the customer, as occured in *Helby v. Matthews.*

(b) The first two roles are combined in one person but the dealer is someone else, *e.g.* in the typical hire-purchase or credit sale agreement where a finance company is involved.

(c) The last two roles are combined in one person, the creditor being someone else, *e.g.* when a bank makes a personal loan to a customer who uses it to buy goods directly from the dealer.

It is useful to bear this analysis in mind when considering the following methods that are used to provide credit.

Bank loan

20–14   This term is usually used to describe an arrangement whereby the customer borrows a fixed sum at a fixed rate of interest and agrees to pay it off by fixed regular (usually monthly) instalments. The repayments will often be made by automatic deductions from the customer's current account at the bank. The loan will usually be unsecured but may be secured, *e.g.* by the assignment of a life policy. A bank loan will invariably be an example of the third possibility (c) above.

Bank overdraft

20–15   This is an arrangement whereby the customer is allowed to overdraw (*i.e.* borrow) on his current account. Like a bank loan, it will fall within the third possibility (c) above. Unlike a bank loan, it will be flexible in a number of ways. First, the interest rate is liable to fluctuate over the period of the loan. Secondly, the debtor may not be required to pay it off at any particular rate but may be trusted to pay it off as and when he can. Thirdly, it may not be for a fixed sum but may simply allow the customer to overdraw up to a maximum amount. Lastly, it may not be restricted to one occasion. The customer is usually allowed, as he pays it off, to overdraw again and again—always subject to a maximum amount.

Bank's revolving credit

20–16   This is simply a version of a bank loan but has one feature of an overdraft—namely that the debtor, as his debt becomes reduced by his regular repayments, is automatically allowed to borrow again up to the original or an agreed figure. He can do this again and again.

Shop's revolving credit

Some large shops and chain stores, *e.g.* men's tailors, operate a **20-17** system whereby the customer agrees to pay so much a month (say, £30) and at the same time the customer can buy goods on credit up to a certain value (*e.g.* 12 times his monthly payments). Thus, in this example the customer could immediately buy £360 worth of clothes and will take about 12 months to pay for them. If that was all that the arrangement was, it would be no more than an ordinary credit sale agreement. However the customer is normally allowed to "top up" his debt, *i.e.* as his repayments reduce his outstanding debt, he can then purchase more clothes so as to bring his debt back up to £360. This sort of arrangement is often termed by the shop a "budget account". It is an example of the first possibility (a) above. The credit is usually unsecured.

Check trading

A trading check is a piece of paper or token or voucher. It is a **20-18** device for providing a fixed amount of credit which is (usually) unsecured. The customer will acquire the check first and then use it to buy goods or services. Suppose the check has a face value of £90. Then the customer can buy goods up to that value at any shop prepared to accept the check. The value of the goods he has bought, say £45, will be marked on the back of the check thus leaving the customer free to spend the rest of the check elsewhere. The shops will actually get payment from the check trading company from which the customer acquired the check. The customer will pay off the check trading company in instalments over a period of weeks, *e.g.* 36 weekly instalments of £3. The total of his instalments will of course be more than the face value of the check, the extra representing the interest. Check trading is an example of the third possibility (c) above. The creditor is one person (*i.e.* the check trading company). The seller and supplier of the goods is another person (*i.e.* the shop which accepts the trading check in payment). The contract between the customer and the shop which accepts the trading check in payment is a contract of sale of goods: *Davies v Customs and Excise* (see paragraph 8–05 above). A trading check can be used only at those shops which are prepared to accept them. There will be an arrangement between the check trading company and a large number of stores whereby the latter agree to accept the checks.

Check trading is more common in the north of England than in **20-19** the south and has traditionally involved quite small sums (*i.e.* up to about £100) and weekly repayments. Trading checks are often acquired from a door-to-door representative of the check trading company, who also will collect the weekly repayments. However, checks are in some instances being used for much larger sums in which case the repayments are usually monthly. Sometimes the check is restricted to the purchase of a specified item from a specified shop. Such checks are usually termed trading vouchers.

A trading check or voucher is not a revolving credit. Once the debtor has spent the value of his check he cannot, as his repayments are made, automatically have more credit. He must apply again to the check trading company (or, rather, to its representative) for another check.

Credit cards

20–20   The credit card system has much in common with that of trading checks. It is a further example of the third possibility (c) above. Again three parties are involved, the customer, the creditor (in this case the credit card company) and the seller/supplier. A credit card is used in much the same way as a trading check. The buyer (*i.e.* the credit card holder), having decided what to purchase, buys it but does not pay either cash or by cheque; instead he uses his credit card. The seller is then paid by the credit card company and the latter within about two to seven weeks sends an account to the customer for payment. The normal arrangement between a credit card company and a retailer is that the retailer gives the card company a discount. Thus if a card holder uses his card to pay for an item costing £100, the card company will pay only about £95 or £96 to the retailer. This discount is part of the card company's profit. The card holder will of course still be required to pay the card company the full amount. Now, those card companies which require the customer to pay the whole amount at once are providing no more than a sophisticated form of general trade debt—debt deferred for a short time to be repaid in one instalment (*e.g.* Diner's Club and traditional American Express cards). Such cards are often termed charge cards to differentiate them from credit cards properly so-called. Some companies, *e.g.* American Express, offer charge card agreements and credit card agreements. With the latter the card holder is allowed to pay the account off in monthly instalments. The best known of these are "Visa" and "Access". Confusingly, the Marks & Spencer Chargecard, despite its name, is a credit card because it allows the card holder to pay off each account in a number of repayments over a period of time!

The legal nature of a typical credit card or charge card **20–21** arrangement was considered in *Re Charge Card Services Ltd* (1988 CA). There were two underlying agreements. One was between the card company and card holder and regulated the basis on which credit could be obtained and was to be paid off. The other was between the card company and retailer; under it the retailer agreed to accept payment by means of the card and was to receive payment, less a discount, from the card company. In the case, a number of card holders had used their cards to pay for petrol at various garages before the card company became insolvent. This left a number of the garages owed money by the card company. Being unable to get it from the insolvent company, the garages claimed it from the individual card holders. The garages claimed that payment by credit or charge card was like payment by cheque. If a customer's cheque had been dishonoured by the bank, the garage would be entitled to claim the price direct from the customer. This is because payment by cheque is conditional upon the cheque being honoured. A number of the card holders had, however, already paid the card company for the petrol in question. So if they now had to pay the garage, they would end up having to pay twice for the same petrol. The Court of Appeal held that payment by means of a credit or charge card is not conditional, but absolute. It is a complete payment by the card holder who is not liable to pay the garage if the card is not honoured. Thus it is the retailer who runs the risk that the card company may become insolvent. It was also held, interpreting the agreement between the card company and the card holder, that the company had the right to claim payment from the card holder irrespective of whether the card company had paid the garages. Thus the neat result was that those card holders who had not yet paid the card company in respect of petrol purchased using their card remained liable to do so, but no card holder was liable to pay the garage for such petrol. It should be added that a card might be dishonoured for a reason other than the card company becoming insolvent, *i.e.* because the person using the card was doing so in excess of his credit limit, or had stolen the card. It might be, under the terms of the agreement between the card company and the retailer, that in those circumstances the card company is not liable to pay the retailer. If so, there is no doubt that the retailer in those circumstances would be entitled to claim payment from the person who had used the card, though probably not the full cash price but only the lesser amount that the retailer had expected to be paid by the card company. This is the only amount the retailer has lost because of the customer's representation (implied by his action of using the card) that he was authorised by the card company to use the card on that transaction.

20–22   There are two significant differences between the credit card system and the trading check system. First, the credit card holder does not actually draw upon any credit (*i.e.* owe any money) until he uses his credit card to purchase something. Thus when the credit card holder obtains his credit card he does not agree to any fixed amount of credit. The amount of the credit he obtains will depend upon the value of what he chooses to buy with the card. However, there will be a credit limit which he must not exceed at any one time. Secondly, a credit card provides a type of revolving credit. Thus the card holder can use the card again and again to obtain mere credit, subject to the promise that his total credit does not at any one time exceed the credit limit stipulated in his credit card agreement. The credit card will normally be valid for two years but on expiry a replacement card will usually be sent automatically to the card holder.

20–23   A credit card provides an extremely useful and flexible form of credit. Even if the card is not used, the card holder has the sure knowledge that he can obtain instant credit. He can use it (or not) as and when he chooses. Although he can use it only at shops and other establishments which have an arrangement with the credit card company, it is true to say that a great many places at home and abroad have made such arrangements to accept both Visa and Access. Further, the debtor can make repayments more or less as he pleases. He can pay it all off when the first account is sent to him or he can pay off some (not necessarily the same amount) each month. The only restriction is that there is a normally minimum amount which he must repay each month. Naturally, the longer he takes to make repayment, the more he will have to pay in interest.

A further point needs to be made. A credit card can usually be used not only to buy goods or services but also to obtain a cash loan from a bank. The bank will then obtain immediate repayment from the credit card company. The latter can be repaid by the card holder in the flexible way described above.

20–24   Visa and Access are cards which can be used by the card holder at any shop which has an agreement with the relevant credit card company enabling the shop to accept that company's cards. However, some large stores or chains of stores have their own credit card schemes under which the card holder is limited to being able to use the card in that company's own stores. Some of these "in-house" credit cards are operated by the company which owns the store. These are therefore sometimes termed in the trade "two party" credit cards. There are only two persons involved in the transaction, the card holder and the company owning the store. This arrangement is an example of the first possibility (a) mentioned at paragraph 20–13 above. The roles of creditor, seller and dealer are all combined in one person. Sometimes one of these "in-house" credit card schemes (*e.g.* the Marks & Spencer Chargecard) will be operated, not by the store itself, but by a subsidary company or by a bank or finance company in arrangement with the store. The main difference between this "three party" type of "in-house" credit card and the more common Visa and Access cards is that the in-house card can be used only in the store (or chain of stores) with which it is connected. Some stores operating in-house schemes also have arrangements with the major operators (*e.g.* Visa and Access) enabling them to accept payment via the major credit cards. Other stores are more exclusive and recognise only their own in-house cards. Besides stores, other large scale retail operators, *e.g.* hotel chains and petrol companies, also operate in-house credit card schemes. These days a respectable man-about-town is perhaps not properly dressed unless he carries an assorted collection of charge cards and credit cards!

Rental agreements

Where goods are hired but the hirer is given no option to **20–25** purchase, the agreement is not a hire-purchase agreement but is simply an ordinary bailment. There is in a sense no element of credit, since the hirer pays each week for what he gets each week (*i.e.* one week's use of the goods). There is no element of "have now, pay later". However, it is becoming quite common with certain types of goods (*e.g.* televisions) for the goods to be hired by the same person for virtually the whole of the useful life of the goods. It is true that the hirer never becomes owner of the goods but he does have them (to keep indefinitely) and pay later. This is in a very real sense never-never, even though it is not a "credit" agreement.

"Credit-hire" agreements

The "credit-hire" agreement, a modern phenomenon, is a hire **20–26** agreement which does involve the provision of credit. The hirer is typically a motorist whose car has been put off the road in an accident caused entirely by the other's driver's fault. The agreement provides for the motorist to hire a replacement car for so long as her own is off the road, and also provides that the hire charges will become payable, not at the end of the hire period but only when the motorist's damages are recovered from the other motorist whose negligence caused the accident. Commonly the credit-hire company (or its chosen solicitor) will pursue that claim on her behalf recover her damages and deduct the credit-hire charges before handing those damages over to her. A credit-hire agreement undoubtedly involves an element of "have now" (*i.e.* the hire of the car) and "pay later". Unsurprisingly, hire charges under credit-hire agreements are much higher than under conventional hire agreements (known as "spot hire"). The higher charges reflect the fact that, under a typical credit-hire agreement, the hirer receives the following benefits not provided under a spot hire agreement: (i) she is relieved of having to lay out money for the car hire; (ii) she is relieved of having to pursue a claim against the other motorist, *i.e.* because normally the credit-hire company does that for her, (iii) she is thus also relieved of having to bear the costs in pursuing litigation against the other motorist. The majority of the House of Lords in *Dimond v. Lovell* (2000) considered, *obiter*, that the cost of these extra benefits was not compensatable in damages obtainable from the other motorist. This, if correct, means that the hirer can recover, in damages from the other motorist, hire charges only at the equivalent spot hire rate. Thus the difference between the credit-hire charges and the lower spot hire rate will have to be borne either by the hirer or by the credit-hire company (*i.e.* if it chooses not to, or cannot, enforce the credit-hire agreement fully against the hirer). If this *obiter dicta* in the House of Lords proves correct, it may well be the death knell of credit-hire agreements, since these are usually "sold" to the innocent motorist on the basis that she will not have to pay anything for the hire of the replacement car, since the credit-hire company will recover all of the hire charges on her behalf from the other motorist. The day after the House of Lords gave judgment in *Dimond v. Lovell*, the shares in at least one credit-hire company were described as having gone into free fall! The extent to which credit-hire agreements are regulated by the Consumer Credit Act is explained later at paragraphs 21–07, 21–17, 21–22, 21–25. (For a detailed and comprehensive account see an article *"Recovery of Credit Hire Charges"* at [1999] C.I.C.C. 25).

PARASITIC BUSINESS

Just as the continued flourishing of businesses retailing   **20–27**
consumer goods and services is the lifeblood of the consumer
credit business, so the continued flourishing of the consumer
credit business is the lifeblood of further subordinate businesses
that now exist. These can be described as parasites which depend
upon the consumer credit business for their existence. Between
the retailers of consumer goods and services and consumer credit
businesses there is a degree of mutual dependence in that the
retailers depend for the continued flourishing of their own
businesses upon the availability to their customers of credit.
However, there is not always the same degree of mutual
dependence between consumer credit businesses and the
subordinate businesses which have just been described as
parasites. These businesses can be broken down into two broad
categories—those which render a service to creditors (or potential
creditors) and those which render a service to debtors (or potential
debtors).

Credit reference agencies
A number of enterprises operate in this field. Their function is   **20–28**
to collect and maintain a register of information about the creditworthiness of individuals. Upon request and the payment of a fee
they will supply to a finance company (*i.e.* potential creditor)
information about an individual (*i.e.* the potential debtor who has
applied to the finance company for credit). Thus these agencies
provide finance companies with a method of assessing the risk
involved in providing credit to a given individual. A bad report
from a credit reference agency can result in the individual being
refused credit.

Credit brokers
A credit broker is someone who acts for a potential debtor for   **20–29**
the purpose of finding him credit. A common type of credit
broker is the mortgage broker, who specialises in putting his
client in touch with a finance company which is prepared to lend
money on the security of a house mortgage (usually a second
mortgage). There is sometimes a fee or commission which the
client agrees to pay the broker for his services.

Credit Insurers

20–30   It is possible for a debtor to take out an insurance policy to cover his repayments. A typical policy will provide for (a) repayment of instalments which are due during any sickness or unemployment of the debtor and (b) repayment of the total outstanding debt if the debtor dies. Sometimes it is an express condition of the credit agreement that the debtor takes out a policy of this kind.

Debt collectors

20–31   Some firms specialise in taking over bad debts from finance companies (and others) and then trying to recover them for themselves. The risk on each bad debt is obviously considerable but the profit for the debt collector on each debt actually recovered is also considerable—because the amount paid to the creditor by the debt collector in respect of each bad debt will be much less than the mount actually owed by the debtor.

Debt counsellors and adjusters

20–32   There are firms who will advise and act on behalf of a debtor who gets into difficulties with repayments. They will of course charge the debtor a fee for their service. Depending upon what the debtor wants they may merely give him advice, or act on his behalf to negotiate with the creditor (*e.g.* to get the repayment period extended) or even actually take over the debtor's obligations under his credit agreement(s) in return for him promising to repay them (perhaps over an extended period).

Apart from credit insurers, each of these businesses which have just been described as parasitic is termed by the Consumer Credit Act an "ancillary credit business".

CREDIT UNIONS

20–33   The Report of the Crowther Committee on Consumer Credit said:

> "A credit union consists of a group of people with some common bond—*e.g.* living in the same locality, working in the same factory, or belonging to the same association—who agree to save regularly, according to their means, in order to create a common fund from which members can borrow on reasonable terms."

The report noted that the credit union movement had not caught on in this country as it had for example in the United States and in Canada. One possible reason was that there was no legal framework for the registration and supervision of credit unions. The Credit Unions Act 1979 was designed to provide that legal framework. It lays down the criteria for registration and provides a supervisory system. It provides that if a society satisfies certain conditions it can be registered as a credit union under the Industrial and Provident Societies Act 1965. The conditions are:

(i) The society's registered office is under the society's rules to be situated at a place in Great Britain.

(ii) The rules contain provisions complying with the Act— *i.e.* regulating such things as the qualifications for membership, the holding of meetings, the taking of deposits and the making of loans.

(iii) The objects of the society are those, and only those, of a credit union—namely,
   (a) the promotion of thrift among members by the accumulation of their savings;
   (b) the creation of sources of credit for the benefit of members at a fair and reasonable rate of interest;
   (c) the use and control of members' savings for their mutual benefit; and
   (d) the training and education of the members in the wise use of money and in the management of their financial affairs.

(iv) There is a common bond between members in consequence of the admission to membership being restricted to persons fulfilling a specific qualification, *e.g.* following a particular occupation, residing in a particular locality, being employed by a particular employer, or being a member of some association or organisation existing for some purpose other than that of a credit union.

20–34 The minimum number of members of a credit union is 21 and the maximum is 5,000. A credit union may receive funds only from members and only in the form of subscriptions for shares (except that it may receive deposits of up to £750 from anyone too young to be a member, *i.e.* under 16).

Section 11 regulates the making of loans. Thus, "... a credit union may make to a member who is of full age a loan for a provident or productive purpose ...". So the credit union ought aways to ascertain the purpose of a proposed loan and to refuse it if, for example, it is wanted to spend on a luxury cruise. The loan must not exceed the member's total paid up shareholding by more than £5,000. Also, any member may not have a shareholding exceeding £5,000. The interest rate on a loan may not exceed 1 per cent per month. The period of repayment may not exceed five years in the case of a secured loan or two years in the case of an unsecured one.

The Act contains rules allowing the credit union to borrow (no more than an amount equal to half the total paid up share capital) and to invest (as authorised by the Treasury). There are further provisions as to the maintenance of reserves, the maintaining and auditing of accounts, taxation, amalgamations, winding-up and the supervisory powers of the registrar. Also, the various financial limitations in the Act can be increased by the chief registrar with the consent of the Treasury.

20–35   Currently only a fraction of 1 per cent of the population belongs to a credit union. Prior to the passing of the Financial Services and Markets Act 2000, the government, as part of its strategy to counter economic exclusion, saw it important to encourage the expansion of credit unons. Hence it announced a number of changes it proposed to make to the law relating to credit unions. Thus the following changes are due to occur.

- Transfer of the regulation of credit unions from the Registrar of Friendly Societies to the Financial Services Authority (FSA).

- Removal of the rule that there must be no more than 5,000 members.

- Increase in the maximum amount which can be held in youth accounts from £750 to £5,000.

- Increase in the maximum repayment period for loans to 3 years for unsecured and 7 years for secured loans. For those credit unions which satisfy certain criteria (to be laid down by the FSA), the periods will be 5 and 12 years respectively.

- Greater operational flexibility allowed, regarding for example: the disposal of re-possessed land; being allowed to charge for ancilimy services.

In addition, the Association of British Credit Unions is working with the main banks to develop, with government encouragement, a Central Services Organisation (CSO) which will help the many volunteers who run credit unions, by spreading administrative and management best practice and helping achieve common standards of competence and reliability.

CHAPTER 21

THE CONSUMER CREDIT ACT 1974

THE Act followed the Crowther Committee's Report on Consumer   **21–01**
Credit (1971) and in large part implemented its recommendations.
The basis of the Report was that consumer credit, although it might
take many different forms, was always basically the same thing.
Thus the Act, which is concerned with providing reasonable
protection for those consumers who obtain credit, brings under one
umbrella consumer credit agreements generally—whatever form
they take. The Act repealed previous Acts which applied only to
particular forms of consumer credit, *i.e.* the Pawnbrokers Acts 1872
and 1960, the Moneylenders Acts 1900–1927, the Hire Purchase
Act 1965 and the Advertisements (Hire Purchase) Act 1967. Two
sets of provisions, however, remain in force—the Bills of Sale Acts
and the Hire Purchase Act 1964, Pt. III. The former means that
chattel mortgages are likely to remain uncommon (see paragraph
20–09 above). The latter was dealt with at paragraph 5–40 above.

The repeal of the Hire Purchase Act 1965 did not mean that   **21–02**
the whole of the law relating to hire-purchase was recast—rather
the reverse. Before 1974 the law of hire-purchase was generally
thought to be satisfactory. Thus, in the new Act, it was largely re-
enacted with little alteration except that much of it applies to
other consumer credit agreements as well. In the new Act the
terms "creditor" and "debtor" are used. The creditor means the
person who provides the credit, *i.e.* in the case of a hire-purchase
agreement, the owner; in the case of a direct loan, the lender; and
in the case of a credit sale agreement, the seller. The debtor
means the person who receives the credit, *i.e.* in the above
examples, the hirer, borrower or buyer.

There are three aspects to the way the Act operates.

(i) It regulates virtually the whole range of consumer credit
agreements. That is to say, it controls the contractual
position, the rights and duties existing between the
creditor and debtor.

(ii) It creates a number of criminal offences designed to prevent unfair and undesirable practices by those engaged in the business of providing or advertising credit and by those engaged in connected businesses such as credit brokerage. These offences are principally concerned with the advertising of credit and the canvassing of customers.

(iii) It gives additional duties to the Director-General of Fair Trading. They are to keep under review the whole of the consumer credit business, to superintend the working and enforcing of the Act and to operate the licensing system. This system is created by the Act and generally requires anyone carrying on a business of providing consumer credit to have a licence.

21–03 The following two chapters will deal with licensing and with criminal offences relating to advertising and seeking business. After that the remaining chapters will be primarily concerned with the first of these three aspects of the Act—namely, those provisions which deal with the rights and liabilities between the creditor and debtor, *i.e.* which deal with the formation, validity and enforcement of a consumer credit agreement.

These provisions of the Act cannot be circumvented. Two sections see to that. First, section 173 prevents the parties contracting out of the effect of the Act's provisions. A term of an agreement regulated by the Act is void to the extent that it is inconsistent with any provision in the Act (or any regulations made under the Act) for the protection of the debtor. Where the Act imposes upon the debtor a duty or liability, that duty or liability cannot be increased by any term of the agreement.

The second section referred to is section 113, which prevents the Act being evaded by the use of security. Thus where an agreement is regulated by the Act, the creditor cannot enforce any security so as to benefit himself to an extent greater than if the debtor carried out his obligations to the full extent that they would be enforced under the Act. The effect of this is that the creditor can take security as an added safeguard to ensure that the debtor carries out all his obligations to the full extent that they would be enforced against him under the Act, but where an obligation would not be enforced under the Act, the creditor cannot use the security to enforce that obligation. This section will be referred to again (paragraph 26–43).

Many regulations have been made under the Act. A number of **21–04** them contain a lot of detailed requirements. This is true, for example, of those which deal with credit advertisements and those which deal with the form and contents of regulated agreements. Others of the regulations exclude specified persons or specified agreements from certain of the provisions of the Act. In this book it is not possible to give all the detail of all these various regulations. Thus although all the more important regulations are referred to, often only a summary of their provisions is given.

The rest of this chapter will deal with the definitions (mainly of different types of agreement which fall within the Act) in sections 8 to 20.

DEFINITIONS

Those agreements that are regulated agreements under the Act **21–05** are of two types—consumer credit agreements and consumer hire agreements.

Consumer credit agreements

The definition of a consumer credit agreement is to be found in **21–06** section 8(2) which, however, is meaningful only in the light of section 8(1). The two subsections read:

> "(1) A personal credit agreement is an agreement between an individual ('the debtor') and any other person ('the creditor') by which the creditor provides the debtor with credit of any amount.

> "(2) A consumer credit agreement is a personal credit agreement by which the creditor provides the debtor with credit not exceeding £25,000."

[For agreements made before May 20, 1985 the figure of £25,000 was £5,000. For agreements made on or after that date and before May 1 1998, the figure was £15,000.]

Section 9(1) completes the picture:

> "(1) In this Act 'credit' includes a cash loan, and any other form of financial accommodation."

Because of the word "individual" in section 8(1), any agreement where the debtor is a company (or any other corporate body) is not a personal credit agreement and is therefore outside the definition of a consumer credit agreement. On the other hand partnerships and other unincorporated associations are treated as individuals.

The definition of a consumer credit agreement does not include rental agreements which are dealt with under the definition of consumer hire agreement (below) but it does include the other types of agreement considered in the last two chapters. Thus it includes credit sale and conditional sale agreements, bank loans, check trading and credit card agreements. Section 9(3) specifically states that it includes hire-purchase agreements.

21–07   No agreement falls within the definition unless it provides "credit". The explanation of "credit" in section 9(1) is less than complete. An element of "have now, pay later" is a fairly good indication of credit. Sometimes it is said that credit involves the "deferment of a debt" or the "deferment of an obligation to pay". Professor Goode, in his *Consumer Credit Legislation*, suggested that credit is provided "whenever the contract provides for the debtor to pay, or gives him the option to pay, later than the time at which payment would otherwise have been earned". *Dimond v. Lovell* (2000) involved a "credit-hire" agreement. As explained at paragraph 20–26 above, this did not require the hirer to pay the car hire charges at the end of the hire period, but allowed her to postpone paying them until the conclusion of her claim against another motorist whose negligence had damaged the hirer's own car. In holding that the agreement thus provided credit to the hirer, the House of Lords applied Professor Goode's test, although Lord Hobhouse thought that it would not always be a satisfactory one to apply. The result is that a credit-hire agreement can be regulated under the Act as being both a consumer credit agreement and, if the hire period was capable of lasting over three months, also a consumer hire agreement. For the definition of consumer hire agreement, see paragraph 21–15 below.

21–08   No agreement is a consumer credit agreement unless it is within the financial limit of £25,000. For the purpose of applying the financial limit, a distinction is made between fixed-sum credit and running-account credit. The idea of a fixed-sum credit is easy. It is a once-only credit, *e.g.* a single loan. It is still a fixed-sum credit even if later the creditor agrees to make a further loan to the debtor and even if he does so before the first loan is repaid. There will then be two fixed-sum credit agreements. Hire-purchase agreements, credit sale agreements, conditional sale agreements, ordinary bank loans and trading checks are all examples of fixed-sum credits. A running-account credit is what is often termed in the credit trade a revolving credit, where the debtor does not have to re-apply for a further credit but automatically as part of his original credit agreement has the right to further credit (usually subject to a credit limit). Examples of running-account credit are bank overdrafts, revolving credits from a bank or a shop and credit card agreements.

If a credit agreement provides fixed-sum credit of £25,000 or **21–09** less then it is within the definition. The relevant figure is not the total amount which the debtor is to pay but the amount of the *credit*. That is, roughly speaking, the capital amount which the debtor is borrowing and it therefore does not include the interest payable by the debtor. To be precise, the amount of the credit does not include any item in the "total charge for credit". What is meant by the "total charge for credit" is considered a little further on (paragraph 21–35). All that can be said now is that the total charge for credit will reflect the cost to the debtor of having the credit. Thus the biggest item in the total charge for credit will be the interest charged to the debtor, which will therefore not be part of the "credit". Thus an agreement would fall within the definition of a consumer credit agreement if it gave the debtor a cash loan of £25,000 to be repaid by him in 50 monthly instalments of £560. The amount of the credit would be £25,000 even though the repayments would total £28,000. The extra £3,000 is interest, falls within the "total charge for credit" and therefore is not part of the "credit". For the definition of a consumer credit agreement, the relevant figure is the credit (the amount borrowed), not what it costs the debtor to borrow it.

With a hire-purchase agreement the calculation is not quite so **21–10** easy but the principle is the same. Suppose Sam wishes to buy a yacht for which the retail cash price is £33,000. Sam has only £8,000 saved up. So he acquires the yacht under a hire-purchase agreement under which he makes an immediate deposit of £8,000 and agrees to pay 50 monthly instalments of £560 each. The agreement gives him an option to buy the yacht for £2 provided he has first paid the deposit and all the instalments. This hire-purchase agreement would fall within the definition of a consumer credit agreement because the amount of the credit is £25,000.

Suppose, however, that the retailer had offered to insure (or **21–11** buy insurance for) the yacht for two years at an additional price of £100. To buy the yacht thus insured would cost £33,100 in cash. However, since Sam still only has £8,000 saved up, he takes it on hire-purchase terms whereby he pays an immediate deposit of £8,000 and agrees to pay 50 monthly instalments of £562 each (the option money still being £2). Now, in this case the agreement would fall outside the definition since the amount of the credit is £25,100. Thus where the credit would otherwise be at or just under £25,000 it is possible to get the agreement outside the definition by persuading the prospective debtor to borrow just a little bit more. This could be done by offering some optional extra item which is sufficiently tempting to persuade the debtor to have it. In the case of a yacht a particularly tempting extra might be the provision of a mooring for a certain number of years. A similar service is sometimes provided in the "mobile home" (*i.e.* caravan) business where one can buy a caravan and sometimes with it also the right to have it on a given site for a given number of years.

21–12 A warning must be given. A point made earlier must be repeated. It is that a distinction must be made in every case between (a) the amount of the credit and (b) the total charge for credit. These terms are mutually exclusive. The amount of the credit does not include any sum which is within the total charge for credit. In the example just given about Sam and his yacht the £100 for the insurance was not within the total charge for credit (see paragraph 21–38 below).

21–13 The £25,000 financial limit applies also in relation to running-account credit agreements. Here the governing figure is the credit limit, *i.e.* the maximum debt which the debtor is allowed to run up. If the debtor's credit limit is £25,000 or less, the agreement is within the financial limit and, providing the debtor is an individual (not a company), it is a consumer credit agreement. The agreement will still be a consumer credit agreement even if the debtor is allowed *temporarily* to exceed his credit limit. However, even where the agreement has no credit limit or has one in excess of £25,000, there are three situations when it will still be within the financial limit. These three situations are where:

(i) The debtor is unable on any one occasion to draw credit in excess of £25,000.

(ii) The terms of the agreement are such that if the debt (the debit balance) exceeds a certain figure (of £25,000 or less) the terms (*e.g.* the rate of interest) become more onerous for the debtor.

(iii) It is probable, at the time the agreement is made, that the debt will not at any time rise above £25,000.

Thus most running-account credit agreements will be within the definition. A clear example of one which would not would be one restricted to large credits of over £25,000 and which could not be used (even on one occasion) to acquire a credit of £25,000 or less.

Generally any credit agreement which falls outside the **21–14** definition of a consumer credit agreement falls altogether outside the Act. However, there is one important exception. There is one set of the Act's provisions which applies not only to consumer credit agreements but also to all personal credit agreements— namely those sections (137–140) which empower the court to reopen an extortionate credit bargain (see paragraph 26–06 below).

Consumer hire agreements

A consumer hire agreement is any agreement for the bailment **21–15** (hiring) of goods which fulfils four conditions (section 15):

(a) It is not a hire-purchase agreement.

(b) It is capable of lasting more than three months.

(c) It does not require the hirer to make payments exceeding £25,000.

(d) The hirer is not a body corporate.

[For agreements made before May 20, 1985 the £25,000 figure was £5,000. For agreements made on or after that date and before May 1 1998, the figure was £15,000.]

The first condition does not, of course, mean that a hire-purchase agreement is not regulated. We have just seen that hire-purchase agreements fall within the definition of a consumer credit agreement. The second condition means that, for example, an agreement to hire a car for two months would fall outside the Act. The third condition excludes from the definition an agreement under which the rental payments are so high that even if the goods are hired for the minimum period allowed by the agreement the payments will exceed £25,000. Thus agreements to hire large industrial plant or machinery are likely to fall outside the definition, even if hired by an individual or partnership.

Consider, however, an example—a hire agreement which is not a hire-purchase agreement and which provides:

(i) That the hirer (an individual) shall pay a deposit of £15,000.

(ii) That the hirer shall pay a monthly rental of £10,000.

(iii) That the hiring shall continue for a maximum of one year but that the hirer shall be able to terminate it at or at any time after the end of the first month.

21–16 This agreement falls within the definition since it might last longer than three months and the payments might not exceed £25,000.

Consider another example—a hire agreement which is not a hire-purchase agreement and which provides:

(i) That the hirer (an individual) shall not pay any deposit but shall pay a rental of £100 per month.

(ii) That the hiring shall last three months.

(iii) That the hirer shall have the right to renew the agreement for a further three months.

This agreement is *capable* of lasting more than three months and is also within the definition.

21–17 It was necessary for the Act to have a separate definition of a consumer hire agreement since, as explained in the last chapter (paragraph 20–25), it does not normally involve any element of credit and thus does not fall within the definition of consumer credit agreement. A "credit-hire" agreement is an unusual type of agreement which involves both hire and credit and thus can fall within both definitions, consumer credit agreement and consumer hire agreement (see paragraph 21–07 above).

It will be found that a great many sections of the Act refer to the "creditor or owner" and the "debtor or hirer". The words "owner" and "hirer" refer to the parties to a consumer hire agreement and not to the parties to a hire-purchase agreement. The words "creditor" and "debtor" include (and refer to) the owner and hirer respectively under a hire-purchase agreement. This is because, as we have just seen, a hire-purchase agreement where the credit does not exceed £25,000 falls within the definition of a consumer credit agreement.

Regulated agreements

A regulated agreement is any consumer credit agreement or **21–18** consumer hire agreement other than an exempt agreement.

Most of the provisions of the Act apply, not to all consumer credit agreements, but only to regulated agreements. This is true in particular of those sections which relate to the formation, validity and enforcement of agreements. The position is similar in relation to the licensing provisions so that someone who carries on a consumer credit business which is confined to giving credit under exempt agreements does not require a licence.

The question of which agreements are exempt agreements will be examined a little later. First, it is necessary to consider certain sub-categories of consumer credit agreement.

Restricted-use and unrestricted-use agreements

Credit will be either restricted-use credit or unrestricted-use **21–19** credit (section 11). It is unrestricted-use credit if it is in fact provided in such a way as to leave the debtor free to use it as he chooses. Thus hire-purchase agreements, credit sale and conditional sale agreements, check trading agreements, credit-hire agreements and a shop's revolving credit are all examples of restricted-use credit agreements. A bank loan or overdraft will almost always be unrestricted-use credit, since the money is usually paid directly to the borrower who is therefore free to use it as he chooses. In this case it is still unrestricted-use credit even if the borrower had agreed to use it only for one particular purpose, *e.g.* to repay a debt to X. It would of course be a restricted-use credit agreement if the bank stipulates that the money is to be paid directly by the bank to X.

A credit card agreement is an example of a multiple agreement, *i.e.* it can be used to buy goods or services at a restricted number (albeit a large number) of shops, etc., and it can be used to obtain a cash loan. This is an unrestricted-use credit agreement with respect to the provision of cash, and a restricted-use credit agreement with respect to the provision of goods or services.

Debtor-creditor and debtor-creditor-supplier agreements

Every regulated consumer credit agreement must be either a **21–20** debtor-creditor-supplier agreement or a debtor-creditor agreement (sections 12 and 13). The former describes the type of agreement where either there is a business connection between the creditor and the supplier of the goods (as occurs in check trading) or the creditor is also the supplier of the goods (as in every credit sale, conditional sale, hire-purchase and credit-hire agreement). In order to determine whether there is a business connection between the creditor and supplier (*i.e.* whether the credit agreement is a debtor-credit-supplier agreement) it must first be decided whether the credit agreement is for restricted-use or for unrestricted-use credit.

The rule can be formulated as follows. The following agreements are debtor-creditor-supplier agreements:

(a) An agreement for restricted-use credit where the creditor and supplier are one and the same person.

(b) A restricted-use credit agreement "made by the creditor under pre-existing arrangements, or in contemplation of future arrangements, between himself and the supplier".

(c) An unrestricted-use credit agreement made by the creditor under pre-existing arrangements between himself and the supplier, in the knowledge that the credit is to be used to finance a transaction between the debtor and the supplier.

Any agreement not in one of these three categories is merely a debtor-creditor agreement.

21–21 In many cases a restricted-use credit agreement will be a debtor-creditor-supplier agreement and an unrestricted-use credit agreement will be a debtor-creditor agreement. These are the common combinations. Thus hire-purchase, conditional sale, credit sale, trading check agreements and credit-hire are all restricted-use debtor-creditor-supplier agreements. Further illustrations are provided by a typical credit card agreement which is, as has been seen, a multiple agreement. In so far as it relates to a cash loan, it is an unrestricted-use credit agreement and is a debtor-creditor agreement. In so far as it relates to goods or services it is a restricted-use credit agreement and is also a debtor-credit-supplier agreement. It is the latter because the supplier of goods or services who accepts payment by means of a credit card does so under an arrangement between himself and the credit card company—an arrangement which either pre-existed, or was contemplated by, the credit agreement.

It is, however, possible for the combination to be different. For example a bank loan may be granted to the debtor to pay off a pre-existing debt of his and it may be payable directly by the bank to the person to be paid off (see paragraph 21–19 above).

This would be an agreement for restricted-use credit but would merely be a debtor-creditor agreement. Exactly the same result would occur where a bank agrees to enable its customer to buy a new car by making him a loan, but at the same time stipulates that the money is to be payable directly by the bank to the supplier (*i.e.* the car dealer). The agreement between the bank (creditor) and its customer (debtor) is clearly for restricted-use credit but it is still merely a debtor-creditor agreement because it is not made under pre-existing arrangements or in contemplation of future arrangements between the bank and the car dealer.

Take one further example, this time of an agreement in the third category (above) of debtor-creditor-supplier agreements— namely, an agreement where the creditor furnishes the credit in such a way as to leave the debtor free to use the credit as he likes but where the creditor makes the agreement under pre-existing arrangements between himself and the supplier in the knowledge that the credit is to be used to finance a transaction between the debtor and the supplier. This situation could arise on facts like these: Shiver wants central heating installed in his house. He approaches Warmitup Ltd who indicate that they will deal only on a cash payment basis and suggest that Shiver gets in touch with Hotmoney Ltd who have an arrangement with Warmitup Ltd whereby Hotmoney Ltd will make loans to potential customers of Warmitup Ltd. After some negotiations, Hotmoney Ltd make a loan to Shiver which is paid directly into Shiver's hands. This is a debtor-creditor-supplier agreement even though it is an unrestricted-use credit agreement.

21–22

The Act nowhere uses the words "business connection". Nevertheless the policy behind the classification into debtor-creditor-supplier agreements and debtor-creditor agreements is to identify the former as credit agreements where there is some business connection between the creditor and supplier. The policy is that where there is that business connection between the creditor and the supplier, both of them (and not just the supplier) should be answerable to the customer if the goods or services supplied do not correspond with representations made to him before he bought them or if the supplier is in breach of contract with the customer. This point will be returned to later (paragraphs 24–23 and 25–03).

Electronic Funds Transfer and debit cards

21–23   In the light of the foregoing, consider one particular development in banking services, namely Electronic Funds Transfer (EFT). This is a modern means of payment in supermarkets, department stores and other places. In the shop at the point of sale there will be a terminal which will have a direct electronic link with the major clearing banks. A bank customer who holds a "debit" card (*e.g.* a Delta or Switch card) is able to hand his debit card to the shop's checkout assistant who will run it through the terminal. That terminal via its electronic link automatically transfers the money (more or less immediately) from the customer's own bank account to the shop's bank account. There is no need for the customer to write a cheque. Unlike a cheque guarantee card, a "debit" card does not enable the customer to obtain an unauthorised overdraft. That being so, the Consumer Credit Act does not apply at all to a "debit" card unless the customer has from his bank an agreed overdraft authority with a credit limit not exceeding £25,000. In the absence of an overdraft (or an agreement of the bank authorising one), there will be no credit agreement.

Consider now the case of an individual "debit" card holder who does have his bank's permission to overdraw—up to, say, £4,000. Clearly in that case, his agreement with the bank is a regulated consumer credit agreement. Is it a debtor-creditor-supplier agreement? The answer is no, because of an amendment made to section 187(3) of the Consumer Credit Act by section 89 of the Banking Act 1987. Since the agreement is not a debtor-creditor-supplier agreement, the customer's bank will not be liable for misrepresentations and breaches of contract by the supplier.

21–24   One piece of plastic may serve several purposes. It may be a "debit" card, a cheque guarantee card, a cash withdrawal token and a credit card. In that case, how can the agreement be classified for the purposes of the Consumer Credit Act? The answer is to regard each aspect of the card as a separate agreement and to classify that. Thus when used as a debit card by a holder who has an agreed overdraft authority it is a debtor-creditor agreement. When used as a regulated credit card to purchase goods or services, it is a debtor-creditor-supplier agreement. When used as a regulated credit card to draw cash it is a debtor-creditor agreement. In short, the agreement is a multiple one and some aspects of it may be regulated and others not; some aspects of it may be within one category of regulated agreement and others within another. (On credit cards and multiple agreements, see paragraphs 21–19 and 21–21. On cash withdrawal tokens and cheque guarantee cards see paragraph 26–34.)

Exempt agreements

Subject to one important exception, exempt agreements are not regulated by the Act. The exception is that the court has power to reopen an exempt consumer credit agreement if it is an extortionate credit bargain. The principal exempt agreements are:

21–25

(i) Consumer credit agreements secured on land (*i.e.* a mortgage) and made by a local authority.

(ii) Certain land mortgage agreements granted by a building society, bank (or wholly-owned subsidiary of a bank) or (providing the body is specified for this purpose in an Order made by the Secretary of State) any of the following bodies—insurance company, friendly society, trade union, employers' association, charity, land improvement company or body corporate named in a public general Act of Parliament, or named in an Order under the Housing Act 1965 or the Home Purchase and Assistance and Housing Corporation Guarantee Act 1978. Not all land mortgage agreements are exempt when made by these bodies, only debtor-creditor agreements financing land purchases or the provision or alteration of dwellings or business premises. Thus, if a bank or building society grants a mortgage loan of £25,000 or less to an individual for some other purpose, *e.g.* to buy a car, the credit agreement will be regulated.

(iii) A "fixed-sum" "debtor-creditor-supplier" agreement under which the debtor is to repay the credit in no more than four instalments and within a period of 12 months. The following is an exempt agreement. Footsore buys a luxury armchair under a credit sale agreement, agreeing to pay 35 per cent immediately and the rest by four equal monthly instalments. The twelve month period begins with, and includes, the date the agreement is made. Thus an agreement requiring the repayments to be made within 12 months *after* the date of the agreement will not qualify for this exemption: *Zoan v. Rouamba* (2000 CA). Some credit-hire agreements stipulate that the hire charges must be paid before the first of the following events: (i) conclusion, settlement or abandonment of the hirer's claim against the other motorist; (ii) expiry of a period of 365 days *beginning* with the date the agreement is made. Such an agreement appears to satisfy the requirements for this exemption and the House of Lords, *obiter*, said as much in *Dimond v. Lovell* (2000). On credit-hire agreements generally, see paragraphs 20–26, 21–07 and 21–21 above. By way of exception, hire-purchase agreements, conditional sale agreements, agreements financing the purchase of land and agreements secured by pledge (*i.e.* pawn) cannot fall within this exemption.

(iv) A "debtor-creditor-supplier" agreement financing the purchase of land where the number of payments to be made by the debtor does not exceed four.

21–26

(v) A "running-account" "debtor-creditor-supplier" agreement where the debtor is required to pay the whole of each periodical account by a single payment. This exemption means that the milk, newspaper and grocery accounts of many households will be exempt. So also are those charge card agreements (*e.g.* Diners Club and American Express) which require the card holder to settle each account by a single repayment. If, however, such an agreement allowed the card holder to draw a cash loan (of £25,000 or less) to use as he wished then the exemption would be lost. The agreement would be a multiple one (see paragraph 21–19 above). In so far as it related to the cash loan it would be a debtor-creditor agreement and thus not exempt. In determining whether an agreement falls within this exemption, some caution is needed because some card issuers (*e.g.* American Express) operate two different kinds of agreement; one which allows extended credit and is a regulated agreement; and another which is exempt because it requires each periodical account to be settled with a single payment

(vi) A "debtor-creditor" agreement which is of a type offered only to a certain class or classes of individuals and not offered to the public generally, where there can be no increase in the charge for credit and where the cost of the credit is low, *i.e.* where the true annual rate of the total charge for credit does not exceed a rate 1 per cent higher than the highest of the base rates operated by the main English and Scottish banks at the close of business 28 days before the making of the credit agreement.

Few business will wish to grant loans at a rate low enough to gain this exemption, since the business would probably then become unprofitable. However, those companies which grant cheap loans to their employees as fringe benefits may well set their rates sufficiently low to gain exemption. A company loan agreement of this sort might well contain a clause providing that if the employee leaves that employment, the rate will rise (*i.e.* above the limits just mentioned). Such a clause will not cause the agreement to lose its exemption.

(vii) A "debtor-creditor" agreement which is of a type offered only to a certain class or classes of individuals and not offered to the public generally, where there is no charge for credit other than interest and where the rate of that interest, though possibly variable, is low, *i.e.* cannot at any time exceed a rate of 1 per cent higher than the highest of the base rates operated by the main English and Scottish banks 28 days earlier.

Loans made under the Student Loans scheme would appear to be exempt under this category. They are, however, subject to their own legislative framework comprising the Education (Student Loans) Act 1990 and the Education (Student Loans) Regulations 1998.

(viii) A consumer credit agreement providing credit to be used by the debtor in connection with overseas trade.

(ix) Consumer hire agreements for the hire of metering equipment (for metering gas, water or electricity) hired from a corporate body (*e.g.* British Gas plc) authorised to supply gas, water or electricity.

The above agreements are exempt by virtue of section 16 and the Consumer Credit (Exempt Agreements) Order 1989.

Small agreements

A regulated agreement which does not exceed a specified financial limit (£50) is a small agreement—section 17. A fixed-   **21–27** sum credit agreement is a small agreement provided the "credit" does not exceed £50 (the credit is the capital amount, *i.e.* excluding the total charge for credit). A running-account credit agreement is a small agreement if it has a credit limit of £50 or less.

There are exceptions to all of this. First, no hire-purchase or conditional sale agreement falls within the definition of a small agreement. Secondly, neither does any agreement which is secured by anything other than a guaranteee or indemnity. Thirdly, it is not possible artificially to contrive to make several small agreements in place of one larger one. If, where one agreement would exceed the £50 limit, two or more agreements are made so as to bring each agreement below the limit, the agreements will be regarded together as one agreement which exceeds the limit.

The object of defining small agreements is so that it is easy for later sections to exclude such agreements (*i.e.* where small sums are involved) from some of the technical requirements of the Act (*e.g.* from the formality and cancellation provisions).

Non-commercial agreements

21–28 Section 189(1) defines a non-commercial agreement as "a consumer credit agreement or a consumer hire agreement not made by the creditor or owner in the course of a business carried on by him". Thus an agreement for a loan between friends or from a father to his son would be a non-commercial agreement. It will be seen that non-commercial agreements are excluded from many provisions of the Act (*e.g.* the formality and cancellation provisions). For an explanation of "carrying on a business" see paragraph 22–05 below.

In *Hare v. Schurek* (1993) the claimant carried on business as a car dealer and did not normally extend credit to his customers. On one occasion, however, he agreed to supply a car to a friend of his on hire-purchase terms. The Court of Appeal held that the word "business" in the definition of non-commercial agreement meant a consumer credit or consumer hire business. It was held that, since the claimant did not carry on a consumer credit business or consumer hire business, this agreement was not made in the course of a business and was therefore a non-commercial agreement; thus the claimant did not need a consumer credit licence. This reasoning was probably wrong, since there is, in the definition of non-commercial agreement, no qualification to the word "business" and the claimant did not need a licence in any event (see paragraph 22–05 below).

Linked transactions

The object of the definition in section 19 is to enable later **21–29** sections to provide for what will be the effect on linked transactions in the event of the debtor or hirer withdrawing an offer to enter a regulated agreement or exercising his right of cancellation of a regulated agreement. The effect will be that any linked transaction is similarly (and automatically) withdrawn from or cancelled—sections 19(3) and 69. It is therefore not possible for a creditor or owner to get around the cancellation provisions of the Act by persuading the debtor or hirer to enter a linked transaction.

The following are linked transactions:

(a) A transaction which the debtor or hirer has to enter as a condition of the principal agreement, *e.g.* if his credit agreement requires him to take out an insurance policy to ensure that the debt will be repaid if he dies.

(b) A transaction financed or to be financed by the credit agreement where the credit agreement is a debtor-creditor-supplier agreement. Thus an agreement to buy goods by using one's credit card is a linked transaction in relation to the credit card agreement.

(c) A transaction which has all the three following characteristics:
  (i) It was suggested to the debtor by someone who knew that the principal agreement had been or might well be made, *e.g.* the creditor or owner himself, the credit broker, or, depending upon the circumstances, the dealer.
  (ii) It was a transaction between the debtor or hirer and a person who knew that the principal agreement had been (or might well be) made or for whom the dealer acted as credit broker in negotiating the transaction.
  (iii) The debtor entered the transaction to induce the creditor or owner to enter the principal agreement or for another purpose related to the principal agreement or for a purpose related to the transaction to be financed by the principal agreement (provided in the last case that the principal agreement was a restricted-use credit agreement).

21–30   There are three further points in the definition. First, no
agreement will be a linked one except in relation to a regulated
agreement. Secondly, no security agreement (*e.g.* one of guarantee
or indemnity) can be a linked agreement. Thirdly, a transaction
which would be a linked agreement if the debtor were a party to
it will still be a linked agreement even though it is a relative who
instead of the debtor or hirer is a party to it.

It will be appreciated that the definition is indeed a complex
one. It may become easier if it is remembered that the definition
is intended to embrace those transactions which, if the debtor or
hirer is allowed to cancel his regulated agreement, ought also to
be automatically cancelled. Assistance may also be gained from a
few examples:

  (i) X agrees to buy on credit sale terms a deep freezer
      from Y, a dealer. X also enters a separate agreement
      with Y whereby Y agrees to install the freezer. X enters
      a further agreement with Y that Y shall restock the
      freezer six months after delivery. The credit sale
      agreement is the principal agreement and the other two
      agreements are linked transactions.

 (ii) The situation is exactly the same as in (i) except that
      the principal agreement is made by X not with the
      dealer Y but with a finance company. The other two
      agreements with Y, the dealer, are still linked
      agreements.

(iii) The situation is the same as in (i) or (ii) except that X's
      wife is the person who makes the installation or
      stocking agreement with Y, the dealer. The installation
      and stocking agreements are still linked transactions.

 (iv) An agreement by a supplier, Z, to sell goods to X for
      which X pays by using a trading check is a linked
      transaction.

  (v) In the example at paragraph 21–22 (above) the
      agreement between Shiver and Warmitup Ltd is a linked
      transaction—the principal agreement being that between
      Shiver and Hotmoney Ltd.

21–31   There are three provisions of the Act which apply directly to
linked transactions. Their effect is as follows. First, a linked
transaction made before the regulated agreement is made is of no

effect unless and until the regulated agreement is made—section 19(3). Secondly, if the regulated agreement is withdrawn from or cancelled, then any linked transaction is similarly withdrawn from or cancelled—section 69(1). Thirdly, if for any reason the debtor's indebtedness is discharged early, the debtor is discharged from any further liability under any linked transaction—section 96(1). To see what all of this means, suppose that the credit sale agreement in example (i) above is one which X has the right to cancel (see paragraph 24–48 below). Then if X were to cancel the agreement before the freezer was installed, he would not be obliged to have it installed and thus would not be obliged to pay for the installation. That is all very sensible since if X has cancelled the credit sale agreement then he is not going to have the freezer. If X did not cancel the credit sale agreement but paid off the whole of his credit within six months of delivery he would not be obliged to have Y restock the freezer. As we shall see later, a debtor has a right to pay off the credit early at any time he wishes (paragraph 26–04).

Three types of linked transaction are exempted from the three provisions (mentioned above) which would otherwise have applied to them—Consumer Credit (Linked Transactions) (Exemptions) Regulations 1983. These three types of transaction will therefore be unaffected by the debtor withdrawing from or cancelling his regulated agreement or discharging his debt under that agreement ahead of time. These three exempted transactions are: **21–32**

   (i) contracts of insurance;

  (ii) written guarantees of goods;

 (iii) any transaction which is (or is made under) an agreement for the operation of a savings, deposit or current account.

The first of these exemptions means that if the debtor cancels the regulated agreement (*i.e.* assuming that it is cancellable), any connected insurance contract will not also automatically be cancelled. There is nevertheless a possibility that the insurance contract, *e.g.* of life insurance, may be cancellable under the cooling off provisions of other legislation, *e.g.* sections 75–77 of the Insurance Companies Act 1982. The second and third of the exemptions require an explanation. The second deals with written guarantees of goods. It seems peculiar and can lead to absurdity. To show this, let us return to the example, given earlier, of X   **21–33** making a credit sale agreement to buy a freezer. Suppose that at the time of the making of the agreement, X makes a written contract with the dealer whereby X undertakes to pay £25 and in return the dealer guarantees to rectify any defects or breakdowns occurring within five years of delivery of the freezer. Now suppose also that the credit sale agreement is one which X has the right to cancel within a few days of making it. If he exercises that right of cancellation he would of course not have the freezer (or, if it had already been delivered to him, he would have to let the dealer recover it from him). Nevertheless, he would still have the guarantee and would still have to pay for it—a guarantee for a freezer he has not got! That is the absurd result of exempting the written guarantee from the rule which would otherwise have meant that the guarantee was cancelled when the regulated agreement was cancelled. The Regulations clearly need to be amended.

21–34 The third exemption is more sensible. It would not be unusual for a bank manager, before agreeing to grant a bank loan to a new customer, to get that customer first to open a current account at the bank. If the customer did so, then that current account would then become effective immediately and would remain so even if the customer then withdrew from the prospective bank loan agreement or if he took the bank loan and then paid it off earlier than the loan agreement required. That is the sensible result of the third exemption.

The total charge for credit

21–35 The Act makes a basic distinction between the credit and the cost to the debtor of having it. The idea behind having a definition of the "total charge for credit" is that the definition should produce a figure which, if stated to the debtor, will accurately tell him the cost of having the credit. The "credit" and the "total charge for credit" are mutually exclusive. Any sum which is part of the total charge for credit cannot be part of the credit. A simple agreement to borrow £25,000 and to repay it at the end of a year with £25,000 + £3,000 interest involves credit of £25,000 and a total charge for credit of £3,000. A creditor may, however, try to conceal his charges. He may require a repayment of only £25,000 whilst at the same time requiring the debtor, as a precondition to getting the loan, to buy a peanut for £3,000. More subtly, he may, as condition of the loan, require the debtor to take out an insurance policy with a particular insurance company—a company which, perhaps, has agreed to pay the creditor a handsome commission on such new business. There are numerous ways in which a debtor may find that he has to pay for having credit. The definition of the total charge for credit is designed to include such costs so that when the total charge for credit is stated, it represents the true cost of the credit.

The amount of the total charge for credit may have to be **21–36** calculated for any one of a number of reasons, including the following:

(i) It is a necessary first step towards the calculation of the annual percentage rate of charge (paragraph 21–39 below).

(ii) It may in some cases have to be included in the agreement in accordance with the formality requirements (paragraph 24–34 below).

(iii) It will be relevant in determining the debtor's liability under a debtor-creditor agreement after cancellation (paragraph 24–58 below).

(iv) In conjunction with the annual percentage rate of charge, it will be relevant in determining whether an agreement is an extortionate credit bargain (paragraph 26–06 below).

The calculation of the total charge for credit is to be made as at the time the credit agreement is made. It is done simply by adding up all the items which fall within the definition. The definition is a two-stage one. First, there is a general rule. Secondly, there are exceptions. An item is within the definition if it is within the general rule and is not excluded by the exceptions. This is all set out in the Consumer Credit (Total Charge for Credit) Regulations 1980, made under section 20 of the Act.

The general rule

By this rule, the total charge for credit includes any interest **21–37** which is payable under the credit agreement and also any charges payable under the five following kinds of transactions:

(i) the credit agreement itself;

(ii) transactions entered into in compliance with the credit agreement;

(iii) transactions required to be made or maintained as a condition of the making of the credit agreement;

(iv) transactions for the provision of security;

(v) any credit brokerage contract relating to the credit agreement.

Charges under these five different types of transaction are within the general rule even if some other benefit is derived from them (*e.g.* the peanut or the benefit of the insurance policy referred to earlier). The charges are still included even though they are payable, not by the debtor, but by a relative of his (*e.g.* if his wife had agreed to buy the peanut as a precondition of the debtor being granted a loan). Furthermore the whole of the charge is included, *e.g.* in the case of the insurance policy, the whole of the premiums. Until the Regulations were amended in 1989, credit brokerage fees were not included in the definition. It is sensible that they are now included (see item (v) above), since a fee that the customer has to pay in order to be introduced to the source of finance is truly part of the cost of getting the credit.

It may occur that an item within the general rule is something upon which the debtor will be entitled to income tax relief, *e.g.* the interest payable on a house-purchase mortgage. Nevertheless the whole of that item must be included within the total charge for credit. To put it another way, the calculation must be made on the assumption that the debtor will obtain no tax relief; the fact that he will obtain tax relief is to be ignored.

The exceptions

21–38 Certain charges are excluded by these exceptions from the total charge for credit. They are:

(a) default charges;

(b) charges that would also be payable by a customer buying the same goods or services for cash instead of on credit terms;

(c) certain charges for the care, maintenance or protection of goods or land;

(d) variable bank charges on current accounts;

(e) certain other charges for transfer of funds and for keeping an account open;

(f) certain club membership and similar charges;

(g) most charges for guarantees;

(h) most insurance premiums.

Default charges are excluded because they are not payable if the debtor honours his agreement. Charges which would be payable by a cash customer (*e.g.* delivery charges payable on a new car) are excluded because, as a matter of common sense, they are not part of the cost of the credit. This rule also means that if a discount is given to cash customers, and not to credit customers, then the discount is part of the total charge for credit: *R. v. Baldwin's Garage* (1988). As to care or maintenance charges, it may be (*e.g.* in a hire-purchase agreement relating to a colour television) that the credit agreement requires the debtor to enter a maintenance contract covering the goods. In that case, the charges payable under this maintenance agreement are excluded from the total charge for credit, provided the debtor is allowed by the terms of his credit agreement (and in practice has) a free choice as to with whom he makes the maintenance agreement. Also excluded are any maintenance charges which are payable only if something goes wrong; these are excluded even if the debtor is not allowed a free choice as to who is to do the maintaining. The exclusion of variable bank charges (other than interest) on current accounts covers the case where a bank manager agrees to grant a bank loan requiring as a condition that the debtor maintains a current account at his branch. Bank charges on the current account which vary according to the use made of the current account are not part of the total charge for credit under the loan agreement. Also excluded are other charges for the transfer of funds and charges for keeping open an account intended to receive payments towards the repayment of the credit (and payment of charges). This exclusion does not apply, however, if the charges are abnormally high and the debtor does not have reasonable freedom of choice in the matter. The exclusion of club membership fees deals with the situation where, for example, a motoring organisation or a trade union has arrangements whereby a member can obtain credit (perhaps on preferential terms) from a particular finance company. It may well be a term of any resulting credit agreement that the debtor remains a member of the club or trade union. However, his membership fee will still not be part of the total charge for credit provided it entitles the debtor to other benefits besides the credit facilities and provided he was a member before applying for the credit.

With one exception, all charges for guarantees and all insurance premiums are excluded. The exception relates to any guarantee or policy which the creditor requires to be made (or maintained) in order to ensure that the creditor is repaid (fully or partially) in the event of the death, invalidity, illness or unemployment of the debtor.

The annual percentage rate (APR)

21–39   Once the total charge for credit has been ascertained, it is then possible to calculate the annual percentage rate. This can be difficult, depending upon the particular type of agreement, because it has to be done according to some rather complex Regulations—the Consumer Credit (Total Charge for Credit) Regulations 1980 made under section 20 of the Act. Nevertheless, the calculation must be made because the APR will often have to be stated in advertisements and in the agreement itself. This is crucial to the achievement of truth in lending, a prime objective of the Consumer Credit Act. Since all traders have to calculate the APR according to these Regulations, a consumer first gets an accurate idea of the cost of having the credit and secondly is able to make a fair comparison between different sources of credit.

The APR is particularly relevant for two further purposes. First, it determines whether a debtor-creditor agreement secures low-rate exemption (see paragraph 21–26 above). Secondly, it is relevant in determining whether a credit bargain is extortionate (see paragraph 26–06 below).

CHAPTER 22

LICENSING

THE licensing system created by the Consumer Credit Act is **22–01** intended to secure consumer protection. The consequences of unlicensed trading are severe for the trader and in the case of malpractices the Director-General has wide powers, including that of taking away the trader's licence. The licensing system is not a means of restricting competition and the Director-General cannot, for example, refuse a licence or withdraw one on the ground that there are already enough credit traders. The Director-General, whose duty it is to administer the licensing system, has the duty of maintaining a public register of licences. Any member of the public can on payment of a fee inspect the register.

There are two kinds of licence, a group licence and a standard **22–02** licence. The vast majority of traders will have to obtain a standard licence. Group licences are not intended for groups of companies. Rather, a group licence is likely to be granted to cover a group of people when it seems unnecessary to ask each of them to apply for a standard licence. This can occur where there is some other means of control over the business practices of members of the group. Thus, for example, the Law Society has obtained a group licence covering all solicitors who hold a practising certificate. The licence is limited to activities arising in the course of the solicitor's practice and does not cover a solicitor carrying on a consumer hire business or operating as a credit reference agency. A solicitor wishing to carry on one of these latter businesses should apply for a standard licence covering those categories (B and F, see below). The rest of this chapter will be concerned with standard licences, which have a duration of 5 years but can be renewed.

The licensing system is intended to be particularly instrumental in **22–03** controlling malpractices in the door-to-door peddling of credit, described in the Act as "canvassing off trade premises". An attempt orally to induce a consumer to enter into a regulated agreement amounts to canvassing off trade premises if (section 48),

(a) it is made during a visit by the canvasser carried out for the purpose of making those oral representations, and

(b) the visit is to somewhere other than where a business is carried on by the canvasser, the creditor or owner, the supplier or the consumer, and

(c) the the visit is not made in response to an earlier request.

The canvassing off trade premises of debtor-creditor agreements (*e.g.* ordinary cash loans) is a criminal offence (see Chapter 23). There is no such absolute prohibition of the canvassing off trade premises of other regulated agreements. Thus the doorstep promotion of the sale of goods or services (*e.g.* the installation of double glazing) on credit terms is permitted. However, for it to be lawful to canvass off trade premises these other regulated agreements (*i.e.* debtor-creditor-supplier agreements and consumer hire agreements), the canvasser must be operating under a licence which specifically and expressly covers such activity. If the Director-General finds that a trader is using unfair doorstep methods he may well either withdraw the licence or else vary it so as to remove the authority to canvass off trade premises.

Shortcomings of the system.

22–04   In a review of the consumer credit licensing system begun in 1999 the government acknowledged criticisms of it, including claims that: (i) checks on the fitness of applicants are insufficiently comprehensive; (ii) there is little compliance monitoring after a licence has been issued; (iii) enforcement action, when taken, is too slow to safeguard consumers. In a consultation exercise in 2000 the DTI floated a number of options for change, including the possibility of scrapping the renewals system, reducing the number of people falling within the licensing system, or scrapping the licensing system altogether. Given that the licensing and enforcement system is wholly funded by the income generated from licence application fees, it is difficult to see how any of these options would address the criticisms!

BUSINESS NEEDING A LICENCE

22–05   Broadly, someone needs a licence if he carries on a business in the course of which regulated agreements are made with customers (debtors and hirers) or if he carries on an ancillary credit business. There are six categories of standard licence:

Category	Business
A	Consumer credit
B	Consumer hire
C	Credit brokerage
D	Debt-adjusting and debt-counselling
E	Debt-collecting
F	Credit reference agency

In each category it is only if a business (which includes profession or trade) is carried on that a licence is required. Thus if someone on one occasion lends money to a friend—even if the friend is to pay interest—the lender would not be regarded as thereby carrying on a business. "A person is not to be treated as carrying on a particular type of business merely because occasionally he enters into transactions belonging to a business of that type" (section 189(2)). A garage proprietor who (more than occasionally) hired out cars under consumer hire agreements would be carrying on a consumer hire business even if the main part of his business consisted of selling cars and petrol for cash. Though a trader's business may fall predominantly outside the six categories, he still needs a licence if a part of it falls within any of the six categories—unless that part amounts to only "occasional" transactions. In *R. v. Marshall* (1989 CA) a double glazing firm had, over a period of 16 months, introduced six customers (or told them that they could be introduced) to a source of credit finance. In determining whether the proprietor was carrying on a business of credit brokerage (*i.e.* whether these six transactions were more than "occasional"), it was immaterial whether the introductions were initiated by the firm (in order to induce customers to buy the firm's products) or by customers simply wanting help. The Court declined to say that the transactions were definitely more than occasional. Similarly, a car dealer who never normally provides credit but who on one occasion agrees to supply a car to a friend on hire-purchase terms will not be carrying on a consumer credit business: *Hare v. Schurek* (paragraph 21–28 above).

If a creditor lends money in order to make a profit, it does not **22–06** necessarily follow that he is carrying on a business. This is because there is a distinction between carrying on a business and being an investor: *Wills v. Wood* (1984 CA). In that case a hotelier had retired, sold his hotel for £26,000 and been advised by his solicitors to invest part of it in buying shares and the remainder in loans secured by mortgage. Thus he gave £11,000 to his solicitors to lend to clients of theirs at about 12 per cent interest. As one loan was paid off it was replaced by another or the money was retained by the solicitors as cash, presumably on deposit with a bank. Taking into account the very small number of loans involved, the lack of advertisement, the restriction of potential borrowers to the clients of one solicitor, the restriction to loans secured on real property and the fact that the interest rate was more comparable to a building society rate than to a money lender's rate, it was held that the retired hotelier was not carrying on a business of money lending but was merely an investor. Although this case was decided under the Moneylenders Acts, the finding that he was not carrying on a business would presumably be the same under the Consumer Credit Act and could mean not only that the creditor need not be licensed, but also that the mortgage loan agreement in question (a £2,000 loan to an individual) would be a "non-commercial agreement" (see paragraph 21–28 above).

Someone carrying on a business in more than one category needs a licence covering all the categories of his business. A separate licence is not required for each address at which a business is carried on. A bank which has many branches need have only one licence. Where a business is carried on under more than one name, all the names used must be specified on the application and also on the licence. Trading under a name not specified on the licence is unlicensed trading and is a criminal offence.

22–07   There are two specific exclusions from the whole of the licensing requirements (section 21). Thus a local authority does not need a licence and neither does a corporate body named in a public general Act of Parliament empowering the body to carry on a business. The latter exception does not excuse companies incorporated under the Companies Act, since that Act does not name companies incorporated under it. The exception does excuse, for example, the Post Office. The fact that these bodies are excused from having to be licensed does not mean that their agreements (*i.e.* which they make with their customers) are thereby rendered exempt from regulation by the Act. Thus a regulated agreement made by a local authority would have to comply with the documentation requirements of the Act. It is only if a consumer credit or consumer hire agreement falls within the definition of exempt agreement that the agreement itself is not regulated (see paragraph 21–18). Subject to the two exceptions just mentioned, someone carrying on a business in one of the six categories needs to be licensed. Because of the overlap between the six categories the OFT encourages applicants to apply for all six categories—the application fee is the same in any event.

Category A—Consumer credit business

This is "any business so far as it comprises or relates to the provision of credit under regulated consumer credit agreements" (section 189(1)). A business which grants credit only to companies or grants credit only in excess of £25,000 is not a consumer credit business, since its agreements are not consumer credit agreements. Similarly a business will not need to be licensed if it grants credit only under consumer credit agreements which are exempt agreements, since these are not regulated agreements. In the definition the words "so far as" make it clear that even if only a small part of the business involves the granting of credit under regulated agreements, still a licence is required. For example a manufacturing company may have nothing at all to do with granting credit except that it operates a staff loan scheme. Nevertheless, unless the loans made to the staff are all either in excess of £25,000 or else made under exempt agreements (*e.g.* because made at a low rate of interest), the company needs a category A licence.

22–08

Category B—Consumer hire business

This is "any business so far as it comprises or relates to the bailment or (in Scotland) the hiring of goods under regulated consumer hire agreements" (section 189(1)). Little explanation is needed here in the light of the points made about category A business. Television rental companies are clear examples of category B businesses. If a given business falls within both categories, the proprietor will need a licence covering both. An example is that of a garage which supplies cars on hire-purchase terms (*i.e.* without involving a finance company) and which also hires cars out under regulated consumer hire agreements. Where a finance company is involved and it is the finance company which

22–09

makes the credit or hire agreement with the customer, then it is the finance company which needs to have a licence covering the relevant category (A or B). However, in that case the dealer, if it was he who put the customer in touch with the finance company, will need a category C licence.

Category C—Credit brokerage business

22–10   This is "any business so far as it comprises or relates to credit brokerage" (section 145(1)). Credit brokerage is "the effecting of introductions" of prospective customers to credit or hire businesses. It is not restricted, however, to the introducing of customers wanting to make regulated agreements. The definition of credit brokerage is wider than that. It also includes the introduction of people wanting house-purchase loans to a building society or to any other business which provides credit secured on land. It also includes the introduction of people wanting credit to a business which makes exempt agreements (unless all the business's agreements are exempt because of the small number of payments to be made by the debtor). Thus it would be credit brokerage to introduce prospective borrowers to a business which grants loans at rates of interest low enough to make the agreements exempt, but it would not be credit brokerage to introduce new customers to the milkman. His agreements are exempt because he requires each customer to pay off each account in single lump sum.

22–11   One tends to think of a broker as offering the customer a choice of possible sources of finance or of goods on hire. However, a broker who only ever effects introductions to the same source of finance is still within the definition. Furthermore, the requirement to be licensed can not be avoided by always introducing customers to another credit broker so that he in turn can make the final introduction to a credit grantor. It is credit brokerage to effect introductions to another credit broker. It is clear then that the definition of credit broker covers all those that one would expect, such as those who describe themselves as finance brokers or mortgage brokers. Also within the definition is the dealer in the hire-purchase transaction where a finance company is the creditor. The dealer will have proposal forms supplied by the finance company. A customer wanting to acquire his goods on credit will be asked to fill in one of these and the dealer will then send the completed form off to the finance company. That constitutes "effecting an introduction". On the other hand, a retailer who is willing to accept payment by means of a credit card is not thereby a credit broker, since he does not introduce the customer to the credit card company. For the same reason a retailer who displays application forms for a credit company's credit cards is similarly not a credit broker: *Brookes v. Retail Credit Cards Ltd* (1985 DC).

Category D—Debt adjusting and debt counselling

The principal businesses falling into this category are those **22–12** which give assistance to debtors (or hirers) who have got into financial straits and are having difficulty maintaining their payments. Debt counselling is the "giving of advice to debtors or hirers about the liquidation of debts due under consumer credit agreements or consumer hire agreements". If it is done by way of business, for example by an accountant, then a licence is required.

Some businesses do more than give advice (see paragraph 20–32). Hence debt adjusting covers certain other activities concerned with the liquidation of debts due under consumer credit or consumer hire agreements. In particular there are two such activities. First, it is debt adjusting to negotiate with the creditor or owner on behalf of the debtor or hirer the terms for the discharge of the latter's debt. Secondly, it is debt adjusting to take over from the debtor or hirer in return for payments by him the obligation of paying off his debt. It is also debt adjusting to engage in any activity which is similar to the two activities just mentioned. It is quite common for a car dealer to seek on behalf of one of his customers a quotation of a "settlement" figure. This often happens when the customer, who has not completed his hire-purchase payments on his car, nevertheless wishes to trade in that car in part-exchange for a newer one. It is arguable that the dealer in obtaining a settlement figure from the customer's finance company is either "negotiating" the terms for the discharge of his debt or else indulging in a "similar activity".

The definitions of both debt counselling and debt adjusting are concerned with help given in relation to debts due under consumer credit or consumer hire agreements, *i.e.* even if they are exempt agreements. On the other hand help given in relation to a debt due under an agreement providing credit in excess of £25,000 will not fall within the definition of debt counselling or debt adjusting because the agreement would not be a consumer credit agreement. Any business "so far as it comprises or relates to" debt adjusting or debt counselling should be covered by a category D licence.

Category E—Debt collecting

22–13   This is "any business so far as it comprises or relates to" the "taking of steps to procure payment of debts due under consumer credit agreements or consumer hire agreements". As with the last category, the business is still within the definition even if the debts it collects are due under exempt agreements. The definition is wide also in that it includes both those who act as agents (usually on high commission) to collect debts on behalf of creditors and also those who first buy up (*i.e.* by assignment) debts from creditors and then collect the debts for themselves.

Category F—Credit reference agency

22–14   This is "any business so far as it comprises or relates to" the "furnishing of persons with information relevant to the financial standing of individuals, being information collected by the agency for that purpose". It is quite common for all sorts of people to be asked about the financial standing of someone they know. Thus a building society may, before agreeing to grant a loan, take references from the customer's bank and his employer. This does not make the bank and employer credit reference agencies, because the information passed on to the building society was not collected by them for the purpose of passing on.

Partial exclusions

22–15   The definitions of the various types of ancillary credit business (categories C, D, E and F above) are given in section 145. Section 146 has the effect of excluding from some or all of those definitions certain people who might otherwise have fallen within them. It follows that if someone is excluded from any given definition, he need not be licensed under that category. None of these exclusions applies to categories A and B (consumer credit and consumer hire businesses).

Barristers acting as such and solicitors engaged in contentious business are excluded from all categories of ancillary credit business. Although a solicitor not engaged in contentious business is not excluded, he will be covered (except as regards categories B and F) by the group licence in respect of any activity arising in the course of his practice (see paragraph 22–02). The creditor or owner is excluded from the definitions of debt counselling, debt adjusting and debt collecting. If this were not so, every time he collected a payment or gave advice to his debtor or hirer, he would need to be licensed in category D or E in addition to his category A or B licence. Also excluded from the same definitions is someone who on purchasing the creditor's or owner's business takes over (*i.e.* by assignment) the debts owed to the business. Of course, in order to carry on the business he has bought, he does need himself to have a category A or B licence. Furthermore, the creditor selling the business can not transfer his licence. The purchaser must apply for his own. He would be wise not to complete the purchase before obtaining it.

Finally there is an exclusion designed to cover a particular type **22–16** of person. This is the person (typically a housewife) who has what is sometimes called a "home catalogue" belonging to a mail order company and who acts as the company's agent in selling goods from the catalogue to her friends and acquaintances. The goods are usually sold on credit sale terms and the housewife is not an employee of the company but receives a commission on each sale. She *should* be effectively excluded from the definitions of credit broker (category C), debt adjuster and debt counsellor (category D) and debt collector (category E). This exclusion (section 146(5)) applies to anyone who is not acting in the capacity of an employee and who

(a) asks someone to enter either a regulated consumer hire agreement or a debtor-creditor-supplier agreement where the creditor is to be the supplier, and

(b) effects the introduction after canvassing off trade premises.

The difficulty arises when the home catalogue housewife concludes the bargain not during a visit by her to a friend's house but during a visit by a friend (the debtor) to her's. This is because an activity is not within the definition of canvassing off trade premises unless the *canvasser* is making a visit when he or she orally asks the customer to enter the regulated agreement (see paragraph 22–03). The housewife could hardly be said to be "visiting" her own house. Thus in this case she is not excluded and falls within the definition of credit broker (and, if she collects payments under the agreements, of debt collector as well). It seems she ought to be licensed if she proposes to conclude bargains when her friends visit her. (For a fuller explanation, see an article at [1980] New L.J. 528.)

UNLICENSED TRADING

22–17   Subject to two qualifications a licence covers all lawful activities done in the course of the business whether by the licensee or by other persons on his behalf (section 23(1)). The first qualification is that the Director-General has power in granting the licence expressly to limit the activities it covers. The second is that the licence does not cover canvassing off trade premises unless it expressly says so. In any case it is the canvassing off trade premises only of debtor-creditor-supplier agreements and regulated consumer hire agreements that can be licensed, it being an offence to canvass off trade premises debtor-creditor agreements. It is unlicensed trading and a criminal offence for anyone to indulge in an activity for which a licence is required, if he is not licensed for that activity (section 39(1)). Thus someone who indulges in canvassing off trade premises when that is not expressly covered by his licence will be guilty of unlicensed trading. It is an offence, and it is also unlicensed trading, to trade under a name not specified in the licence (section 39(2)). Unlicensed trading, besides being a criminal offence, can also result in agreements being unenforceable.

AGREEMENTS RENDERED UNENFORCEABLE

22–18   There are three ways in which unlicensed trading can render agreements unenforceable.

Regulated agreements made by unlicensed creditor or owner

22–19   Section 40 creates a general rule that a regulated agreement made when the creditor or owner was unlicensed is not enforceable against the debtor or hirer. It is the time at which the agreement is made that is the relevant time. If at that time the creditor or owner is not licensed to make that particular agreement, then he can not enforce it. If for example the agreement was made by the creditor canvassing off trade premises and the creditor's licence did not expressly authorise that activity, the agreement will not be enforceable. Section 40 applies only to regulated agreements. Thus other agreements (*e.g.* exempt agreements) made by an unlicensed trader are fully enforceable. Also the section affects enforcement only by the creditor or owner. It does not prevent the debtor or hirer enforcing the agreement.

There are two exceptions to the general rule in section 40:

(i) It does not apply to non-commercial agreements.

(ii) It does not apply where the Director-General makes a validating order, *i.e.* an order that regulated agreements made by a particular trader during a period when he was unlicensed are to be treated as if he had been licensed.

The second exception enables the Director-General in effect to excuse the trader (except for any criminal charge) for not having obtained a licence, if he thinks no harm has been done. In considering any application for a validating order, the Director will take into account:

(a) how far customers were prejudiced by the trader's conduct;

(b) whether the trader would have been likely to be granted a licence if he had applied for one;

(c) the degree of culpability on the trader's part for being unlicensed.

Agreements for the services of unlicensed ancillary credit trader

Any agreement for the services of any unlicensed person **22–20** carrying on an ancillary business is generally unenforceable by the party who should have been licensed (section 148). The relevant time is when the agreement is made. Thus an unlicensed credit broker who makes an agreement to effect an introduction in return for the promise of a fee or commission will be unable to sue for that fee or commission. It may well be the customer looking for credit who agreed to pay the fee and who will therefore benefit. Sometimes, however, the credit grantor has agreed to pay a commission to a broker introducing customers. If the broker was unlicensed when making the agreement with the credit grantor, the latter will benefit from the agreement being unenforceable. The rule applies in the same way to all ancillary credit traders (credit brokers, debt counsellors, debt adjusters, debt collectors and credit reference agencies). The trader must have a licence covering the relevant category. If someone licensed only as a credit broker makes an agreement to act as debt adjuster, he will be unable to enforce that agreement. As under section 40, the trader can apply for an order validating his agreements and the same factors will be taken into account by the Director-General in considering the application.

Regulated agreements made after introduction by unlicensed credit broker

22–21
Section 149, in effect, makes the creditor or owner bear the consequences of his credit broker being unlicensed. A regulated agreement made by a debtor or hirer who was introduced for the purpose of making that agreement by an unlicensed credit broker is unenforceable against the debtor or hirer. There are three differences between the position here and that under section 40 (*i.e.* where the creditor or owner was unlicensed). First, it is the time of the introduction by the credit broker that is relevant and not the time when the regulated agreement is made. Secondly, non-commercial regulated agreements are affected. Thirdly, there are two people entitled to apply for a validating order. Thus the Director-General can grant to the credit broker an order (under section 148, paragraph 22–20 above) validating agreements for the services of the credit broker, in which case that validating order, unless the Director-General states otherwise, will automatically also validate regulated agreements made after introductions by the credit broker. Alternatively the Director-General can grant to the creditor or owner an order validating regulated agreements made by that particular creditor or owner after introductions by the unlicensed credit broker.

The moral of section 149 for creditors and owners is to take all reasonable precautions to see that the credit brokers who introduce customers to them are licensed and are licensed to conduct business in the way that they do (*e.g.* by canvassing off trade premises). If no such steps have been taken, the Director-General may well refuse a validating order. Thus, for example, the finance company which is creditor in the typical hire-purchase transaction (see paragraph 19–08) may find that all its agreements made through a particular unlicensed dealer are unenforceable.Director-General's Licensing Powers

DIRECTOR-GENERAL'S LICENSING POWERS

Besides the power to grant or refuse validating orders, the **22–22** Director-General has powers to refuse, to refuse to renew, to vary, to suspend and to withdraw licences. He does not have a free hand in the exercise of these powers. Thus on receipt of a valid application, he *must* grant a standard licence if two criteria are both satisfied:

(i) The applicant is a fit person to engage in the activities to be covered by the licence.

(ii) The name or names under which he applies to be licensed are not misleading or undesirable.

The sorts of thing likely to make an applicant not a fit person are if he or any of his employees, associates, agents or directors has been guilty of violence, fraud or dishonesty, or otherwise persistently broken the law, practised racial or sexual discrimination or indulged in unfair or improper practices. Exactly the same criteria apply in relation to renewals, variations, suspensions, and withdrawals as they do on an initial application. Before exercising any of these powers against a trader, the Director-General must allow the trader a chance to make representations to him and there is further machinery allowing a trader against whom one of these powers has been exercised to appeal to the Secretary of State and, if that is unsuccessful, to appeal on a point of law to the High Court. There are also similar rights of appeal if the Director-General refuses to grant a validating order.

ADVERTISING AND SEEKING BUSINESS

THE Consumer Credit Act places controls and restrictions upon   **23–01**
canvassing off trade premises, it totally prohibits certain kinds of
promotion of credit facilities and it regulates the content of
advertisements and quotations.

CANVASSING OFF TRADE PREMISES

The Act has a two-pronged method of protecting the consumer   **23–02**
from what can loosely be termed "doorstep selling" of credit. By
one prong, it makes certain agreements cancellable, *i.e.* it gives
the consumer a short "cooling off period" in which he can cancel
the agreement after he has made it. This prong does not, however,
place any restriction or control upon the way in which a customer
may be persuaded to make an agreement. The second prong
places restrictions and controls upon canvassing off trade
premises. The two prongs are entirely independent of each other
and it by no means follows that because an agreement is made as
a result of canvassing off trade premises, it is cancellable.
Similarly, an agreement could be cancellable even though no
canvassing off trade premises was involved. The first prong,
which deals with cancellation, will be considered in Chapter 24
and will not figure any more in the present chapter.

There are two different kinds of canvassing off trade premises.
One is concerned with persuading a member of the public (a
consumer) to make a regulated agreement and the other with
persuading someone to agree to engage the services of an
ancillary credit trader. We shall consider them separately.

Canvassing a consumer to make a regulated agreement

The definition in section 48 of "canvassing off trade premises"   **23–03**
is technical. It deals with oral persuasion aimed at getting a
customer to make a regulated agreement. Making oral

representations in an attempt to induce a consumer to enter into a regulated agreement amounts to canvassing off trade premises if:

(a) the oral representations are made during a visit by the canvasser carried out for the purpose of making them, and

(b) the visit is to somewhere other than where a business is carried on by any of the following—namely the canvasser, the creditor or owner, the supplier or the consumer, and

(c) the visit is not made in response to a request made on a previous occasion.

It is only if the canvassing falls within this definition that it is controlled in the ways shortly to be explained. Thus, there is no control upon visits made to the consumer at the consumer's business premises. A visit made, for example, to a shop in order to persuade the shopkeeper to take a loan is not canvassing off trade premises. Nor would it be canvassing off trade premises if the canvasser, having visited some premises (*e.g.* his golf club) for just one purpose (*e.g.* to play golf), fell, whilst there, into conversation (*e.g.* with another member) during which he found himself suggesting that the other should consider taking credit (perhaps to buy a new set of golf clubs). It is only if the canvasser made the visit for the purpose of making such a suggestion that he will be canvassing off trade premises.

23–04 There are two controls upon activity which does fall within the definition. First, there is a total ban on the canvassing off trade premises of debtor-creditor agreements (*e.g.* ordinary cash loans). It is a criminal offence—section 49. Even if the visit is made in response to an earlier request, it will still be an offence unless that request was in writing and signed. The second control relates to other regulated agreements. These are not totally prohibited. However, for it to be lawful to canvass off trade premises these other regulated agreements, the canvasser must be operating under a licence which specifically authorises canvassing off trade premises—section 23(3). Thus, whilst doorstep attempts to persuade the consumer to take an ordinary loan are totally banned, the doorstep sale of trading checks and the doorstep promotion of goods or services (*e.g.* double glazing) on credit terms is allowed, provided the canvasser has a licence specifically authorising it.

There is one very limited exception to what has been said so far. It arises from a determination by the Director-General under section 49(3). It applies only in the case of an ordinary current account (a cheque book account), only where the canvasser is trying to persuade an account holder to take an overdraft on a current account, and only where the canvasser is the creditor or an employee of the creditor. In this case, there is no ban on canvassing off trade premises and no need for specific authorisation in the licence. Thus, a bank manager can visit an existing customer in the customer's home to try to persuade that customer to take an overdraft on a current account.

Canvassing the services of an ancillary credit trader

An ancillary credit trader is anyone who carries on a business **23-05** as a credit broker, debt collector, debt counsellor, debt adjuster or credit reference agency. The definition here (in section 153) is the same as the definition of the first kind of canvassing off trade premises, except that here the object of the canvassing is to persuade the person who is the target of it to enter into an agreement to engage the services of an ancillary credit trader.

Thus, making oral representations for that purpose amounts to canvassing off trade premises if:

(a) the oral representations are made during a visit by the canvasser carried out for the purpose of making them, and

(b) the visit is to somewhere other than where a business is carried on by any of the following—namely, the canvasser, the canvasser's employer or principal or the person to whom the representations are made, and

(c) the visit is not made in response to a request made on an earlier occasion.

There is just one very strict control upon this second kind of canvassing off trade premises. It is a criminal offence to canvass off trade premises the services of a credit broker, debt adjuster or debt counsellor—section 154. This is a total ban, but there is no ban whatsoever upon the canvassing off trade premises of the services of a debt collector or credit reference agency.

CRIMINAL OFFENCES

Circulars to minors

23–06   It is an offence, with a view to financial gain, to send to a minor (someone under 18) a circular inviting him to obtain credit (or goods on hire) or to seek further information about it—section 50. If, however, a circular is sent to a minor which includes a statement that loans are not available to anyone under 18, then the offence is not committed because the circular does not amount to an invitation to the minor to obtain credit: *Alliance & Leicester Building Society v. Babbs* (1993 DC). The same case decided that if the advertiser had a policy and system to ensure that applications from minors were refused, then also the offence would not be committed, since the advertiser would then clearly not have sent the circular to the minor "with a view to financial gain". In any case information sent to a minor about the Student Loan scheme is not provided "with a view to financial gain"— the Education (Student Loans) Act 1990 (schedule 2).

Unsolicited credit tokens

23–07   It is an offence to issue a credit token to someone who has not asked for it in writing signed by himself—section 51. This is intended to prevent the unsolicited sending out of credit cards (as occurred when, before the Consumer Credit Act was passed, the Access credit card scheme was launched). There is an exception where the credit token is issued as a renewal or replacement for a previous one. For an example of a conviction under this section, see *Elliott v. Director-General of Fair Trading*, paragraph 26–39 below.

ADVERTISING

Advertisements controlled by the Act

23–08   There are three sorts of advertisements controlled by the Act (sections 43 and 151):

> (i) Advertisements issued by anyone carrying on a consumer credit or consumer hire business or by anyone carrying on a business providing credit on the security of land. The advertisements which are controlled are those which indicate that the advertiser is willing to

provide credit or goods on hire. *Jenkins v. Lombard North Central* (1983 DC) concerned an advertisement for a car which bore not only the price of the car but also the words "Lombard North Central Limited" together with that company's logo. This was held not to be a controlled advertisement because, although it suggested that the company might provide credit, it did not state as a fact that the company was willing to provide credit. By way of exception, an advertisement of credit is not controlled if it indicates either that the credit must exceed £25,000 and that no land security is required, or that the credit is available only to a company or other corporate body. The Consumer Credit (Exempt Advertisements) Order 1985 creates further exceptions so that an advertisement is not controlled by the Act if it relates to any of the following exempt agreements—namely agreements (other than agreements financing the purchase of land) which are exempt by virtue of them involving (a) trade with a country outside the United Kingdom, or (b) the hire of metering equipment from bodies such as British Gas Plc or water or electricity companies, or (c) repayments not exceeding a specified number. For details of which agreements are within these three categories of exemption, see paragraph 21–25 above. The last of these means that advertisements for exempt charge cards (*e.g.* American Express) are not controlled by the Act, although advertisements for regulated credit cards are.

(ii) Advertisements issued by any credit brokerage business. Here the advertisements which are controlled are those which advertise the credit brokerage services and those which advertise the services of the credit or hire business to which the credit brokerage business introduces customers.

(iii) Advertisements issued by a debt adjusting or debt counselling business, indicating that it is willing to advise on debts or engage in transactions concerned with the liquidation of debts.

The control

23–09   The control over these advertisements is exercised by a number of criminal offences which it is possible for the advertiser to commit. He commits an offence if the advertisement:

(a) conveys information which in a material respect is false or misleading (section 46), or

(b) indicates a willingness to supply goods or services on credit terms at a time when the supplier is not also prepared to supply the goods or services for cash (section 45), or

(c) infringes the advertising regulations (see below).

The offence in section 46 can be committed if the credit advertisement is in any way misleading. It does not have to be misleading about the credit being advertised. For example, an advertisement for a car would be subject to the control of the Consumer Credit Act if it happened also to include reference to credit being available. It could then be caught by section 46 if it was misleading in what it said about anything, *e.g.* about the car or about the cash price. Thus in *Rover Group Limited and Rover Finance Limited v. Sumner* (1995 Crown Court) the advertiser was convicted under section 46 when the advertisement was misleading in that it indicated the cash price of £5,995 and only in very small print in a footnote indicated that this excluded the cost of delivery and number plates. This means that this provision can sometimes be used where the statutory time limit has expired for the bringing of a prosecution under some other provision, *e.g.* the Trade Descriptions Act (see paragraph 18–33 above).

23–10   The advertiser (*i.e.* the person who runs the business which issued the advertisement) is the principal offender. However, it is also possible for certain other people to be convicted—namely the publisher, the person who devised the advertisement and the person who procured its publication (*e.g.* an advertising agency).

Section 168 provides defences which are modelled on, and virtually identical to, defences available under section 24 of the Trade Descriptions Act 1968 (see paragraph 18–26 above). Thus, anyone charged with an offence under the Consumer Credit Act has a good defence to the charge if he proves two things:

(i) that he took all reasonable precautions and exercised all due diligence to avoid the commission of an offence, and

(ii) that the offence (or what would have been the offence) was due to a mistake, reliance on information supplied to him, to the act or omission of another person or to an accident or some other cause beyond his control.

Advertising regulations

The Consumer Credit (Advertisements) Regulations 1989 apply to advertisements which are controlled by the Act and which indicate that the advertiser is willing to provide credit or goods on hire. The Regulations do not, however, apply to advertisements which on their wording are aimed solely at business, *e.g.* "Hire your office photocopier from us" or "Business loans, £500 to £50,000".   **23–11**

The detail of the Regulations is too great to be given here. Their broad thrust can be outlined. Their aims are to see that the consumer is given sufficient information in such a way that he gains a fair impression of what is being advertised and also can make a meaningful comparison between different sources of credit (or goods on hire). The Regulations require any advertisement to which they apply to be one of three types: a simple advertisement, an intermediate advertisement or a full advertisement. An advertisement will be a simple one provided:

(a) it does not specify any cash price (or other price), and also

(b) it contains no indication that credit or goods on hire are available, other than the name of the advertiser and a statement of his occupation.

Of course, if an advertisement, despite the inclusion of the advertiser's name, contains no indication at all that he is willing to provide credit or goods on hire, then the advertisement is not controlled by the Act or by the Regulations: *Jenkins v. Lombard North Central*, (paragraph 23–08 above). If it does contain such an indication, *e.g.* "Motor finance from Vehicle Credit Ltd", then it will not comply with the requirements of the Regulations as to a simple advertisement if it also contains a price for the goods advertised. The object of the Regulations in relation to small   **23–12** advertisements is really to allow "name" advertising, *e.g.* on ash trays, pencils, calendars, etc.

If an advertisement does not comply with the requirements of a small advertisement, then it must comply with those of either an intermediate advertisement or a full advertisement. The requirements for the latter are comprehensive and require a very full account of what is on offer. In the case of a credit advertisement (but not of course a hire advertisement) one very important requirement is that there be a statement of the annual rate of the APR (Annual Percentage Rate of the Total Charge for Credit). This has to be calculated (within certain very narrow tolerances) in a uniform way by all credit advertisers, *i.e.* according to the Consumer Credit (Total Charge for Credit) Regulations 1980, paragraph 21–39 above. If an advertisement contains a rate of charge calculated on any other basis (*e.g.* a so-called "flat" rate), then the advertisement must give greater prominence to the APR. Thus a potential debtor can truly compare the cost of credit from different sources.

23–13   An intermediate advertisement has to contain some, but need not contain all, of the information required to be included in a full advertisement. It must, however, contain an indication of where full written information can be obtained from.

Quotations

23–14   There used to be regulations governing the form and content of written quotations given in response to requests from prospective customers. It was found that few customers asked for written quotations and the regulations were revoked in 1996. New requirements were introduced by the Consumer Credit (Content of Quotations) and Consumer Credit (Advertisements) (Amendment) Regulations 1999 (as amended in 2000) which do not, however, lay down a comprehensive code for credit and hire quotations; nor do they require a trader to respond to a request for a quotation. They simply require health warnings to be included in advertisements and also in any written quotation given in relation to three particular types of agreement. The first is where there is a chance that the customer will be asked to provide his home as security, in which case the quotation must make that fact clear and must include a warning such as "YOUR HOME IS AT RISK IF YOU DO NOT KEEP UP REPAYMENTS ON A MORTGAGE OR OTHER LOAN SECURED ON IT." The second is where the agreement might be secured on land and the repayments would be made in a currency other than sterling, in which case the quotation must include a warning such as: "THE STERLING EQUIVALENT OF YOUR LIABILITY UNDER A FOREIGN CURRENCY MORTGAGE MAY BE INCREASED BY EXCHANGE RATE MOVEMENTS."

The third is a mortgage of the debtor's home, typically taken out by an elderly householder in order to realise part of the value of his or her house whilst being allowed still to live in it for the rest of his or her life. Thus the quotations must include a prescribed statement where:

(i) the mortgage does not require repayment of credit or interests while the debtor continues to occupy the home as his main place of residence; or

(ii) the mortgage does not require repayment of the credit (though it may require payment of interest) while the debtor continues to occupy the home as his main residence *and* the creditor cannot resell the home to enforce the agreement whilst the debtor continues to occupy the home as his main residence.

The statement which must be included in quotations for such agreements is "CHECK THAT THIS MORTGAGE WILL MEET YOUR NEEDS IF YOU WANT TO MOVE OR SELL YOUR HOME OR YOU WANT YOUR FAMILY TO INHERIT IT. IF YOU ARE IN DOUBT, SEEK INDEPENDENT ADVICE".

FORMATION OF A CONSUMER CREDIT AGREEMENT

BECAUSE different types of consumer credit agreements are made **24–01** in different ways, it will be necessary to deal with the different types to some extent separately. Many of the problems arising in connection with hire-purchase, conditional sale and credit sale agreements are due to the fact that the agreement between debtor and creditor (finance company) is often negotiated through the dealer. Thus these agreements will be considered first. Before embarking upon that, we should note that the formality and cancellation provisions of the Consumer Credit Act apply to regulated agreements of all types. These provisions and also provisions relating to credit brokers' fees and credit reference agencies will be considered at the end of this chapter.

HIRE-PURCHASE, CONDITIONAL SALE AND CREDIT SALE AGREEMENTS

Offer, acceptance and revocation

As we have seen, the customer usually makes an offer to the **24–02** finance company by filling in a form and leaving it with the dealer. That offer will usually be accepted by the finance company posting their acceptance to the customer. In that case the contract will be made when the acceptance is put in the post. It usually takes several days and sometimes much more. At any time before the letter of acceptance is posted (or the offeror is in some other way informed of the finance company's acceptance) the offeror can revoke his offer. Normally, in order for revocation to be effective, it must actually be notified to the other party before the contract is made. So, if the customer (*i.e.* the offeror) posts to the finance company a revocation of his offer, that revocation will be effective only if it actually arrives before the finance company posts its letter of acceptance. However, there is no need for the revocation to be in writing. Furthermore, the dealer is agent of the finance company for the purpose of receiving revocations. Thus, when the customer tells the dealer that he revokes his offer to the finance company, that has the same effect as if he had told the finance company. Provided he does so before the finance company posts its letter of acceptance, there will be no contract between the customer and the finance company.

24–03   In *Financings v. Stimson* (1962 CA) the customer filled in at the dealer's premises a hire-purchase proposal form and he was allowed to drive the car away. The dealer sent the form off in the usual way to the finance company. After four days the customer returned the car to the dealer declaring that he did not want it. Shortly after that the car was stolen from the dealer's premises. It was recovered fairly quickly but in a badly damaged state. The following day the finance company purported to accept the customer's offer and sent him a copy of the "agreement". The Court of Appeal held that there was no agreement and therefore no contract for two reasons: (i) by returning the car to the dealer and declaring that he did not want it, the customer revoked his offer to the finance company. Communication of that revocation to the dealer was sufficient, as the latter was the finance company's agent for the purpose of receiving a revocation; (ii) the customer's offer to the finance company must be taken to have been conditional upon the goods being in substantially the same state at the time of acceptance as they were at the time the offer was first made. Thus for two reasons the customer's offer was, at the time in question, incapable for being accepted. There being no contract, the customer was under no liability to the finance company.

24–04   The position as so far stated is that at common law. The customer's position at common law is strengthened where section 57 of the Consumer Credit Act applies. That section applies to all regulated hire-purchase and conditional sale agreements other than non-commercial ones and it applies to all regulated credit sale agreements other than non-commercial agreements and small agreements. It has two important provisions. First, the dealer is agent of the creditor for the purpose of receiving notice (oral or written) that the debtor's offer is withdrawn. This reinforces the rule in *Financings v. Stimson*. Secondly, the withdrawal of either party from a prospective agreement takes effect as if the agreement:

(i) had been actually made, and

(ii) had been a cancellable one, and

(iii) had been cancelled by the debtor under section 69.

Thus the debtor will be in the same position as he would be in after cancelling a cancellable agreement. As we shall see (paragraphs 24–54 to 24–58) the debtor is in a strong position after cancellation. Thus section 57 has the effect of strengthening his position after withdrawal from a prospective agreement.

A withdrawal from a prospective agreement means that there is no agreement and therefore no obligation under the agreement. If the debtor has taken delivery of any goods he will have to return them and if he has made any payments he will be entitled to recover them. However, where section 57 applies, the effect of treating it as a cancelled agreement is that the debtor has, in addition, a lien over the goods to compel the repayment. This entitles him to retain possession of the goods until he is repaid. This could be very useful where for example the dealer has allowed the customer to drive away the car as soon as the customer had signed the proposal form and paid the deposit. If the debtor then withdrew his offer to the finance company, he could retain possession of the car until his deposit was repaid.

Uncertainty

It is true of any agreement that it is not a contract unless the parties have agreed on the basic terms. We saw in Chapter 2 that an agreement for the sale of goods will not normally constitute a contract if the parties have not agreed on something as basic as the price.   24–05

Similarly, a hire-purchase agreement may be void for uncertainty. In *Scammell v. Ouston* (1941 HL) Ouston had been negotiating to acquire a van from Scammell on hire-purchase terms. They reached an agreement "that the balance of purchase price can be had on hire-purchase terms over two years". Ouston sued Scammell for non-delivery. The House of Lords found Scammell not liable because there was no contract, the agreement being too vague. The parties had not reached any agreement as to what the hire-purchase terms were to be.

Mistake

It may happen that the parties, though believing themselves to have agreed the terms, have not in fact done so. In *Campbell*   24–06

Discount v. Gall (1961 CA) the customer selected a car from the dealer's stock. They agreed that the customer would apply to a finance company to acquire it on hire-purchase terms—the cash price being £265. The customer signed the finance company's proposal form in the usual way and left it with the dealer for the latter to fill in the details and send it off to the finance company. The dealer filled in the cash price as £325. The finance company accepted this proposal. The Court of Appeal held that there was no contract between the finance company and the customer, because they were not agreed on the price. In law one is bound by an agreement made by one's agent. However, the Court rejected any idea that the dealer was, for the purpose of completing the form, agent for either party. Thus, although the dealer is agent of the finance company for the purpose of receiving revocations, it was held that he is not, unless expressly authorised, their agent for the purpose of making a hire-purchase contract. This is the position at common law.

24–07   The rule that the dealer is not normally the agent of the finance company was confirmed in *Branwhite v. Worcester Works* (1968 HL). The facts were the same as in *Campbell Discount v. Gall*. The customer signed the proposal form leaving the cash price still to be filled in. He paid to the dealer the initial deposit (£130) which would be due to the finance company if the proposal was accepted. The dealer filled in the wrong cash price on the proposal form, which he sent off, together with his own offer to sell the vehicle, to the finance company. The finance company accepted both these proposals and sent to the dealer the cash price less the deposit (£130) which the dealer had already received from the customer. It was assumed and accepted that following *Gall*'s case there was no valid contract between the finance company and the customer because they were not agreed on the price. The customer therefore claimed the return from the finance company of his deposit of £130, arguing that the dealer who had received it was agent of the finance company in doing so and that therefore the dealer receiving it was equivalent to the finance company itself receiving it. This argument was rejected. The dealer is not, unless expressly authorised, agent of the finance company for the purpose of receiving deposits. However, the customer was held entitled to the return of his money on a different ground—namely that the finance company had itself received the deposit. Although the dealer had not actually sent the £130 to the finance company, the latter had nevertheless obtained it by deducting it from the purchase money which it had sent to the dealer. There being no contract between the customer and the finance company, the customer was entitled to the return of his initial deposit on the ground of a total failure of consideration.

Branwhite's case (like *Gall*'s case) was decided upon the **24–08** assumption that there was no contract between the customer and the finance company. This assumption was wrong. It does not follow that there is no contract just because the dealer is nobody's agent and sends the finance company a form with figures different from those intended by the customer. This is because of the rule that normally someone who signs a document intended to have legal effect is bound by the terms of that document if the other party (here the finance company) relies upon that signature and is unaware that the document does not accord with the signer's intentions. In *United Dominions Trust Ltd v. Western* (1975 CA) the customer and dealer agreed a price for a car and the dealer produced a finance company's proposal form for the customer to sign. This he did, leaving the dealer subsequently to fill in the agreed figures. He believed it to be a hire-purchase proposal form but it was in fact a proposal for a loan agreement. The dealer did not disillusion him and, unknown to the customer, filled in, not the agreed figures, but inflated figures. He then sent the form off to the finance company, which duly accepted the proposal as it then appeared. The Court of Appeal held that the customer was bound by the terms of the document he had signed, including the figures subsequently inserted by the dealer. Thus the position at common law can be summarised as follows. The dealer (unless expressly authorised by the finance company) is not the finance company's agent. The customer is bound by the terms of the document he signs unless the finance company knows that it does not accord with the customer's intentions. That is so, irrespective of whether he signs a completed document or he signs an uncompleted one leaving it to be completed by someone else. The position would be very different if the dealer were the agent of the finance company. In that case there would be no binding agreement because the finance company would be regarded as knowing what its agent knows, namely that the proposal form does not represent the customer's intended offer.

The common law rule, settled in *Branwhite*'s case, is that the **24–09** dealer, who typically has possession of the finance company's proposal forms and has knowledge of the finance company's charges and who may help the customer complete the form, is not normally agent of the finance company. It is possible, however, that exceptional facts could exist which in a particular case could establish the dealer as agent. That occurred in *Purnell Secretarial Services v. Lease Management Services Ltd* (1994 CA). The dealer was Canon (South West) Limited, from whom the customer had bought several photocopiers over a period of years. During a visit by the dealer's sales representative, the customer made it plain that it was essential that any new machine should be capable of making "paper plates" as indeed the demonstration model was. On this basis the customer signed an agreement to hire a new machine, only to discover after delivery that the machine was incapable of making "paper plates". It transpired that the customer had made the hire agreement not, as the customer had thought, with the dealer, but with a finance company, Lease Management Services Limited. This was a surprise to the customer since the agreement was headed "Canon (South West) Finance" and below that in a large box beside the word "supplier" appeared "Canon (South West) Limited", the word "Canon" being printed in that company's distinctive logo. Much further down, in more tightly typed print, there appeared the words "Lessor/Owner: Leaser Management Services Limited trading as Canon (South West) Finance". It was held that the finance company, Lease Management Services, by customising its form, had chosen to identify itself with Canon (South West) Limited and had thereby misled the customer into thinking the contract was with Canon (South West) Limited. Therefore the finance company was estopped from denying the authority of Canon (South West) Limited's staff to speak for the finance company. The dealer was agent (by estoppel) of the finance company which was thus liable for misrepresentations and breaches of promises made by the dealer. This case involved a hire agreement and not a hire-purchase agreement but the common law principles are the same in relation to each.

24–10 The common law rule that for most purposes the dealer is not the finance company's agent has in the case of regulated agreements, been overturned. Section 56(2) of the Consumer Credit Act provides that antecedent negotiations in relation to the goods shall be deemed to be conducted by the dealer "in the capacity of agent of the creditor as well as in his actual capacity".

The dealer is by virtue of section 56 agent of the finance company in any antecedent negotiations with the customer—and negotiations include any dealings between customer and dealer. That means that any deposit received by the dealer from the customer is received by him as agent for the finance company.

Thus even if there is no binding agreement between the finance company and the debtor, the latter can reclaim the deposit from the finance company; and that is so even if the finance company never received it from the dealer.

Non est factum

Someone who signs a document in the mistaken belief that it is **24–11** of a totally different type can evade liability on his signature provided he was not careless in signing. He can plead *non est factum*—that it was not his deed. If the plea succeeds, his signature is null and void. There are two requirements for the plea to succeed:

(a) The document must be radically different from what the signer believed.

(b) The signer must not have been careless in signing.

A mistake merely as to the details, *e.g.* as to the number of instalments or the dates when due, will not be sufficient. Believing a personal loan agreement to be a hire-purchase agreement is not a sufficient mistake either: *United Dominions Trust v. Western*, above. However, if the signer believes himself to be witnessing a will or to be guaranteeing a friend's debt when he is in fact signing a hire-purchase agreement, that is a sufficient difference: *Muskham Finance v. Howard* (1963 CA).

Even if the signer can establish a sufficient mistake, he will usually fail because it will usually have been careless of him not first to have read what he signed. He will therefore find it easier for the plea to succeed if he is illiterate or blind or if, like the old lady in *Gallie v. Lee* (1970 HL), he had just lost his glasses.

Misrepresentation

If before the contract is made, one party makes an untrue **24–12** statement of fact which induces the other party to make the contract, the latter may have a remedy for misrepresentation. The principles applicable and remedies available were set out in Chapter 6.

A particular problem arises where goods are selected from a dealer's stock and subsequently acquired on instalment terms from a finance company. The problem is that most of the statements made to the customer to persuade him to have the goods are made not by the other party to the instalment contract (the finance company) but by the dealer.

We have already seen that if such a statement proves to be untrue, the customer may have a claim for damages from the dealer for breach of collateral warranty (*Andrews v. Hopkinson*, paragraph 19–10 above). Does the customer have a remedy also against the finance company for misrepresentation? This is an important question because if he does, not only may he be entitled to damages from the finance company, but he may also be able to rescind the contract in accordance with the principles set out in Chapter 6. However, the answer at common law is "NO". There is a remedy for misrepresentation only in respect of statements made by one party or his agent to the other party. For most purposes (other than receiving revocation of an offer) the dealer is not agent of the finance company. Thus when a dealer makes statements about the goods, he is not, unless expressly authorised, doing so as agent of the finance company.

24–13   Although that is the common law position, it has in the case of regulated agreements been reversed by the Consumer Credit Act. By section 56 the dealer is a negotiator in antecedent negotiations and in conducting these negotiations the dealer is deemed to be an agent of the finance company. Antecedent negotiations begin when the dealer and the customer first get into communication and that includes communication by advertisement. The antecedent negotiations include any representations made by the dealer. Section 56 is important in that, in respect of misrepresentations about the goods by the dealer, it confers upon the customer the armoury of the law of misrepresentation with which to attack the finance company. In particular he will be entitled to rescind the regulated agreement. It is sufficient that he gives notice of rescission to the dealer, for by section 102 of the Consumer Credit Act the dealer is agent of the finance company for receiving notice of rescission.

24–14   By the terms of section 56(1)(b), the antecedent negotiations in which the dealer is deemed to be agent of the creditor are those conducted by him "in relation to goods sold or proposed to be sold" by the dealer to the creditor. Consider the following situation. A customer has a car on hire-purchase terms and is still paying off the instalments under her hire-purchase agreement with finance company X. She approaches a car dealer asking to trade in her existing car and to acquire a new one on hire-purchase. Enquiries made of finance company X reveal that the settlement figure needed to pay off the customer's existing debt is £1,000.

The car dealer suggests that the customer acquires the new car under a hire-purchase agreement with finance company Z. The customer agrees and they come to an arrangement. It is that: the cash price of the new car is £6,000; the trade-in allowance for the existing one is £3,000; the customer completes a hire-purchase proposal form of finance company Z proposing to take the new car on hire-purchase terms, make a down payment of £2,000 and pay the balance of £4,000 (plus credit charges) in monthly instalments over three years. The car dealer undertakes to receive the trade-in car, to pay off the £1,000 owing to finance company X and to use the balance of the trade-in allowance as the customer's £2,000 down payment under the new hire-purchase agreement. Finance company Z accepts the customer's proposal and pays the car dealer £4,000 (*i.e.* the cash price of £6,000 less the £2,000 down payment received, as part of the value of the traded-in car, by the car dealer direct from the customer). The customer takes delivery of the new car and subsequently discovers that the car dealer has gone out of business, disappeared and has never kept his promise to pay the £1,000 to finance company X. Can the customer claim that finance company Z is liable for breach of the dealer's (its agent's?) promise to pay the settlement figure to finance company X? Yes. For the customer her buying of the new car and the trade-in arrangement and settlement of her debt on her traded-in car were all one transaction. Thus the dealer's promise to pay off the customer's existing debt was something done "in relation to" the car she was buying: *Forthright Finance Ltd. v. Ingate* (1997 CA).

Legality

24–15   A party who makes such a contract knowing it to be illegal will be unable to sue the other party. In *Snell v. Unity Finance* (1963 CA) the customer made a hire-purchase contract in the usual way with a finance company. He had not enough money to pay the minimum deposit required by regulations then in force. The cash price of the car was £185. The minimum deposit required by the regulations was 20 per cent, but the customer had only £25. The dealer and the customer filled in the forms to show (wrongly) that the customer had paid a deposit of £50 and that the cash price was £210. The finance company accepted the proposals. Later the customer sued the finance company on the ground that the car was defective and not reasonably fit for its purpose. He lost because the Court would not allow him to enforce an illegal contract. Incidentally, there have been no regulations requiring a minimum deposit, since the last regulations were revoked in 1982.

Suppose that in *Snell v. Unity Finance* the customer had defaulted in his payments. In that case the finance company could have enforced the agreement against him and sued him for the arrears, because the finance company was not *in pari delicto, i.e.* as much to blame as the customer. The finance company could also have exercised its right to recover possession of the goods on default by the customer, for the same reason. However, there is also an alternative reason. Under a hire-purchase agreement ownership does not pass until all the instalments have been paid and the option exercised. Until then, the finance company is owner and that ownership gives it the right to recover the goods (or their value) unless the customer can establish a right to retain them: *Bowmakers v. Barnet Instruments* (1944 CA). If, on the other hand, the customer pays off all the instalments and exercises his option, then ownership passes to him and this happens even under an illegal contract: *Belvoir Finance v. Stapelton* (1970 CA). The right (if any) of the creditor (*i.e.* the owner) to recover possession of the goods on default by the debtor (*i.e.* the customer) will be considered further at paragraphs 27–18 and 27–19.

OTHER REGULATED AGREEMENTS

24–16   The contracts we have considered so far in this chapter (*i.e.* hire-purchase, conditional sale and credit sale agreements) have one thing in common—namely that the credit agreement and the contract by which the customer agrees to have the goods are one and the same thing. That being so they are (*i.e.* it is) made at the same time. However, we come to consider a number of other kinds of credit agreement where often the seller and the creditor are two different people, where the customer therefore makes two agreements and where he will usually make one before the other. This fact can be crucial. Usually the credit agreement will be made first so that the debtor then has the funds or the credit facilities to make the purchase. Thus someone who has a credit card will have made his credit agreement (*i.e.* the credit card agreement) when he accepted his card by signing it or first using it. When some time later he uses his card to purchase some goods he will not be making a new credit agreement but simply using the credit facilities available under the credit agreement made earlier. Thus although the dealer who sells him the goods is made by the Act agent of the creditor, he is not the agent of the creditor in the making of the credit agreement. This is because the debtor will not have made contact with the dealer until after the credit agreement was made.

There are two people who are to a greater or lesser extent deemed to be the agent of the creditor or owner—namely the debtor's or hirer's representative in negotiations and the negotiator in antecedent negotiations.

Customer's representative

The Act uses the formula "any person who, in the course of a **24–17** business carried on by him, acts (or acted) on behalf of the debtor or hirer in any negotiations for the agreement". This formula clearly includes those persons who run businesses whereby they arrange loans or other forms of credit for the customer. They do not grant the credit themselves but will negotiate on behalf of the customer with a prospective creditor. They sometimes describe themselves as finance brokers. It is also possible for a customer's own solicitor or accountant to fall within the formula—if for example the customer got him to negotiate a loan for the customer. Anyone falling within the formula is deemed for three limited purposes to be agent of the creditor or owner. Someone falling within the formula will in this book be described as the customer's representative. The customer's representative is of course primarily an agent of the customer and is not agent of the creditor or owner except where the Consumer Credit Act states that he is.

The three purposes for which he is made the agent of the creditor or owner are:

(i) For receiving notice from the customer that the customer withdraws his offer to enter a regulated agreement—section 57.

(ii) For receiving notice of cancellation—section 69 (see paragraph 24–52 below).

(iii) For receiving notice from the customer that the customer rescinds his regulated agreement—section 102.

Section 102 should not be misunderstood. The customer's representative is not the agent of the creditor or owner for the purpose of making representations. Therefore section 102 does not mean that misrepresentations by the customer's representative will entitle the customer subsequently to rescind his agreement with the creditor. It means simply that if for some other reason (*e.g.* a misrepresentation made by the creditor himself) the customer is entitled to rescind a regulated agreement, it is sufficient that he gives notice of that rescission to the customer's representative. Whenever the Act makes someone the agent of the creditor or owner for the purpose of receiving a notice or payment, he is under a duty to the creditor or owner to transmit it to him forthwith—section 175.

Negotiator in antecedent negotiations

24–18   A negotiator in antecedent negotiations is a deemed agent of the creditor or owner. The purpose for which he is deemed the creditor's or owner's agent include and are wider than those for which the customer's representative is a deemed agent. Thus if a customer's representative falls also within the definition of a negotiator in antecedent negotiations, he can be regarded simply in the latter capacity.

There are just three types of person who fall within the definition of a negotiator in antecedent negotiations (section 56):

(a) The creditor or owner. Plainly no question of agency arises here.

(b) The dealer in the case of a hire-purchase, conditional sale or credit sale agreement. This was considered in the earlier part of this chapter.

(c) The dealer (termed by the Act, the supplier) in the case of any other debtor-creditor-supplier agreement.

Our concern here then is with who falls within category (c). Debtor-creditor-supplier agreements other than those mentioned in (b) include credit card agreements and trading check agreements (see Chapter 21). Thus the trader who supplies goods under a credit card agreement (*i.e.* because the buyer uses his credit card instead of paying cash) is a negotiator within section 56.

24–19   Any person (except the creditor) falling within the definition of a negotiator in section 56 is deemed in conducting negotiations with the debtor (the customer) to be an agent of the creditor (section 56(2)). This does not however alter any other capacity he may have. Thus the supplier of goods under a credit card agreement is a seller of goods to the customer as well as being an agent of the creditor in negotiations with the customer. Section 56 gives a wide meaning to the "negotiations" during which the negotiator is agent of the creditor. These negotiations begin when the negotiator and the customer first get into communication (including communication by advertisement). The negotiations include any representations made by the negotiator to the customer and any other dealings between them. Thus statements (*e.g.* about the quality of the goods) made by the negotiator during the negotiations are made by him in two capacities. They are regarded as made not only by the dealer but also by the creditor (because made by his agent). The exact effect of them being so regarded will be considered a little later.

"Antecedent" needs to be explained. Section 56 talks of a **24–20** negotiator in antecedent negotiations. Antecedent means previous or earlier—but previous to what, earlier than what? It is clear from category (c) above that it is possible for a supplier to be a negotiator in antecedent negotiations which occur after the relevant credit agreement has been made, *e.g.* the supplier of goods under a credit card agreement. Thus antecedent sometimes means previous to the making of a credit agreement (*e.g.* in categories (a) or (b) above) and sometimes means previous to the making of an agreement to be financed by an already existing credit agreement.

Let us put it another way. In the case of a hire-purchase agreement antecedent negotiations will occur before the credit agreement (*i.e.* the hire-purchase agreement) is made. In the case of a purchase of goods by use of a credit card, the antecedent negotiations will occur before the purchase but after the credit agreement was made. Although representations made by the dealer to the customer will in both cases be treated as if made also by the creditor, the effect of that will be much more significant when those statements were made before the credit agreement was made (*i.e.* in the hire-purchase case). In that case a misrepresentation by the creditor will entitle the debtor to rescind the whole credit agreement in accordance with the principles outlined in Chapter 6 (and see paragraph 24–12 above). However, a misrepresentation by the creditor after the credit agreement was made (*e.g.* in the credit card situation) will not entitle the debtor to rescind the whole credit agreement. It will, however, entitle him (as we shall shortly see) to rescind that aspect of the credit agreement relating to the purchase in question.

Offer and acceptance

24–21   It is true of any contract that the contract is made at the time when both sides agree to be bound by the same terms, *i.e.* when one side makes an offer which the other accepts.

To discover whether or when an acceptance occurred the communications between the parties must be examined. We have seen (paragraph 19–07) that in the case of a hire-purchase agreement the finance company will require the customer to make an offer by filling in its proposal form containing the terms of the prospective agreement. The agreement (*i.e.* the contract) will be made if and when the finance company communicate to the customer their acceptance of his offer. Other credit agreements are not always made in the same way. Thus a customer who wishes to have a credit card—*i.e.* to enter into a credit card agreement—will no doubt be asked to fill in an application form. He may find, however, that the credit card company, although it is satisfied with the application, regards the application not as an offer but as only a request for the company to make an offer. Thus the customer is likely to receive an offer (together with the credit card) from the company.

The offer will state that the customer will accept the offer when he signs or uses the credit card. The agreement will be made therefore when the customer first signs or first uses the card. Arrangements vary from one creditor to another. Some will insist on the customer making the offer and others will insist on making the offer themselves and leaving the customer to accept it. Yet other creditors will not invariably be insistent one way or the other. Thus a bank manager may make an offer of an overdraft to one customer and from another customer receive an offer to take an overdraft. Whichever party makes an offer, the agreement will be made when the acceptance of it by the other party takes effect. In the case of regulated agreements the exact point of time when the agreement is made has added significance. Not only is it important because a withdrawal of an offer cannot be effective after acceptance of the offer but it also marks the beginning of the seven-day period within which a second copy of the agreement may have to be served upon the customer. This will be dealt with later under the formalities provisions (paragraph 24–32 to 24–47).

Withdrawal of offer

24–22   An offer can be withdrawn at any time before the offer has been effectively accepted. The time when acceptance takes effect was explained in Chapter 2 (paragraph 2–06)—in particular, if the post was expected to be used, the acceptance takes effect upon posting. This is a general rule of the law of contract and applies therefore to regulated agreements. There is also a general rule that a withdrawal of an offer does not take effect upon posting but only upon its receipt or communication to the other party. Thus a withdrawal will have no effect unless it actually arrives before the acceptance is posted. If it does not, both sides are bound and neither can back out (*i.e.* unless it is a cancellable agreement—see later, paragraph 24–48).

Section 57 applies to prospective regulated agreements which are subject to the formalities requirements (see paragraph 24–32 below)—and that includes most regulated agreements. Its effects are twofold as they are in relation to hire-purchase agreements (see paragraph 24–04 above). First, the customer's representative (paragraph 24–17 above) and the negotiator in antecedent negotiations (paragraph 24–18 above) are deemed to be agents of the creditor or owner for receiving notice of withdrawal by the customer. Secondly, where either party withdraws from a prospective agreement, the debtor or hirer will be in the same position as he would be in if the agreement had been made, had been a cancellable one and had been cancelled under section 69. That position will be explained later (paragraphs 24–54 to 24–58).

We will now consider some particular types of regulated agreement in the light of what has so far been said in this chapter.

Credit cards

By section 57 a negotiator in antecedent negotiations—*i.e.* the supplier of goods under the credit card agreement—is agent of the creditor for the purpose of receiving from the debtor notice withdrawing an offer to enter the credit agreement. However, this will be of little importance in practice because an offer cannot be withdrawn once it has been accepted and the debtor is unlikely to attempt to get credit by means of his credit card agreement until after the offer has been accepted (and after the credit card agreement has therefore been made). In any case a great many credit card agreements are made, not by an offer from the debtor which the creditor accepts, but by an offer by the creditor to the debtor (the card holder) which the latter accepts by signing or using his credit card.

24–23

It has already been seen that by virtue of section 56 representations by the supplier to the debtor are made by him also as agent of the creditor. It was also seen that this would not enable the debtor to rescind the whole credit card agreement. It would, however, entitle him to rescind that part of the credit card agreement relating to the transaction in relation to which the misrepresentation was made. This requires explanation. There is no doubt that a credit card agreement (unless it is exempt like certain American Express and Diners Club agreements) is itself a regulated running-account credit agreement. As a matter of ordinary contract law, that agreement is a standing offer under which the credit card company is offering credit to the card holder. The card holder is not committed to take any particular amount of credit or indeed any credit at all. He may keep the card and never use it. When he uses it to pay, say, £40 for a pair of shoes he accepts the standing offer to provide him with credit and he accepts it to the extent of £40 worth of credit. In thus accepting the standing offer he creates a contract with the credit card company for the provision to him of £40 worth of credit. Each time he uses the card he makes a new contract with the credit card company. Suppose the supplier makes a misrepresentation (*e.g.* the shoe seller falsely states the shoes to be 100 per cent leather). If the credit card agreement is a regulated one, that is a misrepresentation by the credit card company, *i.e.* through their agent, a negotiator in antecedent negotiations. It has presumably induced not just the sale of the shoes but also the accompanying use of the credit card. The card holder therefore has the right to rescind the contract for the £40 worth of credit. This is because a misrepresentation by the other party to that contract (the credit card company) induced him to make it. He could exercise this right by informing the credit card company that he is rescinding the transaction. He would then be entitled to refuse to make any payments relating to that particular transaction. Of course, if he had made some repayment of the £40 to the credit card company, he might be regarded as having affirmed the contract and thereby having lost the right of rescission. In an appropriate case the card holder may even wish to claim damages from the credit card company for the misrepresentation. For an explanation of the remedies available for a misrepresentation see Chapter 6.

24–24   As already observed, at common law a credit card agreement amounts to a standing offer and thus each new use of the card creates a new contract between the card holder and the credit card company. It is therefore tempting to regard each such new contract as a new regulated agreement. Such an approach would be wrong, contrary to the scheme of the Act (see [1978] New L. J. 448). Every time a new regulated agreement is made, the formality and documentation provisions have to be complied with. The Act clearly contemplated that with a running-account credit agreement those formalities could be satisfied when the agreement was first made and would not apply each time the agreed credit facility was used. (For a fuller analysis, see *Credit Cards*, an article at [1979] J.B.L. 331.)

In practice it will be in only very rare cases that a card holder will need to rely upon section 56 to make a claim against the credit card company. He has considerable rights against the supplier and will usually get satisfaction direct from him for any misrepresentation or breach of contract by the supplier (see Chapters 6 and 7). Where the supplier agrees to take back the goods and give a refund, he will not usually hand money over to the card holder but will instead credit the card holder's credit card account with the credit card company. Even where he cannot obtain satisfaction from the supplier (perhaps because the latter has disappeared or become insolvent), the card holder will very often be able to make a claim under section 75 against the credit card company for the supplier's misrepresentation or breach of contract. It is only where section 75 does not apply (*e.g.* where the cash price of the item in question did not exceed £100) that the card holder will be forced to rely upon section 56. Section 75 is explained at paragraph 25–03 below. So far it has been assumed that there is just one card holder. Sometimes, however, someone with a credit card agreement has a second person (often the husband or wife) who also has a card which can be used on the same account. Where it is the latter who has used his card on the purchase in question, can he rely on section 56 in the same way as if he were the principal card holder? The answer depends upon the same arguments as apply to whether he may claim under section 75. A similar point is that section 56 probably cannot be relied upon by any card holder who made his credit card agreement before April 1, 1977—though there probably are not too many such credit card agreements which are still operating. Here again there is a similar issue in relation to section 75. See generally the treatment of section 75 at paragraph 25–05 below.

The debtor might not use his credit card as a means of paying **24–25** the dealer, but might instead use his credit card to obtain a cash loan and then use the cash to make a purchase from the dealer. In this case the credit card agreement will, in relation to the loan and subsequent purchase, be for unrestricted-use credit and will be a debtor-creditor agreement (see paragraph 21–21). If in this case the debtor were able to show a misrepresentation or breach of contract by the dealer, that would not give him any claim against the creditor. The dealer would not be an agent of the creditor because he would not in this case fall within the definition of a negotiator in antecedent negotiations. Also section 75 would not apply to give a remedy against the creditor. The debtor would thus be left to his remedies against the dealer.

Check trading
24–26   The supplier will always be a negotiator within the meaning of section 56 and will therefore be agent of the creditor. Also the credit agreement will usually already have been made before the debtor approaches the supplier of the goods or services.

With check trading it can happen that the customer first sees the item in the supplier's showroom, indulges in antecedent negotiations with the salesman and then goes to the creditor to make the necessary credit agreement. This situation is likely to occur with more expensive items in which case the document he obtains from the creditor is likely to be termed a trading voucher and be specifically restricted to the purchase of the specified item (see paragraph 20–19 above). If this sequence of events has occurred, any misrepresentation made by the supplier to the customer before the latter made his trading voucher agreement will entitle the customer to rescind both his agreements, *i.e.* not only the agreement with the supplier but also the trading voucher agreement. Furthermore, in order to rescind the latter (as well as the former) it is sufficient that the customer gives notice of rescission to the supplier since by section 102 the supplier is agent of the creditor for the purpose of receiving notice of rescission.

Section 75 may enable the debtor to bring a claim against the creditor for a breach of contract or a misrepresentation by the supplier.

Cash loan
24–27   It is with a cash loan that there is more likely to be a customer's representative involved, who is agent of the creditor for certain purposes including the receiving of a withdrawal of the customer's offer to enter the regulated agreement. Also, even

though the debtor borrows the cash from the creditor and uses it to buy goods or services from the dealer, it is nevertheless possible for the latter to be a negotiator in antecedent negotiations, *i.e.* agent of the creditor. It would happen where, for example, the dealer has a regular arrangement with the creditor whereby the latter is prepared to make loans to potential customers of the dealer, *i.e.* to put a potential customer in a financial position to make a purchase from the dealer. Such arrangements between dealers and lenders tend to occur where the dealer does not wish (or cannot afford) himself to give credit terms to his customer.

If in pursuance of such an arrangement between creditor and dealer, the creditor agrees to make a cash loan to the customer, the resulting regulated credit agreement will be a debtor-creditor-supplier agreement and the dealer will be a negotiator in antecedent negotiations. This is exactly the situation in the example given at paragraph 21–22 above, where Warmitup Ltd is therefore agent of Hotmoney Ltd in conducting negotiations with Shiver.

However, most cash loans are not made in such circumstances but are mere debtor-creditor agreements. This is certainly the case with the vast majority of bank loans and overdrafts. In these cases the position is as with a cash loan obtained under a credit card agreement. Thus the dealer is not the bank's agent for the purpose of any representations about the goods or services he supplies, *i.e.* section 56 does not apply. That being so, the bank is free of any liability for any misrepresentation or breach of contract by the dealer.

Consumer hire agreements

There is with this type of contract no question of the prospective hirer obtaining the goods from one person (the owner) and credit from another. There is after all no element of credit. Thus in the case of a consumer hire agreement there is only one person who falls within the definition of a negotiator in antecedent negotiations—namely the owner himself. There is therefore no negotiator in antecedent negotiations who is deemed to be the agent of the owner. However, if there is "any person who, in the course of a business carried on by him, acts on behalf of the hirer in any negotiations for the agreement" then that person (the customer's representative) is deemed to be agent of the owner for the purposes indicated earlier (paragraph 24–17).

24–28

Just as with hire-purchase agreements, so with consumer hire agreements, there is sometimes a triangular arrangement whereby the dealer sells the goods to a finance company which contracts with the customer to supply them to him. This process was explained at paragraph 19–08 in relation to hire-purchase. The difference is that here the finance company supplies the goods to the customer on hire instead of hire-purchase terms. We saw (at paragraphs 24–06 to 24–08) that at common law the normal rule is that the dealer is not the agent of the finance company. This is the position at common law in relation to hire-purchase and it is exactly the same where the agreement is a hire agreement: *Woodchester Equipment (Leasing) Limited v. BACFID* (1995 CA). This is so unless, as in *Purnell Secretarial Services v. Lease Management Services Ltd* (paragraph 24–09 above), there is some very exceptional factual material which establishes an agency.

Although the common law position is the same as it is in the case of hire-purchase, the application of the Consumer Credit Act is not the same. This is because where it is a consumer hire agreement instead of a consumer credit agreement, the dealer is not made agent of the finance company: *Moorgate Mercantile Leasing Ltd v. Gell and Ugolini* (1986 CC). As just stated, the owner is the only negotiator in antecedent negotiations, (*i.e.* the finance company).

CREDIT-BROKER'S FEES AND CREDIT REFERENCE AGENCIES

24–29   There are two types of ancillary credit trader who may have a role to play in connection with the making of a regulated agreement, a credit broker and a credit reference agency.

Credit broker's fees

An individual consumer will sometimes go to a credit broker for an introduction to a source of credit. Section 155 establishes a rule designed to prevent the credit broker from charging the consumer more than £5 for any introduction which does not result in the consumer obtaining credit. The rule applies where the consumer wants to make a consumer credit agreement, a consumer hire agreement, a credit agreement (*e.g.* for £30,000) to finance the purchase of a house or flat or a credit agreement secured by a mortgage of land (*e.g.* a second mortgage, whether or not exceeding £25,000 credit). The rule is that if the credit-broker's introduction of the consumer does not result in an agreement (of one of the types just indicated) within six months of the introduction, the consumer cannot be liable to pay the credit broker any fee or commission in excess of £5. If he has already paid such a fee or commission, he is entitled to recover it all back (except the £5). He is of course not entitled to recover it until the six months have elapsed.

Credit reference agencies

The general function and definition of a credit reference agency 24–30 has already been explained in paragraphs 18–25 and 22–14. The bank of knowledge that an agency has about any one person can be formidable and, if it indicates that the person is uncreditworthy, can mean that it is very difficult for that person to obtain credit—except perhaps from the most speculative of creditors who lend without reference to the borrower's creditworthiness and who also charge correspondingly high interest rates.

Concern has been felt at the secrecy with which credit reference agencies have in the past operated. Very often their information has been available only to the trade (*i.e.* finance companies, etc.) so that an individual has been unable to discover the accuracy of reports about his creditworthiness, or indeed whether any such reports have in fact been obtained. The aim of sections 157–159 is to rectify the situation.

Section 157 entitles the debtor or hirer to discover from the 24–31 creditor, owner or negotiator in any antecedent negotiations, the name and address of any credit reference agency which has been consulted as to the creditworthiness of the debtor or hirer. If the creditor, owner or negotiator does not supply that information after receiving a written request for it, he commits an offence. Once that information has been obtained, the debtor or hirer is then in a position to take advantage of section 7 of the Data Protection Act 1998 (or, in the case of a partnership or other unincorporated body, section 158 of the Consumer Credit Act). This entitles an individual (or unincorporated body) to make a written request (plus payment of a small fee for expenses) for details of information relating to the individual (or body) which is kept at the agency. Such a request can be made, irrespective of whether the person making it has obtained credit or has merely tried to obtain it or has not even tried to do so. The agency must comply with the request and failure to comply is an offence.

By section 159, a consumer who considers an entry in the file relating to him to be incorrect and likely to prejudice him if not corrected, can require the agency either to remove the entry or to amend it. Then the agency must within 28 days either do that and notify the consumer that it has done so or else notify him that it has not. If the latter course is taken the consumer can require the agency to add to his file an accompanying notice of correction of not more than 200 words drawn up by the consumer. If the agency refuses to do so, either the consumer or the agency can refer the matter to the relevant authority, who may make such order as he or she thinks fit. Failure to obey the order is a criminal offence. The relevant authority is the Data Protection Commissioner unless the consumer is an unincorporated body, in which case it is the Director General of Fair Trading.

FORMALITIES

24–32 Sections 60–65 deal with formalities which must be complied with in the making of a regulated agreement. The aim is to ensure;

> (i) That the debtor is fully aware of the nature and cost of the transaction he is about to enter (including the cost of the credit).

> (ii) That his written agreement gives him a clear account of his rights and obligations.

Agreements subject to the formalities requirements
24–33 These provisions apply only to regulated agreements. However, they do not apply (section 74) to any non-commercial agreement or to any agreement which fulfils all the following conditions:

> (a) It is a small agreement.

> (b) It is a restricted-use agreement.

> (c) It is a debtor-creditor-supplier agreement.

An example of an agreement which fulfils these conditions is a trading check agreement for £50 or less. Another example is a credit sale agreement under which the credit does not exceed £50. A regulated hire-purchase or conditional sale agreement will always be subject to the formalities requirements unless it is a non-commercial agreement. This is because hire-purchase and conditional sale agreements are excluded from the definition of "small agreements" in section 17. The exception, just mentioned, whereby certain small agreements are not subject to the formalities requirements, does not apply to any agreement which both falls within the Consumer Protection (Cancellation of Contracts Concluded away from Business Premises) Regulations 1987 and also either provides credit exceeding £35 or is a consumer hire agreement requiring payments totalling over £35. For an account of those Regulations, see paragraph 2–18 above.

The reason that non-commercial agreements are not subject to the formalities requirements is that those requirements are intended to protect the consumer against the financially powerful creditor (whether that be the dealer or, say, a finance company). It is however quite possible for two private individuals to enter into what is in fact a regulated consumer credit agreement. For example, the man who sells his car privately (perhaps following a small advertisement in the local paper) may agree to his buyer paying him later—perhaps in instalments.

A similar example would be where a private individual lends money to a friend to be repaid over a period of time. In these cases the law would be unreasonable and unrealistic to insist that the agreement be put into writing and copies of it served on the debtor, etc.

Section 74 enables the Director General also to except from having to comply with the formality requirements two further types of agreement which sometimes have to be made hastily. They are certain agreements to overdraw on a current account and certain agreements to finance payments arising out of a death. The latter might be an agreement to finance the paying of inheritance tax or court fees payable in order to get probate of a will. This exception the Director has limited to agreements where the creditor is a bank and the debtor is someone acting in the course of his trade or profession. As to the former, imagine the situation where the bank manager is presented with a cheque which if he pays it, will put the customer's account into the red. If the manager pays out on the cheque—as often happens in practice—he is in effect agreeing to the customer having an overdraft. It would be plainly unrealistic to require every such agreement to be in writing, etc. The overdraft exception applies to all debtor-creditor agreements for overdrafts on current accounts.

Form and content

The regulated agreement must comply with the Consumer **24–34** Credit (Agreements) Regulations 1983, made under sections 60

405

and 61. These Regulations lay down detailed requirements as to the form, legibility and contents of agreements. In particular an agreement must have whichever is the appropriate one of the following headings: Hire-Purchase Agreement regulated by the Consumer Credit Act 1974; Conditional Sale Agreement regulated by the Consumer Credit Act 1974; Credit Agreement regulated by the Consumer Credit Act 1974; Hire Agreement regulated by the Consumer Credit Act 1974. As to the contents of an agreement the Regulations require the inclusion of such things as:

   (i) names and addresses of the parties;

  (ii) the cash price (though not in the case of hire agreements or of unrestricted-use credit or debtor-creditor agreements);

 (iii) the amount of any deposit or advance payment required of the customer;

 (iv) the amount of the credit (or the credit limit);

  (v) the APR;

 (vi) the total amount payable;

 (vii) the amount of each payment and when payable;

(viii) details of default charges;

 (ix) details of any security provided by the debtor or hirer.

In addition the agreement will have to contain notices, in a precise form laid down in the Regulations, informing the debtor or hirer of certain of his statutory rights and protections. These include: his right of cancellation of a cancellable agreement; his right of early termination if it is a hire-purchase or conditional sale agreement; his statutory protection if he loses a credit-token; his right of early settlement. These rights and protections are explained in later chapters of this book.

Apart from complying with the Regulations, the agreement must embody all the terms of the agreement (other than implied terms)—section 61(1)(b).

Signatures

24–35   By section 61 the agreement must be contained in a document which is signed:

(i) by the debtor or hirer, and

(ii) by or on behalf of the creditor.

Thus the debtor must sign it in person, unless the debtor or hirer is a partnership or other unincorporated body in which case it can be signed by one person on behalf of the debtor or hirer. It is not sufficient that the debtor or hirer signs it when it is still blank. When it is presented or sent to him for signature, it must include all the terms of the agreement (other than implied terms) and it must be readily legible. This means that dealers ought not to follow the practice whereby the dealer persuades the customer to sign the form (say a hire-purchase proposal form) in blank and then the dealer fills in the spaces later—see, for example, *Campbell Discount Co. v. Gall* (paragraph 24–06 above).

The Consumer Credit (Agreements) Regulations 1983 require the agreement to include a signature box in a particular form. The debtor or hirer must sign within that box. Other signatures, *e g* of the creditor or of a witness, must be made outside the box. Normally the date of each signature must be inserted, although this is not necessary if the agreement is not a cancellable one and the date when the agreement becomes an executed agreement is inserted. The agreement becomes executed when the completed document is signed by (or on behalf of) both sides.

Copies

Sections 62 and 63 provide for the debtor or hirer to receive a **24–36** copy or copies of the agreement. Depending upon the circumstances, the debtor or hirer must be given either one or two copies of the agreement. Whatever the circumstances, he should always receive one copy when he signs the agreement. If the agreement is sent to him for his signature then the copy should be sent at the same time. If the agreement is presented personally to him for his signature, then the copy should be given to him there and then.

A further (*i.e.* second) copy must be given to the debtor or hirer if the agreement was not actually made on the occasion when he signed it (section 63). This situation commonly arises. An agreement is not made until both sides accept it—or to be more accurate until one side makes an offer which the other side accepts. Now, often, when a customer signs a finance company's form (*e.g.* for hire-purchase) that is no more than a proposal (*i.e.* an offer) by the customer. There is no agreement and therefore no contract until the finance company accepts the proposal. The finance company will seldom agree immediately. It (or rather one of its officials) will probably sign the form a few days later and post it or a copy of it back to the customer. That will constitute acceptance of the customer's offer and that will therefore be when the agreement is made (*i.e.* when the fully signed, executed, agreement is posted or given back to the debtor). That being so, the agreement will not have been made when the debtor signed the agreement. This will normally be the situation where, as explained at paragraph 19–08 above, the customer signs a finance company's hire-purchase proposal form at the dealer's place of business.

24–37 When a second copy is required it must in the case of a cancellable agreement (see paragraph 24–48 below) be sent by post. In any case the second copy, when required, must be received by the debtor or hirer within seven days following the making of the agreement. Note that the seven days begin to run when the agreement is made, which will not be when the customer signs the agreement, because in that case a second copy would not be necessary. Thus when a second copy is required, the agreement will usually be made when the customer's proposal is accepted. If, as is usual, the means of acceptance is the posting of a duly signed copy back to the customer, that copy (*i.e.* the second) must necessarily reach the customer within the required time (seven days) of the making of the agreement (the posting of the acceptance)!

24–38 The rule as to the time limit for delivery of the second copy (if required) is more lenient in the case of a credit token agreement (*e.g.* a credit card or trading check agreement). In that case the creditor need not comply with the time limit set out above provided the second copy is given to the debtor before or at the time when the credit token itself is given to him.

When an agreement is signed by or on behalf of both parties it is an "executed" agreement. Until then it is "unexecuted". We have just considered those situations where a second copy is required. These situations arise when the agreement was still unexecuted at the time the first copy was given, and when therefore the first copy will necessarily have been a copy of an unexecuted agreement. The second copy, of course, must be a copy of the executed agreement.

In addition to those copies which must be given to the customer at or about the time of making the agreement, the customer is entitled at any time during the currency of the agreement to request a further copy—section 77–79 (see paragraph 26–26 below).

One further point must be made in relation to all copies. Whenever the Consumer Credit Act requires a copy of a regulated agreement to be given or posted, it is part of that requirement that the copy is given or posted together with a copy of any document referred to in the agreement.

Each copy must, in its form and contents, comply with the Consumer Credit (Cancellation Notices and Copies of Documents) Regulations 1983. Those Regulations also contain certain stated exemptions from the requirement that each copy must be accompanied by a copy of any document referred to in the agreement. Otherwise, every copy would have to be accompanied by a copy of the Consumer Credit Act!

Special formalities for cancellable agreements

The question of which agreements are cancellable will be dealt with presently (paragraph 24–48 below). Section 64 lays down additional formalities for them. Every copy of the agreement given to the debtor or hirer under section 62 or 63 must contain a notice telling him of his right to cancel the agreement and giving the name and address of a person to whom notice of cancellation may be given. That notice of cancellation must be in the form laid down in the Regulations mentioned in the last paragraph.   **24–39**

Also, in the case of an agreement where a second copy need not be sent under section 63 (*i.e.* where the agreement is made on the occasion when the customer signs it), a notice must generally be sent by post to him. The time limit for sending it is the same as applies for the sending of a second copy under section 63. That notice must give the debtor or hirer details of his right of cancellation and the name and address of a person to whom notice of cancellation may be given. This notice too must be in the form prescribed by the Regulations.

Special formalities for second mortgages

Sections 58 and 61(2) are intended to protect the debtor against high pressure sales methods of what are loosely termed second mortgage companies, *i.e.* finance companies who will lend money usually for unrestricted-use to any houseowner provided he gives to the finance company security in the form of a mortgage on his land (*i.e.* his house). This need not in fact be a "second" mortgage but in practice usually will be, because the houseowner will probably have created a first mortgage in order to raise the   **24–40** money to purchase the house. Sections 58 and 61(2) do not apply to any mortgage created specifically to finance the purchase of the land which is in fact mortgaged or to any bridging loan connected with the purchase of land.

The effect of section 58 is that the customer must receive a copy of the prospective agreement in advance of receiving the actual agreement to sign. The copy is for his information for him to think about and is not for him to sign. By section 61(2) the agreement (*i.e.* for his signature) must be sent to him by post but must not be sent until a lapse of at least seven days after the earlier copy was given to him. During that lapse of time the prospective creditor or owner must leave the customer alone to make up his own mind. The creditor must not in any way approach the customer during the interval between delivery of the copy and of the agreement for signature. He must continue to stay away until either a further seven days have elapsed after delivery of the agreement for signature or the customer has signed and returned the agreement.

24–41   The aim and effect of these arrangements is that there may be a reasonable period during which the prospective customer is relieved of the "sales" pressure of the prospective creditor or owner. The length of this consideration period will depend upon whether and when the customer signs and returns the agreement. He will have in any case a minimum of seven days and, if he does not sign and return the agreement, he will have at least a further seven days. During the consideration period, the only circumstance in which the prospective creditor or owner will be entitled to approach the customer will be if the customer has during the consideration period specifically requested him to do so. Furthermore, the advance copy must clearly indicate to the customer his right to withdraw from the prospective agreement. It must contain a notice to this effect in the form laid down in the Consumer Credit (Cancellation Notices and Copies of Documents) Regulations 1983.

The advance copy required to be given by section 58 is in addition to those required by sections 62 and 63 (see paragraphs 24–36 to 24–37 above).

Effect of non-compliance with the requirements

24–42   Any agreement which does not comply with all the formality requirements is "improperly executed". The debtor or hirer will not in any way be penalised for this. Thus he can if he wishes enforce the agreement even if it was never signed or never even put into writing. For example he may wish to claim damages under a hire-purchase agreement for breach of an implied condition that the goods will be of satisfactory quality (see paragraph 25–09 below).

It is the creditor or owner who may find it either impossible or difficult to enforce an improperly executed agreement. He will be entirely unable to enforce it (or any security) if the formality requirements have been infringed in any of the following three respects (section 127):

(i) If the debtor or hirer did not sign the agreement or a document containing certain minimum basic terms of the agreement (set out in schedule 6 of the Consumer Credit (Agreements) Regulations 1983).

(ii) If, in the case of a cancellable agreement, the requirements of section 64 were not complied with, *i.e.* if any copy given to the debtor did not contain the required details of the right of cancellation or if a notice of those rights should have been served separately and was not.

(iii) If, in the case of a cancellable agreement, the creditor has failed to serve the copy (or copies) required by sections 62 and 63 and has also not served, at some time before commencing proceedings, a copy of the fully-signed agreement.

Only in these very restricted situations will it be entirely impossible for the creditor or owner to enforce the agreement. In relation to the first of them, the minimum basic terms required are laid down in Schedule 6 to the Consumer Credit (Agreements) Regulations 1983. These are: a term stating how the debtor or hirer is to discharge his obligations to make payments under the agreement; a term stating any power of the creditor or owner to vary the amount payable; plus (in the case of a credit agreement) the amount of the credit (or the credit limit) and the rate of any interest on the credit. Unless the debtor or hirer signed a document containing at least these minimum basic terms, the creditor or owner cannot enforce the agreement against him. It follows that the creditor or owner will not be able to enforce a purely oral agreement unless that agreement was not subject to the formality requirements. The third situation above can be easily avoided by the simple expedient of the creditor or owner serving

24–43

a copy of the fully signed agreement on the debtor or hirer immediately before commencing proceedings against him.

24-44   Even if the creditor or owner does not find himself in one of the three situations above, he may have some difficulty in enforcing an improperly executed agreement. He can enforce it—but subject to five restrictions:

(i)   He can enforce it only by action in court (section 65).

(ii) He cannot, without an order of the court, retake possession of the goods or land associated with the agreement (even if otherwise he would be entitled to) because that would constitute enforcement of the agreement (section 65).

(iii) He cannot enforce any security except to the extent that the court allows him to enforce the regulated agreement (section 113). This is important where the security is provided otherwise than in the regulated agreement itself, *e.g.* in the case of a guarantor or indemnifier.

(iv) The court has power in granting any order enforcing the agreement:

(a) To reduce or extinguish any sum payable by the debtor or hirer (*i.e.* so as to compensate him for any prejudice caused to him by reason of the default)—(section 127).

(b) To exclude from the contract any term not contained in the signed agreement (section 127).

(c) To impose any conditions (*e.g.* the delivery of a further copy to the hirer) (section 135).

(d) To suspend the operation of an enforcement order or any part of it (*e.g.* until certain conditions have been fulfilled) (section 135).

(e) To amend the agreement as the court considers just (section 136).

These powers, especially those given by sections 135 and 136, are very wide and will enable the court in many cases to wipe out or minimise any prejudice caused to the debtor by the non-compliance with the formalities requirements. For example, in *Rank Xerox Finance v. Hepple and Fennymore* (1994) the county court granted an enforcement order but in doing so significantly reduced the amount of money payable by the customer because the agreement had not fully indicated the charges payable upon default.

(v) Before the court will make any order enforcing the agreement, the creditor or owner will have to convince the court that in view of the non-compliance it is nevertheless just and fair that the order be made. The court must consider to what extent the debtor or hirer has been prejudiced by the non-compliance and to what extent the creditor or owner is to be blamed for it (section 127).

Plainly the court has power to waive purely technical **24–45** infringements of the requirements. Moreover, in view of the wide powers given to the court to minimise the prejudice caused to the debtor or hirer, it would seem unlikely that the court will often refuse to grant an enforcement order. It must of course refuse in the three situations mentioned earlier (paragraph 24–42). One rare situation where the court would be also likely to refuse would be where the creditor or owner has knowingly not complied with the requirements with the deliberate intention of prejudicing the debtor or hirer.

Security

Often the security (if any) will be given by the debtor or hirer. **24–46** In that case the security should be described in the regulated agreement or in a document referred to in the regulated agreement—Consumer Credit (Agreements) Regulations 1983.

However, the position is not so simple where the security is given by another person—in the case of a contract of guarantee or indemnity. As we have seen (paragraph 19–12 above) finance companies quite often demand that someone acts as guarantor or indemnifier of a credit agreement—particularly when the prospective debtor is a young person under about 25. Such a guarantor or indemnifier is often a parent or friend and will normally agree to the arrangement at the request of the debtor or hirer—because otherwise the finance company will not agree to the credit transaction.

On the other hand someone may act as guarantor or indemnifier without any request to do so from the debtor or hirer. Recourse agreements made between finance companies and dealers are examples (see paragraphs 19–11 and 19–12 above). The

Consumer Credit Act applies to security only if given at the request (express or implied) of the debtor or hirer—section 189. Thus a recourse agreement does not have to comply with formalities laid down in the Act and will still be enforceable even though the principal agreement between creditor and debtor did not comply with the formalities requirements.

A guarantor or indemnifier who acted as such at the request (express or implied) of the debtor or hirer is given a considerable measure of protection by the Act. First, where the court refuses or would, if asked, refuse to enforce a regulated credit agreement because it was improperly executed, any security (*i.e.* the guarantee or indemnity) will also be unenforceable (section 113, see paragraph 21–03 above).

24–47 Secondly, certain formalities must be observed in relation to the security (guarantee or indemnity) itself (section 105). The person providing the security (the guarantor or indemnifier) is termed the surety. Section 105 requires the security agreement to be in writing and signed by or on behalf of the surety. It authorises regulations to be made as to the form and contents of the written document and it requires copies of that document and of the principal agreement (the credit agreement) to be given to the surety. Those Regulations are the Consumer Credit (Guarantees and Indemnities) Regulations 1983.

If any of the above formalities are not complied with, the security is "improperly executed" and is not enforceable against the surety except on an order of the court. In deciding whether to make an order to enforce the security, the court has to weigh similar considerations to those it must take into account in deciding whether to enforce an improperly executed regulated agreement. To put it another way, sections 127, 135 and 136 apply in both cases. Thus the court has wide powers to put right any prejudice suffered by the surety (*e.g.* by reduction of any sum payable by the surety or by amending the security document). There is one significant difference. Whereas a regulated agreement which, contrary to the formalities requirements is not in writing or not signed by the debtor is never enforceable (see paragraph 24–42 above), there is no such rigid rule in the case of an unsigned or unwritten security agreement. There is simply the rule that the court must have regard to the prejudice caused to the surety and the degree of culpability of the creditor or owner.

At this stage three notes of warning must be sounded. First, the fact that a security document is improperly executed does not affect the validity or enforceability of the credit agreement to which it relates. The credit agreement is still valid even though the security may be unenforceable. (The same is not true vice versa—section 113 (see paragraph 21–03 above).)

Secondly, the formalities requirements in section 105 of the Consumer Credit Act apply only to security given in relation to a regulated agreement. The third warning is that those formalities (which apply to security whatever form it takes) are in addition to formalities laid down by other Acts of Parliament in relation to particular form of security, *e.g.* the Bills of Sale Acts 1878–1882 (mortgages of goods), the Policies of Assurance Act 1867 and the Law of Property Act 1925, s. 136 (assignment of life assurance policies), and the Statute of Frauds 1677 (guarantees).

CANCELLATION

The cancellation provisions (section 67–73) represent an attempt to combat a particularly undesirable selling technique. Door-to-door salesmen used to persuade people to commit themselves to acquire on credit terms goods or services for which the payments might be crippling and the need for which would seem to recede in the cool light of reason after the salesman had left. At one time, certain encyclopedia salesmen were guilty of this. Thus the cancellation provisions are aimed at what might be termed doorstep credit agreements. Where an agreement is cancellable, the debtor has a short period of a few days in which he may cancel the agreement, even after it has been made. These provisions, therefore, create an important exception to the principle that after a contract is made, neither party can back out of it. A contract not cancellable under these provisions (of the Consumer Credit Act) about to be discussed may be cancellable under either the Consumer Protection (Cancellation of Contracts Concluded away from Business Premises) Regulations 1987 or the Consumer Protection (Distance Selling) Regulations 2000. These two sets of regulations extended the principle of a cooling-off period, respectively, to cash agreements made on the doorstep and to contracts made solely via distance selling (*e.g.* by mail or over the internet). The former are discussed at paragraph 2–19 and the latter at paragraph 16–05 above.

24–48

Cancellable agreements

24–49   Section 67 provides that certain regulated agreements can be cancelled by the debtor or hirer. A regulated agreement is cancellable if two conditions are fulfilled:

(i) The antecedent negotiations included oral representations made when in the presence of the customer by or on behalf of the negotiator. It will be recalled that either the creditor or owner or the dealer may be a negotiator in antecedent negotiations (see paragraph 24–18 above)—though in the case of a consumer hire agreement, the dealer will not be a negotiator in antecedent negotiations: *Lloyds Bowmaker Leasing Ltd v. MacDonald* (1993 Sheriff Court) (and see paragraph 24–28 above).

(ii) The customer signed the agreement elsewhere than at certain business premises—namely those of the creditor or owner, of the dealer and of any party to a linked transaction (other than the customer or his relative).

24–50   The first requirement will be fulfilled in almost any case where the agreement is made after the prospective customer has spoken face to face either with the dealer or with the creditor or owner. It would not of course be fulfilled where the agreement was negotiated by the customer entirely through the post. Suppose the only oral representations made to the customer by the dealer or the creditor or owner were made over the telephone. Here again the first requirement would not be fulfilled. Not every statement made during antecedent negotiations will amount to a "representation" for the purposes of section 67. For example a simple greeting, "Good day", or an inconsequential bit of small talk, "Nice day isn't it?" would not suffice. A statement will amount to a representation for the purposes of section 67 only if it is a statement of fact, or of opinion, or an undertaking as to the future, which is capable of inducing the proposed customer to enter into the regulated agreement: *Moorgate Services Ltd v. Kabir* (1995 CA). It is sufficient if there is at least one such statement made in the presence of the customer during the antecedent negotiations.

The second requirement is fulfilled if the customer signed the agreement away from the business premises mentioned, *e.g.* at his own business premises or at his home. Thus a hire-purchase agreement which the debtor signs at the dealer's premises is not cancellable. On the other hand if, after listening to the dealer's sales talk, the customer takes the agreement away and signs it at home, then the agreement will be cancellable. Thus although the cancellation provisions were aimed at what might loosely be termed "doorstep" credit agreements, their net is cast rather more widely than that.

Two categories of regulated agreement are, however, excluded **24-51** altogether from the cancellation provision:

    (i) An agreement involving a land mortgage or credit restricted to being used to purchase land or a bridging loan in connection with the purchase of land—section 67. There is in these cases no need for a cooling-off period after the agreement is made because as we have seen (paragraph 24-40) the formalities provisions provide for a consideration period before the agreement is made. One reason for these special arrangements is no doubt that it can be difficult to unravel a transaction involving land after that transaction has been completed.

    (ii) Any agreement not subject to the formalities requirements (section 74)—namely, non-commercial agreements, small agreements which are debtor-creditor-supplier agreements for restricted-use credit, and debtor-creditor agreements for overdrafts on current accounts and certain agreements to finance payments arising out of a death. These exclusions are more fully explained at paragraph 24-32 above.

The exclusion of certain small agreements involves the exclusion of a great many credit sale agreements by which housewives buy small household items from mail order firms. However, a good many of these mail order firms expressly include in each credit agreement a term that the customer can cancel it and return the goods within so many days of delivery. In any case, the buyer will be entitled to reject the goods if they do not comply with the conditions as to description and quality, etc., implied by the Sale of Goods Act (see Chapter 7 above).

This raises the important question of who is to bear the expense of returning the goods. If the customer rejects goods for breach of condition then he is under no obligation to pay for their carriage but is entitled to wait for them to be collected. This is also the position where he cancels the agreement under the cancellation provisions of the Consumer Credit Act (or under the Consumer Protection (Cancellation of Contracts Concluded away from Business Premises) Regulations 1987). However, if the agreement is outside those provisions and he cancels under an express term of his agreement, then he may well find that the agreement requires him to be responsible for the carriage of the goods back to the creditor or owner.

Notice of cancellation

24–52   To exercise his right of cancellation the debtor or hirer must serve a written notice indicating his intention of withdrawing from the transaction. The notice of cancellation must be served upon one of the following persons (section 69)—the creditor or owner (or his agent), the person specified in the agreement as being a person to whom such notice may be sent, the dealer, any person who in the course of a business acted on behalf of the customer in negotiations for the agreement. The notice can be sent by post and must be sent or served within the time limit in section 68.

Time limit

24–53   After the debtor or hirer has signed the agreement (or prospective agreement) the cooling-off period during which he can serve a notice of cancellation lasts for several days. By section 68 he can serve the notice any time after he signs and before the end of a period of five clear days. However, that period of five days does not begin until the day after he receives his second copy of the agreement (required by section 63, see paragraph 24–36 above). The day after he receives his second copy is the first of the five days. He may serve his notice of cancellation at any time before that day or on that day or on any of the subsequent four days. If posted on the last of these days it will still be effective even though it does not arrive until later (or even if it never arrives at all)—section 69(7).

The exact cooling-off period available to the debtor or hirer will depend upon how long elapses between him signing the agreement (or prospective agreement) and his receipt of his second copy. It is wrong to refer to it as a five-day or a six-day period, because it will almost always be more than that. The second copy has to be sent to him by post after the making of the agreement and need not be sent until several (maximum seven) days later. Furthermore, the agreement may not have been made until some time after the debtor or hirer signed the prospective agreement (*i.e.* the proposal form).

In those cases where a second copy does not have to be sent under section 63, the five-day period begins on the day after the debtor or hirer receives the notice informing him of his rights of cancellation (required by section 64, see paragraph 24–39 above). It can happen that a second copy is not required under section 63 and also that regulations have been made excusing the creditor or owner from serving a notice of cancellation rights under section 64. In that case the cooling-off period lasts until the end of day 14 after the debtor or hirer signed the agreement—the first of the 14 days being the day after he signed.

Effect of the notice

A distinction is drawn between two categories—on the one hand consumer hire agreements and debtor-creditor-supplier agreements for restricted use credit and, on the other hand, other regulated agreements. Thus the following agreements fall within the first category—all hire-purchase, conditional sale and credit sale agreements and also all trading check agreements and consumer hire agreements. A typical credit card agreement is a multiple agreement and will fall within the first category as regards the provision of goods or services and within the second category as regards the provision of cash. The second category will include most ordinary cash loans. Agreements within the second category are postponed for later consideration and the effect of cancellation of agreements in the first category will now be considered.

24–54

Broadly the position is that the parties are freed from any further commitment in the agreement or in any linked transaction. If the agreement or linked transaction has not been made, *i.e.* the offer to enter it has not been accepted—the notice of cancellation operates as a withdrawal of that offer. If the agreement has been made, it is cancelled. The debtor or hirer must return the goods (if any), can get his money back if he has paid any, and need pay no more money. This broad picture will be qualified and expanded in the following paragraphs. One qualification is that the Consumer Credit (Linked Transactions) (Exemptions) Regulations 1983 exclude certain types of linked transactions from the cancellation provisions—see paragraph 21–32. Apart from that, whenever a regulated agreement is withdrawn from or cancelled, so is any linked transaction. It is upon this latter basis that further details of the effect of cancellation will be given.

24–55   The debtor or hirer (and any relative of his) is under no obligation to make any payment under the agreement or under any linked agreement. Any sums he has already paid are with one exception repayable by the person(s) to whom they were paid. The exception is that any money paid as a fee or commission to a credit broker can be recovered only to the extent that it exceeds £5. Although money which is repayable is always recoverable from the person to whom it was paid, in some situations the debtor will have a choice as to the person from whom he recovers it—either from the creditor or from the supplier. This choice is available in the case of a restricted-use debtor-creditor-supplier agreement where the supplier is not the same person as the creditor, *e.g.* trading voucher agreements. This choice is particularly valuable where either the creditor or supplier has become insolvent.

If the debtor or hirer has traded in other goods in part-exchange, he is entitled to their return in substantially the same condition within 10 days of serving his notice of cancellation. If they are not so returned, he is entitled to a sum equivalent to their part-exchange allowance. He is then entitled to that sum as if he had paid it as cash under the agreement. The choice as to whether to return the part-exchanged goods or to repay the part-exchange allowance is that of the person who took the goods in part-exchange (*i.e.* usually the dealer).

The debtor or hirer can enforce his rights upon cancellation by taking action in the courts. In addition he is given a lien over any goods of which he (or a relative of his) is in possession under the terms of a cancelled agreement (or linked transaction). This enables him to retain those goods until he receives the return of any money to which he is entitled and the return of his part-exchanged goods (or their part-exchange allowance).

24–56   Subject to that lien, section 72 requires the return of certain goods which have been obtained—namely goods of which the debtor or hirer (or his relative) is in possession, under:

(a) a cancelled restricted-use debtor-creditor-supplier agreement relating to goods, or a consumer hire agreement, or

(b) a cancelled linked transaction relating to goods.

The duty imposed on the debtor or hirer (or his relative) by section 72 requires him to take reasonable care of the goods.

Unless he is holding the goods to compel repayment of sums due to him, he must hand them over provided he is requested to do so in writing signed by or on behalf of the supplier or owner of them. He is not under any other duty to return them. In particular he need not transport them or arrange for their carriage and is entitled to wait until they are collected. If he does convey the goods (or send them at his own expense) to the dealer or owner, then that is quite satisfactory and he is discharged from any further obligation. If, 21 days after serving the notice of cancellation, he is still in possession of the goods and has received no written request to return them, he no longer has any obligation to take reasonable care of them. Section 72 does not apply to perishable goods, goods supplied to meet an emergency or goods which before cancellation were consumed or incorporated in something else. One example would be materials (*e.g.* spare parts) used in repairs. These exceptions are necessary because it would generally be unreasonable to expect the debtor to return such goods!

Pause and consider the effect of cancellation from the point of view of the person who has contracted to supply the goods or services. That person may be the creditor (*e.g.* in a credit sale agreement) or he may be the supplier under a linked transaction (*e.g.* the supplier under a trading voucher agreement). Often after cancellation he will be no worse off than if the agreement had never been made. This will be so where at the time of cancellation either he has not provided any goods or services or else he has provided only goods which must after cancellation be returned to him. He will not then be out of pocket because, although he will have to refund any money received, he will not have to provide any goods or services and can recover the goods he has supplied.

However, as we have seen, there are certain special categories   **24–57**
of goods which the debtor need not return. Add to that the fact that the debtor need not return any services he has received. It is then obvious that if before cancellation the supplier has already supplied goods in the special categories or any services, he may well be out of pocket. He will have to refund payments received but will not be able to recover anything (either goods or money) in respect of the goods or services he has supplied. This unfortunate position can for example arise whenever an agreement to provide services on instalment credit (of over £50) is cancelled. Those services could be anything, *e.g.* chimney sweeping, repairing a house or car, landscaping a garden, felling trees,

transporting persons or goods. If such an agreement is cancelled, the debtor is under no obligation either to pay any money or to return any goods incorporated in the house, car or garden (*e.g.* building materials, spare parts or plants). Furthermore he can recover payments already made. Obviously a supplier will try to prevent the situation arising where cancellation can occur after such goods or services have been supplied. He could do this by for example:

(i) Refusing to provide the services or goods on credit terms (and also refusing to allow the agreement under which the goods are supplied to be a linked transaction). This will ensure that the agreement is not a regulated agreement and not affected by the Consumer Credit Act—though it could be cancellable under other legislation (see paragraph 24–48 above).

(ii) Allowing credit terms but insisting that the debtor signs the agreement at the supplier's trade premises. This will ensure that although it is a regulated agreement, it is not a cancellable one.

(iii) Allowing credit terms but making it a condition of the agreement that the goods or services will not be supplied until after the cancellation period has elapsed. In this case the agreement may well be a cancellable one but at the time when cancellation can occur no goods or services will have been provided.

These are entirely reasonable methods for a supplier to protect himself. Nevertheless they are liable to result in the customer being forced either to do without credit or wait for his goods or services. There are two situations where the supplier may understandably fail to adopt any of those methods to protect himself, namely

(i) where goods or services are supplied to meet an emergency, or

(ii) where goods are supplied which, by the act of debtor (or his relative), have before cancellation become incorporated in something else.

By section 69(2) there is a special rule in these two cases to prevent the supplier being out of pocket. Thus although the agreement is cancelled and although no goods or services are returnable, nevertheless the debtor remains liable after cancellation to pay for the services or goods.

We come now to consider the effect of cancellation in the case **24–58** of the second category of agreements referred to earlier, *i.e.* unrestricted-use credit agreements and debtor-creditor agreements. The obvious example is of an ordinary cash loan. The rules applicable are basically the same as those already set out in relation to agreements within the first category—but with one important difference created by section 71. Its effect is that although the agreement is cancelled, the debtor must repay (together with interest) any credit which he has already received. To that there are two slight qualifications. First, no interest is payable on any money which the debtor repays either within one month of cancellation or (if there were to be instalments) before the date of the first instalment. Secondly, in a case where the credit is to be repaid entirely in instalments the debtor is not liable to repay it unless he receives a written, signed request from the creditor which states the remaining instalments. That request must be in the form laid down in the Consumer Credit (Repayment of Credit on Cancellation) Regulations 1983. The debtor is under no duty to pay anything beyond what is specified in section 71. Any other payment, if already made, can be recovered (except the first £5 of any agreed credit broker's fee). The provisions of section 71 requiring repayment of credit already received are only fair since there are no goods obtained under an agreement in this second category which have to be returned— and without the rule in section 71 the debtor would be able to avoid repaying a loan by the simple expedient of cancelling the agreement.

CHAPTER 25

CREDITOR'S LIABILITY IN RESPECT OF THE GOODS OR SERVICES SUPPLIED

A DISTINCTION can be drawn between two types of contractual **25–01** terms—those relating to the credit and its repayment and those relating to the goods or services supplied. It is the latter with which this chapter is concerned. These include terms relating to the quality of the goods supplied, the time of delivery, the title of the seller, etc. Sometimes both types of terms (*i.e.* as to the credit and as to the goods or services supplied) are contained within the same agreement—*i.e.* in the case of hire-purchase, conditional sale and credit sale agreements. Most of this chapter will be devoted to dealing with these agreements. However, first we shall consider those situations where there are two agreements—one relating to the credit and a separate one relating to the supply of goods or services. This occurs for example in the case of a bank loan, a credit card purchase or a trade check purchase. The credit agreement is with one person (the bank or finance company) and the agreement to buy goods or services is with another (the supplier). In relation to the latter agreement two questions arise:

(i) What are the terms of the agreement to buy goods or services?

(ii) To what extent is the creditor (as well as the supplier) liable for breaches of those terms by the supplier?

TERMS OF THE GOODS OR SERVICES AGREEMENT

The debtor may use his credit (be it a bank loan, credit card or **25–02** whatever) to buy either goods or services. If he buys goods, then it will be a contract of sale of goods that he makes with the supplier. The terms of that contract will include those which were discussed in Chapter 7. If he buys services then the terms of the

425

agreement will be those that are expressly agreed between him and the supplier plus any terms that are implied. The terms of a contract for services will therefore vary a great deal according to the type of agreement made. He may buy a package holiday or a cruise, have central heating installed or an extension built, have his garden landscaped or his yacht repaired, etc. All these are contracts for services and the terms expressly agreed or implied will be different in each case. There is no room here to consider them all, but only to make some general observations.

In contracts for services the implied terms will include those implied by the Supply of Goods and Services Act 1982. These were explained in Chapter 8 and the circumstances in which they could be excluded were explained in Chapter 10 (paragraph 10–37). Without repeating the detail it might be useful to recall that the following terms are implied by the Supply of Goods and Services Act 1982:

(i) Where the services are provided in the course of a business, there is an implied term that the work will be done with reasonable care and skill—section 13.

(ii) If no time is mentioned in the contract, then there will usually be an implied condition that the services will be provided and completed within a reasonable length of time—section 14.

(iii) Where the contract involves the supply of some goods, there are implied terms as to title, description, quality and sample which are similar to those in sections 12 to 15 of the Sale of Goods Act—sections 1 to 5 of the 1982 Act.

CREDITOR'S LIABILITY FOR THE SUPPLIER'S BREACH

25–03   We are here concerned with the situation where the debtor has two contracts—a credit agreement with the creditor and a contract with the supplier to buy goods or services. It is a basic common law rule that only a party to a contract can be liable for breach of that contract. Therefore, at common law even if the seller who sells the goods or services is in breach of contract, the buyer will have no remedy against the creditor because the latter was not a party to the contract to sell the goods or services. The buyer will have a remedy only against the seller.

However, section 75 has made a considerable inroad into this rule. This section, which applies to debtor-creditor-supplier agreements, has already been quoted in connection with misrepresentation (see paragraphs 24–24 and 24–26). Section 75 provides that if the debtor has "any claim against the supplier in respect of a misrepresentation or breach of contract, he shall have a like claim against the creditor". Thus the debtor can bring the claim against the seller or the creditor or both. Take an example: X uses his credit card to buy an armchair (cash price £145) from a shop. The armchair is not of satisfactory quality and collapses, causing X some injury. By virtue of section 75, X can sue the credit card company (as well as the shop) for damages for injury and damage caused. This right to sue the creditor could be very valuable in the situation where the shop has become insolvent. If X exercises his right to claim against the creditor, the creditor (the credit card company) can claim against the supplier under a right of indemnity. The effect of section 75 is therefore that it is the creditor who stands the risk of the supplier becoming insolvent.

Turning briefly to the new debit cards used in conjunction with Electronic Funds Transfer, these debit card agreements, unlike credit card agreements, are debtor-creditor agreements (see paragraph 21–23 above). Thus section 75 does not apply to them because it applies only to debtor-creditor-supplier agreements.

As just observed, section 75 applies only in the case of a debtor-creditor-supplier agreement, *i.e.* broadly, where there is some business connection between the creditor and supplier, as in the example of Shiver, Warmitup Ltd and Hotmoney Ltd given at paragraph 21–22 above. However, there are two further restrictions upon the operation of the section. First, it does not apply to a non-commercial agreement. Secondly, it does not apply to a claim in respect of "any single item to which the supplier has attached a cash price not exceeding £100 or more than £30,000". So, if X, as well as buying an armchair, had used his credit card to buy a hot water bottle which had burst and ruined his bed, he could not make a claim for that damage against the credit card company because the hot water bottle will not have had a cash price in excess of £100. That is so even if the damage caused was in excess of £100. X would of course still have his remedies against the seller. Section 75 applies to items having a cash price of over £100 but not over £30,000. Of course if the debtor's agreement provided him with fixed-sum credit which exceeded £25,000, the credit agreement would not be a regulated

25–04

one and section 75 would not apply. Section 75 could well apply, however, where a debtor has a regulated agreement providing him with, say, £25,000 worth of credit to help him buy an item having a cash price of £40,000.

25–05   Section 75 probably can not be relied upon by any credit card holder who made his credit card agreement before July 1, 1977. (Similarly, section 56 probably cannot be relied upon by a card holder who made his credit card agreement before April 1, 1977). It seems unlikely, however, that many credit card agreements made so long ago are still active. Thus for a full explanation readers are referred to the fifth edition of this book and to [1978] New L.J. 448.

Whenever a regulated credit card agreement was made, a complication arises where there is a second authorised user. This occurs where someone with a credit card agreement has as part of that agreement an arrangement whereby a second person (often husband or wife) has a card which can be used on the same account. The latter person, the authorised user, is not, however, made liable to pay the debts incurred. Thus there is one account and one person liable to make repayments on that account, but there are two card holders each able to draw on the account. Where it is the authorised user who has used his card on the purchase in question, can that authorised user rely on section 75 in the same way as if he were the principal card holder? Exactly the same question could be asked in relation to section 56 and the answer is exactly the same. At first sight the answer appears to be no, since the wording of both sections makes it clear that they operate only in favour of the *debtor*. Imagine a wife, Joan, who is authorised user of a card on her husband's, Darby's, account. Suppose she uses the card to pay £200 for a coat from Bill's shop. She is clearly the person who makes a contract with Bill's shop. (It is a sale of goods contract—see paragraph 8–05 above.) She is not acting as her husband's agent in making that contract but is clearly herself buying the coat. If the coat is not fit to wear, it is she who has a claim against Bill for the coat not being of satisfactory quality. Is she, perhaps, Darby's agent in using the credit card to debit his credit card account? If she is, then could he (instead of her) rely on the sections? The answer still appears to be no. In relation to section 75, the debtor is given a right to bring against the creditor any claim which he could have brought against the supplier, but *Darby* has no claim against Bill. Joan's problem is that sections 56 and 75 confer rights only on the debtor and the debtor is Darby. In order to succeed under either section, Joan needs to show that she too is a debtor. Perhaps she can. The word "debtor" in the Act does not have the simple meaning of someone who owes a debt. It means the "individual receiving credit under a consumer credit agreement"—section 189(1). Presumably Joan got her card (of which she is the authorised user) by agreement of the credit card company. In that case the card company in making the agreement with her provided her with a financial accommodation, credit upon which she can draw. If that is so, the credit card company has a credit agreement with Darby and also has one with Joan. The difficulty with that is that if the card company has provided a financial accommodation to Joan, then one would have expected Joan to have to be responsible for repaying any credit she draws. It is surely much more accurate to say that in letting Joan have a card on Darby's account, the card company has granted a further financial accommodation to Darby and that Joan when she uses her card is actually acting as Darby's agent to pledge *his* credit. The plain fact is that the legal position of the second authorised card holder needs clarifying, preferably by an amendment to section 75. Clearly, as matter of policy, the law *should* be that the second authorised card holder has exactly the same rights against the credit card company as if she had been the principal card holder. (For a fuller discussion of the position of the second authorised card holder see [1994] Sol. Jo. 1212.)

Leaving the problem of the second authorised card holder, we can turn to another situation in which the card companies have sought to avoid liability under section 75. This is where the card holder has used his card to make a purchase abroad. The contract of purchase abroad may be governed by the law of the country (*e.g.* Japan) in which that purchase occurs. Nevertheless the credit card agreement, if made in England between a card issuer in England and a card holder resident in England, will be governed by English law, including section 75. It should still be possible first to discover whether the card holder has a claim against the supplier (*i.e.* according to whatever law governs the supply contract) and secondly to hold the card issuing company jointly and severally liable for that claim. The credit card companies' attempts to avoid section 75 liability in respect of transactions when the card is used abroad are in each case a "try on".

25–06

In *Porter v. General Guarantee Corporation* (1982 QB) Kilner Brown J. said in relation to a hire-purchase agreement that section 75 was relevant. He was plainly wrong. In fact section 75 does not apply to hire-purchase, conditional sale and credit sale

25–07

agreements. This is, after all, only common sense, since in these cases there are in the credit agreement itself terms relating to the delivery, description and quality of the goods; and if one of those terms is broken the creditor will in any case be liable for what is his own breach of contract. Where a finance company makes a hire-purchase, conditional sale or credit sale agreement with the debtor, the finance company buys the goods from the dealer and contracts with the debtor to supply the goods to the debtor. Thus the finance company supplies the goods on credit terms to the debtor.

25–08   The situation is different, however, where the finance company does not itself buy the goods and then supply them to the debtor, but instead lends the debtor the money to enable the debtor himself to buy the goods direct from the dealer. In this situation the agreement between the finance company and the debtor is not a hire-purchase, conditional sale or credit sale agreement. It is simply a loan contract. If the loan contract is a regulated debtor-creditor-supplier agreement (*i.e.* made as a result of business arrangements between the dealer and the finance company), section 75 will apply. That was the situation in the Scottish case, *United Dominions Trust v. Taylor* (1980) where a finance company lent money to Mr Taylor to enable him to buy a car from Parkaway Cars. The finance company brought proceedings against him to enforce the loan agreement. He based his defence on section 75. He said he had a claim against Parkaway Cars for breach of contract and for misrepresentation because the car had been misrepresented to be in a good condition when in fact it was unroadworthy. It was held that this, if proved, gave him a good defence under the loan agreement. Where the debtor had a right to rescind the supply contract (*i.e.* his contract of sale of goods with Parkaway Cars), he had under section 75 a "like claim" against the finance company; a "like claim" meant a claim to rescind the loan agreement (for an analysis of this case, see [1981] J.B.L. 179). In this situation, where the customer has obtained the loan to buy the car and then rescinds his two contracts, *i.e.* with the dealer and the creditor, then of course he must return the car to the dealer, but presumably the creditor and dealer are left to sort out between them the return by the dealer to the creditor of the loan which the customer had used to buy the car. Despite a certain amount of academic criticism, the decision in *U.D.T. v. Taylor* was followed in another Scottish case, *Forward Trust Ltd v. Hornsby* (1996).

For the general criticism of the policy behind section 75, see [1978] New L.J. 703.

HIRE-PURCHASE

We now come to the terms as to title, description, quality, **25–09** sample and delivery which are implied in hire-purchase agreements. First, a few words must be said about terminology. Traditionally the parties to a hire-purchase agreement have been called "hirer" and "owner". These are the words that have usually appeared in the agreement itself and they therefore have also tended to be used in the judgments of decided cases. However, the Consumer Credit Act has brought about a change. That Act and other Acts of Parliament now use the words "debtor" and "creditor" to describe the parties. This change of terminology has not changed the essential nature of a hire-purchase contract. The debtor under a hire-purchase agreement will still be the hirer of goods with an option to purchase them. Many finance companies continue to use the old terminology in their hire-purchase agreements. There is nothing wrong with that and it is not inaccurate. Indeed it serves to make it clear that the agreement is a hire-purchase agreement and not a credit sale agreement or some other kind of credit agreement. In this chapter, however, the new terminology will be used.

The written hire-purchase agreement seldom contains many terms securing the debtor's interest. Indeed, in the past, such agreements have often included exemption clauses designed to prevent the debtor being able to make a claim for the creditor's breach of the agreement. Parliament has stepped in to protect the interests of debtors. The position is regulated by the Supply of Goods (Implied Terms) Act 1973 and the Unfair Contract Terms Act 1977. The relevant sections of the 1973 Act are sections 8–11 and these apply to all hire-purchase agreements irrespective of whether they are regulated agreements. They imply terms relating to title, description, quality and sample. The Unfair Contract Terms Act 1977 severely restricts the creditor's ability to exclude his liability.

The Supply of Goods (Implied Terms) Act implies terms into hire-purchase agreements which are virtually identical to the corresponding terms implied in sale of goods contracts. The result is that, whether a customer buys goods or whether he takes them on hire-purchase terms, his rights as to title, description, quality and sample are the same. Apart from necessary changes of wording, sections 8, 9, 10 and 11 are identical to sections 12, 13, 14 and 15 of the Sale of Goods Act. Since the latter sections have been considered in detail in Chapter 7, sections 8–11 of the 1973 Act will be considered here only to the extent that there are matters specially relevant to hire-purchase contracts.

Terms implied in a hire-purchase contract at common law have in large measure been rendered redundant and superseded by the terms implied by the 1973 Act. Nevertheless in one or two instances they may be significant and this will be seen as the chapter proceeds—particularly in relation to delivery and acceptance.

Title

25–10   Section 8 of the Supply of Goods (Implied Terms) Act 1973 is virtually identical to section 12 of the Sale of Goods Act. Section 8(1)(a) reads:

> "(1) In every hire-purchase agreement, other than one to which subsection (2) below applies, there is—
>
>> (a) an implied condition on the part of the creditor that he will have a right to sell the goods at the time when the property is to pass."

In hire-purchase contracts, it is usually some time before property passes to the debtor. Property will not pass until the debtor exercises his option to buy and that option will not be exercisable until he has paid all his instalments. Provided the creditor has the right to sell the goods at the time the debtor exercises his option, the creditor is not in breach of the condition in section 8(1)(a).

However, there are three other grounds upon which the creditor may be liable unless he has the right to sell much earlier than the time at which the debtor exercises his option. The first ground is breach of the condition implied by the common law as to title— namely that the creditor will have good title to the goods at the time when the debtor takes delivery. In the situation where goods are handed over as soon as the agreement is made, the creditor must have good title right from the start. On the other hand, where the goods are not to be delivered until some time after the making of the agreement, the creditor will not be in breach of the condition provided he acquires good title to the goods before the debtor takes delivery of them. *Mercantile Guarantee v. Wheatley* (1938 KB) concerned an agreement made by a finance company on February 7 to let out a lorry on hire-purchase terms. On that date the finance company did not own the lorry but subsequently purchased it on February 11. Thus the finance company had good title when, on March 8, the debtor took delivery of the lorry. Goddard J. held that the common law condition as to title was not broken since the relevant time was when the goods were delivered.

The second ground of possible liability of the creditor who does not have the right to sell the goods is for breach of an express term of the agreement. *Barber v. NWS Bank* (1996 CA) involved an agreement which included an express term that until full payment the property in the goods should remain vested in the creditor. It was conceded that this amounted to an express term that at the time of the contract the creditor had good title and it was held that this amounted to a condition of the contract. The case involved a conditional sale agreement but the law is the same in the case of hire-purchase.

25–11

The other ground of possible liability of the creditor who does not have the right to sell the goods is breach of the warranty implied by section 8(1)(b) of the Supply of Goods (Implied Terms) Act—the warranty of quiet possession and freedom from undisclosed charges or encumbrances. This warranty relates to the period of hire, *i.e.* the period before the debtor exercises his option to buy. The warranty of quiet possession (as in sale of goods) also relates to the future, *i.e.* after the debtor has exercised his option and acquired ownership in the goods (see *Microbeads v. Vinhurst Road Markings*, paragraph 7–25 above).

Breach of a condition as title—whether the one implied by section 8(1)(a) or the one implied by the common law or an express one—gives the debtor the right to treat the contract as repudiated and to reclaim all the payments he has made. The reason he can recover all his payments is that he can be said to have suffered a total failure of consideration. This is just a way of saying that the law regards him as having received no benefit from the contract. Because he has received no benefit, he can recover the whole amount that he has paid. We saw in Chapter 7 that this was the position in sale of goods when the seller is in breach of the condition as to title in section 12 of the Sale of Goods Act, *i.e.* the buyer can recover the whole price he has paid (*Rowland v. Divall*). *Rowland v. Divall* has been followed in a hire-purchase case, *Warman v. Southern Counties Finance* (1949 KB). The facts in the latter case were that the debtor had paid all instalments and had enjoyed the use of the goods for some

25–12

months before having to surrender them to their true owner. Finnemore J. said that the true basis of a hire-purchase agreement was that the debtor should be able to acquire ownership of the goods. The debtor was unable to acquire ownership and his Lordship held that therefore the debtor had suffered a total failure of consideration and was entitled to the return of all his payments. The result, as in *Rowland v. Divall*, was that the plaintiff enjoyed the use of the goods for some months at no cost to himself. The basis of these decisions—that the plaintiff derived no benefit from the contract—would appear questionable! Nevertheless these cases, both decisions at first instance, were approved and followed by the Court of Appeal in *Barber v. NWS Bank* (1996).

25–13   The situation could come about that a creditor is in breach of a condition as to title but subsequently manages to cure his defect in title. He could do this, for example, by buying the goods from their true owner. If this occurs whilst the debtor is still enjoying the use of the goods, then the debtor will not subsequently be able to treat the contract as repudiated: *Butterworth v. Kingsway Motors* (see paragraph 7–19 above). Also he will not suffer a total failure of consideration, since the creditor will now be able to give him good title—even if a little belatedly. He will therefore not be able to reclaim all his payments. His claim will be simply for damages for the fact that he did not obtain good title as soon as he should have done. If the creditor cures his defect in title before property is to pass to the debtor, *i.e.* before payment of the final instalment—then the debtor will suffer no delay in obtaining good title. He will acquire it at exactly the time that he should do so, *i.e.* on exercising his option. In this case he will be entitled only to nominal damages. Thus the debtor who discovers that his creditor is in breach of a condition as to title would be well advised to treat the contract as repudiated immediately, *i.e.* before the creditor cures his defect in title. If the debtor does this, he will be able to recover all his payments. If, instead, he waits until after the defect is cured, he may be reduced to a claim for nominal damages. His method of treating the contract as repudiated is to inform the creditor that he rejects the goods and regards the contract as repudiated.

Description

25–14   Section 9 of the Supply of Goods (Implied Terms) Act is virtually identical to section 13 of the Sale of Goods Act. Section 9 reads:

"(1) Where under a hire-purchase agreement goods are bailed or (in Scotland) hired by description, there is an implied term that the goods will correspond with the description, and if under the agreement the goods are bailed or hired by reference to a sample as well as a description, it is not sufficient that the bulk of the goods corresponds with the sample if the goods do not also correspond with the description.

(1A) As regards England and Wales and Northern Ireland, the term implied by subsection (1) above is a condition.

(2) Goods shall not be prevented from being bailed by description by reason only that, being exposed for sale, bailment or hire, they are selected by the person to whom they are bailed or hired."

Where the debtor has agreed to take the goods as a result of a previous inspection, the creditor's obligation may be greater than merely to see that the goods match the description in the written agreement. As Denning L.J. said in *Karsales v. Wallis* (1965 CA),

"When the hirer has himself previously seen and examined the [item] and made application for hire-purchase on the basis of his inspection, there is an obligation on the lender to deliver the [item] in substantially the same condition as when it was seen. It makes no difference that the lender is a finance company which bought the [item] in the interval without seeing it."

The facts in that case were that the debtor had inspected at the dealer's premises a roadworthy Buick car which, after he had made the usual hire-purchase agreement with the finance company, was delivered to him in such a deplorable condition that it was incapable of self propulsion without a major overhaul. The Court of Appeal held the creditor liable for what was in fact a fundamental breach of its obligation—so radically different was the car from that which the debtor had contracted to take.

Quality

Again, section 10 of the Supply of Goods (Implied Terms) Act **25–15** is, apart from changes of wording necessary to make it apply to hire-purchase agreements, identical to section 14 of the Sale of Goods Act.

It may be remembered that the condition that the goods be reasonably fit for a particular purpose is not implied unless that particular purpose, for which the goods are required, is made known before the contract is made. By section 10 it is sufficient that the debtor makes it known either to the creditor or to the negotiator in antecedent negotiations. Thus it is sufficient that he tells the dealer for what purpose he requires the goods. The same is true of a sale of goods contract (*e.g.* a credit sale or conditional sale agreement) by virtue of section 14(3)(b) of the Sale of Goods Act (see paragraph 25–23). This rule does not, however, apply where the debtor is a corporate body, *e.g.* a limited company. Here the particular purpose for which the debtor requires the goods must be made known to the *creditor* before the contract is made. That is so in the case both of hire-purchase contracts and also of sale of goods contracts. (For an explanation of all this see [1983] J.B.L. 312.)

The conditions as to satisfactory quality and fitness for purpose are exactly the same in hire-purchase contracts as they are in contracts of sale of goods.

Sample

25–16   The same can be said of the conditions relating to the hire-purchase of goods by reference to a sample. There is no significant difference between section 11 of the Supply of Goods (Implied Terms) Act and section 15 of the Sale of Goods Act.

Delivery and payment

25–17   There are no statutory implied terms relating to delivery and acceptance. That leaves us to consider what terms are implied at common law. There is a lack of authority but there seems no reason to suppose that the terms are any different from those in sale of goods.

Thus, in the absence of any contrary agreement by the parties, it is the creditor's duty to hand over the goods upon demand, *i.e.* it is up to the debtor to collect them and it is not the creditor's obligation to arrange transport for the goods. If the goods are known to be at the premises of a third party, then those premises will be the place of delivery, *i.e.* it is from the dealer's premises that the debtor must collect them.

If the creditor refuses to deliver (*i.e.* to hand over) the goods, that is a breach of condition and the debtor can treat the contract as repudiated and reclaim any money paid and also claim damages (if he has suffered any).

Where the subject matter of the hire-purchase agreement is a second-hand motor vehicle, the creditor is under an obligation also to hand over the registration document. In *Bentworth Finance v. Lubert* (1968 CA) Lord Denning M.R. said of the debtor,

> "She was entitled to say 'Produce the log book. Until you do, there is no contract'. There may, of course, be circumstances in which the condition may be waived by taking delivery of the car and using it."

The debtor is under a duty to accept the goods, provided that those supplied fulfil the contract. When he fails to do so, the proper remedy for the creditor is not to claim arrears of instalments but to claim damages for the debtor's failure to take delivery: *N.C.R. v. Stanley* (1921). The measure of damages is the same as that in sale of goods—*Inter-office Telephones v. Freeman* (1958 CA), *i.e.* the loss arising naturally from the breach of contract. Thus the creditor will be able to recover his loss of profit on the transaction. That loss will normally include: **25-18**

    (a) the difference between the creditor's purchasing price and the retail cash price of the goods, and

    (b) the creditor's lost finance charges, *i.e.* the extra profit he would have made by disposing of the goods on instalment terms instead of by a cash sale.

However, if the debtor had gone through with the hire-purchase agreement, the creditor would have received his profit over a period of time. Thus, when awarding damages to the creditor for loss of profit the court will make a deduction to take account of the fact that the creditor is then receiving his profit immediately in one lump sum, *i.e.* earlier than he otherwise would have received it.

Remedies

Broadly speaking, the remedies are similar to those in sale of goods. Thus where the creditor is in breach of a warranty the only remedy normally available to the debtor is to sue for damages. Where the creditor is in breach of condition, the debtor has, in addition to a claim for damages, a right to treat the **25-19** contract as repudiated and reclaim money that he has paid. As in sale of goods, the method of treating the contract as repudiated is either to refuse to take delivery of the goods or, if delivery has already been taken, to reject them. He can reject them simply by informing the creditor that he does so. Just as in sale of goods, a debtor who is not dealing as a consumer will not have a right to reject for a breach of an implied condition as to description, satisfactory quality, fitness for purpose or as to sample, if the breach is so slight that it would unreasonable to reject the goods. For this purpose someone buying in the course of a business is not dealing as a consumer (see paragraphs 10–21 to 10–23).

25–20   We saw in Chapter 13 that in sale of goods the right to treat a breach of condition as having repudiated the contract is lost when the buyer "accepts" the goods (section 11(4) of the Sale of Goods Act). When that occurs, the buyer can treat the breach of condition only as if it were a breach of warranty and it follows that his only remedy is a claim for damages. In hire-purchase law there is no exact equivalent to section 11(4) of the Sale of Goods Act. However, there is a somewhat similar rule that, if after the breach of condition, the debtor affirms the contract, he will then be able to treat it only as a breach of warranty. In sale of goods, we saw that the buyer may be taken to have accepted goods if after a fairly short time he has not indicated that he is rejecting them. It may be that in hire-purchase rather more time has to elapse before he will be taken to have affirmed the contract. In any case, if he returns the goods requiring them to be repaired that is quite likely to be interpreted as not being an affirmation. In *Farnworth Finance Facilities v. Attryde* (1970) the subject-matter of the hire-purchase agreement was a new motor cycle. After taking delivery, Mr Attryde found that the motor cycle had a lot of defects and he repeatedly returned it to be put right. The repairs were never satisfactory and eventually, when the rear chain broke, he rejected the cycle. Up to this time he had had the cycle for four months and had driven it some 4,000 miles. Nevertheless the Court of Appeal held that he had not in fact affirmed the contract. His conduct indicated rather the reverse— namely that he was prepared to affirm the contract only if the defects were remedied. It followed that he was within his rights when he rejected the cycle, thereby treating the contract as repudiated. It was further held that he was entitled to recover all of the payments that he had made. No deduction was made for the use he had had of the cycle because that was offset by the inconvenience caused by the defects.

It used to be thought that in hire-purchase, if the debtor **25–21** affirmed the contract and the goods remained unfit for their purpose (or otherwise in breach of condition) after the affirmation, the debtor's right to reject the goods revived. This, however, is not so: *U.C.B. Leasing Ltd v. Holtom* (1987 CA). Once the debtor has affirmed the contract, he has lost for good his right to reject. If he subsequently rejects the goods or otherwise repudiates the contract, he will himself be in breach and liable to pay damages to the creditor. This may not be as disastrous for the debtor as at first appears. It is true that if the goods are not of satisfactory quality (or the creditor is in breach of some other condition) affirmation by the debtor removes the debtor's right to reject the goods. Nevertheless the debtor will still be able to claim damages for that breach of contract. So when the debtor is sued by the creditor for damages for wrongful rejection, the debtor has a counterclaim. The amount of that counterclaim will be assessed on the basis that the debtor is entitled to recover as damages all of his payments already made and all his outstanding liabilities to the creditor. The only deduction that will be made will be in respect of such use as the debtor has had of the goods before they were rejected. In *Charterhouse Credit Co. Ltd v. Tolly* (1963 CA) he was awarded the total of his initial deposit, *the damages awarded to the hire purchase company on its claim* and the cost of new tyres he had had fitted to the car, less a small deduction for the slight use he had had of the car. The same principles were applied in *U.C.B. Leasing Ltd v. Holtom*, where the sum awarded to the debtor included also an amount for inconvenience and distress. These were caused by the fact that, during the time the debtor had it, the car had persistent electrical problems, sometimes suffering a complete electrical failure, which on a couple of frightening occasions could have led the debtor to have an extremely serious accident.

Exclusion

The law relating to exemption clauses in hire-purchase **25–22** contracts is the same as that relating to those in contracts of sale of goods. The common law rules are equally applicable. The Unfair Contract Terms Act 1977 applies to hire-purchase agreements in precisely the same way as it does to contracts of sale of goods. The statutory terms implied by sections 8–11 of the Supply of Goods (Implied Terms) Act are dealt with in exactly the same way as the terms implied in contracts of sale by sections 12–15 of the Sale of Goods Act. There is the same distinction between "consumer deals" and others—the distinction having exactly the same effect.

CREDIT SALE AND CONDITIONAL SALE

25–23   A credit sale agreement is a contract of sale of goods and the terms implied in it are those implied into any other contract of sale of goods. In particular sections 10–15 of the Sale of Goods Act apply equally to credit sale agreements as to other sales. So also do the provisions of the Unfair Contract Terms Act 1977.

One thing explained in relation to hire-purchase (see paragraph 25–15 above) was that, in connection with the statutory implied condition as to fitness for purpose, it is sufficient that the debtor has told the dealer (*i.e.* the negotiator in antecedent negotiations) the particular purpose for which the goods were required. The same is true in relation to contracts of sale of goods. This is the effect of certain words in section 14(3) of the Sale of Goods Act—which words were omitted at paragraph 7–43 above.

With one exception, sections 10–15 of the Sale of Goods Act also apply to conditional sale agreements as they do to credit sale agreements. The exception is that section 11(4) of the Sale of Goods Act does not apply to conditional sale agreements which are "consumer deals" (see paragraph 10–21 above). Thus in these types of agreement the right to reject the goods for breach of condition is not lost by the buyer "accepting" them. This is the effect of section 14 of the Supply of Goods (Implied Terms) Act. Instead, the position is as in hire-purchase agreements. Thus the right to treat the contract as repudiated may be lost not by "acceptance" but by affirmation.

CHAPTER 26

ENFORCEMENT BY THE CREDITOR OR OWNER

THIS chapter falls into three parts. The first part deals with the broad principles of enforcement, the second with subsidiary matters which may affect the enforceability of the credit agreement and the third with provisions relating to the enforcement of security.   **26–01**

BROAD PRINCIPLES OF ENFORCEMENT

This is the most important part of the chapter and deals with certain provisions of the Act which apply to all regulated agreements. Running through them all is Parliament's intention to protect the debtor from harsh terms in the agreement and generally to ensure that he receives fair treatment.   **26–02**

County court

Any court action by the creditor or owner to enforce the agreement or any security for it must be brought in the county court—section 141. Not only must the debtor or hirer be made a party to the proceedings but so also must any surety. While the action is still undecided the court can, on application by the creditor, make any order it thinks just for protecting any property of the creditor or owner, or any property which is subject to any security, from damage or depreciation.   **26–03**

Payment ahead of time

The debtor under a regulated consumer credit agreement is entitled to discharge his debt ahead of time whenever he wishes by giving written notice to the creditor and making full payment of all his payments due under the agreement (section 94). Early payment by the debtor of all sums payable under the agreement will mean that if the agreement is a hire-purchase or conditional   **26–04** sale agreement, the debtor will become the owner of the goods at an earlier date than he otherwise would.

The Consumer Credit (Rebate on Early Settlement) Regulations 1983 provide for a rebate to a debtor who pays off his debt ahead of time. The rebate is calculated according to the Regulations or according to the terms of the agreement, whichever give the higher rebate. The amount required to discharge the debt under section 94 is reduced by the amount of the rebate.

Payment behind time

26–05   It is not uncommon for a debtor to be late in paying off his debt or some instalments of it. In these circumstances the creditor does not receive his money as soon as he ought to. It is quite possible for the agreement to state that in that event the creditor shall be entitled to an additional payment as interest for the period of the delay. However, that interest must not be at a rate higher than that which the debtor was already paying under the agreement. If the agreement stipulates for a higher rate to be payable on default, the creditor will be able to recover only interest calculated at the rate payable under the contract as a whole—section 93.

Extortionate agreements

26–06   Sections 137–140 lie at the very heart of the Act. They apply to personal credit agreements whether or not they are regulated agreements (*e.g.* even if the credit exceeds £25,000). They empower the court on application by the debtor (or a surety) to reopen an extortionate credit agreement. Separate proceedings can be brought to make an application or the application can be made as a form of defence to an action by the creditor to enforce the agreement or any security. Where the debtor (or any surety) alleges that the credit bargain is extortionate, the burden of proof rests upon the creditor to prove the contrary—section 171(7). In 1999 the DTI commissioned some research as a result of which it issued a discussion paper in 2000 in which it proposed a change in the law to enable the court itself (without any application by the debtor) to initiate the re-opening of a credit agreement in proceedings, including undefended proceedings, against the debtor or a surety—though this would not be possible if the debtor or surety objected. This proposal is a response to some concern that the current provisions do not adequately safeguard vulnerable consumers against the charging of unjust interest rates.

A credit bargain is extortionate if (section 138) it requires the debtor or a relative of his to make payments which are "grossly exorbitant" or if the agreement in some other way "grossly contravenes ordinary principles of fair dealing". In deciding whether an agreement is extortionate, the court must take into account the interest rates prevailing at the time the agreement was made. It must also take into account "any other relevant considerations", some of which are set out in section 138.

The rate of interest is obviously a prime consideration. Clearly rates of interest will vary from agreement to agreement as well as from time to time. Some types of agreement will always incorporate a greater rate of interest than other types. It is important therefore to compare like with like; to compare the true annual rate of interest payable under the agreement in question with the true annual rate of interest payable generally under agreements of that type made at that time. So, for example, an annual rate of interest, say, of 104 per cent would be exorbitant in the case of a hire-purchase agreement. Nevertheless, it would seem quite reasonable to charge £2 interest on a loan granted at short notice of £100 for one week—even though that would in fact represent an annual rate of interest exceeding 104 per cent! There is no set rate of interest beyond which any agreement is automatically taken to be extortionate. It is always a question of fact in all the circumstances of the particular transaction. In determining that question the court will look not just at payments due under the credit agreement itself but also at any other payments which enter into the total charge for credit (*e.g.* those payable under certain linked transactions). The question is whether the bargain as a whole (*i.e.* including all transactions which are to be taken into account in computing the total charge for credit) is extortionate. For an account of those transactions which are to be taken into account in computing the total charge for credit see paragraphs 21–35 to 21–38 above.

As well as interest rates, other relevant considerations must be **26–07** taken into account. Take an extreme example—it has to be extreme to satisfy the word "grossly". A frail old lady whose only income is a state pension and whose eyesight is failing is frightened by a door-to-door canvasser into entering and signing an agreement whereby her house is to be treated for woodworm for a price which is higher than that normally charged and is to be paid over a period of three years by instalments which she cannot afford. Factors which would be relevant here are the old lady's age, her lack of business experience, her general state of health and her failing eyesight as well as the degree of sales pressure exerted upon her and the extent to which the effect of the agreement was explained to her. The reader can no doubt imagine other considerations which may be relevant.

Sections 137–140 should be seen as a long stop or safety net to protect the debtor who requires protection but otherwise would have none.

When the court does decide to reopen a credit agreement, it has wide powers (section 139(2)) to relieve the debtor or a surety from payment of any sum in excess of what is "fairly due and reasonable". Not only can the court alter the terms of the agreement and set aside or reduce the obligations of the debtor or surety but it can even require the creditor to repay money already paid under the agreement. It can do this even if the creditor has not received that money, for example, if under a hire-purchase agreement the debtor has paid a deposit to the dealer which the dealer has not transmitted to the finance company (*i.e.* the creditor).

The general rules on limitation, stated in the Limitation Act 1980, apply to applications to re-open an extortionate credit bargain. How they apply is currently a matter of some controversy, discussed in an article at (1998) 142 S.J. 274. Two propositions advanced in that article are now confirmed by the decision in *Rahman v. Sterling Credit Ltd* (2000 CA). First, where the debtor makes an application (which is not merely a defence to a claim by the creditor) to have the agreement amended or his obligation to pay reduced, the period within which he must bring the claim is 12 years starting with the making of the credit agreement (Limitation Act 1980, section 8). Secondly, where he claims a repayment of money already paid, the period is six years (Limitation Act, section 9). Two issues, however, remain to be determined. They *should* be determined as follows: (i) the six years period just referred to starts when the debtor's cause of action accrued, which is when he made the payment which he know seeks to have repaid; (ii) there is no limitation period at all when the debtor's application to have the credit bargain re-opened is simply a defence to a claim by the creditor to enforce the agreement.

Alternative legislative provisions

26–08   Where a debtor is unable to persuade a court to re-open an agreement as being extortionate, he may nevertheless be able to challenge the agreement, or part of it, under other provisions.

Firstly, where the court makes any order under the Act, it has a supplementary power under section 136 to amend the agreement "in consequence of a term of the order". This can, for example, involve reducing the rate of interest, when a time order is granted. Section 136 is discussed at paragraph 26–23 below.

Secondly a contract term can be challenged as being an unfair term under the Unfair Terms in Consumer Contracts Regulations 1999. These regulations were explained at paragraph 10–39 above. Under them the consumer cannot challenge the validity of a core term (*e.g.* one which sets the interest rate under the agreement) but can challenge other terms. In *Director General of Fair Trading v. First National Bank* (2000) the Court of Appeal found a clause to be unfair which had the effect of denying the court the opportunity of considering whether to exercise its power, under section 136, to reduce the contractual rate of interest. For details of this case, see section 136 at paragraph 26–24 below. In *Falco Finance Ltd v. Gough* (1999) a County Court had to consider three aspects of a £30,000 mortgage loan agreement: (i) a "dual rate" clause by which a "concessionary" rate of interest, lower than the normal contractual rate, was charged unless and until the debtor fell into arrears at any point, in which event the normal contractual rate would be payable for the rest of the term of the loan; (ii) a clause providing for a rebate of charges on early repayment to be calculated as if the repayment took place six months later than in reality; (iii) a clause providing for the interest payable under the agreement to be calculated on a "flat rate" basis. Whereas only the first was found to be extortionate, all three clauses were found to be "unfair" within the Unfair Terms in Consumer Contract Regulations—despite the fact that the last of the three appears to be a core term.

Default notice

Section 87 operates where the debtor is in breach of the **26–09** agreement. Its effect is to prevent the creditor from pursuing certain remedies unless and until a default notice has first been served upon the debtor giving him a chance to put right his default. The remedies which the creditor is thereby prevented from pursuing are, broadly, those which would involve the debtor in more than just being compelled to honour the agreement and put right his default, *i.e.* those remedies of the creditor which operate as a sort of threat to induce the debtor to honour the agreement.

Thus by section 87(1) a notice of default must be served before the creditor or owner is entitled:

"(a) to terminate the agreement, or

(b) to demand earlier payment of any sum, or

(c) to recover possession of any goods or land, or

(d) to treat any right conferred on the debtor or hirer by the agreement as terminated, restricted or deferred, or

(e) to enforce any security."

By way of exception to section 87(1), no default notice need be served before the creditor can become entitled to treat the debtor's right to draw upon any credit as restricted or deferred. Thus, for example, a credit card company which discovers that a card holder has exceeded his credit limit can take immediate steps to prevent him using the card to obtain still further credit. No default notice is required where the creditor seeks a remedy which would do no more than compel the debtor to honour the agreement in the normal way. Thus where the debtor is in arrears, no default notice is required before the creditor can sue for the arrears.

When the default notice is required, it must make certain things clear to the debtor (section 88):

(i) The nature of the alleged breach.

(ii) What action is required to remedy it or, if it is not remediable, how much (if anything) is required to be paid in compensation.

(iii) The exact date by which the breach must be remedied or the compensation paid.

(iv) The consequences if the debtor does not comply with the notice.

26–10 The time allowed must be at least seven days from the date the notice is served upon the debtor. If the default notice overstates the amount owing, it will be invalid, unless (possibly) the error was so small as to be insignificant: *Woodchester Lease Management Services Ltd v. Swain* (1999 CA). The default notice must also be in the form prescribed by the Consumer Credit (Enforcement, Default and Termination Notices) Regulations

1983. If the debtor complies with the notice within the specified time by rectifying the breach or paying the stipulated compensation, the breach must be treated as if it had never occurred (section 89).

If at the end of the specified time the breach has not been remedied or the compensation has not been paid, then the creditor is free to pursue any of the remedies in section 87(1), provided that under the terms of the agreement he is entitled to do so. If the default notice included no requirement for the breach to be remedied or for any compensation to be paid, then after seven days the creditor is free to pursue any of the remedies in section 87(1), again, provided that he is entitled to do so under the terms of the agreement. Two points of explanation are required. First, section 87 does not confer any remedies or rights upon the creditor. It simply restrains him from pursuing certain remedies. Thus, when the restraint is lifted, he can pursue any given remedy only if, quite apart from section 87 (*i.e.* under the terms of the agreement), he is entitled to do so. Secondly, the creditor cannot avoid giving the debtor a chance to put things right by the simple expedient of failing to include in the default notice any requirement for the breach to be remedied or compensation paid. If the breach can be remedied then a requirement for that must be included. If it cannot, and compensation is required, then a requirement for payment of compensation must be included.

Consider an example. Flotsam buys a boat under a credit sale **26–11** agreement in which there is a condition that Flotsam will not sell the boat until he has paid all the instalments. The agreement states that if Flotsam breaks the agreement by selling the boat, all the remaining instalments shall fall due immediately. Flotsam does sell the boat. Now, the breach cannot be put right, since the boat now belongs to someone else, and the creditor will not require compensation. In this situation the creditor can serve a default notice without any requirement for the breach to be remedied or for any compensation. After seven days he can commence an action against Flotsam for the whole of the remaining instalments (less any rebate for early payment under section 95, see paragraph 26–04 above).

The default notice requirement is exactly the same where a hirer is in breach of a regulated consumer hire agreement as it is where the debtor is in breach of a regulated consumer credit agreement.

Death of the debtor

26–12   Consumer credit agreements quite often include a clause which provides for what is to be the position if the debtor dies. The agreement may, for example, provide that on the death of the debtor, all the remaining instalments shall immediately become payable in one lump sum. Hire-purchase agreements sometimes provide that the hiring and the agreement shall terminate upon the debtor's death.

Section 86 applies to any regulated agreement where the debtor dies. Its effect depends upon whether the agreement was "fully secured" or not. Where the regulated agreement is fully secured and the debtor or hirer dies, then by section 86(1) the creditor or owner cannot do any of the acts specified in paragraphs (a) to (e) of section 87(1) (see paragraph 26–09 above). There is a complete embargo. In short, this means that, in spite of anything written in the agreement, the death of the debtor or hirer will not affect the operation of the agreement. The debtor's or hirer's personal representatives will simply take over his rights and duties under the agreement.

Where the agreement is not fully secured, section 86 does not place an absolute embargo upon the operation of clauses in the agreement which would, upon the death of the debtor or hirer either (for example) terminate the agreement or cause the remaining payments to fall due immediately. Nevertheless it does severely restrict the operation of such clauses. The creditor or owner can do one of the acts specified in paragraphs (a) to (e) of section 87(1) only if two requirements are both fulfilled:

(i) the creditor or owner applies to the court, and

(ii) the creditor or owner proves to the court that he has been unable to satisfy himself that the present and future obligations of the debtor or hirer under the agreement are likely to be carried out.

In practice this will involve showing that none of the personal representatives or relations of the debtor or hirer is willing to take over the agreement.

26–13   There are three qualifications to section 86. First, the credit agreement may provide that on the death of the debtor or hirer, the outstanding debt (or part of it) shall be paid out of the proceeds of a policy of life assurance taken out on the debtor's or hirer's life for that purpose. Such a provision in the agreement is enforceable and not affected by section 86. Secondly, section 86 does not prevent the creditor from treating the right to draw on any credit as terminated by the debtor's death. Thus, for example, the debtor's personal representatives would not be able to use his credit card or to draw money under his overdraft agreement. Section 86 is concerned only with debts which the debtor had before he died. Thirdly, section 86 does not apply in relation to the termination of an agreement which is of an unspecified duration or where the specified period of duration has expired.

Let us examine the effect of section 86 in some particular examples:

26–14

(i) The debtor dies owing money under an ordinary unguaranteed credit sale agreement. Unguaranteed is used here to mean that the debtor had no guarantor. In this case the agreement will be unsecured. The debtor's personal representatives will be entitled to continue the agreement (*i.e.* to pay the instalments as and when due from the debtor under the agreement). However, if they refuse to do so and the creditor is unable to make satisfactory arrangements with anyone else (*e.g.* the debtor's relatives) for the carrying out of the agreement, then the creditor could ask the court to enforce a term of the credit sale agreement (if it contained such a term) which stipulates that the whole outstanding balance becomes due on the death of the debtor.

(ii) The debtor died owing money borrowed on an unsecured bank loan. If the loan was for a specified period then the result would be exactly the same as with the credit sale agreement. If the loan was not for a specified period and included a term that the creditor (the bank) could terminate it and demand immediate repayment at any time, then there would be no restriction upon the bank doing just that.

(iii) The debtor died owing money under his credit card agreement, which is of unspecified duration and includes a term that on the death of the debtor the agreement shall terminate and the outstanding debt become repayable immediately. Because the agreement is of unspecified duration, section 86 will not apply and the effect of the debtor's death will be as stated in the agreement.

(iv) The debtor died owing money under an unexpired regulated agreement of specified duration (*e.g.* a credit sale agreement) under which the liability of the debtor and of his personal representatives was fully guaranteed by someone who acted as guarantor at the express or implied request of the debtor. Now, such a guarantee is within the definition (section 189) of "security" and therefore such an agreement would be "fully secured". That being so, the creditor (even if satisfactory arrangements could not be made for the carrying out of the debtor's obligations) could not do any act within paragraphs (a) to (e) of section 87(1). Thus the creditor could not regard the agreement as terminated by the debtor's death, nor could he sue for any instalment earlier than it would have been due from the debtor had he lived.

26–15 (v) The hirer under an unguaranteed consumer hire agreement of specified duration dies while the agreement is still running. Under such agreements there is usually no security given for the payments due under the agreement. Nevertheless the owner will be able to regard the agreement as terminated and recover the goods only if he applies to the court and can show that he was unable to satisfy himself that the hirer's obligations under the agreement would be carried out.

(vi) The debtor dies leaving outstanding instalments to be paid under an unguaranteed hire-purchase agreement. A hire-purchase agreement will in practice always be of a specified duration. The debtor's personal representatives will have the right to continue the agreement just as if he had not died. The problem arises if such satisfactory arrangements cannot be made for the carrying out of the debtor's obligations. Is the agreement "fully secured"? If it is, the position is the same as in the case of a credit sale agreement with a guarantor of the liability of the debtor and his personal representatives. If it is not "fully secured", then the creditor (in the absence of satisfactory arrangements) could ask the court to enforce any provisions in the agreement allowing the creditor to terminate it, to take possession of the goods, etc.

The Act nowhere defines "fully secured" which presumably **26–16** describes an agreement where the creditor or owner has taken security which, if realised at the time of the debtor's or hirer's death, would cover the whole of the outstanding payments under the agreement. Section 189 defines "security" as:

"...a mortgage, charge, pledge, bond, debenture, indemnity, guarantee, bill note or other right provided by the debtor or hirer, or at his request (express or implied) to secure the carrying out of the obligations of the debtor or hirer under the agreement."

Has the creditor under a hire-purchase agreement got any "security"? In any ordinary sense of the word he has, because he has the right to the return of his goods (subject to the provisions of the Consumer Credit Act) if the debtor defaults in circumstances entitling the creditor to terminate the agreement (see paragraphs 27–18 and 27–19 below). However, is this right "provided by the debtor"? The answer would appear to be that the agreement is "fully secured" if in the agreement itself the debtor gives the creditor the right to take possession of the goods upon termination of the agreement. If, however, the agreement does not give the creditor such a right then there is no "security" and it follows that the agreement cannot be "fully secured". This is so even though the creditor may still be entitled to recovery of the goods on termination of the agreement (see generally Chapter 27), because in this case the right to recovery of the goods is not "provided by the debtor" but derives from the basic property rights which belong to the owner of goods (the creditor under the hire-purchase agreement). Since most hire-purchase agreements do not today expressly provide for what is to happen to the goods upon termination of the agreement, it follows that in relation to the vast majority of hire-purchase agreements there is no "security" and that they are therefore not "fully secured".

Non-default notice

In the event of the debtor or hirer being in breach of a **26–17** regulated agreement, there is a list of things (in section 87(1)) which the creditor or owner cannot by reason of the breach become entitled to do without first serving a default notice. Sections 76 and 98 contain similar provisions which apply where the creditor or owner is entitled to do one of those things otherwise than by reason of a breach of the agreement by the debtor or hirer. For example, an agreement may provide that the creditor can terminate it at any time or that he can terminate it if the debtor is convicted of an offence of dishonesty or is sent to prison or changes his address, or becomes unemployed, etc.

Section 98 prevents the creditor or owner terminating a regulated agreement without first serving on the debtor or hirer a notice of his intention to do so. Section 76 requires the creditor or owner to serve a similar notice before enforcing a term of regulated agreement by:

"(a) demanding earlier payment of any sum, or

(b) recovering possession of any goods or land, or

(c) treating any right conferred on the debtor or hirer by the agreement as terminated restricted or deferred."

The notice must give the debtor or hirer at least seven days' warning of the creditor's or owner's intention and must be in the form prescribed by the Consumer Credit (Enforcement, Default and Termination Notices) Regulations 1983. Like a default notice, the notice in this case does not prevent the creditor from treating the right to draw on any credit as restricted or deferred.

26–18 Unlike section 87 (default notice), sections 76 and 98 apply only to agreements which have a specified period of duration. Thus they apply to hire-purchase, conditional sale and credit sale agreements. They do not, however, apply for example to an agreement for a bank overdraft for an indefinite period. If such an agreement gives the bank the right at any time to demand immediate repayment of the whole debt then no notice need be served before the bank can do just that.

The Act does not give any name to the notice which sections 98 and 76 require to be served. In this book it is termed a non-default notice to distinguish it from a default notice. It will be appreciated that these two types of notice are very close cousins. In the case of an agreement of specified duration, before the creditor or owner can take certain kinds of action (*e.g.* terminating the agreement) he will have to serve one of these types of notice. Which one he must serve will depend upon whether the creditor's right to take that action derives from the debtor's breach of the agreement (default notice) or some other event (non-default notice). Whichever one it is, service of the notice will entitle the debtor to apply for a time order. With a default notice the debtor normally has an opportunity to put right his default, whereas plainly there is no question of that with a non-default notice.

Time order

The debtor or hirer can ask the court for a time order in any **26–19** court action brought by the creditor or owner to enforce a regulated agreement. Alternatively when the debtor or hirer has been served either with a default notice (under sections 87 and 88) or with a non-default notice (under section 76 or section 98), then he can apply for a time order without waiting for the creditor or owner to sue him.

The power given by section 129 to the court to make a time **26–20** order is twofold. It can allow time (a specified period) for the debtor or hirer to remedy any breach of the agreement other than non-payment. It can also give time for the payment of any sums owed by the debtor or hirer under the agreement. Where the court does make a time order, it can make the payment(s) "payable at such times, as the court having regard to the means of the debtor or hirer and any surety, considers reasonable." The court's power is confined to sums which at the time the order is made have already fallen due. It does not extend to future instalments. Thus the debtor under a credit sale agreement cannot ask the court to alter the amount or dates of future instalments but can ask it to give him time to pay instalments which have already fallen due. There are three exceptions to the rule that the power to make a time order does not extend to future instalments. First, if there has come into operation a term (an accelerated payments clause) of the agreement which stipulates that all remaining instalments are due immediately, the debtor can ask the court to give him time to pay those because they have (owing to that term of the agreement) fallen due already. The second exception arises where a mortgage of land has been granted as security for a loan and, after the debtor's default, the creditor (no doubt after having served a default notice) commences repossession proceedings. It has been held that commencing repossession proceedings amounts to a "calling-in" of the loan, *i.e.* causes the creditor to be entitled to the whole of the outstanding balance: *Southern District Finance plc v. Barnes* (1995 CA). Thus it has the same effect as the operation of an accelerated payments clause and thus the court is empowered to make a time order in respect of the whole debt including future instalments. The third exception arises where the agreement in question is a hire-purchase or conditional sale agreement. In that case the court has special powers when asked for a time order—section 130(2). In particular it can, even in the absence of an accelerated payments clause, make a time order in respect of future instalments which have not yet fallen due and thus is able (if it considers it just and reasonable to do so) to rewrite the whole instalment pattern.

26–21   The court has power to vary or revoke any time order it makes. So, for example, the debtor could come back to the court later and ask that he be given a further extension of time in which to make the payments subject to the time order. Alternatively the creditor could ask that the time order be revoked (*e.g.* if the debtor was not in fact making payments as required under the time order). In that case the creditor might ask for immediate judgment in his favour for the total amount then due or for any other remedy (*e.g.* enforcement of any security).

Court's supplementary powers

Suspended and conditional court orders

26–22   Section 135 gives the court certain extra powers in making any order in relation to a regulated agreement. It can make any order (or any term of the order) conditional upon the doing of specified acts. It can also suspend the operation of any order or term of an order.

The court's powers under section 135 can be particularly useful where the creditor or owner brings an action to recover possession of goods to which the agreement relates (*e.g.* in the case of a hire-purchase, conditional sale or consumer hire agreement). He will probably be bringing the action because the debtor or hirer is in arrears. In that case the court could make a time order (giving the debtor or hirer time to make up his arrears) and could also order the debtor to return the goods. The court could then suspend the operation of the return order so that it will not take effect unless the debtor or hirer fails to comply with the time order. Alternatively it could suspend the order indefinitely, requiring the creditor to return to the court again before being able to enforce it.

This is only an example and the court's power to impose conditions or to suspend the operation of an order apply in relation to any order relating to a regulated agreement.

Amendment of agreement

26–23   Section 136 provides: "The court may in an order made by it under this Act include such provision as it considers just for amending any agreement or security in consequence of a term of the order." Can the court vary the rate of interest when granting a time order? The court clearly has power to vary the rate of interest in the case of an extortionate credit bargain. Apart from that, however, the court when granting a time order can vary the interest rate (under section 136) only where that variation in the interest rate is "in consequence of a term of the time order": *Southern and District Finance plc v. Barnes* (1995 CA). This could come about as follows. It could very well be, for example, that the effect of making a time order is to delay the receipt of payments by the creditor, *e.g.* by the court in the time order providing for a greater number of smaller payments over an extended repayment period. If no reduction were made in the contractual rate of interest, that rate would continue to apply to the monthly deficiency arising between the contractual monthly instalment and the monthly instalment directed by the court. This would result in the creditor on the one hand receiving overall a higher total amount of interest whilst on the other receiving a slower rate of repayment. In the case of an agreement with a high, albeit not extortionate, rate of interest, it would then be appropriate for the court to reduce the rate of interest "in consequence of" the time order. The fact is that if the court is able to reduce the interest rate, that may well be a way of achieving justice. Suppose the court is dealing with a loan secured by a mortgage at a rate of interest which, though not extortionate, is nevertheless very high. The debtor has got into arrears. These are piling up at an alarming rate because interest is accumulating on the arrears. The creditor commences repossession proceedings. The court is then facing a choice of either granting an immediate repossession order or else giving the debtor a chance to catch up by making a time order, a time order being normally made for a stipulated period on account of temporary financial difficulty. The court cannot make a time order unless the debtor has some reasonable chance of keeping up with the payments required under the time order. If the court is able to find a reason to reduce the interest rate, *i.e.* "in consequence of a term of the time order", then that may make all the difference, thereby enabling the court to make a time order for payments which the debtor has some chance of maintaining.

Director General of Fair Trading v. First National Bank (2000) **26–24** involved a clause in a standard form loan agreement. It provided that interest at the contractual rate was payable on outstanding arrears until the arrears were paid off. It provided that this obligation to pay interest did not merge with any judgment and thus interest would continue to be payable even after judgment until the debt was paid. In the absence of the clause, the matter of interest on a judgment debt would be governed by the County Court (Interest on Judgments) Order 1991. Under that order, not only would the relevant rate of interest be lower than that payable under the defendant's loan agreements, but no interest at all would be payable on judgments for less than £5,000 or judgments for money due under regulated consumer credit agreements. Under powers in the Unfair Terms in Consumer Contracts Regulations (explained at paragraph 10–47 above) the Director General asked the court to declare the clause unfair and to grant an injunction to stop the defendant using it. His evidence was that often a debtor against whom the bank brought proceedings would agree to a "consent" order being made by the judge, such judgment being for the outstanding balance to be payable by instalments over an extended period. The consent order would then be made by the judge without any hearing of the merits of the case and, because of the clause, interest at the contractual rate would be payable on the judgment debt. The Court of Appeal held the clause to be unfair because its effect in practice was to impose post-judgment interest without the court considering whether to make a time order or, if it did, whether also to make an order under section 136 reducing the contractual interest rate. A clause which is unfair within the regulations is of no effect (see paragraph 10–45 above).

SUBSIDIARY MATTERS

Unlicensed creditors and credit brokers

26–25   A regulated agreement made by an unlicensed creditor or owner or made following an introduction by an unlicensed credit broker is likely to be unenforceable against the debtor or hirer— see paragraphs 22–19 to 22–21 above.

Subsequent copies of the agreement and information

26–26   Sections 77–79 entitle the debtor or hirer at any time during the currency of a regulated agreement to request a copy of the agreement and a statement of account. The request must be in writing and accompanied by £1 for expenses. Sections 107–110 have similar provisions entitling a surety to ask for a copy or statement of account or both. Section 97 entitles the debtor under a regulated agreement at any time to request in writing (without enclosing any fee) a statement of account showing the amount required to be paid to clear off the whole debt. Under section 103 the debtor or hirer can make a written request to the creditor or owner for a written termination statement acknowledging that the agreement has ceased to have any operational effect and that the debt has been fully paid off. In this case the creditor or owner must either comply with the request or else give a written statement disputing the debtor's or hirer's assertions.

If the creditor or owner does not respond within 12 days to one of these requests, two consequences are likely to follow. First, the creditor or owner will not be able to enforce the relevant agreement (*i.e.* regulated agreement or security agreement) unless and until he rectifies his default by supplying the copy or statement of account. Secondly, if he has not rectified the default within a further month, he commits an offence.

By section 172, a statement of account or termination statement **26–27** given in response to one of the requests mentioned above is normally binding upon the creditor or owner. Thus if he wrongly understates any payment to be made by the debtor or hirer, he will not usually be able to claim any more than that. Similarly, if he states that the debt has been fully paid off he will not normally be able later to assert that it was not. He will be able to do so only if he can convince the court that it is "just" that the statement should not be binding upon him. Section 172 applies only to statements given under the sections mentioned above. Suppose that a creditor under an agreement that is not regulated is requested for a settlement statement and that the statement he sends out understates the amount necessary to pay off the debt. In that case the creditor is free to insist on payment of the full amount owing, unless the debtor has acted in reliance upon the erroneous statement. In the latter case the creditor will be estopped from demanding more than the erroneous settlement figure: *Lombard North Central v. Stobart* (1990 CA).

With the exception of section 97, none of the sections entitling the debtor or hirer or the surety to request a copy or a statement of account or a termination statement (*i.e.* sections 77–79, 103 and 107–110) applies to non-commercial agreements.

Finally, it is to be noted that under a running-account credit agreement, the creditor is under a duty to send the debtor a regular periodic statement of account—section 78(4) and (5). The Act, however, provides no penalty for a failure to do so.

Appropriation of payments

26–28   It may happen that the debtor or hirer has more than one credit agreement with the same person. Alternatively he may have separate agreements with two different persons but have to make payments under them to the same person (*e.g.* if he has to make payments to X who is the agent for both creditors). Suppose the debtor makes a payment. To which agreement does the payment relate? It may not seem an important question because, regardless of which agreement is the relevant one, the total amount still remaining outstanding will be the same. However, the question will be important if one of the agreements is unenforceable for any reason. The rule under section 81 is that, where the debtor or hirer has two or more regulated agreements and has to make payments in respect of them to the same person, the debtor or hirer has the right to appropriate any payment as between the different agreements as he sees fit. If he does not indicate any appropriation, then the payment is automatically appropriated towards the different agreements proportionately according to the sums then due under the different agreements (*i.e.* ignoring any future instalments which have not yet fallen due). Thus, if he wishes, the debtor or hirer can indicate that all his payments are to go to pay off sums due under an enforceable agreement— thereby leaving the creditor to "whistle for" payments under any unenforceable agreements. Even if the debtor or hirer makes no such appropriation, the creditor or owner cannot appropriate all the payments to an unenforceable agreement. The payments must be appropriated proportionately.

There is one qualification to what has just been said. Where none of the agreements in question is a hire-purchase or conditional sale agreement or a consumer hire agreement and where there is no security in respect of any of them, there is no automatic appropriation. The result in that case is that if the debtor does not indicate to which agreement a payment relates, the recipient of the payment can appropriate the payment as he wishes.

26–29   In *Julian Hodge Bank Ltd v. Hall* (1998 CA) the debtor had just one agreement, a regulated hire-purchase agreement. He was in arrears. Ignoring future payments which had not yet fallen due, he owed two sets of money: (i) arrears of payments which he should have made; (ii) default interest which, at the contract rate, had accumulated on the arrears. When he made a further payment which was less than the total of (i) and (ii), the debtor could have made his own appropriation of it as between (i) and (ii). Since he did not, the creditor was free to make such an appropriation. It was held that the creditor's appropriation is not effective until communicated to the debtor and once it is communicated it is irrevocable. It might, for example, be communicated by a letter or invoice, showing the revised amounts of (i) and (ii) owing. Whichever way it is appropriated, it will still have the same effect on the overall amount outstanding. In a hire-purchase case, however, appropriation of the payment to (i) may, as it did in *Julian Hodge*, increase the chances of the goods being "protected goods", see paragraph 27–20 below.

Variation of the agreement

Section 82 applies to variations of agreements. There are **26–30** basically two different ways in which a variation in a regulated agreement can occur. First, the agreement may give the creditor or owner the *right* to vary the agreement. This is particularly common in running-account credit agreements which are likely to continue for some time, where the creditor may in the future need to change the rate of interest. By section 82 any variation by the owner or creditor shall not have effect until notice has been given to the debtor or hirer. Under section 82(1) and the Consumer Credit (Notice of Variation of Agreements) Regulations 1977, the general rule is that any variation by the owner or creditor shall not have effect unless and until he has given at least seven days' notice in writing, *i.e.* seven days from when the debtor or hirer receives the notice. To that general rule there is one exception which applies where the creditor is exercising a right to vary a rate of interest which is determined by reference to the outstanding balance established at daily intervals (*e.g.* in the case of a bank overdraft). The exception allows the creditor an alternative to the giving of written notice to each individual customer. It allows him, instead, to publish notice of the change in at least three national daily newspapers whilst, at the same time, displaying notice of it in the public part of each of the creditor's business premises. One further exception to the general rule allows a consumer hire business (*e.g.* a TV rental company) to make an instant variation in the rental payments under consumer hire agreements where the need to do so is caused by a change in the rate of VAT. A notice giving details of the variation must be displayed at the relevant business premises (*e.g.* the TV rental showroom or shop).

The second way in which a variation may come about is by *agreement* between the parties. This may happen for example if the debtor is having difficulty maintaining his repayments and wishes to spread them over a longer period. By section 82(2) an agreement supplementing or varying an earlier agreement is to be treated as if it revoked the earlier one and substituted a new agreement—the latter being called the "modifying agreement" and having the combined effect of both the earlier agreement and the later one.

26–31 The most important effect of section 82(2) is that the formalities requirements (but not the cancellation provisions) will usually apply to the new agreement (the modifying agreement). Thus the requirements as to signatures and the service of copies will apply. If they are not complied with, the creditor or owner may not be able to enforce the agreement (see paragraph 24–42 above). The Consumer Credit (Agreements) Regulations 1983 contain specific requirements as to the contents of modifying agreements. One exceptional case where the formalities requirements will not apply is where a running-account credit agreement is later varied so as to allow the debtor temporarily to exceed the credit limit (section 82(4)).

A variation can convert an unregulated agreement into a regulated one. Imagine a hire-purchase agreement under which the amount of credit is £46,000 and the instalments are to be paid over four years. Suppose that towards the end of the third year (*i.e.* at a time when £10,000 worth of credit is still outstanding) the creditor and debtor agree to vary the agreement by adding on some more goods involving further credit of £13,500. Then the modifying agreement, having the combined effect of the earlier agreement and the variation, is an agreement providing credit of £23,500. Therefore, provided the debtor is an individual, the modifying agreement is a regulated one. On the other hand a variation (with one exception) can not convert a regulated agreement into an unregulated one—section 82(3). Thus, if, in the hire-purchase example just given, a further variation were agreed, thereby taking to £25,500 the amount of credit provided under the new (the second) modifying agreement, the latter would still be a regulated agreement. The exception is that it is possible for a regulated running-account credit agreement to be varied so as to make the modifying agreement an unregulated agreement, *e.g.* if the credit limit is by agreement increased (other than merely temporarily) to a figure above £25,000.

Misuse of credit facilities

26–32
With certain kinds of credit facilities, there is a particularly high risk that someone other than the debtor will manage to gain access to the facilities and thereby obtain credit. This is so, for example, where the credit is obtained by the production by the debtor of a trading check or credit card. If the check or card falls into the wrong hands then it may be used by someone who is never afterwards found.

The question arises as to whether the original debtor has to pay for that. There are special rules in section 84 relating to credit tokens and they will be dealt with a little later (paragraph 26–35). However, apart from those special rules, there is a general all-embracing rule in section 83 that the debtor under a regulated agreement shall not be liable for any use of credit facilities by another person who is not the debtor's agent and not authorised by the debtor to use them. This section is not confined to trading checks and covers any kind of credit facilities which are provided under a regulated agreement.

26–33
We must now consider two items, either or both of which are sometimes given by a bank to a current account customer—cheque guarantee cards and withdrawal tokens. The purpose of the cheque guarantee card is to enable the current account customer to persuade someone else (*i.e.* other than his own bank) to cash a cheque or accept a cheque in payment. The customer's own bank guarantees that it will honour the cheque up to £100 if the customer produced the guarantee card when writing the cheque. The withdrawal token (usually indistinguishable from a credit card in appearance) enables the customer to obtain cash from his current account outside the bank's opening hours by using the token to operate a machine situated, usually, outside the bank. Normally these facilities are not used to obtain credit. Just like a cheque book, they are provided under a current account agreement. In fact, assuming that the customer has got some money in his current account, he is not a debtor but a creditor (*i.e.* the bank owes him money, not vice versa). When he uses, say, his withdrawal token, that will have the effect of reducing the amount in his current account and he will therefore not be obtaining credit. Rather he will be obtaining money which the bank owes him. However, if the customer uses his cheque guarantee card or his withdrawal token so as to cause his bank to pay out more than the funds in the customer's current account, then he has obtained credit from his bank. When the bank provided him with those facilities whereby it obliged itself to give

him this credit, it made with him a regulated consumer credit agreement. (This point is not absolutely certain; see an article "The Cheque Card as a Consumer Credit Agreement" [1977] J.B.L. 126.) If it is a regulated agreement then it is still a regulated agreement even if in fact the customer never afterwards actually obtained credit under it.

26–34   The result of all this would appear to be that section 83 applies to cheque guarantee cards and the withdrawal tokens. However, there are three things which affect the simplicity of that. First, in relation to the cheque guarantee card there is the rule in section 83 that it does not apply to any loss arising from the misuse of a cheque—and a cheque guarantee card can be used only in conjunction with a cheque. Thus whether the customer or the bank must bear any loss caused by unauthorised use of a cheque guarantee card will depend upon the particular agreement between the bank and the customer. The second complication arises in relation to the withdrawal token (which is used independently), for the withdrawal token falls within the definition of a credit token and is therefore subject to the special rules relating to credit tokens—the effect of which is basically that the customer can be liable for the first £50 of -any loss. The third complication also arises in relation to the cash withdrawal token. It is that section 83 and the special rules (in section 84) relating to credit tokens apply only to misuse of *credit* facilities. Thus they apply to a cash withdrawal token only when it is used to draw on credit. Nothing in the sections prevents the debtor from being made fully liable for a misuse of the cash withdrawal token which merely reduces the amount of money in his account, *i.e.* which occurs when his account is not overdrawn. However, the banking Code of Practice published, and subscribed to, by all major banks and building societies, extends to all cards (*i.e.* even if they are not regulated by the Consumer Credit Act) and has provisions similar to those in sections 83 and 84. By that code of practice the customer cannot be liable for more than £50 of loss occurring before the customer has notified the card issuer that the card has been lost or is liable to be misused, and is not liable for any loss occurring after such notification. Under the code, these restrictions on the customer's liability do not apply if the customer has been fraudulent or the loss is caused by his gross negligence.

Credit token agreements

26–35   A credit token is, broadly, a card, check, voucher, coupon, stamp, form, booklet or other document or thing, which is given to the debtor by the creditor and which can be used by the debtor to obtain cash or services or goods on credit. Thus the following are credit tokens—credit cards, trading checks, and current account withdrawal tokens (see paragraph 26–33). A "debit" card used to make Electronic Funds Transfers will be a credit token, but only if the debit card holder has an agreed authority to overdraw (see paragraph 21–23 above). Cheques and cheque guarantee cards, however, are not credit tokens.

Section 51 is aimed at something which has been known to happen on a large scale, namely the sending of credit cards to persons who have not asked for them. It makes it a criminal offence to supply a credit token to someone who has not asked for it. Except in the case of a small debtor-creditor-supplier agreement the debtor's request must be in a document signed by himself. The exception is designed to allow a trading check for £50 or less to be given when the debtor has made only an oral request. This ties in with the fact that small debtor-creditor-supplier agreements for restricted-use credit are excepted from most of the formality and documentation provisions (see paragraph 24–32). Thus a trading check for £50 or less can safely be given to a debtor who has made a purely oral agreement to have it. The section has a further exception whereby no prior request is needed before a credit card is sent out in renewal or replacement of an earlier one (for credit cards normally expire after a year or so). Section 85, however, requires the creditor to give the debtor a further copy of the credit agreement whenever he gives the debtor a renewal or replacement credit token. If the copy is not given, the creditor cannot enforce the credit agreement until it has been given. If after a month it still has not been given, then the creditor commits an offence.

One particular risk with a credit card is that before it reaches **26–36** the person for whom it was intended, it falls into the wrong hands—*i.e.* someone else might obtain it and use it to obtain credit. By section 66 the debtor (*i.e.* the person who was intended to receive it) will not be liable for any use made of a credit token unless he has himself accepted it. This is so whether the credit token was sent to him unsolicited or after he had requested it or agreed to its being sent. Even if it has actually reached him, it does not follow that he has accepted it. He does not accept it until he either signs it, signs a receipt for it or uses it.

Someone (*e.g.* a thief) may make unauthorised use of the credit **26–37** token after the debtor has accepted it. It is quite likely that in these circumstances the credit agreement will make the debtor liable to the creditor for any loss caused by this unauthorised use. Section 84 permits this but restricts the liability of the debtor in three respects. First, if he has lost possession of the credit token at the time of the authorised use, his liability cannot exceed £50 (or the credit limit if lower) in respect of the whole period that he is out of possession. This restriction does not, however, apply to the debtor's liability in respect of any misuse by someone who obtained possession with the debtor's consent. Secondly, the creditor is not liable for any unauthorised use that is made of the credit token after he has given notice that it is lost or stolen or for any other reason likely to be misused. Notice may be given orally (*e.g.* by telephone) but in that case the notice will be ineffective if the agreement requires it to be confirmed in writing and it is not confirmed in writing within the period stipulated in the agreement (the period allowed must be at least seven days). Thirdly, the debtor will be under no liability at all for unauthorised use unless the name, address and telephone number of the person to whom notice can be given that the credit token is lost or stolen, or is for any other reason liable to misuse, was shown clearly and legibly in the agreement. Nothing in section 84 prevents the debtor being made liable by the terms of his contract for any loss which does not arise from misuse of a *credit* facility, *e.g.* if a cash withdrawal token is used by a thief to withdraw £200 from the debtor's current account at a time when the debtor had £300 in the account. Remember, however, that there is an equivalent protection given by "the banking Code of Practice"— see paragraph 26–34 above.

26–38   Section 171 completes the protection for the debtor by putting the onus of proof of certain matters firmly upon the creditor. In proceedings brought by the creditor under the agreement it is for the creditor to prove that the credit token was lawfully supplied and was accepted by the debtor. Where the debtor alleges that any use of the credit token was not authorised by him, it is for the creditor to prove either that it was or that the unauthorised use occurred before the creditor had been given notice that the credit token was lost, stolen or likely to be misused.

26–39   Finally, observe an oddity. It is possible to have a credit token without there being either a credit token agreement or an offer to make such an agreement. In *Elliott v. Director-General of Fair Trading* (1980 QB) a footwear retailing company instituted a promotional scheme whereby the company sent to members of the public unsolicited plasticised cards which looked very much like credit cards. The idea was that a holder of such a card could use it at an Elliott shop to obtain goods on credit. The company was charged, under section 51, with sending out an unsolicited credit token. Clearly, when a card was received by a member of the public, there was no credit agreement. The sending of the card was either an offer or it was merely an invitation to treat. It was not clear which. The wording on the card was ambiguous. On the one hand it said "This card is available for immediate use" and "credit is immediately available". On the other, it also said "...it can only be used when a signature has been accepted at an Elliott shop" and other literature which was sent out with the cards made it clear that the customer would have to complete further forms and formalities before being able to use the card. The court held that the company was guilty. The card was a credit token irrespective of whether it amounted to an offer. A card is a credit token within the statutory definition (in section 14) if on its face or its reverse side there is an undertaking that on its production credit will be given.

ENFORCEMENT OF SECURITY

There will not be found in this book an explanation of each **26–40** of the different bodies of law relating to the various forms of security. Nevertheless, there is some reference to two forms of safeguard for the creditor. First, later in this chapter there is a very short explanation of the rights of the pawnor and pawnee now regulated by provisions of the Consumer Credit Act which repealed the Pawnbrokers Acts of 1872 and 1960. Secondly, the creditor's right under a hire-purchase agreement to reclaim possession of the goods is considered in the next chapter. In any case, we have already seen that strictly speaking that right is not "security" within the definition of the Act (paragraph 26–16).

We are about to consider certain sections of the Act which apply to rights that are within that definition.

It is useful at this stage to recall (from paragraph 24–46) certain things about the Act's definition of security (section 189(1)):

(i) Security includes a guarantee or indemnity.

(ii) Security does not include anything (whether a guarantee or indemnity or anything else) which is not provided by the debtor or hirer or at his request (express or implied).

(iii) Where security is provided by someone (*e.g.* a guarantor) other than the debtor or hirer, that person is termed a "surety".

It will be remembered that the Act does not apply to recourse agreements between finance companies and dealers. This is because the dealer does not make a recourse agreement at the request (express or implied) of the debtor, paragraph 24–46 above.

Default notice

26–41   When security has been provided by someone other than the debtor or hirer (*i.e.* by a surety) and a default notice is served on the debtor or hirer, a copy of the notice should be served at the same time on the surety—section 111. If this is not done, the security is unenforceable by the creditor or owner except on an order of the court which will have to take into account the same considerations as where the formalities requirements were not complied with—namely the amount of prejudice caused by, and the degree of culpability for, the copy not being served.

Subsequent copies

26–42   Sections 107–109 entitle a surety, upon sending a written request together with a small fee, to receive a copy of the regulated agreement, of the security document and a statement of account. This has already been explained (paragraph 26–26).

Restriction of enforcement of security

26–43   Section 113 makes a rule of wide effect, that any security shall not be enforced so as to benefit the creditor or owner to an extent greater than would be in the case if (in the absence of any security) all the debtor's or hirer's obligations under or in relation to the regulated agreement were carried out to the extent to which they would be enforced under the Consumer Credit Act. This means: where the regulated agreement is unenforceable, the security is also unenforceable; where the regulated agreement is enforceable only on an order of the court, so is the security; and where the court would make such an order for the enforcement of the regulated agreement only upon certain conditions, the same conditions will attach to the security. Thus although it is possible for the regulated agreement to be enforceable and the security unenforceable it is not possible for the regulated agreement to be unenforceable and the security enforceable. Section 113 therefore makes it clear that the security should be regarded as secondary to the debtor's or hirer's obligations under the regulated agreement. Its function is to ensure the performance by the debtor or hirer of his obligations—but only to the extent that they can be enforced against him.

One might be left wondering of what value security can **26–44** possibly be. The answer is that it can be of great value. An obligation to pay may be enforceable at law against the debtor or hirer and yet the creditor may still be unable to obtain the money, *e.g.* if the debtor has not got the means to pay or has disappeared without trace. It is comforting for the creditor to know that if this should occur he could, for example, look to a guarantor or cash in a life assurance policy that has been assigned to him.

There is one exceptional situation where section 113 will allow security to be enforced even though the regulated agreement could not be enforced at law. That is where the security is an indemnity or guarantee and the only reason that the regulated agreement is unenforceable is that the debtor or hirer is not of full age or capacity. We saw in paragraph 2–12 that traders will often not give credit to someone under 18 unless an indemnity or guarantee is given by an adult. This exception to the general rule in section 113 means that the indemnity or guarantee will not be valueless if the young debtor or hirer defaults. If the only reason that the regulated agreement is unenforceable against the debtor or hirer is the fact he is under 18, than the indemnity or guarantee will still be enforceable.

Land mortgages

By section 126 a land mortgage securing a regulated agreement **26–45** is enforceable on an order of the court only.

Pledges

Sections 114–122 deal with the rights and obligations between **26–46** the pawnor (*i.e.* the borrower) and the pawnee (*i.e.* the creditor). Unless otherwise indicated, they apply to all pawns, whether given under a regulated agreement or not.

Broadly, their effect is as follows: the pawnee must give the pawnor a pawn receipt which complies with the Consumer Credit (Pawn Receipt) Regulations 1983. Failure to do is an offence. In the case of a pledge agreement to which sections 62–64 apply (which require copies, etc., of a regulated agreement to be given to the debtor or hirer, see paragraphs 24–36 to 24–39 above) the pawnee commits an offence if he does not comply with the requirements of sections 62–64. In the case of any pawn agreement, the pawnor is entitled to redeem the pawn (*i.e.* pay off the debt, present his pawn receipt and recover his goods) at any time before the last of the following events:

    (i) The end of six months from when the pawn was taken.

    (ii) The end of the last day on which it was agreed between the parties that it could be redeemed.

    (iii) When the pawn becomes the property of the pawnee or, if it does not, when the pawnee realises (*i.e.* sells) the pawn.

26–47   After the end of six months in (i) or the agreed period in (ii), whichever is later, the pawn becomes the property of the pawnee if the maximum credit under the agreement did not exceed, and could not have exceeded, £75. Otherwise it does not become the pawnee's property but he is entitled to sell it. If the amount of the credit (or, if it was running-account credit, the credit limit) did not exceed £100, he can sell it without first giving notice. Otherwise he must first give the pawnor at least 14 days' notice of his intention and asking price. The notice must be in the form required by the Consumer Credit (Realisation of Pawn) Regulations 1983. If he makes a profit on the sale (*i.e.* more than enough to cover both the debt owed to him by the pawnor and the pawnee's selling expenses) he must give the surplus to the pawnor and if he delays in paying over that surplus he will be liable for interest on it during the period of delay: *Matthew v. T. M. Sutton Limited* (1994 ChD).

Normally the pawnee will return the pawn to someone who presents both the pawn receipt and the necessary amount to repay the debt. If this turns out to be someone other than the pawnor (*e.g.* someone who has stolen the pawn receipt), the pawnee will not be liable for having returned the pawn to the wrong person unless he knew or had reasonable cause to suspect that the bearer of the pawn receipt was not entitled to redeem the pawn. If he unreasonably refuses to allow a pawn given under a regulated agreement to be redeemed, he commits an offence.

CHAPTER 27

TERMINATION OF HIRE-PURCHASE CONTRACTS

AT the outset the parties will no doubt expect that the contract will run its full course—that the debtor will pay all his instalments and at the end will exercise his option to purchase the goods. Nevertheless, the hiring may be terminated before the debtor has paid all his instalments. This chapter is concerned with the causes and consequences of such premature termination. It is not, however, concerned with the right of cancellation which is given for the first few days to some debtors who sign the agreement elsewhere than at certain trade premises. That was considered in Chapter 24. **27–01**

Unlike cancellation, termination is seldom in the debtor's best interest. The normal consequences of termination are that the debtor has no right to retain the goods and that he is unable to recover any payments he has already paid; he may even have to make a further payment. Thus it is rarely a positive decision on the debtor's part to terminate the agreement. The most common cause is in fact the debtor's inability or failure to keep up his payments. We shall see, however, that the debtor whose agreement is a regulated agreement has much less to fear from termination. The Consumer Credit Act gives him considerable protection. One set of provisions of the Consumer Credit Act will not, however, be mentioned further in this chapter; those relating to extortionate credit agreements. It should nevertheless be borne in mind throughout that these provisions can be used if the court finds the agreement extortionate and that they are not confined to regulated agreements but can be used in relation to any personal credit agreement irrespective of the amount of the credit (see generally paragraph 26–06 above).

We shall be dealing with the position at common law, *i.e.* where the agreement is not regulated by the Consumer Credit Act, as well as the position in relation to regulated agreements. Although this chapter will be concerned only with hire-purchase **27–02** agreements, the practice will be continued, in line with the Consumer Credit Act, of referring to the parties as creditor and debtor rather than owner and hirer, although it is true that many of the creditor's rights derive from the fact that he is the owner of the goods. This is especially so in relation to his rights against third parties.

This chapter will be devoted to answering five questions, in the following order:

(1) What events cause termination?

(2) What is the effect of an accelerated payments clause?

(3) After termination, is the creditor entitled to recover the goods from the debtor?

(4) After termination, is the creditor entitled to any further payment from the debtor?

(5) After termination, is the creditor entitled to recover the goods if they have passed to a third person?

EVENTS CAUSING TERMINATION

27–03   Broadly, termination may come about as a result of one of four things: subsequent agreement between the parties; exercise by the debtor of a right of termination; breach of the agreement by the debtor; or, lastly, the occurrence of an event stipulated in the agreement as liable to cause termination. When termination occurs it is not always easy to identify which of these things was the cause. It can, however, be important, for the consequences of termination vary according to the cause.

Mutual agreement

27–04   It is quite possible for the creditor and debtor to come to a subsequent agreement whereby they terminate the hire-purchase contract. In practice, this will seldom be done except where a new hire-purchase agreement is substituted for the old one. The debtor will hardly wish to return the goods and also to sacrifice the payments which he has already made. On the other hand, the creditor will not usually be too willing to forgo a substantial part of the payments and also have the problem of disposing of the goods. The creditor is more likely to try to persuade the debtor to replace   his   existing   contract   with   another   hire-purchase agreement, spreading the remaining payments over a longer period of time.

The parties may of course decide that it is not necessary to terminate the agreement and substitute a new one and decide instead simply to agree to vary the first one. However, if they do this then the provisions of the Consumer Credit Act will operate as if they had terminated the first agreement and made a new one producing the combined effect of the first agreement and the later variation (see section 82, paragraph 26–30 above).

Termination by mutual agreement seldom gives rise to any legal difficulty. The problems with which this chapter is concerned are associated rather with termination which comes about in some other way.

Exercise by the debtor of a right of termination

Often a hire-purchase agreement will contain a term expressly **27–05** allowing the debtor to terminate the contract, although there will usually also be a provision to the effect that the debtor must, as the price of doing so, make a further stipulated payment (*i.e.* in addition to payments falling due before termination). Notice in writing to the creditor will normally be required. Since the contract expressly allows him to terminate it, the debtor does not commit a breach of contract by exercising the contractual right. This can be an important point in relation to whether the creditor is entitled to recover the further payment stipulated to be due on the debtor exercising his right of termination (see *Associated Distributors v. Hall,* paragraph 27 33 below). It will be important where the agreement is not a regulated one but not where the agreement is a regulated agreement because in the latter case the amount of money recoverable by the creditor is governed by section 100 (see paragraph 27–34 below).

In the case of a regulated agreement, section 99 gives the debtor a right to terminate the contract by giving notice in writing to the creditor or any person entitled or authorised to receive payments under the agreement. The debtor may have both the above rights of termination, *i.e.* if the agreement both gives to the debtor an express right of termination and is also a regulated agreement. If in that situation the debtor exercises his right of termination, the consequences will be those that are the more lenient and beneficial for the debtor, *i.e.* those in section 100 or those stipulated in the agreement. The reason for this is that by section 173 the agreement cannot increase but can only reduce the debtor's liability as stated in the Act.

27–06   Where the agreement is not a regulated one, the debtor will not have a right to terminate under section 99 but may still have a contractual right of termination. In this case a stipulation for a further payment may be enforceable even though it is excessive. Thus it might exceed the actual loss caused to the creditor by the termination. It might mean that he receives in all more than he would have received if the agreement had never been terminated and had been fully carried out. To put it another way, it could result in the creditor receiving in all (*i.e.* including the sums already paid by the debtor before the termination and the value of the goods returned to the creditor at the time of the termination) more than the whole of the total price (see *Associated Distributors v. Hall*, paragraph 27–33 below). This means that where the agreement is not a regulated one, the consequences of the debtor exercising a contractual right of termination could be very harsh for the debtor. They certainly could be worse than if he broke his contract (*i.e.* simply allowed his payments to get into arrears). For this reason the court will not hold that the debtor has exercised a contractual right of termination unless it is sure that he was fully aware of the consequences. In *United Dominions Trust v. Ennis* (1967 CA) the subject-matter of the agreement was a Jaguar car and the debtor was a London docker who found he could not keep up his payments when the dockers went on strike. He wrote to the creditor saying, "I wish to terminate my agreement with you as I find I cannot fulfil the terms". The Court of Appeal held that the debtor was not exercising his contractual right of termination but was, in effect, giving the creditor notice of his breach of contract. Referring to the debtor's contractual right (option) of termination. Lord Denning M.R. said, "A hirer (*i.e.* debtor) is not to be taken as exercising such an option unless he does so consciously, knowing of the consequences and avowedly in exercise of his option". Since the debtor had not exercised his right of termination, it was the creditor who had terminated, as he was entitled to do, for the debtor's breach of contract. This meant that the creditor had no right to the stipulated further payment which was excessive and therefore void as a penalty (see paragraph 27–33 below).

Breach of the agreement by the debtor

27–07   Not every breach by the debtor will terminate the agreement. Those breaches which may result in termination are:

(i) An act by the debtor wholly repugnant to the agreement, *e.g.* if he sells the goods or otherwise indicates by acts or words that he repudiates the contract. If the debtor does such an act, the creditor is not bound to regard the agreement as terminated but is entitled to do so. If he does so, the law will regard the termination as having been caused by the debtor's repudiation. This fact will tell against the debtor if the creditor claims damages (see paragraph 27–27).

(ii) A breach by the debtor which does not amount to repudiation but which is specified in the agreement as giving to the creditor the right to terminate the hiring. The usual breaches specified in this way are first, failure by the debtor to take reasonable care of the goods and, secondly, the debtor falling into arrears with his payments. Sometimes the contract states that it is automatically terminated on the occurrence of one of the specified breaches. Sometimes it gives the creditor the right of termination after giving notice. When the creditor exercises his right of termination for the debtor's breach then, unless the debtor repudiated the agreement, the law regards the termination as having been caused by the creditor. This fact will be in the debtor's favour if the creditor claims damages (see *Financings v. Baldock*, below, paragraph 27–28).

(iii) A breach of a term which is a condition of the contract. If the contract clearly indicates that a term is a condition (as opposed to a warranty) then any breach of it by the debtor has the same effect as an act by the debtor which is wholly repugnant to the contract. A statement in the contract that a given term is "of the essence" clearly labels it as a condition. Thus where the contract states that punctual payment of all moneys due by the debtor is "of the essence", then, if the debtor is late (even if only by one day) in making one of the payments, he can be treated by the creditor as having repudiated the contract: *Lombard North Central v. Butterworth* (1987 CA). The damages to be paid by the debtor will be assessed accordingly. Thus there is a fine, but important, line between a contract provision that if the debtor is 10 days late in making any payment the creditor has the right to terminate the hiring (*Financings v. Baldock*) and

473

one which states that punctual payment of all moneys due under the contract is "of the essence" (*Lombard North Central v. Butterworth*). Both give the creditor the right to terminate the contract for late payment, but the latter can result in the debtor having to pay greater damages (see paragraph 27–29 below).

27–08   If the agreement so specifies, it appears to be possible for the contract to be terminated if the debtor is late with one instalment. However, in the case of an agreement which is a regulated agreement, this cannot happen without the debtor first being given a chance to bring his payments up to date. Section 87 applies where the debtor is in breach of the agreement. It provides that the creditor cannot (amongst other things) either terminate the agreement or treat any right of the debtor's as terminated without first serving a default notice on the debtor. The section applies to regulated agreements and it applies irrespective of whether the debtor's breach was a repudiatory one or not. Default notices were considered in the last chapter (paragraph 26–09). By way of reminder it may be said here that where the debtor's only breach is non-payment of instalments the default notice must make a number of things clear to the debtor, including:

(i) The exact amount required to bring his payments up to date. If the amount is overstated, the notice is invalid: *Woodchester Lease Management v. Swain* (1999 CA).

(ii) Exactly how long (a minimum of seven days) he has got in which to pay it (*i.e.* the date of expiry of the default notice).

(iii) The consequences of failure to comply with the notice.

(iv) The provision of the agreement (if any) under which the agreement can be terminated.

(v) That if the breach is duly remedied the agreement will not terminate.

27–09   Some of these requirements were not made clear in *Eshun v. Moorgate Mercantile Co.* (1971 CA). The debtor had paid £115 out of a total hire-purchase price of £405 17s. 3d. The default notice served on him stated correctly that he was £23 3s. 6d. in arrears. It then said:

"unless we do hear from you with payment within the course of the next nine days after the date on which you would normally be expected to receive this letter, we shall have no alternative but to assume that you do not wish to continue the hiring under the Agreement and are, in effect, terminating by repudiation."

The Court held that this notice was invalid on three grounds. First, the creditor had no right to assume from the mere non-payment of two instalments that the debtor was in effect terminating by repudiation. The creditor cannot put upon the debtor a repudiation when he has never repudiated. Secondly, the notice did not refer to the provision of the hire-purchase agreement under which it was given and under which the amounts in default were due. Thirdly, it did not clearly state exactly how long the debtor had before the period for payment expired. Since the notice was invalid, the agreement was never terminated and therefore the creditor had no right to recover possession of the goods. The creditor therefore had to pay compensation to the debtor for having done so.

A further interesting point to emerge from the case was that even if the agreement had not been regulated by an Act of Parliament, it still could not have been terminated without a notice of default being served. Lord Denning M.R. said, "I think that even at common law a notice of default may be necessary...the agreement being a one-sided one with stringent terms, the plaintiff was entitled to a reminder that his instalments were in arrear before it could be terminated".

Other stipulated events

Hire-purchase agreements commonly provide for termination on the occurrence of any one of certain stipulated events (other than breach of the agreement), *e.g.* on the death of the debtor, on his becoming insolvent or on his being sentenced to a term of imprisonment. Either the contract will provide that it is terminated automatically by a given event or it will give the creditor the right (option) to terminate it on the occurrence of the event. At common law the effect of such an event occurring is as stated in the contract, *i.e.* either that the contract terminates automatically or that it becomes terminable at the creditor's option.

Where the agreement is a regulated agreement the common law position is modified in two respects. One of these modifications applies where the stipulated event is the death of the debtor. The

27–10

other modification (the requirement for a non-default notice) applies whatever the stipulated event.

Section 86 applies to any regulated agreement where the debtor dies. This section has already been fully considered in the last chapter (paragraph 26–12). It is sufficient to say here that usually the death of the debtor will not cause the agreement to terminate, notwithstanding anything said in the agreement. The result will be that on the debtor's death, his rights and obligations under the agreement will transfer to his personal representatives, *i.e.* those responsible for administering his estate.

Sections 76 and 98 apply to regulated agreements where the stipulated event is anything other than a breach of the agreement by the debtor. Their effect is that the creditor cannot (amongst other things) either terminate the agreement or treat any right of the debtor as terminated without first serving on him a notice (a non-default notice) giving him at least seven days' warning. These sections also have already been considered once (paragraph 26–17). However, there are two remaining questions that need answering in relation both to default and also to non-default notices.

Default notice and non-default notice

27–11   It will be apparent that where termination occurs other than by mutual agreement or by the debtor exercising his right of termination, one of these notices has to be served. Two questions arise in relation to such notices:

(i) Exactly when will termination occur?

When the creditor has a right (*i.e.* option) to terminate the agreement on a breach or other stipulated event, then termination cannot occur before expiry of the notice served on the debtor. That (*i.e.* expiry of the notice) will in practice be when termination will occur—because the notice will state so. However, sometimes a hire-purchase agreement states that the agreement is to terminate automatically upon a certain type of breach by the debtor or upon some other event. At common law, of course, this would mean that termination occurred as soon as (and at the same time as) the stipulated event. Section 87 (default notice) or section 76 (non-default notice) prevents the creditor, until the expiry of the notice, from being entitled to "treat" any right to the debtor as terminated. So we have the position that it is not until the expiry of the notice that the creditor can treat the contract as terminated. At the expiry of the notice he can treat the contract as terminated—but, as terminated when? The answer is that he can then treat the contract as having terminated upon the happening of the event which was stipulated as causing the automatic termination. This is because the sections requiring the notice to be given to the debtor do not (with one exception) prevent automatic termination occurring but only prevent (*i.e.* delay) the creditor treating the termination as having occurred. The exception brings us on to the next question.

(ii) Can the notice requirements ever prevent termination occurring altogether?

In one situation they can. That is where, after a default notice is served and before it expires, the debtor complies with the notice by remedying his breach or paying compensation as required in the notice. If he does this, then the debtor's breach is treated as not having occurred (section 89). In this case it follows that the breach cannot give rise to termination (either automatically or otherwise).

Apart from that one situation, service of a notice will not **27–12** prevent termination. It does, however, give the debtor the opportunity to apply for a "time order" and the court then has power to give the debtor another chance, to allow the debtor to keep the goods, to spread his repayments over a longer period, etc. However, if the court exercises these powers, that will not prevent the agreement being technically terminated. It may seem odd that on the one hand the debtor will in these circumstances be in possession of the goods, paying instalments and having the ability to exercise his option to buy them, while on the other hand the agreement has terminated. The explanation is that the debtor is then in possession of the goods under the time order made by the court. It is true that he will be "treated" as in possession under the terms of the agreement, but this will not alter the fact that the agreement has technically terminated. It may in these circumstances seem irrelevant that the agreement had, technically speaking, been terminated, and so it is, as between the creditor and debtor. However, as we shall see, it may be an important point in the creditor's favour if the debtor's landlord later seizes the goods from the debtor's possession in order to pay for the debtor's rent. More will be said on this later.

One more thing needs to be said at this stage about time orders. The court's power to make a time order includes the power to allow time (a specified period) during which the debtor can remedy a breach (other than one consisting of non-payment). This will cause a postponement of the time when the creditor will be able to terminate the agreement or to treat it as terminated.

OPERATION OF AN ACCELERATED PAYMENTS CLAUSE

27–13   Sometimes a clause of a hire-purchase agreement will provide that in the event of the debtor falling into arrears, the creditor can, by serving a notice, cause all the remaining (*i.e.* future) instalments to fall due immediately upon expiry of the notice unless by then the debtor has paid off all his arrears. The idea is that if the debtor does not pay off his arrears before the notice expires, he can immediately be sued for the whole outstanding balance owing under the agreement. The debtor in effect is to forfeit his right to pay it off over a period of time. Normally the amount payable under an accelerated payments clause will be less than the total of the outstanding instalments. This is because there will be a reduction (or "rebate") to reflect the fact that the creditor will be receiving the remaining instalments earlier than if they had remained payable over a period of time. Under an accelerated payments clause the debtor will become owner of the goods earlier than he otherwise would. Exactly when he will become the owner will depend upon the wording of the clause. It will be either upon expiry of the notice served on him under the clause or else when the debtor pays the outstanding balance which has fallen due because of the clause.

27–14   The original plan of any hire-purchase agreement is that the debtor will pay over a period of time and that, when at the end of that period he has paid all the instalments, he will have the right to become the owner. The operation of an accelerated payments clause involves not an abandonment of that plan, but merely a speeding up of it. The debtor still remains liable to pay the instalments (subject to any "rebate") and he still becomes the owner of the goods. The effect of the clause is that both his liability to pay the instalments and also the transfer of ownership to him are brought forward to an earlier time. The effect is much the same as where the debtor voluntarily chooses to pay off the whole outstanding balance early. The other premature terminations dealt with in this chapter operate very differently. They involve an abortion of the original plan. Thus where, upon a debtor's default, the creditor serves a notice, not under an accelerated payments clause, but under a termination clause, the effect is as follows. It is that upon expiry of the notice, unless the debtor has paid off his arrears, the hiring ceases and normally (*i.e.* unless the court grants a time order) the creditor will become entitled to the return of the goods. Sometimes a hire-purchase agreement will contain both a termination clause and an accelerated payments clause, thereby giving the creditor a choice. In the event of the debtor's default, the creditor could serve a notice under either. Clearly, if the goods had been destroyed or lost or had depreciated to become almost worthless, the creditor would be sensible to opt for the accelerated payments clause.

In the case of a regulated agreement an accelerated payments **27–15** clause, like a termination clause, cannot be activated without the debtor first being given a chance to rectify his default, *i.e.* to bring his payments up to date. Thus, a default notice must be served under section 87 (see paragraphs 26–09 and 27–08) before the creditor can become entitled to any accelerated payment. After service of the default notice, the debtor can apply to the court for a time order. For the debtor there is at this stage, however, an alternative to consider, which would be especially appropriate if the goods have become severely depreciated and are no longer worth very much. This is the exercise of his statutory right of termination under section 99. This right is available in the case of a regulated agreement but must be exercised before expiry of the default notice. This is because the statutory right in section 99 (see paragraph 27–05) is exercisable "at any time before the final payment by the debtor under a regulated hire-purchase or regulated conditional sale agreement falls due". It can be exercised after a default notice has been served under an accelerated payments clause. If, however, upon expiry of such a default notice the debtor has not exercised his right of termination and still has not rectified his default, the whole outstanding balance (less a "rebate") will fall due. That is the final payment required of the debtor under the agreement. Once it has fallen due, *i.e.* upon expiry of the default notice, the debtor cannot subsequently exercise his statutory right of termination: *Wadham Stringer Ltd v. Meaney* (1981 QB).

Upon expiry of the default notice, the debtor under a regulated **27–16** agreement still has, however, the right to apply for a time order under section 129. By granting a time order, the court could reverse the effect of the accelerated payments clause. The debtor would still have to pay the outstanding instalments but instead of him having to pay them all at once as stated in the accelerated payments clause, the court could by granting a time order allow the debtor to pay them in instalments, *e.g.* much as originally planned under the agreement. Time orders were explained at paragraph 26–19.

Now let us turn to the rebate which a debtor is allowed under an accelerated payments clause. In the case of a regulated agreement he is entitled either to the rebate which is expressly allowed in the clause itself or else to the rebate given by the Consumer Credit (Rebate on Early Settlement) Regulations 1983 made under section 95 (see paragraph 26–04 above). He is entitled to whichever is the higher of these two rebates. Of course, if there is no early payment, *e.g.* because the court makes a time order which reverses the effect of the accelerated payments clause, then the debtor loses his entitlement to any rebate. The Regulations just mentioned apply only to regulated agreements. However, any accelerated payments clause, provided it is exercisable when the debtor is in breach of the agreement, is subject to the doctrine of penalties: *Wadham Stringer Ltd v. Meaney* (1981 QB). This doctrine applies irrespective of whether the agreement is a regulated one. Under this doctrine the accelerated payments clause would be void if it provided for no rebate of charges or if it provided for a rebate much less than that provided by the Regulations in relation to regulated agreements. If an accelerated payments clause is void, then, despite the service and expiry of any default notice, no accelerated payment can fall due under it. In that case the hire-purchase agreement will remain unaffected and, if it is a regulated agreement, the debtor will retain his statutory right of termination under section 99.

The remainder of this chapter will be concerned not with accelerated payments clauses, but with premature termination without the debtor becoming owner of the goods.

RECOVERY OF THE GOODS BY THE CREDITOR FROM THE DEBTOR

27–17   Whether the creditor is entitled to recover the goods after termination may depend upon whether the hire-purchase agreement is a regulated agreement within the Consumer Credit Act or not. The common law position, *i.e.* where it is not a regulated agreement, will be examined first.

Common law

27–18   At common law the rule is that once the hiring has been terminated, the debtor has no right to retain possession of the goods. The creditor is entitled to recover possession. This is so even if the contract does not expressly say so: *Bowmakers v. Barnet Instruments* (1945 CA). If on request the debtor refuses or fails to hand over the goods, he commits conversion of the goods. There are two ways in which the creditor can enforce his right to possession. He can either seize physical possession of them or he can commence court proceedings against the debtor for conversion. There may be difficulty in the first method because, if the goods are on the debtor's premises, the creditor may be unable to seize them without trespassing and thus laying himself open to an action by the debtor. For this reason sometimes the hire-purchase agreement will contain a clause expressly authorising the creditor to enter the debtor's premises to recover possession of the goods after termination. If the creditor brings an action for conversion, he is most unlikely to obtain a court order compelling the debtor to return the goods. He will obtain damages instead. The damages will not be the full value of the goods, but only the outstanding balance of the hire-purchase price, *i.e.* the remaining payments which the debtor would have been liable to pay if the agreement had not been terminated: *Wickham Holdings v. Brooke House Motors* (1967 CA). If the result of an award of damages to the creditor is that he gets payment of the balance of the hire-purchase price earlier than he would have got it if the agreement had not been terminated, then a reduction will be made to take account of this accelerated payment.

The Torts (Interference with Goods) Act 1977 allows the creditor, if he wishes, to choose a different judgment in place of a simple award of damages—namely a judgment giving the debtor an option either to pay damages (assessed as just explained) or to return the goods. If the debtor opts to return the goods then the debtor is entitled to receive from the creditor a financial allowance, *i.e.* a sum equal to the amount by which the value of the goods exceeds the alternative damages awarded.

Regulated agreements

The position is different in three ways where the agreement is a regulated agreement: **27–19**

    (i) Section 92 provides that the creditor is not entitled to enter any premises to take possession of the goods except under an order of the court. This means that in practice, unless the creditor can persuade the debtor voluntarily to hand over the goods, the creditor will have to bring a court action to recover them. If he does that then the court has power to make a time order.

(ii) Where the debtor wrongfully retains possession of the goods after termination, the court will normally order the debtor to return the goods to the creditor. The debtor will not be given the option of paying their value instead (section 100(5)). The court may, however, refuse to make an order for the return of the goods if a refusal would be "just". Of course, there would be such a refusal or else the operation of the return order would be suspended where the court makes a time order.

(iii) Where the goods are "protected goods", the creditor is not entitled to recover possession of them without bringing a court action.

It is still the position that where the agreement is terminated otherwise than by the debtor's breach, the creditor is entitled to seize physical possession of the goods without trespassing. The creditor is similarly entitled, even where the agreement has been terminated by reason of the debtor's breach unless the goods are "protected goods". However, no doubt when the court gives the debtor another chance and therefore makes a time order, it will simultaneously deprive the creditor of the right to seize possession while the time order is in force.

Protected Goods

27–20 For the debtor the consequences of termination can be unfortunate in that he may have the goods repossessed by the creditor in spite of the fact that he has paid a considerable amount towards them. He may then find that the creditor claims also a further money payment for termination of the agreement. We shall shortly be seeing that the court, by making a time order, can give the debtor another chance of maintaining payments under the agreement. The effect of the protected goods provision is to see that the creditor has not seized possession of the goods before the court has considered whether to give the debtor that second chance. However, these protected goods provisions apply only where the goods fall within the definition of "protected goods".

The definition

Goods which are let under a regulated hire-purchase agreement **27-21** fall within the definition of protected goods in section 90 if three conditions are fulfilled:

(a) The debtor is in breach of the agreement.

(b) The debtor has paid or tendered to the creditor one-third or more of the total price of the goods.

(c) The property in the goods remains in the creditor.

The last of these will cause no difficulty since property (*i.e.* ownership) will remain with the creditor until the debtor exercises his option to buy (*i.e.* until he has paid all the money due under the agreement).

The first condition is satisfied only if the debtor is in breach of the agreement. If the agreement has been terminated for some other reason the creditor will be entitled to seize the goods, providing he does not trespass to do so, or he can sue for their return under section 100(5) (see paragraph 27–19 above). Where the debtor falls into arrears, the goods will be protected goods provided one-third of the total price has been paid or tendered.

The total price is the total sum payable by the debtor under the agreement, *i.e.* the deposit plus all the instalments plus the option money. The calculation will normally be easy. However, it will be complicated if either the total price includes charges in respect of the installation of the goods or the debtor has more than one regulated agreement with the same creditor.

For the purposes of the calculation, any installation charges have to be separated from the rest of the total price. By section 90(2) the debtor will not be regarded as having paid or tendered one-third of the total price unless he has paid or tendered both:

(i) the whole of the installation charges, and

(ii) one-third of the remainder of the total price.

Section 81 applies where the debtor has, in addition to the **27-22** agreement in question, a further regulated agreement under which he has to make payments to the same person as he does under the agreement in question. The section provides that any payment made by the debtor can be appropriated by him as between the different agreements. If the debtor does not indicate to which agreement any given payment is appropriated, then that payment is appropriated between the agreements proportionately according to the amount of the sums due under each agreement (see paragraph 26–28 above). If on the other hand the debtor has just one agreement under which he owes, both (i) arrears of payments which have already fallen due, and (ii) default interest which has accrued on those arrears, then in the absence of an appropriation by the debtor, there is no automatic appropriation and the creditor can appropriate any payment received to either (i) or (ii): *Julian Hodge Bank Ltd v. Hall* (paragraph 26–29 above). If it is appropriated to (ii) then it will not go towards payment of the one third of the total price, since default interest is not part of the "total price".

Goods will not be (or will cease to be) protected goods if the debtor exercises his right of termination (*i.e.* under section 99). Thus where the debtor falls into arrears, it may be much to his advantage not to exercise his right of termination but simply to do nothing and let the creditor, if he wishes, serve a default notice and terminate the agreement. Since in these circumstances it would not be in the debtor's interest for him to exercise a right of termination, the court would be reluctant to find that he had done so, unless he had done it consciously and was fully aware of the consequences—*United Dominions Trust v. Ennis* (paragraph 27–06 above).

The protection

27–23   The creditor is not entitled, otherwise than by court action, to recover possession of protected goods from the debtor (section 90). Thus he must not seize physical possession of them. It is not a criminal offence for him to do so. However, if, contrary to section 90, he does so, then the agreement is terminated and all payments made under the agreement are returnable to the debtor who is relieved of further liability under the agreement—section 91. There are three significant exceptions to the protection given by section 90, *i.e.* three situations where the creditor can recover physical possession of the goods without contravening section 90:

> (i) If the debtor has disposed of the goods to a third party, the creditor can seize them from the third party without contravening section 90. This is because section 90 prevents him seizing them "from the debtor". (For the creditor's rights as against the third party, see paragraphs 27–38 to 27–49 below.) If the debtor has not

disposed of the goods but has simply, for example, lent them to a friend or left them to be mended by a repairer, the creditor would be contravening section 90 if he seized them. Lord Denning M. R. in *Bentinck v. Cromwell Engineering Ltd* (1971 CA) was referring to the section of the Hire Purchase Act 1965 which has been replaced by section 90 (and which used the word "hirer" instead of "debtor") when he said:

> "In the ordinary way, once goods are 'protected goods', *i.e.* more than one-third has been paid, the finance company cannot recover possession— except by action—from the hirer, nor from any garage or repairer with whom the hirer may have left it. The words 'from the hirer' include all those to whom the hirer has bailed it."

(ii) If the debtor has abandoned the goods, the creditor can seize them without contravening section 90, for he is not then seizing them "from the debtor". In *Bentinck's* case, the debtor paid the deposit and first few instalments before falling into arrears. The car was badly damaged in an accident and he left it at a garage but did not give orders to repair it. Three months later the finance company, the creditor, traced him. He paid none of the arrears, gave a false 'phone number and disappeared without trace. After a further six months the finance company took the car from the garage where it had been left by the debtor some nine months earlier. The Court held on these facts that the debtor had abandoned the car and the finance company had not contravened section 90.

(iii) The creditor does not contravene section 90 if the debtor consents to the creditor repossessing the goods: *Mercantile Credit Co. v. Cross* (1965 CA) and section 173(3). To be effective, the consent has to be given at the time of the repossession. Even then the consent will not be effective unless the debtor knows, or has been informed, what his rights would be if he refuses consent: *Chartered Trust v. Pitcher* (1987 CA). Those rights would (if the creditor brought legal proceedings to recover possession of the goods) be the right to ask the court to reorganise his repayments and let him retain possession under a time order (see paragraphs 27–36 and 27–37).

Court action

27–24   If the creditor wishes to recover possession of protected goods he must bring an action in the county court. Even if he can show that the agreement has terminated he will not automatically be granted a "return order", *i.e.* an order for the goods to be returned. The court may decide that such an order would not be just and may instead grant a time order. The court's powers will be further considered after we have looked at what money claim the creditor can make.

MONEY CLAIM BY CREDITOR FROM DEBTOR

27–25   When termination occurs, the situation is different according to whether the agreement is or is not a regulated agreement. Regulated agreements will be considered second. Turning first to the position at common law, *i.e.* where the agreement is not a regulated one, the creditor may have two alternative claims against the debtor. He may be able to claim damages for the debtor's breach of contract or he may be able to claim the amount stipulated in the agreement as being payable upon termination (*i.e.* the minimum payment).

Damages

27–26   Damages can be obtained for the debtor's breach of contract. Since termination is usually preceded by the debtor falling into arrears, there is usually a reason for claiming damages. The amount, however, will depend upon whether the debtor repudiated the contract or whether he simply got into arrears. If he has simply got into arrears, the amount of damages will depend upon whether punctual payment was of the essence of the contract.

(i) Damages for repudiation

27–27   These are assessed according to the rule in *Yeoman Credit v. Waragowski* (1961 CA) where at the time of termination the debtor had paid only the initial deposit, £72. After termination the creditor recovered possession of the goods, a car, which was then worth £205. The creditor was awarded the following damages:

(a)	Arrears of instalment due before termination			£60
& (b)	A sum arrived at by taking the total hire purchase price and then deducting certain items:		£434	
	payments already made	£72		
	the amount awarded under (a)	£60		
	the option money in the agreement	£1		
	the value of the goods recovered	£205		
		£338	£338	
			£96	£96
	Total			£156

When the creditor is awarded damages assessed on the *Waragowski* basis, he is in effect put in the same position as if the whole transaction had gone through as originally contemplated. Adding up the amounts he receives before termination, the value of the goods he has recovered and the damages awarded, it can be seen that he receives virtually the whole hire-purchase price.

Sometimes when termination occurs early on, the creditor gets this sum earlier than he would have done if the agreement had never been terminated. If it had not been terminated, he would have had to await payment of the instalments as the months went by. If it does occur that the creditor receives payment earlier than he would have, the court will make a deduction from the award of damages to take account of that earlier payment: *Overstone v. Shipway* (1962 CA).

(ii) Damages where the debtor does not repudiate

Where the debtor simply gets into arrears but does not repudiate the contract, the agreement may give the creditor the right of termination. If the creditor exercises that right then the termination is caused not by the debtor's breach but by the creditor exercising his right. That being so, the creditor cannot claim for loss of future payments as damages. He is limited to a claim for arrears of instalments due before termination. This was decided in *Financings v. Baldock* (1963 CA). The debtor had been in arrears; he had told the finance company (the creditor) that he hoped to pay off the arrears. The finance company later terminated the agreement. It was held that since at the time of

27–28

termination the debtor could not be said to have repudiated the contract, he was liable only for arrears of instalments up to the date of termination. It is clear then that a debtor who finds he cannot maintain his payment is best advised not to repudiate the agreement, but to indicate that he hopes and intends to make up the instalments. The court's sympathy in these cases tends to be with the debtor rather than the creditor who is normally a finance company. The court will tend, if possible, to find that the debtor's conduct has not amounted to a repudiation and it will not allow the finance company to put upon the debtor a repudiation when the debtor has not in fact repudiated: *Eshun v. Moorgate Mercantile Co.* (see paragraph 27–09 above). One clear case of repudiation, however, is where the debtor sells or otherwise wrongfully disposes of the goods, in which case the damages will be assessed on the *Waragowski* basis.

Where damages are assessed on the *Financings v. Baldock* basis and the creditor therefore receives only arrears up to the date of termination, there will be added to that amount a sum equal to the creditor's loss caused by the debtor's failure, if any, to take reasonable care of the goods. The hire-purchase agreement will have included a term requiring the debtor to take reasonable care of the goods. If he does not do so then the goods when recovered by the creditor may be worth a certain amount less than if reasonable care had been taken of them. It is that amount which will in the award of damages be added to the arrears due up to the date of termination.

The law as established in *Financings v. Baldock* does not apply where the debtor has broken a *condition* of the contract.

(iii) Damages where debtor's breach is a breach of condition

27–29   In *Lombard North Central v. Butterworth* (1987 CA) the contract provided that punctual payment of instalments under the contract was of the essence of the agreement. This clearly meant that punctual payment was a condition (as opposed to a warranty). In accordance with the general law of contract, the Court of Appeal held that therefore any lateness in payment, even if it did not amount to a repudiation by the debtor, could nevertheless be treated by the creditor as if it were such a repudiation. This meant that the creditor's damages after termination were to be assessed not on a *Financings v. Baldock* basis but on a *Waragowski* basis. This decision may well have resulted in the law in *Financings v. Baldock* becoming a dead letter, since many hire-purchase companies have, after *Lombard North Central v. Butterworth*, drafted their contracts to state that prompt payment by the debtor is of the essence of the contract. Thus, as Nicholls L.J. said in the *Lombard* case, the conclusion in that case "emasculates the decision in *Financings v. Baldock*".

(iv) Claim against a guarantor or indemnifier

As already explained, if, when the debtor has neither repudiated the contract nor broken a condition, the creditor exercises a right of termination, the creditor cannot claim loss of future payments from the debtor. He is entitled only to the return of the goods and arrears which were due before termination. That is what happened in *Goulston Discount Co. v. Clark* (1967 CA) where the creditor recovered from the debtor £157 less than he would have recovered if the debtor had repudiated the contract. The question in *Goulston* was whether the creditor, a finance company, could recover that £157 from the car dealer. Under a recourse agreement between the finance company and the dealer, the dealer had, in consideration of the finance company entering into a hire-purchase agreement with W (the debtor), agreed as follows. He had agreed that he would "indemnify" the finance company against any loss that the finance company might suffer by reason of the fact that W did not, for any cause whatsoever, pay all the amounts which he would pay if he completed his hire-purchase agreement. It was held that since this was an indemnity, the finance company was entitled to recover the £157. If it had been a guarantee, the finance company would have failed in this claim because a guarantor is under no greater liability than the debtor. The decision in *Goulston* would be exactly the same if the facts occurred again today. The claim under the indemnity (the recourse agreement) would not be reduced or affected at all by section 113 of the Consumer Credit Act, since the recourse agreement would not be "security" within the definition in the Act, see paragraph 26–40 above.

27–30

Minimum payments

Hire-purchase agreements commonly contain a provision that on termination the debtor must pay a stipulated amount. From the creditor's point of view, one advantage of claiming this minimum payment instead of damages is that no damages can normally be claimed where the termination has occurred not as a result of the debtor's breach of contract, but as a result of some event, *e.g.* the

27–31

debtor terminating under a right to do so. Another advantage is that the minimum payment clause will usually provide for a fixed sum, whereas in a claim for damages there may be a dispute about the creditor's actual loss. However, the principal advantage is that the minimum payment clause may provide for a larger sum than the creditor could claim as damages. This last fact has caused neither the courts nor Parliament to look with favour upon minimum payment clauses. Thus a minimum payment clause may either (i) be void because of the common law doctrine of penalties or (ii) be ineffective because of the provisions of the Consumer Credit Act relating to extortionate credit bargains (if they apply) or (iii) be ineffective by virtue of the Unfair Terms in Consumer Contracts Regulations 1999. The provisions on extortionate credit bargains and the 1999 Regulations have already been considered (at paragraphs 26–06 and 26–08 respectively).

Penalties

27–32   The common law doctrine of penalties is concerned with a certain type of contractual clause—namely, the sort of clause which stipulates how much will be payable in the event of a breach of contract. Such a clause is a liquidated damages clause and is void if it amounts to a penalty. It will not be a penalty if it was a genuine attempt by the parties to pre-estimate the likely damages in the event of the breach. It will be a penalty if the stipulated minimum payment is large, out of all proportion to the likely damages (see, generally, paragraph 14–21 above). In the words of Lord Dunedin in *Dunlop Pneumatic Tyre Co. v. New Garage Motor Co.* (1915 HL):

> "It will be held to be a penalty if the sum stipulated for is extravagant and unconscionable in amount in comparison with the greatest loss that could conceivably be proved to have followed from the breach."

In *Bridge v. Campbell Discount Co.* (1962 HL) the clause in question required the debtor to pay on termination:

(a) arrears of payments due before termination, plus

(b) an amount which together with payments made and due before termination amounted to two-thirds of the hire-purchase price.

This was in addition to the fact that the creditor was entitled to the return of the goods. The clause was held to be a penalty because, including the value of the returned goods, it would in nearly all cases give the creditor more than 100 per cent of the hire-purchase price, *i.e.* more than damages assessed on the *Waragowski* basis.

Even a clause where the amount stipulated is the same as **27–33** would be awarded as damages assessed on the *Waragowski* basis can be a penalty. It will be a penalty if it provides for that amount to be payable where the damages, if awarded, would be assessed on the *Financings v. Baldock* basis. In *Anglo Auto Finance Co. v. James* (1963 CA) the clause required the debtor to pay:

(a) arrears of payments due before termination, plus

(b) the amount by which the hire-purchase price exceeded the sum of:

    (i) payments made and due before termination, and
    (ii) the value of the goods when recovered and resold.

The Court of Appeal held that this was a penalty and awarded damages instead. Since the debtor had not repudiated the agreement the damages were assessed on the *Financings v. Baldock* basis.

The doctrine of penalties applies where an excessive sum is stipulated to be payable on a breach of contract. However, termination can and does sometimes occur where there is no breach of contract, *e.g.* where the debtor exercises a contractual right of termination or where the contract terminates automatically on some specified event such as the debtor's bankruptcy. The Court of Appeal in *Associated Distributors v. Hall* (1938) held that the doctrine of penalties does not apply where a sum is stipulated payable on a termination which occurs without the debtor being in breach of the agreement. The creditor can sue for the stipulated amount, however great. This decision has proved a controversial one, although it still stands as part of the law. In *Bridge v. Campbell Discount Co.* the House of Lords was evenly split on the question of whether it was correct. The decision leads to the situation where, if the debtor exercises his contractual right of termination, he may have to pay a larger sum than if he breaks his contract, thus causing termination. It is for this reason that the court will not hold that the debtor has exercised his right of termination unless he did so fully aware of the consequences (see *United Dominions Trust v. Ennis*, paragraph 27–06 above). Of course it is now possible that a clause providing for a very high sum to be payable on a termination occurring in the absence of a breach by the hirer would be rendered ineffective by the Unfair Terms in Consumer Contracts Regulations 1999 (see paragraph 10–39 above).

Regulated agreements

27–34   Where the creditor brings a money claim against the debtor, that is an action to enforce the regulated agreement. That being so, the court will have the power to make a time order which is to be considered in the next section of this chapter. However, what money award could the creditor expect if the court were to make an immediate "return order"? The Consumer Credit Act does not state what size of award should be made. Thus the answer is that the award would equal whatever sum would be obtainable by the creditor as damages at common law—unless the agreement stipulated a different amount. However, it should be added that if the agreement stipulated an excessive amount, the court could reduce that amount. Even if the doctrine of penalties did not apply, the court could reopen the agreement as being extortionate (see paragraph 26–06 above).

By way of exception to what has just been said, the Act does state in section 100 how much money award should be made where the termination has occurred by the debtor exercising his right of termination under section 99. In that case the debtor's liability is to pay any loss caused by his failure to take reasonable care of the goods, plus all the arrears due before termination, plus whichever is the smallest of the following three amounts:

(i)   The amount of the minimum payment stipulated in the agreement. If none is stipulated then the amount under this head is zero.

(ii) The amount, if any, by which one-half of the total hire-purchase price exceeds the total of the sums paid by the debtor and the arrears due before termination.

(iii) The amount of the creditor's actual loss arising from the termination by the debtor (*i.e.* the amount of damages assessed on the *Waragowski* basis).

Thus where the debtor exercises his right of termination the most that he will have to pay (assuming he took reasonable care of the goods) is the amount required to clear off his arrears due before termination, plus enough to bring up his payments to one-half of the total price. In calculating one-half of the total price, difficulties will arise if the total price includes installation charges or if the debtor has a further regulated agreement with the same creditor. For the purposes of the calculation, the installation charges have to be separated from the rest of the total price. By section 100(2) one-half of the total price is to be regarded as equal to the whole of the installation charge plus one-half of the remainder of the total price. Section 81 applies where the debtor has, in addition to the agreement in question, a further regulated agreement with the same creditor. Its effect has already been explained (see paragraph 26–28).   **27–35**

POWERS OF THE COURT IN THE CASE OF REGULATED AGREEMENTS

Hire-purchase has been picturesquely described as the fertile mother of litigation. The vast majority of this litigation takes the form of an action by the creditor against the debtor in circumstances where the latter has defaulted on paying his instalments. There can be no doubt that the vast majority of hire-purchase agreements fall within the category of regulated agreements. Thus the court's powers, which we are about to examine, are designed to enable the court to deal with the situation where the debtor has defaulted.   **27–36**

A hire-purchase agreement will usually give the creditor the right to terminate it if the debtor becomes a certain amount in arrears. Thus when the debtor gets into arrears the action brought against him by the creditor will be one of two sorts:

(i) The creditor chooses to regard the agreement as terminated and (after serving the necessary default notice) brings an action claiming repossession of the goods and damages or the stipulated payment.

(ii) The creditor chooses not to regard the agreement as terminated and sues simply for arrears.

In the latter case the court will either give immediate judgment to the creditor for the arrears due or it will make a time order under section 129 allowing the debtor extra time to pay. Time orders were considered earlier (paragraph 26–19) when it was seen that the court can adjust the instalment pattern so as to make it easier for the debtor to maintain his payments.

27–37 If the creditor adopts the first alternative and claims repossession, then the court can make a time order or it can exercise its powers under section 133. A time order will have the effect of allowing the debtor another chance of making his payments—perhaps over a longer period. The court's powers under section 133 are to make either a return order or a transfer order. A return order is an order for the return of the goods to the creditor. The court must make a return order unless it would not be just to do so. Such an order would therefore be made if there were clearly no chance of the debtor paying off the debt. In that case the creditor will be likely to ask for damages also. The amount of such an award has already been considered (paragraph 27–34).

A transfer order is an alternative to making a return order, but one which will in practice be available only occasionally. It is an order that the debtor return part of the goods but which allows him to keep the other part as his own without making further payment. This order can be made only where the court can divide the goods and where the payments already made by the debtor under the agreement are at least equal to a minimum amount. The minimum amount which he must have paid is a combination of (i) that part of the total price which is attributable to the goods he is being allowed to keep and (ii) one-quarter of the rest of the total price. The total price includes the deposit, all the instalments and the option money which were scheduled under the agreement. The reason a transfer order will seldom be available is that the goods cannot very often be divided. It is not common, except perhaps in the case of some items of furniture (*e.g.* a three-piece suite), for one hire-purchase agreement to embrace more than one item.

Even after a return order or transfer order is made, there may be some delay before the creditor enforces the order. In this situation, if the debtor can find the financial resources to do so, he is still entitled to pay the whole outstanding balance of the total hire-purchase price and thereby become the owner of all the goods. He has this right until the creditor actually recovers possession—section 133(4).

RECOVERY BY THE CREDITOR OF GOODS IN THE HANDS OF A THIRD PARTY

We are here concerned with the position where someone other than the creditor or debtor also claims to have an interest in the goods. We have seen that on termination the creditor has a right as against the debtor to possession (subject to the provisions of the Consumer Credit Act). When some third party claims an interest, whose claim takes priority—the creditor's or the third party's? **27–38**

Sale of the goods by the debtor

When the debtor sells the goods before completing his payments, the goods will be in the hands of the purchaser. The general rule is that the creditor is entitled to recover the goods from the purchaser: *Helby v. Matthews* (see paragraph 5–34 above). This is the reason that hire-purchase has proved so popular with finance companies. It gives the creditor this high degree of protection even when the debtor wrongfully sells the goods. The reason for the general rule is that the creditor under a hire-purchase agreement remains the owner of the goods until the debtor has paid off all the instalments and exercised his option to buy. He remains the owner even though the debtor sells the goods. It is his ownership that entitles him to recover the goods from the purchaser and he has that right regardless of whether the hire-purchase agreement has been terminated. Of course, if one of the exceptions to the *nemo dat* principle applies (see Chapter 5 above), then the creditor will lose his rights over the goods and the innocent purchaser will acquire good title. From the creditor's point of view the important thing about hire-purchase is that one exception in particular does not apply, *i.e.* the exception in section 9 of the Factors Act and section 25 of the Sale of Goods Act—because the debtor is not a "buyer" in possession. **27–39**

The general rule then is in favour of the creditor rather than the innocent purchaser. The rule is the same if, instead of selling the goods, the debtor pledges them with a pawnbroker. The pawnbroker is in the same position as the innocent purchaser.

The general rule is very hard on the innocent third party and has been reversed where the subject-matter of the hire-purchase agreement is a motor vehicle which the debtor sells to an innocent private purchaser. In this case the innocent private purchaser acquires good title to the vehicle by virtue of the Hire Purchase Act 1964, Pt. III (see paragraph 5–40 above).

27–40   In a case where none of the exceptions to the *nemo dat* principle applies, the creditor may nevertheless not discover that the debtor has disposed of the goods and may therefore do nothing to recover them. If the debtor continues to pay his instalments, eventually completes his payments and exercises his option to purchase, that will operate to feed the title down to the person who acquired the goods from the debtor: *Butterworth v. Kingsway Motors* (see paragraph 7–19 above). If this happens, it follows that, since the creditor under the hire-purchase agreement is no longer the owner, he has no right to the goods.

Even where the creditor under the hire-purchase agreement is still the owner, as in *Helby v. Matthews*, it does not follow that he will actually recover possession of the goods. If the third party refuses to hand them over, the creditor can bring a court action, *i.e.* a claim for conversion. The refusal of the creditor's demand to hand them over is a conversion. However, the court will not order the goods to be returned but will award damages to the creditor. Now, the damages will not necessarily be the full value of the goods at the date of conversion. The debtor has already paid some sums to the creditor (*i.e.* the initial deposit and perhaps some instalments). If the debtor had not disposed of the goods but had kept them he could have bought them by paying the outstanding balance of the hire-purchase price. Thus, all that the creditor has lost is that outstanding balance. It is that amount which will be awarded to him as damages against the third party: *Wickham Holdings v. Brooke House Motors* (1967 CA). To look at it another way, the debtor, by selling the goods to the third party (albeit wrongfully), has transferred to the third party his (the debtor's) rights—in particular his option to buy the goods for the outstanding balance of the hire-purchase price. The Torts (Interference With Goods) Act 1977 allows the creditor, if he wishes, to choose a different judgment in place of an award of damages—namely a judgment giving the third party (the innocent purchaser) an option either to pay damages (assessed as just explained) or to return the goods. If the third party opts to return the goods then the debtor is entitled to receive from the creditor a financial allowance, *i.e.* a sum equal to the amount by which the value of the goods exceeds the alternative damages awarded.

There is an important qualification to the rule in *Wickham*   **27–41**
Holdings v. Brooke House Motors. It is that the creditor cannot
recover from the third party any more than the value of the goods
at the date of conversion: *Chubb Cash Ltd v. John Crilley & Son*
(1983 CA). It can happen, for example, that at the date when the
third party refuses the creditor's demand to hand over the goods,
their value is less than the outstanding balance of the hire-
purchase price. The amount recoverable by the creditor from the
third party is the *smaller* of the two following amounts: (i) the
outstanding balance owing under the hire-purchase agreement; or
(ii) the value of the goods at the date of conversion, *i.e.* the date
the third party refused the creditor's demand to hand them over.

It should be added that an innocent purchaser who is liable in
conversion to the creditor will have an action against the debtor,
from whom he bought the goods, for breach of the condition as to
title in section 12 of the Sale of Goods Act (see paragraph 7–17
above).

Suppose that the innocent purchaser to whom the debtor sold   **27–42**
the goods has himself resold them to a sub-purchaser. In that case
the creditor may be able to bring a claim against the sub-
purchaser. He will be able to do so provided, again, that none of
the exceptions to the *nemo dat* principle applies. The creditor's
claim against the sub-purchaser will be on exactly the same basis
as that (just explained) against the innocent purchaser who has
not disposed of the goods. It is a claim in conversion. Now
suppose that such a claim is impossible because one of the
exceptions to the *nemo dat* principle does apply. This might occur
where a motor vehicle is involved. Thus, a debtor who has a car
on hire-purchase terms might sell the car to a car dealer who in
turn sells it to an innocent sub-purchaser. Here the innocent sub-
purchaser obtains good title by virtue of the Hire Purchase Act
1964, Pt. III (see paragraph 5–40 above). The Act does not,
however, protect the car dealer. Thus the creditor has the
possibility of a claim against the debtor or against the car dealer,
the latter claim being a claim for damages for conversion. If the
sale by the car dealer was a sale at a car auction, the creditor also
has a claim against the auctioneers for conversion. All of this is
because selling someone else's goods without authority amounts
to conversion. The owner (the creditor) can succeed in a claim
for conversion provided that he was either in possession of the
goods at the time of conversion (unlikely) or else had a right, at
the time of conversion, to immediate possession (more likely).

27–43   *Union Transport Finance v. British Car Auctions* (1978 CA) arose out of facts which occurred before the Consumer Credit Act was passed. A hire-purchase agreement required the debtor not to remove or alter the identification marks on the car and not, without the creditor's permission, to sell it or offer it for sale. The agreement also provided that, if the debtor made any default in his monthly rentals or committed any other breach, the creditor had the right to terminate the agreement by serving a default notice on the debtor. Before completing his payments under the agreement, the debtor altered the car's registration number and without authority took it to a car auction where it was sold. Subsequently the creditor learnt what had happened and brought a claim for conversion against the auctioneers. The auctioneers, in defending the action, asserted that at the time of the conversion (the auction sale) the creditor did not have a right to immediate possession because the creditor had not at that time served a default notice upon the debtor. The defence failed. It was held that the terms of the agreement allowing the creditor to terminate the agreement by serving a default notice on the debtor, conferred rights on the creditor *additional* to his rights at common law. The latter included the right to terminate the hire-purchase agreement without notice if the debtor did any act wholly repugnant to the agreement. When the debtor put the car into the auction the creditor therefore had the right to immediate possession, *i.e.* the right to terminate the agreement without notice. If the facts of this case were to occur again after the coming into force of section 87 of the Consumer Credit Act, the result might well be different. Section 87 (see paragraph 27–08 above) applies to any breach by the debtor and requires the creditor to serve a default notice giving at least seven days' notice before he can be entitled to terminate the agreement or recover possession of the goods. It thus prevents the creditor having a right to immediate possession unless and until a default notice has been served and has expired.

Debtor creates a lien

27–44   At common law a repairer to whom goods are entrusted for repair has a lien over them for his charges. The lien is the right to retain possession of the goods until his charges are paid. A lien does not arise where maintenance alone is involved but only where the work is to improve the goods. Now, it is not uncommon for a debtor to have the goods repaired. This may happen if it is a car that has been in an accident. If the debtor has it repaired and later the hire-purchase contract is terminated, the repairer's lien takes priority over the creditor's right to recover possession. This means that the creditor is not entitled to possession without first paying the repair bill. This is because the essence of hire-purchase is that the debtor shall have the use and enjoyment of the goods and therefore is authorised to have them repaired if need be. It therefore makes no difference that the repairer knows that his customer is hiring the goods on hire-purchase, for the repairer is entitled to assume that the debtor is authorised to have them repaired. This is still so, even if the hire-purchase agreement expressly states that the debtor is not authorised to create a lien. In *Albemarle Supply Co. v. Hind* (1928 CA) the subject-matter of the hire-purchase agreement was a taxi cab. In the agreement the debtor agreed not to create a lien for repairs. The garage where he took it for repair knew that he was hiring it on hire-purchase terms but was unaware of the restriction on the debtor creating liens. The Court of Appeal held that the lien was good even against the creditor. The decision would of course have been different if the garage had known of the restriction in the agreement. In that case the creditor would have been entitled to the taxi free of the lien, *i.e.* without having to pay off the repair charges.

Another situation where the creditor is entitled to recover the **27–45** car free of lien is where the debtor deposits it for repair after the hire-purchase agreement has been terminated. This was the position in *Bowmakers v. Wycombe Motors* (1964) where, since the hire-purchase agreement had been terminated, the debtor had no more authority to use the car or to have it repaired. The garage therefore could not establish a lien against the creditor and this was so even though the garage was unaware that the car was or had been the subject of a hire-purchase agreement. In this case the garage had to surrender the goods to their owner (the creditor) but could of course still sue its customer (the debtor) for the repair charges.

Suppose that at the time the debtor deposits goods for repair, he is in possession of those goods under a time order. Section 130 expressly provides that in such circumstances the debtor "shall be treated as a bailee of the goods under the terms of the agreement, notwithstanding that the agreement has terminated". The position where the debtor deposits the goods for repair after a time order has been made is exactly the same as where he does so during the currency of the agreement before a time order is made.

Debtor's landlord levies distress

27–46   A landlord can levy distress on goods in his tenant's premises if the tenant is in arrears with his rent. This means that he can seize the goods in order to sell them to pay the rent. Those goods may well include goods of which the tenant has possession on hire-purchase terms. The Law of Distress Amendment Act 1908 allows others whose goods have been seized by the landlord to serve on the landlord a notice of ownership. If this is done, the landlord is not entitled to continue with distress in relation to those goods. If the law stopped there, the owner (*i.e.* the creditor) would be in a good position against the landlord provided he discovered that the landlord had seized the goods before the landlord sold them. However, the goods may come within one of two categories in relation to which the creditor is not allowed to serve a notice of ownership. They are:

   (i) Goods bailed under a hire-purchase or consumer hire agreement or agreed to be sold under a conditional sale agreement—but not where the agreement has been terminated.

   (ii) Goods in the tenant's possession with the owner's consent in such circumstances that the tenant is the reputed owner of them.

(i) Goods bailed under a hire-purchase agreement, etc.

Normally, therefore, the creditor will not be able to serve a notice of ownership on the landlord because the goods will fall within this category. However they will not fall in this category if, when the landlord seized them, the agreement had already been terminated. Thus it can be vital to decide exactly when the agreement was terminated. A time order being made may not prevent the agreement from being (technically) terminated (see paragraph 27–10). We have seen that the requirement for the creditor to serve a default or non-default notice will not generally affect the timing of an automatic termination (see paragraph 27–12).

There is one further situation where the goods, even if the agreement has not been terminated, will not fall within this category. That is during the period after a default notice has been served and before it expires or is earlier complied with. If the notice expires and the debtor has not complied with it, the creditor will then be able to terminate the agreement immediately in which case—as we have just seen—the goods will remain outside this category.

(ii) Goods in the tenant's possession with the owner's consent in such circumstances that the tenant is the reputed owner of them

We are here concerned only with the situation where either the **27-47** hire-purchase agreement has been terminated or else a default notice is still current (*i.e.* has been served and has not expired or been complied with). This is because, in the absence of a current default notice or a termination of the hire-purchase agreement, the goods will in any case be within the previous category. The point here is that even after termination, the goods, if still in the tenant's possession, will be assumed to be there with the owner's (*i.e.* the creditor's) consent unless the latter has done some act clearly withdrawing that consent. The effective way of doing this is for him to serve on the debtor a notice expressly withdrawing his consent, at or after termination. It is not sufficient that the agreement has terminated automatically under some clause in the agreement which states that upon termination the creditor's consent to the debtor's possession is automatically withdrawn: *Times Furnishing v. Hutchings.*

Perdana Properties v. United Orient (1982 PC) involved goods which were the subject of a hire agreement (which was not a consumer hire agreement). Before the hirer's landlord levied distress, the owner had written to the hirer making it clear that the owner's consent to the continued possession by the hirer was withdrawn, although the owner had not actually terminated the hiring agreement. It was held that the owner was entitled to have the goods released to him by the landlord. The goods were not within this second category because the owner had effectively withdrawn his consent to the hirer's continued possession, even though he had not terminated the agreement. Of course, if the agreement had been a hire-purchase, conditional sale or consumer hire agreement, the owner would have been unprotected because the goods would have fallen within the previous category.

Sometimes goods will not be in the tenant's reputed ownership because of some well-known custom that people such as the tenant hire goods. Thus it is, or was, apparently a well-known fact that hotel keepers hire furniture: *Re Parker* (1885).

If the landlord levies distress after termination of the agreement or during the currency of a default notice, it seems that the creditor will be able to serve a notice of ownership provided the goods are not in the tenant's possession with the creditor's consent in such circumstances that the tenant is the reputed owner of them.

Debtor goes bankrupt

27–48　As a general rule when someone goes bankrupt all his property passes to his trustee in bankruptcy whose task it is to collect in all the bankrupt's assets and use them to pay off the creditors. This does not, however, affect goods which do not belong to the bankrupt, such as goods he is hiring on hire-purchase terms.

Sheriff levies execution on the debtor

27–49　When a defendant has a judgment entered against him by a court, the claimant can enforce that judgment by having the sheriff or court bailiff execute it for him. The sheriff or bailiff is entitled to enter the defendant's premises and seize his goods so that he can sell them and use the proceeds to pay the amount of the judgment. The risk is that he seizes goods which the defendant is hiring on hire-purchase terms. If he does so unknowingly and sells them, the owner (*i.e.* the creditor) thereupon loses all rights in the goods and the purchaser acquires good title. However, if the creditor becomes aware of the fact that his goods have been seized, then he can recover possession of them at any time before the sheriff disposes of them. If it is too late and they have been sold, he is entitled to the proceeds of sale.

CHAPTER 28

TERMINATION OF CREDIT SALE, CONDITIONAL SALE AND CONSUMER HIRE AGREEMENTS

CREDIT SALE AGREEMENTS

UNDER a credit sale agreement property passes to the buyer **28–01** before he has paid the instalments of the price. If he sells the goods, the person buying them from him will acquire good title. The buyer is free to sell the goods at any time. Some credit sale agreements provide that if he does so, the full outstanding balance of the purchase price shall immediately become payable. This means that the seller can commence proceedings against him immediately for the whole outstanding balance. However, if the agreement is a regulated agreement within the Consumer Credit Act, the creditor (*i.e.* the seller) will first have to serve a default or non-default notice (see paragraphs 26–09 and 26–17 above) and the court will also have power to make a time order under section 129, *i.e.* to allow the debtor (*i.e.* the buyer) to pay the sum off in instalments (see paragraph 26–19).

A credit sale agreement may provide that the whole outstanding balance of the price shall become payable on certain specified breaches by the buyer (*e.g.* if his payments get more than a certain time in arrears). Here again if the agreement is a regulated agreement within the Consumer Credit Act, then the creditor could not sue for that sum until he had first served on the debtor a default notice. Again, the court would have the power to make a time order.

A credit sale agreement does not give the seller the right to recover possession of the goods on default by the buyer. It will not give the buyer a right to terminate it prematurely and section 100 of the Consumer Credit Act does not apply; so the buyer has no statutory right of termination (other than, in the case of a

regulated agreement, to pay off his debt early—section 94). Thus
the question of "protected goods" does not arise and the
protected goods provisions do not apply to credit sale agreements.
From a finance company's point of view, a credit sale agreement
is a device for the company to give what in effect is an unsecured
loan for the purchase of particular goods (see paragraph 20–05
above).

CONDITIONAL SALE AGREEMENTS

28–02   A distinction must be drawn between conditional sale
agreements which are regulated agreements within the Consumer
Credit Act and those which are not. Where the debtor is an
individual, the distinction depends upon the amount of credit
involved (paragraphs 21–08 and 21–09 above).

Agreements that are not regulated agreements
28–03   Under these agreements property does not pass to the buyer
until the stipulated conditions are fulfilled (*i.e.* usually not until
he has paid all the instalments). However, the essence of a
contract of sale is that the buyer either buys or commits himself
to buying, *i.e.* to acquiring property in the goods. Therefore, as
with a credit sale agreement, a conditional sale agreement will
not give the buyer a right of premature termination of the
agreement. It may, however, give the seller a right to recover
possession of the goods and to retain ownership in the event of
the buyer's default, death, bankruptcy, etc. If it does, then the
common law rules relating to penalties and damages (outlined in
the last chapter) will apply.

If the buyer disposes of the goods before property has passed
to him, he may nevertheless confer good title upon the person
who buys them from him. Any of the exceptions to the *nemo dat*
principle might apply (see Chapter 5 above). In particular, the
exception in sections 9 of the Factors Act and 25 of the Sale of
Goods Act might apply: *Lee v. Butler* (see paragraphs 5–34, 19–
03 and 19–04 above).

Regulated agreements
28–04   The scheme of the Consumer Credit Act is to make regulated
conditional sale agreements the same in effect as regulated hire-
purchase agreements. Thus the provisions of the Act apply to
regulated conditional sale agreements as they do to regulated hire-
purchase agreements. That includes not only the provisions of the

Act that apply to regulated agreements generally but also certain provisions which apply only to hire-purchase and conditional sale agreements. It follows that the following provisions are amongst those that apply to regulated conditional sale agreements:

(a) The "protected goods" provisions—sections 90 and 91.

(b) The provisions requiring service of default notice or non-default notice—sections 87, 76 and 98.

(c) The provision preventing termination upon death of the debtor—section 86.

(d) The provision empowering the court to make a time order—section 129.

(e) The provision empowering the court to modify the agreement or to make a return order or a transfer order—section 133.

(f) The provisions giving a statutory right of termination to the debtor and stating the amount payable by the debtor in that event—sections 99 and 100.

The last of these is important because it makes the agreement different in kind from what it is in theory. The agreement involves a commitment by the debtor (the buyer) that he will pay all the instalments and thereby become the owner of the goods. Otherwise it would not be a contract of "sale" at all (see paragraph 1–15 above). The reality is that section 99 gives him (as it does to a debtor under a regulated hire-purchase agreement) a statutory right to terminate the agreement prematurely. As we have seen, this is a right to get out of the agreement without buying the goods which will have to be returned to the creditor.

We come now to the situation where the debtor (the buyer) has **28–05** disposed of the goods to an innocent third party. The problem arises as to who has the better right—is it the third party or is it the creditor (the seller) under the conditional sale agreement? Remember, the creditor is, until property passes to the debtor, the owner of the goods. Here again, statute makes a conditional sale agreement which is a consumer credit agreement the same, in effect, as a hire-purchase agreement. Thus Schedule 4 to the Consumer Credit Act and section 25(2) of the Sale of Goods Act provide that, for the purposes of section 9 of the Factors Act and section 25 of the Sale of Goods Act, a buyer under a conditional sale agreement which is a consumer credit agreement shall be deemed not to be a person who has bought or agreed to buy goods. Thus someone to whom the buyer sells the goods will not acquire good title under either of the two sections mentioned (see paragraph 5–34 above). It should be noted that in the case of a motor vehicle, a "private purchaser" could acquire good title under Part III of the Hire-Purchase Act 1964 which applies to a purchase from the debtor under a conditional sale agreement as it does to one from the debtor under a hire-purchase agreement (see paragraph 5–40 above).

Buyer's landlord levies distress or buyer becomes bankrupt

28–06   These matters are dealt with separately since the relevant law is the same regardless of whether the agreement is a regulated one. We are concerned with the relationship between the seller and the buyer's landlord or trustee in bankruptcy. The position can be put very simply. It is the same as if the conditional sale agreement had been instead a hire-purchase agreement. The seller is in exactly the same position as he would have been if he had let the goods under a hire-purchase agreement instead of agreeing to sell them under a conditional sale agreement. The position in the case where he let them under a hire-purchase agreement has already been explained (see paragraphs 27–46 to 27–48).

CONSUMER HIRE AGREEMENTS

28–07   A consumer hire agreement is in one essential respect different from a hire-purchase, conditional sale or credit sale agreement. The difference is that it is not contemplated that the customer (the hirer) will ever buy the goods.

As in the case of a hire-purchase agreement, termination of a consumer hire agreement can occur in a number of ways—mutual agreement, on breach of the agreement by the hirer, on some other stipulated event or on the hirer exercising a right of termination. Nothing more needs to be said on termination by mutual agreement. After considering the other terminating events in the order just given, consideration will be given to the owner's right to recover possession of the goods and to other rights arising on termination.

Breach by the hirer

As with a hire-purchase agreement so here there are three sorts **28–08** of breach by the hirer, any of which may entitle the owner to terminate the agreement:

(i) A repudiatory breach, *e.g.* a failure (not mere delay) to make payments over such a period that it seems clear that he is not going to keep the agreement.

(ii) A breach stipulated in the agreement as giving the owner a right of termination, *e.g.* the hirer becoming more than 10 days late in making any payment.

(iii) A breach of a condition (as opposed to a warranty) of the contract, *e.g.* late payment when the contract states punctual payment to be of the essence of the contract.

Section 87 applies whenever the owner is entitled to terminate the agreement by reason of the hirer's breach, *i.e.* it applies to regulated consumer hire agreements just as it does to other regulated agreements. Thus the owner cannot terminate the agreement, cannot recover possession of the goods and cannot enforce any security without first serving a default notice. As with other regulated agreements the serving of the default notice enables the customer to rectify his default within the period of notice and it also enables him to apply for a time order. The court's power to make a time order is restricted to payments that have already fallen due. Thus it cannot alter the future payment pattern and can give the hirer extra time only in respect of payments already due. The court has no power to extend the period during which the hirer is entitled under the terms of the agreement to remain in possession of the goods (section 135(3)). It has that power in respect of hire-purchase and conditional sale agreements; for it can make a return order and suspend the operation of the return order for so long as the time order is complied with. Section 135(3), however, prevents the court from doing this so as to extend the period during which the hirer is entitled to possession of the goods under the terms of a consumer hire agreement.

Other stipulated events

The agreement may state that, upon the occurrence of any one **28–09** of certain stipulated events, the owner can terminate the agreement (or, alternatively, that the agreement will terminate automatically). Where the stipulated event is a breach of the agreement by the hirer then section 87, which has just been mentioned, applies. We are now dealing with the situation where the stipulated event is something other than a breach by the hirer, *e.g.* his death, his being sentenced to prison or committing an act of bankruptcy, etc.

Section 86 applies to regulated consumer hire agreements as it does to other regulated agreements, with the result that the death of the hirer under an agreement of specified duration will seldom entitle the owner to terminate the agreement against the wishes of the debtor's personal representatives (see paragraphs 26–12 to 26–16 above).

Also, sections 76 and 98 apply in the same way as they do in relation to other regulated agreements. Thus the owner will not be able to treat an agreement of specified duration as terminated upon any stipulated event without first serving a non-default notice upon the hirer (see paragraph 26–17 above). The hirer will then be entitled to ask the court for a time order.

Exercise by the hirer of a right of termination

28–10   Section 101 gives the hirer under certain regulated consumer hire agreements a right of termination, provided he gives due written notice. Section 101 does not entitle him to terminate the agreement before it has run for 18 months and the hirer must give a minimum period of notice. That minimum period is the lesser of:

    (i) three months, and

    (ii) the shortest interval between the due dates of the hirer's payments under the agreement.

Thus if the agreement provides for the hirer to pay rent monthly, then one month's notice is sufficient. The notice can be given to any person entitled or authorised to receive payments under the agreement. Therefore all the hirer need do is to hand the notice to the person to whom he pays his rent.

The agreement can improve the hirer's rights given to him by section 101 but it cannot diminish them (section 173). It might improve them, by, for example, allowing him to give a shorter period of notice or allowing him to terminate the agreement before 18 months has expired.

Certain agreements are excluded from the application of section 101. They are:

(i) Any agreement under which the hirer's payments are to exceed £1,500 per year.

(ii) Certain agreements involving specialised goods required by the hirer for business purposes.

(iii) Any agreement where the hirer requires the goods so that he in turn can in the course of his business let them out to someone else.

(iv) Agreements, if any, excluded by the Director-General of Fair Trading from the application of section 101.

Recovery of the goods by owner from hirer

The owner under a regulated agreement will not be entitled to **28–11** enter any premises to take possession of the goods unless at the time he obtains the permission of the occupier to do so. This is because section 92 applies to regulated consumer hire agreements as it does to hire-purchase and conditional sale agreements. Apart from that, however, the owner does have the right, after termination of the agreement, to recover possession of the goods. He has this right as soon as he is entitled to treat the agreement as terminated, *i.e.* when the default notice expires. This right is enforceable in the courts, or the owner can alternatively enforce it by seizing physical possession. The latter alternative will seldom be very practicable without the hirer's consent, because of the restriction on entering premises imposed by section 92.

Financial relief for the hirer

Where the owner recovers possession of the goods (whether by **28–12** court action or otherwise) the court can grant the hirer financial relief if it appears just to do so—section 132. The financial relief can take either or both of two forms:

(i) An order that any payment still due from the hirer shall be reduced by an amount stated by the court (even, if the court so decides, reduced to nothing).

(ii) An order that the whole or any part of any sum already paid by the hirer shall be repaid.

The purpose of section 132 is no doubt to enable the court to ensure that when the agreement is terminated the hirer does not end up having to pay or having paid an amount which is equivalent to rent for a much longer period than the agreement actually lasted. Thus in deciding on if and how to exercise its powers under section 132, the court must have regard to "the extent of the enjoyment of the goods by the hirer".

Hirer wrongfully disposes of the goods

28–13　　If the hirer sells the goods then the owner will have a right to recover possession from the purchaser unless the latter acquired them under an exception to the *nemo dat* principle. It will not be very likely, however, that the hirer will sell under any such exception. In particular the hirer is not a buyer in possession and (even if the goods are a motor vehicle) the Hire-Purchase Act 1964 will not apply. (For other possible exceptions to the *nemo dat* principle, see Chapter 5 above.)

Hirer's landlord levies distress or hirer becomes bankrupt

28–14　　The relationship between the owner and the hirer's landlord or trustee in bankruptcy is exactly the same as if the agreement, instead of being a consumer hire agreement, had been a hire-purchase agreement or conditional sale agreement (see paragraphs 27–46 to 27–48 above).

INDEX

Abandonment of goods by debtor
hire-purchase agreement,
27–23
Accelerated payments, 26–10,
26–19, 26–20, 27–12 to
27–16
Acceptance
Consumer Guarantees Directive
and, 13–06
goods, of, 6–03, 7–19, 7–51,
11–08, 13–04 to 13–07,
25–23
non-acceptance. *See* Damages
offer, of—
contract of sale, 2–02, 2–06,
2–07
regulated credit agreement,
24–02, 24–21
Advertising
see also Trade descriptions
consumer credit, 21–02, 23–08
to 23–14
misleading, 18–44, 18–45
Affirmation
breach of condition, after—
conditional sales agreement,
25–23
contract for transfer of goods,
8–02
hire-purchase agreement,
25–20, 25–21
contract of sale, after
misrepresentation, 6–03
Agency
auctioneer as agent, 15–06
contract of agency distinguished
from contract of sale, 1–16,
1–17
customer's representative as
agent, 24–17
dealer as agent of creditor. *See*
Dealer
mercantile agents, sales by, 5–11
to 5–19
negotiator in antecedent
negotiations as. *See*
Antecedent negotiations

Agreement to sell, 1–05
Ancillary credit business
businesses constituting, 20–27 to
20–33, 22–15, 22–16
licence requirement, 22–05,
22–08 to 22–17
Annual percentage rate (APR),
21–39
Antecedent negotiations
generally, 24–10, 24–13, 24–14
negotiator in, 24–10, 24–13,
24–18 to 24–20, 24–22,
24–23, 24–27,
25–15, 25–23
Appropriation of goods to contract
of sale, 3–19 to 3–28
Approval, sale on, 3–17, 3–18,
5–34
Arrears
regulated agreements and, 27–36
Ascertained goods, 3–05, 3–09
Auction
advertisements before sale,
15–02
auctioneer, position of, 15–06 to
15–08
bidding agreements, 15–09
completion of contract of sale,
2–04, 15–03
Directive on Consumer
Guarantees and, 7–52
exemption clauses, 15–05
generally, 15–01, 15–03
mock auctions, 15–10
reserve price, 15–03, 15–04
right to bid, 15–03
rings, 15–09
Automatic vending machines
completion of contract of sale,
2–05

Bailment, contract of
consumer hire agreement as,
21–15
generally, 1–05, 8–08
hire-purchase agreement as,
19–01, 19–02

Bailment, contract of—*cont.*
  implied terms, 8–08
Bank
  cheques. *See* Cheques
  loans, 20–04, 20–05, 20–14,
    21–21, 21–34
  overdraft, 20–15, 23–04, 24–21,
    24–51
  revolving credit, 20–16
  withdrawal tokens, 26–33,
    26–34
Bankruptcy
  conditional sales agreement and,
    28–06
  hire-purchase agreement and,
    27–48
Barter, contract of
  generally, 1–09
  implied terms, 8–02, 8–04
Bill of sale, 20–09, 21–01
Breach of condition
  contract of sale of goods, 7–09
    to 7–12, 7–51, 13–03,
    14–11
  hire-purchase agreement, 25–19
    to 25–21, 27–29
Breach of contract
  classification of, 7–09
Breach of warranty. *See* Warranties
Business
  "in the course of carrying on",
    7–34, 9–19, 10–23, 18–07,
    21–28,
    22–05, 22–06
Buyer
  buyer in possession, 5–32 to
    5–39, 17–04, 17–06
  meaning of, 5–34, 19–02, 19–04
  remedies for. *See* Buyer's
    remedies
Buyer's remedies
  action for damages, 13–12
  additional or alternative
    defendant, 13–14
  creditor, against, 13–14
  recovery of purchase price,
    13–13
  rejection of goods. *See* Rejection
    of goods
  repudiation of contract, 13–10,
    13–11

Buyer's remedies—*cont.*
  specific performance of contract,
    13–01

C.I.F. contracts, 3–29, 11–03,
    11–08, 17–01, 17–02 to
    17–08,
    17–15, 17–16
Cancellable agreements
  Consumer Credit Act 1974 and,
    2–22
  cooling-off period, 2–18, 2–20,
    2–22, 24–53
  distance selling and, 2–23,
    16–14 to 16–18, 16–20
  effect of cancellation, 2–21,
    24–54 to 24–58
  excepted contracts, 2–19, 2–22
  generally, 2–18, 24–49 to 24–51
  notice of cancellation—
    effect of, 24–54 to 24–58
    generally, 24–52
    special formalities for, 24–39
Canvassing off trade premises
  generally, 22–03, 22–17, 23–01,
    23–02 to 23–05
  unlicensed trading, as 22–17
Capacity to make contract, 2–11,
    2–12
Charge card
  see also Credit card
  payment by, 8–05, 12–02
Check trading
  generally, 8–05, 20–18,
    20–19
  misrepresentation by supplier,
    24–26, 25–08
  supplier as agent of creditor,
    24–26
Cheque
  guarantee card, 26–33, 26–34
  payment by, 8–05, 12–02,
    12–04
  thing in action, is, 1–08
Classification of contract of sale,
    3–03 to 3–06
Collateral contracts
  generally, 8–03
  money consideration and, 1–10
  product liability and, 9–02,
    9–03

Collateral warranty, 9–02, 19–10, 24–12
Common law
  generally, 1–03
  sale under when seller not owner, 5–41
Computer software
  contracts to supply, 1–14
Condition
  see also Implied terms
  breach of. See Breach of condition
  generally, 3–12, 7–10, 7–11
Conditional sale agreement
  bankruptcy of buyer, 28–06
  buyer in possession, 5–34, 17–06
  cancellation of. See Cancellable agreements
  credit sale agreement distinguished, 19–06
  distress levied by buyer's landlord, 28–06
  early payment of debt, 26–04
  formalities in making. See Regulated agreements
  formation of agreement, 24–02 to 24–15
  generally, 19–06
  implied terms, 25–23
  passing of property under, 19–06, 28–03
  recovery of goods by seller, 28–03
  regulated, 28–03
  selling of goods by buyer, 5–34, 5–40, 17–06, 28–03, 28–05
  termination of, 28–02 to 28–06
  time order, 2–04
  unregulated, 28–03
Consideration
  failure of, 7–18, 7–19, 13–02, 24–07, 25–12
  part exchange as, 1–09
  price, is, 1–04
Consumer Credit Act 1974, 21–01 et seq.
Consumer credit agreements
  definition of, 21–06 to 21–14
  exempt agreements, 21–25, 21–26

Consumer credit agreements—cont.
  generally. See Regulated agreement
  small agreements, 21–27
Consumer credit business
  definition of, 22–08
  licensing requirement, 22–04, 22–08
Consumer deals, 10–21 to 10–23, 25–22
Consumer hire agreement
  see also Regulated agreement
  bankruptcy of hirer, 28–14
  breach by hirer, 28–08
  default notice, 28–08
  definition of, 21–15 to 21–17
  distress levied by hirer's landlord, 28–14
  financial relief for hirer, 28–12
  formalities in making. See Regulated agreements
  formation of, 24–28
  generally, 28–07
  recovery of goods on termination, 28–11
  termination of, 28–07 to 28–14
  wrongful disposal by hirer, 28–13
Consumer hire business
  definition of, 22–09
  licensing requirement, 22–04, 22–09
Consumer safety, 9–15, 9–16
  see also Product liability
Consumer sales. See Consumer deals
Contract of sale of goods
  capacity and, 2–11, 2–12
  classification of, 3–03 to 3–06
  definition of, 1–04 to 1–10, 1–18
  form of, 2–10
  formation of, 2–01 to 2–12
  generally, 2–01, 7–01
  other transactions distinguished, 1–11 to 1–17
  price and, 2–13 to 2–17
  terms of. See Terms of contract
  time of making, 2–02 to 2–07

Contractual document, 10–04,
  10–05
Conversion, claim for, 5–03
Cooling-off period, 2–18, 2–20,
  2–22, 24–53
Copies of agreement. *See*
  Regulated agreements:
  formalities
County court
  enforcement actions by creditor/
  owner, 26–03
Course of dealing, 10–07
Credit
  ancillary credit businesses,
    20–33, 22–15, 22–16
  fixed sum, 21–08, 21–09
  forms of, 20–01 to 20–12
  methods of providing, 20–13 to
    20–25
  restricted-use agreements,
    21–19
  revolving, 20–16, 20–17,
    21–08
  running-account, 21–08, 21–13
  secured, 20–06
  total charge for credit, 21–09,
    21–35 to 21–38
  unrestricted-use agreements,
    21–19
  unsecured, 20–05
Credit brokers
  fees, 24–30, 24–58
  generally, 20–29
  licensing requirement, 22–04,
    22–10, 22–11
Credit cards
  authorised user, 25–05
  creditor's liability for supplier's
    misrepresentation/breach of
    contract, 6–06, 24–19,
    24–23, 24–25, 25–05,
    25–06
  formation of agreement, 24–23
    to 24–25
  generally, 20–20 to 20–24
  payment by, 8–05, 12–02
Credit facilities
  misuse of, 26–32 to 26–34
Credit-hire agreement, 20–26
Credit insurers
  generally, 20–30

Credit reference agencies
  access to information held by,
    24–30, 24–31
  amendment of incorrect
    information, 24–31
  generally, 20–28, 24–30
  licensing requirement, 22–04,
    22–14
Credit sale agreement
  cancellation of. *See* Cancellable
    agreements
  conditional sale agreement
    distinguished, 19–06
  early payment of debt,
    28–01
  formation of, 24–02 to
    24–15
  formalities in making. *See*
    Regulated agreement
  generally, 19–06, 28–01
  implied terms in, 25–23
  passing of property under,
    28–01
  reselling of goods by buyer,
    28–01
  termination of, 28–01
Credit tokens
  generally, 26–35
  time limits for copies of
    agreement, 24–38
  unauthorised use of, 26–36 to
    26–39
  unsolicited, criminal offence of
    issuing, 23–07, 26–35
Credit unions, 20–34 to 20–36
Creditor
  liability for supplier's breach,
    25–03 to 25–08
  liability in respect of goods/
    services supplied—
    breach by supplier, 25–03 to
      25–08
    conditional sale, 25–23
    credit sale, 25–23
    generally, 25–01
    hire-purchase, 25–09 to
      25–22
    terms of agreement and,
      25–02
  meaning of, 18–13, 21–02,
    21–17

Criminal courts
  powers of, 18–02
Criminal offences
  product liability. *See* Product
    liability
  trade descriptions etc, 18–01,
    18–48
Crops
  sale of, 1–06, 3–04, 3–06, 4–10,
    4–11, 4–14
Cross-border contracts
  applicable law, 16–31
  enforcement of foreign
    judgment, 16–32
  generally, 16–23
  jurisdiction, 16–24 to 16–30
Customer's representative, 24–17,
  24–22

Damages
  contract of sale—
    breach of contract, 7–09,
      7–51, 14–01
    buyer's claim—
      anticipatory breach, 14–07
        to 14–09
      breach of condition, 14–11
      breach of warranty, 14–12
        to 14–14
      generally, 13–12
      late delivery, 14–10, 14–17
      non-delivery, 14–05, 14–06,
        14–15
      sub-sales, 14–15 to 14–18
    measure of damages, 14–01 *et*
      seq.
    misrepresentation, 6–04
    mitigation of damages, 14–19
    penalties, 14–21
    seller's claim—
      buyer's delay in taking
        delivery, 12–02
      non-acceptance of goods,
        12–03, 14–03, 14–04
  hire purchase agreement,
    creditor's claim—
      arrears, 27–23, 27–28
      breach of condition, 27–29
      breach of contract, 27–25,
        27–26
      repudiation, 27–27

Dealer
  agent of creditor, as, 24–03,
    24–04, 24–06 to 24–10,
    24–12,
    24–13, 24–18 to 24–20,
    24–23 to 24–28
  hire-purchase transaction, in,
    19–07 to 19–11, 20–02,
    20–13,
    22–11, 24–02, 24–12
Death of debtor, 26–12 to 26–16
Debit cards, 21–23
Debt adjustors
  generally, 20–32
  licensing requirement, 22–04,
    22–12
Debt collectors
  generally, 20–32
  licensing requirement, 22–04,
    22–13
Debt counsellors
  generally, 20–31
  licensing requirement, 22–04,
    22–12
Debtor
  meaning under Consumer Credit
    Act, 21–02, 21–17, 25–09
Debtor-creditor agreements, 21–20
  to 21–22, 21–25
Debtor-creditor-supplier
  agreements, 21–20 to 21–23,
    21–25
Default notices
  consumer hire agreement,
    28–08
  hire-purchase agreement, 27–11,
    27–12
  regulated agreement. *See*
    Regulated agreements
Defective products. *See* Product
  liability
Deliverable state
  whether goods in, 3–11, 3–13,
    3–15
Delivery
  contract of sale—
    carrier, delivery to, 11–09
    concurrent condition with
      payment of price, 11–02
    damages—
      late delivery, 14–10, 14–17

Delivery—*cont.*
  non-delivery, 14–05, 14–06,
    14–15
    expenses connected with
      putting goods into
      deliverable state, 11–
    generally, 11–01, 11–03
    instalments, delivery by,
      11–08
    place of, 11–04
    time of, 7–13, 7–14, 11–05
    wrong quantity delivered,
      11–07
  hire-purchase agreement, 25–17,
    25–18
  order, 3–24, 3–33, 12–09, 12–10
Deposit
  hire-purchase, 24–06 to 24–10
  sale of goods, 2–17, 12–12
Description
  condition that goods correspond
    with—
    contract for services, 8–09
    contract of hire, 8–08
    contract of sale of goods,
      7–26 to 7–31
    hire-purchase agreement,
      25–14
Director General of Fair Trading
  generally, 18–46, 18–48
  licensing powers, 22–01, 22–22
Disclaimer
  see generally Exemption clauses
  accuracy of trade description, of,
    18–11 to 18–13, 18–26,
    18–27, 18–31
Distance selling
  cancellation of agreement, 2–23,
    16–14 to 16–18, 16–20
  definitions, 16–07
  Directive, 2–09, 16–05
  enforcement of Regulations,
    16–22
  excepted contracts, 16–08,
    16–09
  fraudulent use of payment cards,
    16–20
  information for consumer, 16–10
    to 16–13
  performance of contract, 16–19
  Regulations, 16–05 to 16–22

Distance selling—*cont.*
  restrictions on use of
    communications,
    16–21
Distress, landlord levying
  conditional sales agreement,
    28–06
  consumer hire agreement,
    28–14
  hire-purchase agreement,
    27–46, 27–47
Document of title, 5–06, 5–11,
  5–17, 5–17, 5–27, 5–29,
  5–30, 5–33,
  5–35, 5–37

E-commerce
  Draft Directive on Certain
    Aspects of Electronic
    Commerce, 16–04
  Electronic Communications Act
    2000, 16–02, 16–03
  Electronic Signatures Directive,
    16–02
  Internet sales, formation of
    contract of sale, 2–08
Electronic Funds Transfer, 21–23,
  21–24
Estoppel, 5–04 to 5–09
European law
  Consumer Guarantees Directive,
    7–52 to 7–54, 13–06
  Distance Selling Directive, 2–09,
    16–05
  Electronic Signatures Directive,
    16–02
  Injunctions Directive, 18–52,
    18–53
  Product Liability Directive,
    9–06
  Unfair Terms in Consumer
    Contracts Directive, 10–40
Examination of goods
  buyer's right of, 7–35
Exchange, contract of. *See* Barter,
  contract of
Exclusion clauses. *See* Exemption
  clauses
Excursions organised by traders
  cancellation of agreement and,
    2–18

Execution of judgment, 5–43, 27–49

Exempt consumer credit agreements, 21–25, 21–26

Exemption clauses
auctions and, 15–05
criminal use of ineffective clauses, 10–48, 10–49
generally, 10–01
hire-purchase agreements and, 19–07, 21–03, 25–22
incorporation into contract, 10–02 to 10–09, 15–05
misrepresentation and, 10–10
privity of contract and, 10–11
scope of, 10–13 to 10–17
Unfair Contract Terms Act 1977 and, 10–18 to 10–38
Unfair Terms in Consumer Contracts Regulations 1999 and, 10–39 to 10–47

Extortionate credit agreements, 26–06, 26–07

F.O.B. contracts, 17–01, 17–09 to 17–15, 17–16

Factors
sales by, 5–11 to 5–19

Fair trading. See Director General of Fair Trading

Feeding of title, 5–39, 7–19, 27–40

Finance company
hire-purchase transactions and, 19–07, 19–08
licence requirement, 22–05, 22–08

Fitness for purpose
implied term as to—
contract for services, 1–13, 8–02
contract of sale of goods, 1–13, 7–32, 7–43 to 7–49
hire-purchase agreement, 25–15

Fixed sum credit, 21–08, 21–09

Freedom of contract, 7–02

Frustration of contract of sale, 3–36, 4–08 to 4–17

Future goods, 3–06, 4–04

Goods
ascertained, 3–05, 3–09
future, 3–06, 4–04
purely generic, 3–05, 4–05, 4–11
rejection of. See Rejection of goods
specific, 3–04, 3–08
things constituting, 1–06 to 1–08
unascertained. See Unascertained goods

Guarantee
Directive on Consumer Guarantees, provisions, 7–53
generally, 20–08, 24–46
hire-purchase agreement and, 19–12, 27–30
linked agreements and, 21–30
minors and, 2–11, 24–46, 26–44
product liability and, 9–02, 9–03

Hire-purchase agreement
abandonment of goods by debtor, 27–23
accelerated payments clause, 26–20, 27–13 to 27–16
bailment contract, is, 19–01, 19–02
breach of agreement by debtor, 27–07 to 27–09
cancellation of. See Cancellable agreements
damages, creditor claiming. See Damages
dealer. See Dealer
death of debtor, 27–10
default/non-default notice, 27–11, 27–12
exemption clause, 19–07, 21–03, 25–22
finance company's role, 5–05, 19–07, 19–08, 20–02, 24–02
formalities in making. See Regulated agreements
generally, 1–15, 19–01, 19–08
illegal agreements, 24–15
implied terms in, 25–09 to 25–22

Hire-purchase agreement—*cont.*
  minimum payment on
    termination, 27–31 to
    27–33
  money claims against debtor,
    27–25 to 27–35
  protected goods, 27–20 to 27–24
  reasonable care of goods, debtor
    must take, 27–28
  recovery of goods after
    termination—
    debtor, from, 19–07, 27–17 to
      27–19
    third party, from, 19–04,
      27–38 to 27–49
  regulated agreement, whether,
    21–06, 21–07, 21–10
  return order, 27–19, 27–36,
    27–37
  sale of goods contract
    distinguished, 1–15, 5–34,
    19–02 to 19–05
  termination of—
    breach of agreement by
      debtor, 27–07 to 27–09
    death of debtor, 27–10
    debtor exercising right, 27–05,
      27–06
    events causing, 27–03 to
      27–12
    generally, 27–01, 27–02
    mutual agreement, by, 27–04
    recovery of goods after,
      27–17 to 27–19
    stipulated events causing,
      27–10
    stipulated minimum payment,
      27–31 to 27–33
  time order, 26–19 to 26–21,
    27–36, 27–37
  transfer order, 27–37
  uncertainty, void on account of,
    24–05

Illegal contracts, 24–15
Implied terms
  conditional sale agreement, 25–23
  contract for services, 8–06,
    8–09, 25–02, 25–03
  contract for transfer of goods,
    8–02 to 8–07

Implied terms—*cont.*
  contract of hire, 8–08
  contract of sale of goods—
    description, 7–26 to 7–31
    fitness for purpose, 7–43 to
      7–49
    generally, 7–08, 7–10, 7–15,
      7–16
    quality, 7–32 to 7–42
    sale by sample, 7–50
    title, 7–17 to 7–25
  credit sale agreement, 25–23
  hire-purchase agreement, 25–09
    to 25–22
Indemnity
  generally, 20–08, 24–46
  hire-purchase agreement and,
    19–12, 27–30
  linked agreements and, 21–30
  minors and, 2–11, 24–46, 26–44
Injunctions Directive, 18–52,
  18–53
Innocent purchaser, 5–01 *et seq.*,
  12–09, 19–04
Insolvency
  buyer's, 12–05, 12–11
  debtor's, under hire-purchase
    agreement, 27–10
Instalments
  see also Severable contracts
  delivery of goods in, 11–08,
    12–06
Interest. *See* Total charge for credit
International sales
  C.I.F. contracts, 3–29, 11–03,
    11–08, 17–01, 17–02 to
    17–08, 17–15, 17–16
  F.O.B. contracts, 17–01, 17–09
    to 17–15, 17–16
  generally, 17–01
  other types of contract, 17–16
  payment, 17–17 to 17–21
Invitation to treat
  offer distinguished, 2–03,
    2–04
Interim agreement for sale of
  goods, 2–15
Internet sales
  see also E-commerce
  formation of contract of sale,
    2–08

Labour and materials supplied,
contract for, 1–11 to 1–13,
8–06
Land
contract for sale of, 2–10
mortgage of. *See* Mortgage of
land
"things attached to or forming
part of", 1–06, 1–07
Landlord. *See* Distress, landlord
levying
Legality of contract, 24–15
Licensing of consumer credit
business needing licence, 22–05
to 22–16
Director General of Fair
Trading, powers, 22–01,
22–22
exclusions—
full, 22–07
partial, 22–15, 22–16
generally, 22–01 to 22–03
group licence, 22–02
shortcomings of system, 22–04
standard licence, 22–02, 22–05
unlicensed trading, 22–17 to
22–21, 26–25
Lien
auctioneer's, 15–08
cancellation of agreement and,
24–55
generally, 7–22
hire purchase agreement,
recovery of goods in
possession third party,
27–44, 27–45
rejected goods and, 13–02
unpaid seller's, 5–33, 12–05 to
12–10
Life assurance
assignment of endowment
policy, 20–12
Linked transactions, 21–29 to
21–33
Loans, 20–04, 20–05, 20–14,
20–16, 21–21, 21–26, 21–34,
24–27

Mail order
cancellation of agreement, 2–19
exclusion from licensing, 22–16

Mail order—*cont.*
misleading advertisements and,
18–44
privity of contract and, 10–12
Manufacturers
liability for defective products.
See Product liability
liability for negligence, 9–04,
10–11, 10–12
privity of contract and, 10–12
rights and obligations of,
1–02
Market overt, 5–20
Mercantile agents
unauthorised sales by, 5–11 to
5–19
Merchantable quality. *See* Fitness
for purpose; Quality
Minors
capacity to make contract, 2–11,
2–12
guarantees and, 2–11, 26–44
sending circulars to, criminal
offence, 23–06
Misleading prices etc. *See* Trade
descriptions
Misrepresentation
actionable, 6–02
additional/alternative defendant
and, 6–06
consumer credit agreements and,
6–06, 24–12 to 24–14,
24–17,
24–23 to 24–26
customer's representative, by,
24–17
damages as remedy, 6–04
dealer, by, 24–17, 24–23 to
24–26
estoppel and, 5–04 to 5–09
exclusion clauses and, 10–10
exclusion/restriction of liability
for, 6–05
generally, 6–02, 6–06
liability for, 6–01
negotiator in antecedent
negotiations, by, 24–23 to
24–26
remedies for, 6–03, 6–04
rescission of contract as remedy,
6–03

Mistake
buyer's identity, as to, 5–23 to
5–25
consumer credit agreements and,
24–06 to 24–10
existence of goods of goods
sold, as to, 4–02 to 4–07
Mitigation of damages, 14–19
Money
goods, as, 1–08
Money consideration, 1–09, 1–10,
8–02, 8–04, 8–05
Mortgage of goods, 20–02, 20–09,
20–10, 24–47
Mortgage of land
enforcement, 26–45
exempt agreement, as,
21–25
second mortgage, special
formalities for, 24–40,
24–41
security, as, 20–11
Motor vehicles
disposition under Hire Purchase
Act 1964, 5–40
registration book—
passing of title and, 5–06,
5–15, 5–16, 5–18
supply of vehicle without,
whether breach of
contract, 25–17

Necessaries
contract to purchase, 2–11
Negligence
dealer's liability, hire-purchase
transaction, 19–10
exclusion of liability for, 10–11,
10–12, 10–33, 10–37
manufacturer's liability, 9–04,
10–11, 10–12
risk of damage to goods caused
by, 3–32
Nemo dat quod non habet
principle of, 5–02
Non-commercial agreements
cancellable, whether,
24–51
formalities requirements and,
24–32
generally, 21–28

Non-default notice
hire-purchase agreement, 27–11,
27–12
regulated agreement, 26–17,
26–18
Non-delivery. See Delivery;
Damages
Non est factum, 24–11
Notice of defect in seller's title
buyer in possession of goods/
documents of title, 5–33,
5–38
mercantile agent, 5–19
motor vehicles, 5–40
seller in market overt, 5–20,
5–21
seller in possession of goods/
documents of title, 5–27,
5–30
seller with voidable title, 5–22

Offer
acceptance of—
contract of sale, 2–02, 2–06,
2–07
regulated credit agreement,
24–02, 24–21
formation of contract of sale
and, 2–02, 2–03
invitation to treat distinguished,
2–03, 2–04
regulated credit agreement,
24–02 to 24–04, 24–21,
24–22
Trade Descriptions Act,
definition under,
18–14
withdrawal of offer to enter—
contract of sale, 2–02
regulated credit agreement,
24–02 to 24–04, 24–22
Option to buy, 1–15, 5–34, 19–02
Overdraft, 20–15, 23–04, 24–21,
24–51
Owner
definition under Consumer
Credit Act, 21–17, 25–09
seller not. See Seller not owner
Ownership
meaning of, 1–05, 3–01, 5–01
split, 5–17

Ownership—*cont.*
 transfer of. *See* Passing of
  property

Part exchange, 1–09, 8–0, 24–55
Part payment, 2–17
Passing of property
 generally, 1–05, 3–01, 3–02
 seller not owner, when, 5–01,
  5–02 *et seq.*
 time of, 3–02, 3–07 to 3–29
Passing of risk, 3–02, 3–30 to
  3–36
Pawn
 generally, 18–10
 pawnor not owner, 5–17, 5–18,
  5–24
 rights and duties of pawnee,
  26–46, 26–47
 sale by pawnee, 5–41, 26–46,
  26–47
Payment
 ahead of time, regulated
  agreement, 26–04
 behind time, regulated
  agreement, 26–05
 concurrent condition with
  delivery of goods, 11–02
 generally, 11–10
 hire-purchase agreement, implied
  condition, 25–17, 25–18
 part payment, 2–17
 stipulations as to time of, 7–13
Perishing of goods
 after contract made, 4–08 to
  4–17
 before contract made, 4–02 to
  4–07
 meaning of perish, 4–03, 4–04,
  4–10
 unascertained goods, 4–05,
  4–11, 4–17
Personal credit agreement
 definition of, 21–06
Pledges, 20–10, 26–46, 26–47
 see also Pawn
Possession
 buyer in possession, 5–32 to
  5–39, 17–04, 17–06
 ownership distinguished,
  3–01

Possession—*cont.*
 recovery of possession, hire-
  purchase agreement. *See*
  Hire-purchase
 seller in possession, 5–27 to
  5–31
Possessory title
 sale of, 7–22
Postal communications
 acceptance of offer and, 2–06
Price
 action by seller for, 12–02
 amount of, 2–13 to 2–15
 deposits, 2–17
 recommended, 18–41
 recovery of purchase price by
  buyer. *See* Consideration
 misleading price indications,
  18–34 to 18–43
 valuation by third party, 2–16
Privity of contract
 Contracts (Rights of Third
  Parties) Act 1999 and, 7–03
  to 7–05
 Directive on Consumer
  Guarantees and, 7–54
 exemption clauses and, 10–11
 generally, 7–03, 10–11
Product liability
 grounds for manufacturer's
  liability—
  collateral contract or
   guarantee, 9–02, 9–03
  Consumer Protection Act
   1987, under, 9–06 to
   9–19
  contract of sale, 9–01
  General Product Safety
   Regulations 1994, under,
   9–20 to 9–28
  negligence, 9–04, 9–05
Property
 meaning of, 1–05, 5–01
 passing of. *See* Passing of
  property
 transfer of. *See* Passing of
  property
Protected goods
 hire-purchase agreement, under,
  27–20 to 27–24
Pyramid selling, 18–46, 18–47

Quality
  see also Fitness for purpose
  damages for breach of term as
    to, sub-sales, 14–18
  implied term as to—
    contract for services, 8–02
    contract of sale of goods,
      7–32 to 7–42
    hire-purchase agreement,
      25–15
Quiet possession
  implied term as to—
    contract of sale of goods,
      7–17, 7–24, 7–25
    hire-purchase agreement,
      25–11
Quotations for credit and hire
    agreements, 23–14

Recourse agreement, 19–11,
    19–12, 24–46
Regulated agreements
  amendment of, 26–08,
    26–23
  antecedent negotiations. *See*
    Antecedent negotiations
  appropriation of payments where
    more than one agreement,
    26–28,
    26–29
  arrears—
    suit for recovery of, 27–36
    termination of agreement on
      account of, 27–36
  cancellation of. *See* Cancellable
    agreements
  canvassing off trade premises.
    See Canvassing off trade
    premises
  challenges to, 26–08
  copy of agreement, request for,
    26–26
  court orders, 26–03, 26–08,
    26–22 to 26–24, 27–34
  death of debtor, 26–12 to 26–16,
    27–10
  default notice, 26–09 to 26–11,
    26–41, 27–36
  formalities in making—
    agreements subject to, 24–32,
      24–33

Regulated agreements—*cont.*
  aim of statutory provisions,
    24–32
    cancellable agreements,
      special formalities for,
      24–39
    content of agreement, 24–34
    copies, 24–36 to 24–38
    excepted agreements, 24–32,
      24–33
    form of agreement, 24–34
    non-compliance, effect of,
      24–42 to 24–45
    second mortgages, special
      formalities for, 24–40
    signatures, 24–35
  generally, 21–05, 21–18
  improperly executed, 24–42
  liability of debtor for misuse of
    credit facilities, 26–32
  licence. *See* Licensing of
    consumer credit
  linked transactions, 21–29 to
    21–33
  misrepresentation and, 24–12 to
    24–14
  mistake and, 24–06 to 24–10
  non-default notice, 26–17, 26–18
  offer to enter agreement, 24–02
    to 24–04, 24–21, 24–22
  payment—
    ahead of time, 26–04
    behind time, 26–05
  recovery of goods after
    termination, 27–19
  return order, 27–19, 27–36,
    27–37
  small agreements, 21–27
  statement of account, request
    for, 26–26, 26–27
  termination of—
    arrears, for, 27–36
    money award to creditor,
      27–34, 27–35
  termination statement, request
    for, 26–26, 26–27
  time order, 26–19 to 26–21,
    27–36
  transfer order, 27–37
  uncertainty, void on account of,
    24–05

Regulated agreements—*cont.*
variation of agreement, 26–30,
26–31
Rejection of goods
buyer rejecting—
delivery by instalments and,
11–08
generally, 13–02
partial rejection, 13–07
trival breach of implied
condition and, 13–03
waiver of right to reject,
13–09
debtor rejecting—
conditional sale agreement,
25–23
hire-purchase agreement,
25–19 to 25–21
Rental agreements, 20–25, 21–06
see also Consumer hire
agreements
Repudiation of agreement
see also Rejection of goods
contract of sale of goods—
breaches of conditions and
warranties and, 7–09 to
7–12,
13–10, 13–11
delivery by instalments and,
11–08
delivery date and, 7–13, 7–14
hire-purchase agreement, 25–19
to 25–21
Resale
seller's right of, 12–12
Rescission, 6–03, 24–12, 24–13
Restricted-use credit, 21–19
Retention of title clauses
generally, 3–48
mixed goods and, 3–50
Romalpa case, 3–49
unmixed goods and, 3–51 to
3–55
Return of goods
cancellable agreements and,
2–21
Return order, 27–19, 27–36, 27–37
Revocation of offer. *See*
Withdrawal of offer
Revolving credit, 20–16, 20–17,
21–08

Risk
transfer from seller to buyer,
3–02, 3–30 to 3–36
Romalpa clause. *See* Retention of
title clauses
Running-account credit, 21–08,
21–13

Safety. *See* Consumer safety;
Product liability
Sale of goods
agrecment to sell, 1–05
approval, sale on, 3–17, 3–18,
5–34
common law and, 1–03
contract. *See* Contract of sale of
goods
generally, 1–01
legislation, 1–03
sale or return, 1–17, 3–17,
3–18
sub-sale. *See* Sub-sale
Sale of Goods Act 1979, 1–03
Sample, contract for sale by
implied term as to—
contract of sale of goods,
7–50
hire-purchase agreement,
25–16
sale by description, as, 7–28
Satisfactory quality. *See* Quality
Second mortgage
special formalities for, 24–40,
24–41
Security
definition of, 26–16, 26–40
enforcement of, 21–03, 26–40 to
26–47, 27–30
formalities in relation to, 24–46,
24–47
forms of, 20–07 *et seq.*
generally, 20–06
Seller
in possession, 5–27 to 5–31
not owner of goods. *See* Seller
not owner of goods
remedies. *See* Seller's remedies
unpaid seller, meaning of, 12–04
Seller not owner of goods
buyer in possession, 5–32 to
5–40

Seller not owner of goods—*cont.*
  common law power, sale under,
    5–41
  conversion, claim for, 5–03
  court order, sale under, 5–42
  estoppel, 5–04 to 5–
  factors, 5–11 to 5–19
  generally, 5–01
  market overt, 5–20
  mercantile agents, 5–11 to 5–19
  motor vehicles, disposition
    under Hire Purchase Act
    1964, 5–40
  nemo dat quod non habet
    principle, 5–02
  seller in possession, 5–27 to
    5–31
  signature of owner on document
    authorising sale, 5–10
  statutory power, sale under,
    5–41
  voidable title, sale under, 5–21
    to 5–26
  writ of execution, effect of,
    5–43
Seller's remedies
  actions for the price, 12–02
  damages for non-acceptance,
    12–03
  generally, 12–01
  goods, against, 12–04 to 12–12
  lien, 12–05 to 12–10
  personal remedies, 12–02,
    12–03
  resale of goods, 12–12
  stoppage of goods in transit,
    12–11
Services
  contracts for—
    generally, 1–11, 25–02
    implied terms, 8–01, 8–02,
      8–06, 8–09, 25–02
    false statements as to, 18–15 to
      18–25
Severable contracts, 4–03, 11–08,
    12–06
Signature
  in blank, 5–07, 5–10
  mistake as to nature of
    document and, 24–11
  non est factum, plea of, 24–11

Signature—*cont.*
  owner's, authorising another to
    sell goods, 5–10
  regulated agreements and,
    24–35
Small agreements, 21–27,
    24–32
Specific goods
  generally, 3–04
  time of passing of property and,
    3–08
Specific performance of contract
  buyer's remedy, as, 13–01
Statement of account
  request for, 26–26, 26–27
Stoppage of goods in transit,
    12–11
Sub-sales
  damages for loss of, 14–15 to
    14–18
  good title, sub-purchaser
    acquiring, 12–08, 12–10
Supplier, 20–02, 20–03, 24–18
  see also Dealer
Supply of Goods and Services Act
    1982, 8–01 to 8–09
Surety, 24–47

Telephone conversations
  acceptance of offer and, 2–07
Telex communications
  acceptance of offer and, 2–07
Termination statement
  request for, 26–26, 26–27
Terms of contract
  express terms, 7–06, 7–07,
    7–10
  freedom of contract and, 7–02
  generally, 7–01
  implied terms. *See* Implied
    terms
  stipulations as to time, 7–13,
    7–14
Things in action, 1–09
Third parties
  enforcement of contract by,
    7–03 to 7–05
Time of delivery and payment,
    7–13, 7–14, 11–02, 11–05,
    11–10
Time order, 26–19 to 26–21

Title
  document of title, 5–06, 5–11,
    5–17, 5–17, 5–27, 5–29,
    5–30, 5–33,
    5–35, 5–37
  feeding of title, 5–39, 7–19,
    27–40
  implied condition as to—
    contract of sale of goods,
      7–17 to 7–25
    hire-purchase agreement,
      25–10 to 25–13
  meaning of, 5–01, 5–02
  possessory title, sale of, 7–22
  retention of title clauses. See
    Retention of title clauses
  voidable, sale under, 5–21 to
    5–26, 5–35
Total charge for credit
  duty to disclose amount of,
    21–39, 23–11, 24–34
  generally, 21–09, 21–12, 21–35
    to 21–38
Trade descriptions
  Act of 1968, 18–03 et seq.
  additional or alternative
    defendant, 18–32, 18–43
  defences, 18–26 to 18–31,
    18–41, 18–42
  enforcement, 18–33
  false statements as to services,
    18–15 to 18–25
  limitation of action, 18–33
  misleading price indications,
    18–34 to 18–43
  sale/supply of goods with
    misleading description,
    18–05 to 18–14
Trade usage, 10–08
Trading check. See Check trading
Trading voucher, 20–18
Transfer of goods, contract for
  implied terms, 8–02 to 8–07
Transfer of property. See Passing
  of property
Transfer of risk. See Risk
Transfer of title
  see generally Passing of
    property
  seller not owner, when, 5–01,
    5–02 et seq.

Trespass
  recovery of goods and, 19–07,
    27–18, 27–19, 28–11

Unascertained goods
  generally, 3–05
  identified bulk, from, 3–05,
    3–28, 3–37 to 3–47, 4–17
  perishing of goods and, 4–05,
    4–11, 4–17
  time of passing of property and,
    3–09
Unauthorised seller, 5–01 et seq.
Uncertainty
  hire-purchase agreement, in,
    24–05
  sale of goods agreement, in,
    2–13 to 2–15
Unfair terms in consumer
    contracts, 10–39 to 10–47,
    26–08
Unpaid seller, 12–04
Unrestricted-use credit, 21–19
Unsolicited goods
  formation of contract of sale
    and, 2–09
Unsolicited visits by traders
  cancellation of agreement and,
    2–18

Valuation
  ascertainment of price and,
    2–16
Vending machines
  completion of contract of sale,
    2–05
Void contract, 4–02, 5–23
Voidable title
  sale under, 5–21 to 5–26
Voucher
  payment by contract of sale of
    goods, 8–05

Waiver
  breach of condition and, 7–13,
    7–14, 7–51
  lien, of, 12–07, 12–08
  rejection of goods and, 7–51,
    13–09
  stoppage of goods in transit and,
    12–11

Warranties
  agent's warranty of authority,
    15–04
  auctioneer's, 15–08
  breach of, 7–09 to 7–12, 7–51,
    13–02, 25–19
  collateral, 9–02, 19–10, 24–12
  exemption clause overriding oral
    warranty, 10–09
  manufacturer's, 9–02, 9–03

Warranties—*cont.*
  stipulations as to time as,
    7–13
Weights and measure authorities,
  18–01, 18–33
Withdrawal of offer. *See* Offer
Work and materials supplied,
  contract for, 1–11 to 1–13,
  8–06
Writ of execution, 5–43